BUSINESS HISTORY

Selected Readings

BUSINESS HISTORY

Selected Readings

Edited by

K.A. TUCKER

Fellow, Research School of Social Sciences,
Institute of Advanced Studies,
Australian National University

FRANK CASS & CO. LTD.

First published in 1977 in Great Britain by
FRANK CASS AND COMPANY LIMITED
Gainsborough Road, Gainsborough House,
London E11 1RS, England

and in United States of America by
FRANK CASS AND COMPANY LIMITED
c/o International Scholarly Book Services, Inc.
Box 555, Forest Grove, Oregon 97116

ISBN 0 7146 3030 6

Printed in Great Britain by
JOHN G. ECCLES, LONGMAN, INVERNESS

Contents

Introduction

Many topics could qualify for inclusion in a set of readings on business history. Traditionally, besides coming under the general umbrella of economic history, business history has been a complement to studies and teaching in business administration. More recently, it has become a strong candidate for closer liaison with industrial economics, applied micro-economics and business finance. Business history also covers such subjects as technology, industrial relations, marketing and research and development. Therefore, in selecting articles, one could call on research from labour history, urban history, the history of technology, agricultural history, banking and insurance history, textile history, transport history and marketing history. All of these specialised research areas, in contrast to the usual historical approach of chronological treatment of all aspects simultaneously, suggest an emphasis on structure, decision-making and performance within pre-defined boundaries.

The overriding criterion in selection has therefore been the framework of structure-conduct-performance for the industry, activity or firm. The emphasis is on the technical and organisational relationships between the governing factor input and output conditions and the objectives and control mechanisms of the decision-making personnel. Business history becomes the history of business practice.

The selection of articles in this volume is presented in four main parts. The first three parts are made up of reprinted materials. But in three instances (Readings 1, 2 and 16), the authors of the original articles reproduced here have prepared and agreed to the publication of further explanatory comments. These addenda bring their appraisal of the topic up to date and refer explicitly to additions to the literature since their papers first appeared. A fourth part completes the readings by the addition of previously unpublished commentary on relevant bibliographical sources and material on research problems and procedures.

This set of readings has been planned with three purposes in mind. Firstly it sets out to demonstrate good examples of the writing of business history using a wide range of source material. Secondly, it is intended as an aid to developing a critical perception of the value and uses of research in business history. Finally, it is hoped that it will encourage and facilitate further analysis of business records and the conditions affecting business policy, structure and growth.

The remainder of the introduction has been planned so that each of its four sections relates to one of the four parts of the volume as shown in the table of contents. While each component of the introduction can therefore be read independently in conjunction with its group of readings, the matters discussed in individual papers often do overlap this arbitrary classification.

I

Managers and businessmen have numerous objectives. Similarly, business historians consider that topics for rewarding research and methods of investigation should have different priority and emphasis. Part One (Aims and Methods in Business History) contains articles exploring the nature of business history; its purpose, practice, current limitations and relations with other subjects. Cole's paper (Reading 1) attempts to distil the central objectives of business history research by concentrating on the entrepreneurial function. He concludes with a comprehensive listing of major themes: business enterprises, businessmen's biographies, business instruments, business thought, business systems, business groups and business censorship. In the addendum he argues that an ideal schema of analysis should be based on the sociological basis of institutional change.

The theme of entrepreneurial endeavour may focus on the possible objectives of the businessman, the firm, or other institutions. Many hazards face the business historian in attempting to discover the motivating forces behind the actions of businessmen or firms. Hyde (Reading 2) discusses the range of objectives and the limitations of interpreting business behaviour against the main micro-economic assumption of much of economic theory — profit maximisation.

The theory of the firm has been based traditionally on the assumption that those operating a business entity will attempt to maximise profits, subject to given knowledge of factor prices, technology and a budget constraint. This view has been challenged by theorists, business historians and applied economists. Some have argued that the objective may be to maximise output, but have conceded that this need not conflict with the objective of maximising long-run profits. Others have argued that a firm may attempt to achieve satisfactory or 'satisficing' levels of profit. This objective may dominate when market pressure is weak (e.g. where there are high entry barriers); or it may be a feature of the performance and control mechanism which accepts some trade-off of maximum profits in return for leisure, fringe benefits or psychic returns. Many have suggested that, in reality, firms may elect to have a mixture of objectives, which may also have changing importance over time. For example, firms may attempt to achieve both a target level of growth in share prices and also a target proportion of profits for distribution as dividends. But should the targets, in their extreme or actual values, be mutually inconsistent, a suitable weighting of priorities may be assigned to keep the system in equilibrium.

Growth is one of the long-term objectives commonly attributed to enterprises. The theory of the growth of the firm provides a convenient framework against which to test the experience of surviving organisations or the reasons for the lack of growth or disappearance of firms. Galambos (Reading 3) shows that the possible integration of a theory of growth, based on a progression of stages, with evidence on the changing structure of industries may lead towards a more rigorously tested and enlightening interaction between business history and economic theory.

It may be, however, that the long-term objectives of the firm or organisation are to survive and merely to provide for a continuity of operations. This strategy may, in turn, confer security of employment or prolong the life of key products. Another long-term aim, for example, may be to minimise tax payments, tariff costs, or private operating costs and thereby transfer to the economy at large the incidence of some types of production cost. However, should such strategies be adopted as a basis of operation, commercial or political forces may upset the achievement of the target. For example, a family business which attempts to obtain long-term security and status for its members may risk bankruptcy or a take-over bid. Organisations that avoid responsibilities which are expected of them may find it difficult to attract labour or may induce government intervention. They may attract fiscal levies, less tariff protection, anti-trust action or some form of government control. Employers and directors who wish to maximise their career prospects or salary growth, independently of qualifications and experience (or who wish to maximise the continuity of family income, irrespective of the degree of relative commercial competence), may discover sooner or later that the market or the electorate may challenge their objectives and affect their success in achieving them.

Most of the readings in this selection implicitly contain some discussion of the methods and approaches used by business historians to measure and describe the origins and impact of changes in business structure and the rate of growth of the firms in question. However, recommendations and cautions about the manipulation of business data and presenting the results of research may provide some guidance for future study or enquiry. The editor (Reading 4) also shows how financial ratios, commonly used to assess financial structure, profitability, liquidity and efficiency, may be calculated from historical accounting records. Many of the techniques available to applied economists may similarly prove relevant for historical inference. (For example, see the use of regression analysis in Reading 13).

While business historians and applied economists may ask similar questions, they tend generally to use different methods and data sources. It cannot be denied that historical data is often incomplete by being partially, irretrievably destroyed. However, applied economists often discover that, when dealing with contemporary matters, they cannot use some types of evidence because of their confidentiality. They may be able to estimate the unknown data or substitute a surrogate or proxy variable to take the place of the unobtainable series. The business historian must often make similar estimates, not because of the secrecy of the information but because the records are missing or perhaps were never kept. One can argue, therefore, that the data limitations to which business historians and applied economists are subject must converge in time. Indeed, some readings in this selection are witness to this fact. For example, measures of the costs, prices and outputs of firms may be inferred from secondary material after making suitable adjustments and corrections for unrepresentative observations or even seasonal deviations. (See Readings 6 and 13).

Once the 'raw data' are made available, by direct transcription or indirect estimation and adjustment, the methods of analysis and data manipulation become important. Again, it has been a feature of business economics rather than of business history for statistical analysis and economic theory to be used. But, as already noted, the data sources may be as limited for recent as for distant periods, if the differences in the sources of data used do not in themselves dictate differences in methods of analysis. There is little except the training and time available to the researcher and the inclination and understanding of his audience to prevent the business historian from using available methods of quantitative analysis.

II

Resource allocation, selection of techniques of production, management of labour relations, financing of growth, and adaptation to changes in competition and government intervention are common to all sectors of economic activity. The readings in Part Two (Entrepreneurs, the Firm and Industrial Structure) show the role of business, both within sectors and by integration between sectors, in contributing towards economic growth and structural change. The first four readings (Readings 5-8) refer to examples of primary and secondary industry as well as to the basic elements in a production process. Payne (Reading 5) reconstructs, from an account book of a colliery, key statistics which chart the level of stock, output and cost structure. By contrast, Blaug (Reading 6) focuses on secondary evidence at the industry level. He uses measures of productivity and of the structure of inputs to deduce evidence about forms of technical innovation and the rate and cycles of industrial growth. Each production process requires labour inputs in different proportions. Labour productivity and turnover are influenced by many conditions. Pollard (Reading 7) gives a detailed picture of working conditions and methods of factory discipline during the Industrial Revolution. He uses a variety of examples and types of documentary evidence. Richardson and Bass (Reading 8) consider the relative importance of four features in contributing towards the profitability of an iron manu-facturing company. They evaluate locational or spatial advantages, the rate of technical progress, monopoly power and economies of scale. By reconstructing data on the profit rate and capital structure, and interpreting it in conjunction with detailed evidence on industrial relations, capacity utilisation, output-mix and other features, they conclude that it is difficult to isolate the respective contributions of each possible source of profit. In some instances, advice, planning and management control aided performance, while at other times, chance, unexpected events and uncontrolled constraints determined the outcome. Musson (Reading 9) describes the historical development of techniques of factory lay-out and standardised mass-production processes in the mechanical engin-eering industry. We note not only that economies of scale and learning processes contributed directly to cost-reduction in this industry but also that, by their application to producer goods, they contributed to improved efficiency in other sectors in which the goods were used. There were also beneficial spin-offs from the emulation by firms in related activities of the successful techniques.

The impact of decision-making in allocating labour and capital resources, choosing and developing technology, building up financial reserves and securing and rewarding labour and skills can be seen in changing market shares, competition, government inter-vention, growth strategies, and the provision of intermediate services to meet changing requirements. The six readings (Readings 10-15) making up the remainder of Part Two, illustrate decision-making over time and the process of business growth. The degree of vertical integration in American manufacturing industries for the period 1899-1948 is measured by Livesay and Porter (Reading 10). They conclude that, as regards vertical integration, industry conditions were a more important determinant than size of firm. Nevertheless, there were wide variations in changes in vertical integration among industries. Further research on methods of measuring integration, industry conditions and other related variables may indicate the peculiar and general features of the dynamics of change in this particular feature of business and industrial structure. Dixon (Reading 11) shows how an anti-trust decision against an integrated group of oil companies resulted, over the next fifty years, in these companies developing competitive strategies to increase their individual market shares. By contrast, Glover (Reading 12) describes (from the records of one firm) the role of government demand in the heavy woollen industry in promoting and possibly distorting the efficiency of the industry.

The complexity of feedback relationships and the extent and timing of exogenous influences, often frustrate the desired objectives of entrepreneurs in increasing their profitability or market share. Klein and Yamamura (Reading 13) study variations in the pattern of the financing of railroads and in their profitability. They then deduce, after allowing for differences in the functions and nature of the railroads, the entrepreneurial motivation in the adoption of certain competitive strategies. On a similar theme, Porter and Livesay (Reading 14) consider the role of merchants as providers of different types of capital to various parts of the manufacturing sector. Here the emphasis is on the types of relationship and channels of contact which developed between those marshalling and reallocating capital resources and those utilising these resources as a supplement to internally generated finance. The final reading in Part Two considers a similar type of interaction. But in the case of Siegenthaler's study (Reading 15) the 'input' provided is that of advice. The demand for advice and the structure of the market for associated advisory services is analysed. The value of the service in the hands of the user is measured.

III

Techniques to assist in decision-making, and the control of operations, while continuously evolving, have been available in various forms to businessmen during the past. Part Three (Techniques of Business Management and Organisation) concentrates on studies which examine such techniques and look at the attempts of managers to deal with risk and uncertainty emanating from technical, financial, and extra-economic origins. The first two readings in this section by Yamey (Reading 16) and Johnson (Reading 17) discuss the role of financial and cost accounting methods in influencing management behaviour. Yamey, in a study of the role of double-entry bookkeeping and the rise of capitalism, is sceptical of Sombart's assertion that double-entry accounting was necessary for capitalist enterprise and for entrepreneurial decision-making. His additional comments, on more recent studies and challenges to this view, suggest that this debate may well be carried further and involve closer studies of the use made of accounting and similar records by firms in different economic environments. Johnson (Reading 17) follows such a course for one firm. He describes the development of cost accounting practices and their use. In this case he concludes that the managers did not use their cost accounting records to evaluate economic decisions about alternative factor costs, technology mix or optimal production levels. Instead, the accounting records had a specific internal use in aiding technical or engineering decisions at the plant level.

Business techniques to predict future trends may improve decisions about the purchase, holding and sale of materials or goods. Two articles, by Heaton (Reading 18) and Clapp (Reading 19), are illustrations of methods of forecasting and market anticipation. They demonstrate the behavioural implications of dealing with uncertainty. Heaton describes how market information was compiled and used to aid production and inventory planning and to evaluate changes in demand conditions. The short study by Clapp provides an interesting example of the way in which a business used price-quantity schedules for analysis and control at a time before such an analytical construct had appeared in academic economic literature. The final paper, by a social anthropologist, Cohen (Reading 20), describes the social organisation of credit in a contemporary cattle market in Nigeria. It is an interesting analysis of the importance of social constraints on individual business behaviour, and of the efficiency with which the resulting network of business relationships coped with an environment including a high degree of business risk in various forms. Similar arrangements and methods were to be found in earlier periods of the business history of now more advanced economies.

IV

The selection of twenty readings is supplemented by three appendices. Appendix A (Interpreting Accounting Data and Business Records) presents a list of references and a brief commentary on the methods used and found useful for measuring and appraising business data and relevant secondary material. The interpretation which business historians make of the contents of business records can be affected by changes over time, in the unit of measurement used in such records, and by the lack of uniformity in the definition of terms and concepts used by business firms in their records. Appendix B (Allowing for Changes in the Unit of Account and Measuring Income, Assets and Liabilities) comments on the limitations of accounting methods in these respects, and provides a bibliography, derived primarily from accounting literature, to which business historians may refer for guidance. Appendix C (Select Bibliography for Further Reading) provides, under section headings corresponding to those of the table of contents, additional material which may be consulted for further study of the major topics of business history.

PART ONE

Aims and Methods
in
Business History

1
What is Business History?

Arthur H. Cole*

As one grows old, one becomes increasingly annoyed at confusion of almost any variety; and that which continues to surround the concept of 'business history' chances to impinge frequently enough upon my attention to impel me to try to reduce the disparities in concepts still existent among individuals interested in the field. Diversity of concepts was evident even among men interested enough in the area to come — in some cases, goodly distances — to attend a two-day meeting at the Harvard Business School on the teaching of the subject. Perhaps because I was already teaching economic history before business history was born, because I have known the chief actors in the world created by Professor N. S. B. Gras, and because I have had to give thought to the nature of entrepreneurial history, I may in this connection pretend to pose as a sort of academic *amicus curiae*. And I think that I have made manifest my interest in the field.

THE NATURE OF BUSINESS

Too often young folk start talking about business history without first stopping to secure a clear concept of business itself. They may carry the notion that business is merely buying and selling, huckstering, the hurly-burly of the traditional bazaar of the Middle East; others may hold the image of business as an arena populated by giants of great wealth and great power who buy politicians and generally are up to no good; and the novelists or muckrakers or others have created other impressions. Actually business is much more complex than the concepts which any of these notions convey. It can be visualized on at least three levels or in three patterns.

One level or pattern is the ideational. It is constituted of all the

*From *Business History Review*, Vol. XXXVI, No. (1962) pp. 98-106. Reprinted by permission of the editor of *Business History Review* and the author.

knowledge by aid of which the wheels of production, distribution, advisory service, etc., are established and maintained: how to secure a corporate charter, how to manage a shoe factory, how best to compensate salesmen, etc. — millions and millions of 'bits' of knowledge, accumulated over centuries of experience, and daily being added to. It is the presence or lack of this body of knowledge that really distinguishes the developed from the underdeveloped countries, and it is the slow manner in which such knowledge can be absorbed into an industrial order that spells the slowness with which such underdeveloped countries can rise toward equality with the older business nations.

A facet of this ideational world — ideas transmuted into modes of behaviour — was spoken of recently by Professor Solomon Fabricant:[1]

> Underdeveloped countries are learning that in their rush to reach desired levels of economic efficiency, time must be taken to develop the kind of business ethics, respect for the law, and treatment of strangers that keep a modern industrial society productive. Widening of the concept of family loyalty and tribal brotherhood to include love of man 'in general' is a necessary part of the process of economic development.

Another facet is made a significant portion of Mrs Edith Penrose's theory of the growth of 'the firm' when she specifies experience of men working together in individual enterprises as conditioning greatly the manner in which those concerns would be expected to perform in the future. A firm uses two types of knowledge, she writes, one that may be looked upon as objective and available to everyone, and, the other, knowledge which is born of experience within the particular enterprise. Moreover, 'increased experience,' she asserts, 'shows itself in two ways — changes in knowledge acquired and changes in the ability to use knowledge.'[2]

Again, the importance given to decision-making in some descriptions of primary business processes — even in some definitions of business — is related to this level or feature of business life. Thought processes do precede and condition the decisions of businessmen; and those who participate in the decision-making process are surely important cogs in the business machinery. It is a question merely whether decision-making constitutes a full description of business — surely not.

At all events, it scarcely behoves those of us who have been or are now connected with schools of business to look askance at the notion of business possessing a prime basis in knowledge. Such institutions of learning are founded on the faith that business experience can be observed and generalised into assertions of wider or narrower pertinence to future business action, and that these acquired truths can by oral communication or the perusal of books be somehow made to lodge in the brains of students to a degree adequate to guide them in their own efforts to manage business enterprises or help in that management.

Stemming in large part from this ideational level is the world of institutions — the production enterprises, the construction companies, the banks, the department stores, and a myriad of other forms of organization — through which business operations are carried out. Traditionally such institutions have been viewed as a multitude of independent units — *a* candy factory, *a* hardware wholesaler, *a* bank, *a* railroad, etc. — with the only connection among them being competition of units concerned with the same or overlapping areas of activity. I would propose a different image, that of an interconnected, mutually supporting congeries of business units. For purposes of exposition, the extractive, manufacturing, and construction industries may be conceived to constitute the central core of this business system, while, outside of this primary citadel, one can specify a series of concentric circles in which other business institutions may be held to lie — the complement in each successive circle being perhaps those ancillary or service institutions closely and then less closely connected with the performance of the institutions located in the central region. Purveyors of productive equipment, providers of short-term capital, transporters of raw materials and finished goods, etc., might lie in an inner circle, the publishers of trade periodicals, public accountants, etc., perhaps in a more removed circle, while still further away might lie the interior decorators of executive offices, schools that trained workmen or clerks for the establishments, etc. Perhaps the major industries of steel, rubber, textiles and the like could be envisaged as possessing to some extent separate and distinct institutional worlds — like Innis' 'staples,' perhaps Rostow's 'sectors,' or the Swedes' 'development blocks' — but, inasmuch as some of the ancillary and service institutions — such as railroads, commercial banks, etc. — serve many industries, a good deal of overlapping would need to be envisioned.

Incidentally, attention may be drawn to the circumstance that such a business construct differs essentially from that usually employed by economists. The latter seem content to line institutions up in industries and go no further, except perhaps as required by the modern ideas of monopolistic competition — a rather specialized instance of business interconnections.

Actually, it is somewhat difficult to draw a limit to the series of

concentric circles that I have proposed. Out some distance would
lie perhaps management advisory concerns, commodity exchanges,
and the publishers of trade journals; possibly still farther, schools
of business, architects specializing in industrial buildings, or counsel specializing in antitrust matters; and it might be questioned
whether the Federal Bureau of Standards, the Census Bureau, the
Securities and Exchange Commission, and other governmental
agencies should not be added, since the government is by no means
merely regulatory; it also provides much information useful to the
managers of individual enterprises.[3]

In fact, one may wish to conceive of the outermost ring of the
business circles as merging closely with much that we are inclined
to call 'society.' There are surely many connections between the
business world and the publication of both newspapers and general
periodicals; there are portions of the world of art which affect
business and, in turn, are affected by the latter; there are connections between business affairs and literature, the drama, and
sometimes even poetry. It was actually a consequence of this line of
reasoning that led me to envisage three areas of social action — the
individual business unit, the business system, and the contacts with
the total society — when I ventured to write about the 'business
enterprise in its social setting.'[4]

The third level or pattern of business is that of performance —
bales of cotton goods produced, shares traded on the New York
Stock Exchange, ton-miles of freight carried, and the like. To many
businessmen, this aspect of the business world would seem the
most important; and surely it is the most obvious. I would hold,
however, that this is an area of minor interest to the business historian. When there is a question of the value of the whole business
system, he would undoubtedly desire to indicate the increase in the
output of goods and services which has occurred over the centuries
and decades under the exertions of the private enterprise system;
and, for the short run, he may be concerned with 'volume' as a factor in the determination of diminishing prices. But it seems to me
that, by and large, this counting of output is more properly the
domain of the economic historian. When goods are really produced
or distributed, the work of the businessman is finished.

That the world of business spreads out geographically from
border to border of most countries — with perhaps only small
enclaves of even modestly self-sufficient farmers — needs hardly be
stated. Less common, I believe, is an appreciation of the variety of
economic activity — the provision of goods and services — which
has come under the domain of business action. That the world of
business extends over diverse extractive, manufacturing, con-

struction, distributive, financial, and transportation activities is obvious. However, surely commercial or market-oriented farmers should be embraced, likewise many entertainment and recreational facilities from theatres to bowling alleys, baseball teams to the producers of ski wax, while many of the basic human activities or experiences do not escape the advantages (or disadvantages) of response to business management: materials for the control of pregnancy, presentations of young ladies to society, commercial administrators of weddings, and both funeral homes and huge mausoleums to wind up one's stay on earth.

It is also to be noted that, with the increase of the professional quality in business management personnel, the divergence of business and the professions seems to have become narrowed — at least vis-a-vis some of the professions such as actors and actresses of screen or television, lawyers, architects, and even college professors, thanks to the inroads of foundation funds and the increased opportunity for employment in government service. Our 'business civilization' has lately become even more inclusive than ever before of events in the total society.

COROLLARIES OF THE FOREGOING

It is obvious that the earlier identification of 'business history' with company history is grossly inappropriate. No doubt company history is business history; but the reverse gives an erroneous view of conditions, as if one identified any one architectural style and 'architecture.' The preparation and publication of company histories seem not far different from the drafting and issuance of personal biographies in the area of political history. They are surely of much value, but they can hardly be viewed as pre-empting the whole field.

Secondly, it becomes desirable to look at the forces and instrumentalities which make viable the business system of a nation. Some of the so-called 'business virtues' may be worth noting, such as reliability, promptness, rectitude in business dealings, and the like. Also, one should observe the importance of such instrumentalities as stock certificates, bills of lading, promissory notes, time-payment contracts, and the like.

Since the paths taken by the evolution of the business system will almost inevitably differ from country to country, perhaps even among regions in so large a nation as our own, and since the timing of such developments would surely differ in the several areas, there would appear to be many opportunities for comparative studies. Professor Karl Deutsch used to propose a study of the relative speeds in the adoption of particular technological advances — such

as the adding machine or the Linotype apparatus — in various
countries as likely to make manifest variations in entrepreneurial
character; but surely a comparison of the course, speed, and extent
of achievement in the development of a complex business system
would prove even more revealing of variant national business
characters. This would seem a sort of symphonic form for business
history writing.

However, I am tempted to add two lines of thought pertinent to
economico-business performance. The first is that when one brings
down to earth or — to change the figure — puts flesh on the bare
bones of such economistic phrases as 'capital formation' or the
'international movement of the productive factors,' one is coming
closer to a consideration of realities and, if one wishes to make use
of historical inquiries, one is better equipped to propose public
policies appropriate to the circumstances of the real world. Governments and public censors cannot deal effectively with abstractions;
indeed, in policy administration governments must deal with business institutions and businessmen. I am particularly annoyed when
I read of the 'British export of capital' to the United States or other
countries. One receives the idea unconsciously that British lenders
stood on the street corners of America or Australia or other 'underdeveloped' countries, and tried to press pounds, shillings, and
pence upon unhappy borrowers. The whole point of the activity
seems to me to be obscured by this particular phrase — this
abstraction.

In the second place, I believe it worthwhile to suggest that,
relative to economic growth of nations, the world of business is not
without distinct and separate importance. It seems to me by no
means clear that the innovational activities of businessmen, their
attention to operational improvements — not merely technological
developments — and the internal drives toward at least keeping up
with one's competitors may not constitute a force productive of
economic advance quite apart from the economists' 'supply of the
productive factors.' Businessmen's intellectual efforts, no less than
those of the inventor, the scholar, or the statesman can be creative.

THE THEMES OF A REJUVENATED BUSINESS HISTORY

From the perspective of the foregoing comments, it is possible to
visualize a marked expansion of the area of business history —
'history as written':

> Surely the histories of individual enterprises should be specified —
> and I would suggest the use of the term 'enterprise history' to
> designate this branch of composition.

Businessmen's biographies would still remain worthwhile.

Now would be included the history of the evolution of business instrumentalities: the bill of exchange, the mortgage bond, the through bill of lading, etc. Here business history would rub elbows with legal history.

Efforts can also be made to trace the evolution of business thought — as, for example, relative to accounting, scientific management, budgeting, etc. — and the development of business literature.

Sketches of the development of the business system relative to particular branches of industry or particular geographical areas would become appropriate, and comparative histories of national developments could be attempted.

Last but not least, changes could be investigated as to the attitudes of specific groups in society toward the business world as a whole, to the traits of character perceived in representative figures within that world, to the economic performance of the whole system or specific parts of it, and the like. Contrariwise, so to speak, studies could be promoted of the changing public censors of business, the reasons for the latter's approvals or disapprovals, the competence of their observations, etc.

In point of fact, the individual scholars now interested in the area of business history (as now broadly defined) appear to fall into three groups. One takes a professional point of view — the lessons of past experience in business are valuable for the enlightenment of current business executives and perhaps the training of future executives. In turn this interest can be seen to be two-pronged. One prong tends to relate the developments of the past to continuing business problems. Indeed, a casebook might be compounded for these teachers and scholars along the line perhaps of classic examples of bad and good judgment, or good or bad fortune in the face of uncontrollable circumstances. Cases of beginning business operations at the wrong phase of the business cycle, of excessive optimism, of too great reliance on a single large purchaser of one's products, etc., could be brought together, with all useful historical detail and a knowledge of what actually did happen after the decisions were made.

The second prong in the interest of this group concerns the changing place of business in the whole society. Here the term 'business' is taken as synonymous with the private enterprise system, and the whole process of public appraisal above noted is involved. The business historian is, in fact, not necessarily well qualified to deal with this facet of his field any more perhaps — to take an extreme case — than an obstetrician should be an authority on the population problem. An adequate handling of the inquiry calls for competence in social history and the history of ideas, and familiarity with sociological concepts. However, if this line of analytical history is properly developed, the business executive or the student in the school of business will secure a notion of his position relative to a changing scheme of thought and emotion and will be in a better position, on his own initiative, to influence the future course of such ideas and feelings, or to adjust to them.

This latter approach to business history seems to hold a considerable interest for scholars and teachers outside the schools of business. Students and instructors of college courses on comparative economic systems would have concern with the materials; and so also perhaps scholars and students in the area of ethics, at least if the latter subject were examined in historical perspective. In some measure, likewise, scholars and courses dealing with the changes in social and political thought would have use for these data. Here business history overlaps with general or social history; but I believe that there would be value in the devotion by the business historian of attention to this area. Surely he could place the actions and thoughts of businessmen more fully in their historical setting than a sociologist or general historian unfamiliar with the arena in which the actions or thoughts took place.

Finally, there is a body of scholars who are concerned with business history as an adjunct to their examination of economic growth. It is interesting, for example, that Professor Conrad in his recently compounded sketch of the evolution of the American economy — generally in quantitative terms — finds it useful or necessary to call upon the activities of investment bankers to explain satisfactorily to himself the course of economic change in the post-Civil War decades.[5] (The business historian might be inclined to put to Professor Conrad the question: why were these particular alterations in the business structure important in explanation of economic change and not many others of our colonial, pre-Civil War, or even twentieth-century periods?). Customarily, indeed, economists and economic historians have called upon facts and changes in conditions of the business world to provide explication of events which chance to interest them; and those recently concerning themselves with economic growth are likely to do the same. I believe that the historian of business change can make a real contribution to discussion in this new area of speculation — not the less because I believe changes in the structure of business to effect alterations in economic productivity independent of other conditions and circumstances in the economy and society.

CONCLUSION

In sum, I believe the business historians of the past have been given to intellectual myopia, and to have been thus unfortunate in no inconsiderable part by reason of the identification of the term 'business history' with company history. Since the withdrawal of Professor Gras from the scene, business historians seem much too modest and timid in viewing the potentials of their territory. Perhaps they could be compared with the sort of person whom Philip D. Bradley used to hold to be common in Latin America — a man who would sit on a mountain of iron ore and do nothing creative about it. It appears to me that business history, if properly developed, holds numerous enticing opportunities for research and writing — in a rather diverse rainbow of relationships and themes. Business historians need not abandon enterprise histories, but they can add on other fields of inquiry more fruitful for both the improvement of professional training in the schools of business and for enlightenment of scholars and students engrossed in social history. The future of the area seems exceptionally bright, if these opportunities are grasped by the present and rising generations of scholars working in the field.

NOTES

1 Solomon Fabricant, 'An Economist's View of Philanthropy', in *Proceedings of the American Philosophical Society*, Vol. 105 (April 21, 1961), p. 163.

2 Edith T. Penrose, *The Theory of the Growth of the Firm* (New York and Oxford, 1959), p. 53.

3 In reality, of course, the domain of business has really quite ragged edges. For example, there are cooperative enterprises; there are central banks, sometimes privately owned but devoted to a public function; there are stock, bond, and commodity exchanges; there are professions not much removed from businesses; there are privately endowed colleges and universities — with Harvard College the American business institution with the record of longest continuous existence; and there are business functions evident in governmental agencies, e.g., budgeting, accounting control, purchasing, etc. 'Business' trails off into foundations, hospitals, and other eleemosynary institutions.

4 Arthur H. Cole, *Business Enterprise in its Social Setting* (Cambridge, 1959).

5 Alfred H. Conrad, 'Income Growth and Structural Change', in *American Economic History*, edited by Seymour E. Harris (New York, 1961), pp. 46-54.

ADDENDUM

The lapse of time and the opportunity for much ratiocination offer the potentiality of enlarging the perspective of business history. Traditionally, the term 'business' has been interpreted as somehow related to a single line of entrepreneurial activity, that is, to what the economist has chosen to view as an 'industry'. Such an interpretation might have been adequate for the economist's chief concern, the action of commodity prices. I found the concept a hamper to the study of historical change when, as long ago as the middle 1920s, I was trying to explain the course of evolution in the American wool manufacturing 'industry'. Now with the duty of giving an explanation of total American economic expansion within a regime to which governmental action was relatively incidental, at least until relatively modern times, I have come to postulate a business *structure* based upon active entrepreneurship — not an area of unrestrained competitors, but one where institutions of credit creation, transportation, of communications and commodities, even schools of business management, formed a congregation of integrated business units which *together* could be envisaged as the promoter of economic advance. Indeed, this was the picture which I derived from a fresh survey of American business history from our colonial days up to the present.

To the foregoing concept it was easy to add the element of geographical expansion, an element usually neglected by economists and indeed something which *they* can assume to be constant. Also it seemed appropriate to add the factor of changing intellectual or ideational complement, rather obvious to the librarian of a large collection of business literature — as I served at Harvard for quarter of a century. I would also add the pregnant notion of my predecessor in the field of entrepreneurial activities, Joseph A. Schumpeter, contained in an essay on 'the creative response' of businessmen confronted with specific business situations[1] — a capacity which I would see to extend beyond the launching of the individual enterprises. This element of corporeal behaviour under entrepreneurial leadership would provide the potentiality of continuing adjustment if the initial effort was adequately conceived, by the process that, for financial operations, W. Hastings Lyon called 'trading on the equity',[2] and provided financial institutions stood ready to supply credit. Facilitated by extension of settlement and concurrent business institutions over a relatively empty geographical territory, as was the good fortune of the United States for numerous decades, the advent and extension of a 'national market' for some decades served as a generator of an ever greater spread of the domestic 'business structure', and has continued in some measure so to serve until the present day. The business world of the United States is numerically one of small and medium sized business units mounting in number to the millions despite the advent and enlargement of numerous 'giant' concerns.

Some part of this proliferation of enterprises has formed the means of establishing and enlarging the sweep of business intelligence and acquired wisdom. Early American newspapers in numerous cases carried columns of 'prices current'; this practice permitted local merchants to acquire reprints of such materials for distribution to other areas, sometimes other countries; increase of mercantile activity stimulated the flotation and ensured the continuance of 'journals of commerce' or their equivalent; in time came boards of trade, trade associations and their publications, institutes or companies of management consultants, schools of business, and bureaux of business research. Scholars may with much assurance compare the substantial improvement of professional knowledge for businessmen with that acquired over time and utilised by doctors or architects or other men of action. I once attempted to illustrate or digest the changes in American businessmen by positing a succession of three stages of elevation: empirical, informed and sophisticated.[3] I still believe these descriptions useful as summary statements.

All the foregoing has been rendered possible, at least in the rapidity and magnitude achieved in the United States, by the evolution and persistence of an environment of social thought favourable to entrepreneurial activities, and an entrepreneurial personnel — perhaps aided by continuing immigration of a population of many backgrounds — which penetrated or encouraged entrepreneurial actions of appropriate character and quantity.[4]

It is the possibility of analysis of the historical or time-ruled evolution of business in any area — and probably the decline of such a regime — which allows the employment of this schema of analysis. This sociological schema of institutional change may — at least in fully elaborated form — permit business history or this branch of economics to pursue research and teaching on a truly scientific basis. Business history may be able to break the chain imposed by economists in their primary, often justified concentration upon an unchanging social situation and action by quanta of capital and labour.

NOTES

1 Joseph A. Schumpeter, 'The Creative Response in Economic History', *Journal of Economic History*, Vol. 7 (1947), pp. 149-59.
2 Walter Hastings Lyon, *Corporation Finance* (1912).
3 Arthur H. Cole, 'An Approach to the Study of Entrepreneurship: a Tribute to Edwin F. Gay', *Journal of Economic History*, Vol. 6 (1946), Supplement pp. 1-15.

4 The first of these conditions has been portrayed in its ever changing features by Thomas C. Cochran in his recent volume, *Business in American Life: a History,* 1972. The second line of development will presumably be delineated by Alfred D. Chandler, Jr, in a forthcoming volume. Incidentally, it was in connection with the author's preparation of a volume to accompany those just mentioned that the foregoing theoretical structure was elaborated. The theory *was* a derivative of accumulated facts. [By reason of increased deterioration of eyesight, Professor Cole had to pass the completion of a full manuscript over to Professor Irene D. Neu of Indiana University. For tributes to Professor Cole, who died shortly after this addendum was submitted, see Thomas C. Cochran, 'Arthur Harrison Cole, 1889-1974', *Business History Review* vol XLIX, no. 1 (Spring, 1975) pp. 1-5 and Hugh G. J. Aitken, 'In the Beginning . . . ', *Journal of Economic History*, vol. 35, no. 4 (December, 1975) pp. 817-20.]—Ed.

2
Economic Theory and Business History [1]
A comment on the theory of profit maximisation

Francis E. Hyde*

In the June 1962 issue of *Business History* Dr Barry E. Supple published an article[2] in which he made, *en passant*, some pertinent references to the rather infrequent use made by economic historians of economic theory. He went so far as to say that for most business historians the work of Schumpeter might never have been written, so little impact has it apparently made upon them. While agreeing with this general expression of opinion, it might be of further value if we were to particularise and examine Dr Supple's statements with reference to certain concepts in economic theory of relevance to the business historian. We start, therefore, by accepting the criticism implicit in Dr Supple's excellent article as valid and just.

I

The writing of business history is a hazardous occupation. The records of British firms are rarely adequate for the task and their analysis, perforce being incomplete, leaves gaps which, in the interests of the narrative, have to be filled from a rag-bag of external sources. But having minimised the difficulties of material and its presentation, the historian must, if he is to write a worthwhile business history, ask himself pertinent questions. Why do men and women pursue individual lines of activity in the maintenance of their business and what effects do their actions have upon the economic environment in which they work?[3] The answer is that, for the majority, they do what they do simply in order to make the greatest amount of money. This was undoubtedly true of vast numbers of merchants and manufacturers in the eighteenth and nineteenth centuries. They worked within the circumscription of a philosophy which encouraged them in the belief that their efforts

*From *Business History*, Vol. V (1962), pp. 1-10. Reprinted by permission of the editor of *Business History*.

were of the greatest value to their fellow men, if pursued where profits were at the maximum.

But the mere amassing of wealth can never be the final answer to a fundamental question concerned with the driving force in a man's business career. Such an explanation by itself can satisfy neither the economist nor the business historian. The true facts about a given situation very often indicate a deeper significance to men's motives. The economic concept of maximisation does comprehend the existence of deeper motives such as the desire to achieve security both presently and in the future, or the desire for benefits and satisfactions which money can bring, that is to say, freedom and leisure.

Logically, the theory is a perfect theory. Its validity is not impugned by the fact that businessmen sometimes behave strangely or that, for psychological reasons, they may pursue one course of action rather than another. Whatever end is achieved can, in terms of theory, be regarded as rational. It is not our purpose to question the theory of profit maximisation; we simply intend to demonstrate the range of difficulty confronting the business historian in his endeavour to explain behaviour and motives and draw forth con- clusions from his observations. It is hoped that the implications of this approach will emphasise the additional, though by no means insuperable, difficulty of setting out his findings within the frame- work of economic theory.

Some recent studies in business behaviour can be used to ask a series of questions illustrating these phenomena. For example, Peter Stubs combined the complementary occupations of filemaker and innkeeper. Why did he not occupy himself solely as an inn- keeper.[4] Why did the Booths continue in the shipping business when they could possibly have sustained their fortunes more effectively as leather manufacturers?[5] Why did Lord Leverhulme involve himself in the cares and worries of a vast organisation long after his own personal fortune had been assured?[6] Why did the Rathbones, after creating a successful business in timber, tea, corn and shipping allow their merchant activity to be diverted by other equally excellent much less remunerative occupations, a diversion of interest which finally caused the decline of their firm's prosper- ity?[7] Why did the Holt brothers bring their firm to the verge of ruin by clinging to outmoded ideas of ship construction?[8] Or more simply, what induced Pilkington Brothers to expand their activities beyond the demands of a purely local market?[9] What was the causal nature of the relationship which sustained the production of Spencers in supplying rubber to railways when they might have built up a wider market for rubber goods?[10] Similar questions

could be asked about any firm whose records are worth investigation. Questions easily asked, however, are not usually so satisfactorily answered. Any historian worth his salt should be able, if he
asks questions, to answer them *qua* historian. But Dr Supple quite
rightly suggests that the writing of business history needs more
than the historian's technique. What to the historian may well be
unrelated facts in the growth or decline of a firm, can be given
intelligible interpretation by the economist within a specific
concept. By such interpretation it is claimed that the *raison d'etre*
of human motives can be given a clearer definition; that economic
theory, by reason of its methodological exactitude, can be used to
give a cutting edge to the historian's tools. This may be so, but
whether facts are interpreted by historical analysis or by economic
analysis, their intrinsic value remains unchanged. Nevertheless,
when businessmen are forced, as they often are, to pursue oppor-
tunist policies in the utilisation of their resources, it is the economic
theorist rather than the historian who faces the greater difficulty in
the task of exposition. Economic theory progresses by providing a
series of answers in the explanation of a given dynamic situation.
For example, the theory of profit maximisation has been successfully
qualified, from the classical marginalist concept through the introduction of the security and leisure motives to the wider range of
theory dealing with business decisions.[11] The historian, therefore,
might find justifiable grounds for hesitation in using a process of
reasoning which, by virtue of its complexity, may confuse rather
than elucidate his argument.

II

Presumably, most business historians, at some stage in their
investigations, have to make use of the marginal concept of maximisation. It would be of value to their historical analysis were they
also conversant with Schumpeter's theory of innovation. In dealing
with questions of entrepreneurial behaviour they are almost certain
to be concerned with the elucidation of price and output policies,
investment decisions and political action in so far as these may
have long-run economic significance.[12] Economic analysis now
recognises that the security motive as an element in entrepreneurial
behaviour, is second only in importance to that of profit maximisation.[13] With security at the back of his mind, the businessman not
only attempts to equate costs with revenue but is also exercised by
the possible effect of a particular pricing policy on the attraction of
newcomers into his field of operations; whether such a policy will
provoke retaliation from rivals; whether it will maintain the
goodwill of his customers.

It is always extremely difficult to apply ideas and theories, fashioned and conditioned against the multi-patterned background of twentieth-century technological development, to an understanding of the business behaviour and motives of those who lived in different circumstances in a previous period of history. To attempt to explain the motives of businessmen living in the eighteenth and nineteenth centuries in terms of twentieth-century logic must present the historian with a dilemma. But it need not necessarily be an unprofitable exercise. There will always be individual exceptions to any given set of rules. The desire for security may have led to qualifications in the marginal concept of maximisation, and this refinement of theory may satisfy the economist in its general application. The business historian, however, can nearly always produce an exceptional series of examples. Peter Stubs may have maximised his resources by becoming an innkeeper as well as a file maker but he did not so diversify his activities in the interests of security. Similarly, the Holt brothers, the Rathbones, the Levers and the Pilkingtons all were striving towards a maximisation of resources, but apart from the Rathbones they were far more inclined to take risks hazardous to the safety of their enterprise, rather than to seek a secure employment of their capital. The Holts entered the first China Conference in an endeavour to secure stable conditions and security in the trade; but their stubborn refusal to modernise their fleet brought them, despite the improvement in trading conditions, to the verge of bankruptcy. The Rathbone trading interests were so designed that they might provide security against the worst financial disasters of the mid-nineteenth century; but the obsession of the firm's partners in attempting to anticipate the effects of future depressions led to much diversion of current resources and, in consequence, to a diversion of effort which may have prevented full maximisation of profit. The safeguarding activities of the Soap Makers' Association, designed to bring security to the soap trade, were largely brought to nought by the dynamic individualism of William Lever who preferred the cut and thrust of competition in the winning of markets for his products to a more secure, but less rewarding passivity of a controlled market. Pilkington Brothers raised their firm to a dominant position in the sheet-glass industry by taking decisions which involved them in great risk and by ignoring, for the most part, schemes designed by the Glass Makers' Association for mutual security. In fact the history of glass manufacture is scattered with the ruin of inefficient firms who were constantly being forced out of existence by the exigencies of a trade which could never have achieved maximisation of resources with attendant conditions of security.

In accepting the refinements of modern theory in its application to the concept of maximisation, therefore, the business historian must enter a *caveat*. However logical the argument, however widely spread the empirical tests, there remains the 'irrational' behaviour to be explained;[14] the persistent stubbornness of the human mind, the overcautious use of resources, the ebullient individualism which may destroy others in the process of achieving domination, the faith which enables men to take risks beyond the limit of calculation and which, when it is justified by success, belies the theoretical exposition; these are some of the facts and conditions which help to make the study of business history fascinating and worth-while. It follows, therefore, that as the business historian becomes aware of the limitations in the application of economic theory in his work, the economic theorist ought, by studying the facts presented by business historians, to leaven the argument and, where necessary, continue the process of re-defining the theory.

III

Schumpeter's contribution to the theory of the trade cycle introduced into the system of static equilibrium, a dynamic factor which upset the earlier concept of the equilibrium.[15] This new factor arose from the decision-taking process of the entrepreneur in the expansion of his business activities. According to Schumpeter the businessman, in a new and specific sense, does not merely produce goods in a traditional way for a known market, but is constantly adapting his resources in the creation of new products, new industrial processes and even new industries. The banker advances funds for investment, the limitation on such funds being the extent of the banker's requirements in maintaining liquidity. The entrepreneur, by using these funds acquires control over new factors of production, and, by paying extra wages starts a dynamic process in the economy. Additional purchasing power circulates, wages and prices rise and the boom begins. Once this process has been completed, however, the output becomes larger and cheaper, the bank loans are repaid from the proceeds of the new sales and the volume of purchasing power shrinks. A new state of equilibrium asserts itself and the whole process becomes subject to self regulation.

Schumpeter's conclusion is that business crises are not inevitable; static equilibrium is restored after a movement to a higher plane of economic growth. Crises could be averted by taking steps to avoid the panic which inevitably followed the interruption of a boom period.

In this concept the entrepreneur is given an important and specific role. Through his dynamic activity, initially made possible by his use of bank credit to build up new enterprises, he is, by creating new purchasing power, departing from those conditions which Wicksell considered to be normal;[16] that is, where the available supply of capital was absorbed by those seeking funds for profitable investment, at a rate of interest equal to marginal profit. In Schumpeter's dynamic theory the entrepreneur is employing his resources under conditions wherein interest does not make saving equal to investment as the classical economists held, but in conditions where interest makes investment equal to bank credit. This concept, extended by the Keynesian theory of liquidity preference, gave theoretical status to the nature of the relationship between the businessman and his banker. It made possible the application of other ideas to the process of decision-taking.

In this present context, however, decision-taking becomes a fundamental attribute of the businessman's power to alter the level of economic activity. In so far as the entrepreneur may desire to establish his new investment on a secure basis, his action to achieve security usually takes place *after* he has reached a higher plane of production. Recent refinements to the marginal concept of maximisation recognise that he may be influenced in three ways.[17] First, from a desire to build up financial strength the entrepreneur is induced to plough back his profits beyond the point of optimal return on a purely profit-maximising basis; secondly, the entrepreneur may be forced in the long run to expend an increasing and disproportionate amount of his resources in maintaining the level of sales of his products in a highly competitive market; thirdly, he may be induced to take political action in the pursuit of economic advantages, the cost of such action being inconsistent in the short-run with the principle of profit maximisation but which, in the long-run, may bring greater security to the maintenance of profit. The cost of these activities forms part of the total cost structure of the firm and so affects all decisions related to pricing, output and investment.

Economic theory, therefore, has attempted progressively to build into a concept of the entrepreneur's activities a series of qualifications which can comprehend the unusual or the 'irrational' in human behaviour. The business historian, on the other hand, in reporting events, is not so inhibited. He accepts as normal material for historical analysis the odd and sometimes irrelevant considerations which colour the taking of decisions. He can also, by analysing motives, very often arrive at precise judgments about behaviour. Alternatively, if he cannot arrive at precise judgments, he can, from his interpretation of factual knowledge, offer suggestions as to cause and effect in a much more realistic interpretation than the economic theorist can possibly hope to achieve. For example, it is true that, through fear of subsequent depressions, the Rathbones adopted a cautious approach to the use of their resources. This caution may have reduced their profits in the short-term activity. But when depression came they were able, simply because of inhibiting foresight in time of boom, to make substantially higher profits than their competitors. Similarly, the Holt brothers by their conservatism delayed the rebuilding of their fleet. When the rebuilding finally took place in the 1890s, they were able to take advantage of a long series of technological developments and thus, without the expense of innovation and experiment, to equip their ships with the best and most modern improvements. In this way they achieved a competitive advantage over their rivals and, in the long run, their profits increased beyond their own expectation. In other words, these two firms, by sacrificing maximum profits in the short-run, obtained a greater reward in the long-run. Economic theory may supply a reasonable, if impersonal, explanation of this kind of 'swings and roundabouts' behaviour, but it is the business historian who is more keenly aware of the individual motives and decisions prompting such behaviour. Both reach the same conclusion that maximisation of average profits was ultimately achieved.

Again, the development of the Booth family interests from leather manufacture and shipping and from shipping into a complex of other enterprises in the twentieth century can be similarly regarded. So too, can the process leading to the domination of Unilever in the control and output of their vast range of commodities; and Pilkingtons in the production of sheet glass and Spencers in the supply of rubber mechanicals. Not invariably, however, does the historian accept the refinement of theory in determining the *method* which a firm might use in maximising its profits. It is quite clear from Dr Payne's excellent study that Spencers set their prices more in accordance with the marginalist theory of price determination than with the theory that postulates that businessmen follow a full-cost principle of pricing. In fact, it would appear that this firm's pricing policy reflected the desire to obtain maximum security. The attainment of maximum profits was subordinate to this objective. Even so, the conclusion is reached that 'it may be argued that this is exactly the same thing as saying that Spencers aimed to secure maximum profits in the long run, but *merely* to have said this, it is felt, would have failed adequately to describe the firm's pricing policy'.[18]

IV

The above quotation underlines the significance of the use of economic theory by the business historian. It adds a further dimension to his work even though it may also present him with a second dilemma. A knowledge of theoretical analysis can lift his narrative from the level of the purely descriptive to that of deep perspective. The dilemma confronting him lies in the choice of those particular aspects of analysis which can best serve his purpose.

There is still one important development of the theory of profit maximisation which has to be considered. It has been argued that the course of many a flourishing business has been diverted because, at a precise stage in its history, the entrepreneur has preferred to maximise his satisfactions rather than his profits; that is to say, he prefers to have more leisure and a lower level of income rather than continuous business activity in search of increasing profits. The Rathbone family can be cited as an example of this tendency. In most large firms men may seek more leisure and achieve it, but there are always others to carry forward policies with vigour and determination. Old men retire, young men bring new ideas and new vision. In Schumpeter's strict definition of the dynamic role of the entrepreneur this facet of behaviour need not therefore be considered as being particularly significant. It might well be, however, that the reverse case, where a man stays in control of policy long after he ought to have retired, might have profound and lasting disadvantages for the firm's future growth.

How then, in attempting to assess the behaviour of businessmen can the historian either reinforce or check the validity of economic theory when his observations lead him to believe that, on occasion, the entrepreneur takes decisions inconsistent with the strict premise of theoretical hypothesis! Even when the businessman behaves in the way theory says he should behave, can he, in fact, determine the point at which his profit can be maximised? Most certainly not; but it would be foolish of the historian to ignore the value of a theoretical technique on this account. Modern refinements of the theory of maximisation go far towards helping the historian by recognising that the entrepreneur himself has difficulty in calculating maximum profit. The concept now provides a much more realistic and precise framework in determining this process. Attention is now drawn to the fact that it is entirely unrealistic to suppose that businessmen calculate from imaginary demand schedules. Recent studies of oligopoly suggests that the starting point is not a supposed demand schedule but a realistic, objective and determinable equal profit curve.[19] Although these studies relate mainly to the activities of oligopolists and monopolists, it seems reasonable to assume that many entrepreneurs may have behaved in this way at stated period in their firms' history.

The businessman knows how much he sold last year and the price he received per unit of product. He can, therefore, plot one point on last year's demand schedule. Starting from this point he can estimate two things: first, what the cost would be of producing many different outputs and secondly, what the selling price would have to be at each level of output in order to give him the same amount of profit as he received last year. This can be calculated objectively from his records. Thus, he is able to draw up an equal profit curve. In consultation with his sales manager he may decide to sell a given quantity at a given price, presuming this to be a combination on the curve. The sales manager may feel that they could sell the given quantity at a higher price, in which case future experience would suggest a higher profit than that received last year. The point is that no attempt is made to draw up a demand schedule showing all possible prices and outputs. The range of prices and outputs drawn up simply shows equal profit with that of last year.

Here, at least, is some common ground on which the theorists and the business historian can make use of each other's techniques. The latter knows from his analysis of business records that the entrepreneur has been doing what is described above for a very long time. There is, however, a qualification to be made in respect of a further development of this theoretical exposition. The starting point for price and output calculations is cost of production. The logical conclusion from this is that it is a more realistic explanation of the entrepreneur's behaviour to assume that he bases his strategy on the premise that he must be prepared to adjust his prices in order to sell a given output rather than that he knew how much he could sell at each price and fix the most profitable output accordingly.[20] This is within the comprehension of historical analysis and, providing the data are available, the additional use of a theoretical technique can bring weight and authority to the historian's conclusions.

V

Nevertheless, however much the historian may wish to widen historical analysis by the use of economic analysis, it is obvious that there are areas in which the two techniques cannot be satisfactorily married.[21] Economic theory is not a universal standard of measurement which can be used indiscriminately by the historian. It is a progressive and a developing system of thought. A knowledge of theoretical concepts, however, can give the historian the insight enabling him to pose specific questions which, in turn, gives added perspective in the use of his material. In such matters as cost and pricing policies and decision-taking in Schumpeter's dynamic sense, a knowledge of theory must make him a better historian. On the other hand it can be argued that a knowledge of the business historian's findings can help to make the economist a better theorist.[22] Where it is possible to use both techniques the advantages are, therefore, mutual. We must agree with Dr Supple's statement that every business historian in writing business history should ask himself the question 'What were these men trying to accomplish in embarking upon a business career'? The answers to this question will be varied and surprising. They will certainly not agree that the main purpose was to maximise profits in every aspect of the business undertaking. The Holts, the Booths, the Rathbones and Levers all provided and maintained services which were not strictly economical; the Pilkingtons despite their quest for innovation, held on to traditional methods of production in the pursuance of craftsmanship. All this was done in the interest of goodwill. The businessman, therefore, is very often as much concerned with presenting an image of his activities as with the pursuit of profit. The theory of profit maximisation might, perhaps, take a more realistic view of this phenomenon.

If we examine the firms which have been used as illustration in this article, we find that the question of intention provides a common thread from which depends a multiplicity of behaviour. They were all pursuing an acquisitive policy in maintaining themselves; they developed markets or made products as opportunity offered. They proceeded by trial and error. They built up goodwill for quality of service and excellence of product. In their own way and in accordance with circumstances they were, in Alfred Holt's words, 'striving to build up a firm which should be durable.'

It has been the object of this article to demonstrate that an important economic concept has, in certain respects, been transformed into a tool which the business historian can use. The inherent difficulties of its use due to the inconsistencies of human behaviour have, by reason of the progression of the theory itself, become less formidable. But the dilemma of the business historian in translating the relevant parts of the theory into the terms of his subject matter, still remains. This in no way invalidates Dr Barry Supple's thesis. By the use of theory the historian will escape from the dullness of mere description and make his studies lively and worth-while.

NOTES

1 The author is indebted to Mr H. R. Parker of the Department of Economics, the University of Liverpool, for his critical comment and for permission to make use of material relating to Rothschild's thesis on the security motive.

2 Barry E. Supple, 'The Uses of Business History', *Business History* IV, 2, June 1962, 81-90.

3 A. Fritz Redlich, 'Approaches to Business History', *Business History Review*, XXXVI, 1, Spring 1962, 66. This excellent paper gives a wider interpretation to such questions.

4 T. S. Ashton, *An Eighteenth Century Industrialist: Peter Stubs of Warrington 1756-1806* (1939, reprinted 1961).

5 A. H. John, *A Liverpool Merchant House: Alfred Booth and Company 1863-1958* (1959).

6 Charles Wilson, *The History of Unilever: a Study in Economic Growth* (1954).

7 Sheila Marriner, *Rathbones of Liverpool 1845-73* (1961).

8 Francis E. Hyde (with the assistance of J. R. Harris), *Blue Funnel: A History of Alfred Holt and Company of Liverpool 1865-1914* (1957).

9 T. C. Barker, *Pilkington Brothers and the Glass Industry* (1960).

10 P. L. Payne, *Rubber and Railways in the Nineteenth Century* (1961).

11 There is an extensive literature on this subject. See particularly the work of Veblen, Gamb, Davenport and Brady. The security motive is dealt with extensively in K. W. Rothschild, 'Price Theory and Oligopoly', *Readings in Price Theory*, Selected by a Committee of the American Economic Association (1935), 440-466; this chapter was reprinted from the *Economic Journal*, LVII (1947), 299-320; for later refinements on decision-taking see C. F. Carter, G. P. Meredith and G. L. S. Shackle (eds.), *Uncertainty and Business Decisions* (1957), 60-74; R. A. D. Egerton, *Investment Decisions under Uncertainty* (1960); for the role of the entrepreneur under conditions of technical change see relevant chapter in C. F. Carter and B. R. Williams, *Industry and Technical Progress* (1957).

12 Economic theory recognises a varied interpretation of the word 'entrepreneur' in relation to function. The word is here used in a general sense.

13 K. W. Rothschild, op. cit., 450-60.

14 The word 'irrational' is here used in a non-economic sense. As stated in the text economic theory regards as rational any end which the entrepreneur may achieve; but see A. Fritz Redlich, op. cit., 69.

15 J. A. Schumpeter, *Theory of Economic Development* (1912) and *Business Cycles* (1939).

16 K. Wicksell, *Lectures on Political Economy* (1935).

17 K. W. Rothschild, op. cit., 450-60.

18 P. L. Payne, op. cit., 134.

19 W. J. Eiteman, *Price Determination in Oligopolistic and Monopolistic Situations*: Michigan Business Reports Number 33 (1960), 32-41; see also R. L. Hall and C. J. Hitch 'Price Theory and Business Behaviour', *Oxford Economic Papers*, No. 2 (May 1939), 12-45.

20 *Ibid.*, see also W. J. Baumol, *Economic Theory and Operations Analysis* (1961). 192-205.

21 See Edith Penrose, *Theory of the Growth of the Firm* (1959), 184; also P. L.

Payne, 'The Uses of Business History', *Business History*, V.1, December 1962, 18.

22 See A. H. Cole, *Business Enterprise in its Social Setting* (1959). In his Preface, xiii, Professor Arthur Cole emphasises this point. 'In fact, if economics takes on an evolutionary cast, there seems no area so central for the scientific handling of economic change — stagnation and decline as well as growth — with all relevant factors brought into the models, as entrepreneurial history — business administration dealing with economic forces over time within a framework of social institutions and cultural themes. It would not be economics reduced to a series of algebraic formulae, but it might well be economics more useful to decision-makers concerned with long-run problems in business, in government, and in society'.

ADDENDUM

Since this article was written many excellent business histories have been published. Further work on such large industrial undertakings as Courtaulds, Pilkingtons and Unilever, have provided deep and penetrating insights into the decision-taking process of management. Other works, namely those concerned with shipping companies, have attempted to give a precise definition of the methods by which resources were employed in anticipation of a maximum return. In general, the opening up of primary sources of information has added greatly to our knowledge of individual firms and the function of the controllers of resources. In a more particular sense, however, considerable advances have been made in the use of techniques linking theoretical concepts with a more highly sophisticated analysis of historical data.

If one starts from the premise that a primary objective in the study of Economics is concerned with the allocation of scarce resources and that within this objective may be fitted a theory (now much revised) of maximisation, it follows that the business historian may be equally concerned with these concepts in the analysis of his source material. Let it be emphasised that the business historian must always be the exponent of the role of the individual in a qualitative historical setting. At the same time, he has found it necessary to widen the scope of his presentation through the use of quantitative techniques. Statistical analysis has, therefore, become part of the general stock in trade. In many recent publications where the data could be readily submitted to statistical exercise, the result has been that the actions of individuals have been given a deeper perspective. Over a wide range of business archives the records of shipping companies can, perhaps, provide the material most suitable for statistical analysis. The investment in a ship is a definable quantity; the earning capacity over a period of twenty years can be measured accurately, the depreciation can be assessed in precise terms and actual returns from employment can be compared with anticipated returns. The rate of interest received (representing the marginal efficiency of capital) may be calculated. In short, the application of various quantitative techniques in such an instance, may enable the business historian to make a more accurate judgment about the decision to invest and the worthwhile nature or otherwise of that investment.

If business historians wish to pursue their craft within an analytical framework supported by quantitative assessment, it is a matter of urgency that the records of firms should be preserved intact. In the context of this comment, it is essential that Board Minutes, Directors Reports, annual accounts and business correspondence should provide the core for investigation as it is from this central body of material that statistical information can be compiled. In particular, the annual accounts and balance sheets provide figures for the construction of cost-revenue equations, the return on capital employed, the extent of capital indebtedness, the earning capacity and the control over long and short-term funds. Such information can help the historian to make judgments on the use and allocation of resources within possible limits of maximisation. As a result, a clearer definition of the effectiveness of policy decisions should be made possible. It follows, therefore, that in order to ensure such a method, the historian must equip himself with a knowledge of accountancy techniques and procedures. In other words, the writing of business history now involves the use of historical, theoretical, quantitative and accountancy techniques in the analysis of decision-taking processes.

There is, however, one other aspect of business behaviour (as mentioned in the article above) which still remains unresolved. Two recently published books (B. M. Deakin and T. Seward, *Shipping Conferences* and P. N. Davies, *The Trade Makers*) have emphasised the fact that shipping companies could have earned a much higher rate of return on their capital had they invested in an alternative form of enterprise such as, for example, manufacturing industry. Instead of considering this possibility, however, many companies built up large reserve funds during the 1930s as a bulwark against being forced out of their traditional line of business. This particular attitude was, undoubtedly, governed by preference, technical knowledge and ultimately goodwill in the provision of an efficient service. One must conclude from this that, within the prevailing conditions of the time, it was still possible to employ knowledge and managerial skill in an endeavour to secure a maximum utilisation of resources by taking decisions based on the experience of a fluctuating economic environment; it would have been quite another matter for those same resources to have been used in an alternative form of enterprise requiring the application of an entirely new range of criteria. One of the major conclusions in the article above must, therefore, remain unaltered. Businessmen will always tend to use their capital in those undertakings where their experience and knowledge is most likely to bring them satisfaction and a reasonable reward.

In historical terms, the hypothesis that businessmen within an identifiable group work within the bounds of their own criteria for maximisation of resources or, conversely, that one group has not generally been led into the investment of their capital in the enterprise of another group through the inducement of higher rates of return, can only be tested by the production of many more good business histories. As more business archives are thrown open to investigation, the greater will be the historian's capacity for synthesis. To this end the writing of business history can be given greater precision by making use of theoretical concepts and allied quantitative techniques. A final word of warning needs to be given. Business history deals primarily with the acquisitive instincts of human beings. In this context, they are often imprecise, unreliable and sometimes wayward. Unpredictable actions by individuals must always bring some degree of qualification in the use of the more sophisticated forms of measurement. At best, economic theory can suggest how businessmen ought to behave given certain prerequisites; statistics can be applied to test the effectiveness of behaviour. It is the task of the business historian to pose the questions and seek out the answers to those questions, within the limits of his source material.

3
Business History and
the Theory of the Growth
of the Firm

Louis Galambos*

For some years now business historians have been much per-
turbed about their discipline. This concern springs from very real
problems indeed; it is obvious, for instance, that business history is
producing few generalisations.[1] To all but the* most charitable, it
must be apparent that many of the books and articles in this field
border on antiquarianism. Much of the work that is being done
deals with particular businesses or businessmen, asking only those
questions which can be answered directly from the company
archives that are being used. As a result, most business histories sit
in their well-bound splendour on the shelves of university libraries,
untouched by historians, ignored by economists, unnoticed by the
general reading public. Even many business historians appear
normally to use the books of their colleagues only for reference; I
have a deep suspicion that they seldom read very many of these fat
volumes in their entirety.

The source of these difficulties — as has been clear for some
time — is the lack of a broad and meaningful intellectual framework. The discipline is limping along without the kind of synthesis
that would lend meaning to case studies and would enable its
practitioners to draw general conclusions from their monographic
research.[2] In its early years business history utilised the stage
analysis formulated by N. S. B. Gras.[3] His general history focused
upon the internal administration of business and was particularly
valuable for its treatment of business developments in the early
stages of the evolution of capitalism. His analysis of the changes
which took place in the business system after the end of the nineteenth century was, however, relatively superficial, and this, I think,
is one of the reasons that recent business historians have

*From *Explorations in Entrepreneurial History*, Second Series, Vol. 4, No. 1, pp.
3-16. Reprinted by permission of the editor of *Explorations in Entrepreneurial
History* and the author.

abandoned Gras's stages instead of updating them. In a sense the discipline simply outgrew Gras's concepts, but unfortunately the old synthesis was discarded without building anything to take its place.

During the past few years several conferences and many luncheon meetings have been filled with talk about what the new framework should be — but the plans never seem to get off the drafting board. Eleven years ago, R. Richard Wohl pointed out that: 'The chief problem of business history . . . is to discover some way in which the diverse and separate activities of a multitude of independent firms can be woven together so that the development of the nation, or a region, or of a particular period can be better understood.[4] Four years later (in 1958), at the Harvard Business School's Conference on the History of American Business, the conferees agreed that a synthesis was 'desirable,' and that it was 'possible to proceed, at least in some areas, using available books, monographs, and articles.' Those in attendance were not able to 'produce a blueprint for a history of American business,' but 'there was general agreement that the time has come to attempt one or more syntheses in this field.'[5] But alas, the call to action was completely ignored.

This set the stage for another conference. In 1961, the business historians again gathered on the banks of the Charles River. Once more it was solemnly announced 'that competent scholars, interested in contributing to a wider and better understanding of business through historical research, have frequently failed to achieve their objective, largely because they have lacked a generally accepted analytical framework into which their findings could be fitted.'[6] Summarising the results of this latest get-together, Arthur M. Johnson said that while there were several suggestions about how that framework might be built, there was no consensus as to what, exactly, it would look like.[7] If another meeting were held today, the results would undoubtedly be the same.[8] On the assumptions that this is an unfortunate situation and that it is time to do some positive work on the foundations of a general business history, the following paper attempts a preliminary exploration of the problem. While the author is merely an apprentice or, at best, a journeyman in the field of business history, he has grown impatient with the master craftsman and has decided that the best way to make progress toward a synthesis is to stop having special conferences and to start writing about a general history.

THE BUSINESS UNIT VERSUS THE BUSINESSMAN

As the first step toward a synthesis, business historians might do well to decide whether they are going to focus primarily upon the businessman or upon the business organisation. The failure to make this decision has caused a considerable amount of confusion. This is so, in part, because the problems of abstraction and generalisation for the two subjects are different. Questions about the businessman, qua man, necessarily carry the historian into realms of individual motivation, of environmental influences upon the individual, and of the psychology of decision-making. These are interesting subjects for exploration. But the theorising that they involve is inherently different from that required if the historian's major concern is the business unit as an economic and social organisation. Building a general historical analysis of business behaviour in either of these areas would be a formidable task, but business historians have taken on both at the same time. Furthermore, they have danced back and forth, now emphasising one and then the other, with little apparent concern for the extent to which this has minimised the chances of achieving a synthesis.[9]

Given the necessity to make a choice between emphasising either the businessmen or their organisations, which would be preferable? My own answer is that at the present time the best way to make some progress toward synthesis is to designate historical periods and to formulate an analytical framework which stress the evolution of the business unit. This does not mean that the individual would be ignored; it merely proposes that monographic research and in particular biographical studies should address themselves to a coherent body of questions about business organisations.

Admittedly, this particular approach involves certain liabilities. The history would probably become more technical, the craft more specialised; we would never recapture the general reading public. Moreover, historians and archivists negotiating for access to company records would be handicapped. At present, by stressing the personal element in business history they can appeal to the ego of the businessman and his family. By contrast, history written in organisational terms would probably be less interesting to many of the private and corporate benefactors who have supplied business historians with their manuscripts and with much of their financial support.[10]

There are, however, many advantages to a synthesis formulated around the organisational aspects of business. For one thing, the fundamental problems of generalisation will be somewhat simplified. Group behaviour seems to lend itself to analysis more easily than do the complexities of individual action. Organisations have a structure of authority which can be charted. They do not have the subconscious element which plagues the analysts of individual behaviour. Organised activity, by its very nature, involves a degree of rationality which makes systematic inquiry easier.[11]

Another advantage stems from the fact that the organisational approach will facilitate interaction between business history and two particular social science disciplines which deal with related subjects. Certainly we cannot afford to ignore any body of theory which might be used as a stepping stone to effective generalisation. In the two cases of which I am speaking, social scientists are already working on theoretical constructs which can be useful to business historians. These two fields are the sociological theory of complex organisations and the economic theory of the growth of the firm.[12] The latter, in particular, seems to offer much in the way of stimulating ideas, and the purposes of this paper can be served by treating the economic theory and leaving the sociology for consideration at some other time. Having made my decision to deal essentially in terms of business organisations, I would like now to look more closely at this special branch of theoretical economics to see what it offers to business history.[13]

THE THEORY OF THE GROWTH OF THE FIRM

The theory of the growth of the firm — as distinguished from the traditional theory of the firm — is a new branch of economics. Two of the leading economists who have helped launch this new sub-discipline are Edith Tilton Penrose and William J. Baumol.[14] As their books and articles make clear, they are developing a dynamic micro-theory which attempts by constructing models to understand various aspects of the process by which a firm grows.[15] Before Penrose and Baumol attacked this problem, theory of the firm focused upon such questions as the determination of prices or the level of output for the firm at a particular point or slice in time.[16] Management was considered as a given; it was eliminated by assumption in order to enable the economist to construct a workable, static model; management could only change in the long run and thus was not a justifiable consideration.

The theory of the growth of the firm involves important departures from this tradition. In studying the process of growth, Penrose, for example, makes management and the body of talents that it represents one of the important factors in setting the pace and direction of firm growth.[17] Managerial or entrepreneurial skills which are not fully exploited provide, Penrose says, an internal pressure, a kind of automatic or built-in stimulant, for the firm to expand.[18] Productive resources available to the firm are also important. But as Penrose makes clear, it is the interaction between the material and the human factors which is decisive in shaping an organisation's development.[19]

Baumol also brings the businessman into the study of the process of firm growth. His businessman is a strange type of person to encounter in the literature of theoretical economics. He is a chap who knows very little about his own cost and demand functions. He is prejudiced by past experience to be favourably inclined toward expansion.[20] He does not even maximise profits — and this is a truly appalling departure from orthodoxy — he maximises the rate of growth of sales (meaning total revenue) so long as he can maintain a certain minimum profit level.[21]

The theoretical firm that these businessmen direct is a large, diversified corporation operating under oligopolistic conditions. Attention is fixed squarely upon the successful, the growing firm; this, after all, is what the model is designed to explain.[22] Both economists accept the existence of imperfect competition; both assume that competitive pressure nonetheless remains an important fact of life for the businessman and his business.[23] The men who direct the affairs of these model firms are professional managers. It is assumed that management and ownership are separated as is, indeed, the case in most of our present-day corporate giants.[24]

One of the most interesting questions raised in this quest for a dynamic model involves the time-range of decision-making. How far into the future do businessmen look when they make their entrepreneurial decisions about the allocation of firm resources? Or, to put the question another way, what is the 'expectational horizon' of top management? In dealing with this question on a theoretical plane, some economists have suggested that beyond a certain point in the future, management's expectations become so vague or 'shapeless' that nothing more than normal interest on the firm's assets can be anticipated.[25] Another approach has been to assume that in the modern firm, with its flexibility and high degree of rational planning, management can always expect new opportunities to arise in the future; in reality, then, the expectational horizon reaches out toward infinity.[26] This, of course, is the problem which lends itself rather easily to empirical study, but so far as I know, there has been no systematic treatment of this question either by historians or by institutional economists.

Another aspect of this search for a dynamic model of the firm has involved an effort to determine the logic which explains particular ways of growing. What, for instance, lies behind the process of diversification? Is there any pattern to the situations which

result in a decision to expand through the acquisition of going concerns? Through merger with another business or businesses?
Penrose has been studying those problems; she has stressed the
manner in which the firm's pool of resources influences the route
which growth follows; available managerial talents once more enter
the picture, since it is the managers who must somehow integrate
any new organisation or resources into the old system on an efficient
basis.[27]

I could go on reviewing the hypotheses developed by economists
in this special sub-discipline, but I believe that this brief survey has
already made several points clear: First, the theory of the growth of
the firm has broken sharply with the traditional tenets of the theory
of the firm; by introducing a variety of complex variables and long-
run considerations, the micro-growth theorists have sacrificed the
pleasant predictability of the familiar supply and demand functions
in an effort to develop a dynamic model. Second, this venture into
dynamics is a very recent development, and the economists have
really only begun to lay the foundation for their model. At this
point there is basic disagreement over the most rudimentary
elements in the theory of the growth of the firm. Third, despite
these problems, the economists have already asked a number of
important questions about business behaviour; even the premises
upon which their models are constructed involve assumptions
which business historians cannot afford to ignore. By this last point,
all that I mean is that the economists assume that there are patterns that can be explained rationally; it is also the business
historian's job, I think, to find these patterns or norms, to help
explain them, and to find and explain the actions which diverge
from the norms. The economists do not, in this case, have many
specific answers, but they do have a storehouse of good questions.
Wherever these questions lend themselves to empirical study, I
believe that business historians should be eager to work hand-in-
hand with the theoreticians. Out of this cooperative effort would
perhaps come the general synthesis the business historians have
been looking for during the past decade.

All that I am suggesting is that business historians follow a path
that has already been blazed — with favourable results — by many
economic historians in this country. They have begun to share ideas
and results with the economists who are working on macro-growth
theory. The economists in this branch of dynamics have been
forced to examine a variety of historical problems in their efforts to
construct aggregate growth models. I do not believe that they have
suffered (although the predictability of their models has) from this
encounter with history. On the other hand, the historians — and I

might mention Douglass North as a good example — have obviously benefitted from their contact with economic theory. This is true even though there is certainly no consensus among either economists or historians about the best growth model to use.[28]

Similarly, the entrepreneurial school associated with the Research Centre in Entrepreneurial History achieved outstanding results from a blending of theory and history. In this case the theory was Schumpeter's grand design, centering about the innovator as the prime mover in economic development.[29] Business historians have also been influenced by Schumpeter's concepts, and any general business history would, perforce, include consideration of the entrepreneurial function and the manner in which it is performed within business organisations. At present, however, it would seem best to leave most aspects of macro-theory to the economic historians, while business history matches micro-research with the theory of the growth of the firm, a micro-theory.

BUT HOW CAN THE HISTORIAN USE THE THEORY?

Thus far, however, all that I have given you is some rather vague promises. Before one is able to consummate a marriage of convenience between business history and economic theory, the terms of the contract must be stated more precisely.[30] Perhaps I can briefly suggest what these terms might be. To begin with, the theory of the growth of the firm (despite its limitations) offers a dowry which provides the basic elements from which one can build an historical period around the dominant form of business unit in the present-day American economy. General Motors, DuPont, Standard Oil — these corporations are all similar to the theoretical firm posited by growth analysis. Each of these businesses is very large, has professional management, is diversified and has the ability to move in a wide variety of new directions. The firm exists as an entity separate from its owners and its managers — it has a life (incidentally, a very long life) of its own. These are successful, growing firms; their industries are the oligopolies which play a dominant role in our modern economy. Given their important position in the economy, it seems reasonable to construct an historical period around this type of business: we might call it something like the Era of the Decentralised-Managerial Firm.

In analysing this period, business historians would do well to accept as a starting point a number of the hypotheses advanced by the growth theorists. Let us assume, for instance, that there is a general or average pattern of growth for the Decentralised-Managerial Firm. Moreover, let us posit that the type of managerial resources which characterises this era has an important influence upon the growth of the firm and upon the general configuration of administrative action within the corporation. Another reasonable hypothesis is that the average range of the expectational horizon for the management of this type of business can be determined — at any rate, the average point at which the expectations become shapeless can be found. One economist has suggested that the horizon usually lies from ten to twelve years beyond the present — this, however, is an educated guess which historians should be able to test, perhaps to change, and certainly to refine.[31] Similarly, one would expect to find a pattern of managerial behaviour consistent with certain fundamental goals — such as profit or sales maximisation — and with certain major and minor constraints, such as adverse governmental action.

After having absorbed these hypotheses, however, the business historian must fill out the analysis. Business units which are unsuccessful must be brought into the picture. The smaller firms that surround the large corporations must be included and their functions analysed; growth theory has something specific to offer here, as Penrose has advanced the idea that as the Decentralised-Managerial Firms grow, they leave interstices in the economy and that these gaps are (and will continue to be) the special domain of small business.[32]

Business historians must also give their period a chronological dimension that it thus far lacks. As Alfred D. Chandler, Jr., has already demonstrated, this particular form of business structure has only become widespread during the last quarter of a century.[33] In the years from around 1920 through 1940, the Decentralised-Managerial Firm was being developed, analysed and perfected by such pioneers as DuPont and General Motors. Subsequently, the strategy of diversification and the corresponding decentralisation structure were widely adopted throughout the economy.[34]

Another historical element which must be added to the stage analysis is a treatment of the forces (1) which led to the development of the Decentralised-Managerial Firm; and (2) which shaped its subsequent evolution as a business form. Chandler has also worked on both of these questions and has demonstrated convincingly that in the cases he has examined, the changing nature of the market and the new technology were the major forces at work.[35] Professor Chandler has acknowledged, however, that we can still benefit from research in company records on this aspect of evolving structure of American business. We still need to know more about the forces acting on the structure of businesses that have not yet been studied in detail.

For the moment, however, I think that this outline will suffice to indicate how history and micro-theory could be blended. We have a fairly well-defined historical period built around the dominant form of business enterprise. Our major subjects for study include the forces creating and shaping this type of business and the patterns of business behaviour associated with the Decentralised-Managerial Firm. Other business units are to be analysed in relation to or in comparison to the giant firm.

Once this most recent period and the transitional era are set up, the business historian is inevitably led back into the past. An earlier period can perhaps be discerned: from around 1870 through 1920, the American economy was apparently dominated by a different form of economic organisation — one that we might call the Centralised-Industrial Business. As an archetype of this sort of business unit, one might well mention the Standard Oil Company.[36] For this era, the transitional period is rather poorly defined, but we can hazard a guess that (by ignoring developments in cotton textiles) the limits can probably be set at around 1850 through 1870.[37]

In this period, as in the first one, it seems reasonable to propose that there was a general pattern or patterns of growth. While the management of this type of business certainly differed from the professional managers of the modern era, we can assume that the general characteristics of this earlier class of businessmen had a decisive impact upon the normal styles of growth and business administration of their era. One would imagine that the expectational horizon of the Centralised-Industrial Business would not extend so far into the future as it does for the modern firm, but at any rate the possibility of estimating an average horizon needs to be explored. Historians have already done some work on the basic goals and constraints which guided managerial decision-making in this sort of organisation. But the differences between this pattern and the goals and constraints of the managers of the Decentralised-Managerial Firm have, so far as I know, not yet been systematically examined.[38] A number of different business histories have also described the forces shaping the nineteenth-century industrial unit, although we know all too little about the formative years of this type of business. As yet, a general treatment of the subject remains to be written.[39]

Once this period is tentatively established, the historian will again be carried back in an effort to find the boundaries and characteristics of the preceding time. For the present, we can simplify this task by limiting our survey to America. Then we can perhaps be satisfied with a single period, extending from the founding of the colonies through about 1850; this era was, it seems, dominated by the Mercantile Business.[40] In this instance there can be no introductory or transitional period, since this form of business unit was transplanted in American soil from overseas.

With the dominant form of enterprise determined and the chronological limits tentatively introduced, a set of hypotheses similar to those advanced for the previous two periods can be used. A pattern of growth and administration, an average expectational horizon, a set of goals and constraints, a profile of management and an analysis of the forces shaping the evolution of the primary form of business organisation must be charted. It seems reasonable to suggest that for this type of business, the horizon was considerably closer to the present than it was for the Centralised-Industrial Business. Similarly, in the Mercantile Business, the individual looms large in the normal pattern of business operations — the kinship group appears to have exercised a decisive influence upon the path and pattern of growth.[41] These and related hypotheses await, however, the kind of vigorous but general examination that is beyond the scope of this paper.

CONSEQUENCES OF THE STAGE ANALYSIS AND MICRO-ECONOMIC HYPOTHESES

What would be the advantages, the precise advantages, of this particular analysis framed primarily in terms of the evolving form of the business organisation? Most importantly, it would offer a meaningful synthesis. It would provide business historians with a body of generalisations. Admittedly, a true theory of business history can only be achieved when the forces acting to shift the system from one stage to another are more fully understood, but at least this approach will enable the historians to get at the central problems.

Furthermore it would open the way for comparative studies. Heretofore business historians have, for the most part, done case studies; given the volume of research materials with which they must grapple, they have found it difficult to use the comparative approach. But by using this form of general analysis, it seems that the business historian could be constantly measuring his subject against the pure form or type of the synthesis. Let me give an example of how this might be done, using in this case Thomas Cochran's extremely interesting history of the Pabst Brewing Company.[42] In describing the company's expansion in the latter part of the nineteenth century, Cochran was able to show that this company grew in a particular way. Moreover, he went beyond the level of generalisation attained in most business histories, as he was able to demonstrate that the Pabst growth pattern differed from that of other major companies in the industry.[43] Armed with a general business history, however, I believe that he could have gone one step further, comparing this pattern with that of the norm for this era or at least with the normal pattern for consumer goods industries.

This approach to the problem also opens the way for further cross-fertilisation between economic theory and business history. In the future, the economists will continue to improve their models; historians can counter with their own generalisations about the framework and about the questions it contains. By working within the confines of a general business history, the historians should be able to develop empirical data of a sort that would be extremely valuable to their colleagues in history and in economics.

As a final word, let me say that this hypothesis or set of hypotheses is advanced in the hope that it will draw a particular kind of criticism. I have complete confidence that my critics will be able to tear apart sections or perhaps all of this framework. I would hope, however, that when they do so, they would build something positive to take its place. Then we can make some progress toward our common goal: more meaningful and interesting business history.

NOTES

1 Only two examples come to mind: a number of business historians have contributed to the modification of the robber baron concept; see, Hal Bridges, 'The Robber Baron Concept in American History', *Business History Review*, XXXII, No. 1 (1958), 1-13. Alfred D. Chandler, Jr., has developed a series of important generalisations about the evolution of big business in modern America; see, 'The Beginnings of "Big Business" in American Industry', *Business History Review*, XXXIII, No. 1 (1959), 1-31; and *Strategy and Structure: Chapters in the History of the Industrial Enterprise* (Cambridge, 1962). Hereafter cited as Chandler, *Strategy*. Aside from these contributions, the pickings are slim.

2 I do not mean to imply that this is the only problem facing business history today. See, for instance, George R. Taylor's discussion of the pro-business bias which characterises the so-called revisionist business historians of the 1950s: 'Comment upon a paper by Fritz Redlich', *Business History Review*, XXXVI, No. 1 (1962), 79-85.

3 N. S. B. Gras, *Business and Capitalism: An introduction to Business History* (New York, 1939).

4 R. Richard Wohl, 'The Significance of Business History', *Business History Review*, XXXVIII, No. 2 (1954), 131.

5 Arthur M. Johnson, 'Conference on the History of American Business: A Summary Report', *Business History Review*, XXXIII, No. 2 (1959), 205, 210.

6 Harold Williamson, 'Comment upon a paper by Clarence C. Walton', *Business History Review*, XXXVI, No. 1 (1962), 42-43.

7 Arthur M. Johnson, 'Where Does Business History Go From Here?' *Business*

History Review, XXXVI, No. 1 (1962), 11-20, especially p. 14.

8 In 1962, Peter L. Payne once again said that a major problem facing the discipline was to figure out 'how to add up the present miscellany of enterprise histories to arrive at something significant . . .' 'Uses of Business History', *Business History*, V, No. 1 (1962), 15.

9 At the 1961 conference, Richard C. Overton gave an excellent statement of the methodology which inevitably leads to this result: 'the business historian need start with nothing more than the simple working hypothesis that a given firm deserves investigation. Then, in his research and writing he should concern himself in inductive fashion first with the conditioning factors bearing upon the successive phases of decision-making . . ., next with the policies themselves, and finally with the traceable results. Only when he has put this story together — wherever it may lead him and without concern for preconceived destination points — will a portion of truthful human experience be available for such use as may then seem appropriate'. 'Comment upon a paper by Clarence C. Walton', *Business History Review*, XXXVI, No. 1 (1962), 40.

10 On the other hand, this 'liability' might eventually help business historians solve the problem mentioned in footnote 2, above.

11 As Thomas C. Cochrane has observed: 'Although the *purpose* of business is to organise economic factors in such a way as to secure a profit, the *means* of business is to organise human beings in operational groups'. 'Comment upon a paper by Herman E. Krooss', *Business History Review*, XXXVI, No. 1 (1962), 55.

12 On the former, see Amitai Etzioni, ed., *Complex Organisations: A Sociological Reader* (New York, 1961); and the same author's study entitled *A Comparative Analysis of Complex Organisations: On Power, Involvement, and Their Correlates* (Glencoe, Illinois, 1961). Some of the major contributions to the theory of the growth of the firm are discussed below.

13 At present there is virtually no cross-fertilisation. As economist Edith Tilton Penrose has noted, her ideas on the process of the growth of the firm are 'on the whole, susceptible to empirical testing against the experience of individual firms . . .' But, she said, 'Although there are many business histories and biographies of individual businessmen, only a handful are really good from this point of view . . .' *The Theory of the Growth of the Firm* (New York, 1959), p. 3. Hereafter cited as Penrose, *Theory*.

14 *Ibid.* As the title of her book suggests, Penrose addresses herself directly to the problem of building an economic model that will help economists to understand the growth of the firm. William J. Baumol approaches the problem indirectly in his study of *Business Behaviour, Value and Growth* (New York, 1959). Hereafter cited as Baumol, *Business*. Baumol analyses the static theory of oligopoly, but in the course of doing so, he introduces a number of considerations which veer from the static tradition and which give him, in fact, a dynamic model similar in some regards to that of Penrose. Baumol attempts (pp. 88-100) to fit his modified oligopoly model into an analysis of economic growth, and in this chapter completes his break with the earlier, static theory.

15 On the difference between dynamic and static models, see William J. Baumol, *Economic Dynamics* (New York, 1951), pp. 2-4.

16 For an econometric approach to micro-dynamics, see Edwin Mansfield, 'Entry, Gibrat's Law, Innovation, and the Growth of Firms', *The American Economic Review*, LII, No. 5 (1962), 1023-1050.

17 Penrose, *Theory*, pp. 43-51.
18 *Ibid.*, p. 54.
19 *Ibid.*, pp. 76-79. 'The services that resources will yield depend on the capacities of the men using them, but the development of the capacities of men is partly shaped by the resources men deal with. The two together create the special productive opportunity of a particular firm'. Cf. Penrose's general analysis with the description by Ralph W. and Muriel E. Hidy of the manner in which the Standard Oil Company became heavily involved in the production of crude petroleum. *Pioneering in Big Business: History of Standard Oil Company (New Jersey)* (New York, 1955), Chapter 7. Hereafter cited as Hidy and Hidy, *Pioneering.*
20 Baumol, *Business*, pp. 98-99. Penrose's managers and entrepreneurs seem to be slightly better informed than Baumol's, although they do not have perfect knowledge.
21 *Ibid.*, pp. 45-53. By contrast, Penrose hangs on to the orthodox assumption that the businessmen to seek by maximise profits in he long run. For a fairly elaborate discussion of this particular point, see Henderikus Geert Werkema, 'Profit and Related Objectives in the Theory of the Firm' (Unpublished dissertation, Rice University, 1962), especially pp. 134-149. Hereafter cited as Werkema, 'Profit'. In his book (1959), Baumol suggested that management probably maximised sales, but in an article published in 1962, he altered this by saying that management probably maximised at '*Rate of growth* of sales revenue and not the current *level* of sales'. 'On the Theory of Expansion of the Firm', *American Economic Review*, LII, No. 5 (1962), 1085.
22 Penrose, *Theory*, pp. 9-30.
23 In his article 'On the Theory of Expansion of the Firm', *American Economic Review*, LII, No. 5 (1962), 1078-1107, Baumol explores certain aspects of this subject on the assumption first of perfect, and then of oligopolistic, competition.
24 Baumol, *Business*, pp. 95-97, briefly discusses 'Forces Which Make for Separation' of ownership and management; he adds very little to a subject that was treated carefully in Adolf A. Berle, Jr. and Gardiner C. Means, *The Modern Corporation and Private Property* (New York, 1933).
25 Edgar O. Edwards and Philip N. Bell, *The Theory and Measurement of Business Income* (Berkeley, 1961), p. 35. Hereafter cited as Edwards and Bell, *Theory*.
26 Werkema, 'Profit', pp. 63-66.
27 Penrose, *Theory*, pp. 104-196.
28 Douglass C. North, *The Economic Growth of the United States, 1790-1860* (Englewood Cliffs, N.J., 1961). One can, I hope, approve of this cross-fertilisation without being so wildly enthusiastic as is George G. S. Murphy, 'The "New" History', *Explorations in Entrepreneurial History/Second Series*, II, No. 2 (1965), 132-146.
29 See William Miller, ed., *Men in Business: Essays on the Historical Role of the Entrepreneur* (New York, Harper Torchbooks edition, 1962); and *Explorations in Entrepreneurial History*, I through X.
30 Some historians are concerned that they and their colleagues might 'sell out' to the behavioural scientists. Arthur H. Cole has suggested that 'there has long been a notion prevalent in academic circles that a theoretical hypothesis, however shaky its bases, is somehow superior in intellectual quality to a historical finding, however broad and well supported by evidence; and the deduction has followed that historians should study theory, but theorists may be excused from immersing themselves in facts'. *Business Enterprise in its Social Setting* (Cambridge, 1959), xi. My own assumption is, however, that a joint effort would help history and theory: both hypotheses and evidence are essential to both crafts, but at this

point the economists have a monopoly on the former and the business historians have a surplus of the latter.

31 Edwards and Bell, *Theory*, p. 35, citing B. S. Keirstead, *An Essay in the Theory of Profits and Income Distribution* (Oxford, 1953), p. 37.

32 Penrose, *Theory*, pp. 223-225.

33 Chandler, *Strategy*, pp. 324-382.

34 *Ibid.*, pp. 252-282.

35 *Ibid.*, pp. 383-386.

36 See Hidy and Hidy, *Pioneering*.

37 Chandler, *Strategy*, pp. 19-24.

38 Thomas C. Cochran, *Railroad Leaders, 1845-1890, The Business Mind in Action* (Cambridge, 1953).

39 Judging from an unpublished manuscript that Professor Chandler has shown to me, it is clear that he is working on this exact problem; Alfred D. Chandler, Jr. (assisted by Stephen Salsbury), 'The Role of the Firm in the American Economy: A Historical Analysis.'

40 Bernard Bailyn, *The New England Merchants in the Seventeenth Century* (Cambridge, 1955). W. T. Baxter, *The House of Hancock: Business in Boston, 1724-1775* (Cambridge, 1945). George R. Taylor, *The Transportation Revolution, 1815-1860* (New York, 1951), pp. 10-14.

41 Bernard Bailyn, *The New England Merchants*, especially, pp. 75-111, 143-177. For the manner in which the kinship group's influence carried over into the industrial sector, see Robert K. Lamb, 'The Entrepreneur and the Community', in William Miller, ed., *Men in Business*, pp. 91-119.

42 Thomas C. Cochran, *The Pabst Brewing Company: The History of an American Business* (New York, 1948).

43 *Ibid.*, pp. 59-61.

4
Business History:
Some Proposals for Aims
and Methodology

K. A. Tucker*

I

This article has a dual purpose. First, some of the aims and methods employed in a study[1] of a New Zealand business are discussed. A summary is given of the approach adopted together with some of the unpublished sections of the thesis[2] on which the book was in part based. Secondly, many of the methodological problems encountered are discussed in the general context of what may be considered as appropriate aims and techniques for business history research.

More specifically, it is claimed that a useful approach to business history is that which gives greater emphasis to analytical techniques developed for empirical studies of the firm or industry. A further suggestion is that the presentation of these analytical features and results of business history research is best kept separate from the narrative of events, except perhaps where a serious conflict of information arises, or where an inadequacy of data requires the description to be supplemented from analytically reconstructed evidence. The suggestions that follow and the demonstration as to how these ideas were incorporated in a specific research example, is in no way a claim to superiority of methodology in all respects. Neither is it asserted that the specific example is necessarily a good demonstration of the sort of results that this approach could yield. The results shown could more correctly be regarded as a starting point for more detailed and rigorous analysis. This article does not claim that these suggestions are new and completely unpractised: rather, where these approaches are already recognised as being useful in certain circumstances, it is an argument for these

* From *Business History*, Vol. XIV (1972), pp. 1-16. Reprinted by permission of the editor of *Business History*.

techniques to be more widely used and any framework of analysis to be more clearly specified.

The firm taken as an example was originally a small drapery and millinery business begun by Misses Charlotte and Mary Milne in Auckland, New Zealand in the year 1867. The early business operated as a partnership until 1901; the major changes until then being a shift in location and rebuilding, the addition of a new partner (Henry Charles Choyce, the husband of Charlotte), and a widening range of merchandise and departments.

The business was therefore a department store by the time the partnership became a public company in 1901. Before World War I the organisation had shifted to a new location in a large multi-storied building. A major financial re-organisation was embarked upon in 1951. The firm had already sought to defend itself against competition and widen its merchandise range. It secured sources of supply by purchasing manufacturing subsidiaries and then later undertook a programme of branch expansion in other cities as well as erecting stores on new suburban sites. Up to 1967 the group of Milne and Choyce concentrated on adapting to new environmental and competitive conditions and took various measures during this period to achieve a better record of sales growth and profitability. On the centenary of the firm, relatives of the founders still occupied the top executive positions.

II

Business historians have taken up various postures over the dilemma of how to synthesise or separate presentation and analysis. In prefacing the subsequently acclaimed[3] first two volumes of Unilever's history, Charles Wilson pointed out that ' . . . a history of this kind should be both narrative and analytical, though the attempt to combine the two added seriously to the difficulties of a task already complex enough by the very nature of the business itself.'[4]

In retrospect, after the efflux of a decade of business history research and in view of the ferment in economic history over appropriate aims and techniques, it now seems that this combination was an unwise and almost impossible task. The rigorous analysis of certain features of finance, costs, pricing, market shares and product competitiveness is excessively limited and there is a danger of accepting at face value events reported from source material biased towards what contemporary spokesmen thought was happening or had occurred.

More recently, D. C. Coleman reports that in writing the history of Courtaulds he has had unrestricted access to all material and has been able to 'express responsible judgment upon the firm's achievement. Because it was agreed, during the preliminary discussions, that this was to be an analytical history, 'warts and all', I have enjoyed this freedom and exercised it.'[5] After emphasising the conflicting approaches of the theoretical economist and the orthodox historian Coleman points out that his approach has been 'eclectic'[6] and that the two volumes ' . . . are the product neither of a team of assistants nor of a computer.'[7] Coleman, in avoiding rigorous statistical analysis (as distinct from presenting statistical information), probably fears that the uniqueness and interest of the story may be lost or subjugated to a lifeless and monotonous quantification emphasising trends, components and levels. The 'mixture' he uses would appear to be correct on two grounds; namely that not all information can be quantified and not all readers have an academic interest in business history research. However, the implication that failures are reported as well as successes (ie, 'warts and all') and that interesting irregular occurrences are described as well as regular operations cannot be consistently claimed as being attributable to the actions of businessmen or the events of the business without invoking some specific framework of measurement and testing. Benchmarks must be established and be stated as the criteria before a researcher or author can claim that the veracity of businessmen's statements has been analysed or accepted, or that decisions made and actions performed have been tested against any framework of appraisal.

In pointing out defects in Australian business histories, Merab Tauman[8] has recommended that a more detailed and forceful analysis should be attempted to discover what contributes to growth and change in the firm. Clarence C. Walton[9] went further than this in suggesting that postulates and hypotheses should be developed and tested on an interdisciplinary basis in an effort to try to distil the dominant features of change and growth in business enterprises. But how helpful are these examples and suggestions? Do they present more difficulties than they resolve and do they go far enough in setting up an improved methodology and objectives for business history research?

It is the argument of this article that if we accept that growth and change are intended and planned for, and in a measure achieved, then some schema or framework must be developed for reconstructing and reviewing this interaction of decision-making, implementation and control. Some measure of the degree of control exercised over what was intended must be formulated. Some indication of the unexpected against the predicted must be evaluated and recorded.

In other words, if the business historian is to subject the records of an organisation to an analysis of growth and change, this must be measurable[10] in terms of similar indicators as were or have since become available for an independent analysis of the firm's current or prospective position in any number of respects (e.g. finance, marketing, industrial relations). This will involve an historical reconstruction or 'simulation' of the firm's change and growth using techniques of measurement and evaluation that yield a retrospective basis for objective performance review. Much of the information available to business historians is contained in minute books, special memoranda and reports to shareholders or other financially interested parties. As such, these recorded items and statistics reflect what the directors or management either sincerely thought was the current state of affairs, or alternatively, what they wished interested parties to consider as the measure of the firm's performance and status. This is one area where the imposition of some systematic measurement process would reveal how closely the reconstructed state of affairs accords with the recorded evidence. Some examples may be useful at this stage. First, consider a company that continuously presented its management or share-holders with reports expressed as a percentage change over the previous year for any particular variable.[11] Without labouring the point, it can be clearly seen that the previous year is no benchmark for performance evaluation. In this way, all recorded and reported descriptions of events could, for any one indicator taken in isolation, understate or overstate, without knowing the magnitude, the performance of the firm at any time or over any period. Secondly, consider the practice of accounting in both the timing of report preparation and the effect of this in inducing the control of certain measured variables in a systematically biased manner. A shift in the pattern of seasonal variations or the differential impact of other divisional features (e.g. product range or extent of idle capacity) may seriously misrepresent the phenomena measured should either another method of observing or estimating the variables in question be available or more explicit measures of these features be taken into account.[12] Thirdly, it could be argued that changing money values represent 'fictitious' gains and losses not controllable by management and that these should be separated out from the 'real' measures of sales, cost, assets and profit. The reconstruction of accounts using appropriate indices could yield greatly varying results from those purported to show a 'true and fair' view under the minimum conditions of disclosure to interested parties either before or after company accounting procedure legislation.[13] Finally, profit results are often cited as being attributable to certain circumstances within or beyond the control of the firm. Methods of identifying the cause of this performance must take account of a weighting of controllable and uncontrollable factors as well as a ranking in importance as contributing factors of those variables mentioned or discovered. For example, a firm may have advantages arising from factor market imperfections (e.g. labour costs, interest rates) and wrongly interpret its profit performance as attributable mainly to the efficiency of its inventory policies. Alternatively, the imposition of new taxation structures may be argued as the cause of a profit performance mainly traceable to a lack of recognition by management of changing competitive conditions in the product markets.

It could be argued that the very nature of these recorded and reported events of both a financial and non-financial nature, prevents the application of any rigorous analysis since systematic differences between 'observed' and 'actual' may be perpetuated under virtually any type of reconstruction and review framework. However, this attitude is a shameful retreat from reason and overlooks the dubious validity of any assertion that one can claim to write history 'warts and all' without erecting and stating clearly criteria for deciding what warts are, and, when they appear unmistakable and ugly, why they should have gone unmentioned or un-noticed at the time. It would also allow such features to be described as temporary and inexplicable departures from an otherwise healthy situation, or that they have been wrongly attributed to uncontrollable factors or the wrong weighting of certain causative influences. While the difficulties of setting up such criteria are not to be underestimated, it would seem that business historians are curtailing the development of research and the pedagogic usefulness of their studies unless these points are appreciated and acted upon to a greater extent.

Certain types of analysis and information may be useful as a starting point in evaluating the performance and standing of a business along the lines suggested. We must first accept the axiom that business growth and change is measurable in terms of a 'battery' of financial and other quantitative indicators and that those most appropriate for retrospective analysis are those which are currently useful and applicable.[14] It hardly requires mention that such an approach is constrained by historical problems of data availability and secrecy of information. The second requirement is that the business historian must have available the same information as used by those making the business decisions. Thirdly, it may be necessary to generate or discover information that was not used but which would have been available at the time. Finally, it is possible to make use of information that was not available at the time but has since become available or has been provided by more recently developed techniques of estimation and analysis. Those four facets, either separately or in combination, will yield far more 'objective' evaluations of growth and change than business historians have been traditionally able to achieve.

III

The specific example of Milne and Choyce mentioned earlier is now presented to indicate how some of these types of information were used and to describe various problems encountered. Basing the analysis on the notion that growth and change is measurable in terms of selected indicators and components, a 'model' consisting of a set of identities was developed to reconstruct or historically 'simulate' the financial system of the firm by both monthly and annual measures and to apply well-recognised indicators of trading efficiency and asset structure. Four particular objectives were in mind.

(1) How did the sales levels and composition change over time as between divisions, cash and credit sales and other revenue, and seasonal peaks and troughs?

(2) What changes occurred in gross margins and cost components over time and in the phasing of cash receipts and outlays?

(3) What effects did the above analysed influences have on the trading efficiency and growth of the firm?

(4) What changes in the structure of assets and sources of finance occurred over time and what changes in the liquidity and security of the firm were determined by these features?

It is not possible in the space of this article to provide illustrations of the results for all of these objectives entailed in this analysis of the growth and development of a particular firm. What follows is first a summary, using annual data only, of some of the main features and then comments on what appear to be the major advantages and limitations of the approach. The firm had retained a wealth of detailed monthly and annual data covering a period of over sixty years and the use of a computer proved indispensable for dealing with such a quantity of data. Business historians could wisely make more extensive use of such facilities. A dominant feature of their work is the classification and manipulation of data from a long period and covering many different types of variables.

In Table 1[15] trading profit percentages and the stock-turn ratio are shown as an indication of whether variations in net profits as a percentage of sales were mainly attributable to variations in gross profit margins, inventory policies or a lack of control over certain cost components. In some cases, competition forcing down margins is associated with an unfavourable stock-turn and what may be deduced as excessive cost-component levels. On other occasions, variations in net profit are mainly attributable to either the degree of inventory control or gross margin changes. Table 2[16] shows the major changes in the structure of assets, sources of funds and the liquidity, security and profitability features of the firm over the period 1905-1965. There is little point in describing here the year-by-year changes that these indicators exhibit. More helpful is a discussion as to what it was possible to conclude from an analysis of this type. Several merits and limitations became apparent. First, while it is possible to trace changes and fluctuations in a large number of variables over a long period, it is not always easy or even possible to identify the determinants or causative influences responsible for them. This shortcoming is not necessarily a fault of the approach but is rather the result of a time constraint on the researcher. Further study of consumer credit, changes in the extent of price and non-price competition, changing market shares, and changes in the prices of factor inputs (land, labour and capital) would assist in assessing the relative influence of variables on the supply and demand sides. Various techniques would help separate out the components responsible for the most significant changes in behaviour. Correlation and regression analysis, statistical cost analysis, market share and concentration analysis and indices of capacity utilisation, and competitive environmental features could be used to help identify and specify differential causative influences over time.[17]

Secondly, the measures used have the advantage of completely specifying the asset and liability structure, cash and credit features, and cost and revenue flows and inventory levels of the firm. The identities used, exclusively and exhaustively represent the financial and economic structures of the firm as well as measures of its trading efficiency, asset composition and capital source features over time. Thirdly, this exhaustive and consistent specification of all components of the financial structure and operations of the firm enabled a series of composite ratios to be constructed which together give a comprehensive picture of the business rather than an excessive concentration on one feature at a time. Fourthly, it is possible to construct from these identities, sources and applications of funds estimates, to show how development was financed and what asset composition was achieved. Measures of the rate of change in totals and components were also calculated. Finally, it is possible with the estimation of changes in specific variables to ask questions about management's decision-making on the basis of information available to them at the time. For example, it may be possible to ascertain how far the performance of the company is attributable to planned and expected changes as against unintended or fortuitous exogenous developments. In 1909 the directors of the firm raised a renewable mortgage of £28,000 at a rate of 4¾% for 10 years and debenture finance of £22,000 at a rate of 6% to be redeemed at the company's option. Having finance negotiated before the outbreak of war in 1914, which was then available for later rebuilding, could be interpreted as fortuitous rather than planned.[18] Similarly, a renewal of the mortgage in 1929-30 when £60,000 was raised was probably advantageous retrospectively due to the fortunate timing of events as it enabled the letting of building contracts when building costs were low during the depression years.[19] Conversely, the reluctance by management to pay higher wages in the years 1933-35 could be interpreted as an inadvisable decision considering the high staff turnover and labour shortages and the sales foregone through the undermanning of service areas.[20]

IV

We can now consider briefly the nature of 'counterfactual' questions raised by this approach to business history research. The essence of the theory of the firm is the concept of 'marginal utility' and the related notion of 'opportunity cost'. Expressed another way, the theory of the firm attempts to measure and relate alternative strategies of utilising resources which are designed ostensibly to achieve the same objective. How can this notion be helpful in business history research and is it the same as hypothesising counterfactual conditionals? First, it would seem that one of the major advantages of the more recently developed mathematical and analytical techniques is to set out explicitly the merits and faults, in financial and other measures, of undertaking a range of alternative decisions. The techniques generate information from given data and constructed structural approximations that can be used to evaluate systematically the economic viability of a particular proposal. There is no reason why business historians should not ask this type of counterfactual question about the more distantly collected data in an attempt to measure retrospectively the advisability of the schemes considered or undertaken by management.[21] Where the problems subsequently arise, however, as with all

counterfactual conditionals, is not with the method of enquiry but
with other features, namely, the inadequacy or non-existence of
supporting or alternative data, the intrusion of unforeseen and
uncontrollable variables and the causal repercussions of these
uncertain components in determining an outcome over any
specified time horizon. We can say that hypothesising a counterfactual situation in analytical terms is extremely useful for
indicating what sort of information we should be looking for and
to what extent we can accept as verifiable the performance of
businesses or the reports of businessmen on this. Secondly, once
we come to establishing empirically these alternatives with a view
to making an 'opportunity cost' assessment or some non-financial
judgment about conduct and performance, decisions and control,
then we are on less certain ground.[22] In this case an analysis must
be preferred concerning the interrelationships and repercussions
of the variables, as well as some test as to the appropriateness of
the results, given, limitations on data collection methods, com-
pleteness of coverage and suitablility for the purpose. Any resulting
'judgments' can be rejected on several grounds: namely, incorrect
or insufficient data, over-simplified or wrongly specified structural
relationships, the non-identification of certain supply and demand
features, wrongly argued causal direction and unconvincing error
tolerances. Counterfactual questions can be put in a variety of ways
by other researchers asking different questions as a guide to the
type of information they would look for or generate. The hypotheses
may not in fact be falsified on grounds of logic, but neither need
the axioms be accepted nor the method of acquiring and manipulating the data be agreed to. Econometric historians who have
encouraged us to be more rigorous by using historical 'opportunity
cost' measures have often, to their own eventual discomfort, over-
looked this duality of counterfactual conditions in empirical
research. This has led to both dubious judgments about what
would have happened 'if . . . ', and a reluctance to look for further
information, often of the non-quantitative type, which may have
confirmed or confounded their statistical contortions and theoretical
gymnastics.

There may be other aspects of the theory of the firm which
could be useful starting points for business history research. Bass-
man[23] has suggested that cliometricians could undertake the
testing of 'economic laws' thrown up by economic theorizing. Is
such a role appropriate for the business historian? What type of
analysis would be required for the testing of micro-economic laws
in a retrospective manner?[24] Regression analysis, mathematical
programming and simulation modelling using 'current' data

certainly aid prediction and control. But how far do these techniques, which purportedly 'explain' relationships between variables,
add to our understanding of a particular and unique set of
determinants in the historical situation? To take a time-series on
selected variables for one firm or one businessman's decision
processes presents a very different analytical problem from taking
time-series or cross-sectional data for a sample of units.[25] This
means that 'laws' cannot be tested or formulated for many business
history studies (even given available data) because the aim may not
be to find 'average' or 'frequent' behaviour, but to discover particular divergences from theory or other empirical research and
then to find out why these uncharacteristic deviations are so. Two
points should therefore be noted. A business historian will primarily
seek to falsify the relationships one would expect to be indicated
by the theory of the firm. He would then make an effort to discover
the particular and peculiar determinants of this discrepancy. This
means that 'universal', 'general' or 'large sample' laws will seldom
be proffered or sustained by business historians. Secondly, the lack
of 'lawlike' features is no cause for alarm and information should
not be discarded, as econometricians often do when developing a
predictive model.[26] Rather, this should be a demonstration that
analytical techniques are useful for establishing the degree of
variation and uncertainty surrounding particular observations
and events when considered in their reconstructed context.

V

What conclusions can be drawn about possible appropriate
aims and approaches to business history research? First, while
recognising that data, time and audience constraints are imposed
on business historians, these features do not excuse the rejection
of rigorous techniques that are currently being used in business
performance evaluation. Secondly, and tangential to this, there is a
need for business historians to recognise that special expertise in
some fields of analysis, while losing some audience segments, will
probably yield more useful information than the blanket coverage
of all aspects and all periods of a firm's growth and development.
This could involve the re-writing of parts of published histories of
large organisations by persons of recognised expertise in, for
example, marketing, personnel and industrial relations, and
financial planning and investment policies. Such an approach
would, by being more impartial and informed, give us a clearer
understanding as to how firms operated and grew. Thirdly, the
publication of business histories would benefit from delineating

carefully the public relations and descriptive material from the more rigorous but less integrated sections of analysis; the latter being published in academic journals or even separate chapters or volumes. Fourthly, a more explicit statement on methodology, analysis and measurement should be made and adhered to in demonstrating failures and successes, erroneous and correct decisions and times of prosperity or financial distress. Some measure of the credibility of reports and recorded descriptions can then be made and such an approach will involve statistical and mathematical techniques where appropriate. Fifthly, should techniques of this type be used, they should be a means of indicating both further types of information that may be required as well as testing for the unique, particular and unexpected, and unintended, or uncontrollable. The emphasis should more properly lie here rather than with the frequent, average, certain world of 'lawlike' probabilities that are useful for forecasting, but of little use in reconstructing the particular sequence of events. Finally, 'counterfactual' propositions should be recognised as useful in setting up a range of alternatives for evaluation with a view to such being merely a guide in the 'information search' process. To make judgments involving suspect casual inference, dubious circumstantial relationships and improperly sequenced decisions, is only asking for derision at the clowning antics of hypotheses inventors who say nothing about the world people have lived in and conditions in which businesses have operated.

TABLE 1

Milne and Choyce: Gross Profit Margin, Net Profit and Stock Turn 1905-1965

Year	Gross Profit Margin as a % of Sales (1)	Net Profit as a % of Sales (2)	Stock Turn Ratio (3)	Year	Gross Profit Margin as a % of Sales (1)	Net Profit as a % of Sales (2)	Stock Turn Ratio (3)
1905	25.5	4.9	1.5	1935	30.5	2.7	1.4
06	26.0	5.0	1.6	36	25.4	0.1	1.9
07	25.8	4.3	1.7	37	31.9	3.1	2.3
08	27.1	5.9	1.7	38	33.0	3.7	2.3
09	26.2	4.6	1.8	39	34.1	4.2	2.3
1910	26.0	5.4	2.2	1940	35.7	4.7	2.3
11	24.2	3.6	2.2	41	34.0	3.3	2.4
12	23.1	4.5	2.7	42	32.2	3.1	2.7
13	27.2	8.0	3.0	43	32.1	3.2	3.0
14	25.7	1.1	3.3	44	32.5	3.6	3.3
1915	25.8	1.9	3.0	1945	31.9	3.7	3.4
16	29.2	3.7	2.4	46	29.6	5.0	3.3
17	31.7	3.3	1.9	47	28.4	5.9	3.1
18	29.8	3.7	1.8	48	27.5	5.3	3.1
19	26.6	3.5	1.7	49	26.7	4.3	3.4
1920	28.0	3.0	1.7	1950	27.7	4.6	4.1
21	24.2	1.2	1.9	51	27.3	4.2	3.9
22	24.9	1.9	1.9	52	26.1	3.6	3.2
23	29.0	5.8	2.2	53	26.7	3.5	3.3
24	29.8	5.4	2.0	54	26.8	3.4	3.8
1925	27.7	4.7	2.4	1955	26.1	2.9	3.5
26	28.8	4.2	2.5	56	26.1	2.3	3.3
27	28.7	4.2	2.6	57	25.9	3.0	3.6
28	29.2	4.6	2.8	58	25.9	3.0	3.8
29	30.0	4.5	3.1	59	27.5	2.8	3.5
1930	29.2	4.2	2.9	1960	27.4	2.8	3.8
31	30.8	2.2	2.3	61	27.4	3.1	3.8
32	28.9	0.9	2.1	62	27.4	2.3	3.4
33	30.2	2.6	2.0	63	26.9	2.0	3.6
34	30.6	2.9	1.7	64	27.6	2.0	3.2
				1965	27.6	1.7	3.2

TABLE 2

Milne and Choyce: Measures of Liquidity, Capital Gearing and Profitability 1905-1965

Year	(1) Working Capital Ratio	(2) Quick Assets Ratio	Capital Gearing and Structure (3) %	(4) %	(5) %	Return on Funds (6) %	(7) %	(8) %
1905	2.6	0.8	0.0	54.7	436.7	6.0	9.3	16.9
06	2.9	1.0	0.0	48.3	515.9	6.8	10.1	18.3
07	4.7	1.1	0.0	24.7	584.5	7.1	8.8	16.3
08	4.1	1.6	0.0	29.8	650.0	9.4	12.3	24.2
09	9.7	3.6	136.1	9.0	22.5	2.8	6.9	19.6
1910	2.7	0.5	115.0	34.7	19.3	4.1	10.1	33.8
11	3.2	0.6	101.4	29.8	26.8	3.2	7.5	20.5
12	3.8	0.9	94.5	23.2	26.6	5.1	11.1	32.0
13	3.9	1.0	79.2	21.8	27.0	10.1	19.8	66.6
14	3.6	1.1	79.4	24.1	27.1	1.5	3.0	9.9
1915	3.2	1.0	79.7	30.5	28.7	2.4	5.0	16.4
16	2.5	0.5	75.3	49.8	30.1	4.8	10.6	36.8
17	2.3	0.4	71.4	59.8	30.8	4.5	10.1	36.9
18	1.9	0.3	66.4	83.6	31.6	4.7	11.5	45.3
19	3.7	0.9	121.3	52.8	51.4	4.3	11.5	29.9
1920	3.9	1.2	187.6	65.4	38.8	3.2	11.0	30.2
21	4.8	1.2	237.9	51.9	28.2	1.4	5.2	14.4
22	5.6	1.3	253.3	32.9	20.5	2.2	8.0	21.1
23	2.9	0.4	290.6	69.2	14.5	6.2	27.5	79.6
24	1.3	0.3	276.7	153.8	11.1	5.4	27.3	82.9
1925	1.4	0.3	264.0	145.1	11.1	5.4	26.1	83.0
26	1.4	0.3	271.1	128.3	11.1	4.9	23.1	71.5
27	1.4	0.3	266.8	132.0	11.2	4.9	23.3	73.4
28	1.7	0.4	255.9	98.9	11.7	5.8	24.9	81.7
29	1.4	0.4	244.9	117.6	12.1	6.0	24.2	83.2
1930	1.4	0.3	238.6	123.9	11.6	5.3	22.0	77.3
31	1.7	0.4	259.7	93.4	10.4	2.3	10.3	35.2
32	1.6	0.4	267.1	106.1	10.4	0.7	3.3	11.0
33	1.7	0.5	261.1	96.8	10.7	2.1	9.3	31.2
34	2.2	0.4	169.4	71.0	10.9	2.2	7.2	37.1

TABLE 2 (cont.)

Year	(1) Working Capital Ratio	(2) Quick Assets Ratio	Capital Gearing and Structure (3) %	(4) %	(5) %	Return on Funds (6) %	(7) %	(8) %
1935	2.2	0.4	168.0	70.5	11.2	2.1	6.7	35.1
36	4.0	1.0	174.9	29.3	11.5	0.1	0.2	1.2
37	2.7	0.6	177.3	44.1	11.7	3.1	9.5	45.5
38	2.8	0.7	173.3	42.4	12.1	3.9	11.6	56.6
39	2.0	0.6	163.7	66.8	12.3	4.4	13.6	70.1
1940	3.6	1.1	171.4	43.2	12.6	5.1	17.2	84.4
41	1.5	0.4	162.7	91.6	13.0	3.9	12.4	63.4
42	1.0	0.3	130.4	121.1	13.4	4.1	12.4	64.8
43	0.9	0.3	126.7	133.3	13.8	4.1	12.5	66.9
44	0.5	0.1	117.0	136.3	14.1	4.6	13.7	79.4
1945	0.9	0.3	108.3	137.3	14.5	4.9	14.3	89.6
46	0.9	0.1	92.5	112.1	14.8	6.9	18.2	133.6
47	1.2	0.3	79.2	110.0	14.9	9.1	22.8	195.4
48	1.3	0.2	87.7	131.5	14.3	9.5	27.3	211.8
49	1.3	0.5	67.6	95.1	14.6	7.8	17.8	178.7
1950	1.2	0.4	59.0	92.1	11.4	8.6	18.7	215.0
51	0.9	0.3	54.7	159.9	8.1	7.7	21.4	266.4
52	1.2	0.5	49.1	134.5	7.4	6.4	17.9	247.3
53	1.3	0.6	0.0	62.9	65.4	6.8	10.9	25.4
54	1.5	0.8	0.0	55.9	77.5	5.9	9.1	20.6
1955	1.3	0.8	0.2	70.7	67.8	4.8	8.2	18.9
56	1.5	1.0	1.2	56.3	70.0	4.1	6.3	15.0
57	1.7	0.8	1.1	49.2	72.3	5.5	8.2	20.2
58	1.9	1.3	12.2	50.7	69.1	5.4	8.7	22.3
59	2.0	0.9	16.7	41.8	71.6	4.7	7.4	16.2
1960	1.7	1.1	17.0	44.8	79.0	4.4	7.1	14.5
61	2.0	1.2	29.5	43.8	76.1	4.9	8.4	17.8
62	1.9	1.1	29.7	44.6	74.1	3.5	6.0	12.8
63	1.7	0.9	26.8	64.3	142.9	3.1	5.9	7.0
64	1.6	0.8	34.5	74.9	129.9	3.1	6.5	7.7
1965	1.5	0.9	32.8	82.6	122.5	2.6	5.6	6.7

APPENDICES

APPENDIX A: BASIC IDENTITY EQUATIONS FOR ANNUAL DATA

1 Trading Account:
    (i) $TSV = SB + TPV - SE + GM$
    (ii) $CGS = SB + TPV - SE$

2 Profit and Loss Account:
    (i) $GM + OR = TC + NPB + TAX$
    (ii) $NPA = (GM + OR) - (TC + TAX)$
    (iii) $TC = PUB + WAS + OC$

3 Balance Sheet:
    (i) $P = CR + RR + OS + PS + UPE$
    (ii) $A = CA + FA + INV + IA$
    (iii) $CA = CBE + BBE + SDB + SE$
    (iv) $L = CL + LL$
    (v) $CL = BBE + SCB + TAX + DP$

APPENDIX B: INDICATORS OF EFFICIENCY AND STRUCTURE

A   Trading Efficiency (see *Table 1*):

1 $\dfrac{GM + OR}{TSV}$ (Gross Trading Profit percentage on sales)

2 $\dfrac{NPA}{TSV}$ (Net earnings percentage on sales)

3 $\dfrac{CGS}{(SB + SE)/2}$ (Stock-turn ratio)

B   Liquidity, Capital Structure and Return on Funds (see *Table 2*):

1 $\dfrac{CA}{CL}$ (Working Capital Ratio)

2 $\dfrac{CA - SE}{CL - BBE}$ ('Quick-Asset' Ratio)

3 $\dfrac{LL}{P}$ (Capital Gearing Measures)

4 $\dfrac{CL}{P}$

5 $\dfrac{OS}{FA}$ (Equity Interest in Fixed Assets)

6 $\dfrac{NPA}{A}$ (Net Profit after tax on assets employed)

7 $\dfrac{NPA}{P}$ (Net Profit after tax on Proprietors' Funds)

8 $\dfrac{NPA}{OS}$ (Net Profit after tax on Ordinary Shares)

APPENDIX C: SYMBOLS USED

A   = Total assets
BBE = Bank balance (end)
CA   = Current assets
CBE = Cash balance (end)
CGS = Cost of sales
CL   = Current liabilities
CR   = Capital reserves
DP   = Dividend provision (and payment)
FA   = Fixed assets
GM   = Gross margin
IA   = Intangible assets
INV   = Investments
L   = Total liabilities
LL   = Long-term liabilities
NPA = Net profit after tax
NPB = Net profit before tax
OC   = Other costs
OR   = Other revenue
OS   = Ordinary shares
P   = Proprietorship
PS   = Preference shares
PUB = Publicity expenditure
RR   = Revenue reserves
SB   = Stocks (beginning)
SCB = Sundry creditors balances (end)
SDB = Sundry debtors balances (end)
SE   = Stocks (end)
TAX   = Taxation
TC   = Total costs
TPV   = Total purchase value
TSV   = Total sales value
UPE = Unappropriated earnings
WAS = Wages and salaries

NOTES

1 *Australian Economic History Review*, (September 1969), 197-198 where J. A. Dowie reviews K. A. Tucker, *Milne and Choyce: a one hundred year business history 1867-1967*, (1968).

2 K. A. Tucker, Milne and Choyce: 'An Economic and Financial Analysis'; unpublished M.Com. Thesis, Auckland, 1967.

3 Review by Fritz Redlich, 'Wilson's History of Unilever: A Significant Contribution to Business History', *Journal of Economic History*, XVI, 1956, 56. But note that this review did correctly interpret the result by concluding that '. . . the book is essentially a narrative'.

4 Charles Wilson, *the history of Unilever: A Study in Economic Gorwth and Social Change*; two volumes (1954) ix.

5 D. C. Coleman, *Courtaulds: An Economic and Social History*; two volumes (1969), viii.

6 This approach is vulnerable to the criticism of an inadequately specified frame of reference. A 'phasing theory' has been suggested as an alternative in a review by S. G. Checkland, *Economic History Review*; Second Series, XXIII, No. 3, December 1970, 556.

7 D. C. Coleman, op. cit., x.

8 Merab Tauman, 'A Critical Comment on Australian Business Histories', *Bulletin of the Business Archives Council of Australia*, 1, No. 9, 1961, 59.

9 Clarence C. Walton, 'Business History: Some Major Challenges', *Business History Review*, 36, 1962, 26.

10 In using 'measurable', not only financial or economic variables are assumed to be quantifiable, but also sociological, institutional and ethical phenomena which have features about which some concensus of opinion or code of evaluation can be or has been formulated.

11 Such a practice is by no means uncommon even today, with the particular variable showing a favourable advance given excessive prominence, often to draw attention away from less favourable results of other indicators.

12 For example, the practice of running down inventories at stock-taking time or the minimizing of a bank overdraft figure at balance date by temporarily increasing creditor payment delays will not show the correct average level of stocks or rate of stock turnover or the average reliance on bank advances.

13 See Edgar O. Edwards and Philip N. Bell, *The Theory and Measurement of Business Income*; (Berkeley, 1961) for such a measurement process and D. R. Myddelton, 'The Effects of Currency Debasement', *The Accountant*, 162, No. 4977, May 7, 1970, 689 for a demonstration as to how critical such a reconstruction may be in measuring performance.

14 This is not to assert that businessmen have always had available these techniques, but rather presents a type of counterfactual measurement appraisal as to what they may otherwise have done. Neither does it mean that the full implications of alternatives can be traced out with any certainty over time.

15 See Appendices A, B and C for definitions and the accounting identities used for this part of the annual data analysis.

16 See Appendices A, B and C for definitions and the accounting identities used for this part of the annual data analysis.

17 Using similar techniques, cross-sectional analysis at a point in time could be used to establish differential features between firms in varying trading environments. For an example of this type of analysis, see John R. Meyer and Edwin Kuh, *The Investment Decision: An Emperical Study;* (Cambridge, Harvard University Press), 1957.

18 K. A. Tucker, *Milne and Choyce: a one hundred year business history 1867-1967* (1968).
19 Ibid, 80.
20 Ibid, 84-85.
21 For some possible applications, see Y. Ijiri, *Management Goals and Accounting for Control*; (1965), Richard Mattessich, *Accounting and Analytical Methods*; (1964), L. R. Amey, *The Efficiency of Business Enterprises*, (1969), and for more detailed approaches and proposals William R. Kinney, Jr, 'An Environmental Model for Performance Measurement in Multi-Outlet Businesses', *Journal of Accounting Research*, 7, No. 1, Spring, 1969, 44, V. B. Hall and K. A. Tucker, 'An Optimal Capital-Mix Model Under Conditions of Homogeneous Asset Expansion', *unpublished* (1970).
22 J. D. Gould, 'Hypothetical History', *Economic History Review*, XXII, No. 2, 1969, 202-205 has made a good deal of comment out of not recognizing clearly the distinction between logical operatives and necessary propositions which can be tested by reference to laws or rules of language and/or logic, and empirical or contingent propositions which (a) must be testable *and* (b) must posit verifiable conclusions, incorporating degrees of uncertainty, which could be falsified. The form of either type of hypothesis will be the same.
23 R. L. Bassmann, 'The Role of the Economic Historian in Predictive Testing of Proffered "Economic Laws"', *Explorations in Entrepreneurial History*; II, No. 3, Spring, 1965, 159-186.
24 Louis Galambos, 'Business History and the Theory of the Growth of the Firm', *Explorations in Entrepreneurial History*; IV, No. 1, Fall, 1966, 3-16 makes a similar suggestion.
25 For examples of this contrast of approaches, see G. P. E. Clarkson, *Portfolio Selection: A simulation of Trust Investment*, (New Jersey, 1962), and John R. Meyer and Edwin Kuh, op. cit., or P. E. Hart, *Studies in Profit, Business Saving and Investment in the United Kingdom, 1920-1962*; 1 (London, 1965).
26 A. R. Bergstrom and A. D. Brownlie, 'An Econometric Model of the New Zealand Economy', *Economic Record*; XLI, No. 23, March 1965, 125.

PART TWO

Entrepreneurs,
The Firm and
Industrial Structure

5

The Govan Collieries
1804-1805[1]

Peter L. Payne*

In 1793 the 'respectable inhabitants' who prepared the section on the City of Glasgow for Sir John Sinclair's *Statistical Account of Scotland* rightly emphasised that 'The fossil to which this city owes its greatest advantage is COAL'.[2] Almost certainly the largest and most important of the undertakings exploiting what became known as 'the Glasgow Coal Fields' was the Govan Collieries.[3] Situated on the south bank of the Clyde in the Gorbals — a parish which, it is said, veritably 'abounds with coal'[4] — directly opposite Glasgow Green, these collieries were but a mile from the Old Bridge that gave access to the city.[5] These collieries had been extensively worked since the time of the Restoration[6] and, in the period 1714 to 1731 (when they belonged to the Town, the Trade's House and Hutcheson's Hospital) Robert Dreghorn, tacksman of the colliery, was putting out almost 20,000 loads of coal annually.[7] By the end of the century the Govan Colliery was leased by two directors of Alexander Houston & Co.,[8] Houston Rae and Lieutenant-Colonel Andrew Houston, and so rich were the three seams worked — 'the undermost of which was 14 feet thick' — that contemporaries believed that the Colliery could 'of itself serve the City of Glasgow for 100 years to come'.[9] In the last three years of the century the partners' total profits were £10,166 9s. The lease was valued by William Dixon, the manager, and John Boyd, the book-keeper as some £30,000, being 'from eight to ten years purchase', the usual basis for valuations of this kind.[10]

Already a coal-and-iron-master of considerable consequence, William Dixon rose from managing the Govan Colliery to becoming its proprietor, adding this property to the Calder Iron and Coal Works which he had established with David Mushet in 1801. By the time of this death in 1822 Dixon was one of the

* From *Business History*, Vol. III (1960), pp. 75-96. Reprinted by permission of the editor of *Business History*.

foremost figures in the Scottish coal and iron trades.[11] Among the
records of the Govan Colliery[12] has survived a single account book
dating back to the days when Dixon was still manager. This volume
covers the operation of the undertaking for the two years 1804-
1805, and the colliery accounts still follow the early pattern
described by Professor J. U. Nef: 'all expenses and receipts seem
to have been kept in one ledger. Though the methods adopted may
seem crude to an age in which accounting is almost a science,
these early ledgers have the merit of detail . . . '[13]

The accounts of the Govan Colliery were made up fortnightly
and usually comprised four pages. The first and second of these
give particulars, in sets of hand-drawn columns, of the cost
incurred at each of the three or four pits operating at any one
time. These individual accounts are headed by the 'Amount Paid
to Coaliers as per Output Book', and give the quantity of coal
raised expressed in cartloads of 12 cwt. Following this entry are
listed the names of, and work performed by, the various 'oncost
men' (i.e. all workmen, other than the actual hewers, who were
paid a daily rate of wages[14]) divided into two groups, underground
workers (e.g., roadsmen, bottomers, trapdoor keepers, redsmen,
etc.) and surface workers (e.g. hillsmen, cleeksmen, enginemen,
winders, etc.)[15] Such incidental charges as could be allocated to the
working of a specific pit — gunpowder, shovels, drink money and
the like — end the list. These costs are then totalled and set
alongside the quantity of coal raised. The final set of entries on
these first two pages is labelled 'Incident Charges' and gives the
cost of all work not capable of being assigned to a particular pit:
the wages of the smiths, wrights, masons, engineers, weighers,
carters and grooms, the amounts laid out in equipment and its
carriage to the mines (pit props, rope, candles, tolls, etc.), management expenses, commissions to agents, and a whole host of other
items. In any odd corner where space was available, the costs of the
farm attached to the colliery are enumerated.

The third page sets out in tabular form the daily outputs of
each pit, and the daily sales of the different varieties of coal both
by quantity and value.[16] These data are then summarised in totals.
To the output figure is added the stock on hand at the beginning
of each fortnightly period and the 'overplus', evidently the amount
of coal raised by the 'oncost men' and not therefore embodied in
the hewers' output figures.[17] From the resulting total is substracted
the fortnight's sales to give the stock on hand at the end of the
period.

The fourth, and last, page lists the major purchasers, the quantity
of coal each of them ordered and the total price paid. Only in two

categories is it impossible to ascertain exactly who was taking the coal; these — each of them important outlets — are 'Ready Money Sales', and 'Town Orders' through Andrew Houston, one of the colliery's proprietors and coal agent and shore master at the Broomielaw.

To summarise, the major data given, or capable of calculation, are, on the production side, figures of daily output, the average piece rate per cartload paid to the hewers, the daily wage rates of the oncost men, the special contract prices for extraordinary tasks performed in the mines[18] and the cost of equipment; and, on the marketing side, daily sales, distribution costs (i.e. wages of carters, agents commissions and tolls), the customers, and the selling price of coal. As a new pit was sunk and prepared for working in 1805,[19] it is possible to calculate the capital costs of sinking a pit — such costs being included with the other costs — and, furthermore, by subtracting total costs from total revenue, the colliery's net profits. Indeed, the only matters for which precise details are lacking concern the hewers, since 'the Output Book' referred to in the accounts is lost. Even here, however, the list of bounties, or 'binding' monies, paid to the miners in July 1805, and the details of contract work which they periodically undertook, permit a fairly accurate assessment of their numbers and their distribution between the pits.

It will readily be appreciated that the comprehensive nature of this information provides perhaps a unique opportunity to see exactly how a major Scottish colliery operated during the Napoleonic Wars. This paper presents the findings of an analysis of the statistical and descriptive data contained in the accounts and, at the same time, attempts to provide some impression of what life was like in the most important of the collieries of the Glasgow Coal Field at the beginning of the nineteenth century.

I

There were four pits working in January 1804; Corner Pit, Firrs Pit, Bankhall Pit and Gilliesink Pit, the bulk of the coal being raised from the first two. Gilliesink Pit, producing only about 70 cartloads of coal per week at a cost of over 2s. per cartload (the amount paid to the hewers alone, double that at the much more efficient Corner Pit) was abandoned in April 1804, and until July 1805, when Corner Pit was closed and Quarry Pit came into operation, all the coal was raised from Corner, Firrs and Bankhall pits.[20]

Close to the City and the Broomielaw, well served by roads, and possessing a permanent force of carters, the Govan Collieries were well placed to exploit the expanding Glasgow, coastwise and foreign

markets.[21] Whatever paradoxical seasonal patterns may still have
existed in areas less favourably provided with communications,[22]
the output, sales and price statistics of the Govan Collieries are
quite straightforward.[23] Fortnightly coal production and sales —
particularly the latter — display the seasonal pattern that one
would expect for a colliery serving an easily accessible domestic
market; being relatively high in November and December and low
in June and July, only in the autumn of 1804 is the fairly smooth
swing between the peak and trough of sales distorted, and this is
perhaps due to extraordinary shipments through the Broomielaw.
As the amplitude of the swing is less in the case of coal production
than in sales and as it was possible to build up stocks in the
summer to meet the high winter demands, market prices display a
stability certainly lacking in less fortunately situated enterprises.

A closer investigation of the production figures reveals several
noteworthy features. Total coal output comprised two elements:
first, the amount won by the hewers for which they were paid by
the cartload 'as per the [missing] Output Book' and, second the
'overplus'. The first of these constituent parts was far more important and, moreover, displays greater stability, especially during the
periods March to November 1804, and, somewhat less so, for
February to August 1805. This betokens a stable labour force (evidence for which is apparent elsewhere) and fairly homogeneous
working conditions. The 'overplus', of much less magnitude, is of
great marginal importance. It would appear that at times when
extra coal was urgently needed, during months of peak demand
(particularly December) and when the coal stocks built up during
the summer were all but exhausted, the oncostmen were pressed
into service as hewers and paid their normal day rates plus a bonus
to augment supplies.[24]

Secondly, it is interesting to see that the two fortnights during
which output was at its lowest — despite the contemporaneous
high level of demand — were those that included New Year's Day.
At Hogmanay the miners did very little work and demand was met
from 'stock on hand' which was rapidly run down during the first
few weeks of the year, in 1805 becoming completely exhausted.
This introduces a further point. By comparing the average output
on Mondays with the average daily output (including and excluding
Monday's) some quantitative precision can be given to one of the
more controversial aspects of the Industrial Revolution: the slow
evolution of what is sometimes referred to as 'a disciplined labour
force'.

Contemporary writers — during the progress of their inter-
minable 'tours' — and, later, factory and mines inspectors, rarely

failed to notice that during the progress of industrialisation Sundays and frequently Mondays became increasingly characterised by the 'idle dissipation of the labouring classes'. So demoralised by a 'dull routine of endless drudgery', the worker — particularly the miner — 'was apt to squander his earnings in debauchery'.[25] Since he was usually paid late on Saturday, the crescendo of these excesses was reached on Sunday and by Monday many workers were either incapable of answering the 'despotic factory bell' or were frittering away what remained of their hard won wages in a final riotous fling. As Robert Herron observed during the course of his journey through the western counties of Scotland:

'In the progress of its population, industry and refinement, Glasgow has lost much of its ancient piety. All ranks of its inhabitants seem now to consider Sunday as a day they may lawfully dedicate to amusement. The more licentious part of the labouring artisans spent the evening of Saturday, all Sunday, and the forenoon of Monday, in that dissipation and riot, the means of which, the wages, of the foregoing week have enabled them to purchase'.[26]

Exactly what this weekly revolt against the new discipline meant to the Govan Collieries is apparent in the output figures.[27] During the 613 working days of 1804-5 the average daily production (exclusive of overplus) was 119.50 cartloads; taking only Tuesdays to Saturdays inclusive (513 days), it was 128.87 cartloads. Compared with these figures the average amount of coal raised on Mondays was but 71.42 cartloads, or 60 per cent of the daily average and 55 per cent of the average daily output during the rest of the week. While a proportion of this diminished output was perhaps due to the necessarily enhanced problems of getting the pits working smoothly again following the weekend (for example, it may be assumed that greater problems were encountered in dissipating noxious gases in the workings after a stoppage of some 30 hours than after the short period that elapsed between weekday shifts), the weekend carousal did disrupt normal working and seriously hindered William Dixon's efforts to meet fully the city's growing demands. One cannot generalise from these figures since it is not known how typical they are, but one is tempted to suggest that a possible means of dating the coming of a disciplined labour force is when the average Monday's production equals the average daily production.

II

To obtain the Mossdale, Ell, Main, Humph, Splint and Sourmilk coal lying in seams of between 2 feet 6 inches and 7 feet some 30 to 85 fathoms below the surface,[28] the major pits of the Govan

Collieries were worked by a modification of the long-wall method: only the Bankhall Pit appears to have utilised the wasteful pillar and stall method. The depth of this coal and the manner of its exploitation largely determined the composition and organisation of the labour force.[29]

As Professor J. U. Nef has shown, even as early as the mid-seventeenth century miners were 'separated into several groups or gangs performing different functions',[30] and by 1804 such specialisation was a marked feature of the Govan Collieries. Each pit had its group of 'Coaliers' or hewers, varying in number from about 8 in Bankhall Pit to 24 in Firrs Pit, whose main function was to cut the coal from their alloted 'space' or 'room' of about 10 yards along the coal face. A certain number of these hewers, however, repeatedly emerge from the anonymity of the phrase 'Paid Coaliers as per Output Book', to perform tasks of an exceptional character, the nature of which is briefly described in the Accounts.[31] When it was necessary to sink the main or the stair shaft to a deeper seam, construct new levels, cut 'pavements', break the first of a new series of 'rooms' into a hitherto untouched coal face, overcome a 'hitch', or a dislocation in the strata, hole through a 'gaw' (the narrow veins of igneous rock intersecting the coal beds), make a 'througher' for an air course, and so on, the hewers were paid either by the day at a rate that, it must be assumed, compensated them for the loss of their piece earnings or, more frequently, entered into a special contract to do the job for an agreed sum.[32] In the latter event, and when the task was of some magnitude, a number of miners would join together and constitute themselves into a temporary 'company' — 'the little butty system'[33] — and their agreement with the management would be marked by the payment of 'arles' or 'earnest money'. Experienced 'coaliers' were able to turn to almost any work that was necessary to keep the pits functioning. They constituted the aristocracy of the mines. For cutting the coal — assuming an average total force of 50 hewers — they earned about 18s. a week,[34] and when engaged on other work for which they were paid a daily rate, they received anything from 2s. 6d. to 4s. a day and were doubtless capable of earning a similar amount for tasks subject to special contract, usually at piece-rates.

Although the hewers were often called upon to undertake jobs requiring special skill, by and large their work was made possible by the labours of those oncóst men known as 'roadsmen' and 'redsmen'. There is a certain terminological confusion in contemporary accounts of coal mining, but in the Govan Collieries, at least, it was the duty of the roadsmen to take down the roof and lift the pavement in order to heighten the roads (elsewhere these workers are called 'rippers' or 'brushers'), thus facilitating both the winning of the coal and its conveyance by horse-drawn trams to the bottom of the pit shaft. With the stones produced, the redsmen built and maintained the walls to support the roof, the coal being completely evacuated by the long-wall method of working.[35] When not engaged in this essential work the redsmen would be employed in deepening the main and stair shafts, driving levels and removing obstructions. The senior roadsmen in Firrs Pit was paid 3s. 6d. a day but the usual rate was between 1s. 6d. and 2s. 6d. (according to seniority) in the Corner and Quarry Pits. With the exception of the senior redsmen in Corner pit, who received 2s. 9d. a day, the redsmen received a daily rate of 2s. 6d.

Other oncost men below ground were the bottomers, whose job it was to empty the hutches of coal brought from the face into creels or baskets and hang them on the rope by which they were hoisted to the surface. Bottomers were employed at Corner, Firrs and Quarry Pits at 2s. a day and they were served by the drivers — earning between 1s. and 2s. a day according to seniority — who brought the coal to the pit bottom in horse-drawn trams. In Corner and Quarry Pits a pumpman (2s. a day) attended an underground pump in the ceaseless battle against flooding, and a number of young 'trappers', sat on boards in niches in the walls 'without any light', holding the ropes that permitted the opening and shutting of the trap doors when the wheeled carts passed through.[36] Trappers were paid 5d. a day.

On the surface other oncost men called 'cleeksmen'[37] earned their 1s. 6d. a day by unhooking the baskets of coal from the winding rope and emptying them at the hill, where it became the responsibility of the hillsman, or pitheadman, paid 1s. 8d., 2s. or 2s. 6d. a day at Bankhall, Corner and Firrs Pits, respectively.

So far only those men attached to particular pits have been mentioned. In addition, a number of craftsmen were on the colliery's permanent labour force: these included smiths (2s. 4d. a day), wrights (2s.; later, in the spring of 1805, 2s. 4d.), masons (2s. 6d.) and enginemen (1s. 6d. a day). A weigher was also employed (1s. 8d.), a groom (1s. 6d.; later, in the spring of 1805, 1s. 8d.), and an agent at the Broomielaw (2s. 0d.). The fortnightly earnings of all these employees were entered in the 'Incident Charges' columns, together with those of the standing body of 14-18 carters, all of whom received 1s. 6d. a day until the spring of 1805, when a general rise to 1s. 8d. took place.

The total number on the mine's payroll in mid-1805 — the best period for such a calculation — was 137. Of these, 50 were 'coaliers' or hewers; 22, oncost men below ground; 26, oncost men on the surface; 14 were craftsmen, and 25 carters and others mainly connected with distribution. If the last group be omitted, and if, as seems probable, the labour force was fairly stable, the 112 'miners' — to use the rather loose terminology of the *Old Statistical Account* — raised nearly 40,000 cartloads of coal in 1805 (35,857 cartloads 'as per Output Book', and 4,057 cartloads of 'overplus'), or roughly 210 tons per head.[38]

Despite a rising demand for coal in Glasgow for both domestic consumption and the coastwise and export trades, the coal put out by the Govan Collieries in 1805 was somewhat less than the 1804 figure. The reason for William Dixon's inability to take advantage of the rising market is undoubtedly to be sought in the contemporary acute shortage of miners. On the Tyne and Wear, for example, there was 'a general scramble for hewers', exhorbitant bounties of as much as 20 guineas being paid for fear of not procuring a necessary supply of men',[39] and doubtless many Scottish coalminers — who were much sought after — were enticed south by the advertisements, offering better conditions and high binding money inserted in the Glasgow and Edinburgh papers by English companies.[40] To hold his labour force William Dixon — like other managers and proprietors — was forced to introduce the binding system in July 1805, though the bounties of from half a guinea to two guineas he paid to 64 hewers and underground oncost men in the summer of 1805 were small compared with those offered in the Newcastle area. When binding money had been accepted contracts were rigidly enforced. James McFadyean, who absconded but two months after receiving his two guineas bounty in September, was pursued by Mathew McKenzies and John Wilson, caught, clapped into Paisley Jail, and brought back to fulfil his term.

If Dixon was to take full advantage of the prevailing demand for coal, however, he had not merely to retain what labour he had but make every effort to expand his force of skilled miners. From mid-1805 the fortnightly 'Incident Charges', rarely fail to record the expenses incurred by himself, his son, George Lindsay, and Charles Logan 'in seeking coaliers' in the mining areas of Lanarkshire, the Lothians and even farther afield: two miners from Campbelton, Kintyre, accepted annual bounties in August and their furniture was conveyed to Govan at the Colliery's expense. But, despite the lavishing of drinks on 'stranger coaliers' to get them to sign on, the offer of binding money and free accommodation, and doubtless other blandishments unmentioned in the accounts, Dixon failed to secure any marked expansion in his labour force. Temporarily, at least, the men had become masters[41] and naturally chose to bind themselves for more generous terms and conditions than Dixon was prepared to offer. It is interesting that the daily wage rates of the majority of the oncost men remained stable through 1804-5, though, in the absence of the Output Book, it is impossible to say whether this is true of the hewers' piece-rates.[42]

The odd facets of subterranean life revealed by the accounts can hardly fail to provoke sympathy for the miners' efforts to better their condition. Having descended the special stair shafts (these also served to improve the ventilation) into Corner, Firrs and Quarry Pits, or during, the early months of 1804, having been lowered down the incomplete Bankhall Pit by winding gear operated by a young lad, paid but 4½d. a day,[43] the miners were exposed to a host of dangers. The proximity of the Clyde, invaluable though it was for shipping coals, doubtless aggravated the problem of flooding. Often it was necessary to supplement the steam engine's[44] battle against seepages by constructing dams in the workings and removing the accumulated water by buckets. In Firrs Pit so great was the difficulty that special pumps were installed 'in the levels' in addition to the surface pump.

Despite constant modification of the air courses and the construction of new trap doors in unceasing efforts to ensure good ventilation, choke and fire damp still accumulated. Although Barney Docherty recovered after having been dosed with 'medecene . . . when stiffeled in the Pitt' and Robert Maxwell, overman of Corner Pit, survived to enjoy his £1 compensation for being 'burnt in the Pitt', others were not so fortunate. An expense of 24s. was incurred in November 1805, for 'A Coffin, etc. to Archibald Muir who Died by being Burnt in Bankhall Pitt', and Mrs Harker — like several other miners' wives — figures in the 1805 accounts as the recipient of a cash payment of one guinea 'to help bury her husband when killed in the Pitt 2nd August last'. That fire occasionally swept through the workings is hardly to be wondered at during a period when, in the absence of other means of illumination, lighted candles had to be carried to the work face. Thus, only in exceptional circumstances were fires and explosions worthy of more than a bare mention: such a case occurred in May 1805, when 18 miners were killed in 'a very serious explosion' in the nearby Haugh Pit, Hurlet, and the Govan Colliery contributed £2 2s. 0d. as 'Subscription Money to the Unfortunate Sufferers at Hurlot Colliery (17 men killed in the Pitt)' [Sic].[45]

Yet if the miner at the Govan Colliery had to face these daily hazards, at least he was not badly off during the period covered by the accounts. Fully employed, his work arduous but varied, by contemporary standards well paid, not subject to too rigorous a discipline, living either rent free in a colliery dwelling or having his house rent paid for him,[46] receiving free coal and occasional drink money, he probably counted himself fortunate. If he stayed at the colliery for his entire working life, he could look forward to a small pension of 1s. a week; his wife was sometimes able to supplement the family income by working on the farm attached to the colliery,[47] and his sons (no women or girls were employed at the mines) were soon able to earn their keep by assisting at the face, as hutch fillers, trappers and winders, or by looking after the pit ponies. Not until the railways came in did they put away the horses and use boys as drawers.[48] Life at the Govan Colliery was hard but not without its compensations.

III

In his inquiry 'into the causes of the vast disproportion between the prices of coals at Edinburgh and Glasgow', Robert Bald found that the relative cheapness of fuel in Glasgow was largely to be explained by 'the superior mode in which coal sales are conducted there. 'Each colliery has an agent in the city, who receives orders for coals; these orders are sent out each day to the respective collieries, by which means, the manager appoints each carter his day's work before he leaves the colliery in the morning. By this plan, the delivery of the coals is quite regular; no time is lost; all imposition is avoided, as the carter has nothing to do with the money for the coals, but is answerable for the weight delivered'. [49]

William Dixon maintained a force of 14 to 18 carters to transport the coals raised at the Govan Colliery to the markets of Glasgow and, occasionally, Paisley.[50] These carters must have conveyed 5 tons of coal to the customers each working day at a labour cost of 2½d. per ton-mile.[51] Clearly, the horses had to be fed and looked after, but even this expense was minimised by growing a large proportion of their fodder at the Colliery's farm. However crude these calculations must be, there is no question that Dixon's system was extremely economic and efficient. To these labour costs and the expenses of keeping the horses must be added the toll charges at the Gorbals, Shawfield and other turnpike gates through which the carts had to pass. Over 1804 to 1805 these amounted to £552 1s. 6½d., or only £65 less than the carters' wages (£617 10s. 0d.).

A special account was kept of the costs of 'Cartage to the Broomielaw Etc.', and £472 1s. 3½d. was expended in this way in 1804-05. It would appear that coal for shipment was not carried by the regular carters named in the accounts, though why this was so is not clear. This separate account does, however, give some indication of the quantity of coal exported, for in May, 1804, it is

noted that each 24 cwt. waggon sent to the quayside cost 1s. 3d. in
'cartage, etc.' If it can be assumed that this was a constant figure,
then the total costs of £472 1s. 3½d. represented shipments of about
7,553 24 cwt. waggonloads of coal, or roughly 4,530 tons per year,
slightly more than 18 per cent, of the colliery's total output.

Most of this coal was sold through Andrew Houston, coal agent
and shore Master, at the Broomielaw. The sales accounts contain
many entries of the following kind: 'Andrew Houston for Captain
McDugal — 60 carts, £18'; 'Agnew Crawford for George Mc-
Farlane of the *Mary* — 81 carts, £24 6s. 0d.'; 'John Stewart for
Captain McNeilage — 80½ carts, £24 3s. 0d.'[52] A search through
the advertisements and notices of shipping movements in *The
Glasgow Courier* enables an assessment to be made of the ultimate
destination of this coal. Most of the captains mentioned were the
masters of vessels regularly trading with Belfast and it can be
assumed from the instances where it has been possible to identify
the masters named in the accounts with the vessels whose movements are mentioned in the newspapers that the shipments were
largely for Ireland. Other vessels carrying Govan coal were engaged
in coastwise traffic along the Clyde or, occasionally, with America
and the West Indies. It is possible that the special cwt. sacks of
coal prepared for Robert Bogle & Co. were destined for Jamaica.

The rest of the coal was sold in Glasgow and its vicinity, and
since the major purchases are mentioned in the accounts, a study
of the City Directories provides some idea of its use.[53] The bulk of
the output was clearly destined for the grates of Glasgow householders, and this largely explains the marked seasonal pattern of
sales. Domestic users either purchased directly from the carters or
the pit-head ('ready money' sales were valued at £2,820 18s. 4½d.
in 1804 and £3,346 5s. 9½d. in 1805), or through Andrew Houston
— the value of whose small 'town orders' totalled £1,530 5s. 0d. in
1804 and £1,430 14s. 6d. in 1805 — and such merchants as John
Carmichael, 'coal-grieve, Hutchesonton', and Patrick Playfair &
Co. Exactly what proportion of the coal sold to general merchants
was finally sold to manufacturers cannot be ascertained, but direct
sales to the proprietors of Glasgow's industrial concerns were
fairly substantial.[54]

Over the two-year period, it would appear that about 45 per cent
of the output was being sold to Glasgow householders, either
directly or through Andrew Houston and a number of small commission agents and grocers; about 25 per cent to general merchants,
most of which was also probably for domestic use; about 10 per
cent to manufacturers; and some 20 per cent was exported mainly
to Ireland or shipped to towns along the Clyde, either through

William Scott, the colliery's Broomielaw agent, and Andrew Houston, or other merchants such as Robert Bogle & Co. and R. M. Lowry & Co.

Throughout the years 1804 and 1805, far more coal was sold at 6s. a 12 cwt. cartload than at any other price, though certain qualities fetched anything from 4s. 6d. to 7s. 6d. Not until the closing weeks of 1805 is there any indication of a general rise in prices, to 6s. 6d. and the average price paid for the 87,000 cartloads was 5s. 8½d. per cart, or 9s. 6d. a ton. Whether this stability reflects the operations of a coal combine, such as had existed in the 1790s, or whether Glasgow's growing demand for fuel was just matched by rising output, cannot be ascertained.[55] One thing is known, William Dixon had played a leading role in earlier attempts to stabilise coal prices at a profitable level by the concerted efforts of coal-masters, and was to do so again in the second decade of the nineteenth century.[56]

IV

Compared with labour and distribution costs, the outlay on equipment during 1804-5 was relatively low: so low, in fact, that capital costs were included with the 'Incident Charges' and easily met from current revenue.[57] The major item of expenditure was wood, £362 10s. 2d. being spent mainly on prop wood of Scotch Fir, creel wands and such small items as oak to 'Repair Engine of 24 Inch Cylinder'. The cost of iron castings and 'ironwork' purchased from 'The Clyde Co.' and William Leichman was £249 7s. 5d.;[58] rope from the Glasgow Ropework Co., £130; leather for binding round the edges of trap doors to make them air-tight, for saddlery and for engine buckets, £96 19s. 3d.; and bricks (at 22s. 6d. a thousand), £44 3s. 3d. Large numbers of inexpensive candles were bought, and the other regular purchases included gunpowder, nails, shovels (at 3s. each), riddles for grading the coal, cart grease, 'oil and tallow for the machines', 'putty to boylers' and 'plaiding for pump joints', and drugs for sick horses (though they were more frequently cured by 'drinks of whisky and ale').[59]

The general impression given is one of technological simplicity in an industry in which skilled man power and its organisation was all-important. Coal-getting was a craft, and having been born and bred to it a miner needed but few tools and a sensible manager and overman to perform his task efficiently. If he could be assisted by steam-driven pumps and winding gear so much the better, but basically coal-mining depended principally on the skill, experience and muscles of the hewers and oncost men.

This impression is strengthened by a consideration of the

accounts relating to the sinking of Quarry Pit. The work began on 4 January 1805, by two sinkers and three windlassmen drawn from the colliery's standing labour force and paid by the day. Within a few weeks these men were joined by two bricklayers (paid 3s. 6d. a day), who lined the sides of the deepening shaft with bricks, and four more sinkers and labourers. By March, when the pit was down to 8 fathoms 2½ feet, labour costs of £34 5s. 4d. had been incurred. At this stage the job was taken over by a 'company' of men under the leadership of George Harker, one of the sinkers, who agreed to sink the shaft to the coal seam for £6 10s. 0d. a fathom. The 'Pavement of the Upper Coal' was reached in the fortnight ending 18 May, George Harker & Co. receiving £131 12s. 6d. for their labours (20 fathoms 1½ feet at £6 10s. 0d. per fathom). The entire operation had cost but £165 17s. 10d.

Immediately, a number of men from Corner Pit were engaged in preparing the pit for working, and directly Corner Pit was closed its entire labour force was transferred to the new Quarry Pit and production commenced, nearly 600 cartloads of coal being raised in the fortnight ending 13 July. In the next six months the pit's output was nearly 10,000 cartloads at an average allocatable cost of 1s. 6¾d. per cartload. Even if a more than generous proportion of the colliery's entire 'incident charges' for the second half of the year be added to the costs of sinking and preparation, Quarry Pit had more than paid for itself by October!

The total value of the colliery's capital equipment and plant is *perhaps* indicated by the fact that a premium of £1 16s. 0d. was paid at 'the Sunfire Office' in October 1804, for 'Insurance on £850 from Mich[s]. 1804 to Mich[s]. 1805'; certainly a total capital valuation of around £1,000 would not be inconsistent with the items mentioned in the accounts. It is clear that the major costs of production were variable costs, principally labour charges, and these were so well covered that capital charges could easily be met from sales revenue. There was no need to go to the market for capital. The operations of the mines in 1804-5 provide a glimpse of the process whereby, by utilising revenue that would otherwise have gone to the proprietors in the form of profits, the Govan Colliery was able to become one of the largest and most important mining units in Scotland. In this case, as in so many others, 'Industrial capital has been its own chief progenitor.'[60]

V

During the period under review, the Govan Colliery, near to its main market, well served by existing roads, and possessing an adroit manager and a skilled labour force, was extremely profitable.

Other Scottish collieries were not so fortunate. As Bald observed in 1808, 'it is certain, that since the introduction of the steam-engine, few or no fortunes have been made in this line in Scotland; indeed, it is commonly asserted, that upon the whole, there has been more loss than gain. We have not access to know what the profits precisely have been of late, but there is every reason to conclude, that very little has been cleared per ton upon the annual sales, and that it is so near the losing point, as scarcely to be an object worthy of pursuit . . . No doubt, there are collieries in Scotland that make handsome returns, but they are but few in numbers'.[61] Exactly what degree of accuracy there is in this statement it is not possible to ascertain, but it had long been felt that 'there have been more estates lost than made (especially in Scotland) by working coal mines'.[62]

If this is so, then the Govan Colliery was particularly favoured. In the two years 1804-1805, total sales revenue, £24,731 12s. 10d. (1804, £12,955 3s. 3½d.; 1805, £11,776 9s. 6½d.), exceeded total costs, fixed and variable, £12,815 7s. 4½d. (1804, £6,220 8s. 3d.; 1805, £6,594 19s. 1½d.), by £11,916 5s. 5½d.: for every £1 spent the return was roughly £1 19s. 0d.[63]

The profitability of each pit must partially have determined how much each should contribute to total output.[64] Corner Pit was particularly economic; there, in 1804, the allocatable cost for each cartload raised was but 1s. 7½d. compared with 2s. 2¼d. per cartload at Firrs Pit, 2s. 7d. at Bankhall Pit, and 2s. 2¾d. at Gilliesink Pit. It is not surprising, therefore, that this pit was the major source of the output. In the following year, when Corner Pit was shut down for a reason undisclosed by the accounts, the new Quarry Pit, initially somewhat less economic than Corner Pit, was rapidly developed, the allocatable costs per cartload being 1s. 6¾d. compared with 2s. 2¼d. at Firrs Pit and 3s. 3¼d. at Bankhall Pit. This kind of data must have guided Dixon in the allocation of his resources; influencing his decision to close the labour-costly Gilliesink Pit in April 1804, and to develop the new Quarry Pit rather than Firrs or Bankhall on the abandonment of Corner Pit. Overall each ton of coal raised (by the hewers and as overplus) cost 5s. 1½d. and sold at 9s. 6d. By judicious management and by taking advantage of the contemporary favourable market situation, William Dixon had nearly doubled the colliery's annual net profits in a period of seven years.[65]

VI

The boom in coal-mining inaugurated in the closing years of the eighteenth century continued until 1809, when a fall in prices forced the leading coal-masters to adopt a comprehensive plan for regulating the Glasgow coal trade.[66] An integral part of this arrangement was for a combine to purchase Govan, when it came on the market in 1813, 'because it [had] so much of the superiority of all the works in point of situation, that in the hands of a man of capital and interest it will knock them all out'.[67] The price paid was £30,000 and William Dixon took up — doubtless with the profits of his own coal and iron works at Calder — four ninths of the stock in his own name, the remainder being divided among the other members of the Combine. Six years later, in a time of great distress, when 'several of the more important coal-masters became bankrupt', the remainder decided to put up their joint properties for sale, and the sole ownership of the Govan colliery eventually passed into the hands of the Dixon family, already among Glasgow's most influential citizens.

This is not the place to pursue this story further. Suffice it to say, that the Govan Colliery and its associated ironworks — the first blast furnace being blown in 1837 — became 'one of the sights and wonders of Glasgow.'[68] It figures repeatedly in the early reports of the mines inspectors, who rarely failed to emphasise its size, its efficiency and its unique labour organisation. The second William Dixon was often to be heard before Parliamentary Committees of Inquiry and Royal Commissions. From these and other sources, together with the magnificent collection of Govan Colliery records, the later history of this undertaking will one day be written: this essay has simply attempted to examine some aspects of its story when it operated on a more modest, but no less significant, scale.

TABLE 1A

Govan Colliery: Fortnightly Output, Sales, and Stock on Hand, 1804

Fortnight Ending	Output		Coal Raised Overplus		Total		Sales		Stock[2]	
	Carts	Cwt.	Carts	Cwt.	Carts	Cwt.	Carts	Cwt.	Carts	Cwt.
14 Jan.	1,058	10	171	6	1,230	4	1,892	2	3,529	2[3]
28 Jan.	1,536	6	138	4	1,674	10	1,681	8	3,522	4
11 Feb.	1,544	8	207	6	1,752	2	2,095	2	3,179	6
25 Feb.	1,588	8	138	8	1,727	4	1,894	2	3,012	8
10 Mar.	1,709	2	89	2	1,798	4	1,919	8	2,891	4
24 Mar.	1,473	6	91	0	1,564	6	1,742	10	2,713	0
7 Apr.	1,566	2	160	4	1,726	6	1,649	4	2,790	2
21 Apr.	1,376	2	106	6	1,482	8	1,499	10	2,773	0
5 May	1,405	0	14	4	1,419	4	1,333	4	2,859	0
19 May	1,445	4	15	8	1,461	0	1,349	6	2,970	6
2 Jun.	1,541	10	43	2	1,585	0	1,435	8	3,119	10
16 Jun.	1,356	0	35	8	1,391	8	1,156	10	3,354	8
30 Jun.	1,327	8	23	2	1,350	10	1,370	10	3,334	8
14 Jul.	1,531	0	28	4	1,559	4	913	8	3,980	4
28 Jul.	1,397	8	—	—	1,397	8	1,140	10	4,237	2
11 Aug.	1,422	0	25	6	1,447	6	1,101	2	4,583	6
25 Aug.	1,369	0	6	10	1,375	10	1,900	0	4,059	4
8 Sep.	1,381	8	15	10	1,497	6	2,334	8	3,122	2
22 Sep.	1,262	0	19	2	1,281	2	2,107	4	2,296	0
6 Oct.	1,352	6	29	0	1,381	6	1,610	4	2,067	2
20 Oct.	1,350	4	22	0	1,372	4	1,695	4	1,744	2
3 Nov.	1,348	6	33	2	1,381	8	1,411	8	1,714	2
17 Nov.	1,409	6	39	8	1,449	2	2,080	4	1,083	0
1 Dec.	1,496	0	649	0	2,145	0	2,694	4	533	8
15 Dec.	1,433	4	843	6	2,276	10	2,810	6	—	—
31 Dec.[4]	1,712	10	3,060	8	4,773	6	2,733	6	2,040	0
1804	37,395	10	6,007	8	43,403	6	45,554	8	2,040	0[5]

1 This is the amount of coal raised by the hewers: 'As per Output Book'.
2 'Stock on Hand' on the last day of each fortnightly period.
3 On 1 January 1804, Stocks totalled 4,191 cartloads 2 cwts.
4 This period contains 13 working days, cf. the normal fortnights' 12 working days.
5 Stock on Hand on the last day of 1804.

TABLE 1B

Govan Colliery: Fortnightly Output, Sales and Stock on Hand, 1805

Fortnight Ending	Output[1]		Coal Raised Overplus		Total		Sales		Stock[2]	
	Carts	Cwt.	Carts	Cwt.	Carts	Cwt.	Carts	Cwt.	Carts	Cwt.
12 Jan.	715	2	39	4	754	6	2,327	6	467	0[3]
26 Jan.	1,295	6	234	8	1,530	2	1,997	2	—	—
9 Feb.	1,325	0	199	0	1,524	0	1,524	0	—	—
23 Feb.	1,282	4	193	0	1,475	4	1,475	4	—	—
9 Mar.	1,429	0	165	4	1,594	4	1,594	4	—	—
23 Mar.	1,344	4	161	10	1,506	2	1,346	2	160	0
6 Apr.	1,361	0	165	0	1,526	0	1,460	4	225	8
20 Apr.	1,499	10	127	2	1,627	0	1,693	6	159	2
4 May	1,157	10	35	4	1,193	2	1,329	6	22	10
18 May	1,424	0	117	4	1,541	4	1,509	10	54	8
1 Jun.	1,175	8	239	8	1,415	4	1,415	4	54	8
15 Jun.	1,103	6	123	0	1,226	6	1,219	10	61	4
29 Jun.	1,193	0	12	8	1,205	8	1,123	6	143	6
13 Jul.	1,070	10	149	6	1,220	4	1,220	4	143	6
27 Jul.	1,273	2	—	—	1,273	2	815	4	601	4
10 Aug.	1,068	6	115	10	1,184	4	1,175	4	610	4
24 Aug.	1,510	4	1	10	1,512	2	1,195	6	927	0
7 Sep.	1,542	8	—	—	1,542	8	1,349	4	1,120	4
21 Sep.	1,461	10	—	—	1,461	10	944	4	1,637	10
5 Oct.	1,638	0	20	6	1,658	6	1,360	8	1,935	8
20 Oct.	1,371	4	18	4	1,389	8	1,486	8	1,838	8
2 Nov.	1,446	6	26	6	1,473	0	1,856	6	1,455	2
16 Nov.	1,642	2	36	8	1,678	10	2,162	8	971	4
30 Nov.	1,576	0	649	2	2,225	2	2,487	10	708	8
14 Dec.	1,550	0	566	4	2,116	4	2,374	4	450	8
31 Dec.[4]	2,399	10	659	6	3,059	4	2,784	0	726	0
1805	35,857	4	4,057	10	39,915	2	41,229	2	726	0[5]

1 This is the amount of coal raised by the hewers: 'As per Output Book'.
2 'Stock on Hand' on the last day of each fortnightly period.
3 On 1 January 1805, stocks totalled 2,040 cart loads.
4 This period contains 14 working days, cf. the normal fortnights' 12 working days.
5 Stock on hand on the last day of 1805.

TABLE II

Govan Colliery, 1804-1805:

Statistics Illustrating the Relatively Low Average Output on Mondays

Year	Number of Working Days	Number of Working Mondays	Output (Carts)[1]			Average Output (Carts)			Ratios Expressed As a Percentage	
			Total	Mondays	Tuesdays-Saturdays	Daily	Mondays	Tuesdays-Saturdays	Mondays/Daily	Mondays/Tues.-Sats.
	(1)	(2)	(3)	(4)	(5)	(3)÷(1)	(4)÷(2)	(5)÷(1)—(2)	(7)÷(6)	(7)÷(8)
						(6)	(7)	(8)	(9)	(10)
1804	309	51	37,396	3,761	33,635	121.02	73.75	130.37	60.94	56.57
1805	304	49	35,857	3,381	32,476	117.95	68.99	127.36	58.49	54.17
1804/05	613	100	73,253	7,142	66,111	119.50	71.42	128.87	59.77	55.42

Note:
1 This is the amount raised by the hewers: 'As per Output Book'. Overplus is *not* included.

TABLE III
*Examples of Work of an Exceptional Character
Performed by the Miners of Govan Colliery, 1804-1805*

Fortnight Ending[1]	Pit[2]	Name of Miner or 'Company'	Work Performed, and Rate, as Entered in the A/cs.	Total Pay £	s.	d.
14 Jan.	B	John Walton & Co.	'Widening the door, etc. of Mine'	20	0	0
14 Jan.	C	Wm. Baveridge	'3 Yards bad parting 3d.'			9
28 Jan.	F	Robert Neilson & Co.	'5 fathoms of pavement@3s. 6d.'		17	6
10 Mar.	B	M. Walton & Co.	'To account of sinking Stair Pitt'	3	0	0
10 Mar.	B	Hector McLean	'Reding Road to Stair Pitt 4 days'		11	0
21 Apr.	B	M. Walton	'Blowing down the roof in an Air Course 4 days'		11	0
5 May	C	Stephen Crawford	'Holing through a Stoup'		4	6
14 July	F	John Richmont	'Reding level to Engine 11 days'	1	9	7
3 Nov.	F	James Smith	'At a hitch in N. level 5 days'		12	0
9 Mar.	F	John Neilson	'Reding a fall in the Level'	3	16	0
23 Mar.	B	M. Crawford & G. Urrie	'For Piercing Main Coal'		4	0
6 Apr.	F	Peter Currie	'Causeway road 12 days'	1	8	0
6 Apr.	F	Robert Neilson	'Reding at the Gaw 7 days'	1	4	6
20 Apr.	F	Wm. Barr and M. Strachan	'Arles . . . for Level Room'		2	0
20 Apr.	B	Hector McLean	'1½ fathoms of stone mine@£5'	7	10	0
1 Jun.	C	Robert Baveridge & Co.	'9 fathoms of mine to Quarry Pit Bottom'@4s. per fathom	1	16	0
15 Jun.	F	'Hector and his man'	'Blowing down the roof to place the pump in the level'		10	2
29 Jun	F	Arch. Anderson	'For a througher'		2	6
13 July	F	Hosie & Anderson	'Building a trap door		6	0
13 July	B	George Harker & Hector McLean	'To account of stone mine for an air course up the Cross Hill Gaw'	7	7	0
27 July	B	M. Maxwell	'For going down to let the mason see to put on the trap door and about the damp'		1	6
27 July	B	Geo. Harker & Hector McLean	'At Air Pitt Crosshill Gaw, 6 yards at 21s. per yd.'	6	6	0
10 Aug.	B	Robert Neilson	'Cutting through the dyke 8 days'	1	8	0
7 Sep.	F	Peter Currie & Co.	'Cutting 3 fathoms level room at 4s. 9d. per fathom		14	3
21 Sep.	Q	Wm. Robertson & Co.	'7½ fthms mine at 4s. 3d. each'	1	10	10½
5 Oct.	F	James Gordon and Peter Currie	'9 fathoms Horse Road in East Level @4s. 9d. per fthm and 3½ shifts in West Level'	2	19	0
20 Oct.	B	Thomas Urrie	'Lifting metal and turning road'		1	6

1 Above the horizontal line the dates refer to 1804; below, to 1805.
2 The following abbreviations have been used: B. Bankhall; C. Corner; F. Firrs; Q. Quarry.

TABLE IV
Govan Colliery, 1804-1805:
Costs, Sales Revenue and Net Profits

Year	Costs Allocated[1]	Incident Charges	Total	Average Cost Per Cart[2]		Sales Revenue	Average Selling Price Per Cart[3]		Net Profits (5)—(3)	Average Net Profit Per Cart (6)—(4)		Average Net Profit Per Ton	
	£	£	£	s.	d.	£	s.	d.	£	s.	d.	s.	d.
	(1)	(2)	(1)&(2) (3)	(4)		(5)	(6)		(7)	(8)		(9)	
1804	3,652	2,541	6,220[4]	2	8¾	12,955	5	8¾	6,735	2	11½	4	11
1805	3,640	2,767	6,595[5]	3	2½	11,776	5	8½	5,182	2	6	4	2
1804-1805	7,292	5,308	12.815	3	1	24,732	5	8½	11,916	2	7½	4	2½

Notes:
1 Source, Table V, Col. (4).
2 Col. (3) ÷ total carts raised as in Tables Ia and Ib (i.e. 'As per Output Book' + Overplus).
3 Col. (5) ÷ total sales, as in Tables Ia and Ib.
4 Includes £27 for maintenance of pits not being worked.
5 Includes costs of sinking Quarry Pit (£166) and £23 for maintenance of pits not being worked.
  Any internal inconsistencies in this table are due to rounding.

TABLE V

Govan Colliery, 1804-1805:
Output and Allocated Costs (by Pits)

Year	Name of Pit	Output in Carts[1]	Costs[2]		Average Amount	
			Paid to Hewers	Total Allocated (inc. (3))	Paid to Hewers Per Cart (3) ÷ (2)	Allocated Cost Per Cart (4) ÷ (2)
	(1)	(2)	(3)	(4)	(5)	(6)
			£	£	s. d.	s. d.
1804	Corner	18,478	895	1,506	11½	1 7½
1804	Firrs	13,904	1,013	1,517	1 5½	2 2¼
1804	Bankhall	3,881	330	502	1 8½	2 7
1804[3]	Gilliesink	1,133	118	127	2 1	2 2¾
1804	All Pits	37,396	2,356	3,652	1 3	2 0
1805[4]	Corner	7,306	351	595	11½	1 7½
1805	Firrs	14,717	1,074	1,614	1 5½	2 2¼
1805	Bankhall	4,134	385	678	1 10½	3 3¼
1805[5]	Quarry	9,701	500	753[6]	1 0½	1 6¾
1805	All Pits	35,857	2,310	3,640	1 3½	2 0¼

Note:
1 This is the amount raised by the hewers: 'As per Output Book'. Overplus in not included. Expressed to nearest cartload of 12 cwt.
2 To the nearest £1.
3 Gilliesink Pit ceased production during the fortnight ending 21 April 1804.
4 Corner Pit ceased production during the fortnight ending 29 June 1805.
5 Quarry Pit commenced production during the fortnight ending 13 July.
6 This sum does not include the costs of £165 17s 6d incurred in sinking the shaft. Any internal inconsistencies in this Table are due to rounding.

NOTES

1 I am indebted to Professor T. S. Ashton, Professor S. G. Checkland and Dr J. R. Kellet for reading this article in draft and for contributing a number of valuable suggestions.

2 Sir John Sinclair, *Old Statistical Account of Scotland*, V, 532. (Hereafter cited as *O.S.A.*).

3 *New Statistical Account of Scotland*, VI (1845), 671 (hereafter cited as *N.S.A.*), and H. Hamilton, *The Industrial Revolution in Scotland*, (1932), 198-9.

4 *O.S.A.*, V, 540.

5 See the map by James Barry (1782) and the plan prepared by William Kyle in 1828 to illustrate James Cleland's *Account of the Minerals etc., in the Public Green, Easter and Wester Common, Petershill, etc., belonging to the Corporation of Glasgow* (1836), frontispiece.

6 J. U. Nef, *The Rise of the British Coal Industry* (1932), I, 50, based on the *Privy Council Register of Scotland*, 3rd Series, I, xliv, 258, and *Acts of the Parliaments of Scotland*, VII, 31.

7 James Cleland, *Statistical Tables Relative to the City of Glasgow, Third Edition*, (1823), 186, 189.

8 For the firm of Alexander Houston & Co., see S. G. Checkland, 'Two Scottish West Indian Liquidations after 1793', *Scottish Journal of Political Economy*, IV, 128-135.

9 *O.S.A.*, V, 540-541.

10 Report of the Select Committee on Mr McDowall's Petition, *Parliamentary Papers*, April, 1800, 13, 16.

11 For William Dixon and the Dixon family, see H. Hamilton, op. cit., 173, 184, 186, 194 *et seq.; Memoirs and Portraits of One Hundred Glasgow Men*, I, (1886), 103-5, and below, 89.

12 The Dixon Records, numbering over 400 volumes plus numerous maps and papers, were presented to the University of Glasgow by Colvilles Ltd., on the raising of the site of Dixon's Govan Ironworks in 1959. I am deeply indebted to Mr Ralph Hillis for arranging for the preservation of these records which would otherwise have been pulped.

13 J. U. Nef, op. cit., I, 372, 6n.

14 In all cases where terminological difficulties have arisen James Barrowman's invaluable *Glossary of Scotch Mining Terms* (1886) has been consulted.

15 The tasks performed by these miners are described below, 69-71.

16 Although such varieties as Upper, Main, Humph and Splint Ell were being raised from the pits, the qualities are only distinguished by their different prices. These ranged from 4s. 6d. to 7s. 6d. per cartload of 12 cwt. See below, 75.

17 The meaning of 'overplus' is discussed below, 68, 3.

18 See Table III, below, 83.

19 See below, 76-77.

20 See Table V. Corner and Firrs Pits are clearly shown on Kyles' Plan, *loc. cit.*

21 H. Hamilton, op. cit., 170-71.

22 Among others, Professor T. S. Ashton has pointed out that 'It may be thought that the coal-miners would have been at their busiest in the winter when the demand for domestic fuel was at its peak. In fact, the pits were most active in the summer and autumn . . . When winter rain turned the roads into bogs, and frost or flood put an end to traffic on the rivers, land-sale collieries could supply only customers close at hand, and hence the pit-head price of coal was depressed just when the price in the towns was at its highest'. *Economic Fluctuations in England, 1700-1800*, (1959), 5. See also, for example, A. H. John, *The Industrial Development of South Wales, 1750-1850*, (1950), 14, and W. H. B. Court, *The*

Rise of the Midland Industries, 1600-1838 (1938), 157-8.

23 See Tables 1A and 1B. For prices see below, 86-7.

24 It is possible that 'overplus' represented an amount of coal cut by the hewers that was not credited to them. Barrowman observes, in his *Glossary*, that 'the cart' ("by which miners were formerly paid") was supposed to measure 12 cwts. of riddled coal, but in practice frequently contained an amount in excess of this figure. This would mean that for every 'cart' raised, the proprietor would receive an unpaid increment, for in selling the coal more exactitude would be enforced. The fluctuating quantity of 'overplus' and its steep rise in the period of peak demand, however, makes it extremely improbable that in the case of the Govan Colliery 'overplus' was solely an increment to the proprietor for which the hewers were not paid, though this does not preclude the possibility that this was one element in its composition. Barrowman does not mention the term, nor have enquiries made of National Coal Board officials and miners yielded any explanation. What *is* known is that the accounts frequently record amounts paid to oncost men 'for coals put out . . . on shift wages', such entries do *not*, however become most numerous at times of relatively high 'overplus' production (*e.g.* the last fortnight of 1804, see Table 1A) as one would expect them to do if this were the complete explanation.

25 See, for example, Dr J. Kay, *The Moral and Physical Conditions of the Working Classes Employed in the Cotton Manufacture in Manchester* (1832), First Edition, 7-8; quoted by Frederick Engels, *The Condition of the Working Class in England*, translated by W. O. Henderson and W. H. Chaloner (1958), 200.

26 R. Heron, *Observations Made in a Journey Through the Western Counties of Scotland* (1799), II, 381-2. I am indebted to Miss Barbara Crispin for this reference.

27 See Table II.

28 The coal measures named in the accounts. The average thickness of each of these seams at the Govan Collieries is given in the *New Statistical Account* (1845), VI, 671, and the depths by St. John V. Day, 'The Iron and Steel Industries', *British Association Handbook for the Glasgow Meeting of 1876*, Table X, 24. See also the *Old Statistical Account*, (1793), V, 532-3, and J. Cleland, *Account of the Minerals, passim.*

29 As A. J. Taylor has observed: 'The longwall system, by contrast with pillar and stall or square working, makes work at the face essentially a collective operation. Thus even in the larger collieries, where it was found necessary to commit the overall direction of the mine workings to the hands of the salaried manager, it proved expedient to maintain a system of collective piecework at the face — the so-called "Little butty system".' 'The Sub-contract System in the British Coal Industry', L. S. Pressnell, ed., *Studies in the Industrial Revolution*, (1960), 220.

30 J. U. Nef, op. cit., I, 348.

31 See Table III.

32 As was the case in the Derbyshire Colliery the records of which form the basis for the article by G. W. Daniels and T. S. Ashton, 'The Records of a Derbyshire Colliery, 1763-1779', *Economic History Review*, II, (1929-30), 126.

33 See above n.2.

34 In the absence of the 'Output Book' it is impossible to determine exactly how many hewers were employed at any particular time. However, between July and September 1805, 63 miners, all named, received bounties or binding money. Twelve of these men are named elsewhere in the accounts as oncost men (Redsmen, drivers, bottomers, etc.) and since the accounts indicate that only underground workers received bounties, it may fairly be assumed that the other 51 were hewers. Other evidence — for example, the names of men under special contract, the recipients of drink money and those who received a rent allowance

in lieu of free housing — supports this conclusion. The repetition of names in
the accounts emphasises the stability in the labour force and hence a belief that
little variation in the numbers took place in the period under review.

35 The labour costs involved in the long-wall method must have been more than
compenstated for by the elimination of waste. In the Whitehaven Collieries, for
example, where, by 1800, the bord and pillar system was exclusively employed,
it was possible to extract only about one-third of the coal, the other two-thirds
being required to support the roof in huge 18-20 yard square pillars. See J. Dixon,
An Account of the Coal Mines near Whitehaven, (1801) 101; the definitions given
by J. Barrowman, op. cit.; and, for a later description of work in the Govan
Collieries, the *Children's Employment Commission* (1842), Appendix to the First
Report of the Commissioners, Part I, Thomas Tancred's Report, 319-20, 326,
and the evidence of James Allen, 'manager of the Govan Colliery since 1822, and
connected with the works 26 years,' 356.

36 Based on the evidence given by Francis Conery, aged 9, a trapper at the Govan
Collieries before the *Children's Employment Commission*, Appendix, Part I, 360.

37 From the Scottish word for hook.

38 Cf. the Barrachnie and Sandyhills coal-works '4 miles east of Glasgow', where, in
1793, 150 colliers, bearers and boys, raised about 233 tons per miner per
annum (*O.S.A.*, VII, (1793), 389), and a colliery at Cambuslang where '62 men,
young and old . . . 42 below ground, and 20 above, put out about 290 tons per
miner per annum (*O.S.A.*, V (1793), 257). Both these cases are cited by J. U. Nef,
op. cit., II, 138, n.6.

39 R. L. Galloway, *Annals of Coalmining and the Coal Trade*, (1898), 440; and A. J.
Taylor, op. cit., 229.

40 For example, John Bateman, manager of the large Whitehaven Collieries, was
advertising for men in the Scottish papers at this time; see O. Wood, 'A Cumberland Colliery During the Napoleonic War', *Economica*, N.S. XXI, (1954) 55.

41 John Bateman's anguished complaint in 1804 in a letter to the proprietor of the
Whitehaven Collieries, Viscount Lowther, later Earl of Lonsdale. O. Wood, op.
cit., 56.

42 In this case an average is almost meaningless since although the hewers' piece
rate was basically determined by output, the rate varied not only from one pit to
another, but also in different seams in the same pit according to the difficulty of
working.

43 The dangers of entrusting the raising and lowering of men to 'a mere boy' are
emphasised by Thomas Tancred in his report to the *Children's Employment
Commission*, (1842), Appendix, Part I, 327.

44 In 1793 it was noted by the Rev. Mr William Anderson that 'The Govan Colliery
has two excellent machines, the one for drawing up the water, the other a steam
engine for bringing up coals 100 fathoms, which saves a number of horses',
O.S.A., V, 540. Indeed, the Govan Colliery was the first of the Glasgow pits to
employ 'a fire engine'. *N.S.A.*, (1845) VI, 225.

45 Entry in accounts for fortnight ending 18 May 1805. This disaster is mentioned
by Peter Boag, bottomer of Mr J. Wilson's Haugh Pit, Hurlet, in his evidence
before the *Children's Employment Commission*, Appendix, Part I, 367; and see
R. L. Galloway, op. cit., 406.

46 The accounts contain many entries similar to the following: 'House Rent to Hugh
Neil to Whitsunday last — 10s. 6d.', fortnight ending (hereafter given as f/e) 1
June 1805.

47 Many of the names of the women employed at the farm — the accounts for which
are kept in the ledger — are identical with those of the oncost men working in
the pits.

48 *Children's Employment Commission* (1842), Appendix, Part I, evidence of George

Lindsay (sometime at Dixon's Govan Colliery) 363. See T. S. Ashton and J. Sykes, *The Coal Industry of the Eighteenth Century* (1939), 68.

49 R. Bald, *A General View of the Coal Trade of Scotland*, (1812), 29, 32.

50 The mode of selling coal was apparently strictly regulated by the town council. See J. Cleland, *Statistical Tables*, 192. In June 1805, 'A Fine (of 10s.) was paid in Police Office for not having the Co's. Name on Thomas Zuill's Cart large enough'.

51 The calculation whereby the figures are arrived at is necessarily somewhat complicated. Of the 43,500 12 cwt. cartloads sold annually about 75 per cent went to the city, the centre of which was 1½ miles away, the remainder being taken to the Broomielaw by special 24 cwt. waggons or sold at the pit-head. On average, therefore, each of the 15 carters usually employed carried 1,305 tons of coal to the market per year. The accounts show that each carter worked an average of 10 days per fortnight or 260 a year, at somewhat less than 1s. 7d. a day. This is equal to about 2½d. per ton mile in labour costs. Cf. R. Bald, op. cit., 34.

52 From the accounts for the fortnights ending 11 August 1804, 7 April 1804, and 7 September 1805, respectively.

53 Positive identification was often frustrated by the sparse details contained in the early directories, the erratic spelling of the colliery's book-keeper, and the failure, in both accounts and directories, to provide more than an initial to pinpoint the exact buyer; where so many 'J. Campbells' exist, it is impossible to determine which one is referred to.

54 Among these were several cotton spinners (James Cook & Co., of Gorbals, and Todd & Stevenson, of Springfield), dyers and printers (James & D. H. McDowall & Co., of 39 Virginia Street, and Andrew Campbell & Co., of Greenhead) a number of iron founders (T. Edington & Sons, Phoenix Foundry, 42 Queen Street, and John & James Robertson, engineers, Tradestown, and iron-founders, Gorbals), and such manufacturers as Archibald Blair, japanner, 9 Argyll Street; William Dudgeon, brickmaker, Hangingshaw; and R. B. Niven & Co., soap and candle makers, of the Gorbals and Trongate.

55 See H. Hamilton, op. cit., 196.

56 Ibid., 196-204, and see below, 89.

57 Though how much the already installed 'fire engines' for pumping and winding had cost is not known; no provision was made for their depreciation.

58 In the fortnight during which Gilliesink Pit was abandoned (f/e 21 April 1804) 5 men were employed in 'drawing and lifting the metals' from the pit. This probably refers to cast-iron plates affixed to wooden rails on which laden corfs, or 'whirleys', were pulled by horses from the working face to the pit bottom, though it is possible that already Dixon was using rails made entirely of cast iron. That he was always ready to adopt new and better methods is clear from his rapid adoption of Curr's flat rope, special pulley wheels for which were brought from England in April 1805. For methods of winding and drawing, see T. S. Ashton and J. Sykes, op. cit., 54-69.

59 For example '2 Drinks of Whisky and ale, etc., to Sick Hourse — 2s.', accounts, f/e 25 February 1804.

60 T. S. Ashton, *The Industrial Revolution, 1760-1830*. (1948), 97. A similar instance of balancing *all* costs against revenue in the mining industry is given by G. W. Daniels and T. S. Ashton, op. cit., 129. In this case a net loss of £577 8s. 9d. was incurred over the period 1763-1779.

61 Bald, op. cit., 25-6.

62 *O.S.A.*, (1793), VIII, 616 n.

63 See Table IV.

64 See Table V.

65 It will be recalled, see above, 65, that Dixon certified that the average net profits

for the years 1797-1799 were £3,388 16s. 4d. in his evidence to the Select Committee on Mr McDowall's Petition. For the years 1804-1805, the average annual net profits were £5,958.

66 This paragraph is based on H. Hamilton, op. cit., 196-204.

67 Colin Dunlop to James Dunlop, 1 September 1813. Quoted by H. Hamilton, op. cit., 199. This letter was among the Clyde Iron Works MSS., the bulk of which were unfortunately destroyed in the early 1930's. (Professor H. Hamilton in a letter to the author).

68 See *Memoirs and Portraits of One Hundred Glasgow Men*, I, 104.

6

The Productivity of Capital
in the Lancashire Cotton Industry
during the Nineteenth Century[1]

M. Blaug*

The growth of the Lancashire cotton industry has supplied generations of historians with illustrative material to depict labour-saving technical change. Capital-saving innovations, it is said, were hardly very important until the close of the nineteenth century. Whatever the facts for the modern period, technical improvements in the heyday of the cotton industry surely raised not only capital per man but also capital per unit of output. In the absence of reliable statistics on the capital stock this can only be surmised, but it is not on that account any less widely held.

Shall we ever be able to verify such beliefs? We have few enough over-all estimates of capital formation in Great Britain prior to 1865 and even those for the latter half of the century are not broken down into individual sectors other than residential housing, railways and utilities.[2]

For manufacturing there is in fact no data to indicate the rate of growth of the capital stock in any particular industry. The cotton industry, however, proves to be a singular exception to this generalisation: here we have a number of contemporary estimates by informed observers for six benchmark years between 1834 and 1886. Moreover, owing to the provisions of the Factory Act of 1833, increases in capacity in this industry can be gauged by the returns of spindles, looms, and motive-power installed. The annual value of output of the industry can be computed with a fair degree of accuracy for purposes of comparison to the trends in capital and labour. With the aid of the capital and labour coefficients it may be possible to go beyond the purely descriptive treatment of technical change which characterises so much of the literature on the history of the cotton manufacture. Although no industry has been so

*From *Economic History Review*, 2nd series, Vol. XIII (1960-61), pp. 358-81. Reprinted by permission of the editors of *Economic History Review* and the author.

frequently investigated and written about as the cotton industry, surprisingly little is known about productivity changes in spinning and weaving.

I

According to the 1841 census classification, the cotton industry included all persons employed in the preparation and spinning of raw cotton into yarn and the weaving of yarn into cloth: in 1834 this would have meant some 200,000 factory operatives in England, another 35,000 in Scotland and Ireland, and approximately 200,000 hand-loom weavers. But the early historians of the industry, such as Edward Baines and Andrew Ure, would have included an additional 237,000 persons employed in bleaching, dyeing, calico-printing and the manufacture of lace and hosiery. Other writers were wont to add cotton warehousemen, cotton textile engineers, yarn agents, cloth merchants, and even cotton brokers and dealers.

For my purpose the narrow product-classification of the 1841 census is to be preferred. Quantitative information about the finishing branch of the industry is hard to come by; the finishing of cloth was carried on quite separately from the manufacturing process and was not brought under legislative control until the 1860s. As much is true of lacemaking and hosiery where the bulk of output was still being produced by outworkers or in small workshops as late as 1870. Furthermore, not all hosiery and lace products were made of cotton; in the 1830s they were more often made of silk and wool.[3] The merchanting section, on the other hand, is clearly outside my purview. Hence, for practical reasons, I follow present custom in defining the Lancashire cotton industry as bounded at one end by the Liverpool cotton exchange and at the other end by the Manchester market for unbleached cloth, sold 'in the grey'. But insofar as imperfect statistics allow we shall have occasion to allude to the cotton industry as a whole, inclusive of the finishing section.

In summary form, the findings are as follows:

	1834	1856	1860	1871	1886
Total capital — £ m.	22	45.5	57	87	83
Fixed capital — £ m.	15	31	35	57	58
Ten years moving average of net output — £ m.	11	18	17	28	28
Total capital (constant prices)	22	43	56	85	109
Fixed capital (constant prices)	15	30	34	56	76
Man-hours — m. hrs. p.a.	1570	1254	1432	1404	1586
Ten year moving average of net output — £ m.	11	31	24	42	58
Total capital/net output	2.0	2.5	3.3	3.1	3.0
Fixed capital/net output	1.4	1.7	2.1	2.0	2.1
Capital/output (constant prices)	2.0	1.4	2.3	2.0	1.9
Fixed capital/output (constant prices)	1.4	0.9	1.4	1.3	1.3
Man-hours/real output	143	40	34	33	27
Real capital/man-hours	0.014	0.03	0.04	0.06	0.06

Expressed in current prices, capital invested per unit of (net) output shows a marked rise up to 1860, followed by a gentle decline down to 1886. The ratio of fixed capital to (net) output likewise ceases to rise in the years after 1860. It is evident that the period 1860-86 was marked by significant economies in the use of working capital. But so long as capital and output are measured in current prices there is no way of distinguishing between a fall in the capital/output ratio caused by pecuniary rather than technical economies, by forces external to rather than internal to the industry. Lower equipment prices owing to improvements in the machine goods industry, or, say, lower freight charges and reductions in delivery time produced by technological progress in transportation, will release capital in cotton just as effectively as factor-saving innovations in spinning and weaving. For this reason I have made an attempt to deflate both capital and output. And when both numerator and denominator are measured in constant prices, no rise whatever in the ratio of capital to output is revealed over the whole period: apparently, the price of yarn and grey cloth fell faster than that of machinery and building materials. This finding is particularly striking in view of the fact that the rate of growth of physical output slackened in the 1870s, with the onset of 'the great depression'.

The cotton industry as a whole exhibits very much the same tendency manifested in the spinning and weaving section. Estimates of the capital invested in the three main branches of the finishing trade are available for some years. The results for the industry, defined in the inclusive sense, are given here for comparison to spinning and weaving.

	1834	1845	1856	1860	1886
Total capital — £ m.	34	47	75.5	87	108
Ten years m.a. of net output — £ m.	29	31	39	35	62
Total capital/net output	1.2	1.5	1.9	2.5	1.7
Capital/output (constant prices)	1.2	1.2	1.1	1.5	1.1

In the earlier period (1834-60) the course of technical change seems to conform to the labour-saving bias popularly attributed to nineteenth century development. Not only did the working capital/output ratio rise but labour inputs per unit of output fell violently, reflecting the steady contraction and eventual disappearance of the hand-loom weaving trade. But as the average productivity of capital began to rise after 1860, the productivity of labour grew less rapidly, so that capital per man-hour increased but slightly. Without venturing upon any recondite classification of innovations, we may conclude that the data indicates that capital-saving improvements were prevalent in the decades, following the 'cotton famine'.[4] Indeed, if we could assume that the underlying production functions show diminishing returns to scale we might have concluded that capital-saving innovations predominated throughout the fifty-year period. For such production functions, capital accumulation necessarily raises capital per unit of output; technical change which is biased towards labour-saving improvements cannot offset the upward tendency of the capital/output ratio in constant prices. But we have seen that, on the contrary, the ratio exhibits remarkable stability over the period under consideration. Without pressing this point it is clear that, whatever the nature of the underlying production functions, the slant of technical change *after* 1860 was largely capital-saving. The upward trend in labour's share of net output after 1860 supports this inference.[5] It is interesting to note that the aggregate capital coefficient of the British Economy as a whole also declined from 3.7 in the 1870s to 3.3 in the 1890s.[6]

II

The materials and methods of estimation are described in the appendix but some general remarks about the character of the data is in order before proceeding to discuss their implications.

1. The figures for fixed capital are based upon estimates, sometimes by several independent observers, of the average current value per spindle and per loom of separate spinning and weaving mills; they include the value of land-rights, buildings, machinery, steam engine, and shafting. This ignores the possibility that the capital value per machine in combined spinning and weaving concerns, accounting for about one out of every three or four cotton mills, may have been quite different from those of specialised mills. The problem is aggravated by the fact that the practice of combining yarn and cloth production in one factory grew rapidly between 1825 and 1856 and then declined in relative importance.[7] It is, however, impossible to assess the importance of this deficiency in the data.

2. The figures for working capital must be treated with more caution than the corresponding figures for fixed capital. The standard method of estimating the stock of working capital was to apply an average turnover rate to the flow of annual outlays on wages and raw cotton. Estimates of the turnover rate are difficult to verify. Apparently, the level of raw cotton stocks, not only in the hands of spinners and dealers but also in the ports, was responsible for the prevailing impression that working capital turned over two or three times a year.[8] In a few cases, it was possible to check estimates of fixed plus working capital by applying capital/labour

ratios obtained from surveys of particular districts or from small samples of mills. Some available estimates had to be discarded as not subject to any independent verification.

3. All the capital estimates, with the possible exception of the 1871 figures, value buildings and equipment at current prices, net of depreciation. Depreciation quotas seem to have varied little over the period under consideration. Detailed cost statements for individual mills in the 1830s and in the 1880s show a standard charge of 7.5 per cent for replacement of machinery and 2.5 per cent for maintenance of buildings and steam engines.[9] This seems hard to believe but accounting practices are notoriously slow to alter. (Of course, the effect of falling prices through 1815-52 and 1874-86 was to raise the real value of depreciation allowances). At any rate, if depreciation equalled replacement, capital can be assumed to have grown at the same rate in gross as in net terms. The ratio of gross capital to gross product, however, does not reveal the two-phase movement of the capital net output ratio: it rose continuously over the half-century under review; fixed capital per unit of gross product, on the other hand, increased only up to 1871. This is due to the fact that total output at first grew faster and then fell behind net output.

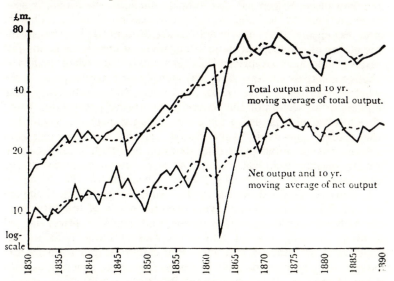

£m.

Total output and 10 yr. moving average of total output.

Net output and 10 yr. moving average of net output

log-scale

The differential rates of growth of gross and net output were due, not to alterations in techniques of production, but to swings in the gap between the prices of raw cotton and finished cloth under the pressure of changing demand and supply conditions abroad. The capital to gross output ratio, measured in constant prices, once again shows a slight decline throughout the period under review.

4. Ideally, the benchmark years for which we have capital estimates should occupy the same position in the trade cycle so as not to distort the calculation of the long-term trend. On balance, it would seem that the benchmark estimates are sufficiently comparable in cyclical position, taking into account the long-lived character of fixtures and implements.

1834 — about midway between trough and peak
1845 — cyclical peak
1856 — about midway between trough and peak
1860 — cyclical peak
1871 — about midway between trough and peak
1886 — slightly past cyclical trough

5. Continuous series for textile machine prices are not available prior to 1885. Hence, capital was deflated by means of a substitute index of the price level of capital goods. Prior to 1870, it was necessary to resort to an index of wholesale prices.[10] I do not think that this produces a serious bias in the results. Broadly speaking, an index of capital goods prices will vary in the same proportion as an index of prices in general if technical change in the economy as a whole is neutral. For an overall labour-saving slant in technical progress implies that cost-reductions are concentrated in the finishing stages of production; hence, the prices of consumer goods fall faster than machine prices. The reverse is true when technical change is largely capital-saving. By identifying machine prices with wholesale prices I have in fact assumed that productivity rose equally in all sectors of the economy, an absurd assumption to be sure but the most plausible under the circumstances. To argue that the machine goods industry always led the race for technical advances is to make the strong assumption of an overall capital saving bias in technical change, since *all* cost-reductions in the making of machines release capital involved in the using of machines. If, on the other hand, we assumed that technical change was predominantly labour-saving over the whole of the fifty years 1834-86 we would have to suppose that machine prices lagged behind in the sharp fall of the general price level after 1873. In that case we would reach a still lower real capital output ratio for the end of our period than is shown above. The same conclusion holds if we accept the argument that any index of machine prices should be given an upward trend to take account of the improved quality of equipment.

6. Real output is estimated as follows: first, the weight of yarn

produced is derived by deducting the loss of weight in spinning — the unsaleable short fibres removed by the carding engines — from official statistics of retained imports of raw cotton adjusted for changes in total stocks. An allowance is made for the fact that the proportion of 'waste' was permanently reduced in the 1860s due to the improved quality of imported cotton and the more careful preparation of fibre. The weight of piece goods produced is then derived by deducting the weight of yarn exports from the volume of yarn produced. The resulting series for yarn consumed in the weaving branch of the industry is equated to the weight of grey cloth manufactured, although in fact the weight of yarn was somewhat increased in the weaving process by the application of sizing to reduce friction in the power-looms. In addition, an intermediate amount of yarn was absorbed by the cotton thread, hosiery and lace trades. There is some tentative evidence to suggest a secular increase in the relative importance of these consumers of cotton yarn, at least up to the late 1870s.[11] To that extent, the rate of growth of output of grey cloth was less, and the trend in the real capital/output ratio was greater, than is indicated above.

7. The money value of output is obtained by multiplying the volume of cloth produced by the average price of grey cloth quoted on the Manchester market, to which is added the value of yarn exports as declared by British shippers. Net output is derived by deducting the value of raw cotton consumed. Cotton was of course only one of the raw materials used up, albeit the most important. Oil, leather, flour, tallow, and coal were others; in addition there were fixed expenses for depreciation, interest on borrowed capital, rents, local rates, taxes and insurance. Unfortunately, there are no aggregate figures for these expenditures in any year during the nineteenth century. Thus, the figures for net output presented here are in excess of the true value added. But whether the upward trend in net value added was greater or lesser than that of net output so-called we can not say.

8. The output of finished piece goods, as distinct from grey cloth, consists of the known value of piece goods exports and the esti- mated value of the home trade. The pounds' weight of goods retained for the home market is obtained by deducting the volume of goods exported, as recorded in the trade accounts, from the volume of grey cloth produced. There are no reliable price-series for finished goods other than the average declared value of exports. According to common opinion at the time, cotton piece goods sold at home were of better quality and hence dearer than goods shipped abroad. It was often held that the average price of home traded fabrics was about a third above that of exported goods. I have

followed contemporary practice in estimating the value of the home trade accordingly. Some observers thought that there had been a secular increase in the magnitude of this price-differential.[12] This would produce an even sharper fall in the capital/output ratio for the industry as a whole through 1860-86 than is shown above.

9. Net output is estimated once again by deducting cotton consumption from gross output. The movements in the two net output series — that of grey cloth and that of finished piece goods — is remarkably similar both in cyclical turning points and in secular rates of growth. Still, there is every reason to believe that such improvements as the introduction of aniline dyes and the complete replacement of block-printing by cylinder printing must in time have reduced the finishing-margins. In the absence of reliable evidence on the cost of finishing such tendencies are ignored in our net output series. But we err on the side of scepticism: cost-reducing improvements in finishing would lead to a rate of growth of value added in excess of the rate of growth of net output so-called. This would mean that the 'true' capital/output ratio for the industry as a whole fell even more than our figures suggest.

III

The trends in capital, labour and output are compared below with the increase of capacity as revealed by the Factory Returns, all expressed in percentage changes from the base 1834.

	1834	1839	1845	1850	1856	1860	1861	1867	1870	1871	1874	1878	1886
Total capital	100	—	—	—	205	257	—	—	—	392	—	—	374
Fixed capital	100	—	—	—	210	236	—	—	—	373	—	—	371
Gross output	100	119	119	133	190	224	238	305	338	333	319	305	305
Net output	100	109	127	136	164	155	155	190	245	255	255	255	255
Wages Bill	100	100	—	91	117	—	144	144	170	—	201	198	212
Real Capital	100	—	—	—	194	252	—	—	—	383	—	—	491
Real fixed capital	100	—	—	—	200	230	—	—	—	386	—	—	513
Man-hours	100	90	91	85	80	—	91	80	90	—	95	96	100
Real output	100	121	210	202	315	399	422	380	426	484	500	445	569
Factories	100	158	—	167	181	—	250	221	215	—	230	232	228
Spindles	100	—	162	194	260	—	281	317	349	—	388	409	410
Power-looms	100	—	250	250	299	—	400	379	441	—	465	515	561
Hand-looms	100	67	30	21	12	0.04	—	—	—	—	—	—	—
Horse-power[13]	100	146	—	201	237	—	100	69	105	—	—	—	—

The break in the upward trend of the capital/output ratio which occurred in the 1860s suggests a qualitative change in the technical structure of the cotton industry. The obvious factor at work was the successful mechanisation of weaving, almost half a century after the introduction of the first practical power-loom. Frequent breakage of yarn from mechanical handling made the early power-looms expensive to operate and unsuitable to anything but the coarsest fabrics. It was not until the 1820s that steam-weaving began to threaten the hand industry. In 1834 there were still twice as many hand-looms as power-looms but thereafter the hand-loom trade fell off rapidly; by 1860, the stock of hand-looms numbered only 7,000. No startling improvements seem to have taken place in mechanical weaving during this period: the increased capacity of the power-looms was barely sufficient to make up for the decline in the volume of hand-woven cloth.

At the same time, spinning capacity was rising very much faster than spindleage, reflecting substantial improvements in technique. Spinning had been a factory industry since 1800. Nevertheless, partly hand-operated mules and jennies were still required for the spinning of finer yarn. It was the introduction of the self-acting mule, power-driven in every movement, which seems to be responsible for the rapid increase of productivity in the spinning section. Patented in 1792 it had not been sufficiently perfected to make it practical before 1825 or thereabouts. At first it had been adopted to medium counts. Further refinements in the 1860s made it suitable to virtually all counts.

Differences in the tempo of productivity advances in the spinning and in the weaving section show up in the trend of product-prices. Between 1830 and 1860 the price of plain piece goods exports declined at almost the same rate as that of yarn exports, suggesting that weaving costs remained relatively constant. Output data for yarn and cloth, after 1860 once again show a rising trend in production per spindle without a corresponding increase in the production of cloth per loom.[14]

	Yarn produced per spindle (lbs)	Cloth produced per loom (lbs)
1867	28	1950
1870	30	1880
1874	32	2110
1878	29	1810
1885	32	1850
1890	38	2130

The early period 1834-60 saw the introduction of a series of labour-saving innovations. There were conspicuous advances in the mechanical handling and preparation of raw cotton. In yarn manufacture, the self-acting mule eliminated the need for a highly skilled spinner who used to work one pair of the old hand mules, assisted by two or three children. The strong bargaining power of the adult spinners seems to have provided the chief stimulus for the introduction of the automatic mule.[15] One of its attendant benefits, however, was a greater evenness and strength of yarn, thereby reducing the time lost by breakage. As a result, the traverse of the mule was lengthened, the number of spindles in a single frame was raised and one man was made to work four instead of two carriages by 'double-decking'.[16] In weaving the same forces were at work. A hand-loom weaver could tent only one loom. When power-looms were first enumerated by the Factory Inspectors in 1835, two looms per weaver was the usual number; by 1860 it had risen to 2.5-3; and by 1887 most weavers were tenting four looms.[17] This does not fully indicate the increased productivity of labour in the making of intricate designs — using the Jacquard device, a hand-loom weaver would have needed as many as three assistants.

The separate trends in labour-productivity in spinning and weaving cannot be determined statistically, owing to the failure of the Factory Inspectors to distinguish spinners from weavers in combined concerns. But if Ellison's estimates of the distribution of the cotton labour force between the two sectors is accepted, the figures for output per man-hour reveal a continuous rise, although at a diminishing rate, despite a 20 per cent reduction in hours worked.[18]

Three Year Averages	Spinners (ooo's)	Yarn produced (m. lbs) per man-hour of spinning	Weavers by hand and by power (ooo's)	Goods produced (m. lbs) per man-hour of weaving
1830	140	0.4	275	0.2
1845	190	0.8	210	0.7
1860	248	1.2	203	1.1
1881	240	1.9	246	1.5
1892	220	2.3	310	1.4

In contrast to the appearance of dramatic labour-saving devices, there were no inventions in the period that were themselves particularly capital-saving, barring ring-spinning which was not widely introduced in England until the 1890s. But the mechanisation of spinning and weaving required a smaller outlay of capital than might have been expected at first: for instance it was soon found that a hand-mule could be converted to a self-actor merely by replacement of the headstock, costing about one-fifth of the price of a new mule.[19] In addition, capital was being continuously released by the greater intensity of utilisation of the new equipment and by piecemeal improvements in their details of construction and accuracy of adjustment. In spinning more spindles were mounted on each carriage at little extra expense and their speed of working was steadily increased. At the time when Baines and Ure published their histories, 350-400 spindles per mule was the common number; both knew of some modern mills in which the mules already carried as many as 1,000 spindles. By the 1850s, 500 had become the average number; this rose to 750-900 by 1875, and in 1876 the upper limit of fifty years' earlier had become the norm. Through 1839-62 the number of revolutions per minute of mule spindles rose 20 per cent. No similar figures are available for the later years but there is no doubt that the same process made itself felt.[20] These developments rested in turn upon improvements in the carding and scutching engines, which cleaned the cotton, and the other pre-paring frames, such as the slubbers and rovers.[21] For instance, the adoption of 'differential motion' for the slubbing and roving frames around 1850 markedly reduced the liability to breakage of yarn when subjected to high-speed spinning.

With yarn becoming more uniform in twist and wound more evenly on the cops, it became possible to raise speeds of working in weaving. The number of picks per minute — the standard measure of the number of throws of the shuttle — increased from about 100 in 1834 to 130 in 1850, to 175 in 1873, reaching 200 in 1885. The development of inventions like the automatic temple and weft-stop motion, which made their way slowly over the years, seem to have contributed towards the quickened pace of weaving.[22] 'There are power-looms made today', wrote one observer in 1887, 'which run more than double the speed of the power-looms fifty years ago, and ten times the speed of the hand-loom'.[23]

It is true that greater speeds required the application of additonal steam-power. But this was usually obtainable gratis from the increased pressure at which the old Watt engines were operated. Sometimes the addition of a boiler was sufficient to raise the work-duty of an engine by 50 per cent. At the same time, the extraction of more power from engines of a given bulk was accompanied by savings in fuel costs: coal consumption for a ten-hour day fell from 72 lbs. per horse-power in 1835 to 52 lbs. per horse-power in 1887.[24]

G. H. Wood, writing in 1910, concluded that the speeding-up of machinery in the cotton industry had proceeded at a compound rate of one per cent from 1833 on. At this rate it would take about 70 years to double the speed of operations. Everything else remaining the same, this alone would have cut in half the amount of working capital which had to be carried for a given output. The working capital/output ratio actually rose through 1834-60, despite the reductions in inventories of yarn and the saving in time which must have accompanied the replacement of hand-loom weaving in scattered homes by power-weaving in factories. But through 1860-86 the increased speeds at which mules and looms were run released capital tied up in goods-in-process: the working capital/net output ratio fell from 1.3 in 1860 to 0.8 in 1886. Faster ocean and railway carriage contributed to this result. Unfortunately, no separate statistics on the proportion of cotton stocks in the hands of manufacturers are available after 1852. But the trend in total cotton stocks held in England, measured in weeks of consumption at the current annual rate, was strongly downward after 1865.[25]

With respect to fixed capital, the years 1825-60 may be regarded as the installation period of the self-acting mule and the power-loom. The process of assimilating these innovations was capital-using because they accelerated the rate of replacement of equipment through obsolescence and created expectations of windfall profit. The years 1860-86 may then be viewed as the operation-period of the installed equipment, cutting costs per unit of output. This distinction, made long ago by Oskar Lange, over-simplifies matters but is nevertheless a useful way of contrasting the two phases in the movement of the fixed capital/output ratio over the years under review.

IV

It is easier to describe what happened that to explain why it happened. One of the essential links is missing: we know next to nothing about variations in the rate of return on capital invested. The best we can do is to piece together some bits of information suggesting the relevant forces at work.

The wage rates of factory workers, which had been falling since the beginning of the century, stabilised in the thirties and forties. Except for an upward bulge in 1845, they did not begin to rise until 1850, after which they moved upwards along an almost constant trend-line. The wage rates of hand-loom weavers tended downward of course, falling permanently below those of factory workers in 1816. If 1834 = 100, Wood's index of the weighted average of weekly wages of spinners and weavers stood at 140 in 1861 and 185 in 1886.[26] It is piece rates, not time rates, however, which provide the motivation for labour-saving innovations. Labour costs per unit of output fell steadily until 1860. Thereafter, hourly wage rates seem to have risen faster than (net) output per man-hour, as shown by the secular increase in labour's share of output. But as the price of yarn and of piece goods fell faster than the price of imported cotton, labour costs as a proportion of all costs probably fell. Hence, the impetus towards labour-saving improvements diminished. And indeed, even in spinning, the period 1860-86 did not witness the same dramatic increases in labour-productivity that had marked the earlier years.

It is worth noting that the tendency to replace dear adult labour by cheap juvenile labour resisted the efforts of factory reformers until the last decades of the nineteenth century. Skilled workers in the cotton industry were almost always adult males; semi-skilled work was done by women and boys 13-18 years old; the unskilled tasks were performed by children under 13. In the eighteenth century, Hargreaves' jenny and Crompton's mule had substituted skilled for unskilled labour.[27] The increased use of Arkwright's water-frame, and its successor the throstle-frame, in the nineteenth century reversed the process, and the coming of the automatic mule increased the demand for female labour at the expense of children and adult males. Once the agitation over the Ten Hours' Bill had died down, child labour once again grew faster than adult labour and this trend continued until 1874.

Percentage of each class of workers employed in cotton mills[28]

	1834	1839	1847	1850	1856	1861	1867	1870	1874	1878	1885	1890	1895
Children under 13	13.3	4.7	5.8	4.6	6.5	8.8	10.4	9.6	14.0	12.8	9.9	9.1	5.8
Males 13-18	12.5	16.6	11.8	11.2	10.3	9.1	8.6	8.5	8.0	7.2	7.9	8.2	7.9
Females over 13	47.9	53.8	55.3	55.5	55.8	55.7	55.0	55.9	53.9	54.7	55.8	55.8	55.7
Males over 18	26.4	24.9	24.9	28.7	27.4	26.4	26.0	26.0	24.1	25.3	26.4	26.9	27.6

These variations seem to have taken place within limits set by technological requirements. The striking constancy of the female labour-force — even when girls aged 13-18 are eliminated — and the small range of variation in the proportions of adult male labour suggests that the distribution of skills was largely governed by the technical characteristics of equipment rather than by relative wages. The evidence is inconclusive because the influence of wage-differentials for labour of different skills may have made itself felt in the choice of goods manufactured: the finer yarns and fabrics required more skilled handling.

While wage rates were rising in the later years there is no reliable evidence to show that the profit rate was falling. It is true that the margin between the price of raw cotton and the price of cotton manufactures fell continuously through the whole of the nineteenth century — this accounts for the different rates of growth of gross and net output of grey cloth. But the downward trend in the general price level, while much less than the downtrend in cotton prices, may have reduced overhead charges. There were complaints about a declining rate of profit per unit of turnover but little is heard about the rate of profit on capital. Still, the price of raw cotton governed the price of output. All available indices show a high correlation in the movements of the prices of raw cotton and of yarn and piece goods.[29] The squeeze in the margin, therefore, stimulated the search for cost-reducing innovations and the rising capital/output ratio up to 1860, implying a higher share of amortisation and interest charges in total cost, invited capital-saving rather than labour-saving changes. If this sounds like *post hoc ergo propter hoc* it is all the available facts will permit us to say.

One may take some comfort from the fact that all explanations of factor-saving improvements in terms of rational optimising behaviour come to grief upon the imponderable element of the state of demand for a product of given quality. Some innovations, such as the comber, patented in 1851, facilitated the spinning of fine yarn with inferior raw material previously unusable. It is impossible to explain its introduction merely by pointing to changes in factor-rewards. And again, the slow adoption of certain cost-reducing innovations must be attributed to their poor efficiency for the finer yarns and fabrics. A notorious example is the failure of ring-spinning to gain a foothold in Lancashire until the last decade of the century, although ring-spinning for warp yarn was already an established practice in the United States by the 1850s. The ring frame was a simpler machine requiring less skill to operate, its output per spindle was twice that of the mule spindle, it saved floor-space and could be driven at higher speeds without extra vibration, thus lengthening the life of the plant, and it spun a stronger yarn. But the mule frame produced a softer and finer quality yarn from a given grade of cotton and, in view of the existing pattern of demand for British cotton goods, the introduction of ring-spinning had to wait upon further technical improvements.[30]

V

The relative constancy of the real capital/real output ratio of the cotton industry in the years 1834-86 should occasion no surprise. Still less surprising is the fall in the capital/output ratio, measured in current prices, through 1860-86. The industry reaped external economies, both pecuniary and technological, through localisation in the Lancashire district. Chief amongst these were the economies of vertical disintegration: the textile machinery industry, which was hardly in existence in 1800, grew rapidly in the second and third quarters of the nineteenth century. As Joseph Nasmith, the famous consulting engineer, declared in 1890:

A spinning mill of 40,000 spindles, which in 1835 would be looked upon as a large one, cost, at that time, from 24 to 26 shillings per spindle to erect, including the building and accessories. At the present time, mills are built to contain as many as 110,000 spindles and these are filled ready for work at a cost not exceeding 21 shillings per spindle . . . Considering the great increase in the productive power of the machinery the fact that it is so much less expensive to work, and that each machine is of much greater capacity, the figures given show that the tendency towards diminished cost is owing very largely to the efforts of machine makers.

In 1833, manufacturers testifying before a Parliamentary Committee concurred in the view that it would cost no more, perhaps even less, to put up a cotton mill in 1833 than at the time of Waterloo.[32] Henry Houldsworth, inventor and spinner, summed up majority opinion:

Q.5262: Has the price of machinery fallen? — I think the price of machinery is reduced, or rather the nominal price per spindle is reduced considerably, and the workmanship of it has increased at least 50 per cent, so that it is not as good a trade for machine makers as it was.

Q.5263: Supposing a manufacturer to spin a certain number of pounds weight of cotton in a year, in 1815, and to spin the same number of the same quality at the present time, what would be the difference in the expense of establishing all the machinery for the manufacture in 1815, as compared to the present time?

I think it would not be greater; at present we are spinning 20 per cent more upon the same number of spindles than in 1815, and at the same time the present mode of spinning required 15 per cent more machinery in order to effect that improvement in quality which enables us to do that extra quantity.

Q.5264: Then, upon the average, you think that, as far as the cost of machinery goes, there is no considerable saving to the manufacturer? — Comparing the sum that a factory will cost now with what it cost in 1815 to do the same work, I would say that the expense of the mill is as much now as it was then.

May we conclude that fixed capital requirements per unit of output were constant between 1815 and 1833? This should warn against the easy assumption that capital-using innovations dominated technical change in the heyday of the Industrial Revolution. After all, a good many of the crucial inventions of the age on balance released rather than absorbed capital: from the smelting of iron with coal, Cort's puddling and rolling process, Watt's vacuum engine, and chlorine bleaching in the eighteenth century, to Neilson's hot blast and Woolf's compound engine in the nineteenth, not to speak of the canal era and the coming of railroads with their effect in reducing the prices of coal, timber and iron. It may be true that an industrial economy uses not only more capital per man but more capital per unit of output than a pre-industrial economy. The question is whether, for Great Britain, the line should be drawn in 1780, in 1800, in 1815, or in 1851. The history of the cotton industry suggests an earlier date than has hitherto been thought reasonable.

APPENDIX A — CAPITAL

a) *Estimates prior to 1834*

The year 1812 saw the first estimate of capital invested in the cotton industry.[34] In a petition to Parliament from 'the merchants, cotton spinners and manufacturers of Manchester' it was stated that 'ten millions sterling fixed capital was invested in cotton mills and machinery.' Several prominent spinners personally endorsed this figure.[35]

No estimates appeared between 1812 and 1832, the year that Samuel Greg testified before the Children's Employment Commission. With five mills and 2,000 employees, spinning 1.5 per cent of the yarn produced and goods woven in the United Kingdom, Greg and Co. held first rank among the cotton firms of the day. The five mills, Greg argued convincingly, were sufficiently representative to form a basis for generalisations about the industry. Having put the labour force in cotton mills in England and Wales at 160,000, he applied the capital-labour ratio obtained in the five plants (93.75), reaching a total figure of £15m., i.e. fixed capital = £10m. and working capital = £5m. Since the cotton-work force in Scotland and Ireland was then approximately 36,000, the same method yields £18.4m. for the capital stock of the industry in the United Kingdom, £12.25m. of which was sunk in machinery and buildings. Two other spinners, testifying before the same committee, estimated fixed capital at £12.35m.[36]

b) *1834*
McCulloch's estimate for 1834 is as follows:[37]

	£m.
Capital to purchase raw materials	4
Capital to pay wages	10
Capital vested in equipment, buildings and stock	20
	34

McCulloch put the total expenditure on raw cotton for the year at £8m. and the total wage bill at £20m. By supposing that circulating capital turns over twice a year, he reached the first two figures cited above. No explanation is given for the estimate of fixed capital.

Cotton consumption in 1834 amounted to £11.5m., not £8m. The wage bill in spinning and weaving alone was £9.5m.; Baines's figure for the wage bill of the whole cotton industry is £16.6m., not £20m.[38] McCulloch had estimated the output of the cotton industry at £34m. Probably, the figure for fixed capital was reached by deducting £14m. for circulating capital from £34m. For the belief that the ratio of capital to total sales was close to unity in the cotton industry was widely shared at the time. This conviction was based partly upon data for the American cotton industry, later confirmed by the American census of manufacturing in 1839 — but it was supported by British experience as well.[39] The five plants of Greg and Co., for example, show an average capital-sales ratio of 1.07.

Baines accepted McCulloch's estimate of total capital after some discussion of its reliability.[40] According to Burn's *Commercial Glance*, an oft-quoted annual circular compiled by a Manchester commission merchant, the current capital value of a typical cotton mill spinning medium counts in 1832 was 17s.6d. per spindle. The estimated number of spindles in 1834 was 12,000,000. Hence, fixed capital in spinning alone was £10.5m. We may add that power-looms are known to have cost about £21-25 each in 1836;[41] there were over 100,000 of such looms in 1834. Fixed capital in spinning and weaving mills, therefore, amounted to at least £12.6m. Baines quoted 'a highly respectable and intelligent cotton-spinner,' who estimated that the capital-labour ratio in combined spinning and weaving firms was approximately 100. This gives a figure of £23.7m. for total capital in the manufacturing branch of the industry. Capital in bobbin-net lace and hosiery was put at £3m. (fixed capital = £1m. and working capital = £2m.) by W. Felkin, who had just completed a private survey of the two trades.[42] Capital in bleaching, dyeing, and printing, although unknown, might reasonably be put at £8.9m. On the whole, Baines was satisfied that McCulloch's figure of £34m. was more or less correct.

I have separated spinning and weaving from the rest of the industry by applying the capital-labour ratio of 93.75 obtained from the plant of Greg and Co. This yields a conservative estimate since capital-intensity must have risen through 1832-4, a period of extensive building of cotton mills.

	£m.
Fixed capital in spinning and weaving 14.8	
Circulating capital	7.4
Fixed capital in bleaching, dyeing, printing,	
hosiery and lace-making	5.4
Circulating capital	6.4
	———
	34.0

c) *1835-8*

The figure of £3.75m. is sometimes cited as the amount of investment in the cotton industry between 1835 and 1838.[43] Actually, this is the amount which Ure predicted would be spent on cotton mills and machinery through 1835-7. A questionnaire circulated in 1835 asking cotton manufacturers to estimate planned additions to steam-power up to 1838 produced the figure of 7,507 h.p. (in fact, the power installed through July 1835-January 1838 was 13,226 h.p.[44]) In Ure's opinion 'the outlay in buildings and machinery necessary to bring this horse-power into operation may be safely estimated at £500 per horse-power'; hence, he concluded that £3,753,000 would be invested in the industry over the next two years.[45] He did not explain how he had arrived at £500 as the amount of capital required per h.p. But since installed h.p. in 1834 was 41,056, the ratio 500:1 was obviously derived from McCulloch's estimate of £20m. for fixed capital in the cotton industry — this ignores the fact that the spinning and weaving section accounted for only £15m. The *Circular to Bankers*, however, surmised that 'the additional machinery brought into play (since January, 1835), for the manufacture of cotton, in England and Scotland . . . is equal to ¼ of all that was at that period in action.'[46] If we take this statement seriously it does imply a fixed capital stock of £15m. in 1834.

It is worth noting that h.p. figures were at no time an accurate index of additional investment in the industry. The increased speeds at which mules and looms were run meant that more power was required unaccompanied by a proportionate increase of equipment. Thomas Ashton, a leading spinner of the day, testified to the reduction in fixed capital per unit of h.p. of 'new establishments' from £500 in 1835 to £400 in 1842. He attributed this to 'altered cost of the mills and machinery, and the application of more power to the same number of spindles or looms.'[47]

d) *1845*

McCulloch's estimate for 1845 was as follows:[48]

	£m.
Capital for purchase of raw materials	4
Capital for payment of wages	8
Capital in equipment, buildings and stock	35
	47

McCulloch estimated gross output in 1845 at £36m.; apparently he had abandoned the notion of a capital/gross output ratio of unity. The figure for fixed capital is not improbable, and that is about all one can say of it. Thomas Ashton put the average capital cost of spinning mills in 1841 at 24-25s. per spindle.[49] At this valuation, fixed capital in spinning in 1845 amounted to £21m. The price of some 250,000 power-looms would add at least another £5m. When we include the finishing branch, hosiery and lace, the figure of £35m. does not seem unreasonable. McCulloch calculated that £10m. was spent on raw cotton; 542,000 spinners, weavers and bleachers earned £13m., to which he added £4m. for the wages of 80,000 engineers. Assuming an annual turnover rate of approximately 2, circulating capital required was £12m.

e) *1856*
   Alderman Baynes's estimate for 1856 formed the basis of several later efforts:[50]

	£m.
Spinning mills: 28m. spindles costing 24s. new, now valued at 17s. 6d. per spindle	25
Weaving sheds: 300,000 looms, costing £24 new, now valued at £20 per loom	6
Floating capital	14.5
	45.5

The numbers of spindles and looms are derived from the Factory Returns of 1856. The wage bill in that year was £11m.; cotton consumption equalled £22m.; circulating capital is assumed to turn over about two and one half times a year. To this estimate by Baynes, Mann added £30m. for capital in the finishing trades and £9.5m. for the floating capital of importers and shipowners; the source for these figures is not supplied.[51]

f) *1860-2*
   Chadwick revised Baynes's estimate in 1860:[52]

	£m.
Spinning mills: 28m. spindles at 18s. per spindle	25.2
Weaving sheds: 300,000 looms at £24 per loom	7.2
Floating capital	20.0
	52.4

The increase in the valuation per loom since 1856 is explained by the unprecedented boom in power-weaving which took place in the late 1850s: betweeen 1856 and 1861 the number of spindles rose 7 per cent but power-looms increased 33 per cent. The significant increase in working capital over the 1856 figure is likewise plausible in the light of the sharp rise in cotton stocks through 1859-60. The cost of cotton used in 1860 was £28m.; the wage bill was approximately £13m.

Chadwick's estimate pertains to England and Wales, not the United Kingdom. The figures for numbers of spindles and looms are his own; the returns of 1861 show that looms were underestimated. I have recalculated the figures to apply to the United Kingdom. Spindles and looms are estimated by linear interpolation of the returns of 1856 and 1861. Working capital is raised by the proportion of the industry carried on in Scotland as measured by spindles, looms, and employment.[53]

	£m.
Spinning mills: 29m. spindles at 18s. per spindle	26.1
Weaving sheds: 378,000 looms at £24 per loom	9.1
Floating capital	21.4
	56.6

g) *1871*

The Factory Inspectors put the value of buildings and machinery in 1871 at £57m. and floating capital at £30m.[54] The figure for fixed capital seems to have been reached as follows:

	£m.
38,120,000 spindles at 24s.	45.7
446,176 looms at £24	10.7
	56.4

The Returns for 1870 give the number of spindles as 37,719,000; the increase in spindles from 1870-1 was 400,000.[55] There were 440,676 looms in 1870; by linear interpolation of the two adjacent returns of 1870 and 1874, their number rose 5,500 through 1870-1.

The valuation per spindle, however, seems to be too high. Platt and Bros., a leading manufacturer of cotton textile machinery, estimated the cost of a modern mill for spinning 32's in 1866 at 18s. per spindle.[56] Machine prices probably rose somewhat in the late 1860s but this hardly accounts for the discrepancy. In all probability, the estimate values equipment at original cost, not at current prices.

h) *1886*
Ellison's estimate for 1886 was as follows:[57]

	£m.
Spinning mills: 47m. spindles costing 24s. new, now valued at 20s. per spindle	47
Weaving sheds: 550,000 looms costing £24 new, now valued at £20 per loom	11
Floating capital	25
Capital in printing, bleaching and dyeing	18
Capital in cotton lace and hosiery	7
	108

The number of spindles in 1885, according to the official count, was 44.3m. 1886 was a bad year in the trade and the number of spindles fell between 1885 and 1886.[58] I have not adjusted Ellison's figure, however, because the Factory Returns did not count spindles standing idle; there was a 13 weeks cotton strike in the Oldham District in 1885. The number of looms in 1885 was 561,000, and their number fell to 550,000 in 1886.

The capital value per spindle of 20s. is verified by Ellison for 71 joint-stock companies in the Oldham District. A year later an independent survey of the 90 incorporated mills in the Oldham district, representing about one-quarter of the whole spinning trade, confirmed this figure. Again, the Superintendent Inspector of Factories estimated that the cost of erecting a mill in 1885 was about 21s. per spindle, 'being 20 per cent lower than it was 10 years ago.'[59]

The value of cotton consumption in 1886 was £33m.; the wage bill for spinning and weaving was £20m. We notice that once again working capital is thought to turn over a little more than twice a year.

For the first time we have a fairly detailed estimate for the capital of printworks, although it is for the year 1889. The figure is £5m.[60]

An estimate slightly higher than that of Ellison's for the year

1885 was furnished by the Manchester Chamber of Commerce to a Royal Commission.[61]

	£m.
Spinning mills: 48m. spindles at 21s. per spindle	50.4
Weaving sheds: 565 looms at £23 per loom	13
Floating capital	25
Capital in bleaching, printing and dyeing	18.7
Capital in cotton lace and hosiery	7
	114.1

The outstanding disagreement is about the value per loom. There is no material to guide our choice of the two estimates. I have preferred Ellison's as being, on the whole, the more authoritative source: his books and his *Annual Review of the Cotton Trade* (1870-1911) repeatedly demonstrate his careful handling of data.

i) *Ratio of fixed to working capital*
The capital estimates given above yield the following ratios of fixed to working capital in spinning and weaving.

1834	1856	1860	1871	1886
2	2.1	1.6	1.9	2.3

It is curious that most trade opinion in the 1830s put the ratio as high as 4 or 5.[62] Manufacturers, testifying in protest against factory legislation, insisted upon the preponderance of fixed costs in their outlays, making short-time working unprofitable. They translated a high ratio of fixed to variable costs into a high ratio of fixed to working capital, although the two are of course quite different things: heavy overhead charges in current operating periods are compatible with a 'low' ratio of fixed to working capital if working capital turns over 'slowly'.

j) *Price deflator*
Cotton machine prices were not published until 1885. There are some figures for machine prices in the literature but these are not adequate to construct an index. For the period 1870-86 the best available alternative is an index for the price level of capital goods constructed by Phelps Brown and Handfield-Jones.[63] It is made up of Jones's index of building costs in London. Sauerbeck's index of raw materials' prices, Schlote's index of the prices of finished export goods and an index of the average declared value of iron and steel exports. Of these only the prices of finished export goods are available back to 1834. Even the prices of pig iron, coal,

bricks and timber, which might have been used to gain an impression of fluctuations, are not continuously available over the period 1834-70. Under the circumstances, I have fallen back on the Jevons-Sauerbeck index of wholesale prices on the assumption that the prices of capital goods varied in the same way as the level of wholesale prices.[64] I have spliced the Jevons-Sauerbeck index with the Phelps Brown index in 1870. For the relevant years, the index numbers are as follows:

$$1834 = 100$$
$$1845 = 95$$
$$1856 = 105$$
$$1860 = 102$$
$$1871 = 102$$
$$1886 = 76.5$$

	1.	2.	3.	4.	5.	6.	7.	8.	9.	10.	11.	12.	13.
27	176	131	22.0	19	14	—	—	65	17	34	29	—	—
28	184	143	21.4	16	10	—	—	77	19	36	30	—	—
29	195	134	19.2	15	10	—	—	61	14	31	26	—	—
1830	221	156	17.1	16	8	—	—	75	17	37	30	—	—
31	234	170	19.6	18	11	—	—	93	20	37	30	—	—
32	247	170	18.9	18	10	19	10	86	16	33	25	37	28
33	256	185	19.6	20	9	20	10	94	18	36	25	38	28
34	270	194	20.6	22	11	21	11	93	17	38	27	39	29
35	284	201	22.3	24	10	22	11	99	20	42	28	40	29
36	309	221	21.9	26	11	23	12	105	21	45	30	41	29
37	326	223	17.1	23	12	24	12	126	22	43	32	41	29
38	371	256	18.5	28	15	24	12	130	21	46	33	42	29
39	340	234	19.0	25	12	25	12	100	16	41	28	42	30
1840	409	291	16.0	27	14	25	13	147	22	47	34	43	31
41	390	267	16.0	25	13	26	14	130	19	43	31	44	32
42	387	250	13.3	22	11	26	14	116	15	37	26	44	32
43	461	321	13.7	26	15	25	14	153	19	42	31	43	31
44	484	346	13.7	27	15	25	14	155	19	45	34	43	31
45	539	404	13.1	29	18	25	14	205	25	51	40	43	31
46	547	385	11.7	27	14	25	14	190	22	48	35	43	30
47	369	249	12.1	19	16	26	14	77	10	33	20	43	30
48	514	379	10.5	23	13	27	14	179	19	41	31	45	32
49	561	412	11.5	26	12	28	14	168	17	44	30	47	33
1850	523	392	13.2	28	10	28	15	144	16	44	26	48	33
51	587	443	12.6	30	14	29	15	161	17	47	31	48	33
52	662	517	12.1	33	16	30	15	239	25	55	38	50	33
53	677	530	12.8	35	17	32	15	239	26	59	41	52	35
54	691	544	11.9	34	16	34	15	235	24	55	37	54	35
55	746	581	12.8	38	18	37	16	227	22	57	37	57	36
56	793	612	11.8	38	16	40	18	241	25	63	41	61	39
57	735	558	13.6	40	14	42	19	197	21	60	34	64	41
58	806	606	13.1	43	17	42	18	182	18	61	35	63	38
59	887	595	14.0	50	22	44	17	227	24	72	44	62	36
1860	965	768	14.4	56	28	47	17	261	28	80	52	64	35
61	996	818	14.0	57	26	50	17	350	36	83	52	67	34
62	407	314	20.1	33	6	54	19	12	2	38	11	71	36
63	462	388	27.7	53	10	58	20	76	8	55	12	75	39
64	510	435	30.6	65	16	60	21	115	21	76	28	79	40
65	672	569	24.6	69	20	61	21	201	21	78	29	81	41
66	829	690	22.8	79	29	62	21	220	36	111	61	84	42
67	909	740	17.9	70	30	64	21	223	31	101	61	87	44
68	932	761	15.7	65	24	68	24	218	27	95	54	93	50
69	883	716	16.6	64	20	70	26	192	25	92	48	100	55
1870	1010	826	15.7	69	26	71	27	290	35	107	64	103	60
71	1134	942	14.0	70	32	70	28	318	36	109	71	105	63
72	1105	894	15.9	77	32	69	29	248	30	110	65	104	63
73	1171	958	14.6	74	29	68	29	322	39	117	72	104	64
74	1190	971	14.1	71	30	67	28	313	34	109	68	103	64
75	1157	943	13.5	66	28	66	28	293	32	104	66	102	64
1876	1198	967	12.3	62	27	65	28	297	31	99	64	101	65
77	1163	940	12.6	62	29	65	28	239	25	95	63	100	64
78	1106	863	11.3	54	24	64	28	202	20	86	56	100	64
79	1103	874	10.6	51	23	63	27	194	18	82	54	99	64
1880	1290	1084	11.6	64	28	62	27	264	25	101	65	96	63
81	1353	1106	11.7	67	29	61	27		22	101	64	96	62
82	1374	1143	11.5	68	30	61	26	349	32	108	70	96	61
83	1408	1151	10.7	65	26	61	26	323	29	105	66	96	61
84	1387	1124	10.6	63	25	62	27	318	27	100	62	98	61
85	1273	1035	10.2	56	23	63	27	237	19	86	53	98	62
86	1410	1164	10.0	60	28	64	28	279	23	92	60	98	62
87	1420	1177	10.2	61	27	—	—	282	23	94	60	—	—
88	1452	1205	10.4	64	28	—	—	285	23	95	59	—	—
89	1449	1206	10.8	66	31	—	—	293	24	94	59	—	—
1890	1559	1308	10.8	70	30	—	—	373	31	105	65	—	—

APPENDIX B — OUTPUT

1. *Yarn produced*

Derived by deducting loss of weight in spinning from raw cotton entered for consumption, i.e. net imports of raw cotton adjusted for changes in mill-stocks and stocks in the ports.[65] Through 1828-61 waste is reckoned at 11 per cent of cotton consumed; through the years 1862-5 it is reckoned at 10, 9, 8, and 7 per cent respectively; after 1865 it is taken at 6 per cent.

The underlying series for cotton consumption raises certain difficulties which have been discussed by others.[66] The practice of estimating yarn production by deducting 6 per cent for unsaleable waste from raw cotton consumed, was first used by Ellison in his *Annual Review of the Cotton Trade* (1870-1911). The first Census of Production in 1907 confirmed his procedure.[67] J. W. F. Rowe, therefore, used the same percentage deduction for his output series down to 1923,. G. T. Jones then applied it back to 1845, and W. G. Hoffman in turn carried it back to the eighteenth century on the grounds that 'some random checks' had verified the procedure for the whole of the nineteenth century.[68] But, in fact, authorities writing in the 1830s agree in estimating waste at 10-11 per cent of cotton entered for consumption.[69] Subsequently, the improved 'ginning' of cotton in the country of origin as well as refinements in the design of carding machines reduced the initial weight lost in spinning. In addition, it became increasingly the practice to work up some of the wasted short fibres into very coarse yarns or to mix them with wool for special uses. Thus, Ellison notes that the amount of unsaleable waste fell in the 1860s from 11 to 6-7 per cent of cotton consumed.[70] To avoid underestimating the rate of growth of real output I have followed Ellison and have assumed that the reduction in waste was accomplished during the cotton famine (1862-5) when the unusually high price of raw cotton encouraged stringent economy measures. After 1865 my series is identical to that of Jones. A contemporary series for yarn production through 1814-76 by Thomas Bazley has been rejected because it assumes a constant proportion of waste over the whole period and seems to make idiosyncratic allowances for changes in stocks.[71]

2. *Yarn consumed or cloth produced*

Yarn produced (1) — net exports of yarn = yarn consumed. Yarn exports are derived from Board of Trade Returns as given by Ellison. There are very slight discrepancies between the Board of Trade series and the Trade and Navigation Accounts series as given by Robson.[72]

Some yarn was diverted in the form of sewing cotton, hosiery and bobbin-net lace. In 1834 less than 2 per cent of cotton consumed was absorbed by the hosiery trade. Cotton lacemaking was even less important and cotton thread manufacture was in its infancy. All three trades, however, expanded rapidly later in the century. This is apparent from the fraction of spindles used to double the yarn for manufacture of thread, hose and embroidered goods which rose from 6 per cent of all spindles in 1867 to just under 10 per cent in 1885. Although the cotton hosiery trade for one declined rapidly after 1875,[73] we are left with the general impression that the identification of yarn consumption with cloth production somewhat overestimates the actual rate of growth of the output of cloths.

3. *Price of grey cloth*

Through 1845-90 the average annual price per lb. of a composite bundle of six representative grey cloths based upon the weekly returns from the Manchester market is recorded in the *Economist*. The prices in shillings were summed for each year and divided by the indicated total pound weight. These are the same quotations used by Jones to construct his index of the price of grey cloth.[74] Through 1827-45 the price has been estimated on the basis of a series for a particular type of grey cloth, on the assumption that its movements are indicative of changes in the average price of all grey cloths.[75] The cloth in question (27in. 72 Reed Printers) is one of the six cloths reported in the *Economist* and its price after 1845 does behave similarly to that of the bundle as a whole. The price of 72 Reed Printers in 1845 was 12.3d per lb.; the price of the bundle of six cloths was 13.1d per lb.; the two series have been spliced in 1845 by multiplying the first by 1.065.

4. *Gross output*

(Yarn consumed (2) x the price of grey cloth (3)) + the declared value of yarn exports = gross output.

5. *Net output*

Gross output (4) — value of raw cotton consumed = net output. The cost of cotton used up is calculated by multiplying Holt's series for raw cotton consumption by the average price, inclusive of insurance and freight, of raw cotton imported. The average declared value per lb. (c.i.f.) of raw cotton imports is available from 1854 on;[76] prior to 1854 it can be estimated from knowledge of the proportions of various kinds of cotton imported and their prices, after making a reasonable allowance for insurance and freight. Imlah's index of the price of East Indian and American cotton, with due allowance for the changing proportions of the supplies taken, was used as a check. Through 1836-60 my estimates agree with a contemporary series.[77]

6. *Ten years' moving average of gross output*

7. *Ten years' moving average of net output*

8. *Home trade (all cotton)*
Cloth produced (2) — lbs. of piece goods exports = lbs. of goods for the home trade. Up to 1920 only the linear yardage of piece goods exported (divided into the categories white or plain and dyed or printed) was recorded in the trade accounts. Figures in yds were subsequently converted to 3 lb. equivalent at 1 lb = 5.47 yds, a ratio which pertained through 1870-1910.[78] It should be noted that the cloth is stretched in the course of each finishing process; to reckon the same linear yardage for cloth, whether unfinished, bleached, dyed or printed, is to understate the amount of grey cloth exported. This would not matter if the proportions of finished and unfinished cloths in total exports did not vary through time. Probably they did vary but since grey cloth was not distinguished from bleached cloth in the trade accounts we can say nothing about it.

9. *Value of the home trade (all cotton)*
Weight of goods retained for the home trade (8) x ⅓ of the average declared value of cotton goods exports = value of the home trade. The average declared value of piece goods exports in pence per yd is available from 1814 on;[79] these have been converted to pence per lb. according to the lb-yd ratio given above. I have followed Mann and Ellison in estimating the value of the home trade upon the assumption that goods sold at home were 33 per cent dearer than goods sold abroad.[80]

10. *Gross output (all cotton)*
The value of the home trade (9) + the declared value of piece goods exports = gross output of the cotton industry as a whole. The declared value of piece goods exports is given in the trade returns.[81] My figures for gross output are virtually identical to Mann's estimates, continued by Ellison. There are divergences prior to 1845 due to the fact that Mann uses his own series for cotton consumption.

If Ellison is to be believed the rate of growth of total output was actually greater than that indicated by Mann's series. Although Ellison extended Mann's estimates in his *Annual Review*, he based his own estimates of output in his book on the cotton industry upon a gradually increasing price-differential between home and foreign markets. He assumed that home-consumed goods were 14 per cent dearer than goods exported in 1830, 38 per cent dearer in 1845, 70 per cent dearer in 1860, and twice as dear through 1871-85.[82]

I have found no evidence, however, that bears directly upon Ellison's conjecture. It is sometimes said that the average count of yarn rose through the nineteenth century. Since the count of yarn relates its weight to its length, the higher the count the greater the value of yarn in proportion to its weight. Contemporary opinion on the matter, however, is conflicting and the evidence is too scrappy to support any generalisations.[83]

Nevertheless, despite significant differences in the price assumptions, my estimates of gross output do not differ much from Ellison's, owing to the fact that he used, for some unknown reason, a lower lb.-yard ratio than is indicated above to estimate the weight of goods exported.[84]

An additional check upon our estimates is provided by the calculations submitted to a Royal Commission in 1886 by the Manchester Chamber of Commerce.[85] It makes no allowance whatever for loss of weight in spinning or for the admittedly higher price of home consumed goods. Since these considerations are opposite in effect upon the value of output there is once again a close agreement with my estimates (with the exception of the period 1875-80 where the Manchester Chamber of Commerce reckons cotton consumption at 20 per cent below the figure given in Holt's *Circular*).

R. C. O. Matthews, using a different method of estimation — a method that could not be applied to more than a decade or two — has recently computed the value of output of the cotton industry between 1825 and 1842.[86] His figures are generally about 10 per cent below mine.

11. *Net output (all cotton)*
Gross output (10) — value of raw cotton consumed = net output.

12. *Ten years' moving average of gross output.*

13. *Ten years' moving average of net output.*

APPENDIX C — MISCELLANEOUS DATA

Unless stated otherwise, the source of the statistics are the Factory Returns: P.P. 1836, XLV; 1839, XLII; 1842, XXII; 1843, LVI; 1846, XX; 1847, XLVI; 1849, LIV; 1850, XLII; 1857, (Sess. 1),

XIV; *Miscellaneous Statistics*, 1857-8, LVII; 1862, LV; 1867, LXIV; 1868-9, LXII; 1871, LXII; 1875, LXXI; 1878-9, LXV; 1884-5, LXXI; 1890, LXVII.

The area to which the data refers is the United Kingdom. But, in fact, the industry was already highly concentrated in Lancashire and two or three other Northern counties by 1830 and the Scottish industry steadily contracted through the nineteenth century. The cotton industry in Ireland was never large enough to matter.

	1	2 (000's)	3 (000's)	4 (000's)	5	6 (000's)	7 (000,000's)	8 (£ m)	9 %
							(850)	(5.8)	
1834	1154	10,800	100	200	41,056	237	1570	9.5	95
							(929)	(7.3)	
1839	1819	—	—	135	59,805	259	1413	9.5	70
							(1220)		
1845	—	17,500	250	60	—	340	1435	—	—
							(1188)	(7.9)	
1850	1932	20,977	250	43	82,555	331	1342	8.6	72
1851	—	—	—	—	—	—	—	—	—
							(1182)	(10.6)	
1856	2210	28,010	299	23	97,132	379	1254	11.0	70
							(1410)	(13.6)	
1861	2887	30,387	400	7	294,130	452	1432	13.7	69
1867	2549	34,215	379	—	201,062	401	1251	13.7	50
1870	2483	37,719	441	—	308,870	450	1404	16.1	61
1871	—	—	—	—	—	—	—	—	—
1874	2655	41,882	465	—	—	480	1498	19.1	66
1878	2674	44,207	515	—	—	483	1507	18.8	74
1881	—	—	—	—	—	—	—	—	—
1885	2635	44,348	561	—	—	504	1586	20.1	79

The exact date at which the Factory Returns are drawn up is never made explicit by the Inspectors. For example, the returns for 1885 were submitted to the printer on March 6, 1885. Were the figures collected in the winter of 1884 or in the opening months of 1885? I have followed Page[87] in the choice of relevant years, usually the year preceding the publication of the returns.

1. *Factories*

The 1834 figure was obtained from the Factory Inspectors by Baines. Baines regards it as complete, unlike the corresponding figure for horse-power.[88] This is confirmed by the fact that the returns for 1835 give 1262 working mills and another 42 mills standing idle. Prior to 1850, both idle and working mills were enumerated; thereafter only mills at work were recorded. All figures given here are for working mills. No total figures are available for 1845 since one of the inspectors failed to return for his district.

A 'factory' is designated in the Factory Returns as a separate building, irrespective of whether the building housed several distinct firms or was owned entirely by a multi-plant firm. In the 1830s, the numbers of mills exceeded the number of firms by 10-20 per cent.[89]

2. *Spindles*

Spindles were not enumerated officially until 1850. Usually, only working spindles were recorded; but in 1874 the figure given refers explicitly to spindles 'running and standing'. From 1867 on spinning and doubling spindles were reported separately. Since the figures through 1850-61 include doubling spindles,[90] the figures after 1861 given here represent spinning and doubling spindles.

The 1834 figure is based upon Ure's estimate of 25 lbs of yarn for the annual output per spindle in 1835 and my estimate of yarn production in 1834. Baines estimates that there were 9,333,000 spindles in 1832 on the basis of Burn's figure of 26.6 lbs of yarn per spindle. Burn's figure seems excessive inasmuch as spindle capacity was 28 lbs in 1867. Kennedy of M'Connel & Kennedy put it at 21.6 lbs p.a. in 1830. Ellison's estimate for 1845 is 26.8 lbs.

The figure for 1845 was supplied by Messrs. du Fay & Co., a firm of Liverpool cotton brokers.[91]

3. *Power-looms*

Baines estimated the number of power-looms in 1834 on the basis of a questionnaire sent to 300 mills by a Manchester accountant. The official returns for 1835 give 109,319 power-looms in operation. The estimate for 1845 is Ellison's. The 1870 figure includes 35,554 looms 'standing but not working.'[92]

4. *Hand-looms*

There are no official statistics for hand-looms. Their number in 1883 was estimated by several manufacturers. The figures for the other years are Wood's linear interpolations, using Ellison estimates for 1845 and 1860.[93]

5. *Horsepower*

Incomplete returns were obtained by the inspectors in 1834. Baines added to this an estimate for the horsepower of the English mills for which no returns were obtained. Clapham cites Baines's total figure but incorrectly adds 15 per cent to an already corrected figure for Lancashire and Cheshire and a complete return for Scotland.[94]

Steam and water-power were enumerated separately. Water-power accounted for about 33 per cent of the total in 1834 but for less than 3 per cent in 1870.

The figures for motive-power, particularly those for years prior to 1861, must be used with great caution. For example, the enormous increase between 1856 and 1861 is illusory, being the consequence of a change in measurement from nominal to indicated h.p. Nominal h.p. was calculated by a formula devised by Watt based upon the given mean effective pressure and piston speed of a low pressure condensing engine. In the 1840s pressures were systematically increased by the addition of new boilers to the same engine; frequently, cotton engines of the Watt type were converted to compounding by 'M'Naughting'; the addition of a high-pressure cylinder at the other end of the beam. Piston speeds were likewise advanced. According to Inspector Horner, the combined effects of these improvements by the 1850s was to increase the real h.p. of existing engines by 25 per cent over the nominal h.p. returned. This was partly outweighed, he thought, by the fact that not all the enumerated power was actually employed at any time.[95] At any rate there is no doubt that the Watt formula had then become obsolete and the change in 1861 to measuring indicated h.p. was long overdue. Unfortunately, there seems to be no reliable method for splicing figures of nominal and indicated h.p. Rankine in his famous *Manual of the Steam-Engine* (1859) asserted that 1 N.H.P. $=$ 3.3 I.H.P. but seven years later he gave the ratio as 1:6[96]. Neither formula makes sense of the later figures in view of other information. The Factory Returns ceased to count installed motive-power after 1870.

6. *Number of persons employed in cotton factories*

The Factory Returns for 1834 are incomplete. Baines corrected the official figure of 220,825 to make up for the total number for the United Kingdom. The figure for the boom year of 1845 is given by Ellison.[97] The inspectors returned 316,327 in February 1847, a year of severe depression in the industry.

I have ignored census data for employment in 'cotton manufacture' because of the treacherous shifts in the classification of occupations in the succeeding censuses between 1851 and 1891.

7. *Man-hours of employment*

Weekly hours of work of women and children fell from 69 in the 1820's to 60 hours after the Act of 1847, to 56.5 hours after the Act of 1874. The work day of adult males, although not subject to legislative control, was gradually adjusted to the hours prescribed for women and children. It appears that the struggle over the relay system postponed the introduction of the 60 hour week until 1856.

Similarly, 56.5 hours did not become the norm until 1879-81.[98] Man-hours of labour inputs were obtained accordingly from the figures for factory employment and hand-loom weavers. The bracketed figures represent factory workers only.

8. *Wage bill of spinners and weavers*

The average weekly wage of factory operatives and handloom weavers is given by Wood on the basis of detailed wage statistics from a large number of sources.[99] The bracketed figures represent the wage bill of factory workers only.

9. *Labour's share in net output*

Owing to the uncertain date at which employment was enumerated, 3 year averages of net output were used.

NOTES

1 This paper was prepared during the tenure of a Guggenheim Fellowship. Some of the material was gathered under a grant-in-aid from the Social Science Research Council. Mr D. E. Chapman assisted with the calculations.

2 For the first half of the century see R. Giffen, *The Growth of Capital* (1889), ch. V; A. D. Gayer, *et. al. The Growth and Fluctuation of the British Economy 1790-1850* (Oxford 1952), Microfilm Supplement, pp. 1574-81. For the second half of the century see E. H. Phelps-Brown, S. J. Handfield-Jones, 'The Climacteric of the 1890's,' *Oxford Economic Papers* (October 1952).

3 J. Clapham, *An Economic History of Modern Britain* (Cambridge, 1950), II, pp. 32-3, 85-7, and see below App. B2.

4 I follow Harrod in classifying technical improvements as labour-saving, capital-saving, or neutral according to whether they raise, lower, or leave unchanged the ratio of capital to output. This despite the fact the capital/output ratio is influenced not only by the factor-saving slant of innovations, but also by the composition of output and by investment designed to expand the capacity of existing plant and equipment.

5 See below App. C.

6 E. H. Phelps-Brown, E. H. Weber, 'Accumulation, Productivity and Distribution in the British Economy, 1870-1938,' *Economic Journal* (June 1953), p. 266.

7 J. Jewkes, 'The Localisation of the Cotton Industry,' *Economic History* (Jan. 1930); A. J. Taylor, 'Concentration and Specialisation in the Lancashire Cotton Industry, 1825-50', *Economic History Review*, 2nd ser. I (1949), Nos. 2 and 3.

8 Through 1834-52 we have statistics on mill-stocks but none at all on stocks in the ports (see J. A. Mann, *The Cotton Trade of Great Britain* (Manchester, 1860)). After 1860 we have data on port stocks but none on mill-stocks. It seems that as much as 80 per cent of total stocks were normally held in Liverpool. This makes the level of total stocks a poor index of the working capital required by spinners and weavers.

9 H. Ashworth, 'Statistics of the Present Depression of Trade at Bolton', *Journal of the Royal Statistical Society* (April 1842); T. Ellison, *The Cotton Trade of Great Britain* (1886), pp. 46-338 (subsequently referred to as Ellison); G. V. Schulze-Gaevernitz, *The Cotton Trade in England and on the Continent* (1895), p. 158.

10 See below App. A, i.
11 See below App. B, 2.
12 See below App. B, 10.
13 Horse-power series after 1861 are not comparable to those for previous years. See App. G, 5.
14 Spinning spindles were first distinguished from doubling spindles in the Returns of 1867; prior to that year yarn output per spindle cannot be precisely determined. (Ministry of Labour estimates give practically the same figures cited above: see G. T. Jones, *Increasing Returns* (1933), p. 114). It must be remembered that, despite the growth of combined spinning and weaving mills, spinning was also carried on as a final stage of production; owing to the large export trade in yarn, spinning plants were not always balanced by corresponding weaving plants within the country.
15 S. J. Chapman, *The Lancashire Cotton Industry* (Manchester, 1904), pp. 69-70; A. Ure, *The Cotton Manufacturers of Great Britain* (1861), II, 152-8 (subsequently referred to as Ure): G. H. Wood, *The History of Wages in the Cotton Trade* (1910), p. 27 (subsequently referred to as Wood).
16 *Reports of the Inspectors of Factories*, 1842, XXII, 26-8.
17 S. Andrews, *Fifty Years of the Cotton Trade* (Oldham, 1887), p. 2; Schulze-Gaevernitz, *op. cit.*, p. 108; Wood, pp. 30-1, 79-80.
18 Ellison, pp. 68-9; F. Merttens, 'The Hours and Cost of Labour in the Cotton Industry at Home and Abroad,' *Manchester Statistical Society* (1893-4). The fact that power-weavers increased faster than spinners through 1860-92 is only partly attributable to more pronounced labour-saving changes in yarn manufacture. Owing to the decline of the yarn export trade in the later years, the demand for cloth rose faster than the demand for yarn.
19 J. Montgomery, *The Theory and Practice of Cotton Spinning* (Glasgow, 1833), pp. 78-80; Ure, II, 155-6; *Rep. Insp. Fact.* 1842, XXII, 26.
20 E. Baines, *History of the Cotton Manufacture* (1835), reprinted by Frank Cass, London, p. 202 (subsequently referred to as Baines); Ure, II, 154; Wood, pp. 140-1; *Rep. Insp. Fact.* 1874, XIII, 62; Schulze-Gaevernitz, *op. cit.* pp. 88-90.
21 The evidence can not be set down briefly, but compare the detailed technological descriptions of current machinery in Ure's book, published in 1836, with E. Leigh, *The Science of Modern Cotton-Spinning* (Manchester, 1873) and J. Nasmith, *Modern Cotton-Spinning Machinery* (Manchester, 1890).
22 Ellison, pp. 37, 142; Wood, pp. 142, 161.
23 Andrews, *op. cit.* p. 6.
24 See below App. C, 5; Ure, I, 309-12; Andrews, *op. cit.* p. 7.
25 See Ellison, Table 1.
26 Wood, pp. 127-8.
27 Chapman, *op. cit.* pp. 53-60.
28 *Ibid.*, p. 12.
29 T. S. Ashton, 'Some Statistics of the Revolution,' *Manchester School* (May 1948); Gayer, *op. cit.* II, 838-9; A. H. Imlagh, 'The Terms of Trade of the United Kingdom, 1789-1913,' *Journal of Economic History* (November 1950), pp. 188-90; Jones, *op. cit.* p. 116; R. C. O. Matthews, *A Study in Trade Cycle History* (Oxford, 1954), pp. 129-30.
30 Chapman, *op. cit.* p. 70; Clapham, *op. cit.* III, 176; R. E. Naumburg, 'Two American Textile Pioneers,' *The Newcomen Society Transactions*, VI, (1925-6).
31 J. Nasmith, *op. cit.*, p. 7.
32 P.P. *Manufactures, Commerce and Shipping, Sel. Cttee.*, 1833, VI, QQ. 476, 1896, 2438, 9059-72, 11008-11014.
34 An earlier estimate, made in 1788, must be rejected as guess-work. Cf. P. Colquhoun, *An Important Crisis in the Calico Manufacture Explained* (1788); Bains,

pp. 216-9; Ure, I, 298; see also M'Connel and Co., *A Century of Fine Cotton-Spinning* (Manchester, 2d. ed. 1913), p. 30.
35 Quoted in G. French, *Life and Times of Samuel Crompton* (Manchester, 1860), p. 285.
36 P. P. *Employment of Children. R. Comm. First Rep.* 1833, XX, D2, pp. 36-8, 95.
37 J. R. McCulloch, *Commercial Dictionary* (1834), p. 443.
38 Baines, p. 412. McCulloch later pared down his employment figure, *op. cit.* (1852 ed.), p. 457.
39 P. P. *S. C. on Manufactures*, 1833, VI, QQ. 2293-60, 2683, 5440; *Economist*, 1844, p. 1357.
40 Baines, pp. 414-5.
41 P. P. *Hand-Loom Weavers. Asst. Comm.* 1840, XXIV, 435.
42 Quoted in Baines, pp. 342-5.
43 From *Circular to Bankers*, cited in L. H. Jenks, *The Migration of British Capital in 1875* (1927), p. 362; Matthews, *op. cit.*, p. 135.
44 P. P. *Population of Stockport. Asst. Poor Law Comm.* 1842, XXXV, 53-4.
45 Ure, I, 413-4.
46 *Circular to Bankers*, 4 August 1837, p. 33.
47 P. P. *Population of Stockport, Poor Law Comm.* 1842, XXXV, 114.
48 McCulloch, *op. cit.* (1852 ed.), p. 457.
49 P. P. *Exportation of Machinery*, 1841, VII, 25.
50 A. Baynes, *The Cotton Trade. Two Lectures* (London, 1857). I have omitted a mysterious item of £10 m. for 'cash in hands of bankers'.
51 Mann, *op. cit.* p. 93.
52 D. Chadwick. 'On the Rate of Wages in the Manufacturing District of Lancashire, 1839-59', *Journal Royal Stat. Soc.* (March 1860).
53 An estimate of £59 m. for 1861, based upon Chadwick's calculations, but made without benefit of the 1861 returns, is given by P. L. Simmonds in his supplement to Ure, II, 393.
54 *Rep. Insp. Fact.* 1874, XIII, 118.
55 A. K. Cairncross, *Home and Foreign Investment, 1870-1913* (Cambridge, 1953), p. 167.
56 Andrews, *op. cit.*, p. 6.
57 Ellison, p. 70.
58 Cairncross, *op. cit.*, p. 167.
59 Ellison, pp. 39, 46, 139; Andrews, *op. cit.*, p. 7; Rep. Insp. Fact. 1884-5, XV, 93.
60 G. Turnbull, *A History of the Calico-Printing Industry* (Altrincham, 1951), p. 115.
61 P. P. *Depression of Trade and Industry. R. Comm. First Rep.* 1886, XXI, App. A, Pt. I, p. 427.
62 P. P. *R. C. on Employment of Children. First Rep.* 1833, XX, Dl, p. 69; P. P. *Hand-Loom Weavers. R. Comm. Rep.* 1841, X, 32; H. Ashworth, *op. cit.*; N. W. Senior, *Letters on the Factory Act* (1834), pp. 3-4.
63 *Oxford Econ. Papers* (October 1952), p. 305.
64 W. T. Layton, G. Crowther, *Introduction to the Study of Prices* (3d. ed. 1938), p. 237.
65 G. Holt's *Annual Circular* as given in Ellison, Table I.
66 See Gayer, *op. cit.*, microfilm supplement, pp. 884-5.
67 P. P. *Census of Production. Final Report*, 1907 (Cd 6320), p. 288.
68 J. W. F. Rowe, *The Physical Volume of Production* (London and Cambridge Econ. Service. Memorandum No. 8, 1924); Jones, *op. cit.*; W. G. Hoffman, *British Industry, 1700-1950* (Manchester, 1956), pp. 225-6.
69 Baines, p.367; Montgomery, *op. cit.*, p. 33.
70 Ellison, pp. 58, 307.

71 'Cotton Manufactures', *Encyclopaedia Britannica* (8th ed. 1854, 9th ed. 1877), VI.
72 R. Robson, *The Cotton Industry in Britain* (1957), table 1.
73 F. A. Wells, *The British Hosiery Trade* (1935), p. 133.
74 Jones, *op. cit.*, pp. 101-2.
75 A. Neild, 'An Account of the Prices of Printing Cloth and Upland Raw Cotton, from 1812 to 1860', *Journal Royal Stat. Soc.* (December 1861).
76 P. P. *Report on Wholesale and Retail Prices*, 1903, LXVIII, 45.
77 Mann, *op. cit.*, p. 91.
78 Robson, *op. cit.*, table 1.
79 P. P. 1903, LXVIII, 48.
80 Through 1836-60, Mann, *op. cit.*, p. 104; through 1863-85, Ellison's *Annual Review*, 1872, p. 8; 1885, p. 3.
81 Robson, *op. cit.*, table 1.
82 Ellison, pp. 59, 308.
83 Andrews, *op. cit.*, p. 7; Ellison, p. 69. The problem is complicated by cyclical swings in the average count produced; mills were set up to produce a range of at least 10 counts so as to permit adjustment to changing cotton prices. See *Economist*, 1849, p. 1328.
84 Ellison, pp. 58-9.
85 P. P. R. C. *on Depression of Trade. First Report*, 1886, XXI, App. A, p. 104.
86 Matthews, *op. cit.*, p. 151.
87 *Commerce and Industry* (1919), II.
88 Baines, pp. 384-94.
89 H. D. Fong, *Triumph of the Factory System in England* (Tsientsin, China, 1930), p. 28.
90 *Rep. Insp. Fact.* 1863, XVIII, 60.
91 Ure, II, 312-5; Baines, pp. 367-8, 353; Ellison, pp. 68-9; Baynes, *op. cit.*, p. 39.
92 Baines, pp. 235-7; Ellison, pp. 65-6.
93 Baines, pp. 237-9, 382-4; Ellison, pp. 65-6; Wood, pp. 127-8.
94 Baines, pp. 384-94; Clapham, *op. cit.*, I, 442.
95 *Rep. Insp. Fac.* 1852-3, XL, 26; 1856, XVIII, 13-4, 24; 1863, XVIII, 60-1.
96 W. J. M. Rankine, *Useful Rules and Tables* (1866), p. 289.
97 Baines, pp. 396-7, Ellison, pp. 65-6. Chapman and Wood ignore the fact that the 1834 returns are incomplete: *op. cit.*, p. 12; p. 127.
98 See G. H. Wood, 'Factory Legislation', *Journal Royal Stat. Soc.* (June 1902).
99 Wood, pp. 127-8.

7
Factory Discipline in the Industrial Revolution[1]

Sidney Pollard[*]

It is nowadays increasingly coming to be accepted that one of the most critical, and one of the most difficult, transformations required in an industrialising society is the adjustment of labour to the regularity and discipline of factory work.[2] Current interest in this process has led to a certain amount of re-examination of the experience of Britain during the corresponding period of her development.[3] Much more requires to be known, and only detailed research can add to our knowledge. The present article is less ambitious: it seeks to further the discussion by examining briefly the evidence available so far, and drawing some tentative conclusions. The subject will be treated analytically rather than historically, that is to say, the first generation of factory workers will be examined, irrespective of its appearance at different times in different industries.

I

The worker who left the background of his domestic workshop or peasant holding for the factory, entered a new culture as well as a new sense of direction. It was not only that 'the new economic order needed . . . part-humans: soulless, depersonalised, disembodied, who could become members, or little wheels rather, of a complex mechanism'. It was also that men who were non-accumulative, non-acquisitive, accustomed to work for subsistence, not for maximisation of income,[4] had to be made obedient to the cash stimulus, and obedient in such a way as to react precisely to the stimuli provided.

The very recruitment to the uncongenial work was difficult, and it was made worse by the deliberate or accidental modelling of

*From *Economic History Review*, 2nd series, Vol. XVI (1963-64), pp. 254-71. Reprinted by permission of the editors of *Economic History Review* and the author.

many works on workhouses and prisons, a fact well known to the working population. Even if they began work, there was no guarantee that the new hands would stay. 'Labourers from agriculture or domestic industry do not at first take kindly to the monotony of factory life; and the pioneering employer not infrequently finds his most serious obstacle in the problem of building up a stable supply of efficient and willing labour'. Many workers were 'transient, marginal and deviant', or were described as 'volatile'. It was noted that there were few early manufacturers in the seaport towns, as the population was too unsteady, and Samuel Greg, Jr. complained most of the 'restless and *migratory* spirit' of the factory population. Thus it was not necessarily the better labourer, but the stable one who was worth the most to the manufacturer: often, indeed, the skilled apprenticed man was at a discount, because of the working habits acquired before entering a factory.[5] Roebuck and Garbett left Birmingham for Prestonpans in order, *inter alia*, to escape the independence of the local workers for the 'obedient turn of the Scots', while Henry Houldsworth found hand spinners to have such irregular habits that the introduction of machine spinning in Glasgow 'rendered it desirable to get a new set of hands as soon as possible.'[6]

Elsewhere in Scotland even the children found the discipline irksome: when the Catrine cotton mills were opened, one of the managers admitted, 'the children were all newcomers, and were very much beat at first before they could be taught their business'. At other mills, 'on the first introduction of the business, the people were found very ill-disposed to submit to the long confinement and regular industry that is required from them'. The highlander, it was said, 'never sits at ease at a loom; it is like putting a deer in the plough'.[7]

In turn, the personal inclinations and group *mores* of such old-established industrial workers as handloom weavers and framework knitters were opposed to factory discipline. 'I found the utmost distaste', one hosier reported, 'on the part of the men, to any regular hours or regular habits . . . The men themselves were considerably dissatisfied, because they could not go in and out as they pleased, and have what holidays they pleased, and go on just as they had been used to do; and were subject, during after-hours, to the ill-natured observations of other workmen, to such an extent as completely to disgust them with the whole system, and I was obliged to break it up.'[8]

As a result of this attitude, attendance was irregular, and the complaint of Edward Cave, in the very earliest days of industrialisation, was later re-echoed by many others: 'I have not half my people come to work today, and I have no great fascination in the prospect I have to put myself in the power of such people.'[9] Cotton spinners would stay away without notice and send for their wages at the end of the week, and one of the most enlightened firms, McConnel and Kennedy, regularly replaced spinners who had not turned up within two or three hours of starting time on Mondays, on the reasonable presumption that they had left the firm: their average labour turnover was 20 a week, i.e. about 100 per cent a year.[10]

Matters were worse in a place like Dowlais, reputed to employ many runaways and criminals, or among northern mining companies which could not guarantee continuous work: 'the major part of these two companies are as bad fellows as the worst of your pitmen baring their outside is not so black', one exasperated manager complained, after they had left the district without paying their debts. Elsewhere, ironworks labourers, copper and tin miners and engineering labourers deserted to bring in the harvest, or might return to agriculture for good if work was slack.[11]

'St Monday' and feast days, common traditions in domestic industry, were persistent problems. The weavers were used to 'play frequently all day on Monday, and the greater part of Tuesday, and work very late on Thursday night, and frequently all night on Friday'. Spinners, even as late as 1800, would be missing from the factories on Mondays and Tuesdays, and 'when they did return, they would sometimes work desperately, night and day, to clear off their tavern score, and get more money to spend in dissipation', as a hostile critic observed.[12] In South Wales it was estimated as late as the 1840s that the workers lost one week in five, and that in the fortnight after the monthly pay day, only two-thirds of the time was being worked.[13]

As for the regular feasts, 'our men will go to the Wakes', Josiah Wedgwood complained in 1772, 'if they were sure to go to the D—l the next. I have not spared them in threats and I would have thrash'd them right heartily if I could'. Again, in 1776, 'Our men have been at play 4 days this week, it being Burslem Wakes. I have rough'd & smoothed them over, & promised them a long Xmass, but I know it is all in vain, for Wakes must be observed though the World was to end with them'. Soho was beset by the same troubles.[14]

Employers themselves, groping their way towards a new impersonal discipline, looked backwards sporadically to make use of feasts and holidays, typical of the old order in cementing personal relationships and breaking the monotony of the working year. Thus John Kelsall noted in 1725 that Charles Lloyd was 'abroad this day with the workmen etc, coursing' and about the same time, the famous Derby silk mill had an annual feast and dancing at Michaelmas, financed by contributions of the curious visitors in the course of the year. The Arkwrights and the Strutts, standing on the watershed between the old and the new, had feasts in Cromford in 1776, when 500 workers and their children took part, and annual balls at Cromford and Belper as late as 1781, whilst in 1772 the Hockley factory had an outing, led by the 'head workman' clad in white cotton, to gather nuts, and be regaled to a plentiful supper afterwards.[15]

Other examples from industries in their early transitional stages include Matthew Boulton's feast for 700 when his son came of age, Wedgwood's feast for 120 when he moved into Etruria, Heathcote's outing for 2,300 from Tiverton, and the repast provided by the Herculaneum Pottery at the opening of its Liverpool warehouse in 1813.[16] Conversely, the Amlwch miners organised an ox-roast in honour of the chief proprietor, the Marquis of Anglesea, when he passed through the island on his way to take up the Lord-Lieutenancy of Ireland.[17] 600 workmen sat down to a roasted ox and plenty of liquor at the Duke of Bridgewater's expense to celebrate the opening of the canal at Runcorn,[18] and feasts were usual thereafter at the opening of canals and railways, but within a generation it was the shareholders that were being feasted, not the workers, whose relationship with the employers had by then taken on an entirely different character.

Once at work it was necessary to break down the impulses of the workers, to introduce the notion of 'time-thrift'. The factory meant economy of time and, in the Webbs' phrase, 'enforced asceticism'. Bad timekeeping was punished by severe fines, and it was common in mills such as Oldknow's or Braids' to lock the gates of the factory, even of the workrooms, excluding those who were only a minute or two late. 'Whatever else the domestic system was, however intermittent and sweated its labour, it did allow a man a degree of personal liberty to indulge himself, a command over his time, which he was not to enjoy again.'[19]

By contrast, in the factories, Arkwright, for example, had the greatest difficulty 'in training human beings to renounce their desultory habits of work, and identify themselves with the unvarying regularity of the complex automaton'. He 'had to train his workpeople to a precision and assiduity altogether unknown before, against which their listless and restive habits rose in continued rebellion', and it was his great achievement 'to devise and administer a successful code of factory diligence'. 'Impatient of the slovenly habits of workpeople, he urged on their labours with a precision and vigilance unknown before'.[20] The reasons for the difference were clear to manufacturers: 'When a mantua maker chooses to rise from her seat and take the fresh air, her seam goes a little back, that is all; there are no other hands waiting on her', but 'in cotton mills all the machinery is going on, which they must attend to'. It was 'machinery [which] ultimately forced the worker to accept the discipline of the factory'.[21]

Regular hours and application had to be combined with a new kind of order in the works. Wedgwood, for example, had to fight the old pottery traditions when introducing 'the punctuality, the constant attendance, the fixed hours, the scrupulous standards of care and cleanliness, the avoidance of waste, the ban on drinking'. Similarly, James Watt had to struggle to introduce cleanliness into the Albion Mills.

Finally, 'Discipline . . . was to produce the goods on time. It was also to prevent the workmen from stealing raw materials, putting in shoddy, or otherwise getting the better of their employers'. It allowed the employer to maintain a high quality of output, as in the case of John Taylor and Matthew Boulton in Birmingham, and of Samuel Oldknow at Stockport.[22]

Works Rules, formalised, impersonal and occasionally printed, were symbolic of the new industrial relationships. Many rules dealt with disciplinary matters only,[23] but quite a few laid down the organisation of the firm itself. 'So istrict are the instructions,' it was said of John Marshall's flax mills in 1821, 'that if an overseer of a room be found talking to any person in the mill during working hours he is dismissed immediately — two or more overseers are employed in each room, if one be found a yard out of his ground he is discharged . . . everyone, manager, overseers, mechanics, oilers, spreaders, spinners and reelers, have their particular duty pointed out to them, and if they transgress, they are instantly turned off as unfit for their situation.'[24]

While the domestic system had implied some measure of control, 'it was . . . an essentially new thing for the capitalist to be a disciplinarian'. 'The capitalist employer became a supervisor of every detail of the work: without any change in the general character of the wage contract, the employer acquired new powers which were of great social significance.'[25] The concept of industrial discipline was new, and called for as much innovation as the technical inventions of the age.

Child work immeasurably increased the complexities of the problem. It had, as such, been common enough before,[26] but the earlier work pattern had been based on the direct control of children and youths, in small numbers, by their parents or guardians. The new mass employment removed the incentive of learning a craft, alienated children by its monotony and did this just at the moment when it undermined the authority of the family, and of the father in particular. It thus had to rely often on the unhappy method of indirect employment by untrained people whose incentive for driving the children was their own piece-rate payment.

In the predominantly youthful population of the time, the proportion of young workers was high. In the Cumberland mines, for example, children started work at the ages of five to seven, and as late as 1842, 200-250 of the 1,300-1,400 workers in the Lonsdale mines were under eighteen. At Alloa collieries, 103 boys and girls of under seven were employed in 1780. In the light metal trades, the proportion was higher still. Josiah Wedgwood, in 1816, had 30 per cent of his employees under eighteen, 3.3 per cent under ten years of age.[29] The greatest problems, however, were encountered in the textile mills.

The silk mills were dependent almost exclusively on child labour, and there the children started particularly young, at the ages of six or seven, compared with nine or ten in the cotton mills. Typically from two-thirds to three-quarters of the hands were under eighteen but in some large mills, the proportion was much higher: at Tootal's for example, 78 per cent of the workers were under sixteen.[30] Adults were thus in a small minority.

In the cotton industry the proportion of children and adolescents under eighteen was around 40-45 per cent. In some large firms the proportions were higher: thus Horrocks, Miller and Co. in 1816 had 13 per cent of their labour force under ten years of age, and 60 per cent between ten and eighteen, a total of 73 per cent. The proportion of children under ten was mostly much smaller than this, but in water mills employing large numbers of apprentices it might be greater: New Lanark, under David Dale in 1793, had 18 per cent of its labour force nine years old or younger.[31]

In the flax and the woollen and worsted industries, the proportions of workers under eighteen were rather higher than in cotton, being around 50 per cent. Again individual large works show much higher figures. In John Marshall's Water Lane Mill in 1831, for example, 49.2 per cent were under fifteen, and 83.8 per cent altogether under twenty-one.[32] Further, in all the textile branches the children were largely concentrated in certain sections, such as silk throwing and cotton spinning. In such departments, the difficulties of maintaining discipline were greatest.

II

These, then, were the problems of factory discipline facing the entrepreneurs in the early years of industrialisation. Their methods of overcoming them may be grouped under three headings: the proverbial stick, the proverbial carrot, and, thirdly, the attempt to create a new ethos of work order and obedience.

Little new in the way of the 'stick', or deterrent, was discovered by the early factory masters. Unsatisfactory work was punished by corporal punishment, by fines or by dismissal. Beatings clearly belonged to the older, personal relationships and were common with apprentices, against whom few other sanctions were possible,[33] but they survived because of the large-scale employment of children. Since the beating of children became one of the main complaints against factory owners and a major point at issue before the various Factory Commissions, the large amount of evidence available is not entirely trustworthy, but the picture is fairly clear in outline.

Some prominent factory owners, like Benjamin Gott, Robert Owen and John Marshall, prohibited it outright, though the odd cuff for inattention was probably inevitable in any children's employment. More serious beatings were neither very widespread, nor very effective. Robert Blincoe's sadistic master was untypical, and large employers frowned on beatings, though they might turn a blind eye on the overlookers' actions. 'We beat only the lesser, up to thirteen or fourteen . . . we use a strap', stated Samuel Miller, manager of Wilson's mill in Nottingham, one of the few to admit to this to the Factory Commission, 'I prefer fining to beating, if it answers . . . (but) fining does not answer. It does not keep the boys at their work'. The most honest evidence, however, and the most significant, came from John Bolling, a cotton master. He could not stop his spinners beating the children, he stated, 'for children require correction now and then, and the difficulty is to keep it from being excessive . . . It never can be in the interest of the master that the children should be beaten. The other day there were three children run away; the mother of one of them brought him back and asked us to beat him; that I could not permit; she asked us to take him again: at last I consented, and then she beat him.[34]

Dismissal and the threat of dismissal, were in fact the main deterrent instruments of enforcing discipline in the factories. At times of labour shortage they were ineffective, but when a buyers' market in labour returned, a sigh of relief went through the ranks of the employers at the restoration of their power. Many abolished the apprenticeship system in order to gain it,[35] and without it others were unable to keep any control whatsoever. Where there were no competing mill employers, as at Shrewsbury in the case of Marshall and Benyon's flax mills, it was a most effective threat.

In industries where skill and experience were at a premium, however, dismissals were resorted to only most reluctantly. At Soho Watt lost his temper quickly with engineers who made mistakes and demanded their discharge, but Boulton quietly moved them elsewhere until the storm had blown over. Similarly, John Kelsall, being accused of leniency at his Welsh ironworks, defended himself in his diary with the excuse that 'being strangers in the Country and divers necessities upon us at times', he did well to keep his labour together at all.[36]

Fines formed the third type of sanctions used, and were common both in industries employing skilled men, and in those employing mostly women and children. They figure prominently in all the sets of rules surviving, and appear to have been the most usual reaction to minor transgressions. Where the employer pocketed the fine there was an additional inducement to levy it freely, and in some cases, as in the deductions and penalties for sending small coal or stones up in the corves from the coal face, these became a major source of abuse and grievance.

Their general level was high and was meant to hurt. Typically, they were levied at 6d. to 2s. for ordinary offences or, say, two hours' to a day's wages.[37] Wedgwood fined 2s. 6d. for throwing things or for leaving fires burning overnight, and that was also the penalty for being absent on Monday mornings in the Worsley mines. At Ferley's Stockport mill, swearing, singing or being drunk were punished by a fine of 5s. and so was stealing coal at Merthyr. Miners were fined even more heavily: average weekly deductions were alleged to be as high as 1s. or 2s. out of a wage of 13s.[38]

Deterrence as a method of industrial discipline should, strictly, also include the actions taken against workers' organisations, but as these are well known, they need only be noted briefly here. The law could usually be assumed to be at the service of the employer, and was called into service for two types of offence, breaches of contract and trade-union organisation and rioting. Workmen's combinations were widely treated as criminal offences in employers' circles, even before the law made them explicitly such, and in turn, the legal disabilities turned trade disputes easily towards violence, particularly before the 1790s.[39] In the Scottish mines, serfdom was only just being eradicated, and in the North-East the one-year contract, coupled with the character note, could be used also to impose conditions akin to serfdom; opposition, including the inevitable rioting, was met by transportation and the death penalty, not only in the mines, but even in such advanced centres as Etruria as late as 1783.[40]

Where their powers permitted, employers met organisation with immediate dismissal: 'any hands forming conspiracies or unlawful combinations will be discharged without notice' read one rule as late as 1833.[41] More widespread, however, was the use of blacklists against those who had aroused the employer's disfavour. Little was heard of them, even in contemporary complaints by workmen, but their importance should not be underrated: as more evidence is becoming available, it is increasingly obvious that they were a most important prop of that reign of terror which in so many works did duty for factory discipline.[42]

By comparison with these commonly used examples of the 'stick', more subtle or more finely graded deterrents were so rare as to be curious rather than significant. John Wood, the Bradford spinner, made the child guilty of a fault hold up a card with his offence written on it; for more serious offences, this punishment was increased to walking up and down with the card, then to having to tell everyone in the room, and, as the highest stage, confessing to workers in other rooms. Witts and Rodick, the Essex silk-mill owners, made their errant children wear degrading dress.[43] These measures presuppose a general agreement with the factory code on the part of the other workmen which today few would take for granted. There was no serious discussion on the techniques of maintaining discipline until after 1830.[44]

III

Employees were as conservative in the use of the carrot as they were in the use of the stick. For a generation driving its children to labour in the mills for twelve to fourteen hours a day, positive incentives must indeed have been hard to devise and, for the child workers at least, were used even less than for adults. Much better, as in the case of at least one flax mill, to give them snuff to keep them awake in the evenings.[45] The extent of the predominance of the deterrent over the incentive in the case of the factory children is brought out in the returns of the 1833 Factory Commission, in replies to item 57 of the questionnaire sent out: 'What are the means taken to enforce obedience on the part of the children employed in your works?' In the following tabulation, the number of answers does not quite tally with the number of factories who sent replies,[46] as doubtful, meaningless and obviously formal answers, e.g. 'scolding', 'persuasion', 'kind words', have been omitted, while some firms gave more than one reply. Bearing in mind that most respondents were merely concerned to deny that they beat their children, and that many replied with the method they thought they ought to use, rather than the one actually in use, the following proportion may appear even more surprising:

Number of firms using different means to enforce obedience among factory children, 1833[47]

Negative		Positive	
Dismissal	353	Kindness	2
Threat of dismissal	48	Promotion, or higher wages	9
Fines, deductions	101	Reward or premium	23
Corporal punishment	55[48]		
Complaint to parents	13		
Confined to mill	2		
Degrading dress, badge	3		
Totals	575		34

The contrast is surely too strong to be fortuitous, especially since the bias was all the other way.

For adults, there were two positive methods which formed the stock-in-trade of management in this period. One was sub-contract, the transference of responsibility for making the workers industrious, to overseers, butty-men, group leaders, first hands and sub-contractors of various types. But this solution, which raises, in any case, questions of its own,[49] was not a method of creating factory discipline, but of evading it. The discipline was to be the older form of that of the supervisor of a small face-to-face group, maintained by someone who usually worked himself or was in direct daily contact with the workers.

The other method was some variant of payments by results. This provided the cash nexus symbolic for the new age. It was also a natural derivation from the methods used in earlier periods in such skilled and predominantly male trades as iron-smelting, mining, pottery or the production of metal goods.[50] In 1833, of 67,819 cotton-mill workers in 225 mills, 47.1 per cent were on piece-work and 43.7 per cent were paid datally, the method of payment for the remainder being unknown.[51] Labourers, children and others under direct supervision of a skilled pieceworker, and some highly skilled trades in short supply, such as engineers and building craftsmen, did, however, remain on fixed datal pay.

In many enterprises the 'discovery' of payment by results was greeted as an innovation of major significance, and at times the change-over does seem to have led to marked improvements in productivity. In 1688 piecework was said to have transformed the character of northern lead-mining and of copper-smelting at Neath some years later; Benjamin Gott spread piece payment from the overlooker to all men at Bean Ing and noted that 'the men consequently feel that they are as much interested as he and cease to look upon him as their master'. In Soho the near-bankruptcy of 1773 was diagnosed to have been caused partly by the lax supervision of the datal workers in the button and related trades, and Scale, the manager, proposed universal piece-work, though it was only the establishment of the Soho Foundry in 1796 under the senior partners' sons, with their newer and tighter management structure, which permitted the general change-over to piece-work among the engineers.[52]

Many of the older systems of payment by results, as in copper or tin mines, or in sinking colliery shafts, consisted of group piece-work, in which the cohesion and ethos of the group was added to the incentive payment as such to create work discipline. The newly introduced systems, however, were typically aimed at individual effort. As such, they were less effective, unless they were made as sharply graded as that of Blincoe's overlooker, who was sacked if he produced less than the norm, and received a bonus if he produced more,[53] and they were often badly constructed, particularly for times of rapid technological change. There were many examples of the usual problems of this type of payment, such as speed-up and rate cutting, as at Soho and Etruria,[54] loss of quality, and friction over interpretation and deductions. Nevertheless, it represented the major change and forward step in the employer's attitude towards labour, not only because it used cash as such but more specifically because it marked the end of the belief that workers were looking for a fixed minimum income, and a rate of earnings beyond this would merely lead to absenteeism,[55] or Sombart's principle of 'subsistence',[56] and the beginning of the notion that the workers' efforts were elastic with respect to income over a wide range.

The rise in the belief in the efficacy of incentive piece payments coincided with a decline in the belief in the efficacy of long-term contracts. These contracts were largely a survival of the pre-industrial age, adopted by many employers even during the Industrial Revolution at times of acute shortages of labour. In the north-eastern coalfield, the one-year binding had become almost universal since the beginning of the eighteenth century and it had spread to salters, keelmen, file-workers and others.[57] Ambrose Crowley bound his men for six months, Arkwright for three months, Soho for three to five years, some potteries for seven years, some cotton mills for five up to twenty-one years and the Prestonpans chemical works for twenty-one years.[58] But any hope that these indentures would ensure discipline and hard work was usually disappointed, and the system was quickly abandoned as a disciplinary method,[59] though it might be continued for other reasons.

A few employers evolved incentive schemes with a considerable degree of sophistication. In their simplest form, overseers bribed

children to work on for fourteen or fifteen hours and forego their
meal intervals, and John Wood paid them a bonus of 1*d*. weekly if
they worked well, but hung a notice of shame on them if they did
not.[60] At Backbarrow mill, apprentices received a 'bounty' of 6*d*. or
1*s*., to be withdrawn if offences were committed, and in silk mills
articles of clothing were given to the children as prizes for good
work; at one silk mill, employing 300 children aged nine or less, a
prize of bacon and three score of potatoes was given to the hardest
working boy, and a doll to the hardest working girl, and their output then became the norm for the rest.[61] Richard Arkwright, in
his early years, also gave prizes to the best workers.

Later on, these bonuses were made conditional on a longer
period of satisfactory work, or modified in other ways. In the early
1800s the Strutts introduced 'quarterly gift money' — one-sixth of
wages being held back over three months, and paid out at the end
only after deductions for misconduct. At John Marshall's the best
department received a bonus each quarter, amounting to £10 for
the overlooker and a week's wage for the hands, and some Dowlais
men, at least, also received a bonus of £2 every quarter, conditional
upon satisfactory performance.[62] At the Whitehaven collieries, the
bonus to the foremen was annual and was tied to net profits: when
these exceeded £30,000, the salary of the two viewers was nearly
doubled, from £152 to £300, and those of the overmen raised in
almost like proportion from a range of £52-82 to a range of
£90-170 — a particularly effective and cheap means of inducing
industry. In other coal mines, the ladder of promotion to overmen
was used effectively as an incentive.[63] It was left to Charles Babbage to work out in 1833 a more detailed analysis of the effect of
monetary incentives on work, and to stress the importance of
norms, of specific awards for exceeding them, and of accurate calculations of costs, of savings and of payments for them. But this
remained on paper only, and another half century was to elapse
before incentive schemes began to be made integral with general
efficiency schemes.[64]

Compared with the ubiquity of financial rewards, other direct
incentives were rare and localised, though they were highly significant. Wedgwood at times appealed directly to his workers, in at
least one case writing a pamphlet for them in which he stressed
their common interests. Samuel Greg, Jr. attempted to create a
settled community spirit at Bollington. Arkwright gave distinguishing dresses to the best workers of both sexes and John Marshall
fixed a card on each machine, showing its output.[65] Best known of
all were the 'silent monitors' of Robert Owen. He awarded four
types of mark for the past day's work to each superintendent, and

each of them, in turn, judged all his workers; the mark was then translated into the colours black-blue-yellow-white, in ascending order of merit, painted on the four sides of a piece of wood mounted over the machine, and turned outward according to the worker's performance.[66]

There is no doubt that Owen attached great importance to this system, entering all daily marks in a book as a permanent record, to be periodically inspected by him. There is equally no doubt that, naive as they might seem today, these methods were successful among all the leading manufacturers named, Robert Owen, in particular, running his mills, both in Manchester and in Scotland, at regular high annual profits largely because he gained the voluntary co-operation of his workers. Why, then were these methods not copied as widely as the technological innovations?

The reasons may have been ignorance on the part of other masters, disbelief or a (partly justified) suspicion that the enlightened employers would have been successful with or without such methods, enjoying advantages of techniques, size or a well-established market; but to limit the reasons to these would be to ignore one of the most decisive social facts of the age. An approach like Owen's ran counter to the accepted beliefs and ideology of the employing class, which saw its own rise to wealth and power as due to merit, and the workman's subordinate position as due to his failings. He remained a workman, living at subsistence wages, because he was less well endowed with the essential qualities of industry, ambition, sobriety and thrift. As long as this was so, he could hardly be expected to rise to the baits of moral appeals or co-operation. Therefore, one would have to begin by indoctrinating him with the bourgeois values which he lacked, and this, essentially, was the third method used by employers.

In their attempts to prevent 'Idleness, Extravagance, Waste and Immorality',[67] employers were necessarily dealing with the workers both inside the factory and outside it. The efforts to reform the whole man were, therefore, particularly marked in factory towns and villages in which the total environment was under the control of a single employer.

IV

The qualities of character which employers admired have, since Weber's day, been to some extent associated with the Protestant ethic.[68] To impart these qualities, with the one addition of obedience, to the working classes, could not but appear a formidable task. That it should have been attempted at all might seem to us incredible, unless we remember the background of the times which included the need to educate the first generation of factory workers to a new factory discipline, the widespread belief in human perfectibility, and the common assumption, by the employer, of functions which are today provided by the public authorities, like public safety, road building or education. All these raise questions which it would lead us too far to pursue here [69]; but one of their consequences was the preoccupation with the character and morals of the working classes which are so marked a feature of the early stages of industrialisation.

Some aspects of this are well known and easily understandable. Factory villages like New Lanark, Deanston, Busby, Ballindaloch, New Kilpatrick, Blantyre, and Joseph Stephenson's, at Antrim, had special provisions, and in some cases full-time staff, to check the morals of their workers.[70] Contemporaries tended to praise these actions most highly, and it was believed that firms laying stress on morals, and employing foremen who 'suppress anything bad' would get the pick of the labour.[71] Almost everywhere, churches, chapels and Sunday Schools were supported by employers, both to encourage moral education in its more usual sense, and to inculcate obedience. Drink and drunkenness became a major target of reform, with the short-term aim of increasing the usefulness of scarce skilled workers such as Soho's engineer erectors, who were often incapacitated by drink, and the long-term aim of spreading bourgeois virtues.

In this process much of the existing village culture came under attack. 'Traditional social habits and customs seldom fitted into the new pattern of industrial life, and they had therefore to be discredited as hindrances to progress.'[72] Two campaigns here deserve special mention.

The first was the campaign against leisure on Saturdays and Sundays, as no doubt, examples of immoral idleness. 'The children are during the weekdays generally employed', the Bishop of Chester had declared solemnly in 1785, 'and on Sunday are apt to be idle, mischievous and vitious.' This was not easily tolerated. Thus Deanston had a Superintendent of streets to keep them clear of immorality, children and drink. Charles Wilkins of Tiverton formed an 'Association for the Promotion of Order' in 1832 to round up the children and drive them to school on Sundays. All the hands at Strutt's and Arkwright's under twenty had to attend school for four hours on Saturday afternoons and on Sundays to 'keep them out of mischief'. Horrocks' employed a man 'for many years, to see that the children do not loiter about the streets on Sundays'. At Dowlais the chapel Sunday school teachers asked J. J. Guest in 1818 to order his employees to attend, otherwise there was the danger that they might spend the Sabbath 'rambling and playing'.[73] Even Owen expressed similar sentiments: 'if children [under ten] are not to be instructed, they had better be employed in any occupation that should keep them out of mischief', he asserted.[74]

The second was the prohibition of bad language. At the beginning of the eighteenth century, Crowley's 'Clerk for the Poor', or teacher, was to correct lying, swearing, 'and suchlike horrid crimes'; while at the same time Sir Humphrey Mackworth, at Neath, fined 'Swearing, Cursing, Quarrelling, being Drunk, or neglecting Divine Service on Sunday, one shilling', and the Quaker Lead Company, at Gadlis, also prohibited swearing in 1708.[75] Later this became quite regular, wherever rules were made: at Darley Abbey, in 1795, the fine was 9d. or 1s.; at Mellor, 1s.; at Nenthead, 6d.; at Galloway's where 'obscene and vulgar language' was prohibited, the men themselves levied the fines. At Marshall and Benyon's also, according to Rule 4 of 1785, a jury of seven was to judge the offence of striking, abusing or harming another workman.[76]

Again, the rules of Thomas Fernley, Jr., Stockport, cotton mills, stated: 'while at work . . . behaviour must be commendable avoiding all shouting, loud talk, whistling, calling foul names, all mean and vulgar language, and every kind of indecency'. Swearing, singing, being drunk were fined 5s.; overlookers allowing drink in the mills were fined 10s. 6d. Gott's Sheepshanks and other large works had similar rules in the West Riding.[77]

This preoccupation might seem to today's observer to be both impertinent and irrelevant to the worker's performance, but in fact it was critical, for unless the workmen *wished* to become 'respectable' in the current sense, none of the other incentives would bite. Such opprobrious terms as 'idle' or 'dissolute' should be taken to mean strictly that the worker was indifferent to the employer's deterrents and incentives. According to contemporaries, 'it was the irrationality of the poor, quite as much as their irreligion, that was distressing. They took no thought of the morrow . . . The workers were by nature indolent, improvident, and self-indulgent.'[78]

The code of ethics on which employers concentrated was thus rather limited. Warnings against greed, selfishness, materialism or pride seldom played a large part, sexual morals rarely became an important issue to the factory disciplinarians (as distinct from outside moralists) and, by and large, they did not mind which God was worshipped, as long as the worshipper was under the influence of some respectable clergyman. The conclusion cannot be avoided that, with some honourable exceptions, the drive to raise the level of respectability and morality among the working classes was not undertaken for their own sakes but primarily, or even exclusively, as an aspect of building up a new factory discipline.

V

Any conclusions drawn from this very brief survey must be tentative and hesitant, particularly if they are meant to apply to industrial revolutions in general.

First, the acclimatisation of new workers to factory discipline is a task different in kind, at once more subtle and more violent, from that of maintaining discipline among a proletarian population of long standing. Employers in the British Industrial Revolution therefore used not only industrial means but a whole battery of extra-mural powers, including their control over the courts, their powers as landlords, and their own ideology, to impose the control they required.

Secondly, the maintenance of discipline, like the whole field of management itself, was not considered a fit subject for study, still less a science, but merely a matter of the employer's individual character and ability. No books were written on it before 1830, no teachers lectured on it, there were no entries about it in the technical encyclopaedias, no patents were taken out relating to it. As a result, employers did not learn from each other, except haphazardly and belatedly, new ideas did not have the cachet of a new technology and did not spread, and the crudest form of deterrents and incentives remained the rule. Robert Owen was exceptional in ensuring that his methods, at least, were widely known, but they were too closely meshed in with his social doctrines to be acceptable to other employers.

Lastly, the inevitable emphasis on reforming the moral character of the worker into a willing machine-minder led to a logical dilemma that contemporaries did not know how to escape. For if the employer had it in his power to reform the workers if he tried hard enough, whose fault was it that most of them remained immoral, idle and rebellious? And if the workers could really be taught their employers' virtues, would they not all save and borrow and become entrepreneurs themselves, and who would then man the factories?

The Industrial Revolution happened too rapidly for these dilemmas, which involved the re-orientation of a whole class, to be solved, as it were, *en passant*. The assimilation of the formerly independent worker to the needs of factory routine took at least a further generation, and was accompanied by the help of tradition, by a sharply differentiated educational system, and new ideologies which were themselves the results of clashes of earlier systems of values, besides the forces operating before 1830. The search for a more scientific approach which would collaborate with and use, instead of seeking to destroy, the workers' own values, began later still, and may hardly be said to have advanced very far even today.

NOTES

1 This paper is part of a wider study of management in the Industrial Revolution, made possible by a grant from the Houblon-Norman Fund of the Bank of England.

2 C. Kerr, John T. Dunlop, F. H. Harbison, C. A. Myers, *Industrialism and Industrial Man. The Problems of Labour and Management in Economic Growth* (1962), pp. 193 ff.

3 Neil McKendrick, 'Josiah Wedgwood and Factory Discipline', *Historical Journal*, IV (1961).

4 Werner Sombart, *Der Moderne Kapitalismus* (Leipzig, 3rd ed., 1919), pp. 809 ff., 829-31; and *Das Wirtshaftsleben im Zeitalter des Hochkapitalismus* (Munich and Leipzig, 1927), I, 424-30.

5 A. Redford, *Labour Migration in England, 1800-50* (Manchester, 1926), pp. 18, 20; Neil J. Smelser, *Social Change in the Industrial Revolution* (1959), p. 105; T. Garnett, *Observations on a Tour Through the Highlands* (1811 ed.), I, 23; A. Ure, *The Philosophy of Manufactures* (2nd ed. 1835), pp. 15, 20-1; R. S. Fitton and A. P. Wadsworth, *The Strutts and the Arkwrights, 1758-1830* (Manchester, 1958), p. 221; Charles Wilson, 'The Entrepreneur in the Industrial Revolution in Britain', *History*, XLII (1957), 115; Frances Collier, *The Family Economy of the Workers in the Cotton Industry During the Period of the Industrial Revolution, 1784-1833* (M.A. Thesis, Manchester, 1921), p. iii, Dipak Mazumdar, 'Under-employment in Agriculture and the Industrial Wage Rate', *Economica*, n.s. XXVI (1959), 334 ff.

6 Fitzmaurice, *Life of William, Earl of Shelburne* (2nd ed. 1912), I, 278; *Select Committee on the Children Employment in the Manufactories of the United Kingdom*, Parl. Papers, 1816, III, p. 234.

7 *Factories Inquiry Commission* (referred to henceforth as 'Factories Commission'), First Report, Parl. Papers 1833, XX, A. 1, p. 83, ev. Hugh Miller; Richard Ayton, *A Voyage Round Great Britain* (1815), II, 214; M. G. Jones, *The Charity School Movement* (Cambridge, 1938), p. 208; Anon. 'Some Glasgow Customers of the Royal Bank around 1800', *The Three Banks Review*, 48 (1960), 39.

8 *Committee on the Woollen Manufacture of England*, P.P. 1806, III, ev. Robert Cookson, p. 70, Wm. Child, pp. 103-4, John Atkinson, p. 116; H. D. Fong, *Triumph of the Factory System in England* (Tientsin, 1930), pp. 180-1; also A. P. Usher, *An Introduction to the Industrial History of England* (1921), p. 350; Herbert Heaton, *The Yorkshire Woollen and Worsted Industries* (Oxford, 1920), p. 353.

9 A. P. Wadsworth and Julia De L. Mann, *The Cotton Trade and Industrial Lancashire: 1600-1780* (1931) p. 433.

10 *Lords' Committee on the Bill for the Preservation of the Health and Morals of Apprentices*, P.P. 1818, XCVI, pp. 147, 168, 175. Also cf. Oliver Wood, *The Development of the Coal, Iron and Shipbuilding Industries of West Cumberland, 1750-1914* (Ph.D. Thesis, London, 1952), pp. 138-9; R. H. Campbell, *Carron Company* (Edinburgh and London, 1961), p. 65. Turnover was lower in the country: Strutt's was only 16 per cent a year, and John Marshall's, in a Leeds

suburb, 20 per cent. Fitton and Wadsworth, *op. cit.*, p. 239; W. G. Rimmer, *Marshalls of Leeds, Flax Spinners, 1788-1886* (Cambridge, 1960), p. 106; Redford, *op. cit.*, p. 20.

11 Charles Wilkins, *The History of the Iron, Steel, Tinplate and Other Trades of Wales* (Merthyr Tydfil, 1903), p. 258; *William Brown's Letter Book 1749-56* (MS. North of England Inst. of Mining and Mech. Eng., Newcastle), Leonard Hartley to Brown, 16 Feb. 1755; A. Birch, 'The Haigh Ironworks, 1789-1856', *Bull. of the John Rylands Library*, XXXV (1953), 331; John Rowlands, *A Study of Some of the Social and Economic Changes in the Town and Parish of Amlwch, 1750-1850* (M.A. Thesis, Wales, Bangor, 1960), p. 302; A. H. Dodd, *The Industrial Revolution in North Wales* (Cardiff, 1933), p. 330; John Rowe, *Cornwall in the Age of the Industrial Revolution* (Liverpool, 1953), p. 19.

12 *S.C. on Children in Manufactories*, P.P. 1816, p. 259, ev. Wm. Taylor; A. Ure, *Cotton Manufacture of Great Britain* (1835-6), II, 448; also *Factories Commission*, Second Report, D. 2, p. 36, ev. Peter Ewart; Usher, *op. cit.*, pp. 349-50; J. F. C. Harrison, *Learning and Living, 1790-1850* (1961), p. 39.

13 A. H. John, *The Industrial Development of South Wales, 1750-1850* (Cardiff, 1950), p. 71.

14 Josiah Wedgwood, *Letters to Bentley, 1771-1780* (Priv. Circ. 1903), p. 88 (19 Aug. 1772), p. 295 (5 July 1776). Also McKendrick, *loc. cit.*, pp. 38, 46; *S.C. on Children in Manufactories*, ev. Josiah Wedgwood, p. 61; *Boulton and Watt Correspondence* (MS. Birmingham Assay Office), Watt to Boulton, 30 Oct. 1780.

15 *Kelsall MSS.* (Friends' House, London), Diary, 13 Sept. 1725; William Bray, *Sketch of a Tour into Derbyshire and Yorkshire* (2nd ed. 1783), p. 108; Fitton and Wadsworth, *op. cit.*, pp. 99-102, 259; Ure, *Philosophy*, p. 344.

16 Erich Roll, *An Early Experiment in Industrial Organisation, being a history of the Firm of Boulton and Watt, 1775-1805* (1930), p. 222; H. W. Dickinson, *Matthew Boulton* (Cambridge, 1937), p. 179; E. Meteyard, *The Life of Josiah Wedgwood* (1865-6), II, 126; W. Felkin, *A History of the Machine-wrought Hosiery and Lace Manufactures* (1867), p. 263; *Herculaneum Pottery Minute Book* (MS. Liverpool Central Library, 380. M.D. 47), 3 Dec. 1813. Also, e.g. Collier, *Family Economy*, p. 175.

17 *Mona Mine MSS.* (University College, Bangor), nos. 1005, 1009.

18 Wadsworth and Mann, *op. cit.*, p. 313.

19 *Ibid.*, p. 391; N. S. B. Gras, *Industrial Evolution* (1930), p. 84; John Brown (ed.), *Memoirs of Robert Blincoe* (Manchester, 1832), p. 59; *Factories Commission*, First Report, A. 1, p. 37, A. 2, p. 8; Campbell, *Carron Company*, p. 71. For freedom in the Welsh Slate Quarries, see Dylan Pritchard, *The Slate Industry of North Wales* (M.A. Thesis, Wales, 1935), p. 71.

20 Ure, *Philosophy*, p. 15; and *Cotton Manufacture*, pp. 259, 269; Paul Mantoux, *The Industrial Revolution in the Eighteenth Century* (1961 ed.), p. 376.

21 *Committee on the Labour of Children in the Mills and Factories of the United Kingdom* (Sadler's Committee), P.P. 1831-2, WV, QQ, 1881-2 6065-9; Usher, *op. cit.*, p. 350; also Gras, *op. cit.*, pp. 85-6.

22 J. Kulischer, *Allgemeine Wirtschaftsgeschichte* (Munich, 1958 ed.), II, 459; W. H. B. Court, 'Industrial Organisation and Economic Progress in the Eighteenth-Century Midlands', *Trans. Royal Historical Society*, 4th ser. XXVIII (1946), p. 94; *Mona Mine MSS.* no. 2633, pp. 44-5; McKendrick, *op. cit.* p. 83; J. Lord, *Capital and Steam Power* (1923), pp. 197, 201; Kerr *et. al. op. cit.* p. 200; John Kennedy, *Miscellaneous Papers* (Manchester, 1849), p. 18; E. Surrey Dane, *The Economic History of the Staffordshire Pottery Industry* (M.A. Thesis, Sheffield, 1929), p. 14; Llewellyn Jewitt, *The Wedgwoods* (1865), p. 129.

23 The best-known codes were those of Josiah Wedgwood (1780), the Soho Foundry (1796), Heathcote's at Tiverton, the Wear Cotton mills, Stockport, Alexander Galloway, and John Marshall.

24 Rimmer, *op. cit.* p. 119. Belper Round Mill was built like a Benthamite Panopticon prison: an overseer at the centre had a clear view of what went on in all the eight segments. Fitton and Wadsworth, *op. cit.* p. 221.

25 Usher, *op. cit.* p. 348; Kerr *et al. op. cit.* p. 193.

26 E.g. *House of Lords Committee on Apprentices*, P.P. 1818 (V) and 1819 (I and II), App. 34.

27 *Committee on Woollen Manufacturers* (1806), ev. Joseph Coope, p. 49; R. M. Hartwell, *The Yorkshire Woollen and Worsted Industry, 1800-1850* (D. Phil. Thesis, Oxford, 1955), pp. 444-6; Smelser, *op. cit.* pp. 190 ff. 231, 269-72. According to the Parliamentary returns of 1816, only 17.7 per cent of the work force in cotton were adult males.

28 *Sadler's Committee*, P.P., 1831-2, QQ. 497, 9607-8, 10286; *S.C. on Children in Manufactories*, P.P. 1816, pp. 61, 132, 135, 268; John Thomas, *The Economic Development of the North Staffordshire Potteries since 1730, with Special Reference to the Industrial Revolution* (Ph.D. Thesis, London, 1934), p. 553; John Fielden, *The Curse of the Factory System* (1836), pp. 5, 9.

29 O. Wood, *loc. cit.* pp. 130-3; *S.C. on Children in Manufactories*, P.P. 1816, p. 60; D. F. MacDonald, *Scotland's Shifting Population, 1770-1850* (Glasgow, 1937), p. 71.

30 *Factories Commission*, First Report, B. 1, pp. 77 ff; *S.C. on Children in Manufactories*, P.P. 1816, pp. 76, 191; *Observations on the Ages of Persons in the Cotton Mills in Manchester* (Manchester, 1819), p. 8; G. B. Hertz, 'The English Silk Industry in the Eighteenth Century', *English Historical Review*, XXIV (1909), 724; Sir F. M. Eden, *The State of the Poor* (1928 ed.), p. 171; *Factories Commission*, First Supplement, D. 1, p. 149, D. 3, p. 257; G. R. Porter, *The Progress of the Nation* (1838 ed.), p. 261; *Select Committee on the Silk Trade*. P.P. 1831-2, XIX, Q. 9591, ev. Henry Tootal.

31 Ure, *Cotton Manufacture*, pp. 398-400; *Factories Commission*, First Report, D. 2, p. 107, First Supplement, D. 1, pp. 136A, 123; D. 3, pp. 259-68; *S.C. on Children in Manufactories*, P.P. 1816, pp. 52, 236-7,258, 261; Sir John Sinclair, *(Old) Statistical Account of Scotland* (Edinburgh, 1795), XV, 37; Porter, *op. cit.* p. 273; John Wade, *History of the Middle and Working Classes* (3rd ed. 1835), p. 570, Thomas Ellison, *The Cotton Trade of Great Britain* (1886), p. 72.

32 *Factories Commission*, Second Supplement, C. 1: the average of the 19 large West Riding woollen mills with over 200 workers each was 50.5 per cent under eighteen, of whom 14.3 per cent of the total were under twelve. *S.C. on Children in Manufactories*, P.P. 1816, p. 237; Rimmer, *op. cit.* p. 316.

33 E.g. *Factories Commission*, First Report, B. 1, p. 9, E, p. 9; Llewellyn Jewitt (ed.), *Life of William Hutton* (1872), p. 105.

34 *Factories Commission*, First Report, C. 1, pp. 44-5, D. 1, pp. 133, 173-4.

35 Ure, *Philosophy*, p. 365; *Factories Commission*, First Report, A. 1, p. 84; *Sadler's Committee*, P.P. 1831-2, Q. 1049; *S.C. on Children in Manufactories*, P.P. 1816, pp. 364-5.

36 T. H. Marshall, *James Watt (1736-1819)* (n.d.), p. 125; *Boulton and Watt MSS.* (Birmingham Central Library), Watt to Boulton, 26 Jan. 1789; John Kelsall, *Diary* (MS.), II, end of 10 Mo. 1719; *Sadler's Committee*, P.P. 1831-2, QQ. 5312, 5343.

37 G. Unwin *et. al. Samuel Oldknow and the Arkwrights* (Manchester, 1924), p. 198; Jean Lindsay, 'An Early Industrial Community. The Evans' Cotton Mill at Darley Abbey, Derbyshire, 1783-1810', *Business History Review*, XXXIV (1960), 299; British Transport Commission (York) Archives, MSS. SAD. 8/107 (Stockton and Darlington); Marshall Papers (MSS. Brotherton Library, Leeds), no. 43; D. Glyn

John, *Contributions to the Economic History of South Wales*, I (D.Sc. Thesis, Wales, 1930), Sect. 3, p. 19.

38 T.S. Ashton, 'The Coalminers of the Eighteenth Century', *Economic History*, I (1928), 320; V. W. Bladen, 'The Potteries in the Industrial Revolution', *ibid.* I (1926), 130; *Factories Commission*, Second Supplement, D. 1, pp. 69-70; Madeleine Elsas (ed.), *Iron in the Making: Dowlais Iron Company Letters, 1782-1860* (Glamorgan Records Committee and Guest, Keen Iron and Steel Co., 1960), 28 Feb. 1829; *S.C. on Children in Manufactories*, 1816, p. 356; *Nevill MSS.* (National Library of Wales), Charles Nevill Sr.: Diary (no. 3), 18 Aug. 1797; Hylton Scott, 'The Miners' Bond in Northumberland and Durham', *Proc. of the Society of Antiquaries of Newcastle-upon-Tyne*, 4th ser. XI (1947), 71; R. L. Galloway, *Annals of Coalmining and the Coal Trade* (1898), pp. 269-70.

39 E.g. *Boulton and Watt MSS.* (Birmingham City Library), Watt to Boulton, 11 Oct. 1781, Watt to Garbett, 12 Oct. 1781.

40 Campbell, *Carron*, pp. 68, 69; McKendrick, *op. cit.* p. 52.

41 *Factories Commission*, Second Supplement, D. 1, pp. 69-70.

42 E.g. Fitton and Wadsworth, pp. 238-9; J. L. and B. Hammond, *The Skilled Labourer, 1760-1832* (2nd ed. 1920), pp. 13 ff.; Elsas, *op. cit.* pp. 36, 66; *Select Committee on Artizans and Machinery*, P.P. 1824, V, p. 25; *Dowlais MSS.* (Glamorgan County Record Office) from Penydarran 20 Sept. 1803, from Birmingham Metal Co. 23 Sept. 1820, from Aberdare Iron Works 15 Jan. 1828, W. Lewis to J. Guest, 6 Oct. 1800.

43 *Sadler's Committee*, P.P. 1831-2, Q. 3061; *Factories Commission*, Second Supplement, B. 1.

44 The earliest, and very limited attempt, was that of J. Montgomery, *The Theory and Practice of Cotton Spinning* (Glasgow, 1833), pp. 251-2.

45 *Factories Commission*, First Report, A. 2, p. 89.

46 595 replied, from four districts: A. 1 (Scotland: 173), C. 1 (North-Eastern: 51), B. 2 (Western: 129), D. 1 (Lancashire: 242).

47 *Factories Commission*, Second Supplement.

48 Obviously too low, see above, p. 132.

49 I hope to deal with them elsewhere.

50 R. H. Mottram and Colin Coote, *Through Five Generations: The History of the Butterley Company* (1950), p. 62; A. H. John, *The Industrial Development of South Wales, 1750-1850* (Cardiff, 1950), pp. 72, 86; *Mona Mine MSS.* nos. 1274, 1599, 2254-65, 3738; H. Louis, 'The Pitmen's Yearly Bond', *Trans. of North of England Inst. of Mining* (1930), pp. 1-2; William Brown, *Letter Book 1749-56* (MS.), to Carlisle Spedding, 24 Jan. 1750/1, Crawcrook Colliery, *Cost Book of Sinking, 1821-5* (MS. North of England Inst. of Mining and Mech. Eng., Buddle Collection, no. 40); W. H. B. Court, 'A Warwickshire Colliery in the Eighteenth Century', *Econ. Hist. Rev.* VII (1937), 227; *Factories Commission*, First Report, B. 2, pp. 80, 81; *Wentworth Woodhouse Muniments* (MSS. Sheffield City Library), A. 1389, Staff Instruction Book, paras, 8, 32; Peter L. Payne, 'The Govan Collieries, 1804-1805', *Business History*, III (1961), 79-80; *Spencer-Stanhope Muniments* (MSS. Sheffield City Library), no. 60481; John Rowlands, *Amlwch*, p. 226; John Thomas, *op. cit.* p. 553; *Select Committee on Manufactures, Commerce and Shipping*, P.P. 1833, VI, Q. 10269, ev. Anthony Hill.

51 Edward Baines, Jr. *History of the Cotton Manufacture in Great Britain* (1835), reprinted by Frank Cass, London, pp. 369-75; Fitton and Wadsworth, p. 240; W. B. Crump (ed.), *The Leeds Woollen Industry, 1780-1820* (Thoresby Society, Leeds, 1931), p. 268; Francis Collier, 'Workers in a Lancashire Factory at the Beginning of the Nineteenth Century', *Manchester School*, VII (1936), 53-4; *Factories Commission*, First Report, D. 2, p. 128, B. 1, p. 14; *Sadler's Committee*, Q. 496; *S.C. on Children in Manufactories*, P.P., 1816, pp. 28, 367; J. Montgomery,

op. cit. p. 225.
52 Roll, *op. cit.* pp. 64, 191, 193, 209-15; Edward Hughes, *North Country Life in the Eighteenth Century* (1952), p. 44; Crump, *op. cit.* p. 38; J. E. Cule, *The Financial History of Matthew Boulton, 1759-1800* (M.Com. Thesis, Birmingham, 1935), pp. 39, 290; *Boulton and Watt Accounts* (Birmingham City Library MSS.), Wages Books, 1828, 1829, 1830; John W. Hall (ed.), 'Diary of a Tour by Joshua Field in the Midlands, 1821', *Trans. Newcomen Society*, VI (1925-6), 9; J. R. Immer, *The Development of Production Methods in Birmingham, 1760-1851* (D.Phil. Thesis, Oxford, 1954), pp. 182-3; William Waller, *An Essay on the Value of the Mines, late of Sir Carbery Price* (1698), 'Epistle Dedicatory'.
53 Brown, *Robert Blincoe*, p. 21.
54 Roll, *op. cit.* p. 206; Wedgwood, *Letters to Bentley*, pp. 89-90, 23 Aug. 1772.
55 See my forthcoming article on 'The Factory Village in the Industrial Revolution', and E. S. Furniss, *The Position of the Labourer in a System of Nationalism* (New York, 1957 ed.), pp. 100-107, chapter 6.
56 See p. 126 above.
57 Hammond, *Skilled Labourer*, pp. 13 ff.; Galloway, *Annals*, pp. 269-70; H. Louis, *loc. cit.* Miners' Bonds (MS. North of England Inst., Newcastle, Forster Coll. vol. 2); Ashton, 'Coalminers', p. 310; Rowlands, *Amlwch*, pp. 228-9; H. Scott, 'Miners' Bond', pp. 55-6.
58 Fitton and Wadsworth, *op. cit.* p. 233; Roll, *op. cit.* pp. 65, 202; Wm. Bourn, *History of the Parish of Ryton* (Carlisle, 1896), p. 122; A. and N. Clow, *The Chemical Revolution* (1952), p. 138; *Boulton and Watt Correspondence* (MS. Royal Polytechnic Society, Falmouth), Watt to Wilson, 27 Aug. 1793; *Lords' Committee on Factory Bill*, P.P. 1818, p. 197; Elsas, *op. cit.* 26 Apr. 1827; John Thomas, *op. cit.* p. 520.
59 *Lords' Committee on Factory Bill*, P.P. 1818, pp. 75-6; E. Kilburn Scott (ed.), *Matthew Murray, Pioneer Engineer, Records for 1765-1826* (Leeds, 1828), p. 40; 'Alfred', *The History of the Factory Movement* (1857), I, 284; Birch, 'Haigh Ironworks', pp. 320-1.
60 See above. *S.C. on Children in Manufactories*, P.P. 1816, p. 135; *Sadler's Committee*, Q. 3061.
61 *S.C. on Children in Manufactories*, P.P. 1816, p. 288; *Sadler's Committee*, QQ. 7292, 7304, 10072.
62 Fitton and Wadsworth, *op. cit.* p. 233; Rimmer, *op. cit.* p. 120; Elsas, *op. cit.*, 26 Apr. 1827.
63 O. Wood, *op. cit.* p. 150; A. Raistrick, *Two Centuries of Industrial Welfare. The London (Quaker) Lead Company, 1692-1905* (1938), pp. 73-4.
64 Charles Babbage, *On the Economy of Machinery and Manufactures* (3rd ed. 1833), p. 255. Also e.g. Horace Bookwalter Drury, *Scientific Management: a History and Criticism* (2nd ed. 1918), pp. 24-5.
65 McKendrick, *op. cit.* pp. 47, 52-4; Fitton and Wadsworth, *op. cit.* p. 100; J. D. Chambers, 'Industrialisation as a Factor in Economic Growth in England, 1700-1900', in *Contributions to the First International Economic History Conference, Stockholm* (Paris, 1960), p. 207; E. S. Dane, *op. cit.* p. 14; Rimmer, *op. cit.* p. 121.
66 Robert Owen, *Life of Owen* (1920 ed.), pp. 111, 189; G. D. H. Cole, *Robert Owen* (1925), p. 78.
67 From the Standing Instructions to the Staff Supervisor, *Wentworth Woodhouse Muniments* (MSS. Sheffield), no. A 1389.
68 Max Weber, *The Protestant Ethic and the Spirit of Capitalism* (1930); Sombart, *Hochkapitalismus*, I, 427-30.
69 See my forthcoming article, 'The Factory Village in the Industrial Revolution', to be published in the *English Historical Review*.
70 Cole, *Robert Owen*, p. 78; *Factories Commission*, Second Supplement, A. 1; *S.C.*

on Children in Manufactories, P.P. 1816, pp. 40, 164.
71 Smelser, *op. cit.* p. 106; Ure, *Philosophy*, pp. 415-16.
72 Harrison, *Learning and Living*, p. 40. Mercantilist writers had been waging a similar campaign for at least a century in the national interest, but had made little impact. The local employer could make his wishes much more effectively heard. Furniss, *op. cit.* pp. 150 ff.
73 Fitton and Wadsworth, *op. cit.* pp. 103, 256; A. P. Wadsworth, 'The First Manchester Sunday Schools', *Bull. John Rylands Library*, XXXIII (1951), 310; *Factories Commission*, First Report, E, p. 24, A. R. Strutt; Elsas, *op. cit.* p. 71; *S.C. on Children in Manufactories*, P.P. 1816, p. 260, ev. Wm. Taylor.
74 *Ibid.* p. 23. Compare Charles Hall: 'Leisure in a poor man is thought quite a different thing from what it is to a rich man, and goes by a different name. In the poor it is called idleness, the cause of all mischief.' *The Effects of Civilization on the Peoples of European States* (1805), p. 24.
75 Hughes, *North Country Life*, p. 342; D. J. Davies, *The Economic History of South Wales Prior to 1800* (Cardiff, 1933), p. 82; Raistrick, *Two Centuries*, p. 78; A. Raistrick, *Quakers in Science and Industry* (1950), p. 174; also his 'London Lead Company, 1692-1905', *Trans. Newcomen Soc.* XIV (1933-4), 136; D. G. John, *loc. cit.* p. 19.
76 Elsewhere, fines might go into the employer's pockets. Lord, *Capital and Steam Power*, p. 206; Hammond, *Town Labourer*, p. 21. Cf. also Lindsay, *op. cit.* p. 299; Unwin, *Samuel Oldknow*, p. 198; *S.C. on Artizans and Machinery*, P.P. 1824, pp. 25-6; *Marshall Papers*, no. 43, Raistrick, 'London Lead Company', p. 157.
77 *Factories Commission*, Second Supplement, D. 1, pp. 69-70. All workers had to attend church at least once every Sunday; *Sadler's Committee*, Q. 994.
78 T. S. Ashton, *An Economic History of England: The Eighteenth Century* (1955), p. 201.

8

The Profitability of Consett Iron Company before 1914[1]

H. W. Richardson and J. M. Bass[*]

Consett Iron Company was founded in 1864 by acquisition of the site and works of the Derwent Iron Company which had been in operation since 1840 (though from July 1858 as the Derwent and Consett Iron Company). The Derwent Iron Co. had been famous only for its size (with 18 blast furnaces the largest ironworks in England) and for its inability to make a profit. It had survived with the aid of lavish credit from the Northumberland and Durham District Bank. By the time of its collapse in the 1857 financial crisis, the bank had advanced £966,831 on the strength of £250,000 of promissory notes from the company's directors and a £100,000 mortgage on the plant (the bank's managing director, Jonathan Richardson, was himself a partner in the company).[2] The firm naturally went bankrupt along with the bank, and the works were in danger of being broken up. This fate was avoided by the intervention of the bank's creditors and shareholders of the North Eastern Railway Co. (with annual freight receipts from the firm of £250,000 the railway had a strong interest in its continued existence), and although the company of 1858 failed to complete the purchase the new company was firmly established in April 1864.

The contrast between the success of the new firm and the failure of the old Derwent Iron Co. could not have been sharper. The company started modestly, for this was a period of depression in the iron industry. Moreover, distributed profits were held down by heavy capital expenditure on replacing obsolete blast furnaces and erecting a new puddling mill. But soon afterwards, Consett Iron Co. became very profitable indeed. The comments of the local press on the firm's progress give an impression of continuous prosperity.

[*]From *Business History*, Vol. VII, no. 2 (1965), pp. 71-93. Reprinted by permission of the editor of *Business History*.

Already in 1875 it was 'the largest iron plate works in the world' and twenty years later held 'probably the premier position amongst the steelplate makers of the world'. One newspaper described its profits as 'prodigious', and an investigation of the firm's position by the Joint Stock Companies' Journal in 1900 concluded that 'Consett has a prosperous record with few to compare with it in England, Europe or even in the United States'.[3] Another newspaper stated that the 'Consett Iron Co. . . . is more a romance of trade than any other organisation in the North' and marvelled that at its foundation 'the undertaking was almost picked off the scrap heap, and seemed a very hopeless enterprise'.[4] Such eulogies read like journalistic exaggeration, but they were substantially true. In the first half century of its history, the company always made a profit and never paid a dividend below 7½ per cent, and then only in the early years 1867-69; dividends of 33⅓, 40, 50 or even 60 per cent were not uncommon, while the average dividend over the period 1864 to 1914 was about 23½ per cent. After the early years the annual profit (after tax and interest) never fell much below £56,000 (in the slump year 1879) and rose as high as £672,000 in 1900. Profit expressed as a percentage of capital employed fluctuated markedly between limits of 8.6 per cent in 1885 and 1895 and 49.2 per cent in 1873; the average over the whole period was 19.1 per cent.[5]

The arguments of this paper rest on the presumption that Consett Iron Co. was more profitable than other steel companies before 1914. To show this conclusively would require too much detail, but three points may be mentioned in its support. One can refer to contemporary newspaper accounts: in 1886 for example the *Newcastle Daily Chronicle* commented that whilst 'other companies lament small returns the Consett Iron Co. has increased its profits in the year just concluded' and a year later stated that 'the company . . . is the most prosperous in the North of England'.[6] Secondly, Consett continued to make substantial profits in periods described as deep depression and as unprofitable in the histories of the steel industry. For instance, Consett's profit figures (see Table 1) scarcely support Burn's view that the early 1890s were 'universally years of reaction' or the generalisation of Burnham and Hoskins that 'during the seventies the dividends diminished and in the late nineties practically disappeared'.[7] Thirdly, direct comparisons of profit between Consett and other firms suggest that Consett was probably Britain's most profitable steel producer. Taking the period 1908-13 and using the percentage dividend paid on ordinary shares as a rough guide to profitability, among the large steel companies Consett's annual average dividend of 35.7 per cent was more than three times higher than the next best, South Durham with 11.7 per cent and Guest, Keen and Nettlefolds with 10.0 per cent. Baldwins, Bolckow Vaughan, Dorman Long, Ebbw Vale and the Steel Co. of Scotland paid average dividends in the range 5 to 8 per cent.

The modest aim here is to give some pointers to explaining this high profitability. Pointers only they must be, because a rigorous analysis is impossible. For one thing, there is no theoretical framework available which could be applied to an analysis of why some businesses are very profitable and others are not. Existing theories of profit (for example, Schumpeter's explanation of profit as the reward to innovators or Frank Knight's theory of profit as being an indicator of the degree of uncertainty) are too general to be useful in the study of one firm in a particular industry. In the absence of a theoretical framework it is difficult to judge the importance of any one factor in profitability relative to another. Investigations may be made to see if synchronisation is possible between the time period during which a particular factor is in force and periods of very high or low profits in an attempt to assess the degree of the factor's influence on the firm's prosperity. A more fruitful inquiry might be to compare the relative profit performance of similar firms in the same industry and to analyse possible causes of variations in profitability (difference in capacity for innovation, quality of management, accessibility to cheap factors of production and other locational aspects, productivity of technical processes in use, monopoly power, size of plant and other economies of scale, sales techniques and commercial acumen, etc.). If sufficient empirical data were available, if all the relevant variables could be measured in some way and if the sample of firms was large enough, the firms could be ranked according to profitability and according to their standing for each variable and the findings correlated; such results would be significant for understanding the causes of profitability in individual firms. For instance, if the best-profit firm headed the table as an innovator and was low down the lists for all other factors it would be a reasonable inference that its capacity for innovation was a vital element in its prosperity. The lack of sufficient individual studies within a single industry rules out this approach at present.

For many reasons, such as differences in market structure and technology, to name but two, the influences on profitability will vary markedly from industry to industry. In iron and steel, one might expect a number of factors to have been historically important. The choice of these is derived from empirical generalisation about the character of the industry and from *a priori* reasoning. The influences are:—

(i)   Locational advantages. Because raw material inputs are large
      and transport costs have been an important item in total costs
      it is probable that the siting of plant in relation to raw
      material supplies has been a significant element in the capacity
      of a steel firm to make a profit. Also, market orientation has
      been important since demand was concentrated within certain
      sectors of the economy which in turn were not uniformly
      dispersed. This view is supported by the industry's history
      since extensive shifts in location have occurred more often
      than in most other industries.

(ii) A high rate of technical progress. Comparative studies of the
      steel industry in different countries have usually suggested
      technical progressiveness as an indicator of relative success.
      How justified this view is it is difficult to say. But over a
      long period of time the industry has on several occasions been
      transformed by revolutionary technological changes, and at
      least some of the pioneers of innovations must have found
      them profitable. Another point is that the production of steel
      is not one or two processes but many involving the use of
      several raw materials, and economies, particularly in fuel,
      are gained by linking one stage of production with another.
      Technical refinements in one stage of production may lead
      to substantial economies or give rise to further technical
      improvements in another. Technical progress may thus be
      cumulative, resulting in larger 'pay-offs' than might appear
      on first sight.

(iii) Monopoly power. This is, of course, a potential cause of high
      profits in every industry, but there are at least two reasons why
      it might be especially important in iron and steel. Firstly,
      the capital costs of constructing an economical steel plant,
      even in the nineteenth century, may have been so high as to
      form a sizable barrier to new entry. Secondly, because iron
      and steel products are, in general, intermediate goods the
      price elasticity of demand for iron and steel is probably low.
      In times of high activity in the steel-consuming industries the
      scope for the exercise of monopoly power by steelmakers will
      be great.

(iv) Economies of scale. The steel industry lends itself to a small
      number of plants each of large size. In modern times the
      capacity of a plant which will operate efficiently has to be
      very large.[8] In the nineteenth century the optimum plant size
      was, of course, much smaller, but because few industries were
      operating on a large scale the steel industry ranked very high
      in the list of industries where economies of scale were

significant. For instance, steel firms in the late nineteenth century were able to exploit some of the gains from closer integration of different sections of the works.

The evidence suggests that none of these factors can account for Consett's prosperity before 1914. The location of the works was not particularly suited to the production of iron and steel. The original Derwent Iron Co. had been set up in 1840 to exploit local ironstone deposits but even by 1849 the costs of working these were too high for economical production, and Cleveland ore had to be brought from more than fifty miles away. In 1852 the company ceased to work the local supply altogether. The siting of the plant on the Durham coalfield ensured the essential supply of good coking coal, and Sir David Dale (who was closely associated with the company for almost fifty years) believed that its prosperity rested on the proximity of this supply of good fuel. But there were many other possible sites equally well placed for fuel supplies, yet nearer to the coast to cut down carriage costs on imported ore (imports became large after the 1860 and 1870s). It is significant that all the other firms in the North East supplying the shipbuilding industry were located on the coast itself. In 1869 Consett's 'isolated position was alleged to be fatal to it being any other than an ordinary coal-producing establishment' by 'an eminent authority in the iron trade'.[9]

On the existing transport system the works were about 32 miles from the coast. In the 1880s the North Eastern Railway's freight rates for iron ore were about 1d. per ton-mile making a considerable difference to the cost of Bilbao ore, priced about 7s. per ton f.o.b. at Bilbao.[10] Consett's location was regarded as so disadvantageous that the company from time to time considered the possibility of moving the whole works to the coast. In 1899 for example, when the company was building shipping wharves on the Tyne at Derwenthaugh, it was stated that 'rumours even go so far as to say the Tyneside development means the ultimate abolition of the Co.'s Consett premises, and their total transference to Derwenthaugh'.[11] The proposal was repeatedly discussed in later years but nothing came of it, apart from the acquisition of the derelict Palmer shipyards for the purpose of building a rolling mill at Jarrow in the late 1930s. A shift in location would have been economical but other considerations prevailed, the foremost probably being the company's feeling of responsibility for the town of Consett and its inhabitants.

It is generally assumed that high profits accrue to the most technically efficient firms, and that pioneers in innovation reap the rewards for their enterprise. The experience of this very prosperous firm does not confirm this view, as Consett was rarely in the van of technical progress. The company was cautious in switching from iron to steelmaking. Only in 1880 was £10,000 experimental expenditure laid aside for steelmaking, and not until June 1883 were the first steel furnaces tested. This was long after steel production had been adopted in South Wales (in the 1860s) and in the North East itself (Bolckow Vaughan's decided to go in for steel in 1871). Nevertheless, Consett were in the lead in substituting steel for iron plates in the North East, by the late 1880s steel plates production exceeded that of iron, and by 1890 the company had built 18 steel smelting furnaces with a capacity of 4,000 tons per week.

Consett adopted the Siemens open hearth process, and never turned to the more recent innovations such as basic Bessemer steel. This was reasonable, since the firm's main customers — the shipbuilders — refused to use basic Bessemer steel, and Consett's interests in Spanish hematite ores would have prevented adoption of basic Bessemer steelmaking even if desired. A similar show of caution was in evidence early in this century when Consett built coke oven by-product plants at the end of the first decade, years after a boom in the building of these plants (concentrated between 1904 and 1908); a possible explanation of this delay was that in the earlier period the company's energies were devoted to blast furnace construction. In the half century of this study Consett was responsible for no major innovation, and the first instance of Consett leading the British industry technically was during the major reconstruction of the early 1920s when batteries of American type ovens were installed; no ovens of this type were installed by other British firms until 1928-9.[12]

This does not mean that the company was technically backward. The plant was always kept up to date by periodic reconstruction and the replacement of obsolete equipment; in 1890 output per furnace was higher than elsewhere in England. In the early 1890s the Consett steelworks were modern enough to be visited by German experts.[13] William Jenkins, general manager from 1869 to 1894, kept in touch with the latest technical developments. Before the switch to steel he visited several steel plate works before perfecting his plans. His letters reveal several instances when he wrote to other firms enquiring about their experience with new techniques.[14] He sometimes tried new devices himself. In 1892, for example, he tried a new steam jet patent but rejected it on technical grounds after three months trial.[15] On another occasion Jenkins had two men down in the works with a technical device for improving the performance of shears in the plate mill. He was unable to give it an extensive trial because this would have necessitated a check to the output of plates, but he referred it to the Dowlais steelworks where new plate mills were being laid down.[16] Before the major reconstruction of 1903-9 the General Manager George Ainsworth and the Chief Engineer James Scott toured the United States to examine the most up-to-date American practice, and an American blast furnace engineer was consulted during the reconstruction. All this does not suggest a firm slumbering peacefully in a backwater and out of touch with modern technology, but neither does it give the impression of a daring pioneer innovator. Broadly speaking, Consett was content to keep its plant efficient enough to produce steel competitively, was satisfied to let other companies take the risks (and the potential profit) associated with revolutionary new ideas, and was happy to wait until these were tried and tested before adopting them. Particularly in the Jenkins' era, the company left development to the dictates of demand rather than trying to lead the market. Jenkins himself was much more concerned with the commercially profitable than the technically possible. It is reasonable to conclude that Consett Iron Co. was average rather than exceptional in regard to technical progress.

Is there any evidence to suggest that Consett's prosperity followed from the exercise of monopoly power? Obviously, control of a sizable share of the market is a necessary but not sufficient condition for the exercise of such power. For one thing, the term 'market' is subject to different definitions. What share of the market gives rise to the possibility of monopolistic control is arbitrary (varying under different conditions and for different products), but here it is convenient to take the Monopolies Commission criterion of one third of the total market as the minimum limit. The maximum share of British steel output held by Consett was 7.1 per cent in 1894, and generally Consett's share was much lower than this. It grew from .02 per cent in 1883 (the first year of steel production at Consett) to 4.3 per cent in 1889, then averaged 5½-6 per cent in the 1890s, 5 per cent in the 1900s and 4.2 per cent between 1910 and 1914. These figures are not conclusive, however, for one might argue that the question of a regional monopoly or monopoly of particular products is more relevant. But the company's share in these markets fell below a monopoly share. For example, in 1886 Consett produced 35 per cent of open hearth steel output in the North East (44,000 out of 124,000 tons), but the district also produced 399,000 tons of Bessemer steel. Consett specialised in products for the shipbuilding industry, particularly plates. If one makes the very generous assumption that all Consett output went into shipbuilding, the firm's production as a proportion of steel consumption by the shipbuilding industry never rose to

30 per cent (at its peak in 1897, 1909, and 1910 the proportion was 28.9 per cent, 28.3 per cent and 28.6 per cent respectively, and the average between 1890 and 1914 stood around 22-23 per cent). This overstates Consett's contribution to shipbuilding, since ship plates were by no means her sole product; in 1890 for instance, plates amounted to three-quarters of the output of finished goods.

The one remaining possibility is that Consett's share of plates production *in the North East* might have been high enough to give the firm a regional monopoly in this line of business. Since Tyne shipbuilding accounted for little more than one-fifth of UK output, it was theoretically possible for Consett to have a full monopoly here. For this to be so, it would be necessary to assume that there were no other plate producers in the area and no interchange of products between plate producers in different districts. Neither of these assumptions is tenable. According to the 1907 *Census of Production* there were six producers of plates in the North East. Consett sold plates extensively in other areas, particularly on the Clyde,[17] and producers in other districts sold on the Tyne. Even in the early period before the rapid expansion of some of the important North East steel firms Consett's share of iron plates produced in the North of England was modest; in 1883 111,000 out of 440,000 tons. Finally, Jenkins' letters do not give the impression that Consett was a price leader in any of the products in which the firm dealt. In April 1887 he wrote: 'There seems to be a disposition on the part of the East Coast makers to sell at lower prices and we must do the best to get the best prices we can, consistent with keeping work for our mills'.[18] A few months later he lamented: 'There does not seem to me to be much spirit in our pig iron business or in our finished steel and iron plates. Some people must be competing very stiffly with Consett in pigs'.[19] In a letter to his Chairman, David Dale, in 1893 he admitted that Consett was being undersold by Colvilles.[20] Consett's relatively small share of the market and the repeated grumbles of its managers about keen competition from other firms belie any suggestion that the company's prosperity could have been due to monopoly power.

As for economies of scale, it is difficult to draw a firm conclusion because of the shortage of evidence. The lack of costing information makes it impossible to work out the trend of costs for Consett Iron Co. as the scale of output rose. But although large the company's works were by no means the largest, and there were other firms which produced on a larger scale yet earned much lower profits. In view of this, it is reasonable to infer that although Consett may have gained economies of scale as output expanded in this period the firm did not benefit from economy of scale advantages denied to all other firms. Moreover, the large scale producer rarely managed to reap the full benefit from economies of scale. For in periods of high demand when he might work to full capacity, the gains from technical efficiency were partly offset by having to pay more for scarce labour.

Having rejected the above possibilities as major factors in Consett's high profitability, it is necessary to inquire into the real causes. A starting point may be found in contemporary explanations. A newspaper report in 1886 inquiring into the causes of Consett's increased profits in a period of depression stated: 'The secret is that it has a comparatively small capital, cheap minerals, and very good management. Its shareholders are judicious in creating large reserve funds and they deserve the prosperity they have achieved'.[21] A year later the same paper stated: 'It was cheaply bought, wisely developed, marches with the demand, and has excellent management'.[22] Another factor in its success was suggested to be the habit of 'improving the position of its capital out of revenue', and it was argued that its prosperity was to some extent a reflection of activity in shipbuilding.

The quality of management is generally accepted to be an important determinant of whether or not a firm is prosperous, and the experience of Consett Iron Co. provides no exception to this rule. The policy of the directors of the company was to leave the internal management of the firm to the general manager, and to interfere as little as possible. Consett had three general managers before 1914: Jonathan Priestman from 1864 to 1869 (he was joint managing director along with David Dale, but seemed to have sole day-to-day control), William Jenkins from 1869 to 1894 and George Ainsworth from 1894. David Dale, too, was an important figure as he was directly involved in an advisory capacity from the beginning, and was Chairman of the company from 1884 to his death in 1906. Of Jonathan Priestman little is known, especially about his ability to manage an ironworks. He was not trained as an ironmaster, his period of control was short and in 1869 he asked to be released from his connections with the company (he may have been pressed to resign). Certainly, Consett's profits were modest during his years of control, considering the limited competition the firm had to face in these early years. On the other hand, all the necessary reconstruction of obsolete plant which the company took over from its predecessor was carried out under him. But Jenkins' opinion of Priestman's ability was low; as he put it: 'with all due deference to Mr Priestman he was not the right man for to manage iron and steel works. There was no discredit to Mr Priestman in saying this, because if I went to manage a draper' shop, I would prove an utter failure'.[23]

William Jenkins was a professional manager, literally cradled in the atmosphere of an ironworks. He was born at Merthyr Tydvil in 1825, son of Thomas Jenkins, headmaster of the Dowlais schools. He entered Sir John Guest's Dowlais ironworks as a boy and worked through all the departments of the company until in 1852 when Sir John died he was appointed commercial manager. Jenkins was just one of many masters who had learnt their business at Dowlais; the others included John Vaughan, manager of the rolling mills of Losh, Wilson and Bell at Walker, E. Windsor Richards of Bolckow Vaughan and Ed. Williams, manager of Bolckow Vaughan's for a time but later proprietor of Linthorpe Ironworks. After long experience at Dowlais, Jenkins was persuaded to manage Consett in 1869 by David Dale (Sir David was later reported as saying that 'never had director of a company done a better day's work than he did that day'). It is perhaps significant that the firm's prosperity dates (to the year) from Jenkins' arrival at Consett. Jenkins was mainly responsible for the decision to specialise in plates after the collapse of the rail trade in 1876, and for the decision to go in for steel in 1883. As suggested above, he was interested in the latest technical developments without being over-anxious to adopt them until proved. He always kept the company's plant up-to-date, and gross capital expenditure on fixed assets over the quarter century of his management averaged £56,000 per year. Contemporaries regarded him as being particularly shrewd in two respects: in his judgment of what was profitable business, and in his choice of men for managerial posts. George Ainsworth was selected by Jenkins as blast furnace manager, and Ainsworth later proved a thorough and efficient general manager himself. As for his commercial shrewdness, his letters reveal a very keen interest in the prices ruling in the markets in which the company was interested. He would seek out the most detailed information about prices, then use this information to cut prices in times of low activity to keep the works going, or to discriminate between the prices quoted on the Clyde and on the Tyne in order to expand sales. He believed that long order books were the key to successful expansion, and worked hard to obtain orders even when working at capacity; the need to fulfil long-standing orders is one explanation of Consett's stability of output even in depression periods. He tried to cut costs by selling direct to regular customers and bypassing the merchants, but his attempts were sometimes thwarted as in 1892 when the Barrow Shipbuilding Co. insisted on placing their order through the merchants as usual.[24] His wages policy was always based on the most complete information obtainable from other firms. For example, in one day in 1887 he wrote to Bolckow Vaughan asking for suggestions on how to meet wage demands from steel melters, and wrote to Colvilles and to the Steel Co. of Scotland asking for details of the wage increases they had just granted.[25] On this occasion he decided that the wage claims were justifiable, and followed the line set by the Clyde firms. This was typical of him; in his dealings with labour he was always fair. In cases of stoppages he always refused to employ backleg labour. Yet his views were not exceptionally progressive. A typical nineteenth century liberal, he condemned Trade Unions as an interference with the liberty of the individual, and in general thought that labour was too highly paid.[26] Nevertheless, he would concede a wage claim if he thought that justice and the company's honour required it. Like many other nineteenth century industrialists, he did not confine his activities to the management of the works but was a great paternalist and played an important role in running the town. For seventeen years Chairman of Consett Local Board, the company under him was the dominant force in the provision of public amenities, building many hundreds of houses, schools and churches and even laying out a public park. His letters reveal a patriarchal concern with the welfare of his workers: making provision for a soup kitchen for distressed workers when the works were operating much below capacity; giving support to the establishment of Sciences and Art Classes; securing a series of extension lectures by Cambridge and Durham Universities (these had to be dropped later because of the poor response); supporting an applicant for the Consett post-mastership; arranging for holly to be delivered at Xmas to the infirmary (also built by the company); making arrangements for a children's tea on Jubilee Day in 1887, and for a miners' trip to the coast; dealing with the problem of a drunken and abusive woman tenant; ordering grate brushes for the infirmary. No problem was too minor or petty to figure in his letter books. Yet the demands of this paternalism do not seem to have interfered with the running of the steelworks. The contrast between the works as he found them in 1869 and when he retired a year before his death in 1895, and between the substantial profits made by Consett in the depressed years of the late 1870s, mid 1880s and early 1890s and the low profitability of other iron and steel concerns makes the conclusion that Jenkins was an important factor in the company's prosperity during this quarter century inescapable.

On the other hand, Consett Iron Co. was no one man show. The part played by David Dale should also be mentioned. David Dale (great nephew and namesake of the founder of the New Lanark cotton mills) was born in 1829, and acquired his early business training in the office of the Stockton and Darlington Railway. He later became secretary of the Middlesbrough and Guisborough Railway, and at 26 entered a partnership in a locomotive firm, the Shildon works. Many years later, he was to be appointed Managing Director of the North Eastern Railway, and in 1872 was made a director of Joseph Pease and Partners, the colliery and iron ore mining firm. From 1858, as a shareholder in the Northumberland and Durham District Bank and a creditor of the Derwent Iron Co., he became interested in the iron trade. He was a managing inspector during the transitional period after the collapse of the bank, Joint Managing Director from 1864 to 1873, a director of the company from the beginning and chairman from 1884 until his death in 1906. He also served on the board of Barrow Steelworks. Dale was the perfect complement to Jenkins, playing the role of financial adviser to Jenkins' man of business. The sound financial policy which the company pursued, placing regular and large sums of profit to reserve and caution in payment of dividends, owed much to his judgment. He was responsible for the choice of Jenkins as general manager in 1869, and was instrumental in setting up the Consett Spanish Ore Co. in 1872 to secure new regular ore supplies from Spain at a time when domestic hematite prices were soaring. His greatest service of all may have been within the field of industrial relations. He pioneered industrial arbitration and conciliation in the North of England, and was an acknowledged expert on labour problems, being Chairman of one section of the Royal Commission on Labour, 1891-95.

Of Jenkins' successor, George Ainsworth, little direct information is available. Three points are worthy of mention. Before his appointment, Ainsworth had served under Jenkins as sub-manager for a long period, and accumulated a great deal of experience. His ability was shown in the carrying through of the major reconstruction of 1903-09 which cost the company about £750,000, and was undertaken only after a thorough inspection of new works overseas. Most important of all, the firm's profitability shows no slackening off under his control; indeed, profits earned and dividends paid were on average higher than in the Jenkins' era. Admittedly, depressions after 1894 were not as serious as before, but even in bad years such as 1909 when profits generally fell, the level of profits and dividends paid remained high.

An undoubtedly important element in Consett's prosperity was the fact that the company was a backwardly integrated concern, and that this resulted in economies in raw material and fuel costs. Of course, backward integration was by no means exceptional in the iron and steel industry, but Consett went further in this than most other firms. From the very beginning the company was an extensive coal and coke producer (it was said of the old Derwent Iron Co. that it could mine coal at a cost equivalent to what other firms were paying in royalties alone), and from 1872 held a quarter share in a large profitable Spanish iron ore concern. The economies gained in raw material and fuel costs were considerable and important, for such costs form a sizeable proportion of total steelmaking costs. At the same time, flow of production was made easier by the more regular supplies resulting from control of raw material and fuel sources. Most important of all was that the company was spared for the most part the substantial increase in costs resulting from shortage of supplies in times of high demand.[27] In average years, the ownership of large coal mines and ore supplies might be a very marginal advantage as the price of coal, coke and iron ore on the open market might approximate to the cost of these materials to Consett from its own sources, but in boom periods the free market price would surge forward making a substantial difference to production costs. The ability to keep costs down may be as vital a factor as expanding sales. In addition, because of external sales of coal the diversification resulting from the coal producing capacity of Consett stabilised the firm's profits. The fluctations in demand for coal and coke on the one hand and pig iron and steel on the other were not of exactly the same periodicity, so that expansion in one line of activity sometimes relieved depression in another. Thus in 1873 boom conditions in the coal industry relieved a slight weakening in the market for iron rails.

The fuel ouput of Consett Iron Co. was considerable throughout this period. Coal output rose from some 750,000 tons per annum to 1,500,000 tons (in 1909-10 for example, *sales* of coal reached a record of 1,100,000 tons), while coke output ran consistently around half this level. Of the coke produced, about half was consumed in the steelworks and the rest sold, much of it abroad. In return for the ore obtained, the company annually sent some 50,000 tons of coke to Spain. Expanding exports required periodic reconstruction of the company's shipping facilities, for instance, the remodelling and extension of Derwenthaugh Quay in 1897 and again in 1911. In addition, the firm produced other products, such as fire bricks (capacity for 50,000 per week in the early 1870s) and coke by-products. In 1911 a by-product recovery plant was installed near one of the collieries at Templetown for extracting crude benzol, and two years later another plant was erected at Langley Park, producing tar and sulphate of ammonia as well as benzol.

Assurance of adequate coal and coke supplies appears to have been a continuous benefit to Consett. In spite of heavy demands on the coal produced, dwindling resources were avoided by an energetic policy of acquiring new royalties and opening up new mines. Throughout this period the company's coalfields were being exhausted at an average rate of over a million tons of coal per annum, but this had no adverse effects on the company's supply position. In the 1870s and 1880s more than £200,000 were spent on the acquisition of new coalfields.

The other aspect of Consett's backward integration, the interests in Spanish ore mines, was again not unusual, for ownership of foreign ore mines by British firms was common in the late nineteenth and early twentieth centuries; in fact, fully one-half of imported ore came from such mines in 1903. But Consett was involved at a very early stage and in the most important area of supply — the Bilbao district of Spain (of 5½ million tons of iron ore imported into the UK in 1901, four-fifths came from this area). In the 1860s Consett had used mainly hematite, drawing its supplies from Cleveland (the Derwent Iron Co. had owned mines in this area from 1851, but these had been disposed of when the new company was formed), the North West and to a lesser extent from Spain. The maintenance of supplies of high quality hematite was vital for Consett, and the carriage costs from Cleveland were not inconsiderable. At the beginning of the 1870s the price of Cumberland hematite was fluctuating violently, mostly in an upward direction, mainly because of growing demands for this ore for the Bessemer steel trade (the annual average price of Cumberland hematite rose from 12s. 1d. per ton in 1870 to 30s. 3d. per ton in 1873). David Dale realised the scope offered from obtaining a foothold in the market for Spanish supplies, and in 1872 Consett united with three other firms (the Dowlais Iron Co. (note the link with Jenkins), Krupps of Essen and the Ybarra Co. of Spain) in acquiring mines at Bilbao and building the necessary railways and wharves under the title of the Orconera Iron Ore Co. This venture required an outlay of £200,000, each party contributing one-quarter. The ore mined was to be apportioned between the four firms, and any surplus sold. Consett's articles of association did not permit it to hold a direct interest in any other company, so a new company, the Consett Spanish Ore Co., was established. The decision to move into foreign ore mines was not immediately profitable for it took some years before regular supplies could be tranported from Bilbao to Consett. Meanwhile, the market for hematite weakened drastically, and after 1875 there was a remarkable drop in hematite prices. This was due to the effect of new sources of supply, particularly Spain, becoming important at a time when the pressure on home demand was relieved by the development of basic steel production. By 1877 the average price of Cumberland hematite was down to 12s. 1d. per ton, though it had risen again to 23s. 6d. in 1880. When prices were high, however, the company gained, since they were supplied with ore by the Orconera Co. under contract 'at a small unalterable rate of profit'. This assured a supply 'at a moderate price' and prevented high profits, except on the surplus not required by the interested companies. Regular supplied were not received from Orconera until 1876 because of civil war in Northern Spain, but the delay did not cause the company much difficulty as large stocks of hematite had been accumulated at Consett.

The Company was very satisfied with the purchase. Jenkins visited Bilbao in 1877 and reported that the ore was of the best quality. The railway and docking facilities were proving to be more expensive than the original estimates, but were well constructed. Jenkins' conclusion was that 'the property is a valuable one' and would 'ultimately yield a fair return'. In that year 26,400 tons of ore were sent from Orconera to Consett; by 1880 the output of the mines totalled 750,000 tons, almost all of it being supplied to the interested firms. From about this time Consett Spanish Ore Co. began to reap dividends from its shares in Spain. The 10 per cent dividend of 1881 rose to 42½ per cent in 1886, and high dividends were maintained up to the First World War; after 1886 the lowest paid was 37½ per cent (in 1889), and dividends of 50 per cent or more were paid in 19 of the 25 years, 1890-1914. The highest paid was 75 per cent in 1904. The accumulated funds of Consett Spanish Ore Co. built up from these large dividends became in effect a long-term low interest loan to the parent company, a factor reducing the need for bank borrowing. In November 1896 Orconera Iron Ore Co. extended its interests by acquiring a number of mines near Santander, complete with railways, staithes, washing plant, etc. The output of the new mines was modest (about 1500 tons per week), but was later expanded substantially. No increase of capital was required for this venture.

Consett relied on the Orconera Co. for almost all its Spanish supplies, and the quantity bought on the open market at Bilbao over the 12 years 1880-91 amounted to a mere 189,129 tons. Other ore imported to Consett came from Africa and Elba rather than from Spain.[28] The happy experience with the Orconera Co. encouraged Consett to extend its foreign ore interests. In 1902 the company invested in an ore concern in Norway, and in 1908 joined a syndicate to work ore in Algeria. Although both these investments failed, it is interesting to note that Consett's stated justification for these ventures was the desirability that a company using half a million tons of ore yearly should be independent of market fluctuations.

Consett's consistently sound financial position aided the company's prosperity. To some extent, the soundness of its finance *reflected* the firm's early profitability. A company earning large profits which can be used for expansion or set aside for security is much less likely to get into debt to the banks or to have any required capital reconstruction held up because of currently depressed sales. But there was more to it than this. A significant contribution in the early years was the fact that the works were purchased so cheaply. Consett was thus spared the burden of over-capitalization which dragged down so many other firms in the iron and steel industry. The original works and estates of the Derwent and Consett Iron Co. were bought for the paltry sum of £295,318 8s. (including £25,000 for an affiliated company, the Bishopwearmouth Ironworks at Sunderland). The properties purchased included 18 blast furnaces with blowing engines, plate, rail, angle and bar mills with puddling furnaces (an annual capacity of 150,000 tons of pig iron and 40-50,000 tons of finished iron), coke ovens, 500 acres of freehold land, more than 1,000 freehold cottages, and Managers' houses and offices. The property would not have been bought so cheaply had it not been for the circumstances surrounding the purchase; namely, that the alternative was for the works to be broken up and for Consett to become a 'ghost town', and the value of the works would then have been limited to the scrap value of the plant and equipment. Not that the purchase was quite the bargain it seemed at first sight, for much of the plant was obsolete and urgent reconstruction was required. This was carried out in the first few years of the firm's existence. The Bishopwearmouth works being unprofitable were soon disposed of, and in 1866, 6,000 additional £10 shares were created in order to buy the nearby Shotley Bridge works for £55,000. This consisted of 3 plate mills, puddling mills and most important of all a colliery nearer to Consett than the company's own. The original blast furnaces had been located on three different sites, but those at Crookhall were scrapped and new ones built at Consett. By 1870, in fact, all the old plant had been pulled down and new works were under construction.

The capacity to make large profits does not necessarily lead to sound finance; much depends on the kind of financial policy which the firm pursues. Consett's dividend policy was always conservative, *if judged by contemporary standards.*[29] Only in very depressed periods (such as the early 1890s) was more than 90 per cent of the profit distributed in the hope that a reasonable dividend might help to stabilise Consett's shares value. A distribution of between 60 per cent and 80 per cent of profits was much more common. Sizeable sums were always placed on one side to finance future expansion. Even as early as 1868 the directors' report stated that 'it will probably be prudent to continue to place to Current Account from time to time Special Expenditure on improvements and additions'. Current expenditure on reconstruction and the creation and building up of a reserve fund were given priority over the distribution of dividends. This meant that the company only very rarely had to create additional capital, or to borrow extensively from the banks (the contrast between Consett and the old Derwent Iron Co. could not have been sharper in this respect). The only case of substantial outside borrowing was between 1876 and 1883 when the directors were granted powers to borrow up to £250,000, but the circumstances were exceptional as this was a period of relative depression and high capital expenditure. Even this power was never fully exercised. Ignoring capitalisation issues, the nominal share capital was increased on comparatively few occasions. The original £400,000 shares were only three-quarters paid up. The capital was increased in 1866 (as noted above) to purchase Shotley Bridge works and new coal royalties, in 1886 by £264,000 to help finance extensions to the new steelworks, and in 1891 by £500,000 of 8 per cent preference shares which were allotted mainly to members of the company (see Table 2).

The main advantage accruing to the company from its sound financial position was the fact that it was able to keep its plant up-to-date very easily without having to look around for outside sources of finance. To the extent that Consett needed to borrow capital this could be obtained without difficulty. The firm's stable financial situation also reduced the cost of borrowing: in 1881 for example, the directors were able to get the rate of interest on bonds reduced from the customary 4½ per cent to 4 per cent. The directors' reports repeatedly gave supporting evidence to this view of Consett's financial position. Even in the gloomy year of 1879 the directors reported that the 'company's financial position is not merely thoroughly sound but easy, and your directors have been able to assure enquiring shareholders that no call is at all likely to be made'. The Company added to its reserve even in depressed years such as 1886, and adhered to its cautious policies in years of great prosperity. In 1900, the year of greatest absolute profit in this period, it was announced that appropriation was to be 'governed by the same considerations as in the past have contributed to the stability and status of the company, viz. dividends proportionate to profit after prudent reserves have been made' (the percentage of profit distributed that year was 61.7). On the rare occasions when, in order to pay a reasonable dividend, the company had to draw on what it would have preferred to set aside for other purposes deficiencies were later made up; thus in the period 1891-95 an average distribution of over 90 per cent was paid but by 1900 reserves had been built up again. In 1898 alone £100,000 was transferred to a Reserve Fund. The company's reserves were so large relative to the demands upon them that by the turn of the century Consett had to look around for long-term investment to make profitable use of its idle funds; in 1900 for instance, an investment of £150,000 was made in Consols. That the investors appreciated the soundness of Consett's finances can be seen from the variations in the gross yield of the company's shares. After a decade of violent fluctuations, the percentage gross yield settled to exceptional stability after 1875, an indication perhaps that the company had 'arrived' as a sound and secure investment in the share market. When Jenkins remarked in 1888 that 'there was no ironmaking concern he knew which occupied such a favourable condition in the share market',[30] he was being more accurate than immodest.

Consett specialised in certain lines of business, and this was possibly another factor in the firm's prosperity. For most of this period the bulk of the finished products turned out consisted of ships' plates. This specialisation gave Consett competitive advantages over firms of a similar size producing a wide range of products and over small plate producers. In 1875 Consett was described as the largest iron plate works in the world; by 1887 (despite the late start in steel production) it was already the largest steel plate producing works in England. This lead in plate production gave Consett plates a world-wide reputation, and the export market was consequently sizeable, Consett plates being exported all over the world (even as far as the Far East — India, Australasia and China). The company's specialisation on plates production was not uniformly high throughout this fifty year period. The Derwent Iron Co. had produced plates in the 1850s, but the production of rails was also large. In the first thirteen years of the new company's existence rail output doubled, reaching a level fo 2,000 tons a week in boom periods. But in 1876 the rail trade collapsed and Consett began to rely increasingly on plates. Both the collapse and the substitution of plates for rails were rapid. In the north of England as a whole rails production in 1873 totalled 324,400 tons and plates production 165,600 tons; by 1877 the output of rails had slumped to 36,800 tons while the output of plates had risen to 214,700 tons.

At Consett already in 1877 plates capacity stood around 1200-1300 tons a week compared with a capacity of 600-800 tons for rails, and over the next few years the firm devoted almost its entire plant to making plates. The switch from iron to steel plates was almost as rapid. Consett's capacity for iron plates in 1882 was around 1,900 tons per week. Then in 1883 the company went in for steel. By 1887 more steel than iron plates were produced (1,000 as against 755 tons per week), and by 1890 steel plates capacity had risen to 2,500 tons a week and iron plates capacity fallen to 500 tons. Although two iron plate mills were still in use in 1892, by the following year no iron plates were being made.

The company was by no means entirely dependent on the demand for plates. A wide and expanding range of goods was produced, from angles to steel pit props. Moreover, the company did not sell only finished products. About 50 per cent of the coal and coke produced was sold, and pig iron was disposed of in substantial quantities mainly to mills and forges in the vicinity. The danger of specialisation is excessive instability. Consett avoided this on the whole because of the shipbuilding industry's steady growth through the late nineteenth and early twentieth centuries. In spite of the fact that Consett's profitability was affected by other circumstances such as the state of the coal and iron industries, the most important factor in year-to-year variations seems to have been the level of activity in shipbuilding. This can be seen by comparing changes in the amount of annual profit with changes in the value of new mercantile construction over the period 1870-1914 (see graph). The fluctuations in the two series show a remarkable degree of synchronisation. This is particularly true in regard to periodicity; in almost every case shipbuilding output and Consett's profits moved in the same direction at the same time. It is not as easy to generalise about the amplitude of the cycles. The booms in the firm's profits were usually more intense than the booms in shipbuilding construction, perhaps reflecting the tendency for steel prices to soar in periods of high demand. The main exception to this was in 1882 and 1883 when there was a great boom in shipbuilding in which Consett did not fully share, primarily because the projected transfer from iron to steel temporarily checked the firm's output.

There are grounds for thinking that industrial relations at Consett were rather better than at most other steelworks, and this too might have played a role in the firm's prosperity. In the very early years the relations between managers and workmen were not good. Strikes were fairly frequent, the labour force was large and to some extent migratory (at this time Consett employed 5-6,000 men, fully

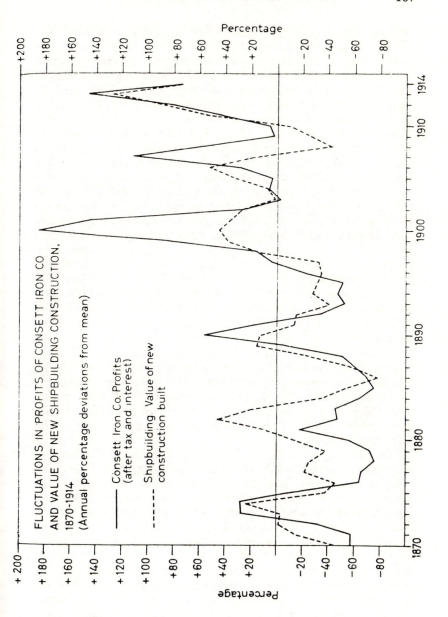

Percentage

FLUCTUATIONS IN PROFITS OF CONSETT IRON CO
AND VALUE OF NEW SHIPBUILDING CONSTRUCTION.
1870-1914
(Annual percentage deviations from mean)

———— Consett Iron Co. Profits
        (after tax and interest)

- - - - Shipbuilding. Value of new
        construction built

Percentage

half of whom were Irish), and the first generation of workers was described in contemporary reports as 'a rough lot'. Later, the position was much improved. All strikes were not avoided, especially those organised at the regional or national level in the coal mining section (such as the three months strike of Durham miners in 1892 or the national strike of miners in March-April 1912). But there is little evidence of any serious internal trouble, a marked contrast with many other steel firms which were often plagued by strikes in this period. The major explanation of this better performance in the field of industrial relations is in terms of the personalities involved, particularly that the pioneers of arbitration and conciliation were linked with Consett. David Dale, as President of the North of England Board of Arbitration and Conciliation set up for the iron industry in March 1869, was the key figure in the spread of arbitration in the North of England. After he resigned as President in 1875, he often acted as Arbitrator. His arbitrations were scrupulously fair, and he often decided in favour of the men. Dale was also responsible for drawing up the sliding scale of October 1871 which operated intermittently throughout this period, though in various revised forms. On the employees' side the pioneer of arbitration was John Kane, the leader of the Amalgamated Ironworkers Union which chiefly represented ironworkers in the Midlands and the North-East. He had been pressing for a conciliation board for at least five years before its establishment, and he served as its secretary until his death in 1876. The interesting point is that Kane had originally been a worker in the Consett works. That the pioneers of methods of conciliation on both the management and union sides were connected with Consett is unlikely to be mere coincidence.

The other aspect of the good industrial relations at Consett was the character and views of William Jenkins. The orthodoxy of his views on trade unions has been noted, and he was very often firm in his dealings with the men. For example, in a dispute with the steel melters in 1887 he wrote: 'my attitude therefore is firmness with no relaxation whatever! The men talk again of arbitration, but we turn a deaf ear to this'.[31] On another occasion he wrote to a fellow employer: 'It is a pity that you do not unite with the other employers in aiming at something like strength on the part of the employers to meet the superior wisdom and strength of the operatives themselves'.[32] This last reference suggests an attitude of respect towards the men rather than stubborn obstinacy. Jenkins had a keen sense of justice and fairmindedness. He willingly granted wage increases when conditions demanded them, or when steel makers in other areas had already moved, or when a reduction had been agreed to in a previous spell of bad trade which had passed. His letters reveal a close knowledge of the workmen at Consett, and aspects of his paternalism were mentioned earlier. Strength and consistency if he were in the right and the feeling that the men always knew where they stood with him combined with fairness, sympathy and an interest in their welfare make him, in the opinion of contemporaries, 'one of the most lenient masters to be found in the North'.

A final point of interest is that Consett was never, in a real sense, a family firm. Of course, family connections did exist between members of the firm at different periods of time — in the early days the Priestmans, father and son, several members of the Fenwick and Henderson families, Sir David Dale and his son. But never in the firm's history did one family have control of the firm. Most of those who played leading roles in the firm's development were either professional managers or men with active business interests outside the firm. Very few cases, if any, can be found of men with a place in the firm which they owed simply to being the sons of their fathers. Too many examples of degeneracy in family firms are known to rule out this fact as a possible influence on the firm's prosperity. A company which, from the outset, owes its responsibility to a body of shareholders is likely to make the right decisions more often than a company whose first obligations are to the dynastic and social ambitions of one family.

It is impossible to assess the relative importance of these influences on the profitability of Consett Iron Co. Some were almost accidental, such as the low capitalisation resulting from the cheap purchase price and the specialisation on products for shipbuilding — an obvious choice to be made by a firm long producing rails and plates once the rail trade had collapsed. But many called for positive managerial decisions: the early acquisition of ore interests in Spain which proved such a vital factor in raw material economies, for example, or the prudent financial policy and the more than adequate provision for re-equipment of plant which followed from it. It may seem a banal conclusion to state that everything depends upon the quality of the management, but in this case there is some justification for the view that the prosperity of Consett Iron Co. was built upon the commercial sense of William Jenkins and the sound financial advice of David Dale. This conclusion is of more than limited significance. When comparing the performances of the British and foreign steel industries in the late nineteenth century, it is fashionable to ascribe the slower rate of growth in the home industry to a failure of British enterprise. Here, at least, is one case which does not support this view. It appears that too many of the steel industry's observers have taken a perverse delight in totting up the failures and ignoring the successes. Dare we speculate that the generalisations will require modification when we have more studies of individual firms?

TABLE 1

Consett Iron Co. — Profits 1864-1914

Year	Profit per year (after tax and interest) £	Per Cent of Profit Distributed (a)	Ordinary Dividend Rate per cent p.a.	Gross yield on ordinary shares per cent (b)	Profit on capital employed per cent (c)
1864	21,062	66.0	9⅓	—	9.2
1865	39,096	76.7	10⅓	8.9	12.0
1866	35,872	66.8	10	8.0	10.9
1867	31,605	74.2	7½	6.9	8.9
1868	38,413	67.2	7½	6.4	10.4
1869	39,786	65.0	7½	6.7	10.8
1870	101,791	58.4	17⅕	12.0	24.5
1871	101,208	45.5	13⅓	7.6	23.5
1872	160,194	39.5	18⅓	7.9	31.7
1873	302,505	73.0	53⅓	17.8	49.2
1874	304,128	81.7	60	18.6	47.1
1875	215,102	77.0	40	12.9	33.7
1876	86,257	72.0	15	5.9	13.9
1877	83,289	74.6	15	6.0	12.9
1878	57,996	89.2	12½	5.3	9.3
1879	55,995	73.9	10	4.6	8.9
1880	104,497	79.2	20	6.4	15.6
1881	195,071	75.5	26⅔	7.8	27.1
1882	128,495	85.9	20	5.6	18.9
1883	130,219	77.7	18⅓	5.6	18.5
1884	85,631	86.0	13⅓	5.6	11.8
1885	60,123	91.8	10	4.2	8.6
1886	72,502	76.1	10	4.5	9.9
1887	95.752	69.2	11⅓	4.8	11.9
1888	117,746	70.2	13⅓	5.2	13.5
1889	220,389	59.7	20	6.0	24.8
1890	366,410	63.2	33⅓	8.9	38.6
1891	275,689	86.8	31⅔	7.8	26.4
1892	157,623	93.3	16⅓	4.8	14.3
1893	110,971	96.9	10	3.7	8.8
1894	124,786	91.8	10	3.6	9.5
1895	114,973	93.5	9	3.3	8.6
1896	182,383	76.8	13⅓	4.6	13.2
1897	246,771	77.0	20	6.1	17.4
1898	272,885	69.6	20	5.2	18.5
1899	433,900	65.8	33⅓	6.8	29.0

TABLE 1 (continued)

Consett Iron Co. — Profits 1864-1914

Year	Profit per year (after tax and interest) £	Per Cent of Profit Distributed (a)	Ordinary Dividend Rate per cent p.a.	Gross yield on ordinary shares per cent (b)	Profit on capital employed per cent (c)
1900	672,585	61.7	50	9.4	38.7
1901	575,088	72.2	50	11.0	30.5
1902	299,996	88.3	30	6.8	15.8
1903	231,324	98.4	25	6.4	12.4
1904	250,067	91.0	25	6.5	13.5
1905	244,825	92.9	25	5.9	13.6
1906	303,181	81.2	27½	5.9	17.0
1907	498,468	68.2	40	8.2	27.5
1908	374,019	77.5	33⅓	6.9	20.8
1909	243,579	78.0	20	4.5	13.6
1910	221,326	94.3	22½	5.4	12.4
1911	338,501	85.7	33⅓	7.4	18.6
1912	427,007	88.4	45	9.2	24.0
1913	581,998	84.2	60	11.4	32.1
1914	408,014	77.0	30	7.5	22.6

(a) Profit distributed after 1894 includes £40,000 per annum as dividends on £500,000 of 8 per cent preference shares (during the period 1891-94 when the shares were in the process of being paid up smaller sums were distributed).

(b) This is calculated by comparing the dividend paid for the company's financial year (ending June 30) with the Stock Exchange middle price on, or nearest to, June 30 of each year.

(c) This column compares profit earned (including interest payable) with the capital employed (the total of share capital, reserves, long-term loans and undistributed Profit). This is a much more meaningful measure of profitability than comparing profit earned with the company's issued share capital. For example, in a company such as this, where many additions to share capital were made by means of capitalization (or bonus) issues from reserves built up from past profits, any measure of profitability usuing share capital as the basis makes year-to-year comparisons misleading, especially immediately before and after each capitalization issue. Moreover, the measure adopted avoids the problem of whether or not preference share capital, because the returns on such shares are limited to a fixed percentage, should be treated in the same way as ordinary share capital.

TABLE 2

Consett Iron Co. — History of Capital Structure

		8 per cent Preference Share Capital Authorised, issued and fully paid (£)	Ordinary Share Capital Authorised and Issued. (a) (£)
1864-65	40,000 Ordinary Shares of £10 issued for cash		400,000
1867	6,000 Ordinary Shares of £10 issued for cash		460,000
1873	9,200 Ordinary Shares of £10 issued as a capitalisation of profits		552,000
1881	18,400 Ordinary Shares of £10 issued as a capitalisation of profits		736,000
1886-91	26,400 Ordinary Shares of £10 issued for cash		1,000,000
1891-94	100,000 Preference Shares of £5 issued for cash	500,000	1,000,000
1914	Preference and Ordinary Shares converted into shares of £1 each fully paid	500,000	1,000,000

(a) During the period 1864 to 1913 only £7.10.0 per share was called up on the Ordinary Shares. In spite of this some of the shares (3342 in 1881) were fully paid and in 1882 the company, under a capital reduction scheme, repaid to the holders of those shares the amount in advance of calls. In 1914 when the division of shares took place the company declared a bonus dividend of 5s per £1 Ordinary Share, the proceeds of which were used to pay up these shares.

The figures in the column represent, of course, the issued and not the paid up share capital.

NOTES

1 We should like to thank the Directors of Consett Iron Co. for their co-operation and, in particular, for their permission to quote from the letter books of William Jenkins.

2 As the Select Committee of 1858 into the 1857 crisis put it: 'It appears that the concern has been worked extremely badly; that it has never made any profits at all, even in the finest years for the ironmasters, and it has gone on absorbing the money of the bank unchecked by the directors', *Select Committee on the Operation of the Bank Act of 1844, and the Causes of the Recent Commercial Distress* (1857-8), xix, 50.

3 *Joint Stock Companies' Journal*, 7 November 1900.

4 *Northern Echo*, 30 April 1906.

5 See Table 1.

6 *Newcastle Daily Chronicle*, 5 August 1886 and 13 October 1887.

7 D. L. Burn, *Economic History of Steelmaking, 1867-1939* (1940), 81 and T. H. Burnham and G. O. Hoskins, *Iron and Steel in Britain, 1870-1930* (1943), 249.

8 An American survey of steelmakers in the 1950s suggested an efficient plant required a capacity of between one and two-and-a-half million tons. J. S. Bain, *Barriers to New Competition* (1956), 158, 236.

9 G. Neasham, *The History and Biography of West Durham* (1881), 38.

10 British Iron Trade Association, *Annual Statistical Report of the Home and Foreign Steel Industries in 1884* (1885), 10, 155, 178-9. The rate for carrying finished goods from the works to the ports averaged about 0.8d per ton-mile. Of course, it must be remembered that, because coal input per ton of iron bulked larger than ore input, location near to supplies of coal was more important than nearness to supplies of iron ore.

11 *Newcastle Daily Leader*, 1 July 1899.

12 Consett was the first ironworks, however, to install Whitwell's hot blast firebrick stoves in the blast furnace instead of the more usual cast iron stoves (in the period 1868 to 1872).

13 W. Jenkins to J. Scott (Engineer), 18 August 1892: 'I dislike bringing Germans here, expecting to see our new plant, but I fear I cannot escape letting this gentleman see the place when he comes'.

14 For example, W. Jenkins to A. Cooper, North Eastern Steelworks, 23 September 1892: 'You mentioned to me some weeks ago that you were about starting your vertical soaking furnace. Quite at your convenience can you kindly tell me what success you have had with it, and whether it is gas-heating or coal-heating. If it is in pretty good trim, would you have any objection to our Mr Parnaby coming down to see it'.

15 W. Jenkins to H. W. Hollis, 20 July 1892.

16 W. Jenkins to E. P. Martin, Dowlais, 15 November 1889.

17 W. Jenkins to A. D. Tolmie, Glasgow, 21 January 1887 and 29 April 1887.

18 W. Jenkins to A. D. Tolmie, 29 April 1887.

19 W. Jenkins to I. Williams, Middlesbrough, 17 June 1887.

20 W. Jenkins to D. Dale, Darlington, 9 October 1893.

21 *Newcastle Daily Chronicle*, 5 August 1886.

22 Ibid. 1 August 1887.

23 Reported in the *Consett Guardian*, 31 October 1890.

24 W. Jenkins to D. Dale, 26 July 1892.

25 25 January 1887.

26 W. Jenkins to C. W. C. Henderson, a director of the company, 5 May 1887: 'I quite agree with you that in the enormous competition going on in the country labour of all classes is too highly paid in relation to capital concerned'.

27 On the other hand, it faced the danger of being unable to buy cheaply in a slump. Consett did not suffer much from this disability.

28 W. Jenkins to D. Dale, 13 May 1892.

29 The qualification is important. Consett's dividend policy was cautious for the nineteenth century, but looks reckless to those accustomed to the mammoth proportions of profit retained by firms in the post 1945 era.

30 *Newcastle Daily Chronicle*, 20 August 1888.

31 W. Jenkins to D. Dale, 2 May 1887.

32 W. Jenkins to C. J. Bagley, 13 December 1889.

9

James Nasmyth and the Early Growth of Mechanical Engineering

A. E. Musson*

Credit is nowadays usually given to the Americans for the pioneering of standardised mass-production and assembly-line manufacture, and there is no doubt that from the mid-nineteenth century onwards they did take the lead in many aspects of mechanical engineering.[1] There is evidence, however, that in some fields they were preceded in the application of such methods by certain early British engineering firms. This is not surprising in view of the fact that these methods were made possible by the invention of automatic machine-tools, most of which were brought out in Britain in the late eighteenth and early nineteenth century.

This country, as is well known, led the world in the early years of the Industrial Revolution, in the development of new methods of manufacturing and working iron and in the production of steam engines and machinery for the growing factory system. The increasing demand for iron machinery could not have been met without a revolution in the methods of making machines, without the development, in other words, of mechanical engineering.[2] Most of the early machinery was made of wood and leather, later of cast iron, since the working of wrought iron was a labourious and costly hand process, using hammer, chisel, and file. The early 'engineers' were recruited from many trades — smiths, carpenters, iron-founders, locksmiths, clockmakers, and above all the versatile millwrights — all manual craftsmen, usually with experience of working with metals. It was impossible to get any very great accuracy in the manufacture of machines by manual methods. The terrible difficulties which Watt at first encountered in the making

* From *Economic History Review*, 2nd series, Vol. X (1957-58), pp. 121-7. Reprinted by permission of the editor of *Economic History Review* and the author. (An expanded version of this article appears in A. E. Musson, *Science and Technology in the Industrial Revolution* (Manchester University Press, Manchester), 1969, pp. 489-509. Ed.).

of his steam engines are well known.[3] 'Nearly everything had to be done by hand. The tools used were of a very imperfect kind. A few ill-constructed lathes with some drills and boring machines of a rude sort, constituted the principal furniture of the work-shop'.[4] Cylinders, pistons, and valves, however, required work of hitherto unattainable accuracy. Wilkinson's cylinder-boring machine solved one of the main problems, while a skilled labour force was gradually built up in the Soho Foundry to manufacture the more intricate machine parts.

Similar problems had to be faced in the manufacture of machinery for the iron, textile, and other industries. Each machine, like each screw or nut and bolt, was a separate piece of engineering; there could be no accurate standardisation, and parts were not inter-changeable. Indeed, it was often a most difficult job fitting together the parts of one machine and getting it to work.

This situation persisted into the first two decades of the nineteenth century. William Fairbairn stated that when he first came to Manchester, in 1814, 'the whole of the machinery was executed by hand. There were neither planing, slotting, nor shaping machines; and, with the exception of very imperfect lathes, and a few drills, the preparatory operations of construction were effected entirely by the hands of the workmen'.[5] James Nasmyth has left similar testimony.[6] 'Up to within the last thirty years', he wrote in 1841, 'nearly every part of a machine had to be made and finished . . . by mere manual labour; that is, on the dexterity of the *hand* of the workman, and the correctness of his *eye*, had we entirely to depend for accuracy and precision in the execution of such machinery as was then required; consequently, the enormous expense [as well as the inaccuracy] . . . proved a formidable barrier'. The progress of the Industrial Revolution, Nasmyth points out, was impeded by this 'almost entire dependence upon manual dexterity'.[7]

These problems were tackled by a number of brilliant engineers, led by Bramah, Maudslay, and Clement, all of London, which was at first pre-eminent in mechanical engineering. Maudslay, according to James Nasmyth and others, was the greatest of these pioneers. It was in his workshop that some of the leading figures in the second generation of mechanical engineers received their early training, including Roberts, Nasmyth, and Whitworth. These men, and others like William Fairbairn, established themselves in Manchester, which, with the rapid growth of the cotton industry and of railways, became perhaps the most important engineering area in Britain, producing not only textile machinery, but water wheels, steam engines, boilers, railway locomotives, machine tools, and a mass of miscellaneous engineering products.

These London and Manchester engineers gradually solved the problems of mechanising machine-making, inventing machines to make machines — self-acting or automatic machine-tools, such as lathes, planing machines, drilling machines, grooving, slotting, and paring machines, punching and shearing machines — which, as Nasmyth pointed out, made possible 'almost mathematical accuracy and precision' in the manufacture of machinery. The basic principle in all such machine-tools was that of the slide-rest, 'the substitution of a mechanical contrivance in place of the human hand, for *holding, applying,* and *directing* the motions of a cutting tool to the surface of the work'. Such machines could be operated 'with such absolute precision' that they could produce objects of any required shape with 'accuracy, ease, and rapidity'. These machine-tools made possible 'the great era in the history of mechanism':[8] without them the enormous possibilities of steam power and mechanisation could never have been developed. They form, in fact, the very basis of the modern machine age, making possible cheap, standardised mass-production.

The first steps in invention are always the most difficult, and the early progress of machine-tool making was comparatively slow.[9] Apart from the technical difficulties and expense, there was a good deal of secrecy maintained by some inventors, while manual craftsmen displayed hostility to mechanisation.[10] Nasmyth states that, after the invention of the lathe slide-rest, that of the planing machine was of most fundamental importance. It 'has done more within the last 10 or 15 years for reducing the cost, and for extending the use of perfect machinery, than had been the case by all the improvements in mechanism for the last century. There is no form which is so frequently required and essential to any piece of mechanism as the plane surface . . . The vast expense attendant on the production of such, by the tedious and unsatisfactory process of chipping and filing, caused every engineer to avoid by all means any arrangements which rendered such forms necessary, however essential they might be to the perfect action of the machine . . . The introduction of the planing machine at once altered the entire system, inasmuch as forms and arrangements became practically possible, which formerly the engineer dared not think of using'. The result was the production not only of 'most strikingly superior' machinery for general manufacture, but also of greatly improved machine-tools at a 'very much reduced cost'. Hence 'in a very short time a most important branch of engineering business, namely, toolmaking, arose'.[11] Professor Willis, writing on machine-tools in 1851, the year of the Great Exhibition, also described the metal planing machine as 'the greatest boon to constructive mechanism since the invention of the lathe'. Its actual invention, however, is shrouded in obscurity. 'We can only learn that, somewhere about 1820 or 1821 [or a few years earlier], a machine of this kind was made by several engineers', including Fox of Derby, Roberts of Manchester, Clement and Rennie of London, Murray of Leeds, Spring of Aberdeen, and perhaps others.[12] Its use seems to have spread slowly at first, but soon it was improved and manufactured in increasing numbers by such as Nasmyth and Whitworth, with revolutionary results.

A parliamentary report in the early 1840's gives evidence of the striking effects of these developments. It stated that 'tools have introduced a revolution in machinery, and tool-making has become a distinct branch of mechanics, and a very important trade, although twenty years ago it was scarcely known'.[13] James Nasmyth soon became vividly aware of the possibilities. He is best known, of course, for his invention of the steam hammer in 1839, but he was also one of the leading engineers of his day in the invention or improvement of machine tools.[14] After serving as personal assistant to Henry Maudslay for a few years in London, Nasmyth decided to establish his own firm in Manchester, starting in an old factory flat in Dale Street in 1834, as 'a mechanical engineer and machine tool maker'. Engineering was by that time well established in Manchester, growing up with the mechanisation of the textile industry in the late eighteenth and early nineteenth century.[15] Some famous names were already to be found in the Manchester directories, such as William Fairburn, Richard Roberts, and Joseph Whitworth. With the expansion of industry, however, there was more than enough work for all, especially for machine-tool makers. 'Shortly after the opening of the Liverpool and Manchester Railway', Nasmyth wrote in his *Autobiography*, 'there was a largely increased demand for machine-making tools', as 'every branch of manufacture shared in the prosperity of the time'. Nasmyth also states that the scarcity, exorbitant demands, irregularity, and carelessness of skilled engineering workers 'gave an increased stimulus to the demand for self-acting machine tools'. These favourable factors resulted in a spate of orders for Nasmyth's 'planing machines, slide-lathes, drilling, boring, slotting machines, and so on'.[16]

It was not long, therefore, before Nasmyth had to seek larger premises. He decided to build a big works at Patricroft, near Manchester, on land leased by himself and his brother George from Thomas Joseph Trafford, Esq., and George Cornwall Legh, Esq., very favourably situated at the junction of the Liverpool-Manchester Railway and the Bridgewater Canal, from which the works derived its name, the Bridgewater Foundry. To secure additional capital for the undertaking, he formed a partnership with Hollbrook Gaskell (formerly with the iron-merchanting and nail-making firm of Yates and Cox, in Liverpool), who assisted him in the administration side of the business, and with Messrs Birley and Co., the large Manchester cotton spinning and manufacturing firm, which apparently had spare capital to invest outside the textile trade.[17]

Some very interesting light is thrown on Nasmyth's ideas at this time by surviving letters which he wrote to his partner Holbrook Gaskell while the Bridgewater Foundry was building.[18] These clearly show that Nasmyth was keenly alive as to the possibilities of standardised production in advance of orders. 'These are indeed glorious times for the Engineers', he wrote, for he was overwhelmed with customers. 'I never was in such a state of bustle in my life, such quantity of people come knocking at my little office door from morning till night . . . The demand for work is really quite wonderful and I will do all in my power to bring about what I am certain is the true view of the Business viz. to have such as planing machines and lathes, etc., etc., all ready to supply the parties who come every day asking for them. If we had such a stock ready made we could in every instance sell them at 20 per cent better prices and please the parties much more and avoid all sort of unpleasant work of hurrying on the work. I could fill 20 pages with my views on this head . . . for I am quite up in the clouds about the prospect it opens. We could at once take the lead in the Business if we put it into force. It is *now* as foolish to wait for orders for such machines as to wait for orders for a ton of iron bars and tell the parties when they apply to you that you must have 4 months as the ore has to be got out of the ground before you can supply and that you will write to the mine to smelt their order. Such machines are now become as much articles of current demand as files or anything else of that nature'.[19]

In a letter to Gaskell on the following day, Nasmyth again enthused on this subject. 'What a noble business we might become if we only could establish the *ready made* concern. Depend [on it] it's the true view of the business, and we would make twice the returns with not ½ the annoyance arising from being made to promise time for Delivery with the continual risk of Disappointing the parties'.[20]

It seems clear from these letters that the idea of having ready-made machine-tools was a novel one, though other types of machinery, especially textile machines, for which there was a huge demand, had been mass-produced for some years before this date. Nasmyth put his idea into practice in the new Bridgewater Foundry (started in 1836, completed in 1837), and instead of waiting for orders sent out printed catalogues describing the various types, sizes, and prices of machine-tools that were available for sale to customers. Two such catalogues, one of 1839 the other of 1849, have survived.[21] The later catalogue included not only cutting machine-tools such as lathes and planing machines, but also Nasmyth's famous steam hammer, invented in 1839, but not patented till 1842. This enabled forgings to be made not only of larger size, but also more quickly and cheaply, especially when used for stamping masses of hot iron into moulds or dies. The steam hammer was, in fact, another type of machine-tool.[22]

Clearly this production of standardised machine-tools — to be used in making standardised machinery for the mass-production of standardised 'end products' — heralds the modern machine age. All these tools were self-acting and could be worked by easily-trained semi-skilled labour. 'The machine tools . . . did not require a skilled workman to guide or watch them. All that was necessary to superintend them was a well-selected labourer.'[23] Nasmyth recruited many of his original workmen from among the labourers in the neighbourhood.[24] Those who showed some mechanical aptitude were put to working machine-tools. He also trained boys to work them. Nasmyth was a believer in 'Free Trade in Ability' and refused to put up with the restrictions of the skilled mechanics' trade societies.

There is little doubt that, as a result of these developements, Britain led the world in the mid-nineteenth-century manufacture of machine-tools. That the U.S.A. were inferior in this department was revealed by the reports of Commissions which visited America in the early 1850s.[25] Whitworth found that 'engine tools' there were 'similar to those in use in England some years ago, being much lighter than those now in use, and turning out less work in consequence'.[26] The Ordnance officials also considered that American machine-tools 'were generally behind those of England'.[27] On the other hand the Americans led the way in the mechanisation of many manufactures, especially of light metal goods.[28] Nasmyth testified to their superiority in the mass-production of small arms, after visiting the factory established by Colt at Pimlico in the early fifties, where he found 'perfection and economy such as I have never seen before'. He contrasted the American innovating energy with the 'traditional notions and attachment to old systems' that were widespread in England.[29]

Machine-tools were not the only products of the Bridgewater Foundry. In 1839, the year of the steam hammer's invention, Nasmyth started the manufacture of railway locomotives, of which

he built 109 by 1853, for many different railway companies.[30] Locomotives engines, in fact, were eventually to become the main
concern of the later firm of Nasmyth, Wilson & Co. Another
speciality of Nasmyth's was his manufacture of small high-pressure
steam engines, which he made in considerable numbers for a
variety of purposes, but especially for the direct driving of machines,
instead of by shafting and gearing from one large engine.[31] He also
specialised in the production of small pumping engines for feeding
boilers. We even find Boulton, Watt & Co. ordering from Nasmyth
'one of your little steam engines and pumps for feeding boilers,
which Mr Blake was informed by Mr Nasmyth you had *always
ready*.'[32] When supplying such a pumping engine to the Great
Western Railway Company in the same year, Nasmyth stated that
'We make a vast number of them for feeding Boilers . . .'[33] It is
clear that these engines were being mass-produced by Nasmyth, in
advance of orders, like his machine-tools. He similarly turned out a
large number of hydraulic presses (worked by his steam pumping
engine), for which he took out patents in 1852 and 1856. In a
description of the Bridgewater Foundry in the latter year we read of
the assembly, ready for sale, of 'a regiment of donkey pumps all in
a line . . . marshalled columns of ambidextrous lathes and grooving
machines; hydraulic presses for making lead pipes; wrought-iron
cranes for forges, etc.', in addition to steam hammers and other
machines.[34]

This mass-production of machinery necessitated planned factory
lay-out, and Nasmyth appears to have been one of the pioneers of
assembly-line production. In one of his letters to Holbrook Gaskell
while the Bridgewater Foundry was being built, he proposed that
the buildings should be '*all in a line* . . . In this way we will be able
to keep all in good order'.   What Nasmyth intended by this plan
is clearly shown in a description of the works which appeared in a
little-known booklet, *Manchester As It Is*, published in 1839. 'With
a view to secure the greatest amount of convenience for the removal
of heavy machinery from one department to another', this account
runs, 'the entire establishment has been laid out with this object in
view; and in order to attain it, what may be called the straight line
system has been adopted, that is, the various work-shops are all in
a line, and so placed, that the greater part of the work, as it passes
from one end of the foundry to the other, receives in succession,
each operation which ought to follow the preceding one, so that
little carrying backward and forward, or lifting up and down, is
required . . . By means of a railroad, laid through as well as
all round the shops, any casting, however ponderous or massy, may
be removed with the greatest care, rapidity, and security'.

'The whole of this establishment is divided into departments, over each of which a foreman, or responsible person, is placed, whose duty is not only to see that the men under his superintendence produce good work, but also to endeavour to keep pace with the productive powers of all the other departments. The departments may be thus specified:—The drawing office, where the designs are made out; and the working drawings produced . . . Then come the pattern-makers . . . next comes the Foundry, and the iron and brass moulders; then the forgers or smiths. The chief part of the produce of the last named pass on to the turners and planers . . . Then comes the fitters and filers . . . in conjunction with this department is a class of men called erectors, that is, men who put together the framework, and the larger parts of most machines, so that the last two departments . . . bring together and give the last touches to the objects produced by all the others'. Altogether the firm employed at this time, only three years after starting, 'about 300 men'.

This extremely interesting description of the Bridgewater Foundry shows that Nasmyth clearly appreciated the advantages of line-production and a smooth flow of work. We are also fortunate in still having a sketch dated 1840, among the surviving Nasmyth drawings, of the inside of what appears to have been the erecting shed, where the various components were being finally assembled to form the finished product, in this case locomotive engines, which are shown progressing in line down the shed. Nasmyth sought by every means to save time and labour. In addition to the railroad which ran through and round the works, he made considerable use of cranes and blocks and pulleys for lifting and moving heavy work. A good deal of his machinery remained in use until fairly recent times: some of his machine-tools, for example, were still working in the shops of Nasmyth, Wilson and Co. in 1920,[36] and the actual buildings are still, for the most part, standing and in use today as part of a Royal Ordnance factory. While these survivals are perhaps a criticism of later failure to modernise, they are also evidence of the excellence and enduring quality of Nasmyth's designs. It was no wonder that when the *Engineer* decided to make 'A Tour of the Provinces' in 1856, its first visit was to the famous Bridgewater Foundry at Patricroft.[37] Later that same year Nasmyth retired. In twenty years he had made a fortune. When he died in 1890, he still had nearly a quarter of a million pounds[38] — testimony to his engineering genius, his business judgment, and the tremendous profits to be made in those pioneering days from the sale of machine-tools, steam hammers, and railway locomotives.

NOTES

1 See D. L. Burn, 'The Genesis of American Engineering Competition, 1850-1870', *Economic History*, Jan. 1931.

2 There is no good modern history of the early growth of mechanical engineering. There is a mass of neglected contemporary literature (periodicals, encyclopaedias, and books), on which see J. B. Williams *A Guide to the Printed Materials for English Social and Economic History, 1750-1850* (1926), II, 'Invention and Engineering', 1-35. A great deal of interesting information is contained in the evidence and reports of the Select Committees which enquired into the export of machinery in 1824-5 and 1841 (Parl. Papers, 1824, V; 1825, V; 1841, VII). An early article which is still particularly useful is that of R. Willis, 'Machines and Tools, for Working in Metal, Wood, and other Materials', *Lectures on the Results of the Great Exhibition delivered before the Society of Arts, Manufactures, and Commerce* (1852), pp. 291-320. The fullest, and still to a large extent unsurpassed, accounts of the work of the early engineers are contained in Samuel Smiles' volumes first published in the 1860's: *Lives of the Engineers* (1861-2) and *Industrial Biography* (1863). The various books of the eminent nineteenth-century engineer, Sir William Fairbairn, also contain a great deal of interesting information, e.g., *The Rise and Progress of Civil and Mechanical Engineering* (1859), *Iron: Its History, Properties, and Process of Manufacture* (1861) and *Treatise on Mills and Millwork* (2 vols., 1861-3). The autobiographies of such engineers as Fairburn and Nasmyth are full of interest (W. Pole edited and extended that of Fairbairn in 1877, Smiles that of Nasmyth in 1883). Of later literature, the following are useful: J. W. Roe, *English and American Tool Builders* (1916); A. P. M. Fleming and H. J. S. Brocklehurst, *A History of Engineering* (1925); J. H. Clapham, *An Economic History of Modern Britain* (1930), I, 151-5. There are also many valuable articles in the Newcomen Society's *Transactions*. The *Victoria County History* contains sections which often throw light on the early development of engineering in particular areas, and so do regional studies like G. C. Allen's *Industrial Development of Birmingham and the Black Country* (1929). This brief bibliographical note, of course, is by no means comprehensive.

3 See S. Smiles, *Lives of the Engineers*, IV, *Boulton and Watt* (1878 edn.) pp. 86-89, 100-101, 170, and *Industrial Biography* (1876 edn.), pp. 179-81; H. W. Dickinson and R. Jenkins, *James Watt and the Steam Engine* (1927), pp. 93-106; H. W. Dickinson, *James Watt* (1936), pp. 43, 58, 87.

4 *Industrial Biography*, p. 180.

5 Presidential address to the British Association at Manchester, 1861.

6 J. Nasmyth, 'Remarks on the Introduction of the Slide Principle in Tools and Machines employed in the Production of Machinery', in R. Buchanan, *Practical Essays on Mill Work* (revised 3rd edn., 1841), pp. 393-418.

7 *Op. cit.* pp. 394-5.

8 Nasmyth, *op. cit.* pp. 395-402.

9 As Willis (*op. cit.* p. 317) pointed out.

10 On the other hand, of course, such opposition, and the high cost of manual labour, were incentives to mechanization in many instances.

11 Nasmyth, *op. cit.* pp. 403-4.

12 Willis, *op. cit.* p. 314. See also Smiles, *Industrial Biography* (1876 edn.), p. 178.

13 *S.C. on Exportation of Machinery, 2nd Report*, P.P. 1841, VII, vii.

14 See his *Autobiography* (ed. Smiles, 1883), Smiles *Industrial Biography* (1876 edn.), pp. 275-98, and articles in the *Engineer*, 23 May 1856, 9, 16, and 23 May 1890, 18 and 25 Sept. 1908, 19 March 1920, and 23 May 1941. Nasmyth has a place in the *D.N.B.*, and there are also some brief notes about him in a pamphlet by H. Richardson, *James Nasmyth: A Note on the Life of a Pioneer Engineer* (Man-

chester, 1929), and in an address delivered by C. A. Gibb to the Watt Club, Edinburgh, 16 Jan. 1943, on *James Nasmyth, Engineer, 1808-90.* Many of Nasmyth's technical drawings of machine-tools, steam hammers, etc., together with his rough sketch-book, are still preserved in the Library of the Institution of Mechanical Engineers, where I have been kindly allowed to examine them.

15 On the early growth of engineering in Lancashire, see *V.C.H., Lancaster,* II, 367-74, and G. H. Tupling, 'The Early Metal Trades and the Beginnings of Engineering in Lancashire', *Trans. of the Lancashire and Cheshire Antiquarian Society,* LXI (1949).

16 Nasmyth, *op. cit.* pp. 199-200.

17 Information regarding these leases and partnerships is obtained from deeds the Lancashire Record Office.

18 These letters have very kindly been made available to me by Mr R. H. Gaskell (grandson of Holbrook Gaskell), of Wheatstone Park, Codsall Wood, near Wolverhampton.

19 Letter dated 11 July 1836.

20 Letter dated 12 July 1836.

21 The 1849 catalogue has been kindly donated by Mr R. H. Gaskell to Eccles Public Library; the other is in the possession of a firm which does not desire publicity, but there is a copy in Eccles Library.

22 The history of the invention and development of the steam hammer is being made the subject of a special article.

23 *Autobiography,* p. 308.

24 *Ibid.* pp. 216-7.

25 *New York Industrial Exhibition: Special Reports of Mr George Wallis and Mr Joseph Whitworth,* P.P. 1854, XXXVI. *Report of the* (Ordnance Department's) *Commission on the Machinery of the United States,* P.P. 1854-5, L.

26 *Loc. cit.* 112.

27 *Loc. cit.* 578.

28 See D. L. Burn, *op. cit.*

29 *S.C. on Small Arms,* P.P. 1854, XVIII, Q. 1367. See also Nasmyth's *Autobiography,* p. 362.

30 Maker's List, Stephenson Locomotive Society. S. Rendell, 'The Steam Locomotive Fifty Years Ago and Now', *Transactions of the Manchester Association of Engineers,* 1906, pp. 5, 8. Nasmyth, *Autobiography,* pp. 237-8.

31 *Autobiography,* pp. 313-5.

32 Letter dated 13 April 1846, *Boulton and Watt Collection,* Birmingham Public Libraries (My italics).

33 Letter to Daniel Gooch, engineer of the G.W.R., dated 16 May 1846, *British Transport Commission Archives,* H.R.P. 1/8.

34 *Engineer,* 23 May 1856.

35 Letter dated 11 July 1836 (Nasmyth's italics).

36 *Engineer,* 19 March 1920.

37 *Ibid.* 23 May 1856.

38 According to the probate, dated 6 August 1890, in Somerset House.

10
Vertical Integration in
American Manufacturing, 1899-1948[†]

Harold C. Livesay and Patrick G. Porter[*]

As part of a long-range project compiling data and source materials for American business history, we recently completed an extensive examination of vertical integration in a cross section of American manufacturing firms in the period 1899-1948. The purpose of this examination was to determine when, where, and why vertical integration occurred in the period after the giant mergers and before the conglomerates. The purpose of this note is to present a summary of the conclusions drawn from the mass of data assembled in the study.

Before presenting the conclusions, however, a brief description of the methodology is necessary. We obtained our sample of firms by making a collated list of the one hundred largest American industrial firms in 1899, 1909, 1919, 1929, 1935, and 1948. This list was compiled from A. D. H. Kaplan's *Big Enterprise in a Competitive System*[1] and contains all firms listed by Kaplan except those mining, transportation, finance, realty, motion picture, and publishing companies which we excluded as non-manufacturing.[2]

The sample firms were classified by principal product into the twenty major manufacturing categories defined in the 1957 *Standard Industrial Classification Manual* and one additional category which we called "Retail Stores." In order to obtain clusters of firms large enough to permit meaningful trend analyses over time we combined categories 24 (lumber and wood products) and 26 (paper and allied products) and added some firms not on Kaplan's list to various categories.[3] The additional firms were chosen on the basis of national prominence and data availability. The total sample is so

[*] From the *Journal of Economic History*, Vol. 29 (1969), pp. 494-500. Reprinted by permission of the editor of the *Journal of Economic History* and the authors.

[†] We wish to thank the Alfred P. Sloan Foundation for financial support which made this study possible.

composed that information is available for a minimum of four firms in each manufacturing category for the years 1929, 1935, and 1948. We checked all the firms in the sample for integration in all the sampling years, regardless of whether they qualified for the top 100 in those years.

In order to determine the extent of integration in the sample firms we divided the industrial production and distribution process into seven stages, defined as follows:

(1) Extraction or production of raw materials: the mining of coal or ores, the growing of agricultural products, etc.

(2) Refining of raw materials: the breaking of coal, conversion of iron ore to pig iron, etc.

(3) Semifinished manufacturing : the processing of raw materials or manufactured products to a stage that requires further processing (other than assembly before final use). A company which engages in stages (2) and (4) is assumed to engage in stage (3) unless there is contrary evidence.

(4) Finished manufacturing: the production of finished components for synthesis or assembly and/or the assembly of such components into finished consumers' or producers' goods.

(5) Transportation: the ownership of transportation equipment and/or transportation companies whose services are directly supportive of the manufacturing or distribution operations. This stage does not include in-plant transportation facilities.

(6) Wholesale distribution: the operation of permanent agencies and/or companies whose principal function is the sale and distribution of products to consumers other than the general public.

(7) Retail distribution: the sale of products to the general public. This stage does not include company general stores.

Using this framework we then checked all sample firms to determine the extent of vertical integration and the direction of change (i.e., integration backward or forward, if any) since the previous sample year. The principal sources employed included *Moody's Industrials, Poor's Industrials*, corporate annual reports in the Corporate Records Division of the Baker Library, Harvard University, and such relevant secondary sources as Harold Williamson's *The American Petroleum Industry*.[4]

CONCLUSION

In the period 1899-1948 there was a general trend toward greater vertical integration in American manufacturing. The prevailing direction of vertical integration was forward, as manufacturers chose more often to integrate forward into wholesaling and retailing then backward toward raw materials. See Table 1.

Most of the vertical integration which took place in the period was apparently motivated by a desire to rationalise flows by assuring efficient facilities for sales and distribution or assuring needed raw materials rather than from any widespread tendency to add the profits of suppliers or distributors to the profits of manufacturing.

TABLE 1

Percentage of Firms Integrating Forward or Backward since Previous Sample Year

Percentage	1909[a]	1919	1929	1935	1948
Integrating forward	21	11	26	18	18
Integrating backward	9	7	6	3	7

a The previous sample year in this case is 1899.

Backward integration was essentially a defensive strategy designed to protect firms which feared that raw material supplies might become controlled by competitors or independent suppliers. In general this meant firms whose inputs came from mineral deposits, forests, or overseas sources. As Table 2 shows, most firms in the lumber and paper; chemical; petroleum; rubber (until the advent of synthetics); stone, glass, and clay; and primary metals industries (all of them dependent on such raw materials) integrated back to raw materials early in the period, and the trend throughout was to increase such control.

In industries where the supply of raw materials was diffuse and plentiful there was little tendency to integrate backward. Thus firms in the food, tobacco, textile, leather, machinery, fabricated metal, electrical machinery, and transportation equipment industries rarely attempted to control supplies of manufacturing inputs. Such backward integration which took place in these fields was usually confined to those inputs originating in mine, forest, or overseas. Meat packers such as Swift and Armour controlled phosphate supplies for their fertiliser production but never engaged in cattle raising. American Sugar Refining owned timber lands, stave mills, and barrel factories at a time when it owned no sugar-producing lands. United Fruit built its Central American empire to insure its banana supply. Leather firms bought hides in the open market but often controlled tanbark forests.

Some firms found integration a useful method of avoiding exploitation by independent suppliers. International Harvester's ownership of iron ore properties, blast furnaces, and rolling mills was an effective lever against United States Steel despite the small

TABLE 2

Percentage of Sample Firms Engaged in Stages 1 (Raw Material), 6 (Wholesaling), or 7 (Retailing), 1899-1948

Stage	Group 20 Food Products 1	6	7	Group 21 Tobacco 1	6	7	Group 22 Textiles 1	6	7	Group 24 & 26 Lumber, Paper 1	6	7	Group 28 Chemicals 1	6	7	Group 29 Petroleum 1	6	7	Group 30 Rubber 1	6	7	Group 31 Leather 1	6	7
1899	15	54	8	100	—	—	—	—	—	50	—	—	29	29	—	67	82	50	—	—	—	—	—	—
1909	13	73	7	50	50	50	—	—	—	50	17	17	62	25	—	90	80	50	40	20	—	50	—	—
1919	31	63	6	—	—	20	—	33	—	67	17	17	55	45	—	96	68	60	33	67	33	25	—	—
1929	33	72	22	—	20	20	—	25	—	75	25	12	54	46	—	100	96	92	67	82	33	25	75	—
1935	39	78	22	—	20	—	—	75	—	75	62	25	69	69	—	100	95	90	67	82	50	25	100	—
1948	44	100	22	—	—	—	—	80	—	89	78	44	69	92	—	100	100	95	50	82	67	25	100	—

Stage	Group 32 Stone, Glass, and Clay 1	6	7	Group 33 Primary Metals 1	6	7	Group 34 Fabricated Metals 1	6	7	Group 35 Machinery (nonelectric) 1	6	7	Group 36 Electrical Machinery 1	6	7	Group 37 Transportation Equipment 1	6	7	Group "R" Retail Stores 3-4	6	7	All Industries 1	6	7
1899	100	100	100	79	—	—	—	100	—	—	—	20	—	—	—	—	—	—	—	—	100	38	22	11
1909	67	33	33	87	6	—	50	50	—	14	43	43	50	—	—	—	33	33	50	—	100	51	31	17
1919	40	40	20	93	10	—	33	33	—	22	67	44	—	50	25	—	42	42	33	11	100	51	39	26
1929	80	40	20	92	48	—	25	75	—	22	67	56	—	75	25	17	67	42	62	23	100	52	59	36
1935	80	60	20	92	59	—	25	75	—	22	78	56	—	75	25	17	75	42	62	15	100	53	68	34
1948	80	100	20	96	80	4	25	75	—	22	78	56	—	75	25	17	75	42	62	23	100	55	79	38

a For Group "R" (retail stores), stages (3) and (4) (semifinished and finished manufacturing) are substituted for stage (1).

capacity of International's furnaces. Sears, Roebuck bought stock in some of its suppliers for similar reasons.[5] In such cases, backward integration could play a major role in controlling input factor costs, even if the capacity of the integrated facilities was small in proportion to the total output of all firms operating on the integrated level. In general, however, it is obvious that most firms saw no need to achieve integrated control of inputs produced by American agriculture, or by the primary metals industry.

Forward integration on the other hand usually began as an offensive competitive strategy. Manufacturing firms first entered wholesaling and/or retailing only when the existing distribution network proved inadequate. This usually occurred for one of the following reasons: the existing mercantile system was unable to provide the mass distribution facilities demanded by mass production; the complexity of the product required technical expertise not available in mercantile houses; the high unit costs of products required consumer credit which exceeded financial capabilities of independent distributors; the product was a new one for which no relevant distribution system existed.

All these limitations were bottlenecks in the flow of goods from producers to consumers. Some firms encountered more of these problems than did others, depending on the nature of their products. The evidence indicates that forward integration is therefore very complex, for a single multiproduct firm often employed several methods of distribution simultaneously. General Electric, for example, maintained sales offices in large cities staffed with specialists in each of its major product lines. This was necessary because customers required expert technical assistance when buying expensive and highly complex electrical machinery. At the same time, however, General Electric continued to market simple consumer products such as light bulbs through independent whole-sale houses in areas of the country where volume was small.[6] In general, then, a manufacturer integrated forward only in those product lines or geographic areas in which constrictions in distribution flows made it necessary. Once one manufacturer in an industry moved forward, others rapidly followed suit in order to remain competitive.

Firms in most industries found it unnecessary to integrate beyond the wholesaling level, for in industries such as lumber and paper, textile mill products, chemicals, primary metals, fabricated metal products, machinery, and electrical machinery, the majority of products were producers' goods which required no retail distribution. In those industries associated with the older, agrarian economy — food, tobacco, and leather goods — change came slowly. The long-established retail network adjusted to increase volume and provided adequate outlets. No manufacturer in these industries integrated into retailing.

In only two groups of industries did firms find it necessary to engage in large-scale retailing. The first and more important group was associated with the automobile, a new product for which no adequate means of distribution existed. Ford, Durant, and others built nationwide dealer networks to provide volume distribution, consumer financing, and parts and service. The huge new market created by the automobile led rubber firms to establish first wholesale, then retail outlets to distribute tires. Before the advent of this new market, rubber manufacturers had engaged in no forward integration. The petroleum industry also built dealer networks for the retail distribution of gasoline.[7]

The other group of industries which engaged in extensive retailing were those which manufactured technically complex and expensive consumer durables. The classic examples of this were the typewriter, sewing machine, and harvester makers, who met the problems of consumer credit, parts, and service by establishing chains of dealerships in a pattern later adopted by automobile firms. In these industries, as in others, forward integration began as an offensive strategy devised by one firm to eliminate obstacles in the flow of its products to the consumer. Other manufacturers in the field then followed suit in self-defence.[8]

The evidence indicates that the dynamic at work in the growth of vertical integration is the firm's need to stabilise and minimise costs by rationalising flows of raw materials and finished products. The velocity and limits of integration are determined by the specific market conditions faced by a particular industry and by the need to remain competitive within that industry. Since changing technologies and markets affect various industries at different times, it is understandable that, as our study shows, the general trend toward increased vertical integration proceeded at a very uneven pace within individual industries in the manufacturing sector. Throughout the period studied, our sample of firms included both highly integrated and relatively unintegrated firms; however, we never found these coexisting within the same industry. All firms within a single industry group were similarly integrated at any point in time, while wide variations existed between the average integration levels of whole industry groups.

Industry conditions were a far more important determinant of integration than firm size. In order to test the proposition that vertical integration is a function of size we obtained the assets of all sample firms active in 1948 from *Moody's Industrials*. Comparison of assets to integration levels shows that (1) variations in integration levels which do exist within industry groups are not, in general, proportionate to the size of the firms in the group, and (2) small firms in highly integrated industries are usually more highly integrated than giant firms in unintegrated groups. For example, American Ice, with assets of $12 million, was operating on all seven of our integration levels in 1948, while American Tobacco with assets of $687 million was operating on only two levels.

This is not to say that size plays no part in determining the degree of integration, for clearly the small, marginal firms in any industry group must concentrate on a single-function, single-product operation. It is apparent, nevertheless, that the firms in both the 'peripheral' and 'center' economies[9] behave in a manner similar to the other firms in the same industry.

Using data compiled in other studies we checked for correlations between concentration and integration and found no general relationship. Nor did we find, as Michael Gort has suggested, that there is an inverse relationship between integration and diversification.[10] This does not seem to have been generally true between 1899-1948. American Tobacco also serves as an example here, for in 1948 it operated in a highly concentrated industry, and was neither highly integrated nor diversified.

Our findings show that it is difficult to make generalisations about vertical integration in the manufacturing sector of the economy as a whole. The phenomenon can be most profitably studied within the context of specific industry categories or groups of similar categories. It seems reasonable, however, to conclude that the overall trend of increased forward integration among American manufacturing firms is evidence that success in the complex American economy continues to depend more on solving the problems of mass distribution than on developing integrated facilities for mass production.

NOTES

1 A. D. H. Kaplan, *Big Enterprise in a Competitive System* (Washington: The Brookings Institution, 1964), chap. 7. Since there is no list for 1899 we used Kaplan's 1909 list for 1899.

2 Also excluded were International Match and Eastman Kodak.

3 Classification of the sample firms into S. I. C. groups revealed none in Group 23 (apparel and related products), Group 25 (furniture and fixtures), Group 27 (printing and publishing), Group 38 (instruments), and Group 39 (miscellaneous). Consequently these groups do not appear in Table 1.

4 Harold F. Williamson, Arnold R. Daum, et. al., *The American Petroleum Industry* (2 vols.; Evanston, Ill.: Northwestern University Press, 1959-63).

5 John A. Garraty, *Right Hand Man* (New York: Harper & Brothers, 1957), pp. 127-28; Boris Emmet and John E. Jeuck, *Catalogs and Counters: A History of Sears, Roebuck* (Chicago: University of Chicago Press, 1950), p. 244.

6 Harold C. Passer, "Electrical Manufacturing Around 1900," *Journal of Economic History*, XII (Dec. 1952), 378-95; also General Electric *Annual Reports* in Baker Library, Harvard University.

7 The petroleum industry had, of course, integrated into retailing before the arrival of the automobile, but the integrated retailing network which developed in the twentieth century was a result of the market for gasoline, not for illuminating oil.

8 The development of integrated marketing facilities in harvesters, typewriters, meat packing, cigarettes, and other industries is summarized in Alfred D. Chandler, Jr., "The Beginnings of 'Big Business' in American Industry," *Business History Review*, XXXIII (Spring 1959), 1-31. Chandler also shows the necessity for competitive imitation of integrated distribution facilities.

9 These terms are Robert T. Averitt's. The center economy includes those firms which are large, diversified, integrated, decentralized competitors in national and sometimes international markets. Firms in the center economy are rich in managerial and technical talent and financial resources. The peripheral economy is composed of relatively small firms with narrower horizons, a small line of related products, centralized management, poorer credit, and a tendency to focus on short-run problems. See R. T. Averitt, *The Dual Economy* (New York: W. W. Norton, 1968), pp. 1-2.

10 Michael Gort, *Diversification and Integration in American Industry* (Princeton: Princeton University Press, 1962), pp. 6-7. For 1948 concentration information we used the Census Bureau's concentration ratio data in United States House of Representatives, Judiciary Committee, Subcommittee on Study of Monopoly Power, *Study of Monopoly Power, Part 2-B* (Washington, D.C.: U.S. Government Printing Office, 1950), pp. 1436-56, and Carl Kaysen and Donald F. Turner, *Antitrust Policy: An Economic and Legal Analysis* (Cambridge: Harvard University Press, 1959), pp. 273-331. For the prewar years we used our own studies of concentration in manufacturing which are based primarily on decennial Censuses of Manufactures. For diversification data we used another of our own studies.

11
The Growth of Competition among the Standard Oil Companies in the United States, 1911-1961[1]

D. F. Dixon*

In 1911 one of the most significant U.S. anti-trust decisions resulted in the dissolution of the Standard Oil trust which had dominated the oil industry of the United States since the 1870s. A half century later, eight of the original members of the trust ranked among the eighteen largest oil companies in the nation. This paper traces the development of these companies which emerged from the trust, showing the growth of competition as they expanded their marketing areas beyond the territories originally assigned to them under the trust agreement, and came into direct competition with one another.

I

John D. Rockefeller was engaged in oil refining as early as 1863, but it was not until seven years later that the Standard Oil Company (Ohio) was formed. Subsequently, the company purchased other refiners, pipelines, and marketing companies and, by 1875, the larger Eastern refiners had joined the Standard Oil group. In the following years, additional companies joined, or were bought out, so that by 1882 the Standard Oil Company (Ohio) was a member of an alliance of forty separate oil companies, representing about three quarters of the refining capacity of the United States, and a larger proportion of the pipeline facilities. At this time, to simplify the operations of the group, an agreement was entered into by the component companies, in which all securities of the participants were held and administered by trustees. The resulting Standard Oil trust dominated the oil industry of the nation. The tactics employed to gain and maintain this dominance, together with the mere size of the group, aroused public animosity, which in turn led to various attempts to curb its power.

*From *Business History*, Vol. IX, no. 1 (Jan. 1967). Reprinted by permission of the editor of *Business History*.

In 1892, the Ohio courts ruled that the original charter of the Standard Oil Company (Ohio) did not allow it to operate under a trust agreement. As a result, the trust was abandoned in favour of a less formal 'community of interest' arrangement. But this arrangement had disadvantages, and some of the member companies came under legal attack. Accordingly, in 1892 the group established a holding company structure. The charter of the largest member of the group, the Standard Oil Company of New Jersey, was broadened to permit it to become the primary holding company, and its name was changed to Standard Oil Company (New Jersey).

This holding company, in turn, was sued by the Federal Government in 1906 under the Sherman Anti-Trust Act. By 1911 the case had reached the Supreme Court, where the majority opinion was that the Standard Oil Company, and the other members of the group, had been conspiring 'to restrain the trade and commerce in petroleum, commonly called "crude oil", in refined oil, and in the other products of petroleum.[2] The court ordered that the company divest itself of stock holdings in subsidiaries, with the result that thirty-four separate companies were formed with no common officers or directors. Among these, separate companies were producing, pipeline, manufacturing and marketing units, but this paper is concerned only with the subsequent development of those which have come to be important marketers of gasoline. Only fifteen of the thirty-four newly independent companies were involved in domestic marketing, and of these, five were distributors of specialty products, and hence are of no immediate interest here.[3] One of these five, Vacuum Oil Company, later became important for our purpose, because it merged with the Standard Oil Company of New York to form Socony Vacuum, now the Mobil Oil Company.

Prior to the dissolution, the United States had been divided into eleven marketing districts, each the exclusive territory of a particular company:

1	Atlantic Refining Company	Pennsylvania and Delaware
2	Continental Oil Company	Rocky Mountain Region
3	Standard Oil Company (California)	Pacific Coast
4	Standard Oil Company (Indiana)	North Central States
5	Standard Oil Company (Kentucky)	South East States
6	Standard Oil Company of Louisiana	Louisiana and Tennessee
7	Standard Oil Company (New Jersey)	East Coast
8	Standard Oil Company of New York	New York and New England

 9 Standard Oil Company (Nebraska)   Nebraska
10 Standard Oil Company (Ohio)   Ohio
11 Waters-Pierce Oil Company   Arkansas, Oklahoma,
                                        Texas

The subsequent discussion will be concerned with eight of these eleven companies. Because the Standard Oil Company of Louisiana remained a subsidiary of Standard Oil (New Jersey) after the dissolution, references to Jersey Standard will subsume the Louisiana subsidiary. Further, Standard Oil (Nebraska) was affiliated with and was largely supplied by Indiana Standard.[4] The Indiana Company, in turn, obtained a controlling interest in the Nebraska Company in 1939. Hence references to Indiana Standard will subsume the Nebraska Company. Finally, the Waters-Pierce Oil Company, whose stock was sixty per cent or more owned by Jersey Standard at the time of the dissolution, is not of interest here, for the Jersey Standard holdings in this firm were purchased by the Pierce Oil Company in July 1913. At this time, the area formerly assigned to Waters-Pierce was divided among Indiana Standard, Jersey Standard and Standard of New York.[5] Figure 1 indicates the resulting 'original territories' of the eight companies, as they are discussed in this paper.

The activities of the eight companies will be traced throughout the half century following dissolution. This time span will be divided into four periods, 1911-1919, 1920-1926, 1927-1939 and 1946-1961. The choice of these particular time periods is due in part to dominant trends of development within the industry, and in part to the dates for which materials are available.

II

Immediately after the dissolution there was little outward sign of competition among the former members of the trust. Each company retained its original corporate name, and most corporation officers remained. Former executives became officers of the newly independent companies, and those who had held responsible positions in the old companies were made directors of the new. However, managerial reorganisation was slow-moving and confused, in part, because the new managers had not been in higher management positions in the trust. Thus, these executives for some time followed closely the policies of their predecessors, and continued existing working arrangements with other former members of the trust.

Moreover, much business continued to be transacted essentially as it had been before. No changes were required by the dissolution

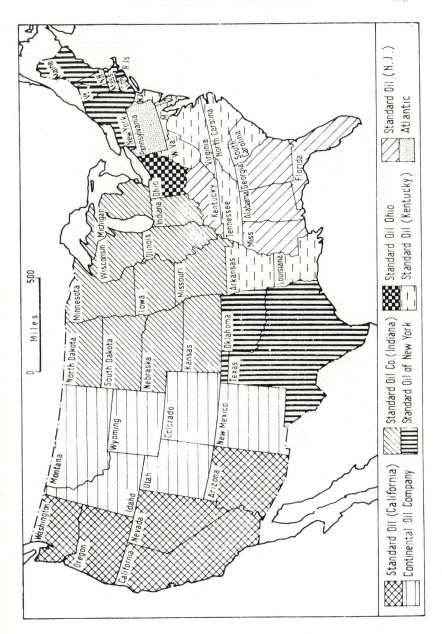

TABLE 1

Extent of Integration of Original 'Standard' Companies

	Production	Refining	Marketing	Transport
Atlantic Refining Company		×	×	
Continental Oil Company.			×	
Standard Oil of California	×	×	×	×
Standard Oil (Indiana)		×	×	
Standard Oil (Kentucky).			×	
Standard Oil (New Jersey).	×	×		
Standard Oil (New York).		×	×	×
Standard Oil (Ohio).		×	×	

decree, and the economic links of the former economic whole remained, despite the change in corporate structure. These links were especially strong because dissolution had not been along lines which provided each company with an integrated operation (Table 1). Atlantic had been essentially a refining company, with no oil production, pipelines or tankers. Moreover, although sixty per cent of its sales had been in foreign markets, it was left without a sales force abroad. Continental was a large marketing company without crude production, refineries or pipelines. Indiana Standard owned three refineries and marketed in ten states, but owned no production or pipelines. Jersey Standard had several large refineries on the East Coast, but only limited domestic marketing facilities since its sphere had been largely foreign business. Yet the company had little crude or pipeline transportation, and no tankers. Only Standard of California was a full integrated company. Thus, until new marketing patterns could be established, each company continued buying or selling its requirements through its original associations with other former members of the Trust.

Despite these restraints, there was competition among the various Standard Oil Companies. There has been much confusion on this point, because the various companies initially respected the old territorial divisions to the extent of generally not constructing marketing facilities or using their brand names in one another's original territories.[6] However, some of these companies did sell surplus gasoline in the territories of former members of the trust, both on the open market and through jobbers. The activity of Atlantic is clear from a statement by J. W. Van Dyke, then president of the company: 'There has been no time during the four years of our independent existence that we have not sold our products for delivery to the states adjacent to, and even remote from, Pennsylvania, and to wholesale buyers other than the so-called Standard Oil Companies in such outside territories.'[7]

The failure of the original companies to expand their marketing facilities into the territories of other Standard Oil companies was partly because of a problem with respect to trademarks. Under the trust arrangement each marketing subsidiary had used its own brand name in its territory exclusively; the use of these brands in other areas was not mentioned in the dissolution decree. Also, many state corporation laws prohibited a corporation from doing business if its name was similar to that of a corporation already registered in that state. Hence, each Standard company recognised the right of each of the others to use its trade marks exclusively in its original territory, so that invasions of the territory of others had to be through the use of less well-known brands, which put the invader at a disadvantage.[8]

Moreover, because many of the former subsidiaries were also supplying gasoline to others for sale in their original territories, an invasion by the 'outsider' might have resulted in the loss of those sales. Milburn, then counsel for Standard of New Jersey, stressed this point: 'I have heard it said, for instance, "How easy for the Standard Oil Company of New Jersey, which is not in the city of New York, to enter business in that city . . ." Now, the Standard Oil Company was a great wholesaler in the city of New York. it had no marketing plant there whatsoever and never had . . . There was a business question to decide. Would it throw up a large and lucrative or profitable wholesale business, and erect there, at a great expense, another marketing plant . . . with a net result of a

TABLE 2

Inter-Company Sales of Gasoline, 1915
(Thousands of Gallons)

Seller	Atlantic	Kentucky Standard	Jersey Standard	Standard of New York	Ohio Standard	Total
Atlantic	—	6.5	2,009.1	23.0	975.7	3,014.3
Magnolia	—	3,503.1	6,999.1	3,510.4	—	14,012.6
Indiana Standard	1,570.4	12,543.6	2,752.8	1,255.0	37,817.4	55,939.2
Jersey Standard	—	20,230.9	—	53,729.0	273.9	74,233.8
Standard of N.Y.	100.9	—	—	—	308.5	409.4
Vacuum	—	—	—	13,612.3	—	13,612.3
Total	1,671.3	36,284.1	11,761.0	72,129.7	39,375.5	161,221.6

Source: Adapted from *Report on the Price of Gasoline in 1915,* op. cit., 8.

loss of advantage to the company itself?'[9] At this time Jersey
Standard was selling over 53 million gallons of gasoline annually to
Standard of New York. (Table 2).

There may also have been in the minds of some in the various
companies the fact that competition between two standard companies might result in losses to others in the market. One writer
explained this point: 'Active competition of two or more of them in
business in the same territory would have much the same effect as
a combination between them to suppress competition, and might
well create the suspicion that this was its purpose.'[10]

Later, after competition among the various Standard companies
had become more vigorous, the danger to independents was spelled
out in an address, 'Cross Competition of Standard Oil Units
Menaces Independent Jobbers', given by an independent oil company executive. The thrust of the argument was that the Standard
companies' rivalry could lead to the independents' 'Total and
complete elimination from the industrial scheme of things.'[11]

In addition to various factors limiting the interest of the 'Standard'
companies in expanding their territories, there were other pressures

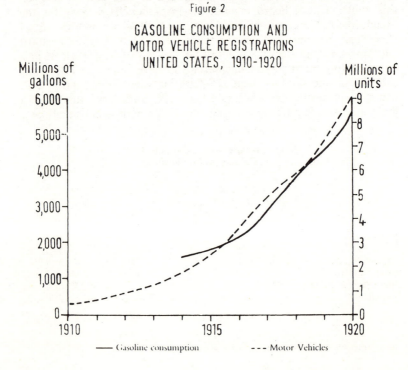

Figure 2

GASOLINE CONSUMPTION AND
MOTOR VEHICLE REGISTRATIONS
UNITED STATES, 1910-1920

——— Gasoline consumption   - - - Motor Vehicles

limiting the ability of these companies to carry out such expansion. The dissolution decree nearly coincided with the boom in gasoline demand; the Model T Ford, first produced in 1908, was manufactured on an assembly line by 1914. Motor vehicle registrations grew at an explosive rate after this time, and gasoline sales grew commensurately. (Figure 2). As a result of this rapid expansion, oil companies were forced to devote much energy to the construction of a new type of distribution system for this new product, and to adapt to the new types of demands made by the motorist.[12]

Moreover, by 1915 the growth in demand for gasoline exceeded the rate at which crude oil could be produced, so that domestic stocks were run down and imports from Mexico were necessary to fill the gap. By 1917, when the US entered World War I, the output of petroleum was beginning to lag conspicuously behind domestic consumption. The war brought increased demands, and a feeling in the industry that a serious shortage in crude was impending. In 1919 one writer stated that: 'The entire automobile industry is expanding so rapidly that it is open to question whether the means for producing motor fuel is keeping pace'.[13] Concern over the adequacy of crude supplies was not voiced solely within the industry; in 1919 the Director of the US Bureau of Mines stated that: 'Within two to five years the oil fields of this country will reach their maximum production, and from that time on we will face an ever-increasing decline. We thus see the domestic oil fields unable to meet our home demands under present methods of utilisation and manufacture. This startling fact cannot be ignored'.[14] Hence, during this period, attention was focused largely upon increasing supply to meet a rapidly growing existing demand, rather than attempting to increase sales by vigorous rivalry for new customers.

The supply problem was accentuated for the Standard companies as a group, because none but the California and Jersey companies had any production facilities at the time of dissolution. Van Dyke of Atlantic expressed his concern about balancing that company's operations: 'We have felt the necessity of investing our profits in directions which will insure that future existence of the company, such as oil-producing properties and tank ships for securing crude oils and disposing of export products.'[15]

Further accentuating the problem were two recessions of 1910-11 and 1912-15 which severely limited the funds available for investment. The money market had begun to tighten in 1909, and by the following year a downward movement in the economy began. Although the trough was not deep, it was the longest since the mid-1880s. A recovery occurred in 1912, but it was one of the shortest expansion periods on record. The Balkan crisis in Europe kept money markets tight, and by early 1913 another moderate downturn had begun. By the end of the year, the contraction reached a deeper trough than had the 1910-1911 recession. In August 1914, Europe was plunged into war, and a world-wide financial crisis resulted; the New York Stock Exchange closed on 31 July. The decline then gathered momentum and continued until the end of 1914. An expansion, due to increasing exports to Great Britain and France, began in 1915, reaching its peak in 1918. However, during the autumn and winter of 1918-1919, a moderate recession occurred as the reconversion process was begun.

As a result of these various factors, by 1919 the various Standard Oil companies generally remained within their original territories. There are few instances of a Standard Oil Company invading the territory of another before the First World War. In 1913, Indiana Standard entered Oklahoma, then the territory of Magnolia (which would become a subsidiary of Socony in 1918). Magnolia, in turn, entered Louisiana in 1914 and New Mexico in 1915, thus entering Jersey Standard and Continental territory. Atlantic was also making some sales in New England by 1916.

The public seemed to have viewed the lack of more general territorial expansion as evidence of continued monopoly control of the industry, and conscious avoidance of the terms of the dissolution decree by the various Standard Oil companies. There was even misunderstanding within the industry itself, for one publication, when discussing Atlantic's financial report for 1920, remarked that the company was a subsidiary of Standard Oil (New Jersey).[16] During this period, there were numerous investigations of the industry by governmental agencies. One report suggested that the public apprehension was without foundation in fact, and concluded that: 'The weight of evidence accumulated as a result of keen and almost constant surveillance by several departments of the government is entirely in support of the conclusion that the dissolution decree has been scrupulously observed.'[17]

Summarising this investigation, the writer commented that 'It is plain that companies in establishing their prices and practices are individualistic in the extreme'.[18] Further, 'As much difference exists between the prices of the several Standard Oil Companies as between the Standard Companies and others. There are scarcely any two Standard Oil Companies with the same basic prices or policies. Methods of marketing and prices vary according to locality, the mental attitude of different executives, and the fluctuations in costs . . .'[19]

It would seem then that rather than monopoly, the appropriate model to employ in analysing the behaviour of the various Standard Oil companies immediately after dissolution would be that of oligopoly, with a 'conjectural variation of zero'. That is, each company believed, or conjectured, that there would be no response by other Standard companies to any action taken in its own territory. There were, in fact, instances during this period in which one Standard company raised prices in its territory, while a Standard company in a neighbouring territory simultaneously lowered prices.

III

The business upswing which followed the trough of July 1921 carried the economy into a protracted period of nearly uninterrupted prosperity. Within this framework of economic expansion the various Standard Oil companies intensified their efforts to integrate and further balance their operations to include production, refining, marketing and transportation facilities. In particular, efforts were made to obtain crude oil supplies, because concern over the adequacy of crude production continued until the mid-1920s. In many instances acquisitions of production or refining facilities brought with them marketing facilities in the territories of other Standard companies, and thus initiated more general competition among them.

In 1919, California Standard entered Texas and the mid-continent area for crude supplies, and also obtained a refinery connection which sold to independent jobbers, who competed with Indiana Standard and Continental. Two years later the California company also entered western Idaho, thus coming into conflict with Continental there as well. Also in 1919, Jersey Standard acquired a 50 per cent interest in Humble Oil and Refining, primarily to obtain crude supplies. However, in addition to crude production, Jersey also obtained marketing facilities in south-east Texas, which meant an invasion of Socony's territory.

Socony's purchase of a controlling interest in Magnolia in 1918 was also primarily designed to improve Socony's crude supply, but at the same time, it brought additional refining capacity and marketing outlets. Because Magnolia entered Arkansas in 1918, Socony was thus in competition with Jersey Standard in that state. Further, Socony purchased the General Petroleum Company of Los Angeles in 1926 to obtain crude for its far eastern markets. With the subsequent discovery of oil in Sumatra, this crude source was no longer required, but General also had a 50,000 b/d refinery, wholesale distribution, and 1,500 retail outlets in California, Oregon, and Washington. This brought Socony 7.4 per cent of this market, all of which was in California Standard's original territory.

The most important example of backward integration, which brought with it extensive marketing facilities, was the expansion of Indiana Standard. From 1911 to the close of World War I, Indiana had remained essentially a marketing and refining company. Throughout this period nearly all of its crudge was obtained through purchase agreements, largely with the Prairie Oil and Gas Company, which had been the Mid-Continent crude supplier for the Standard Trust before 1911. The shortage of crude at the close of World War I indicated the dangers of such dependence upon others; in early 1918 the Whiting refinery was forced to operate at half of capacity because the necessary crude was not available.[20] Although the company obtained its first crude-producing property as early as 1917, the most important development came in 1925 with the acquisition of a controlling interest in the Pan American Petroleum and Transport Company, one of the largest crude producers in the world. Pan American's marketing susidiaries (including the American Oil Company) had facilities along the Atlantic and Gulf Coast. This resulted in an invasion by Indiana Standard into the territories of three of the original Standard companies: Jersey Standard (in D.C., Maryland, New Jersey, Virginia, Louisiana and Tennessee), Socony (in Connecticut, Maine, Massachusetts and Rhode Island) and Kentucky Standard (in Alabama, Florida, Georgia and Mississippi). This acquisition was heralded by the oil press as 'By far the biggest occurrence in Standard Oil Circles since the dissolution suit' and as having a 'more far reaching effect' than that suit'.[21] The significance of Indiana's expansion can be suggested by the fact that this company now distributed in a larger portion of the United States than any other oil company, with the exception of the Texas Company.

Continental, which had been solely a marketing organisation under the trust, for some time after the dissolution continued selling in the Rocky Mountain area the products of the Indiana, Kansas and California Standard companies. However, in 1916 Continental acquired a refinery in Colorado, through the purchase of the United Oil Company, and two years later began acquiring producing properties in Wyoming.

In 1924 the company began breaking out of its original territory through a merger with the Mutual Oil Company, a leading producing and marketing company in the Mid-West.[22] This merger provided the marketing outlets needed by Mutual to balance its producing and refining capacity, and at the same time balanced Continental's operations which were inadequate in producing and refining. This combination added the states of Kansas, Nebraska and South Dakota to Continental's Rocky Mountain marketing territory, and brought the total number of bulk and filling stations served by Continental to 1,000. In the following year Continental purchased the B. & L. Oil Company in Nebraska, thus increasing its position here to second after Nebraska Standard (representing Indiana Standard).

In 1926, Continental purchased the Texhoma Oil and Refining Company, which had producing, refining and marketing facilities in Texas and Oklahoma. The company's position in this area was further strengthened by the purchase of the Constantin Oil Company of Tulsa, and the Sapulpa Refining Company of Sapulpa, Oklahoma.

Thus, by 1926, Continental had expanded its territory from the original six states to fifteen. The company was competing with Socony in Oklahoma, Socony and Jersey Standard in Texas and Arkansas, Indiana Standard in Kansas, Nebraska, Missouri and South Dakota and California Standard in Washington and Oregon.

Part of Atlantic's market expansion in the 1920s also followed from backward integration. By 1920, producing properties had been acquired in the southern United States, especially from Superior. Presumably to provide an outlet for a portion of this production, the company built a refinery in Brunswick, Georgia, and distributed gasoline through jobbers in the Carolinas, Georgia and Florida. This brought Atlantic into conflict with both the Jersey company and Kentucky Standard. On the other hand, some of Atlantic's expansion was the direct result of excess refining capacity in Pennsylvania. The company's Philadelphia refinery alone had a capacity of over 40,000 barrels a day, and existing outlets could not absorb this output. The expansion of sales in the traditional areas of Pennsylvania and Delaware was difficult because at this time Atlantic had approximately 70 per cent of this market, so that additional sales effort would have been subject to diminishing returns. Moreover, legal difficulties might have arisen from the resulting injury to competition, which consisted entirely of independent sellers. Thus new markets were required in the states surrounding Pennsylvania.

It has been mentioned above that Atlantic began some sales in New England as early as 1916 or 1917. New England was apparently chosen as a starting point for expansion because under the trust agreement Atlantic had supplied the products sold by Standard of New York in this area, and because this market could be reached inexpensively by rail and water from the Philadelphia refinery. Atlantic's sales appear to have been small here, for it was not until 1920 that these activities were mentioned in the trade press, or Moody's. It was also in the 1920s that Atlantic began selling in

New Jersey, New York, West Virginia and Ohio. In these instances sales were made through jobbers, and probably not under the Atlantic brand.

In addition to the development of competition among the original marketing subsidiaries of the trust, there also developed rivalry with former Standard Oil Companies which had not previously engaged in marketing activities. The most important of these was the Ohio Oil Company, which in the years following 1911 confined its operations to crude oil production, purchasing and transportation. In 1924, Ohio bought a controlling interest in one of its customers, the Lincoln Oil and Refining Company.[23] At this time, Ohio formed a refining and marketing division to sell both at wholesale and through a chain of stations in Illinois, Kentucky, Missouri, Iowa and Indiana. In this fashion the Ohio Oil Company came into competition with Indiana Standard over a wide area, and Kentucky Standard as well.

Thus, by 1926, rather than there being one Standard Oil company in each state, there were in nineteen states at least two, and in seven instances, more than two Standard Oil companies competing with one another. (Table 3). Despite this initial activity, it is apparent that the depth of the invasions of each other's areas was not great in most instances. The available data indicate that the most severe losses were suffered by Standard of California (losing 7.4 per cent of its territory's sales to Socony) and Sohio (losing 6.1 per cent of its territory's sales to Atlantic) (Table 4).

IV

By the mid-twenties, the dominant pressures in the industry were in marketing rather than crude production or refining. One reason for this shift of emphasis was that during the early 1920s the anxiety over potential crude shortages rapidly changed into concern with the problem of marketing the crude produced from newly-discovered oil fields. Moreover, increased refinery capacity, and changes in refining methods which made possible a higher percentage yield of gasoline from each barrel of crude oil, led to expanded gasoline output. Well-established companies began to branch out into new territories, and new independent companies grew rapidly. As new competition put pressure on their traditional territories, the Standard companies in turn pushed outward in an effort to offset these inroads.

In 1927, Jersey Standard extended its operations into Delaware through the construction of bulk plants and service stations. In the same year the company also entered Pennsylvania, through a subsidiary, the Pennsylvania Lubricating Company. Initially a river

TABLE 3
Marketing Areas 1926

	Atlantic Refining Co.	Continental Oil Co.	Std. Oil Co. (California)	Std. Oil Co. (Indiana)	Std. Oil Co. (Kentucky)	Std. Oil Co. (New Jersey)	Std. Oil Co. of New York	Std. Oil Co. (Ohio)	No. of Companies per State
Alabama				×	+				2
Arizona			+						1
Arkansas		×				+	×		3
California			+				×		2
Colorado		+							1
Connecticut	×			×			+		3
Delaware	×								1
District of Columbia				×		+			2
Florida				×	+				2
Georgia				×	+				2
Idaho		+	×						2
Illinois				+					1
Indiana				+					1
Iowa				+					1
Kansas		×		+					2
Kentucky					+				1
Louisiana				×		+			2
Maine				×			+		2
Maryland				×		+			2
Massachusetts	×			×			+		3
Michigan				+					1
Minnesota				+					1
Mississippi				×	+				2
Missouri		×		+					2
Montana		+							1
Nebraska		×		+					2
Nevada			+						1
New Hampshire							+		1
New Jersey				×		+			2
New Mexico		+					×		2
New York							+		1
N. Carolina						+			1
N. Dakota				+					1
Ohio								+	1
Oklahoma		×		×			+		3
Oregon		×	+				×		3
Pennsylvania	+								1
Rhode Island	×			×			+		3
S. Carolina						+			1
S. Dakota		×		+					2
Tennessee				×		+			2
Texas		×				×	+		3
Utah		+							1
Vermont							+		1
Virginia				×		+			2
Washington		×	+				×		3
W. Virginia						+			1
Wisconsin				+					1
Wyoming		+							1
Total Number of States	5	15	6	26	5	11	14	1	

Original Territories +

TABLE 4

Market Share Gained by 'Standard Oil' Companies from the Original Territories
of other 'Standard Oil' Companies by 1926
(Percentages)

Losses in Original Territories

Gained by	Atlantic	Continental	Std. (Cal.)	Std. (Ind.)	Std. (Ky.)	Std. (N.J.)	Std. of N.Y.	Std. (Ohio)
Atlantic.................	—	0	0	0	1.5	2.9	3.1	6.1
Continental..............	0	—	n.a.	.03	0	n.a.	n.a.	0
Standard (California)......	0	n.a.	—	0	0	0	0	0
Standard (Indiana)	0	0	0	—	n.a.	n.a.	n.a.	0
Standard (Kentucky)......	0	0	0	0	—	0	0	0
Standard (New Jersey).....	0	0	0	0	0	—	n.a.	0
Standard of New York.....	0	1.4	7.4	0	0	1.3	—	0
Standard (Ohio)	0	0	0	0	0	0	0	—

Source: Adapted from Federal Trade Commission, *Petroleum Industry, Prices, Profits and Competition* U.S. Senate Document No. 61, 70th Congress, 1st Session (Washington: Government Printing Office, 1928), 225-227.

terminal was established in Pittsburg, where sites for retail stations were also secured. At about the same time the company secured a contract with the Mitten interests, owning a fleet of buses in Philadelphia, to supply 15 million gallons of gasoline annually. The purchaser's trucks were required to call at Jersey Standard's Camden bulk plant, however, so that Jersey's trucks would not have to cross into Pennsylvania. During the following year the Standard Oil Company (Pennsylvania) was formed and sales were begun in earnest.

The Jersey Company had been supplying refined products to Socony, but as the latter increased refining capacity, its purchases from Jersey Standard fell. Hence, to maintain a position in the New England states, in 1929 Jersey Standard acquired control of the Beacon Oil Company, which owned a 25,000 b/d refinery in Everett, Massachusetts, together with 73 bulk plants and 350 service stations in New England and northern New York.

In 1933, the 28,000 retail outlets of Jersey Standard's various subsidiary companies, except Humble, became 'Esso' stations. At this time the company marketed in all states east of the Mississippi, except for the original territories of Indiana Standard, Ohio Standard and Kentucky Standard. Moreover, through Humble, Jersey also marketed in Arkansas, Louisiana and Texas. An effort to invade Indiana's territory was made in 1935, when Jersey opened three stations in Missouri, but Indiana obtained a court decision prohibiting the use of the 'Esso' trademark in its territory.

As a result of its acquisitions in the earlier 1920s, Socony had marketing operations in the south-west and the west coast, in addition to its New England market. A first attempt to fill the resulting gap in the mid-west, was made in 1930 by the purchase of the White Eagle Oil Company. This company owned a small amount of crude production and refineries in Kansas and Wyoming. Moreover, White Eagle had 1,800 service stations in fourteen central states, which gave it slightly more than one half of one per cent of the nation's gasoline sales. The purchase of White Eagle brought Socony into both Continental and Indiana Standard territories.

Further, in 1932 Socony merged with the Vacuum Oil Company, a former member of the Standard Oil trust. Vacuum, which had a large lubricating oil refinery in Rochester, New York, had specialised in the manufacture of all kinds of lubricants which were sold by other members of the trust. After the dissolution Vacuum continued these sales to the now independent companies. Moreover, the by-products of Vacuum's lubricating oil production, including gasoline, were sold largely to Socony and in some instances, Kentucky Standard. As these companies expanded their own refining capacity, however, they began to supply their lubricant requirements, and Vacuum lost much of its business. Moreover, as oil companies generally succeeded in developing close ties with service stations during the 1920s, Vacuum found that motor oil could not be successfully sold directly to the retail trade in competition with gasoline marketing companies.

As a solution to its problems, Vacuum began to integrate forward into marketing. In the mid-1920s, Vacuum began selling some gasoline to Metro Stations, Inc., one of the largest independent marketing companies in the east, with a chain of stations in Pennsylvania and western New York. In 1927, Vacuum purchased an interest in Metro. Two years later Vacuum was making truck deliveries of gasoline to dealers in Philadelphia, and subsequently began building a chain of stations there, as well as purchasing distributing companies in Philadelphia and Scranton. In 1929 and 1930, Vacuum also acquired the Commonwealth Oil Corporation and Great Western in Ohio; Wadhams Corporation, a large marketer in Wisconsin, Illinois, Minnesota and Michigan; Lubrite Refining Company, marketing in Missouri and Illinois, and the White Star Refining Company with two refineries and distribution facilities in Michigan, Indiana, Illinois and Missouri.

Thus, by 1931, and its merger with Socony, Vacuum had become an important marketing company, and its facilities in the mid-west clearly complemented those of Socony. The resulting company, Socony-Vacuum had marketing facilities in every state except those of Kentucky Standard's original territory. Because of the terms of the dissolution decree the companies were required to obtain approval of the merger from the Federal court. The US Attorney General attempted to stop this merger, but the court ruled in favour of the companies, holding that the main business of each was in different fields, and hence there was too little competition between them to prohibit the merger on the grounds of restraining competition. Further, the court argued that the resulting integrated company's competitive position would be stronger than that of either alone, and hence the outcome of the merger would be an increase in competition, by creating 'an additional competitor in states and localities where neither company is now substantially located.'[24]

During this period, Continental's marketing territory also expanded, through a merger with the Marland Refining Company of Oklahoma. Again the Continental name survived the company's purchase by another firm. Marland was originally a producer selling to Jersey Standard and others, but in 1918 the company constructed a refinery and began marketing operations. Early in 1929 Marland purchased the Prudential Refining Corporation, which operated a refinery at Baltimore, the National Oil Company of Richmond, and the Mylex Oil Company of Washington, D.C. National and Mylex owned and operated service stations in several states along the Atlantic Coast. Later in 1929, Marland acquired Continental. Together, Marland and Continental marketed in twenty-one states, through 800 stations, and the resulting company had a nucleus of a marketing organisation throughout most of the nation, except for the West Coast.

Several other Standard Companies also added marketing operations in the 1920s, although to a less dramatic extent than those mentioned above. In 1928, Indiana Standard obtained marketing facilities in Colorado and New Mexico through the purchase of the Vickers Petroleum Company, and in Wyoming and Montana through the acquisition of the Arro Oil and Refining Company. This brought the Indiana company into the largest part of Continental's original territory.

Standard of California constructed a refinery in El Paso in 1928, making the first important move to expand its marketing and refining facilities. Subsequently, the company marketed in Texas and New Mexico. In the thirties, California Standard expanded its sales still further, but then the company marketed solely through jobbers, first in Montana (1936) and then Wyoming, Colorado, North and South Dakota and Nebraska in 1937.

In 1928, Standard of Ohio acquired the contracts of Spears and Riddle, who were marketing under the Fleet-Wing brand in Ohio, Pennsylvania and West Virginia. Subsequently the Fleet Wing Corporation was formed as a subsidiary, to permit the sales of products to jobbers in Ohio and elsewhere. In the 1930s Standard of Ohio sold gasoline under the Fleet-Wing name through jobbers, first in New York, and later in Maryland, Michigan, Indiana and Kentucky.

Atlantic differed from the other Standard companies mentioned above, for it was not under pressure to find outlets for crude production, since it did not own much crude. However, Atlantic was forced to enter the competition for marketing facilities because other companies, seeking outlets for crude, were causing losses to Atlantic. Along much of the East Coast Atlantic was selling gasoline through jobbers, but during the late 1920s much of this business was lost as jobbers were purchased by competitors, or offered contracts which Atlantic could not profitably match. Thus, the company began building its own facilities, as well as buying existing companies. For example, in 1926, the company purchased the Richmond Oil Company in Virginia, and in 1927, the Red 'C' Oil Company, which had marketing outlets in Maryland, West Virginia, Virginia and North and South Carolina. A chain of seventy service stations, largely in New York, was purchased in 1929 from the Mahaffery Oil Company, of Corning, New York.

In the late twenties and early thirties, there was also an expansion of the marketing activities of former members of the Standard Oil trust which had not previously been engaged in marketing. Between 1927 and 1930 the Ohio Oil Company purchased marketing facilities selling approximately 16 million gallons of refined products per year. These facilities were largely in Indiana, but small jobbers and retailers were also acquired in Michigan, Ohio, Illinois, and Kentucky. This region remained for many years Ohio's principal marketing area. In 1930, Ohio bought Transcontinental to obtain crude production, but also obtained some marketing facilities in Iowa, Nebraska, Minnesota, South Dakota, Kansas, Oklahoma, Arkansas, and Texas. However, Ohio sold largely in small towns and suburbs rather than the large urban markets and hence the company's market share remained small.[25]

Thus, by 1939, there had been wide spread expansion by the Standard companies. Standard of New York had become a nation-wide marketer; Indiana Standard and Continental had also expanded significantly, so that they were each marketing throughout most of the nation. (Table 5). Standard of New York had made the greatest inroads upon the original territory of several of the other 'Standard Companies'. As in 1926, the company had a large share of California Standard's area, but had also gained a large portion of Indiana's area, as well as that of Atlantic and Ohio Standard. (Table 6). Indiana Standard had made equally significant inroads upon the original territories of Atlantic, Continental and Jersey Standard. Continental, although entering the territory of each of the other companies, in no case seems to have made a serious impact, for the average market share gained was approximately 2 per cent. Atlantic, expanding into the original territories of four other companies, in no case gained more than 3 per cent of the market.

V

The period following the Second World War[26] was characterised by efforts of Socony and Indiana Standard to consolidate the territorial gains made before the war, and by the rapid expansion of the Jersey and California companies. All of these activities were the result of intensified competition, in part caused by the crude surpluses throughout the world. Competitive pressures can be met both by more efficient operation, and by wider markets. To achieve both of these goals, these companies sought to become national marketers.

California Standard's discoveries of crude reserves in Saudi Arabia in the immediate post war years resulted in an immense supply overbalance for this company. To help provide a market for this crude, in 1946 California purchased and expanded the 15,000 b/d refinery of the Barber Asphalt Corporation in New Jersey. This provided the basis of California's entry into five north-eastern states, in which 'Calso' and unbranded gasoline was sold through jobbers.[27] This resulted in California's entry into parts of the original territories of Socony, Jersey Standard, and Atlantic.

However, the California company also had large crude production in the Gulf states, and needed a market for this as well. In 1958, when the Justice Department sued to break the contract under which Jersey Standard supplied 83 per cent of the gasoline sold by Kentucky Standard, California began negotiations toward forming a link with the Kentucky company. A merger was worked out, with the agreement of the Government, and announced in June 1961. Simultaneously, a consent decree was entered, requiring the Jersey company to sever its supply contract with Kentucky Standard within five years. California subsequently announced

TABLE 5
Marketng Areas, 1939

	Atlantic Refining Co.	Continental Oil Co.	StdOil Co. (California)	Std. Oil Co. (Indiana)	Std. Oil Co. (Kentucky)	Std. Oil Co. (New Jersey)	Std. Oil Co. of New York	Std. Oil Co. (Ohio)	No. of Companies per state
Alabama				×	+				2
Arizona		×	+				×		3
Arkansas		×				+	×		3
California			+				×		2
Colorado		+	×	×			×		4
Connecticut	×	×		×		×	+		5
Delaware	+	×		×		×	×		5
District of Columbia		×				+	×		3
Florida	×	×		×	+				4
Georgia	×	×		×	+				4
Idaho		+	×	×			×		4
Illinois		×		+			×		3
Indiana		×		+			×	×	4
Iowa		×		+			×		3
Kansas		×		+			×		3
Kentucky					+				1
Louisiana		×		×		+	×		4
Maine				×		×	+		3
Maryland	×	×		×		+	×	×	6
Massachusetts	×			×		×	+		4
Michigan		×		+			×	×	4
Minnesota		×		+			×		3
Mississippi				×	+				2
Missouri		×		+			×		3
Montana		+		×			×		3
Nebraska		×		+			×		3
Nevada			+				×		2
New Hampshire	×			×		×	+		4
New Jersey	×	×		×		+	+		5
New Mexico		+	×				×		3
New York	×	×		×		×	+		5
N. Carolina	×	×		×		+	×		5
N. Dakota		×	×	+			×		4
Ohio	×	×		×			×	+	5
Oklahoma		×		×			+		3
Oregon		×	+				×		3
Pennsylvania	+	×		×		×	×	×	6
Rhode Island	×			×		×	+		4
S. Carolina	×	×		×		+	×		5
S. Dakota		×	×	+			×		4
Tennessee				×		×	+	×	3
Texas		×	×			×	+		4
Utah		+	×	×			×		4
Vermont	×			×		×	+		4
Virginia	×	×		×		+	×		5
Washington		×	+				×		3
W. Virginia	×	×		×		+	×	×	6
Wisconsin		×		+			×		3
Wyoming		+		×			×		3
Total Number of States	17	38	12	39	5	20	44	6	

Original Territories +

Source: Adapted from T.N.E.C. Investigation of Concentration of Economic Power, Monograph No. 39, *Control of the Petroleum Industry by Major Companies* (Washington: Government Printing Office, 1941), 88-89.

TABLE 6

Market Share Gained by 'Standard Oil' Companies from the Original Territories
of other 'Standard Oil' Companies by 1939
(Percentages)

Gained by	Atlantic	Continental	Std. (Cal.)	Std. (Ind.)	Std. (Ky.)	Std. (N.J.)	Std. of N.Y.	Std. (Ohio)
					Losses in Original Territories			
Atlantic...............	—	0	0	0	1.7	3.0	2.3	2.7
Continental.............	n.a.	—	n.a.	2.6	n.a.	1.9	2.0	n.a.
Standard (California)......	0	n.a.	—	0	0	0	n.a.	0
Standard (Indiana)........	8.5	8.3	0	—	6.4	8.8	3.8	1.1
Standard (Kentucky)......	0	0	0	0	—	0	0	0
Standard (New Jersey).....	n.a.	n.a.	0	0	0	—	8.6	0
Standard of New York.....	6.8	5.4	9.9	7.9	0	2.4	—	5.9
Standard (Ohio)..........	1.6	0	0	n.a.	0	n.a.	0	—

Source: Adapted from T.N.E.C. Monograph No. 39, 91-93.

plans to construct a refinery at Pascagoula, Mississippi. Thus, during the post-war period California Standard entered the entire Eastern U.S. Market, and by 1961 was selling in seventeen states which were originally the territories of Standard of New York, Jersey Standard, and Atlantic.

While the California company was expanding on the East Coast, Jersey Standard was entering new markets in the West. In 1942, through its subsidiary, Carter, the Jersey company gained control of the North-west Refining Company of Montana, which included bulk plants and retail outlets in that state. In 1946 Carter also bought the Yale Corporation and the Consumers Oil Company, which had refineries at Billings and New Castle, respectively, and marketing facilities in South Dakota. Carter also expanded further, into the Pacific Northwest, during 1955. These activities brought Jersey Standard into the original territories of both Continental and California Standard.

Jersey entered Indiana Standard's territory for the first time when, in 1946, Penola, a subsidiary, began selling unbranded gasoline to large wholesale buyers in the mid-west. In 1956, the company obtained the Pate Oil Company in Wisconsin, in exchange for 85,000 shares of Jersey stock. Pate was a successful independent marketer, selling approximately 35 million gallons of gasoline yearly through 104 stations within a fifty mile radius of Milwaukee. During the same year Jersey bought South Side Petroleum Company and Perfect Power Corporation, independent marketers in the

Chicago area, with a total of 115 stations. Oklahoma, another important seller in the Chicago area, with approximately 155 stations, was acquired the following year for 122,000 shares of Jersey stock. The Globe Fuel Products Company, also an independent distributor in Illinois, was purchased in the same year. In 1958 Jersey purchased Gaseteria, a chain of 263 stations operating in four mid-west states. By 1960 the Jersey Company had also entered Nebraska through the purchase of the Lincoln Oil Company.

At the same time Jersey was encroaching upon the original territories of Continental and California Standard in the South West. In 1956 Jersey entered New Mexico, and during the next three years gained nearly 4 per cent of this market. Late in the summer of 1959 Jersey purchased approximately 140 stations in Arizona, and in the following year opened 35 outlets in the Los Angeles area, largely by purchasing an existing distributor. In 1960, Jersey entered Nevada and began marketing in Utah and Oklahoma through distributors.

Also in 1960 Jersey entered Sohio's area, and in early 1961 acquired the service station business of the Sun Flash Oil Company in the Columbus area. By the end of the year Jersey had approximately 100 stations in Ohio. Moreover, after California's purchase of Kentucky Standard, Jersey entered Mississippi, Georgia, Florida, Alabama and Kentucky.

This rapid post-war expansion gave Jersey Standard a widespread, but uncoordinated, marketing operation. Thus, in May 1960, the Humble Oil and Refining Company was formed to bring together the many operating subsidiaries — Esso, Carter, Oklahoma, Pate, especially — into a single administrative structure. The 'Esso' brand name was retained in the East and South East, but a new brand 'Enco' was introduced throughout the remainder of the nation, because another 'Standard' brand could not be introduced into the original territories of Indiana Standard, Continental or California Standard.

The activities of the Indiana and New York companies could not be as dramatic as those of Jersey and California, simply because the former had achieved so much in the pre-war period. Of course, there was some expansion by these companies. Indiana entered Oregon and Washington in 1953, but sales there were not large until 1959 when the True Oil Company, with 106 retail outlets in Washington, Oregon and Idaho, was purchased. Some sales were also made in the mid-1950s in California, New Mexico, Arizona and Texas, but again these were not important. Probably the most far reaching development for the Indiana company was its effort to

TABLE 7
Marketing Areas, 1961

	Atlantic Refining Co.	Continental Oil Co.	Std. Oil Co. (California)	Std. Oil Co. (Indiana)	Std. Oil Co. (Kentucky)	Std. Oil Co. (New Jersey)	Std. Oil Co. of New York	Std. Oil Co. (Ohio)	No. of Companies per state
Alabama		×		×	+	×			4
Arizona		×	+	×		×	×		5
Arkansas		×		×		+	×		4
California		×	+			×	×		4
Colorado		+	×	×		×	×		5
Connecticut	×		×	×		×	+		5
Delaware	+		×	×		×	×		5
District of Columbia	×		×	×		+	×		5
Florida	×	×		×	+	×			5
Georgia	×			×	+	×			4
Idaho		+	×	×		×	×		5
Illinois		×		+		×	×		4
Indiana		×		+		×	×	×	5
Iowa		×		+		×	×		4
Kansas		×		+			×		3
Kentucky		×		×	+	×		×	5
Louisiana		×		×		+	×		4
Maine			×	×		×	+		4
Maryland	×		×	×		+	×		5
Massachusetts	×		×	×		×	+		5
Michigan				+		×	×	×	4
Minnesota		×		+			×		3
Mississippi		×		×	+	×			4
Missouri		×		+			×		3
Montana		+	×	×		×	×		5
Nebraska		×	×	+		×	×		5
Nevada		×	+	×		×	×		5
New Hampshire	×		×	×		×	+		5
New Jersey	×		×	×		+	×		5
New Mexico		+	×			×	×		4
New York	×		×	×		×	+	×	6
N. Carolina	×			×		+	×		4
N. Dakota		×		+		×	×		4
Ohio			×		×	×	+		4
Oklahoma		×		×		×	+		4
Oregon		×	+	×		×	×		5
Pennsylvania	+		×	×		×	×	×	6
Rhode Island	×		×	×		×	+		5
S. Carolina	×			×		+	×		4
S. Dakota		×	×	+		×	×		5
Tennessee		×		+		×	×		4
Texas		×	×			×	+		4
Utah		+	×	×		×	×		5
Vermont	×		×	×		×	+		5
Virginia	×		×	×		+	×		5
Washington		×	+	×		×	×		5
W. Virginia	×			×		+	×	×	5
Wisconsin		×		+		×	×		4
Wyoming		+	×	×		×	×		5
Total Number of States	17	30	27	46	5	46	44	7	

1 Purchased by Standard Oil of California.
Source: National Petroleum News, Fact Book Issue, Mid-May, 1961-62, 68-71.

consolidate its operations. On 1 January 1961, the company combined its refining, product transportation, and operating assets with those of its subsidiaries. Standard Oil of Indiana became a parent company with responsibilities for broad management policies and coordination; American became a national marketing and manufacturing company. Again, because of the trade mark problem, a national brand employing the Standard name could not be employed, so that the American name was used, although in Indiana's original territory its stations maintained the Standard identification.

Continental's post-war activities are perhaps best described as retrenchment rather than consolidation. In 1949, the company disposed of its retail marketing outlets in the Eastern part of the U.S., reducing its gasoline marketing area to 23 states.[28] Subsequently, the company expanded westward. In the Southeast it sold largely through a wholly-owned distributor, the Kayo Oil Company. In 1960, Continental purchased the Douglas Oil Company of California which sold gasoline in California, Nevada and Oregon.

Although the Standard Oil Company (Ohio) sold some products in other states before the Second World War, the Fleet Wing name was used rather than the company's 'Sohio' brand. After the war, increased crude and refining capacity increased the pressure on the company to expand its marketing activities. Additional effort within Ohio was clearly not the answer, for the company already

TABLE 8

Market Share Gained by 'Standard Oil' Companies from the Original Territories of other 'Standard Oil' Companies by 1960

(Percentages)

Gained by	*Atlantic*	*Continental*	*Std. (Cal.)*	*Std. (Ind.)*	*Std. (Ky.)*	*Std. (N.J.)*	*Std. of N.Y.*	*Std. (Ohio)*
					Losses in Original Territories			
Atlantic................	—	0	0	0	.7	2.3	2.7	*
Continental.............	0	—	.1	1.4	.3	1.3	1.7	0
Standard (California)......	1.3	8.7	—	*	0	.8	3.0	0
Standard (Indiana)	6.7	13.3	.4	—	6.0	10.0	2.4	*
Standard (Kentucky)......	0	0	0	0	—	0	0	0
Standard (New Jersey).....	14.7	4.3	.5	n.a.	0	—	12.9	*
Standard of New York.....	6.9	3.7	9.4	5.5	0	3.8	—	2.3
Standard (Ohio)..........	n.a.	0	0	*	*	0	*	—

* less than 1 per cent.
Source: Calculated from company market share estimates.

had approximately one third of the market, and further expansion would not only have been difficult, but also might have been subject to attack under the anti-trust laws. Expanding in other states under the Fleet Wing name was less than satisfactory, for this name did not have the acceptance of the 'Sohio' brand.

The company attempted to test the legality of using the 'Sohio' name in neighbouring states by selling its branded products in four stations near Detroit. In May 1954, Indiana Standard brought suit, contending that the 'Sohio' brand was clearly derived from the 'Standard Oil' name, and thus infringed upon Indiana Standard's brand. The court upheld Indiana Standard in a decision rendered in June 1955. During the interval, Ohio Standard introduced a new gasoline with a boron additive, and initiated an intensive advertising campaign to link the name Boron to the Standard name. In 1954, the company established a subsidiary, the Boron Oil Company, and began marketing in Kentucky under the Boron name. By 1961, the activities of the Boron subsidiary were extended to Pennsylvania.

Thus during the post-war period, Jersey Standard had joined Standard of New York and Indiana Standard as a nation wide marketer, and California Standard (when its purchase of Kentucky Standard is included) had expanded to a thirty-two state market. (Table 7). Continental reduced its marketing area somewhat, but remained in thirty states. Ohio Standard also began expanding outside Ohio. Atlantic, however, remained confined to its pre-war territory along the East Coast.

The impact of this expansion upon the original territories of some companies was not great, especially that of Ohio Standard. (Table 8). In other instances, shares of 'invading' Standard companies had actually fallen because of the increased importance of other expanding companies. In only a few cases, such as that of Indiana Standard in the original Jersey territory, and Jersey in the original Atlantic and Standard of New York territories, did the invader obtain ten per cent or more of the market. However, the stage was clearly set for further expansion.

VI

During the fifty years following the dissolution, all of the original Standard companies, with the exception of Kentucky Standard, expanded their marketing territories. Indiana Standard and Standard of New York became essentially nationwide sellers before the Second World War, and in recent years both the Jersey and California companies have been approaching this goal rapidly. Moreover, Ohio Standard is clearly searching for a means of achieving more significant growth beyond Ohio. The geographical extent of expansion by the various companies was suggested by Table 7, where it was seen that in 1961 there were twenty-seven states, and the District of Columbia, which had five or more former members of the Standard Trust competing with one another. Forty-six states had four or more of these companies selling within their boundaries.

The extent of changes in the market areas of individual companies may also be observed in Table 8, but another manner of viewing these developments is to examine the portion of each company's total sales in the United States which have been obtained from their original marketing areas during the period studied. Table 9 indicates that the importance of sales in these original areas generally has declined, or remained constant, as in the case of the Ohio and Kentucky companies. The sole exception here is that of Atlantic, where there has been a significant increase in the importance of the original territory. That is, although Atlantic was one of the first of these companies to strike out into new areas after the dissolution, during the bulk of the past half century the company has come to rely more heavily upon its original marketing area. At the opposite extreme is Standard of New York, which has experienced the greatest proportionate decline, nearly fifty per cent, in its dependence upon its original area. The decline in dependence upon initial territories is also relatively large in the cases of the Indiana and California companies, but small for Jersey Standard, largely because of the recent nature of this company's growth.

TABLE 9

Percentage of Total U.S. Gasoline Sales obtained from Original Territory by Company, 1926-1960

	1926	1938	1954	1960
Atlantic.................	27.1	54.6	48.8	50.4
Continental..............	81.8	26.9	26.8	33.2
Std. (Cal.)...............	99.7	n.a.	73.1	73.0
Std. (Ind.)..............	86.0	59.9	59.8	56.5
Std. (N.J.)	55.1	57.2	51.2	50.1
Std. (Ky.)...............	100.0	100.0	100.0	100.0
Std. of N.Y.............	89.6	49.7	n.a.	40.7
Std. (Ohio)	100.0	87.2	99.1	99.9

Sources: 1926—F.T.C., *Petroleum Industry, Prices of Profits and Competition*, 225-227.
  1938—TNEC Monograph No. 39, 91-94.
  1954—M.G. de Chazeau and A. E. Kahn, *Integration and Competition in the Petroleum Industry* (1959), 90-91.
  1960—Company estimates.

It has been seen above it was not until after the First World War that there was a general expansion of marketing territories, and until the late 1920s much of this appears to have been almost accidental. That is, the shortages, or threatened shortages, of crude oil led to backward integration to assure crude supplies. A great deal of this integration was achieved by acquisition or merger, and some of the companies thus acquired were integrated or semi-integrated, so that marketing facilities were obtained along with crude supplies. Since some of these marketing facilities were in areas outside the original territory of the acquiring company, competition was initiated with former members of the trust. The acquisition of Pan American by Indiana Standard is perhaps the best illustration of this type of expansion.

Not until the late 1920s or early 1930s did there appear widespread efforts to acquire marketing facilities by forward integration. Much of this activity was caused directly, or indirectly, by surplus crude supplies, for which markets had to be found by the various companies. It is notable, however, that the rate of expansion varied significantly among the companies. Before the Second World War, Standard of New York grew rapidly, especially with the merger with Vacuum, which had been integrating forward itself in a search for market outlets. On the other hand, Jersey Standard was particularly slow in expanding, probably because of the company's conservative management, which in turn was partly due to a deep concern that such activity might lead to public animosity toward the company.

After the Second World War, California Standard continued expanding, again largely because of a crude imbalance. However, the Jersey company offers the most dramatic example of market

TABLE 10

Percentage of Shares of U.S. Gasoline Sales by Company, 1926-1960

	1926	1935	1938	1954	1960
Atlantic.	4.2	2.5	2.7	2.2	1.9
Continental.	1.4	1.8	2.2	1.6	1.4
Std. (Cal.)	3.4	2.7	n.a.	4.4	3.8
Std. (Ind.)	10.6	8.5	9.5	7.7	7.4
Std. (Ky.).	2.5	1.4	n.a.	1.6	1.6
Std. (N.J.)	5.4	6.1	6.9	7.8	7.9
Std. of N.Y.	9.6	8.7	9.4	7.8	6.7
Std. (Ohio)	2.4	1.5	1.6	1.7	1.6

Sources: 1926 & 1935—J. G. McLean and R. W. Haigh, op. cit., 104.
1938—F.T.C., *Distribution Methods and Costs*, 26, 51-54.
1954—M. G. De Chazeau and A. E. Kahn, op. cit., 30.
1960—Company estimates.

expansion, although here it appears that it was not crude imbalance at work, but largely an effort to increase marketing efficiency. There was a need for nationwide marketing to improve advertising efficiency in particular. Without nationwide sales, especially under a single brand, it was difficult to use national media. In extreme cases, radio or television commercials on stations located near the fringe of a company's market area might actually have the effect of promoting the product of a rival Standard company in the adjacent territory. It is significant that to achieve this goal of a national brand, Jersey Standard gave up locally important brands throughout much of the nation, in favour of an unknown 'Enco' name. During the same period other companies, which previously achieved nationwide marketing areas, also adopted new brands which could be employed nationally without infringing upon the trade mark rights of other Standard companies in their original territories.

TABLE 11

Percentage Share of Total Gasoline Sales in Original Territories by Company, 1911-1960

Company	1911	1915	1926	1938	1954	1960
Atlantic..........	—	70	44.5	21.9	19.4	16.4
Continental.......	—	63	47.2	98.0	11.8	12.9
Std. (Cal.)........	71[1]	48	28.7	17.7	22.3	21.3
Std. (Ind.)........	85[2]	60	35.0	19.7	17.4	16.2
Std. (N.J.)........	—	60	41.2	27.4	26.5	24.1
Std. (Ky.).........	—.	50	33.3	23.8	18.7	n.a.
Std. of N.Y........	92[3]	70	37.5	20.4	18.0	13.6
Std. (Ohio)	70[4]	70	37.6	23.9	31.4	28.5

Sources: 1911—1 G. T. White, *Formative Years in the Far West* (1955), 489.
   2 P. H. Giddens, *Standard Oil Company* (Indiana) (1962), 136.
   3 *Socony Mobil, A Short History*, booklet published by the company, 13.
   4 Estimate by the company.
1915—*Report on the Price of Gasoline*, 144.
1926—Petroleum Administration Board, *Final Report of the Marketing Division* (Washington, Government Printing Office, 1936), 7.
1938—TNEC Monograph No. 39, 91-94.
1954—M. G. de Chazeau and A. E. Kahn, op. cit., 30.
1960—Company estimates.

Despite the general expansion of market areas, the former Standard companies, as a group, did not maintain their share of the United States gasoline market. In 1926 these companies sold 39.5 per cent of the nation's gasoline; in 1960 this figure had fallen to 32.3 per cent. Nor have the individual companies generally been able to maintain their respective shares of total national consumption. Only Jersey Standard has gained substantially since 1926, and California Standard appears to have gained slightly

(Table 10). Moreover, it is clear that those companies which have not expanded their market areas have experienced proportionately greater losses than have their rivals. Atlantic's loss in share is approximately 55 per cent of its original share, and Kentucky Standard's is 36 per cent, while the losses of both Indiana Standard and Standard of New York have been approximately 30 per cent.

At the same time, these companies' shares of the market in their original territories has also declined (Table 11). This has been due to the invasion of these territories by other Standard companies as well as the growth of other competitors. Actually, the growth in competition from others has been of greater significance in all cases, than that originating from former members of the Trust (Table 12). This implies that although a very large proportion of the growth by the various Standard companies was by merger or acquisition, this has, on balance, led to more intense competition. Moreover, there is no indication that the growth of independent rivals has been seriously retarded by the growth of the Standard companies.

TABLE 12
Loss of Market Share in Original Territory since 1911, by Company, and Source of Rivalry
(Percentages)

	Share held by Original Company in 1960	Share Gained by Standard Rivals	Share Gained by Other Rivals
Atlantic....................	16.8	29.8	53.6
Continental.................	12.9	30.0	57.1
Std. (Cal.)..................	21.3	10.4	68.3
Std. (Ind.).................	16.2	6.9	76.9
Std. (N.J.)	16.2	7.0	77.0
Std. (Ky.)..................	24.1	18.2	57.7
Std. of N.Y.................	13.6	22.7	63.7
Std. (Ohio)	28.5	2.3	69.2

In all instances since the dissolution, the various Standard companies have lost market share in each of the states comprising their original territories, and this has generally been a consistent trend throughout the entire period (Table 13). During the past twenty-five years, however, there have been a few exceptions: California and Jersey Standard have each held their market shares, or increased them slightly in three states: Indiana has increased in two states, and Ohio in its home state.

Despite the general loss of market share, these companies on the whole have continued to rank first in each of the states comprising their original territories.[29] The California, Jersey and Ohio companies remain first throughout their respective 'home' states; Indiana and Kentucky have lost first place in only one state in each case. The major exception to this situation is that of Continental, which continues to hold first rank in only one of its original states, and ranges from second to fourth in the remainder. Standard of New York ranks second in two of the New England States which made up its original territory. Thus, the ranking of these companies in their home states is the sole vestige of the monopoly position which they held a half century before.

TABLE 13

Percentage Share of Gasoline Sales by Company, and States in Original Territories,
1926-1960

		1926	1935	1938	1960
Atlantic.........	Delaware........	44.5	18.0	19.7	13.6
	Pennsylvania	44.5	21.7	22.0	16.8
Continental.......	Colorado.........	47.2	18.4	18.3	14.2
	Idaho...........	47.2	17.1	20.8	12.3
	Montana........	47.2	20.3	15.1	12.8
	New Mexico	. 47.2	25.2	20.8	10.5
	Utah	47.2	21.1	15.3	11.7
	Wyoming	47.2	29.8	20.0	14.4
Std. (Cal.)	Arizona..........	28.7	22.3	n.a.	19.3
	California	28.7	19.5	n.a.	20.9
	Nevada	28.7	24.8	n.a.	24.9
	Oregon	28.7	24.6	n.a.	24.5
	Washington	28.7	27.3	n.a.	17.4
Std. (Indiana).....	Illinois...........	35.5	21.7	21.6	19.8
	Indiana..........	35.5	23.6	23.7	17.0
	Iowa	35.5	21.1	21.2	16.4
	Kansas	35.5	12.7	11.7	13.3
	Michigan	35.5	20.5	18.8	16.8
	Minnesota........	35.5	17.6	20.1	15.3
	Missouri	35.5	16.0	16.2	10.9
	Nebraska	23.6	10.9	9.4	10.0
	N. Dakota........	35.5	29.2	30.3	26.1
	S. Dakota	35.5	24.4	24.5	19.8
	Wisconsin........	35.5	19.8	21.3	15.5
Std. (Kentucky) ...	Alabama.........	33.3	22.6	n.a.	17.7
	Florida	33.3	23.3	n.a.	15.1
	Georgia..........	33.3	20.6	n.a.	13.6
	Kentucky	33.3	29.1	n.a.	20.5
	Mississippi	33.3	21.2	n.a.	16.5
Std. (New Jersey) ..	Arkansas.........	35.5	22.1	20.9	18.4
	District of Columbia	43.2	29.7	27.8	31.1
	Louisiana	35.5	24.8	26.0	23.4
	Maryland	43.2	22.3	23.5	23.9
	New Jersey	43.2	28.0	26.6	26.6
	N. Carolina.......	43.2	27.3	28.4	22.8
	S. Carolina	43.2	31.6	28.7	22.4
	Tennessee........	35.5	25.9	25.4	20.4
	Virginia..........	43.2	28.9	30.8	25.7
	W. Virginia.......	43.2	34.0	37.1	29.3
Std. of New York ..	Connecticut	46.1	28.0	23.3	14.2
	Maine	46.1	27.8	24.2	15.6
	Massachusetts	46.1	27.5	31.2	15.6
	New Hampshire ...	46.1	29.3	25.3	17.5
	New York	46.1	27.5	25.7	19.2
	Oklahoma........	18.1	6.4	13.1	6.9
	Rhode Island	46.1	19.3	19.8	14.5
	Texas............	18.1	12.6	13.1	8.8
	Vermont.........	46.1	28.3	25.9	15.7
Std. (Ohio)	Ohio	37.6	23.0	23.9	28.8

Sources: 1926 and 1935—J. G. McLean and R. W. Haigh, op. cit., 103.
    1938—Calculated from TNEC Monograph No. 39, 91-94.
    1960—Company estimates.

NOTES

1 The factual details upon which this study is based were largely obtained from an issue-by-issue examination of trade periodicals for the years encompassed by the study. Some company representatives have contributed additional material, and the writer wishes to express his appreciation of their assistance.

2 *Standard Oil Company of New Jersey v. U.S.,* 221 U.S. I (1911).

3 The remaining companies consisted of four, largely concerned with the production of crude oil, two of which were entirely devoted to foreign marketing, two refining companies, and eleven which were solely in the transportation field.

4 The President of Indiana Standard stated that the Company did not sell in Nebraska in competition with the Nebraska Company. *High Cost of Gasoline and Other Petroleum Products,* Senate Report No. 1236, 67th Congress, 4th Session, 67th Congress (Washington, Government Printing Office, 1923), 778-9.

5 Indiana Standard extended its operations into southern Missouri; Jersey Standard entered Arkansas and the western part of Louisiana. The balance of the Waters-Pierce area was occupied by Magnolia Oil Company. Until 1918 Magnolia apparently was operated to some extent independently of other former subsidiaries although over 70% of its stock was held by the presidents of Jersey Standard and Socony. Moreover, in 1918 control of Magnolia went to Socony, and thus in this paper the states of Oklahoma and Texas will be considered part of Socony's 'original territory.'

6 The available evidence suggests that this lack of vigorous rivalry at first was largely a result of economic factors. There appears to be only one instance of a formal arrangement precluding competition in a particular area. Indiana Standard prohibited licensees of its cracking patents from selling gasoline in the states which comprised its home territory, plus Montana, Wyoming, Colorado and Oklahoma. *High Cost of Gasoline,* op. cit., 375.

7 Federal Trade Commission, *Report on the Price of Gasoline in 1915* (Washington, Government Printing Office, 1917), 152.

8 The brand-name problem was not tested in the courts until 1935. In March of that year, Jersey Standard opened three service stations in St Louis. Indiana Standard filed suit charging trade-mark infringement and unfair competition. In 1938 the U.S. Circuit Court of Appeals upheld a lower court decision in favour of Indiana Standard, and the Jersey company was perpetually restrained from using its 'Esso' brand in any of Indiana's fourteen state marketing area. More recently, Indiana has obtained a court decree enjoining Ohio Standard from using the 'Sohio' brand name in Michigan.

9 *Report on the Price of Gasoline in 1915,* op. cit., 151.

10 A. G. Maguire, *Prices and Marketing Practices Covering the Distribution of Gasoline and Kerosene Throughout the United States,* U.S. Fuel Administration, Oil Division (Washington, Government Printing Office, 1919), 7.

11 *National Petroleum News,* 16 March 1927, 23.

12 In 1912 the value of gasoline output in the U.S. exceeded that of kerosene, formerly the dominant product.

13 J. E. Pogue and I. Lubin, *Prices of Petroleum and its Products During the War,* U.S. Fuel Administration, Oil Division (Washington, Government Printing Office, 1919), 20-21.

14 *National Petroleum News,* 29 October, 1919, 21.

15 *Report on the Price of Gasoline in 1915,* op. cit., 152.

16 In a subsequent issue, a letter from the secretary of the company was published, explaining that since the dissolution Atlantic had been operating 'independently and competitively, not only in America, but particularly in the foreign markets.' *National Petroleum News,* 23 February 1921, 101.

17 A. G. Maguire, op. cit.
18 Ibid., 11.
19 Ibid., 8-9.   8
20 John G. McLean and Robert Wm. Haigh, *The Growth of Integrated Oil Companies* (1954), 256.
21 *National Petroleum News*, 1 April 1925, 34.
22 It should be noted that Mutual controlled Continental as a result of this merger, although Continental's name survived.
23 Hartzell Spence, *Portrait in Oil* (1962), 235.
24 *U.S. v. Standard Oil Company of N.Y.*, 47F. 2nd 288 (E.D. Mo. 1931).
25 H. Spence, op. cit., 240-42.
26 The years 1939-1945 necessarily saw little change in marketing activities and thus are omitted here.
27 Before the war, California Standard had sold between 100-150 million gallons of gasoline to the Sun Oil Company for distribution in the East under Sun's brand. After the war, Sun's increased refining capacity enabled it to supply its own requirements.
28 The company continued to market a full line of industrial and automotive lubricants on the Atlantic seaboard. Continental withdrew from the eastern gasoline market rather than engage in the extensive investment programme required to establish a strong position in this area. A partial withdrawal from Pennsylvania, New Jersey, and New York was reported even before the Second World War (*Fortune*, June 1939, 94).
29 In seven of the twelve states in which the original company is no longer first in rank, the position has been taken by another Standard company.

12
Government Contracting, Competition and Growth in the Heavy Woollen Industry

Frederick J. Glover*

The highly competitive, atomistic character of the *woollen* (as distinct from the *worsted*) textile industry of the West Riding of Yorkshire in the early nineteenth century is well recognised in the accepted economic history of the period, but the fact that an oligopolistic market structure was also strongly established in an important branch of the industry's activity before 1850 seems to have received scant attention in the published literature. The purchase of blankets and heavy woollen cloths for public use by the government departments (chiefly the Navy Board and the Board of Ordnance) represented an important segment of the domestic demand impinging upon the industry during the three decades following 1820,[1] but the special features of the public buying of woollen textiles were such that only a relatively small number of cloth-making enterprises were induced to share *regularly* in the risks and profits associated with direct tendering. The primary and secondary economic effects flowing from this development were by no means negligible, and it is the purpose of this article to examine some of the important aspects of government contracting in this industry, as revealed by the surviving business archives of a large Yorkshire blanket-making firm;[2] to assess the influence exerted by the government buyers in promoting or retarding the efficiency of the industry; and to draw some general conclusions pertaining to competition and economic development.

I

The partnership of Hagues and Cook, later Hagues, Cook and Wormald, a condominium of landowning, merchanting and banking families, was founded at Dewsbury Mills 2 miles south of Dewsbury

*From *Economic History Review*, 2nd series, Vol. XVI (1963-64), pp. 478-98. Reprinted by permission of the editor of *Economic History Review* and the author.

in the Calder Valley in 1811, primarily as a woollen-spinning and cloth-fulling business but with some hand-loom weaving carried on by employees in their own homes.[3] In 1815 the partners also commenced the direct manufacture of blankets and heavy woollen cloths on a large scale at Dewsbury Mills, which they vended at home and abroad.[4] After 1820 the firm, under the agressive leadership of Thomas Cook, the junior partner in the undertaking, made a powerful bid to secure a large and regular trade with the United States, and by the late 1830's the firm had become the principal British exporter of blankets to that market.[5] The first government orders were procured by Cook and his partners as sub-contracts from London cloth factors in 1818 and 1819, but although great care seems to have been taken in the completion of these initial contracts the ventures proved far from profitable.[6] Cook and his partners thereafter sought direct government orders, but these were not quickly obtained.

It is evident from the firm's correspondence books that the determination with which Cook fought for a share in the government trade was prompted by a trilogy of important considerations. He was anxious to obtain large orders for standard goods in the hope of providing some stability of employment for his labour force and to realise any potential economies of scale;[7] he was aware that his near neighbour, Benjamin Gott of Leeds, had regularly and profitably engaged in this trade;[8] and he was resolved to break down what he, and other West Riding manufacturers, regarded as a grossly unfair prejudice against Yorkshire cloths displayed by the public buying authorities. In 1820 he was writing to a business associate: 'We are determined to have our fair share of these London orders. We do not believe that the Witney people can always *oust* us, either in price or quality, and we must rid the trade of this favouritism. We stand much in need of the employment and profits that these contracts may afford us.'[9]

The 'Witney people' do not seem to have felt as secure in the enjoyment and maintenance of their favoured status as Cook seems to have believed, for some years earlier a partner in the firm of John Early and Sons, the leading Witney blanket producers at that time, was writing to his brother from London: 'It is the general opinion that these Yorkshire blades will do us and something must be attempted to prevent the same if possible.'[10]

Despite the trepidation with which this nascent Yorkshire competitiveness was apparently being received in Witney, however, Cook continued to experience difficulty in gaining public contracts until 1823 (see Table 1), and the general tenor of his comments on this subject in the firm's correspondence books suggests that his

TABLE 1

Hagues, Cook and Wormald, tenders and government contracts, 1820-50[11]

	No. of tenders submitted	No. of contracts received[12]	No. of blankets	No. of yards of cloth[13]
1820	4	0	—	—
1821	5	0	—	—
1822	4	0	—	—
1823	4	1	22,000	—
1824	5	1	20,000	5,000
1825	5	2	30,000	10,000
1826	4	1	35,000	5,000
1827	5	3	30,000	15,000
1828	5	3	35,000	10,000
1829	5	3	30,000	8,000
1830	6	4	65,000	12,000
1831	6	4	45,000	10,000
1832	7	4	32,000	10,000
1833	7	5	65,000	8,000
1834	6	3	35,000	5,000
1835	7	5	80,000	8,000
1836	3	1	60,000	15,000
1837	7	4	45,000	—
1838	7	5	55,000	5,000
1839	8	4	50,000	—
1840	8	3	50,000	5,0000
1841	9	3	45,000	10,000
1842	10	4	62,000	5,000
1843	9	4	20,000	100,000
1844	7	3	60,000	15,000
1845	4	2	65,000	—
1846	9	3	65,000	40,000
1847	4	0	40,000	25,000
1848	9	5	52,000	20,000
1849	10	6	80,000	25,000
1850	10	5	60,000	50,000
Total	199	91	1,323,000	421,000

Yorkshire rivals, Gott excepted, also experienced similar disappointments. The firm of Hagues, Cook and Wormald, however, enjoyed large advantages of capital strength, merchanting skill, and general business connexions, attributes generally denied to the great majority of their West Riding competitors,[14] and it might have been expected that Cook's attempts to cross this particular threshold warranted more tangible success than was manifest in the firm's order books in the early twenties. The Witney manufacturers may have proved more efficient competitors in terms of adherence to promised delivery dates, and they certainly enjoyed a

long-standing reputation for quality in the heavy woollen trade, but
the meagre evidence available supports the view that there was a
pronounced, although not a total, reluctance to award government
contracts to new tenderers — the majority of whom were West
Riding firms — in the decade following Waterloo.[15] It may be
added that this was not entirely disadvantageous to the West
Riding trade, in so far as it provided a stimulus to the Yorkshire
export drive in overseas markets in these years, and probably
explains in part the greater success of Yorkshire cloths *vis-a-vis*
their Witney rivals in the United States.

The Navy Board and the Board of Ordnance invited competitive
tenders for specified quantities and qualities of a dozen types of
heavy woollen blankets and uniform cloths in the spring and
autumn of each year (see Table 2), the former authority normally
contracting for the major portion of its annual requirements in the
earlier season.[16] In addition to specifying measurements, the
contracts also defined the weight, type of wool, quality of manufacture, and colour of the finished fabrics, as well as dates of
delivery to the departmental stores at Deptford and the Tower. The
official buyers did not bind themselves to accept the lowest tenders,
but invariably did so, providing they were satisfied of the capacity
of the tenderer to deliver the goods. Following delivery the cloths
were subject to inspection to ascertain 'their conformity in all
respects to the official sample'. Goods rejected were required to be
replaced by the manufacturer within a reasonable period of time,
and in cases where a large proportion of the contracted quantity
was declared deficient or where there was general failure to deliver
goods on time the contracting authority reserved the right to
impose heavy financial charges upon the contractor. No right of
appeal or days of grace were normally provided for in the contract,
but suppliers aggrieved by decisions of official inspectors were
permitted to petition the authority for an extension of delivery time
or for a reduction in the financial penalties.[17] It was generally
believed in the trade, however, that petitioning was detrimental to
future success in tendering: 'We are most reluctant to resort to a
petition and we prefer to accept our loss on the rejected blankets —
which will amount to about 4*d* per blanket on the whole of the
contract — for you know it will not help us in future tenders.'[18]

The woollen manufacturer had three major obstacles to surmount
in the government trade: in gaining contracts; having his goods
accepted; and in obtaining payment. After much persistent
application in solving the first of these problems, Cook was able to
report in 1825 that: 'The Navy Board is decidedly better disposed
to us Yorkshire tykes now and we think the Board of Ordnance

TABLE 2

Typical heavy woolen fabrics purchased by public departments, 1823-50[*]

	Size	Weight	Price range
Board of Ordnance			
Blankets			
Army barrack	56in x 92in	8lbs	14s 0d—19s 6d
Hospital	56in x 96in	4lbs 12ozs	5s 0d—6s 6d
Single	56in x 92in	3lbs 12ozs	3s 9d—5s 3d
Coverlets	51in x 36in	4lbs	4s 3d—6s 0d
Cloth			
Grey kersey[†]	54in width	25ozs per yd	4s 6d—7s 0d
Grey convict[†]	54in width	20 ozs per yd	2s 3d—3s 6d
Navy Board and Admiralty			
Blankets			
Navy	64in x 85in	9lbs	10s 0d—15s 0d
Transport	65in x 82in	8lbs	7s 0d—11s 0d
Hammock	56in x 76in	3lbs 4ozs	3s 6d—5s 0d
Lightweight	64in x 85in	4lbs 8ozs	5s 0d—7s 0d
Cloth			
Serge (white and navy)[‡]	29in width	5.4ozs per yd	6s 6d—9s 0d

[*]Information from H. C. & W., 'Correspondence Books'.
[†]Delivered in pieces 45 yards in length plus an additional customary yard.
[‡]Delivered in pieces 41 yards in length plus customary one inch per yard.

cannot long resist our just claims for a moderate share of the public business.'[19]

Thereafter, his energies were more concentrated upon the problems of acceptance and payment, although the winning of contracts continued to involve him in a very careful appraisal of his own and his rivals' costs of production and, later, led him into collusive agreements and tendering strategies.

After 1828 Cook found that his trading experiences with the two government departments were markedly contrasted. While he found it relatively difficult to obtain naval contracts, once he did so it was fairly easy to receive approval for his deliveries at Deptford; conversely, he gained orders much more readily from the Board of Ordnance but had the greatest difficulty in moving his fabrics past (what he considered to be) the jaundiced eyes of the inspectors at the Tower: 'We have the utmost suspicion of the conduct of Messrs Wickens and Pew in respect of their treatment of our goods. We do not think that they understand the work.'[20]

It was the practice of the Witney manufacturers to send a representative to the receiving depots whenever their consignments were being subjected to inspection, an action which not only succeeded in expediting the flow of goods into approved stores, but also permitted useful explanatory discussions to take place with the inspectors whenever there was a threat of rejection in the air.[21] Robert Nicholson was appointed by the partners to act in a similar capacity for them in 1823, when Cook successfully tendered for 22,000 Navy blankets. Nicholson, a London resident with cloth merchanting experience, had been handling the general London business for Hagues and Cook, from a warehouse in Coleman Street, from 1819 on a commission basis and, until he was discharged in 1839, he undoubtedly acted to mitigate substantially the losses of the partners arising from rejected consignments and gave them a decided advantage over many of their Yorkshire rivals: 'We do not see how this government business can be at all a profitable one without a regular agent in the City who knows about wool and human nature.'[22]

The correspondence books teem with instructions to Nicholson during the early 1830's. He was invariably given ample warning of the imminence of 'invitations to tender' emanating from the departments and urged to procure the official samples quickly; he was bombarded with specific instructions on the timing and presentation of the contract documents; and he was pressed at all times to: 'Keep a sharp eye on the Witney contingent and on Falkner and the London people. It is always useful to know what they are about.'[23] But the majority of letters he received from Dewsbury Mills were usually exhorting him to: 'Go down to the Tower and get for us a clear statement as to the reason for this monstrous rejection. Nobody puts wool together into these goods as faithfully as we do and we cannot understand why this consignment is so troublesome.'[24] Or else requesting his attention to the hastening of payments: 'It is now three months since we had these blankets passed and there is still no sign of our money. Pray see what you can do to rouse them at Deptford in this matter and let us know their attitude.'[25]

This sluggish flow of remittances for government supplies was a major factor in dissuading many small woollen manufacturers from entering the trade as regular participants although, as noted below, its effects were moderated to some extent by the activities of cloth factors. The delays also threatened to reduce further the already narrow profitability of the trade, but most contractors endeavoured to circumvent this adversity by adding a margin to their basic tender price to cover the anticipated losses arising from rejected goods and delayed payments.[26] In so far as this practice raised supply prices generally, the government was thus paying for departmental inefficiencies of inspection and payment in the form of higher contract prices.

II

The number of firms regularly engaged in heavy woollen cloth contracting does not seem to have varied greatly in the period 1820-50 except during the years of deep general business depression in the early 1840s, which brought many desperate bidders into this market, and structurally the trade had the appearance of a concentrated core of enterprises of efficient size with a more or less competitive fringe of smaller firms continuously fluctuating in size and composition. Cook estimated in 1852 that during the preceding thirty years the partners had had to contend with approximately a score of competitors in securing naval and military orders of whom a dozen were vigorous contestants.[27] Six of these were Witney enterprises led by the house of John Early and Sons, which Cook regarded as a single competitor; five of them were large London cloth factors having no direct manufacturing interests and relying on subcontracting methods to deliver the goods;[28] while the rest were all Yorkshire traders, with Gott of Leeds, Halliley and Sons of Dewsbury, and Firth and Company of Heckmondwike providing the main rivalry.

By sub-letting contracts the London cloth factors diffused their government business throughout the Yorkshire heavy woollen area and the Witney region, while Gott, the Hallileys and the Firths regularly added to their production capacity by purchasing unfinished blankets and cloth from independent clothiers and by putting out wool for fabrication to smaller enterprises. Thus, large numbers of blanket and cloth producers were invariably drawn into the supply process whichever of the twelve major protagonists succeeded in gaining the actual orders. Cook also resorted at times to this method of expanding output, but he disliked bidding for orders which exceeded the productive capacity of Dewsbury Mills, due to the difficulties of exercising satisfactory quality control over batches of cloths made in various establishments and his perennial *angst* regarding rejection: 'We do not want more than 30,000 of the Barrack blankets this time, as we do not relish a repetition of the trouble we had last year with outside makers and slipshod work. For you know that the rejection of one consignment can lose the profit of a whole contract, and profit is the end of business.'[29]

Cook's penchant for repeating this latter phrase throughout his business correspondence was wedded to a strong conviction that the term 'profit' could only be properly employed when the net surplus accruing to the firm did not fall below 2½ per cent of the total sales value, or gross turnover, of goods supplied to customers. The partners struck this 'net profit' after due provision for rent, stock valuation changes, depreciation, and interest on capital in trade during each year.[30] Their accounting methods were arbitrary and not always consistent by modern standards and the data shown in the tables below must be interpreted in the light of this qualification, but '2½ per cent on sales' constituted the minimum profitable return, in Cook's view, if the 'ends of business' were to be attained.

The firm's profits from sales to the public departments and from general sales sank below this 'floor' in the late 1820's (see Tables 3-5), and this led the partners in 1830 to introduce a major change in pricing policy. Their profit mark-up per unit of output was drastically reduced.[31] The volume of sales in all markets responded sharply and favourably to this innovation and the partners received a substantial share in an enlarged government trade in that year. This momentum was not maintained, however, in the first quinquennium of the 1830s, although trade was extremely buoyant in 1833, and in 1834 the value of net profits declined to 1.1 per cent of turnover.[32] The trading difficulties of this year also carried into bankruptcy their local rivals, Halliley and Sons of Dewsbury and disrupted the partnership of Halliley and Carter of London, a blanket-contracting subsidiary.

During the first ten years in which the firm engaged in the government trade, the partners were puzzled by the high degree of competitiveness which they encountered. It was readily conceded that Benjamin Gott's reputation necessarily made him a formidable competitor, but he had forged special arrangements with the buying departments and was not often to be found tendering directly in opposition to Hagues, Cook and Wormald; it was also reluctantly accepted that the Witney producers continued to enjoy the benefits of 'irrational' preferences for their fabrics. But how could the London contractors tender at keen prices when they had to buy the products from many less efficient (in Cook's opinion) manufacturers in the West Riding and then add their own not inconsiderable imposts to make the trade profitable? In the case of Halliley and Carter, Cook found it hard to admit that the Halliley establishment could secure the use of factors of production on cheaper terms than those ruling at Dewsbury Mills, estimating that any such superiority could at best be only marginal and more than offset by the costs of maintaining Jeremiah Carter as a permanent trading associate in London.[33]

Cook finally found the answer to this conundrum by dint of a careful appraisal of the inspection procedures operated at Deptford and the Tower: 'It is now clear to us that Carter and some of the London houses can pass cloths which others cannot. The wool used must be 1½d or 2d per lb less than ours and if their goods can

TABLE 3

Hagues, Cook and Wormald, capital and profits, 1820-50*

	Partners' capital in the business £	Total net profits[†] £	Value of total net profits as % of capital employed	Index of wool prices[§§]
1820	30,521	2,010	6.6	100
1821	n.a.	n.a.	—	91
1822	27,991	2,723	9.7	85
1823	25,524	4,990	19.5	74
1824	28,943	6,436	22.3	82
1825	35,886	3,867	10.8	92
1826	42,157	3,353	7.9	75
1827	42,781	4,394	10.6	74
1828	39,325	1,810	4.6	67
1829	39,460	1,219	3.2	71
1830	33,734	7,019	20,8	80
1831	40,871	4,247	10.3	84
1832	41,234	3,800	9.2	81
1833	42,711	7,600	17.8	81
1834	44,579	1,600	3.6	97
1835	46,872	11,000	23.4	94
1836	73,477	‡14,400	19.6	100
1837	85,418	2,522	2.9	88
1838	73,234	7,400	10.1	85
1839	83,666	3,589	4.3	80
1840	83,056	3,600	4.3	77
1841	85,806	4,400	5.1	71
1842	88,991	3,351	3.8	71
1843	89,464	5,000	5.6	68
1844	94,088	7,200	7.7	71
1845	88,863	7,600	8.6	77
1846	93,934	3,600	3.8	74
1847	76,897[ɡ]	4,233[//]	5.5	65
1848	68,238	7,800	11.4	56
1849	60,966	10,500	17.2	59
1850	69,722	10,500	15.0	65

*Compiled from data in H., C. & W., 'Balance Sheets', 'Ledgers', and 'Private Ledgers'.
†Net of provision for interest on capital, rent, depreciation and changes in value of wool stocks.
‡Influx of capital from banking wind-up.
ɡ Withdrawal of capital following Edward Hague's death.
// Gorton Hodges loss of £4,691.
§§ Price paid for a typical quality of blanket wool by Thos. Cook.

pass, then rest assured that all contest with them is hopeless.'[34]

In the summer of 1838 Cook responded to his discovery of the real nature of the competition facing the partners by negotiating an alliance with Jeremiah Carter.[35] In the course of these negotiations the partners found, to their chagrin, that: 'Carter is already in league with the Witney folk and it is surprising that we have not

TABLE 4

Hagues, Cook and Wormald, sales and profits, 1820-50[*]

	Value of total sales at current prices[†] £	Net profits as % of value of total sales[‡]	Index value of total sales at constant prices[§]	Index value of net profits at constant prices[§]
1820	74,000	2.7	100	100
1821	93,100	n.a.	146	—
1822	126,400	2.2	225	180
1823	119,200	4.2	213	295
1824	110,600	5.8	170	365
1835	171,400	2.3	236	200
1826	106,500	3.1	165	190
1827	120,300	3.6	189	255
1828	115,800	1.6	137	105
1829	110,300	1.1	133	70
1830	248,100	2.8	409	425
1831	192,000	2.2	313	255
1832	165,700	2.3	283	240
1833	230,100	3.3	404	495
1834	140,000	1.1	252	105
1835	252,800	4.3	465	755
1836	309,400	4.6	508	880
1837	161,200	1.6	266	150
1838	169,400	4.4	269	435
1839	217,000	1.7	326	200
1840	140,200	2.6	213	200
1841	130,400	3.4	207	260
1842	98,600	3.4	128	215
1843	130,700	3.8	252	360
1844	222,000	3.2	429	515
1845	239,000	3.2	449	530
1846	146,000	2.5	263	240
1847	274,300	1.5	441	250
1848	341,200	2.3	649	550
1849	381,000	2.8	804	820
1850	432,200	2.4	913	820

*Compiled from data in Table 2 and from information in H., C. & W. 'Private Ledgers'.
†Total sales includes sales to public departments.
‡Total net profits as shown in Table 2.
§Sales and profits deflated by Gayer, Rostow and Schwartz's index of wholesale prices (domestic and imported commodities). Cf. *Growth and Fluctuations of the British Economy in the Nineteenth Century* (Oxford, 1953), I, 468.

fared very much worse during these last few seasons. We propose to join him and hope for an improvement in our returns as a result.'[36]

It was finally agreed that Carter should take charge of the submission of final tenders, using pricing data supplied by Cook supplemented by his own judgment and discretion, and that he

TABLE 5

Hagues, Cook and Wormald, sales and profits on government contracts, 1823-50[*]

	Value of sales to public depts. at current prices £	Net profits at current prices £	Net profits as % of sales to public depts.	Index value of sales at current prices	Index value of net profits at current prices	Sales to public depts. as % of total sales	Value of profits on sales to public depts. as % of total profits
1823	9,820	244	2.5	100	100	8.2	4.9
1824	9,632	220	2.3	95	88	8.7	3.4
1825	9,504	357	2.5	127	128	7.7	9.3
1826	9,050	315	2.3	135	126	12.7	9.4
1827	12,460	378	2.0	188	153	15.5	8.6
1828	10,752	328	2.0	166	136	13.9	18.1
1829	13,960	265	1.9	146	111	12.7	21.7
1830	37,520	864	3.8	238	367	9.1	12.3
1831	21,024	414	2.0	219	174	10.9	9.7
1832	13,208	590	4.5	145	260	8.0	15.5
1833	25,440	1,588	6.2	286	718	11.1	20.9
1834	11,482	352	3.1	133	163	8.2	22.0
1835	42,688	1,782	4.2	506	851	16.9	16.2
1836	27,680	1,752	6.3	292	745	8.9	12.2
1837	15,500	437	2.8	164	186	9.6	17.3
1838	20,544	1,040	5.1	209	426	12.1	14.1
1839	15,672	856	5.5	151	331	7.2	23.8
1840	15,858	964	6.1	154	371	11.3	26.8
1841	14,260	1,202	8.4	145	493	10.9	27.3
1842	17,860	1,501	8.4	247	671	18.1	44.8
1843	17,700	1,700	9.1	223	858	13.6	34.0
1844	27,872	1,796	6.6	345	894	12.6	24.9
1845	28,952	1,951	6.7	348	944	12.1	25.7
1846	28,342	1,904	6.7	386	885	19.4	52.9
1847	22,936	1,354	5.9	236	562	8.4	31.9
1848	25,872	1,262	4.9	315	619	7.6	16.2
1849	24,440	1,359	3.7	496	739	9.6	12.9
1850	27,992	1,203	2.9	568	655	9.7	11.4

[*]Compiled from data in H., C. & W., 'Balance Sheets', 'Ledgers', and 'Private Ledgers'.

should continue to collude with the Witney producers without any direct involvement of Hagues, Cook and Wormald. For his pains he was to receive a commission of 1 per cent on the value of all contracts gained for the partners and he also agreed to 'observe' the passing of the cloth and blanket deliveries through the official inspection processes at the receiving depots. Robert Nicholson continued to act as the general London agent for the partners, until in 1839 Cook discovered irregularities in his accounts and his employment was terminated. Thereafter, the London agency duties were performed nominally by a John Dobson and Company, but effective representation of the firm was the major function of Jeremiah Carter, behind the screen of his own small manufacturing interest in the supply of heavy woollens.

The earlier recognition by the Witney producers of the value and importance of Carter's influence with the inspecting officials and their subsequent coalition with him suggests that they had also found themselves working in an increasingly competitive environment in the late thirties. It also indicates that the preference for Witney goods which had earlier been such a marked feature of the trade was by now of much reduced market significance. Thus, the establishment of Carter in a pivotal position between Witney and Dewsbury was a welcome development to the Earlys and their associates as well as to the partners at Dewsbury Mills, in so far as it strengthened the oligopolistic character of the trade and promised to reduce risk and uncertainties.[37] This collusive association forged in 1838 (henceforth referred to as 'the alliance') survived for eleven years, during which time the principals were concerned to mould their relations with the public buying departments in the pursuit of 'regular trading, fair shares, and reasonable profits'.[38]

III

In the formation of tendering strategy the alliance evolved a system of full-cost pricing augmented by consultation. Cook built up a target price on a foundation of prime and indirect costs to which he added a gross margin to cover depreciation, commission payments, interest on capital and profit. The amount of profit built into the price was a variable factor dependent upon agreement with the Witney manufacturers (who assessed their prices in a similar fashion but whose costs of production were rarely identical with Cook's and seem in general to have been a little higher); on a careful appraisal of the eagerness of the buying authorities; and upon an assessment of the likely strength of competition stemming from the London houses and from fringe bidders. The general aim was to prevent the net profit on turnover from falling below 2½ per cent and to push it as high above that figure without arousing either the suspicions of the authorities or an influx of new competition.

Carter's views on the amount of profit which the traffic would bear, although necessarily empirically determined, were usually decisive for Cook and his partners: 'We are reluctant to agree to raising the price by 2d, as you suggest, for we already see a good profit on our first calculations, but if the Witney people are with you we are disposed to trust your judgment.'[39]

Carter also arbitrated between Witney and Dewsbury as to the size of orders to be won for the respective parties, and Cook's target price was then adjusted above or below its Witney counterpart in an attempt to gain the agreed market shares: 'Our order book is full just now and we do not want more than a small share, say 5,000 of the Transports, this time. You will please adjust our tender price accordingly so as to achieve this.'[40]

The Witney firms fixed their target price after discussion among themselves and, in order to present a competitive face to the buying departments, this price (following consultation with Carter) was then marginally elevated or depressed on the half-dozen separate tenders which were usually submitted so as to steer contracts to different members of the Witney group in turn.[41] The orders received were then shared by mutual agreement in the light of the other current demands playing upon the respective productive capacities of the member firms: 'You do not say in your last letter which of the Earlys is to have the lowest bid this time and at what figure — you must always tell us this so that we may correctly judge the outcome.'[42]

The success of the Cook-Witney alignment rested almost wholly upon this price-fixing and market-sharing agreement, the parties retaining their autonomy to vary the grades of fibre used and the general quality of manufacture. In respect of the higher value fabrics, the Witney producers possessed a slight superiority over the Dewsbury makers in the finishing process and this was sometimes reflected in the contract-awarding behaviour of the buying departments. Chiefly for this reason, the *ex post* results did not always match the *ex ante* intentions of the alliance, but an important by-product of the collusion was the opportunity afforded for the precise comparison of manufacturing costs incurred at Dewsbury Mills and at Witney for standard fabrics, the observable divergencies invariably provoking a critical review: 'It seems to us that the cost of spinning the Hospital Blanket yarn at Witney is unjustifiably high, pray tell the Earlys of this as soon as you can.'[43]

Cook was also very mindful of the fact that the London contractors bought their goods mainly in Yorkshire,[44] and providing the alliance could hold production costs at or below the prevailing level achieved by the most efficient West Riding producers it was rendered very difficult for these other important tenderers to underbid the alliance strongly, unless they were prepared to accept very low rates of profit or to encourage the use of shoddy by their sub-contractors.[45] This practice was, however, distinctly at variance with the contractual specifications, which always insisted on the

employment of 'virgin wool', and it therefore greatly enlarged the
risk of wholesale rejection of the goods.

There is no evidence of any use of shoddy by the Witney
producers during the period of collusion, and Cook refused to
countenance the incorporation of secondary fibres in any products
at Dewsbury Mills, in spite of frequent exhortations to do so from
Carter: 'We have set our face against shoddy at all times and we
shall not risk our trading reputation in this or any market by
emulating our neighbours as you suggest. We know that you and
some of the London people can sometimes pass such goods, but we
think the risk inordinately high.'[46]

Expenditure on raw wool constituted a large proportion of the
prime costs in the heavy woollen trade, and the relative certainty of
securing contracts enabled the alliance to buy suitable fibres in
advance of the receipt of orders from the public departments at
times when prices were at their most favourable.[47] By purchasing
large quantities, Cook and the Earlys also invariably stimulated the
wool markets, thus often raising the future price of raw materials
for their competitors. Cook's exceptional acuity in evaluating fibres
and his flair for timing purchases successfully often brought
substantial advantages. In this regard Cook and his partners
undoubtedly enjoyed an economy of scale at Dewsbury Mills, in so
far as they manufactured a large variety of cloths for many diverse
markets and almost any type of wool purchased could usually be
blended and utilized so as to squeeze the utmost cost advantage
from its use.[48]

A particularly successful method of allaying the competition
from the London houses which Cook employed opportunely was
that of placing orders for blankets suited to the export trade with
the firm's more important smaller West Riding rivals just prior to
tendering time. This had the effect of temporarily tying up their
liquid capital in stocks of wool and of reducing their capacity to
accept additional large commitments, so that the metropolitan
contractors then found them less keen to enter into new engage-
ments: 'We have put out some sizeable orders for blankets for the
States to the Batley Carr, Earlsheaton and Heckmondwike makers,
which should keep them busy for the next two months and I should
be surprised if they were much interested in any government work
from the London houses at the prices they are usually offered.'[49]

Nevertheless, during the severe trading depression of the early
1840s this policy was rendered unusable owing to the sharp decline
in American orders, and there developed a particularly virulent
competition for the public business. Judging by the number of new
tenderers referred to by Cook in his correspondence in these years

the government market for many medium-sized concerns must have appeared deceptively easy to enter;[50] but as these firms generally lacked the technique and scale of operations necessary to survive profitably in regular contracting they suffered an extremely high rate of mortality, indicating that *ease of exit* was an even stronger feature of the trade.[51] At least two of these new entrants, however, John Chadwick and Son of Rochdale, and Howard and Company of Leeds, survived to present the alliance with a troublesome and pervasive opposition.[52]

The Chadwicks were primarily flannel manufacturers, but at times they tendered successfully for the supply of naval serge, securing some of the major contracts in 1838 and in the two succeeding years. Howard and Company specialised in the making of horse blankets and rugs and proved highly competitive in gaining orders for coverlets from the Board of Ordnance. The disruptive impact of these newcomers threatened to spread to embrace other types of service fabrics and Cook was persuaded by Carter in the autumn of 1840 to seek 'an understanding with these intruders'.

Although they were not initially brought fully into membership of the alliance, Cook obtained a gentlemen's agreement with the two parties, which provided for a mutual exchange of information as to prices and quantities before the submission of tenders. He was also able to inform Carter that: 'They have both agreed to acquaint you of their intentions before the calling of tenders and have further promised to negotiate if we seem to be cutting each other's throats. They seem disposed to go along with us in securing regular trade and I am inclined to think that they can be trusted.'[53]

In the first 'season' following the acceptance of these mutual provisions, Cook's sanguine view was strongly confirmed by events, and in the summer of 1841 the loose compact was turned into a tight market-sharing arrangement. The alliance agreed to withdraw entirely from the coverlet trade in favour of Howard and Company, with Cook continuing to submit 'competitive' bids as part of the collusive apparatus, while a 'guaranteed' annual yardage of serge was conceded to the Chadwicks.[54] In return, Cook and the Earlys were assured of control over the submission of tenders for the enlarged oligopolistic grouping, which strengthened their ability to maintain the price structure already erected and provided a protective shield for their supply of other classes of cloths to the public departments.

Having secured its position by these means, the alliance found itself in a strong condition to withstand the brisk, but often temerarious, competition which flowed from a multiplicity of new adversaries in 1842 and the succeeding year. To be sure there were frequent crises, and Carter's correspondence with Cook often contained anxious passages reflecting the tension associated with a sharp contest and high stakes, but the very conditions which stimulated in the heavy woollen trade this increased propensity to tender engendered in Witney and at Dewsbury Mills a more determined attachment to the benefits of collusion.[55] The profitability of this policy is well confirmed by a consideration of the dimensions of economic performance revealed in the account books of Cook and his partners.

IV

During the three decades 1820-50, the value of partners' capital employed in the business at Dewsbury Mills increased approximately threefold (measured at current values). The relatively large increase in 1836, following the cessation of banking by the partners, was offset by an equivalent decrease in 1847 as a result of the death of Edward Hague (Table 3). In response to changes in trading conditions the net profits gyrated considerably in value, varying from 3 to 23 per cent of the capital employed during the period and registering an average value slightly greater than 10 per cent.[56] This was achieved against a background of highly volatile movements in wool prices. It is notable that the firm survived severe business depression without experiencing any year of negative returns, and that more than 50 per cent of the total profits earned in the crisis year of 1847 was wiped out in the single loss sustained by the failure of the Manchester merchants, Gorton Hodges and Company.[57]

The current value of *all* sales grew ninefold over the same period, with nearly a third of this rise achieved in the late forties, and the value of net profits averaging a little more than 3 per cent of this total (Table 4). The value of sales to government departments formed approximately 11 per cent of the value of *all* sales during these years, while the value of net profits earned on government contracts accounted for nearly 20 per cent of the total net profits (Table 5). This enhanced profitability of government contracting in relation to general trade is also reflected in the fact that the average net profits on sales to the government departments was 4.6 per cent, or nearly 50 per cent greater than the average net profit of 3.1 per cent earned on *all* sales.

These results were substantially improved during the years of collusion, 1838,-48, when the net profits on sales to public departments increased to an average of nearly 27 per cent of the total net profits earned. In relation to the value of sales to the naval and military authorities in these years, net profits averaged 6.7 per cent which, when contrasted with the average of 4.6 per cent earned on such sales over the 30-year span, represents an increase in net earnings during these ten years of some 45 per cent when profitability is measured in these terms.[58] The pecuniary advantages of collusion for Cook and his partners may thus be succinctly expressed as a near doubling in the net profitability of engaging in the public business during this decade,[59] the first half of which coincided with a period of extreme and widespread economic depression with 'defence being of more importance than opulence'.[60]

There were other benefits flowing from collusion, but these are more difficult to measure precisely. The regular and microscopic examination of costs of production incurred by the various colluders; the receipt from Carter of a persistent and varied flow of intelligence relating to the fabrics and trading practices of competitors, and the inspection techniques and idiosyncracies displayed by the government officials at the receiving depots; the experience gained in coping with large orders executed to close specifications and rigid delivery dates; the frequent opportunity to engage in large-scale and oligopsonistic purchasing of wool; the firm link with the commercial and mercantile practices of the large London wool and cloth factors;[61] all these elements combined to improve the general manufacturing and trading performance of the Dewsbury enterprise, and particularly enabled Cook to sap the vigour and attenuate the competitiveness of many of the firm's Yorkshire rivals in the American market.[62]

The bulk of the earnings on government orders, like that derived from trading in other markets, was reinvested at Dewsbury Mills and the general compound rates of growth attained in sales, profits, and capital over the period 1820-50 are expressed in Table 6. These rates are not indicative of rapid development, but when related to the marked economic fluctuations prevailing during these 30 years they clearly illustrate Cook's ability to snatch a rising income from an adverse environment and to facilitate the expansion of the firm's productive organisation. The gains from collusion were spread all round the marketing compass and, in the mid-forties, Cook was able to report that: 'We have found our government work quite profitable in recent years and we intend to employ an increased capital in the New York and Philadelphia trade and also in our long trade to Canton and the Australian and New Zealand markets.'[63]

Although tacit agreements operated sporadically for a few 'seasons' after 1848, the overt collusion between Cook and the Earlys was terminated in that year. The death of Jeremiah Carter

TABLE 6

Hagues, Cook and Wormald, average annual rates of growth of sales, profits and
capital in real terms, 1820-50*

Gross value of *all* sales	5.1
Gross value of sales to public departments	5.1†
Total net profits	3.2
Net profits on sales to public departments	5.2†
Partners' capital employed	4.5

*Computed from data in Tables 2 and 3, deflated by Gayer, Rostow and Schwartz index of wholesale prices
(domestic and imported commodities), using average values of first and last five years of the period and the
compound interest formula.
†1823-50.

was the initial precipitating cause of the break — all efforts made
to replace his unique skills as an intermediary proving unsuccessful
— but the fundamental explanation of the rupture of the monopolistic accord at this time lies in the fact that the balance of power
in the heavy woollen industry was moving steadily away from
Witney to the West Riding after the mid-thirties, and was
becoming strongly manifest in the late forties. The technological
dynamism of the Yorkshire trade was fully confirmed in the fifties
by the successful and widespread introduction of the power loom in
the weaving of broad fabrics. Cook and his partners were pioneers
in this innovation, installing the new mechanisms at Dewsbury
Mills in 1844 a few years earlier than most of their Yorkshire rivals
and nearly two decades before their adoption at Witney.[64]

By 1848 Cook had also gained a number of important trading
advantages which considerably diminished his interest in tendering.
He was by now in receipt of regular direct orders from the
Admiralty and beginning to attain a privileged position as a
government supplier akin to that formerly held by Benjamin Gott;
his blanket orders from North America were increasing yearly;[65] his
supply of goods to the United States government was becoming
regular and substantial; and his home market for blankets and
cloths was growing steadily.[66] Furthermore, in the late forties the
whole business milieu in the West Riding was changing and in
response to these expansive stimuli Cook began to devote his
energies to a thorough overhaul of the entire ensemble of productive
techniques at Dewsbury Mills and to the betterment of his
marketing methods. In sum, his propensity to monopolise which
had been nourished by a security motivation during the years of
severe economic stringency was reduced to zero by a growing
enthusiasm for efficiency and risk-taking as the basis of profitable
activity in an environment of growing demand.[67]

The restrictive agreement, however, had well served its purpose. It furnished employment and profits to the colluders and, in so far as government buying methods were not very dissimilar from those employed by the East India and Hudson's Bay Companies and the larger London wholesalers, by artificially hoisting contract bids above their competitive level Cook, in effect, held a price umbrella over many of the small manufacturers in the West Riding trade which materially assisted their survival. Intensity of competition, especially in a period of deep depression, does not always automatically ensure the furtherance of the public interest and,[68] although the actions of Cook and the Earlys in their decade of market manipulation lend strong support to the view that 'competition is something of which producers have only as much as they cannot eliminate',[69] the entrepreneurial behaviour of Cook after 1848 suggests that in times of buoyant demand he found economic rivalry a welcome and generally exhilarating experience.

V

In exploring one firm's recorded business experience (even if this be highly monopolistic) we are confined, as Rostow has reminded us, to a 'Marshallian world of partial equilibrium',[70] and general conclusions pertaining to macro-economic movements must be drawn, if at all, with extreme caution. In relation to the blanket-making industry, however, the oligopolistic alliance of Hagues and Cook and the Earlys had strong repercussions beyond the immediate confines of Dewsbury and Witney. Capital formation was enhanced by collusion and utilised chiefly to improve old products and to introduce new ones and to explore and extend the North American and other markets for heavy woollens, this, in turn, reflecting itself favourably in the general export performance of the economy and the balance of payments. At Dewsbury Mills, profits were also turned to good account in financing technological improvements in weaving, finishing and dyeing, innovations which were diffused throughout the West Riding heavy woollen region.

In the absence of this monopolistic behaviour the government buyers would almost certainly have secured their supplies of blankets and uniform cloths at a lower real cost, and there may well have been a more efficient allocation of resources with a larger number of producers allowed to participate in the trade. Such a wider spreading of real income during the years of depression would undoubtedly have constituted a positive social gain, but it may have militated against the capital accumulation, which brought such large gains in foreign trade in the fifties. The short-term advantages flowing from a highly competitive government trade might thus have been more than offset by long-term disadvantages resulting from the fragmentation of capital resources. This is not to argue that the large established firms are inherently the best guardians of surpluses and economic progress, but the first law of development 'to him that hath shall be given' is a pervasive historical feature of economic activity and,[71] on balance and taking a long view, the policies of the alliance were probably not seriously inimical to the public interest. Indeed, although the alliance gained not inconsiderably from collusion at the expense of competitors and taxpaying public, such profits and losses were probably marginal in relation to the wider gains accruing to the community from the economic growth flowing from increased capital accumulation and its subsequent beneficial deployment.

There are many relevant questions relating to government contracting in this industry in the first half of the nineteenth century, which the available records no not permit us to answer. For example, were the buying authorities ever aware or even vaguely suspicious of the tendering malpractices operated against them? It is pertinent, and not a little puzzling, that there is not the slightest reference to collusive practices in the mass of evidence presented to official committees examining the procedures relating to public supplies in the late forties and the fifties.[72] The government departments could certainly have deployed their own undoubted monopsonistic power drastically against blanket producers during the years 1838-43, but seem to have been loth to do so. In fact, blankets being highly durable products, it would have been economically wise — even if budgetarily difficult — for the departments to have antedated blanket purchases considerably to take advantage of the lower prices ruling in the early forties, and this seems to have occurred to some extent. This constituted a mild form of pump-priming and the government buyers were thus led nesciently into fulfilling a minor contra-cyclical economic function during this period of deep depression.

Or, again, were the authorities hidebound in their entrustment of the public business to the larger and entrenched establishment rather than to newcomers? In brief, what was the net effect of government buying policy upon the efficiency of the blanket trade? Did it hamper innovation or enterprise? Did it stimulate or retard the improvement of manufacturing and commercial techniques or did it play a neutral role? Although complete and unequivocal answers cannot be given to these questions they have been partly resolved in the discussion above. Despite inefficient methods of inspection, the insistence of the buying authorities on the maintenance of weight, quality and finish of fabrics and the heavy premia placed upon skilful wool buying almost certainly had a favourable impact upon the efficiency of the industry, which further assisted the ascendancy of cheap English blankets in overseas markets.

A more searching analysis and elucidation of the strength of these factors, however, waits upon a comprehensive examination of the whole gamut of government trading in the nineteenth century, which would shed much light upon the development of many industries as well as upon the general growth experience of the British economy.

NOTES

1 The available data do not permit a precise evaluation of the magnitude of the trade, but the value of official purchases of these fabrics probably fluctuated within a range of 6 to 12 per cent of the total output of the heavy woollen industry during the thirty years. In real terms, Army expenditure was running at approximately 12 per cent higher in the 1840's than it was in the 1820's, with a 10 per cent fall recorded in the 1830's. Naval disbursements followed a similar course, but with a steeper fall in the 1830's followed by a sharp increase in the last ten years of the period which carried the expenditure to a level some 35 per cent higher than it was in the 1820's. The average total expenditure on Army supplies was approximately 50 per cent greater than the comparable Naval spending during the period. Cf. *H. of C. Accounts and Papers*, XXXIV (1850), 187; XXX (1852), 11.

2 The records are the property of Messrs Wormalds and Walker Ltd. of Dewsbury and, with the exception of a small collection of legal and personal documents, are in the custody of the Brotherton Library of the University of Leeds.

3 In 1818 the partners employed 48 such weavers, 37 of whom resided within 2 miles of Dewsbury Mills. At this date some 60 per cent of the looms used by these employees were owned by Hagues and Cook. Regular purchases of unfinished cloths from independent weavers were also made by the partners in the Leeds and Heckmondwike Cloth Halls, and to a small extent in the Huddersfield area.

4 Thos. Cook refers in his Diary to '900 pairs of blankets which we made in one week', 15 July 1820.

5 For a fuller discussion of the early history of the firm and of its success in the American market see F. J. Glover, 'Thomas Cook and the American blanket trade in the nineteenth century', *Business History Review*, XXXV (1961), 226-46; and 'Philadelphia merchants and the Yorkshire blanket trade, 1820-1860', *Pennsylvania History*, XXVIII, (1961), 121-41.

6 Cook calculated that his losses on these early orders amounted to 'about two per cent on the capital used'. These may be regarded as costs of entrance to the trade arising mainly from inexperience. Cf. Joe S. Bain's discussion of 'shake-down losses' for new entrants in his *Barriers to New Competition* (Cambridge, Mass. 1956), pp. 149-66.

7 There are numerous references scattered throughout the firm's papers to the 'responsibility of providing for our workpeople' and Cook obviously envied the situation of the smaller woollen manufacturers 'who do not have the large distress to contend with that the larger masters must meet in times of bad trade'. There were probably 200 operatives at Dewsbury Mills in 1819 which may be compared with the 600 workers engaged at Gott's Bean Ing factory in the same year.

8 Gott built up his government connections throughout the period of the Napoleonic Wars, overcoming considerable opposition to his goods in the process, and came to enjoy (after 1808) a special relationship with the buying departments which other Yorkshire manufacturers were not able to emulate. Cook makes no reference to this kind of 'favouritism', however, and he seems to have subscribed to the view that Gott's special privileges were fully deserved. Cf. Herbert Heaton, 'Benjamin Gott and the Industrial Revolution in Yorkshire', *Economic History Review*, 1st ser. III (1931), 64; *The Leeds Woollen Industry, 1780-1820*, ed. W. B. Crump (Leeds, 1931), pp. 245-7.

9 Thos. Cook to Robert Nicholson, London, 15 Feb. 1820.

10 From a letter dated December 1814, quoted in A. Plummer, *The Witney Blanket Industry* (1934), p. 237.

11 Compiled from information in Thos. Cook's 'Diary', Hagues, Cook and Wormald (H., C. & W.), 'Correspondence Books', 'Ledgers', 'Private Ledgers', and 'Government Contract Books'.

12 Excluding direct orders from departments.

13 Excluding serge contracts and flannel orders negotiated by the partners on behalf of John Chadwick and Sons, Rochdale, after 1834.

14 John Hague, the senior partner at Dewsbury Mills was a member of an old-established Dublin firm of wool and cloth merchants. He sustained a loss of £50,000 in a country banking enterprise at Malton in Yorkshire in 1826 with little diminution in his subsequent business activities. The Wormald family had a substantial interest in the London banking house of Childs and Company, while the partners at Dewsbury Mills themselves carried on a country banking business in Dewsbury, Bradford and Wakefield until 1836. There is no evidence that this was used to provide financial support for the manufacturing enterprise, although it clearly must often have provided useful short-term benefits.

15 The Witney manufacturers retained their special position in the contracting trade for a longer period in the case of the East India and Hudson's Bay Companies, both of which institutions obtained their cloth requirements by methods identical to those employed by the government departments. Hagues, Cook and Wormald did not gain a regular footing in the East India trade until the middle of the 1830's and, apart from a few sporadic orders received in the early 1820's, did not become established suppliers to the Hudson's Bay Company until 1845.

16 The Navy Board was abolished in 1832 and the purchasing functions concentrated directly within the Admiralty, but the Board of Ordnance was not reorganized until 1855.

17 Rejected cloths were difficult to dispose of profitably through normal commercial channels, due to the fact that their weights, dimensions, and texture departed considerably from those of typical fabrics entering domestic and overseas markets.

18 Thos. Cook to Nicholson, 19 Nov. 1826. The loss reduced the firm's net profit on 20,000 blankets from 4 to 2½ per cent and is reflected in the data summarized in Table 5.

19 Thos. Cook to Thos. Dixon, New York, 31 Dec. 1825.

20 Thos. Cook to Halliley and Sons, Dewsbury, 15 Sept. 1827. Wickens and Pew were inspectors at the Board of Ordnance depot. They examined cloths on a sampling basis and, as they apparently had no technical knowledge of wool or the woollen manufacture, their duties were exercised with a high degree of subjective judgment. This extract is typical of a number of such complaints occurring in the correspondence in the thirties and forties and it indicates a kind of buyer's ignorance working to the disfavour of Cook.

21 This practice was far more prevalent at the naval stores at Deptford than it was at the military stores at the Tower and it gave rise to frequent allegations of bribery and corruption made by aggrieved contractors. There was some reorganization of

the inspection system at Deptford in 1832, but no drastic changes were forthcoming until 1858.

22 Thos. Cook to John Mollett, London, 12 Dec. 1830. Nicholson's commission was 1 per cent on the value of all sales handled for the partners.

23 Thos. Cook to Nicolson, 2 Apr. 1833. Falkner was a leading London contractor.

24 Thos. Cook to Nicholson, 4 Nov. 1835. Cook estimated, in 1839, that the proportion of finally rejected cloth and blankets in their total government trade to that date had been restricted to 'only a little more than one per cent', with another 1 per cent of the total securing approval at an abated price.

25 Thos. Cook to Nicholson, 26 Sept. 1834.

26 The partners were adding 6 per cent to their prime costs to cover such contingencies after 1828.

27 H., C. & W., 'Private Ledger, 1821-1870', fo. 63.

28 Falkner, John Maberley and Gillespie, Moffatt and Company, were the leading houses in this group in the decade of the period, while Dolan and Company, Hebbert and Company, and Isaacs, Campbell and Company were the strongest members of the group in the 1840's.

29 Thos. Cook to Nicholson, 16 March 1831.

30 The partners allowed a conventional 5 per cent per annum of gross sales value for interest on capital employed and made provision for 4 to 6 per cent to meet depreciation.

31 The profit margin added to total production costs was reduced by 75 per cent.

32 Reduced profits were the general experience of Yorkshire woollen manufacturers in these years. Cf. *Select Committee on Manufactures* . . . Parl. Papers 1833, VI, esp. the evidence of John Brooke, p. 152.

33 The Halileys were consuming approximately half the quantity of wool which was processed at Dewsbury Mills in the 1820's and Cook would be the more likely to benefit from any economies of large scale.

34 Thos. Cook to Nicholson, 28 May 1838.

35 Carter had partially retrieved his fortunes after 1834 and re-entered the contracting business with the establishment of his own manufacture of woollen cloths at Ossett, a few miles east of Dewsbury Mills.

36 Thos. Cook to Nicholson, 18 June 1838.

37 The historian of the Witney industry reports the finding of 'only loose alliances between the Witney firms for government contracts', but when the principal houses are seen to be John Early and Company, Richard Early, Edward Early, Richard Early Junior, and Early Brothers it seems clear that highly formal price-fixing agreements and written records could probably be dispensed with. Cf. Plummer, *op. cit.* pp. 101-2.

38 Thos. Cook in a letter to John Wormald, 10 February 1839. The use of the word *collusive* is not intended to impart any moral opprobrium to the polices pursued by the alliance, but rather to convey clearly the degree of co-operation achieved by the respective parties. Furthermore, no attempt is made here to classify very strictly the type of oligopoly — which is a many-faceted market phenomenon — developed in this trade. Cf. Fritz Machlup, *The Economics of Sellers' Competition* (Baltimore, 1952), esp. pp. 359-67.

39 Thos. Cook to Carter, 14 March 1839.

40 Thos. Cook to Carter, 24 March 1839.

41 In varying the tender prices the group worked to limits of a hundredth of a penny per yard of cloth, or per blanket.

42 Thos. Cook to Carter, 20 April 1839.

43 Thos. Cook to Carter, 16 June 1840.

44 The Gotts also bought a large proportion of their blankets in this way in the 1840's.

45 Shoddy was being increasingly utilized in the West Riding during this period.
46 Thos. Cook to Carter, 10 April 1842.
47 Cook told the H. of L. *S.C. on the Wool Trade*, 1828 (515), VIII, that the cost of wool generally represented 52 per cent of the selling value of his fabrics, but he also often reiterated in his correspondence that 'government cloths required 7 per cent more wool than general trade goods'.
48 Cook often bought lots of unsorted wools at advantageous prices in which the grades of quality ran all the way from 'very coarse' to 'fine' and this could only be profitable for an enterprise with a protean range of manufacture.
49 Thos. Cook to Carter, 4 April 1839.
50 'They come and go like flies . . .' Thos. Cook to John Mollett, London, 22 November 1842.
51 Illustrative of the pertinence of the observation that 'the obstacles standing in the way of competing with well-established firms remain substantial and frequently formidable'. W. Fellner, *Competition Among the Few* (New York, 1949), p. 310.
52 Both of these firms seem to have been established for more than ten years before they involved themselves in government contracting.
53 Thos. Cook to Carter, 28 Oct. 1840.
54 Any actual orders received by Cook as a result of this strategy were re-routed to Howard and Company, and when the Chadwicks received orders in excess of those agreed upon there was some sub-contracting to Dewsbury Mills. In addition the parties materially assisted each other to meet delivery dates or to overcome any unexpected manufacturing emergencies.
55 The alliance had a few disputes over market shares, but these were issues of degree rather than of principle, and even the most serious of these conflicts seems to have required little more for their solution than an express coach journey to London by Thomas Cook. Pricing difficulties were also very infrequent, reflecting Carter's aptitude for negotiation, but it must be stressed that the correspondence books of Cook and his partners can at best only partially reflect the true nature and operations of the collusive agreement, and much of the inevitable polemic between the parties probably went unrecorded.
56 The median and modal values, however, are 8.5 and 5.1 per cent respectively.
57 The partners received £59 of the total of £4,750 outstanding to their credit in respect of goods supplied to this house.
58 These benefits of collusion stemmed largely from the fact that the sensitivity of finished fabric prices to changes in the price of raw wool was effectively blunted. The price of fibre used at Dewsbury Mills was generally falling throughout the period (Table 3) and Cook's understanding with the Earlys enabled him to improve his 'terms of trade' significantly.
59 It is, of course, conceded that the necessarily arbitrary assessment of profitability, based on the unsophisticated techniques then prevailing, precludes the use of these data for any reliable calculation of the degree of monopoly power attained by the alliance in this period. In this connexion, see the illuminating discussion in Joe S. Bain, 'The Profit Rate as a Measure of Monopoly Power', *Quarterly Journal of Economics* (1941), LV, 271-93.
60 Cf. R. C. O. Matthews, *A Study in Trade Cycle History* (Cambridge, 1954), esp. pp. 152-5.
61 The heavy woollen trade of the West Riding was largely in the hands of Leeds and Huddersfield merchants until the middle of the nineteenth century.
62 Cook also began to supply point blankets and heavy cloths to the United States Government in 1841, through the agency of A. and S. Henry and Company of Manchester, and by 1845 he had largely wrested this trade from the Gotts.
63 Thos. Cook to John Bibby and Sons, Liverpool, 11 January 1845.
64 Cf. Plummer, *op. cit.* p. 93.

65 They were twice as valuable in 1848 compared with those received ten years earlier.
66 The firm was employing a commercial traveller from 1843.
67 Like many people who work closely with wool, Cook was very much a short-run pessimist and a long-run optimist.
68 Cf. Lesley Cook, 'Orderly Marketing or Competition', *Economic Journal*, LXXI (1961), esp. pp. 497-9.
69 Cf. D. Lynch, *The Concentration of Economic Power* (New York, 1946), p. 109.
70 W. W.. Rostow in National Bureau of Economic Research report on *Capital Formation and Economic Growth* (Princeton, 1955), p. 646.
71 Cf. A. Cairncross, *Factors in Economic Development* (1962), p. 205.
72 Cf. *Select Committee appointed to inquire into the Expenditure on the Navy, Army and Ordnance*, Parl. Papers 1849, IX, X; 1850, X; 1851, VII; *Select Committee appointed to inquire into the principle adopted or making contracts for the Supply of the Public Departments*, Parl. Papers 1856, VII; 1857, II, XIII; 1858, XVI.

13

The Growth Strategies of
Southern Railroads, 1865-1893[*]

Maury Klein and Kozo Yamamura[†]

The importance of railroads as a leading sector or as a part of
social overhead capital in the process of economic development
requires little emphasis. Economic historians of various persuasions
have examined the development of railroads descriptively,
quantitatively, and even counter-factually, while business historians
have provided illuminating sketches of patterns of growth and
entrepreneurial activities for several individual roads. The purpose
of this article is to suggest a link between the pattern and rate of
growth of railroads and the entrepreneurial rationale behind it.
The focus of the study will be upon railroads in the American
South during the period 1865-1893.

In the first section we present a series of data on total assets,
capital, debt, and earnings for twenty southern railroads in the
form of linear regression equations to depict the pattern of
financing these railroads and to obtain measures of profitability.[1] The
use of these simple regression equations permits us to present an
otherwise unmanageable quantity of data with great economy of
space. With them we can also discover and evaluate trends and/or
relationships existing in the data and discriminate what is observed
to be of statistical significance for the purpose of intra-sample

[*] From *Business History Review*, Vol. XLI, no. 4 (Winter, 1967), pp. 358-77.
Reprinted by permission of the editor of *Business History Review* and the authors.

[†] The writers wish to thank Professors Ralph W. Hidy, Arthur M. Johnson and
James P. Baughman for useful comments received while this paper was in
preparation. Much of the central theme and organisation of this paper were
inspired especially by insightful and critical comments provided by Jim Baughman
as editor and patient friend. We are also grateful for the Harvard Graduate
School of Business Administration, which made the writers' collaboration possible
by providing the Harvard-Newcomen Society Fellowship in Business History to Mr
Klein as well as its facilities and a year of intellectual stimulation. The writers
alone, however, are responsible for the shortcomings of this article.

comparisons. The sample of twenty, representing 14,241 out of 31,653 miles of ten southern states in 1893, was chosen for relative availability and reliability of the data from a universe of well over 200.[2] Economic historians familiar with the development of railroads in the late nineteenth century will undoubtedly find that the data confirm most of their expectations. It is hoped, however, that these data, as presented here, will provide a quantitative foundation for hitherto qualitative generalisations. In addition, some of our findings may surprise the non-specialist.

Our central focus, however, lies in the second section, which attempts to use these data to examine entrepreneurial strategy. Since the data as given here enables us to observe intra-sample variations in patterns of financing and profitability, it becomes possible to evaluate these variations against what might have been the strategy of individual entrepreneurs involved in the various railroads. The crucial question to be asked is, why did these entrepreneurs choose the course they did? Or, putting it differently, what entrepreneurial rationale lay behind a leading sector of the South in the process of post-Civil War recovery and growth?

The answer to this question requires not only an evaluation of the data, but a consideration of several interrelated factors as well. For example, not all southern railroads experienced the same pattern of development. Nor did all perform the same functions. We have, therefore, tried to categorise our sample roads according to their nature and function. This approach allows us to evaluate intrasample variations of the data against the nature and function of each road, which in turn enables us to discover possible varieties of entrepreneurial strategy. A purely aggregate study does not permit the luxury of distinguishing between types.

I

In Table 1 we observe that growth of the sample roads in terms of total assets (A) was indeed rapid and steady. The positive slopes (b) for all sample roads indicate that the annual growth rate of total assets was positive in all cases, and generally observed high coefficients of determination (r^2) indicate that the rate of growth was steady. Moreover, when each magnitude of intercept (a) is evaluated vis-a-vis that of slope (b), it is evident that investment activity in these railroads proceeded feverishly during the period. The statistically significant t-test results along with the high values of r^2 in all cases indicate that the annual increase in total assets followed a steady pattern to boost the magnitude of total assets to the level observed for all roads in 1893.[3] When we remember that some of the sample roads had very large negative intercepts, the rate of growth of total assets could only be said to have experienced an accelerated 'spurt'.[4]

More will be said of this table in the following section. Here it suffices to note that our non-aggregate approach serves to show the existence of noteworthy variations in the rate of 'spurt' within the sample. For example, the trend line for the East Tennessee, Virginia & Georgia (17) rose from an extremely large negative value of its intercept at a large annual rate of almost $5.7 million, while the Georgia (1) grew at the annual rate of about $188,000 from its intercept of $3.6 million. Though both roads grew steadily (note r^2 of .66 and .95 for each road, respectively), the former grew at a much faster rate than the latter.

Capital stock (K) and funded debt (F) comprised the two major sources contributing to the rapid increase of total assets. Table 2 shows the relative composition of these two sources. The ratio of the rate of increase in funded debt (F) over that of capital (K) — b_f/b_k — was less than unity for three railroads (1, 13 and 17), extremely large for two (11 and 18) and ranged between 1.29 and 11.37 for the rest.[5] The mean of b_f/b_k for those eleven roads in which r^2 for both b_f and b_k are significant at the .05 level was 2.96.[6] In general, then, the figures indicate that for our sample roads debt grew on the average nearly three times as rapidly as equity.

This result should not seem surprising in view of existing conditions. The growth of southern railroads into large systems did not occur at a leisurely pace. The sudden burst of expansion, and the scale on which it took place, necessitated large amounts of ready capital in a short time. For all the enthusiasm generated by eager promoters, many investors could be coaxed to supply funds only on the basis of a guaranteed return. Moreover, the nascent period of southern railway growth coincided with the loss of local control to bankers and financiers from outside the region. The self-interest of these financiers naturally found a preference for bond issues handled by their own firms.

Tables 3 and 4 pertain to earnings and dividends. In Table 3 net earnings (N) equal gross earnings (G) minus operating expenses.[7] Calculation of trend lines for gross and net earnings garnered the following results. Coefficients of determination significant at the .05 level were obtained for seventeen of twenty for G and fourteen of twenty for N. The observance of high r^2's for G in so large a proportion of the sample indicates that G rose consistently. On the other hand, N reveals a weaker pattern. The number of significant r^2's at the .05 level is smaller and the r^2's for N, with three exceptions, are lower than those for G.

By taking the ratio of b_h/b_g for the eleven cases in which both

TABLE 1

Trend Lines of Growth of Total Assets (A)

No.[1]	Railroad	Initial Amount of Total Assets (Intercept: a)	Annual Rate of Increase of Total Assets (Slope: b)	Statistical Test on Slope[2] (t-test)	Coefficient of Determination (r^2)	Period Observed & Sample[3] Size (n)
1	Georgia	3,599,435.1	187,612.1	46.866	.946	66-93 (28)
2	Cincinnati, New Orleans & Texas Pacific	1,125,411.3	135,412.8	25.070	.547	82-93 (12)
3	Chesapeake, Ohio & Southwestern	13,466,002.0	356,124.0	48.530	.819	82-93 (12)
4	Elizabethtown, Lexington & Big Sandy	5,192,733.5	106,901.7	28.230	.587	82-91 (10)
5	Richmond & Danville	-2,444,363.4	996,622.4	24.080	.821	66-93 (28)
6	Nashville, Chattanooga & St Louis	2,015,649.1	791,606.6	63.072	.948	73-93 (21)
7	Louisville & Nashville	-16,702,578.0	4,788,589.7	37.630	.923	65-93 (29)
8	Wilmington & Weldon	-1,649,408.7	393,514.9	24.033	.786	69-93 (25)
9	Alabama Great Southern	4,227,148.4	450,394.6	45.043	.776	83-93 (11)
10	Charlotte, Columbia & Augusta	3,475,419.3	86,452.0	35.715	.890	69-93 (25)
11	Savannah, Florida & Western	3,094,844.0	432,164.8	23.987	.891	67-93 (27)
12	Norfolk & Western	-112,170,050.0	7,631,739.5	58.341	.880	81-93 (13)
13	Chesapeake & Ohio	-13,066,287.0	4,357,840.0	59.614	.954	70-93 (24)
14	Mobile & Ohio	12,694,685.4	488,771.1	14.291	.618	66-93 (28)
15	Central of Georgia	873,197.7	1,001,794.5	63.321	.969	66-93 (28)
16	Virginia Midland	8,758,704.1	369,659.9	24.385	.560	81-93 (13)
17	East Tenn., Virginia & Georgia	-43,931,977.0	5,663,729.8	15.941	.664	69-93 (25)
18	Georgia Pacific	-40,330,653.0	2,543,993.4	156.152	.960	87-93 (7)
19	South Carolina	5,327,642.4	402,611.2	52.250	.977	66-93 (28)
20	Memphis & Charleston	5,921,576.3	343,417.6	22.538	.921	66-93 (28)

Notes:
1 These numbers are used to refer to each respective road hereafter.
2 All of t-test and r are significant at .01 level.
3 The number in parentheses is the sample size, and the numbers preceding them are time periods. For example, numbers 66-93 are from 1866 to 1893, inclusive, i.e., for 28 years.
Sources Based on data compiled from annual reports of the companies and Henry V. Poor, Manual of the Railroads of the United States (New York, 1867-1894).

TABLE 2

Trend Lines on Capital Stock (K) and Funded Dept (F)[1]

Railroad	Capital Stock			Funded Debt			b /bk
	Intercept (a)	Slope (b)	Coefficient of Determination^2 (r^2)	Intercept (a)	Slope (b)	Coefficient of Determination^2 (r^2)	
1	2,640,449.5	606,189.0	.895	−293,981.8	111,103.8	.860	0.18
2	2,511,497.0	15,598.5	.472	−982,989.6	58,144.8	.880	3.73
3	8,942,768.9	19,438.5	(.197)	4,947,338.5	221,038.8	(.328)	11.37
4	2,911,245.3	20,896.0	(.369)	456,068.9	130,560.6	(.198)	6.25
5	1,968,821.7	116,230.1	.887	2,464,886.7	546,758.7	.880	4.70
6	3,482,825.3	152,820.5	.601	−1,621,069.1	654,674.3	(.047)	4.28
7	−7,004,001.3	1,668,703.8	.832	−12,062,945.0	2,977,730.0	.909	1.78
8	310,312.7	84,579.0	.917	−1,770,198.9	267,315.1	.674	3.16
9	8,626,496.8	86,508.1	(.315)	−5,741,540.4	363,876.4	.882	4.21
10	1,724,153.4	32,229.5	.869	543,408.1	94,582.5	.862	2.93
11	2,023,890.5	151.9	.891	452,932.6	230,103.7	.940	1520.10
12	−40,136,878.0	3,136,827.5	.887	−65,480,961.0	4,039,031.6	.874	1.29
13	−18,231,736.0	2,841,128.1	.901	770,521.3	1,485,965.3	.743	0.52
14	1,606,082.7	203,584.0	.864	4,694,145.3	473,124.8	.894	2.32
15	3,164,638.1	179,934.1	.788	−3,271,337.0	625,953.3	.919	3.48
16	4,120,112.9	66,837.1	.373	4,001,558.2	310,662.6	.631	4.65
17	−26,490,048.0	3,128,092.9	.838	−10,574,387.0	1,716,251.8	.607	0.55
18	7,945,569.3	13,057.3	(.208)	−29,521,147.0	1,687,168.0	.785	129.21
19	3,296,153.2	128,470.5	.984	1,879,471.3	179,140.1	.969	1.39
20	3,384,869.5	74,894.4	.891	1,420,266.6	232,477.1	.891	3.10

Notes
1 Sample sizes are the same as in Table 1.
2 Except for those in parentheses, all r^2s and t-tests on regression co-efficients are significant at 0.05 level.
Sources Same as Table 1.

TABLE 3

Trend Lines on Gross Earnings (G) and Net Earnings (N)

Railroads	Gross Earnings			Net Earnings			
	Intercept (a)	Slope (b)	Coefficient of Determination (r²)	Intercept (a)	Slope (b)	Coefficient of Determination² (r²)	bn/bg
1	658,512.6	32,928.0	.775	380,133.7	6,900.8	(.271)	(0.21)
2	1,120,789.4	191,910.0	.882	337,693.4	32,889.5	(.335)	(0.17)
3	1,082,546.9	122,494.5	.940	682,950.9	55,440.2	.772	0.45
4	154,319.9	28,183.4	(.244)	42,756.9	9,985.7	(.171)	(0.35)
5	1,213,598.7	213,391.6	.805	441,173.5	103,351.5	.381	0.48
6	1,035,574.5	75,018.9	(.206)	−188,609.8	58,993.4	.939	(0.79)
7	2,535,900.2	748,473.6	.922	855,518.7	278,173.1	.917	0.37
8	16,629.6	43,760.9	.826	−34,327.4	20,590.7	.730	0.47
9	−1,216,287.1	112,127.4	.964	−276,613.9	27,065.1	.614	0.24
10	217,616.7	23,426.7	.782	150,674.0	4,242.8	(.211)	(0.18)
11	314,819.8	47,391.7	.753	11,595.7	14,900.9	.551	0.31
12	−4,741,214.2	439,331.9	.797	−1,443,729.2	144,834.8	.894	0.33
13	−10,697,723.0	1,005,075.0	(.188)	−685,864.9	89,097.1	.754	(0.09)
14	1,179,158.9	60,807.9	.714	322,468.0	19,050.3	.363	0.31
15	1,265,493.6	51,543.9	.591	499,053.5	17,609.5	.342	0.34
16	−234,897.9	81,560.0	.876	25,685.5	22,644.9	.602	0.28
17	−1,626,782.5	260,101.2	.884	−438,593.5	80,672.0	.794	0.31
18	−2,406,531.6	153,665.5	.904	669,203.8	−17,784.2	(.067)	(−0.12)
19	798,067.6	19,200.3	.670	404,693.5	−1,886.3	(.031)	(−0.10)
20	68,105.1	30,820.6	.666	213,188.0	7,283.0	(.243)	(0.23)

Notes
1 Sample sizes are identical to Table 1.
2 Except for those in parentheses, all r^2's and t-tests on regression co-efficients, are significant at 0.05 level.
Sources Same as Table 1.

r^2's were significant, we obtain a mean of 0.35. For these eleven roads at least, this figure suggests an important conclusion. Gross earnings (G) rose much faster than net earnings (N), or, bearing in mind the method used in obtaining the figure 0.35, almost three times as rapidly as (N). Though not given here, our calculation of trend lines for operating expenses support this notion that operating expenses were increasing sharply. The reasons for this increase were numerous and complex, and cannot be treated here. Nevertheless, the results of our calculation suggest that the much maligned railroad men had some justification behind their unceasing demands for higher rates once regulation had commenced.

The widening gap between gross earnings (G) and net earnings (N) could not help but adversely affect returns on capital. The upward spiral of operating expenses put an increasingly severe squeeze on operational profits. At the same time, fixed charges were rising with no less alacrity.[8] The growing burden of debt shown in Table 2 brought with it a heavy rise in interest charges. By the late nineteenth century, many southern roads had lost their original tax exempt status, and tax payments became another claim upon earnings. And while expenses and charges mounted, income suffered important setbacks. Increased competition conspired with growing state and federal regulation to drive rates steadily downward.[9] All these factors help to explain the results shown in Table 4, which deals with dividend payments.

Table 4a includes those railroads that paid less than ten dividends and 4b those paying more than ten dividends during the period. The seven roads not included in either table paid *no dividend at all*. For convenience they are listed in Table 4c. In Table 4a it should be noted that the mean dividend rate was low, the Richmond & Danville's 6.63 per cent being near the going rate of interest. The higher payment frequency after 1880 can be attributed to several factors. For one thing, the period after 1880 witnessed the first major consolidation movement among southern railroads. As once independent roads coalesced into large systems, several companies, such as the Georgia, allowed themselves to be leased on terms that guaranteed a specific dividend to its stockholders regardless of its earnings record. In these cases, the lessee absorbed the loss when dividends were not earned.[10]

Secondly, this same amalgamation of roads into large systems was accomplished by bankers and financiers from outside the region. In their often desperate need for funds they sometimes forced subsidiary lines to pay dividends that were not actually earned to the stockholding parent company. The subsidiary company usually suffered serious financial disruption from this

TABLE 4A

Railroads Paying Less than Ten Dividends, 1865-1893

	Name	No. Paid	Mean Div. Rate	Range	Distribution Before 1880	After 1880
5.	(R & D)	8	6.63	10.0-3.0	0	8
10.	(CC & A)	1	9.0	9.0	0	1
20.	(M & C)	1	6.0	6.0	1	0
9.	(AGS)	9	6.17	7.5-6.0	0	9
2.	(CNO & TP)	6	2.92	4.0-1.5	0	6
12.	(N & W)	8	3.31	8.5-1.0	0	8
11.	(SF & W)	8	4.88	7.0-2.0	0	8
19.	(SC)	2	1.50	2.0-1.0	2	0

TABLE 4B

Railroads Paying More than Ten Dividends, 1865-1893

	Name	No. Paid	Mean Div. Rate	Range	Distribution Before 1880	After 1880
17.	(ETV & G)	13	3.85	6.0-2.0	5	8
15.	(CG)	19	7.74	12.0-2.5	8	11
1.	(Ga)	26	8.77	11.0-6.0	12	14
7.	(L & N)	22	5.70	8.0-1.5	12	10
6.	(NC & SL)	17	3.74	5.0-2.0	6	11
8.	(W & W)	21	6.21	8.0-3.0	7	14

TABLE 4C

Railroads Paying No Dividends at All, 1865-1893

3.	(CO & SW)
4.	(EL & BS)
13.	(C & O)
14.	(M & O)
16.	(VM)
18.	(GP)

policy, but the parent company received badly needed cash. The one dividend paid by the Charlotte, Columbia & Augusta provides a classic example of this technique.[11] The ¹prepondrance of payments after 1880 for the roads in Table 4a has two basic explanations: this group contains more roads that endured the conditions described above; and half of the roads in the group, the Alabama Great Southern, the Cincinnati, New Orleans & Texas Pacific, the Norfolk & Western, and the Savannah, Florida & Western, were either built or reorganised out of bankruptcy after 1880.

Table 4b contains those roads with fairly respectable dividend rates and, most important, relatively regular payments over the period. The data indicates that these roads probably were the soundest investments among southern railroads. Analysis of the historical background seems to bear out this conclusion. Of the four best paying roads, the Central of Georgia, the Georgia, the Louisville & Nashville, and the Wilmington & Weldon, only one encountered serious financial difficulties during the depression after 1893. That road, the Central of Georgia, slid into receivership in 1892 when it was discovered that the company had not earned the high dividends it was paying.[12]

From the standpoint of dividends, then, only three of the roads in Table 4b could be considered strong, reliable companies. Yet even their returns on investment do not seem especially attractive when considered against the prevailing rate of interest or the market rate of return for the period (about 7.5 per cent). In short, the returns did not compensate investors for the considerable degree of risk involved.

Dividend rates alone, however, do not provide a meaningful indicator of economic performance, especially in view of the diverse human and institutional factors that influence them. A more reliable measure is needed to appraise the effect of additional investment upon *net* earnings.

Table 5 presents the results of regression equations calculated in the form of $N = a + bA$, and $N/A = a + bt$, where N is net earnings, A is total assets, t is time (in year unit), and, of course, a and b are intercept and slope. The former was calculated to ascertain how rapidly increasing total assets contributed to the increase of net earnings. A total of dividends paid and internal reserves accumulated would have served better than N, which includes several types of fixed charges already described in relation to Table 3, for the purpose of observing 'profitability' as defined by economists. Since this data could not be disaggregated for the purpose of meaningful comparison among the sample roads, N was

TABLE 5
Regression of Net Earnings (N) on Total Assets (A)
and Trend Lines of Ratio of Net Earnings Over Total Assets[1]

Railroads	For: N = a + bA			For: N/A = a + bt		
	Intercept (a)	Slope (b)	Coefficient of Determination[2] (r²)	Intercept (a)	Slope (b)	Coefficient of Determination[2] (r²)
1	231,437.6	.393	.327	.0946	.001	.310
2	—170,613.1	.293	.701	.1975	.002	(.080)
3	—1,945,889.6	.118	.537	.0221	.002	.651
4	—683,377.2	.099	(.325)	.0133	.001	(.110)
5	66,784.9	.084	.305			*
6	—303,224.5	.072	.935	.0330	.001	.571
7	135,087.9	.058	.981	.0784	.001	(.128)
8	56,482.2	.051	.897	.0855	.001	(.192)
9	—296,132.6	.044	(.193)	.0097	.001	(.205)
10	7,073.5	.044	(.187)			*
11	—19,833.3	.039	.794			*
12	362.878.7	.023	.894	.0399	.001	(.119)
13	—513,851.8	.022	.819	.0026	.001	.508
14	231,409.2	.019	(.141)			*
15	477,317.6	.018	.369	.1028	.003	.606
16	261,572.6	.017	(.085)			*
17	227,464.8	.012	.894	.0572	.002	.376
18	484,211.5	.010	(.130)	.0666	.002	(.355)
19	429,680.9	—.004	(.036)	.0682	—.003	.809
20	526,316.9	—.031	(.093)	.0569	—.003	.420

Notes:
1 Sample sizes are the same as in Table 1.
2 Except for those in parentheses, all r²'s and t-tests on regression co-efficients are significant at 0.05 level. * indicates r² was less than .00001.
Sources: Same as Table 1.

used to obtain a pattern of earnings. By this we mean loosely the performance of railroads, i.e. gross earnings minus operating expenses. The same reasoning applies to the trend lines calculated for N/A.

Bearing this proviso in mind, the findings of Table 5 are revealing. For twelve roads for which coefficients of determination were significant at the .05 level, the slope (b) ranged from .327 to .012; in other words, the net earning on each additional dollar added to total assets ranged from 32.7 cents to 1.2 cents. The mean of these twelve slopes is .098, which means that, on the average, the net earnings of these roads increased less than 10 cents per dollar of increase in total assets. It should be noted that only three roads did better than 10 per cent, while five roads failed to reach even 5 per cent on each added dollar. As noted earlier, these net earning figure do not include fixed charges. When these charges are deducted it becomes clear that the rapid increase in total assets yielded very little rise in profits. The findings in Table 3 hinted strongly at this conclusion; the evidence in Table 5 unmistakably confirms it.

The trend lines for the ratio of net earnings over total assets (N/A) are more telling. Of the twenty equations calculated, five yielded slope (*b*) of less than .001 (in Table 5 they appear as .001 because of rounding). Of the remaining fifteen, only eight roads had significant r^2's at the .05 level. For those eight roads, the slopes ranged between —.003 and .003. Two inescapable conclusions follow from these results. First, the ratio of net earnings to assets behaved erratically over the period, as indicated in the large number of statistically-insignificant-to-low r^2's. In other words, an increase in assets had no predictable effect upon the course of net earnings. Secondly, for the eight roads with significant r^2's, the slope (*b*) of their trend lines were either negative or barely above zero. That is, an increase in total assets for those lines had the effect of either reducing the ratio of net earnings over total assets (N/A), or, at best, increasing it very slightly. In none of the twenty sample roads, therefore, did additional investment guarantee an increase in the rate of net earnings.

With such small slopes, the intercepts take on added meaning. We can now regard them as the prevailing ratio of N/A for the period. To put it differently, if the slope (*b*) is close to zero in N/A = *a* + *bt*, N/A could not vary appreciably from *a*, regardless of *t*. The range of these intercepts for eight statistically significant trend lines went from .1028 to .0026, with a mean of .0544. In short, N/A tended to be mired around 5 per cent throughout the period. By any standard this is a rather dismal performance.

According to all the measures of performance and patterns of financing growth suggested here, southern railroads can only be regarded as poor investments during the late nineteenth century.[13] Obviously, then, return on equity does not seem a primary motivation for inducing investment in rapidly growing southern rail systems. Even the traditional explanation of sanguine investors hopeful of large returns does not seem to us adequate to explain the sustained pouring of capital into southern lines. What motives, then, lured this capital into southern transportation?

II

The answer to this question requires a brief explanation of the course of southern railroad development. In broad terms, two distinct eras can be discerned: the Territorial Era, 1865-1880; and the Interterritorial Era, 1880-1883. During the territorial era, southern lines functioned much as they had before the Civil War.

Each road served a specific territory and tended to be dominated by the merchants and financial interests of its principal terminus. Conceived primarily as a potent weapon in the growing commercial rivalry between leading southern ports and interior distributing centres, the roads became servants to local economic aspirations.[14]

During the postwar years, however, a variety of factors forced these provincially oriented roads to expand, largely for defensive reasons. The escalation of expansion brought with it a need for more capital than could be provided locally. At this point, in the late 1870s, money and men from outside the region began to involve themselves deeply in southern transportation. Unfettered by local loyalties, these financiers transformed once provincial roads into the nucleii of large systems sprawling through the entire South. The sudden spurt of growth after 1880 reflects the momentum of this tendency toward interterritorial systems.[15]

A significant shift in investment behaviour provides another barometer of this change. Recently Arthur M. Johnson and Barry E. Supple have distinguished between two kinds of investment motivation, which they term opportunistic and developmental.[16] The former emphasises short-term profit maximisation as the main objective; the latter stresses long-term commitment in order to realise maximum ultimate return. In practice, the difference between the two often shaded into subtle distinctions, and frequently the opportunistic plunge led unexpectedly into a developmental commitment to protect the investment. Nevertheless, mindful of the limitations of generalisation, it can be said that investment in southern roads was primarily developmental during the territorial era and opportunistic during the interterritorial era.

These two conceptual frameworks help explain the nature of southern rail growth. Broadly speaking there were four basic patterns of development for major lines: (1) the road grew and became the centre of a major system; (2) the road grew but was absorbed by a major system; (3) the road developed as a link in a major system; and (4) the road began as a sizeable and important line but did not grow. In this last case the road might have remained independent, like the Mobile & Ohio, or been absorbed by a major system, like the Memphis & Charleston.

If the categories are not imposed too rigidly, our sample roads fall into them reasonably well. By using the concepts outlined above, we can visualise these four patterns of development by means of simple diagrams. In Figure 1, let T stand for territorial, I for interterritorial, D for development, and O for opportunistic.

It should be stressed that the diagrams represent the most prevalent course for each general category. Specific roads could be

Figure I

PATTERNS OF DEVELOPMENT FOR SOUTHERN RAILROADS
1865-1893

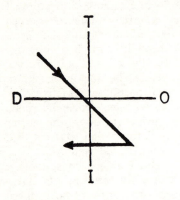

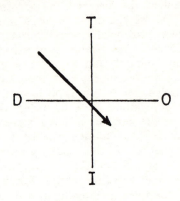

I. NUCLEUS OF MAJOR SYSTEM   2. ABSORBED BY MAJOR SYSTEM

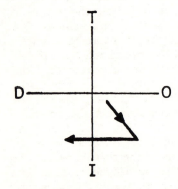

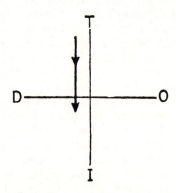

3. LINK IN MAJOR SYSTEM   4. SIZABLE NON-GROWTH LINES

D = Developmental   T = Territorial
O = Opportunistic   I = Interterritorial

TABLE 6
Summary of Preceding Tables and Figures

Railroad	Name	Rank Order of b in $N = a + bA$ and Magnitude[1] (1)	Rank Order of b'/bk and Magnitude[2] (2)	Dividend Class[3] (3)	Category of Nature[4] (4)
1	Georgia	.393	20	.18	C	2
2	Cincinnati, New Orleans & Texas Pacific	.293	9	3.73	(I)	4
3	Chesapeake, Ohio & Southwestern	.118	3	(11.37)	O	3
4	Elizabethtown, Lexington & Big Sandy	(.099)	4	(6.25)	O	3
5	Richmond & Danville	.084	5	4.70	(I)	1
6	Nashville, Chattanooga & St. Louis	.072	7	(4.28)	(C)	2
7	Louisville & Nashville	.058	15	1.78	(C)	1
8	Wilmington & Weldon	.051	11	3.16	C	1
9	Alabama Great Southern	(.044)	8	(4.21)	(I)	4
10	Charlotte, Columbia & Augusta	(.044)	13	2.93	(I)	4
11	Savannah, Florida & Western	.039	1	1520.10	(I)	1
12	Norfolk & Western	.023	17	1.29	I	1
13	Chesapeake & Ohio	.022	19	0.52	O	1
14	Mobile & Ohio	(.019)	14	2.32	O	4
15	Central of Georgia	.018	10	3.48	(C)	2
16	Virginia Midland	(.017)	6	4.65	O	4
17	East Tennessee, Virginia & Georgia	.012	18	0.55	C	1
18	Georgia Pacific	(.010)	2	(129.21)	O	3
19	South Carolina	(—.004)	16	1.39	(I)	4
20	Memphis & Charleston	(—.031)	12	3.10	(I)	4

Notes:
1 The magnitudes in parentheses indicate that the co-efficient of determination of the regression equation was not significant at the .05 level (See Table 5).
2 Magnitudes in parentheses indicate that co-efficients of determination of one or both of trend lines (for K and F) were not significant at the .05 level (See Table 2).
3 Those dividend classes in parentheses indicate that co-efficients of determination calculated for dividend data were not significant at the .05 level. The fact that only in three cases (two C's and one I) were the trend lines statistically significant only reinforces our observation made in regard to Table 4. The trend lines on dividend data are not presented in this article.
4 See Figure 1.

fitted into the proper diagram according to their individual
histories, and fairly precise dates assigned to each line segment.

Bearing these diagrams in mind, Table 6 seeks to investigate
possible relationships between the patterns of development and the
results of Tables 2, 4 and 5. The numbers in column 1 indicate the
rank order and the magnitude of the slope (b) of the regression
equations $N = a + b$A. These could be regarded as indicators of
profitability for each road. Column 2 shows the rank order and the
magnitude of the ratio of the rate of increase of funded debt over
that of capital, i.e. b_f/b_k, and is used here as an indicator of the
sample roads' dependence upon debt financing. Column 3
summarises the findings of Table 4. The letter C represents those
roads that paid consistent dividends, I those paying irregularly, and
O those paying no dividends during the period. Column 4 classifies
the sample roads according to the four development categories
described earlier.

One important observation to be drawn from Table 6 is that it
lends credence to our four patterns of development shown in Figure
1. Those roads classified in categories 1 (flourishing systems) and 2
(budding systems) in column 4 would be expected to have the most
sustained and regular patterns of growth. This is born out by the
fact that all of the t-tests on regression coefficients of $N = a + b$A for
these roads (column 1) are significant at the .01 level, and
coefficients of determination for equations are significant at the .05
level for three roads and at the .01 level for the rest. In contrast, all
but one road in each of categories 3 and 4 have coefficients of
determination not significant at the .05 level, reflecting less regular
and consistent patterns of growth for roads in these categories.

In another area, the relationship between dividend performance
and the categories, we find that the roads classified in categories 1
and 2 contain all C's, while all the O's except one (C & O) belong
to categories 3 and 4. (See columns 3 and 4, Table 6).

Note also in columns 1 and 3, that four dividend class O's are
found for those roads ranked below thirteenth (in terms of the
ranking of the magnitude of the slope (b) of $N = a + b$A), while only
two dividend class O's are found above the thirteenth. Though
these results require much more detailed individual examination in
view of the diverse factors that determine dividend performance, it
would seem that these results support, rather than contradict, our
categorisation of the sample roads.

However, examination of the b_f/b_k ratios and the magnitudes of
regression coefficients of $N = a + b$A against our categorisation of
roads in the light of statistically insignificant results yields little
discernible relationship. Six out of the ten roads classified in

categories 3 and 4 have statistically insignificant regression coefficients. This indicates weak responsiveness of increasing total assets to net earnings and lends support to the nature of our classification.

But, in general, the most we can claim from the regression coefficients (column 1) and the ratio of the rate of increase of funded debt over that of capital (column 2) is that the patterns of responsiveness between net earnings (N) and total assets (A), and of the relative rate of increase between capital (K) and funded debt (F), proceeded along fairly undifferentiated lines for all sample roads regardless of category (column 4).

The observations on Table 6 have important if indirect implications for the question asked earlier at the end of Part I. It seems clear that during the period southern railroads could only have been regarded as poor investments. No amount of promotional fanfare could conceal the poor return on equity. Yet money continued to flow into these projects, and the conclusion must be that it was coaxed by other factors than direct return on investment. Capital kept moving into southern rail ventures because the financiers mobilising it found sources of profit outside rail operations. These sources of profit can be divided into three general categories: (1) bond yields; (2) secondary investments or linkages; and (3) transactional profits.

The role of bond yields has already been mentioned. It constitutes the other side of the investment process. To mobilise large amounts of capital in a short time, bond issues seemed the only feasible alternative. If equity investment promised low returns at considerable risk, the less speculative investor would have to be induced by a guaranteed return. It is entirely possible that bond yields on southern roads exceeded those of other and less risky projects elsewhere, but much research needs to be done to establish any such comparison.

The question of secondary investments also deserves extensive investigation. Few if any of the financiers who went into southern railroads limited their investments to the line itself. Most of them poured capital into real estate, mining and mineral lands, express companies, manufacturing, industrial development, and more exotic and risky projects such as the Lenoir City Company originated by several of the financiers involved in the East Tennessee, Virginia & Georgia.[17] The linkage went in both directions: investment preceded construction of the railroad (or a branch of it), in some cases, and at other times followed completion of the line. On every occasion, however, the commitment of capital assumed the presence of a road to assure connection with outside markets. Often these external projects motivated entrepreneurs to get into railroads in order to influence not only expansion policy but rate differentials as well. Regardless of whether these investments preceded or followed involvement in railroads, the outside projects came ultimately to dominate the financiers' attentions simply because they tended to be more profitable.

Transactional profits comprised the third important motivation for getting into southern railroads. The financiers who mobilised the burst of expansion after 1880 found lucrative business in such varied activities as construction of new lines, speculation in the securities of the roads, transactions involved in the acquisition of other lines (in which they often held personal interests), and the handling of bond issues and short term debt for the lines. The high degree of consolidation prevalent after 1880 offered choice opportunities to buy smaller lines cheaply and sell them to one's own road at an inflated price.[18] In such cases, the company incurred harmful over-capitalisation and an extra financial burden that further weakened its ability to pay a good return on its equity, but the individual financiers profited handsomely. Under these circumstances growth tended not to bring additional net earning power with it; rather it proceeded at the expense of the company's future welfare.

III

In this concluding section, the preliminary nature of this study must be emphasised. There exists a real need to investigate further the rapid development of southern railroads during the late nineteenth century. Our current research has examined theoretically expected relationships among a larger set of variables. Some multiple regression equations, calculated by using rates of change of selected series of available data, offer a promising avenue for better understanding of the process of this multifaceted growth.[19] The changing patterns of financing, competition, and regulation also require further investigation along with a closer evaluation of the entrepreneurial personalities and talents involved.

At this stage, however, a few provisional conclusions seem warranted on the basis of our preceding observations. In addition to the value inherent in the quantitative evidence on patterns of financing and profitability, we have shown that a study of railroad development requires close attention to social and institutional aspects and to entrepreneurial strategies and goals rather than to searching for simplistic cause-effect relationships among faceless entrepreneurs bent on maximising profits.

In the case of our sample roads, aggregate data, manipulated in however sophisticated manner, could not by themselves hope to present an accurate pattern of development for these roads. Nor could they reveal the motivations behind that growth. These roads possessed the common denominators of net earnings below the going rate of interest and heavy reliance on debt financing. They shared common problems, confronted largely similar environments, and probably pursued fairly homogeneous goals. But the strategies they evolved and the policies they adopted to attain their goals depended greatly upon their individual situation and produced a broad spectrum of subtle differences and shadings. Such differences, small but often meaningful for an understanding of the entrepreneurial function, slip undetected through the wide mesh net of quantitative analysis alone. In this respect, our study has reinforced the old saw that problems are general, solutions individual.

Our study also reaffirms the importance of what might loosely be called the business practices of the time in exploring the financing of growing roads and the diverse goals of investors, which are unfathomable in any quantitative study. The interests of managing financiers are more apt to ignore the interests of investors. Certain investors, who hoped for cheaper transportation for their products, access to new markets, or higher value of the land they owned, could easily find 'profits' in the impact of railroads upon their region rather than in dividends. These are old questions. Short-run interests of one group often conflict with long-run interests of another. The simplest quantitative analysis offered here supports the prevailing notion that for the post war South, social gains resulting from developing railroads often outweighed the lack of profits suffered by individual investors. For this reason, the importance of further research on the development of the American railroad in the nineteenth century, without losing sight of entrepreneurial functions and strategies, cannot be stressed too often.

NOTES

1 All the data used in this article are in real terms using 1860 as the base year. That is, the data have been inflated to take account of the postwar deflation. The index used was taken from Ethel D. Hoover 'Retail Prices after 1850,' in National Bureau of Economic Research, *Trends in the American Economy in the Nineteenth Century* (Princeton, 1960), 142, 162. A definition of total assets in nineteenth century railroad accounting would be worth an article in itself. In broad terms total assets included all tangible assets such as property, equipment, materials on hand, and a host of other items. It also included construction accounts, securities of other companies owned, accounts due, cash and bills on hand, and special items. Not surprisingly, the total assets of weaker roads often included dubious and spurious items.

2 These figures are calculated from Henry V. Poor, *Manual of the Railroads of the United States for 1894* (New York, 1894), xv and *passim*.

3 For those who might not be familiar with some terms used in this article, the following brief note might be of some use.

In linear regression analysis, which is in the form of $Y = a + bX$, b (regression coefficient) is the slope which indicates the rate of change in Y per unit of X. The intercept (a) is a magnitude of Y when X is zero. In both a and b, they are not *actual* or "observed" values but values calculated by the linear regression equation fitted by the standard least squares method. Coefficient of determination (r^2) indicates the 'goodness of fit' and its value ranges from —1 to 1. The term 't-test' refers to the test of the 'reliability' of the regression coefficient (b) and is obtained by dividing the value of b by the standard error of b.

In terms of Table 1, the equations were calculated in the form of $A = a + bt$, where A is total assets and t is time in year unit. The term 'trend lines' in the heading of the table is a standard expression for those regression equations in which X is t. The expressions used for intercept and slope (initial amount of total assets and annual rate of increase of total assets) are, of course, calculated and not actual values. The *Notes* to Table 1 state that both the results of t-tests and r^2's are significant at the .01 level. This simply means that the "confidence coefficient" was 99 per cent, i.e. there is only a one out of hundred chance of obtaining such high values for t-test and r^2 had the original data been entirely random. Later in this article, the .01 level is replaced by the .05 level. This means that those values of t-test and r^2 have a lower value of 'confidence coefficient,' i.e. 95 per cent. All through the article, the standard expression 'at given n (sample size)' is eliminated.

4 The negative intercepts seen for seven roads indicate that the total assets in those roads rose sharply from the calculated value of the initial year. As the original data confirm, this is due to an accelerated growth in later years which has an effect of tilting the slope upward and tending to understate the value of earlier years. But given the observed high r^2, the fit of these lines was generally good.

5 The three roads in which rate of increase for equity exceeded that for debt deserve special explanation. For two of the roads, 13 and 17, the data are misleading. Both actually had a considerably higher ratio of increase for debt than for equity, but financial re-organizations caused a massive rescaling of the ratios in favour of equity. In the case of road 13, two such reorganisations took place during the period. Road 1 is a somewhat unique case paralleled by only a few southern roads. Its debt was so small that it could generate enough internal capital to supply its growth needs during the territorial era. In 1881 on the verge of the great expansion era, it was leased to another system on highly favourable terms.

6 Note also that all t-test results are significant at the .05 level. It should be added here, for those readers who might object to our particular regression coefficients, that they are used because of their intuitive appeal. Theoretically, it would be desirable to evaluate each b after allowing for a specified confidence interval; i.e., after evaluating each b by, say, a two-tail test at t. .025 level. We use the ratios we do, however, because our sole purpose is to depict general trends and not to test econometric propositions. It goes almost without saying that a critical test for a trend line is the t-test. Our discussions in the text are done in terms of r 's again because of their intuitive appeal at no cost to the substance of our discussions.

7 Normally, operating expenses referred to those current expenses necessary to keep the road a going concern, such as supplies, salaries, materials etc. But accounting procedures varied widely among individual roads and at different points in the time period. For example, many roads sometimes included capital account expenditures in the current expense account. Other lines began including tax payments in operating expenses later in the period. Numerous exceptions to the general statement can be found, with each requiring its own explanation.

8 Here, as with operating expenses, the term 'fixed charges' has a general explanation not always applicable to individual cases. Basically, it constituted all fixed

obligations against the road, such as interest and tax payments. These might also include such things as lease payments, payments on endorsed bonds of other companies, and any regular annual obligation. The company's profit was thus figured by deducting all fixed charges from net earnings.

9 The Literature on regulation and the rate problem is voluminous. For the southern roads in particular see William H. Joubert, *Southern Freight Rates in Transition* (Gainesville, 1949) and David M. Potter, 'Historical Development of Eastern-Southern Freight Rate Relationships', *Law and Contemporary Problems*, XII (Summer, 1947), 416-48.

10 A survey of eighteen leased roads connected with our sample roads revealed only three cases in which the leased road earned enough to meet its guaranteed dividend after paying all expenses and fixed charges. Even the Georgia Railroad met its guaranteed 10 per cent dividend only once in twelve years.

11 Study of the data makes it clear that the Charlotte, Columbia & Augusta dividend was not the product of unexpectedly high earnings or reduced expenses. Other sample roads where doubtful dividends were declared are the Central of Georgia, the East Tennessee, Virginia & Georgia, and the Lousville & Nashville.

12 For sketchy and somewhat inaccurate accounts of the Central of Georgia's plight, see Stuart Daggett, *Railroad Reorganisation* (Cambridge, 1908), 169-88, and E. G. Campbell, *The Reorganisation of the American Railroad System* (New York, 1938), 96-106.

13 Recall that the data are all in real terms.

14 This concept will be developed in more detail in another article to be published in a forthcoming issues of the *Business History Review*.

15 This broad pattern of growth is traced in John F. Stover, *The Railroads of the South, 1865-1900* (Chapel Hill, 1955), which emphasises the thesis that southerners were losing control of their railroads to 'northern men and money'. While true to some extent, the couching of the struggle for control in such vague sectional terms seems to miss the point of what is happening and makes use of Stover's thesis limited and crude.

16 For explication of these terms, see Arthur M. Johnson and Barry E. Supple, *Boston Capitalists and Western Railroads* (Cambridge, Mass., 1967), 8-10, 181-91, 333-46.

17 An excellent insight into the nature and diversity of these linkage investments, including the Lenoir City Project, can be gained by studying the Charles M. McGee Papers (Lawson-McGee Library, Knoxville, Ohio). McGhee was involved in numerous southern roads, especially the East Tennessee, Virginia & Georgia and the Memphis & Charleston, over the entire period.

18 There are numerous examples of this practice. The most notorious case, perhaps, was the Georgia Company swindle. See Campbell, *Reorganisation*, 97-104, and Daggett, *Railroad Reorganisation*, 162-66, 177-78.

19 The variables we have considered include those discussed in this article and several others, including net worth, tonnage, mileage, operating expenses, fixed charges, cost per ton-mile, earnings per ton-mile, and operating ratios. Though we intend to evaluate the data for each railroad, a few results calculated for the aggregate data (twenty roads), as shown below, suggest our line of thought.

(1)   Net Earnings (N) $= 260,180.62 + 1,314.12M + .00224T - 124,830.56$ Ct.
$$(217.43) \quad\quad (.200215) \quad (54,787.31)$$
$$r^2 = .769$$
$$n = 28$$

M is Mileage, T is tonnage, and Ct is cost per ton-mile. The numbers in parenthesis are standard errors.

$$(2) \quad \Delta K = 822{,}593.01 + 77{,}870.84r - 8{,}887{,}477.90 \; \frac{N}{K+F} \qquad \begin{array}{l} r^2 = .0171 \\ n = 28 \end{array}$$

$$(173{,}805.27) \quad (6{,}792{,}186.5)$$

Where all notations (K, N, F, n) are the same as in the text; where ΔK is $K_t - K_{t-1}$; and where r is the weighted mean rate of dividend.

As seen in equation (1), T is much less meaningful than Ct (with the expected negative sign) in explaining N, while M is the most important of the three variables. Though there are various difficulties involved in making Ct comparable within the sample roads, the differences in explanatory value for the Ct of each road is an important item for further investigation. Equation (2) yields the expected result. As seen in our Table 4, dividends are unimportant in explaining ΔK and N/K + F yields a 'Wrong' sign. For many roads, this form of equation yields statistically insignificant results. But this is another item that needs to be evaluated carefully *vis-a-vis* the entrepreneurial functions of various lines.

14
The Merchant as Catalyst:
Financing Economic Growth

Glenn Porter and Harold C. Livesay*

The years after 1815 presented ambitious American mechanics
and artisans with steadily increasing opportunities. The rapid
growth of population — it quadrupled between 1815 and 1860 —
created an ever larger market for manufactures. Much of this
market remained accessible (as it had been in the colonial period)
to ships that plied the coastal waters and the navigable rivers of the
seaboard. As territorial expansion drew more and more people
farther inland, proliferating transportation networks — turnpikes,
canals, and then railroads — tied the new interior settlements to
the nation's commerce.

Those men who possessed the mechanical knowledge necessary
to operate a manufacturing facility had a choice: they could
continue to produce for local customers, or they could create larger
units, expand output, and try to take advantage of the emerging
national market. As previously discussed, manufacturing entrepreneurs who chose expansion quickly encountered distribution
problems that only the mercantile expertise of urban middlemen
could solve. For most fledgling manufacturers, expansion also
involved an excruciatingly difficult set of financial perplexities.
First, there was the need for capital. Fixed (or long-term) capital
was required for the purchase of land, buildings, and machinery,
and fixed assets necessary for production. Successive moves toward
expansion, or the need to replace obsolete plants and equipment,
required repeated commitments of long-term capital.

An even more vexing difficulty was the need for short-term
(working) capital with which to buy raw materials, pay wages, and

*From Glenn Porter and Harold C. Livesay 'Merchants and Manufacturers: Studies
in the Changing Structure of Nineteenth-Century Marketing'. The Johns Hopkins
Press, Baltimore and London (1971), Chapter IV. Reprinted by permission of Johns
Hopkins University Press.

meet other current operating costs such as taxes, advertising, transportation, loan interest, and the like.

Finally, doing business in distant markets with customers whose probity was unknown involved severe risks not encountered in selling locally. These included the dangers of extending credit to distant clients and of securing payment in funds or notes negotiable at or near par locally. Most manufacturers were so poorly equipped to resolve these dilemmas of capital and finance as they were to handle volume distribution in widespread markets.

LONG-TERM CAPITAL

Most early manufacturing firms were proprietorships or small partnerships. The owners were usually men of limited means. Assembling the fixed assets to commence or expand production often absorbed all the proprietors' resources. Additional fixed capital was extremely difficult to raise. Equity financing through the mass sale of securities did not begin in the United States until the introduction of the railroads, and it did not play a significant role in manufacturing finance before the Civil War.

The legal foundation for equity financing existed long before it found widespread employment in manufacturing. Prior to the Civil War many states had general incorporation laws embodying limited liability; however, for a variety of reasons, manufacturers seldom took advantage of them.[1] Among the reasons were lack of precedent, public scepticism toward such investments, lack of institutions to market shares, and entrepreneurial unwillingness to share ownership and control with 'outsiders'. Indeed, the correspondence and autobiographies of early American businessmen document the intensity with which the men identified themselves with their firms. Driven by pride, they laboured continually to keep their affairs under their own control. This attitude often manifested itself in a reluctance to accept partners, and it certainly was not conducive to the adoption of financing methods that would have diluted ownership even further by selling shares in the business to the general public.

Financial institutions such as banks and insurance companies were of limited utility as sources of long-term capital. Banks would occasionally make long-term loans to manufacturers, but only on strong collateral. They did not make unsecured loans on business prospects, however glowing. In the first decade of the nineteenth century, for example, the Bank of New York supplied capital for the construction of a Paterson, New Jersey, textile mill, but the entire amount of loan was secured by U.S. government bonds.[2]

A mortgage on real estate was another acceptable form of security. In the 1820s and 1830s, Washburn and Godard obtained long-term capital from a Worcester savings bank. The bank in turn held a mortgage on the firms's machine shop and on the millowners' real estate.[3] In 1856 the Baltimore ironmaster S. S. Keyser obtained funds to build a warehouse by mortgaging his family's property to a local bank.[4] Such conservative lending policies seem to have been typical of most sound eastern banks throughout the period. In 1856, for example, the Savings Bank of Baltimore had $190,000 outstanding in long-term industrial loans, all of which was secured by real estate, bank stock, or US government bonds.[5]

Insurance companies, like savings banks, were in the business of pooling individuals' savings and investing them at a profit. Insurance firms were, however, even less inclined than banks to make manufacturing loans. Refusing a loan request submitted by the Shawmut Fibre Company of Shawmut, Massachusetts, an officer of the Union Mutual Life Insurance Company commented that his firm had stopped making such loans 'long ago'. He added, 'It is the custom of our company, which has become practically a law with us, that we do not loan on manufacturing establishments'.[6]

Massachusetts Hospital Life Insurance Company, which opened for business in 1818, invested heavily in the stock of New England textile mills and made large loans to individual stockholders in textile firms, but it made few other investments in manufacturing. Massachusetts Life's participation in textile financing is doubtless explained by the fact that its list of stockholders consisted of names such as Lawrence, Lowell, Jackson, Cabot, Appleton, and other prominant New England merchants.[7] These were, of course, the same families that owned controlling interest in the textile mills, and the merchants were, in effect, lending to themselves by siphoning funds from one family enterprise into another. This pattern of a merchant-controlled financial institution underwriting its stockholders' industrial investments while refusing loans to other manufacturing proprietors and partners was commonplace in the period. It was one of the principal ways in which merchants were able to control antebellum manufacturing developments.

Modern industrial firms secure long-term capital for expansion or modernisation by tapping the savings of the general public. They do so through mass sales of securities, or through loans from financial institutions such as banks and insurance companies. Since neither of these methods was open to pre-Civil War entrepreneurs, growth depended upon personal resources and retained earnings (both of which were usually inadequate), or upon financial assistance from wealthy merchants. In such circumstances it is not surprising that many of the most successful firms were either those founded by the merchants themselves or those in which the entrepreneur was able to secure funds for fixed capital assets through an alliance with members of the mercantile community.

The outstanding examples of the first case were the Waltham and Lowell textile mills and such integrated rail mills as Cambria and Bethlehem — the largest manufacturing enterprises of their times. All of these firms were originally created through merchants' initiative. The merchants raised fixed capital by forming a corporation and selling stock privately to limited numbers of their colleagues.[8] Because many of these firms prospered, and because many of their histories have been written, this method of finance is best known, but it was in fact the least often used.[9]

The second case, in which an established manufacturer financed expansion through an alliance with wealthy merchants, occurred far more often. Sometimes these alliances took the form of a closely held stock corporation; often they were a formal or informal partnership. Whitaker Iron (the forerunner of Wheeling Steel) illustrates the corporate method. In the 1840s George and Joseph Whitaker, the Maryland ironmasters who controlled Principio Furnace, financed their firm's growth by securing capital from the Baltimore merchants Thomas Garrett and William Chandler. The new firm issued 4,000 shares of stock, of which the Whitakers owned 2,400, the merchants 1,600.[10]

Often a firm sought to acquire investment capital by inveigling the merchants who distributed its products into buying shares in the firm, or into becoming partners. The Mount Hope Iron Company (Massachusetts), for example, tried to increase its capitalisation in 1858 by selling shares to several iron commission merchants in Boston.[11] The most dramatically successful example of the partnership method was Jones and Laughlin of Pittsburgh, a firm built through the union of manufacturing entrepreneurs and merchant capital.[12]

The firm began in 1853 as a partnership between Benjamin Lauth, Francis Lauth, Benjamin Jones, and Samuel Kier. The Lauths were immigrant German metalworkers who had built a rolling mill on the south side of the Monongahela River in 1850. Although the Lauths were mechanically ingenious (they perfected a cold-rolling process that produced a very hard iron with a smooth, shiny exterior surface),[13] they quickly encountered the financial difficulties that were the bane of all western Pennsylvania ironmasters' existence before the Civil War.[14] By 1853 they were floundering, and they began to seek added capital in the Pittsburgh mercantile community. This search eventuated in the alliance with Jones and Kier, who contributed $10,000 cash to the business, paid the Lauths $2,700 for their previous efforts, and became equal partners in the business.[15]

Jones and Kier were specialised freight commission brokers who had operated the 'Mechanics' Line of Packets' between Philadelphia and Pittsburgh over the Main Line Canal and Portage Railroad. When the Pennsylvania Railroad reached Pittsburgh in 1852, Jones and Kier shrewdly perceived that the heyday of the freight commission broker had passed; they sold out, opened an iron commission business, and became partners with the Lauths.[16]

Under the terms of the partnership, Jones and both Lauths received salaries of $1,500. The partners agreed to draw no other funds from the business; all profits were to be added to the firm's capital. The Lauths ran the rolling mill; Jones had charge of 'warehouses, books, accounts and finances'.[17] Jones soon proved a singularly nimble financial manager. He saved the business, for, despite the fresh injection of cash and the agreement to plough profits back into the business, the new firm almost immediately needed additional long-term and working capital. Jones was able to arrange for both; moreover, he did so on extremely favourable terms in a region where dozens of manufacturers competed for the limited quantity of capital available. The 'angel' was a Pittsburgh commission merchant, James Laughlin.

Laughlin was an Irish immigrant who had made his fortune as a pork packer and a seller of provisions to settlers passing through Pittsburgh on their way west. In the 1850s he operated commission houses dealing in iron and groceries in Pittsburgh and in Evansville, Indiana. Laughlin sold iron from the Jones and Lauth works, and he apparently had great faith in the future of the firm, for he soon became its financial backer. By March, 1855, he had already contributed $8,200 cash to the firm's capital. In that year he contributed $40,000 more and became a partner in the business.[18] As a partner Laughlin was a manufacturing entrepreneur's dream. He took no part in the active management of the business,[19] but he backed the firm with his entire financial resources through the crucial first decade of its existence. He contributed his personal wealth to the firm's long-term capital and used his personal credit standing to arrange for adequate working capital.

Whether Jones and Laughlin could have survived without Laughlin's all-out support is debatable. It was the only pre-Civil War iron firm, other than integrated rail mills, that survived to become one of the giant twentieth-century steel producers; and it

TABLE 1
Capital Invested in Jones & Laughlin Steel Corp., 1853-1861

Year	Total Capital ($)	Capital Added ($)	Capital Added from Profits ($)	Capital Added by Cash from Laughlin ($)
1853	20,000	—	—	—
1853-1856	127,000	107,000	55,000	52,000
1856-1861	176,000	49,000	30,000	19,000
Total	323,000	156,000	85,000	71,000

Source: Computed from data in various articles of partnership cited previously, the partnership agreement of 1861, and a table of earnings and dividends in H. S. Geneen, Comptroller of Jones & Laughlin, to W. R. Compton, Assistant Chairman of the Board, December 2, 1952, all Jones & Laughlin Steel Corp. Papers.
Note: After 1861 the firm continued its policy of financing expansion with retained earnings. From 1861 to 1908, the firm's profits totaled $70,000,000. Eighty per cent of this was plowed back into the business.

was one of the few unintegrated antebellum iron firms that succeeded in adopting the integrated, high-volume structure. As described in the previous chapter, the integrated mill required large sums of capital. The rail mills obtained theirs from the pooled resources of several merchants. In the 1850s, Jones and Laughlin transformed the Lauths' small, single-stage bar mill into a large, integrated unit. By 1857 the firm had its own blast furnaces to furnish pig iron, thirty-one puddling and heating furnaces to refine the iron and prepare it for rolling, five trains of steam-driven rolls to produce bar iron and shafting, and twenty-five nail-making machines.[20] As a result of expansion and integration, capital invested rose from $20,000 in 1853 to $176,000 in 1861. The increase came entirely from profits and James Laughlin's cash contributions. Retained earnings alone fell far short of supplying the total additions to capital, as Table 1 indicates.

As great as Laughlin's contributions to the firm's long-term capital were, they were probably less important to its ultimate success than his ability to secure adequate working capital. He was able to do so because his endorsements enabled Jones and Laughlin to discount its own and its customers' short-term notes for cash to meet operating expenses. Working capital not only was far more difficult for most manufacturers to come by, but the annual requirements for it greatly exceeded the average annual additions to fixed assets. In 1860, for example, when Jones and Laughlin's fixed assets totalled about $176,000, it had short-term obligations of $200,000 to the Pittsburgh Trust Company.[21]

The firm was able to secure such extensive credit only because its paper carried the endorsement of Laughlin, a merchant and a stockholder in several Pittsburgh banks.[22] Jones could never have secured such advances on the strength of his own (or his firm's) credit alone. Virtually all antebellum manufacturers faced similar requirements for short-term capital relative to total investments; very few had a James Laughlin to obtain it for them. Their ability to secure such funds often determined their success or failure, and the way in which the funds were obtained often determined the conduct of the business.

PROBLEMS OF WORKING CAPITAL

Working capital presented particularly perplexing problems to early manufacturers because of the large quantity required and the paucity of agencies, formal or informal, prepared to supply it. The quantity required was primarily a result of high operating costs and of the credit, banking, and monetary systems that prevailed in the United States prior to the Civil War.

The Jones and Laughlin case cited above, in which short-term obligations incurred in meeting operating costs roughly equalled the fixed assets accumulated through the entire life of the business, was not at all unusual among pre-Civil War American manufacturing firms. For example, E. I. du Pont de Nemours, the Wilmington, Delaware, powder firm founded in 1802, had capital assets of $500,000 in 1860. Its operating expenses during the same year were $440,000. In smaller firms the ratio of current expenses to capital assets were often much higher. John Foebling's wire rope factory at Trenton, New Jersey, had fixed assets of $20,000 in 1850; labour and material costs totalled $42,000.[23]

The bulk of current operating expenses consisted of the cost of raw materials and wages. Both of these were 'variable costs', which rose and fell with the level of production. When an entrepreneur decided to expand production, he almost immediately encountered increased payroll expenses. Raw-material costs also rose, but these could often be deferred to some extent by purchasing on credit. Suppliers, however, had payrolls of their own to meet, and they persistently pressed for punctual payment. Transportation costs (another variable) also had to be paid in cash or on short-term credit (usually within thirty days or less). All of these factors combined to present manufacturing entrepreneurs with a critical shortage of operating capital with which to meet production expenses.

Income, on the other hand, came from sales almost invariably made on long-term credit.[24] The average term of credit in most manufacturing lines was six months, but this often fluctuated. In competitive markets, manufacturers often had to offer more generous terms. The prevalence of extended credit terms was a function not so much of the money supply as of the predominantly agricultural nature of the economy. The best available estimates indicate that manufacturing contributed about one-quarter of the total value added in all American industries in 1839. By 1850, manufacturing's share had risen to about one-third.[25] In such an economy, manufacturing credit terms were necessarily tied to agricultural credit terms. The latter, of course, were a function of the harvest cycle. In either case there was considerable delay before suppliers received payment in full.

Customers paid for their purchases by sending a note — in effect, a post-dated cheque payable at the expiration of the credit period. The manufacturer needed immediate cash to meet expenses. If the note came from a local resident of good credit standing, it could sometimes be cashed at a local bank for a fee (discount), which varied according to the prevailing demand for money. The discount, of course, reduced the profit on sales and added to the cost of doing business.[26] To avoid this cost, manufacturers sometimes accepted payment in produce, which they foisted off on employees as partial payment of wages.[27]

These methods broke down as production increased and markets expanded geographically. Banks refused to accept out-of-town notes, or would accept them only at prohibitive discounts.[28] Even if the manufacturer could afford to hold the note until its payment date, and even if the note did not prove worthless, his troubles were not over, for cheques drawn on distant banks, or notes issued by them, also were subject to discount. Manufacturers therefore tried to insist on payment in local funds, or in paper that traded at face value locally.[29] All the while, of course, their suppliers were making similar demands on them. Factory owners generally were ill-equipped to deal with these perplexities; they had neither the time nor the experience. What they needed were financial intermediaries capable of supplying reliable credit information, rationalising payments in order to minimise discount costs, and furnishing operating cash either by discounting notes, making advances on accounts receivable, or lending on inventories.

In the modern economy a complex network of formal institutions performs all these functions. National and local credit agencies abound. Banks discount reliable manufacturers' notes and lend on receivables. Two types of companies specialise in industrial finance: commercial credit companies discount notes and lend on receivables; factoring companies buy accounts receivable outright and lend on inventories.[30] Before the Civil War no such salubrious conditions obtained. Credit-rating agencies existed, but they primarily served mercantile clients. Banks grew progressively more reluctant to discount notes bearing a manufacturer's endorsement; they rarely (if ever) lent on receivables. Commercial credit and factoring companies were twentieth-century developments; it is thought that the first of each type appeared in 1903 and 1925 respectively.[31]

The late development of formal fiduciary institutions geared to manufacturers' needs, together with the enduring reluctance of banks to provide working capital or to finance transactions, was, like the prevalence of long-term credit, largely attributable to the pre-eminence of the agricultural sector of the economy. Not until the 1880s did the total annual value of manufacturing production exceed the total of agricultural output.[32] Credit institutions (particularly commercial banks) were therefore oriented toward financing the movement of crops to market at home and abroad. They tended to remain so for two reasons.

The first reason was a philosophical conservatism which deeply influenced banking policies. Early nineteenth-century banks were not in business to take 'risks' in the sense that we understand the term today. Savings banks were in business to accept deposits, pool them, and use the resulting fund of capital to invest in mortgages or government bonds. The value of the property or the credit of the U.S. government eliminated the element of risk.

Most commercial banks had been founded by merchants to service the needs of the agricultural and commercial economy. They facilitated commerce at home and abroad by discounting notes and serving as clearing houses for bills of exchange. These transactions were not considered hazardous, because the value of the goods for which notes and bills were issued, together with the personal assets of the merchants involved in the transaction, protected the bank against losses. Because banks were not accustomed to extending these services to manufacturers, and because most early producers were men of limited means, bankers tended to regard manufacturing finance as unknown and risky, and therefore beyond the scope of sound banking practice. It took decades of manufacturing growth to alter this conservative philosophy.

The second reason for the delayed entry of formal institutions into manufacturing finance was the fact that early manufacturers, finding no formal agencies willing or able to assume the financial risks of expanding production and markets, turned to merchants for help. Merchants supplied the needed capital and expertise, and in the process became so deeply entrenched in the manufacturing sector that they were extremely difficult to supplant.

Merchants handled most of the financial transactions of the expanding national market as they managed the growing flow of goods throughout the economy. They were able to do so because, in contradistinction to manufacturers, they were appropriately equipped in resources, temperament, and training.

Throughout the pre-Civil War period, merchants controlled most of the available capital in the United States. Many merchants had large sums of personal cash available[33] and had access to additional funds through credit at home and abroad. Unlike manufacturers, who could obtain bank loans only on tangible collateral, prosperous merchants could borrow extensively from commercial and savings banks, often on their signature alone. This seeming paradox is explained by the prevailing banking philosophy and by the fact that merchants usually *were* the banks. An analysis of the directors and officers of the banks of New York, Philadelphia, and Baltimore in 1840, 1850, and 1860 reveals that more than two-thirds of the officials were or had been merchants. The same was true of virtually all the private bankers in those cities.[34] Middlemen therefore had ready access both to accumulated mercantile profits and to the savings deposits of the populace.

Merchants not only had resources, they were temperamentally inclined to use them to finance commerce. They were professional risk takers. Men who did not hesitate to send ships from the East Coast of the United States around the world, on voyages that lasted for years, were not as likely to be defeated by the financial intricacies of a transaction between Baltimore and Pittsburgh as was a manufacturer accustomed to dealing locally. In addition, as many historians have noted, successful merchants seem perpetually driven to find profitable employment for surplus funds.

In previous centuries this drive led merchants such as the Fuggers and Rothchilds into banking. Others poured their profits back into trade, buying and selling more goods, and building more ships to haul them in. Of necessity, expanded trade required larger markets, and this dynamic led Nicolo Polo and his successors to travel about the world themselves and to finance explorations in search of trading routes and markets in the Indies.

Many American merchants followed these traditional paths in the early nineteenth century. Stephen Girard of Philadelphia became an enormously wealthy private banker. Merchant families such as the Jacksons and Lees of Boston built world-wide trading networks with branch houses in India and China. The need for greater market coverage made merchants the driving force behind such early internal improvements as the Erie and Chesapeake and Delaware canals.

Many merchants, however, found an outlet for their surplus capital in manufacturing finance. Some, like Francis Cabot Lowell, did so at first because the Napoleonic Wars and the War of 1812 made reinvestment in foreign trade impractical. Lowell had been to England, and he realised that potential profits lay in textile manufacturing. Once he and his associates demonstrated the profitability of textile enterprises, other merchants were quick to make similar investments.

Some of these traders turned to manufacturing investment because of the changing American market. Population growth presented greater trading opportunities at home, and the advance of mechanisation widened the market for manufacturers. In selecting their investments, merchants used their knowledge of expanding domestic markets and usually financed those manufacturing fields for which their own trading regions were particularly suited in terms of natural resources, skilled labour, and transportation facilities. For example, the Pennsylvania merchants who underwrote the state's iron industry included the Trotter family, which dealt in tin and copper, but invested heavily in the Lehigh Crane Iron Works; Richard Wood, Charles Wood, and Edward Townsend, Philadelphia dry goods merchants who took over the bankrupt Cambria Iron Works and hired John Fritz to resuscitate it; and, of course, the pork packer turned iron dealer, James Laughlin.

Many specialised merchants invested in firms that produced the particular types of goods they sold. In effect, this was a loose form of backward integration which assured continuing supplies in expanding markets and decreased the merchants' dependence on overseas producers. Anson Phelps supplemented his supply of copper and brass wares by supporting factories in the Connecticut River valley. David Reeves used his profits from importing British rails to start the first integrated American rail mill, Phoenix Iron. Specialised merchants also supplied working capital and became financial agents for their clients.

In so doing they brought their experience and skill to bear on the assortment of capital, credit, banking, and monetary woes which beset ambitious manufacturers. Problems that defied solution by manufacturing entrepreneurs were often resolved by merchants through the application of traditional techniques. Traders since the Middle Ages had had to assemble capital, evaluate investment risks, maintain a flow of credit information, function as investment and commercial bankers, and master the art of doing business over long distances with a polyglot assortment of currencies and commercial paper. In short, merchants routinely performed all the functions later institutionalised in formal agencies such as banks, credit bureaus, and factoring companies. Their financial versatility, developed through the centuries in a preindustrial economy, proved readily adaptable to manufacturing. Entrepreneurs who sought outlying markets were pioneers in American manufacturing, but the commission merchants and jobbers who distributed their products functioned as they and their predecessors always had in arranging and financing transactions.

In the process, commission merchants and jobbers naturally kept current records on the credit standing of clients, and, as previously shown, brokers such as Cabeen and Kemble, and jobbers such as the Troths, relieved manufacturers of credit risks by guaranteeing payment. They also brought some measure of order to the chaos of notes and currency. Through widespread connections in the trading and banking community they were able to absorb and dispose of commercial paper at much less loss than manufacturers. Commission merchants customarily rendered payment in their own notes, which discounted more readily. This accelerated the cash flow and decreased the pressure for working capital. They also furnished short-term funds in other ways. Some, like Laughlin, endorsed notes so that banks would accept them. Unlike Laughlin, most brokers were not partners in the business and therefore charged a fee for the service.

Other merchants acted as note brokers, using their own funds to discount manufacturers' paper. The risks in such dealings were high, but so were the returns. Merchants' discount rates often were not subject to usury laws, or the laws were evaded. In a period when 6 per cent or less was the normal bank interest rate to preferred borrowers, note brokers often charged as much as 30 per cent and rarely less than 12 per cent.[35] In such circumstances it is not surprising to find that many merchants borrowed heavily from banks to underwrite their discounting activities. For example, the Baltimore iron brokers John Gittings and E. J. Stickney borrowed hundreds of thousands of dollars from the Savings Bank of Baltimore in the period 1845-66. During that time they made loans and discounted notes for several iron manufacturers, including Gibbons and Huston, and for the Locust Point Furnace (Maryland).[36] Some measure of the profitability of such operations when prudently managed can be seen in the career of the Philadelphia metal dealer Nathan Trotter. Trotter habitually put his surplus funds into discounting. Between 1833 and 1852 he cleared almost half a million dollars from such deals.[37]

With such widespread demand for discounting, and such great profits to be made, many merchants quit dealing in merchandise altogether and became specialised note brokers. Their services were expensive, but, because they were available nowhere else, note brokers proved indispensable to many manufacturers. As the volume of trade increased, so did specialisation. Note brokerage as a speculation by commission merchants with surplus funds was commonplace by 1830. Specialised note brokers appeared by 1840. By 1850 some of them had become further specialised and handled only one kind of paper — for example, iron or dry goods.[38] Thus, volume brought disintegration of the merchants' cluster of financial competencies, just as it had transformed the manifold mercantile functions of the all-purpose merchant into specialised fields such as dry goods jobbing. In time the process of disintegration produced specialists in every sphere of financial responsibility, and these were the precursors of the formal institutions that appeared after the Civil War.

Commission merchants also supplied working capital by making advances on sales. Brokers paid producers some portion of the total value of the goods as soon as they had been shipped. Baltimore commission merchants Ballard and Hall wrote Jacob Haldeman after receipt of a shipment of iron, 'You are at liberty to value on us payable in 90 days and your draft will meet due honour.' The commission house declared itself 'always willing to make advances to any desired extent on goods in hand . . . if you continue your shipments of iron.'[39]

The merchants, it is important to note, did not make these payments and advances in cash. As in the case of Ballard and Hall, wholesalers issued notes payable at some later date, usually from three to six months after issuance. They did so by authorising manufacturers to 'draw' on them. The manufacturer then filled out a promissory note showing the amont and the date of maturity. He sent the note to the merchant, who signed ('accepted') and returned it. The manufacturer then discounted the note for cash, or used the note itself to pay current bills. The notes of many prominent, wealthy merchants, such as Enoch Pratt, circulated at near face value, and they formed an important addition to the money supply in an era of chronic shortages of currency.

From the manufacturer's point of view, the advantages of receiving advances were negated to some extent by the fact that sales revenue was reduced by the amount of the discount cost; nevertheless, the practice was universal before the Civil War and was not restricted to proprietorships like Haldeman's. Equity-financed firms used it as well. Advances from selling houses supplied crucial working capital to textile mills, and Whitaker Iron often kept its Wheeling mill running on advances from Pratt.[40] Sometimes a firm's success or failure depended upon its ability to make arrangements with a wholesaler for guaranteed advances. To obtain such guarantees, a producer often had to agree to consign his output to a single merchant, thus sacrificing a large measure of control over his business.

Agreements on guaranteed advances and marketing rights were often formalized by a contract between a manufacturing firm and a commission house. Typical of such agreements was one between Robeson, Brooke Company, blast furnace operators of Berks County, Pennsylvania, and the Philadelphia iron brokerage house Whitaker and Coudon. The brokers bound themselves to "undertake the sale of your iron for two years . . . charging you 5% commission and guarantee on the entire product of said furnace [plus] the usual charges for weighing, wharfage etc., and will advance you either in cash or our paper — monthly, the amount of sales, fast as made less charges and interest." Whitaker and Coudon thus assumed the role of exclusive manufacturer's agent for Robeson, Brooke, as did Cabeen for Cornwall Furnace. In return for exclusive sales rights, the brokers promised to supply working capital. 'We will agree to loan you our paper to the amount of Thirty thousand dollars for which we will charge you two and one half per cent.'[41]

Several important stipulations were involved. First, the furnace had to supply 5,000 tons of pig iron annually. If it failed to do so, the interest on the loan jumped to 5 per cent. Second, the brokers reserved the right to discount their own paper (thereby adding brokerage fees to the interest charges), and the furnace could cash it elsewhere only with permission. Third, if the loan was not repaid within a year, 'We will charge you over and above the commission the street rate or charge for the money.'[42]

Whitaker and Coudon's loan was, in effect, an advance against future production. As such, it represented another classic mercantile technique developed for the pre-industrial economy in the form of advances against crops, a technique practiced throughout the nineteenth century by cotton and grain factors.[43] Sometimes such bargains paid off. Gibbons and Huston weathered the slump of 1857 with the help of advances from Curtis Bouve, a Boston commission house, and went on to renewed prosperity. Samuel Colt's suppliers, including Naylor and Company of New York, financed him until his first government contract in the 1840s assured him of success. On other occasions the gamble proved unwise. The Columbia, South Carolina, commission firm of Polock, Solomon, and Company lost $9,000 when an iron furnace went bankrupt.[44]

Middlemen also engaged in barter transactions with manufacturers, thereby reducing the need for cash operating capital. John Wood, the Conshohocken, Pennsylvania, rolling mill operator, shipped sheet iron to Anson Phelps in return for copper and brass. Fall River Iron regularly paid Enoch Pratt and E. J. Stickney for pig iron by shipping them nails.[45] Such transactions were often advantageous for both parties, for the manufacturer disposed of his products and secured raw materials without adding to his debts or undergoing discount costs. Brokers, of course, profited on the sale of both raw materials and finished products.

Through the application of their financial expertise concomitantly with their role as distributors and suppliers, merchants made it possible for American manufacturers to function in expanding markets. Their control of finances often allowed them to dictate policy to manufacturers. Some merchants became partners in, or owners of, producing firms as a result to their advances. In this way Joseph Anderson became president of Tredegar Iron in Richmond, Virginia. The New York commission merchant Augustus Moen joined the wire-making firm of Washburn and Godard.[46] Similar examples abound in the histories of antebellum manufacturing firms.

CONCLUSION

Thus, most early American manufacturing firms existed as partnerships (formal or informal) between technically knowledgeable factory owners or managers and mercantile capitalists. Sometimes (as in the case of rail and textile mills) these alliances developed when merchants, perceiving a new market and seeking a profitable outlet for unused resources, pooled their funds to construct a factory, engage a supervisory staff, and commence production. On other occasions (as in the case of Jones and Laughlin) established manufacturers took in merchant partners in order to secure capital. Jobbers and commission merchants became involved as a logical consequence of their roles as distributors and suppliers.

Whatever the particular circumstances, the ultimate effect of these relationships was to open a channel through which capital poured from the mercantile sector of the economy into the manufacturing sector.

Merchants were the agents of transfer, a role which resulted naturally from their position at the nexus of American commerce.

The growth of American markets for manufactures in the early nineteenth century presented an incentive and a compulsion for mercantile participation in manufacturing finance. The incentive was the profit potential of trade in domestic products; the compulsion derived from the need to control large and dependable supplies in order to maintain control of trade flows. Some merchants found their role as capitalists and financial manipulators so profitable that they dropped marketing to specialise in finance. These private bankers and note brokers were the forerunners of formal agencies specialising in commercial credit which appeared in a subsequent era.

By bringing their capital resources and financial expertise into the manufacturing sector, merchants played an indispensable part in American industrialisation. All but a handful of antebellum American manufacturers who produced for outlying markets and operated successfully for at least a generation received some form of financial assistance from merchants. Nowhere was this more true than in the group of industries which sprang up as a result of the coming of the railroads.

NOTES

1 Thomas R. Navin and Marian V. Sears, 'The Rise of a Market for Industrial Securities, 1887-1902'.
2 Joseph J. Klein, 'The Development of Mercantile Instruments of Credit in the United States', p. 437.
3 Washburn & Godard Bill Book, Inventory and Record, 1822-48, American Steel & Wire Papers.
4 Credit Report on S. S. Keyser & Co., Baltimore, Md., Dun & Bradstreet Collection, 8: 12, 397. Many similar examples could be listed.
5 Peter L. Payne and Lance E. Davis, *The Savings Bank of Baltimore*.
6 Josiah Drummond to Alexander H. Rice, October 21, 1889, Shawmut Fibre Co. Papers.
7 Gerald T. White, *A History of the Massachusetts Hospital Life Insurance Company*, pp. 41-55, 85-104.
8 A firm in which all the stock is closely held by a few individuals is called a 'close corporation'.
9 Victor S. Clark commented: 'Commerce supplied capital to manfuacturing in two ways: by direct investment and by credits to industrial companies. The latter way, although less conspicuous, was probably the more important of the two' (*History of Manufacturers in the United States*, 1: 368).
10 Minutes of Stockholders Meeting, 1842, 1843, 1844; Statement of Stock, Principio Furnace, 1841; both in Principio Furnace Papers.
11 Minutes of Directors' Meeting, October 4, 1958, Mount Hope Iron Co. Papers. This method was more often used to obtain working capital.
12 Jones & Laughlin is particularly interesting to study because it is the only one of the modern 'Big Steel' firms which grew entirely through internal expansion. It absorbed no other producing firms until 1943.

13 Thomas E. Lloyd, 'History of Jones and Laughlin Steel Corporation', mimeographed copy dated 1938, Old History Papers, Jones & Laughlin Steel Corp. Papers.

14 Capital shortages in Pittsburgh are elaborated in Louis C. Hunter, 'Financial Problems of the Early Pittsburgh Iron Manufacturers', *passim*. See also Willis L. King, 'Speech Delivered Before Aliquippa Engineers Institute on the History of Jones and Laughlin Steel Corporation', mimeographed copy in Jones & Laughlin Papers. King was Benjamin Jones's nephew.

15 Agreement between Benjamin Lauth and Francis Lauth with S. M. Kier and B. F. Jones, December 3, 1853, Jones & Laughlin Papers.

16 Kier was never an active partner in the rolling mill. In 1856 he made a spectacular error in judgment by trading his one-quarter interest in the firm in exchange for Jones's share of their commission business. Kier was a fabulous, multifaceted character. In addition to his freight, iron, and commission business, he also owned a fire-brick and pottery factory. In a more exotic vein, he drew off the crude oil that seeped into his father's salt wells near Tarentum, Pa., and bottled it as a panacea called 'Kier's Rock Oil'. He developed a following for this wondrous concoction by sending a 'Medicine road show' around the country in the 1840s. When a steady demand arose, he sold through regular drug channels. In the 1850s he developed a method of distilling crude oil for use as an illuminant, as well was a patent lamp in which to burn it. See Release: Benjamin E. Jones from All Liability to Co-Partners in Firms of Grover, Kier & Co. and Jones, Kier & Co., and Samuel M. Kier from All Liability to Co-Partners in Jones, Lauth & Co., January 17, 1856, *ibid.*; Allen Johnson *et al.*, eds., *Dictionary of American Biography*, 5: 371-72.

17 Article of Partnership between Benjamin Lauth and Francis Lauth with S. M. Kier and B. F. Jones, December 3, 1853, Jones & Laughlin Papers.

18 Agreement between James Laughlin and Jones, Lauth & Co., March 8, 1855; Limited Partnership: Benjamin F. Jones, Benjamin Lauth, and James Laughlin (James Laughlin Special Partner), Term Five Years from August 1, 1856, *ibid.* Francis Lauth had already dropped out of the business. His brother sold out in 1864 for $10,000, went back to Germany, and made a fortune in iron and steel there.

19 His sons did, however; two of them became partners in 1861. Others joined in 1870. With one or two exceptions, a member of the Jones and Laughlin families has headed the firm since its inception.

20 Lloyd, 'History of Jones and Laughlin'; J. P. Lesley, *The Iron Manufacturer's Guide*, pp. 247-48. The mill's capacity rose from 15 tons per day in 1853 to 100 tons in 1869; see King, 'Speech before the Aliquippa Engineers', Jones & Laughlin Papers.

21 Acknowledgment of Obligation of James Laughlin and Benjamin F. Jones to the Pittsburgh Trust Co. to the Extent of $200,000, March 16, 1860, Jones & Laughlin Papers. Laughlin was president of Pittsburgh Trust when he first became interested in the rolling mill.

22 In order to get the bank of Pittsburgh to discount the firm's notes and bills, Laughlin (in his role as endorser) submitted a statement of his personal wealth. In addition to a 13/32 interest in the iron works, he had $50,000 in real estate, $75,000 cash capital in his commission houses, and $25,000 in bank stock. See James Laughlin to President and Cashier, Bank of Pittsburgh, August 26, 1857, *ibid.*

23 US Census Office, *Eighth Census of the United States, 1860: Manufactures*, pp. 53, 55, *et passim*; D. B. Steinman, *Builders of the Bridge*, p. 147.

24 Cash payment was extremely rare, despite the considerable savings it afforded through the avoidance of discount costs. Manufacturers and merchants usually

offered price reductions of up to 10 per cent for payment in cash. Despite these inducements, the only antebellum firm (among the dozens whose papers we have seen) that habitually paid cash, in good times and bad, was the Conshohocken, Pa., rolling mill of James and John Wood. Not only did the Woods pay cash for supplies, but they invariably held their customers' notes until maturity, a remarkable feat at the time. See the Correspondence and Account Books in the Alan Wood Steel Co. Papers.

25 US Bureau of the Census. *Historical Statistics of the United States*, p. 139. An explanation of the term 'value added' appears on p. 133 in the same volume.

26 Discount and interest costs often absorbed as much as 20-25 per cent of gross revenues in the period 1830-60. Presumably the most successful entrepreneurs took this into account when setting prices.

27 This questionable practice was later outlawed by some states, but was institutionalised in company stores in others. Payment in produce continued in small firms for many decades; however, it had pretty well disappeared by 1840 in the firms with which we are concerned here.

28 This was particularly true after the demise of the Second Bank of the United States rendered the transfer of funds difficult and diminished the reliability of state bank notes.

29 See George R. Taylor, *The Transportation Revolution, 1815-1860*, pp. 312-23 and chap. 15, for a lucid description of monetary and banking practices, their hazards and abuses.

30 Terris Moore, 'Unsecured Bank Loans as Permanent Workings Capital for Industry', pp. 116-17; William T. Rhame, 'Competitive Advantages and Disadvantages of Agencies Making Short and Medium Term Loans to Industry', pp. 5-42.

31 Moore, 'Bank Loans as Working Capital', pp. 116-17; Joseph E. Hedges, *Commercial Banking and the Stock Market Before 1863*, p. 86.

32 Bureau of the Census, *Historical Statistics*, pp. 139-40.

33 A forceful demonstration of the profitability of mercantile trade is the fact that Baltimore merchant Robert Oliver made a net profit of $775,000 in 1806-7 in his trade with Vera Cruz alone; see Stuart Bruchey, *Robert Oliver, Merchant of Baltimore, 1783-1819*, chap. 6.

34 Based on data taken from appropriate city and commercial directories. Among the many biographies of merchants who turned bankers are Richard H. Hart, *Enoch Pratt*, and John B. McMaster, *The Life and Times of Stephen Girard*.

35 Don M. Dailey, 'The Early Development of the Note Brokerage Business in Chicago'; Lance E. Davis, 'The New England Textile Mills and the Capital Markets'; Elva Tooker, 'A Merchant Turns to Money-Lending in Philadelphia'; and Klein, 'Mercantile Instruments of Credit', p. 603.

36 Payne and Davis, *Savings Bank of Baltimore*; Credit Report of Locust Point Furnace, Baltimore, Md., Dun & Bradstreet Collection, 8: 348. On occasion Baltimore banks were reportedly unable to discount any kind of paper because the entire supply of loanable funds was in the hands of merchants and note brokers; see Klein, 'Mercantile Instruments of Credit', p. 603.

37 Elva Tooker, *Nathan Trotter*, p. 182. Not all the paper Trotter handled was manufacturers'. He also dealt in bills of exchange and the like.

38 Klein, 'Mercantile Instruments of Credit', pp. 533-35.

39 Ballard & Hall to Jacob Haldeman, May 18, 1819, and February 24, 1820; Andrew Hall to Haldeman, December 31, 1819; and David Wizer to Haldeman, March 24, 1820; Jacob Haldeman Papers. Frequently such advances were subject to interest charges.

40 Davis, 'New England Textile Mills', pp. 6-7; Nelson Whitaker to George P. Whitaker, November 17, 1868, Whitaker Iron Papers; Klein, 'Mercantile Instru-

ments of Credit', pp. 526-28.

41 Whitaker & Coudon to Robeson, Brooke C., March 8, 1858, Whitaker Iron Papers.

42 *Ibid.*

43 This mercantile technique was traditionally employed in agriculture, but it was used for centuries in other industries as well. In the seventeenth century, British wool merchants made advances to weavers, and London coal merchants financed the operations of mining entrepreneurs in order to assure future supplies of coal. See William Hillyer, 'Four Centuries of Factoring'; and John U. Nef, 'Dominance of the Trader in the English Coal Industry in the Seventeenth Century'. As later happened in U.S. manufacturing, the London coal merchants' advances of short-term capital often led to their ownership of the producing property.

44 Curtis Bouve to Charles Huston, October 8 and December 11, 1857, and January 15, 1858, Lukens Steel Co. Papers; Correspondence, 1847-50, Samuel Colt Papers; Ernest M. Lander, Jr., 'The Iron Industry in Ante-Bellum South Carolina', p. 348.

45 Correspondence, 1840-50, Alan Wood Papers; Correspondence, Iron Invoices, and Richard Borden to E. J. Stickney Co., February 18, 1848, Fall River Iron Works Papers.

46 Kathleen Bruce, *Virginia Iron Manufactire in the Slave Era*, chap. 4. The Washburn & Moen Papers are part of the American Steel & Wire Papers.

15
What Price Style?
The Fabric-Advisory Function of the
Drygoods Commission Merchant, 1850-1880

Hansjörg Siegenthaler[*]

It is well known that mid-nineteenth-century New England textile mills paid a good deal of money for the services of the dry-goods commission houses which marketed their products. A large cotton mill with a wholesale value of output of $1,000,000 per year spent at least $15,000 per year on commissions. In comparison, the same corporation paid its top manager, the treasurer, a yearly salary of $5,000 to $7,000 for general supervision of operations and finance, for buying stock, and for dealing with labour problems; its top technician, the mill superintendent, was paid a salary of less than $5,000 per year to supervise production.[1]

The relative share of total expenditures on managerial services which went to the marketing agency was thus large and indicates that the latter furnished a valuable bundle of relatively scarce services. It is the object of this paper to show that, indeed, the bundle of services provided by the marketing agency was crucial to the success of the mill; and to show that the one service of outstanding importance was the giving of advice on the choice of fabrics to be produced.

Choice of fabrics to be produced was a decision of increasing importance in the textile industry, from the middle of the nineteenth century to the 1880s. The spread of technical knowledge and skill and easier access to the technical equipment with the development of a textile-machinery industry led to increasing competitive pressure in the 1840s. At the same time, changes in demand, induced by both economic and sociological developments related to increasing per capita income, increasing social mobility, and urbanisation, opened opportunities to escape competitive pressures by securing, at least for a short period of time, some

* From *Business History Review*, Vol. XLI, No. 1 (Spring 1967), pp. 36-61. Reprinted by permission of the editor of *Business History Review* and the author.

profitable business in response to some peculiar new taste.
Both the woollen and cotton industries reflected these trends;
but the latter less so. Woollen goods were of greater potential
variety and combination. The bulk of output in the cotton industry
consisted of quite standard goods, but the share of output
represented by style conscious printed cotton fabrics was growing
and by 1870 accounted for a considerable portion of total output.[2]

There was no organised fashion market, no seasonal openings
revealing dominant trends and guiding the production lines of
many mills into the same direction. There was, however, a general
willingness on the part of buyers to buy something new and
eagerness on the part of manufacturers to remain ahead of
competitors by meeting that desire with an almost uninterrupted
flow of new designs.

In 1850, for example, the Cocheco Manufacturing Co. introduced
new cotton-print styles throughout the year regardless of the
seasonal concentration of sales: two new styles in September; six in
July; and more than six in all other months with a high of thirteen
in October.[3] At the end of our period, cotton-print seller Amory A.
Lawrence, of Lawrence & Co., observed, 'to be successful we must
be on the alert all the time and constantly making new brands and
kind; the old 64 x 64 print seems to be about as dead a piece of
merchandise now as there is: had we not gotten largely off into
other things I do not know where our mills would have been.'[4]

It is also clear that in those lines of production where a single
producer contributed a substantial percentage of total output, the
sales volume of *each* producer at a given price could fluctuate
considerably (even in the absence of any changes in aggregate
demand) according to the sum of all competitors' decisions on
output quantities. Thus, the individual producer had to adjust his
production programme not only to fashion trends but also to
changes in *his* individual sales opportunities caused by output
decisions by his competitors.

The drygoods commission merchant was the key as he largely
controlled the production programmes of the mills.[5] The manufacturer had to know how to produce. The commission house,
according to a salesman who proved his knowledge, had to know
'just what to tell [the mills] . . . to make and what there is sure to
be a demand for'.[6]

Of course, the role of the marketing agency in developing the
production programme of the mill varied from case to case. It
ranged from mere approval or rejection to creative leadership.
Bagnall reports cases at the two extremes of behaviour.[7] In the first
instance, the mill took the initiative for product innovation.

Damon, a small woollen manufacturer in Concord, Massachusetts, was advised by his marketing agency to produce satinet, a fabric made of cotton warp and woollen filling. When the business became unprofitable, Damon himself decided to put part of his machinery on woollen flannels; again without much success. In both fields he met strong competition. He then combined properties of each of his fabrics and brought out something completely new: a cotton-wool fabric with a flannel finish, the Domet Flannel. Damon's marketing agency merely examined the result, anticipated its success, encouraged its production, and introduced it to the trade.

In the second case, the marketing agency took the lead. The manufacturer was ready to enter flannel production but his commission house was already selling flannels produced by a competing mill. To avoid a market clash between his clients, the agent suggested a slight modification in the newcomer's fabric (an increase in the number of picks to the inch). The manufacturer took the advice and the new fabric sold well — notably under the marketing agency's name (as true creator of the new fabric) and not under the mill's brand. Whether or not the new fabric was actually created by the marketing agency, the decision to produce depended upon its advice, because only the marketing agency was in touch with the trade and in a position to judge prospective sales opportunities.

THE HYPOTHESIS TO BE TESTED

If the success of a product could thus depend largely on the judgment of the marketing agency, then the agency was entitled to share in the benefits of success. This share should show up in the price which a mill was willing to pay for advice on the choice of fabrics and, indirectly, in the compensation the marketing agency received for the whole bundle of services which it performed. Were it possible to isolate the price of the advisory service, we would gain one pecuniary measure for evaluating the choice of fabrics as a variable in the success of textile firms during our period. We would also gain further insight into the importance of those structural elements in the textile industry which are related to choices of fabric. We should not expect to arrive at an exact figure for the price of the *fabric-advisory service*; rather, we intend to show that its magnitude was considerable.

Isolation of the price of the *fabric-advisory service* requires several steps. First, we must separate from the other costs and profits of the commission house those we will call the *normal costs*. To this end, we shall use Lawrence & Co. of Boston as our commission-house example. These *normal costs* are meant to cover only those spendings on human skills which were incurred by all commission houses in providing three *basic services* common to them all. These *basic services* include: first, the *selling service* proper, that is, bringing the seller into contact with buyers and soliciting sales; second, the *bookkeeping service*, that is, keeping track of all sales and monetary transactions; and third, the *transportation service*, that is, organising and supervising the transit of goods from the mill to the wholesale markets.

We will find that for large agencies, the *normal costs* of these *basic services* were small compared with other costs and profits. And, since these large firms handled the bulk of total business, *normal costs* can thus be assumed to be small in the average; that is, small for all commission houses as a group. It will also be suggested that the performance of the *basic services* was not likely to yield considerable rents or profits to the commission house.

In a second step, we shall look at the *additional services* performed by most of the commission houses and at both the costs incurred and the rents and profits realised in their performance. Specifically, we shall consider: *credit service*, that is, the security against losses provided to the mill through the commission house's expert knowledge of the credit standing of buyers; *financial service*; and finally, the *fabric-advisory service*.

We shall find that these *additional services* could introduce a monopolistic element into the marketing mechanism: by offering a package of *additional services* different from that of a competitor, a commission house could attach a mill to itself and influence the mill's demand for its services, pushing up the price of this package and/or gaining additional business. Even if the price were very inflexible, the commission house could at least realise a benefit from economies of scale involved in decreasing its average *normal costs*.

A mill's spendings on additional services, that is, its payments above *normal costs*, could reflect any or all of three elements: first, an outlay on a factor of production representing a change in the *basic services*, for example, on a salaried employee with special skills or on a partner working in a particular capacity; second, additional elements of profit because of a marketing agency's ability to exploit a factor of production or its temporary leading position in the performance of a special service or mixture of services; third, an element of rent accruing to an agent whose package of services was no better than most but who provided his services at less cost than could his average competitor.

We shall try to estimate the value each of these three elements had for each of the distinguishable *additional services* — an estimation which involves more judgment than measurement. These values changed over time, because rent and profit elements changed, or because the competitive price of a factor of production changed, or because the need of a service changed. The package of *additional services* most likely to attract a mill and to bind it to the commission house was not the same in 1850 as it was in 1880. The *fabric-advisory service*, however, gained in relative importance throughout the period.

In a third step, we shall again make use of the accounting data of Lawrence & Co. in order to get more directly at the value of this crucial *fabric-advisory service*. This case study yields a figure for the price one had to pay in the market for the special skills involved in giving such advice.

Before entering upon this three-step argument, however, we must resolve a preliminary problem: payments by a mill to its marketing agency would not reflect the true value of the package of basic and additional services provided by the agency if either controlled the other through financial ties, collusive arrangements, or other factors barring a free bargaining process.

WAS THE MARKET FOR SERVICES COMPETITIVE?

Our argument depends upon the assumptions that the drygoods commission houses offered their services in a competitive market and that the mills purchased these services under competitive conditions as well. The first assumption may be questioned; the second appears to rest on safer ground, as follows.

A large number of textile mills was selling in a few wholesale centres; for example, 304 woollen and 250 cotton producers in Maine, New Hampshire, and Massachusetts alone were competing for the services of commission houses by 1870.[8] In spite of the collusive disposition of the industry, actual agreement on selling terms was apparently never reached between producers and marketers as groups.[9] Cases of mills controlling commission houses by ownership were also exceptional.[10]

The number of competing marketers was also high — 74 houses in Boston alone by 1870.[11] There is fragmentary evidence of a competitive spirit among established houses: Mason & Lawrence, for example, was ready to undersell competitors by 1843; Henry A. Page of Faulkner, Page & Co. tried to change a mill's allegiance by 1877.[12] More important, however, newcomers' competition was always effective: competition from importers turning to a domestic business or from retailers or jobbers changing over to a commission business or combining the latter with wholesaling or retailing.[13]

The rise of new drygoods centres also offered alternatives to existing channels.[14] Thus, concentration of business in the hands of the leading houses was not particularly impressive: the mills for which the eighteen leading Boston commission houses sold by 1870 represented 59 per cent of the total capital invested in the woollen and cotton industries of Maine, New Hampshire, and Massachusetts.[15] It does not appear, therefore, that the mills as a group were tied to any exclusive group of commission houses. Yet mills may have been (and partly were) individually controlled by their commission houses through ownership.

Mercantile interests continued to be important in textile-mill ownership throughout the nineteenth century.[16] But did commission houses generally own the mills for which they sold? A comparison of the total amount of funds available to the Boston commission houses for investment with the capital invested in the mills they served reveals that the commission houses could hardly have purchased a controlling interest in a majority of the mills, much less actually have owned them.

Our estimation of total capital available to the commission houses for investment is based on figures for the total 'worth' of seventy-four Boston houses as given in the credit-rating reports of R. G. Dun & Co. for 1870. It is granted that estimation of this 'worth', that is, the total amount of capital at the risk of business plus capital actually invested in the mercantile firm and the property of the partners in whatever way it happened to be invested, would have been difficult even on the basis of complete inside information — which the credit-rating agency did not have. The latter's figures were based largely on interviews, correspondence, and guesswork. We take them only for a rough approximation of the order of size.[17]

Dun's figures indicate a total commission-house 'worth' of $31,000,000. The capital requirements (of a commission business proper were small and this left the bulk of the total 'worth' of a commission house to be disposed of at will; for example, to be invested in manufacturing property. We estimate (disregarding for a moment the *actual* investment policies of the commission houses) that roughly $30,000,000 of the $31,000,000 'worth' *could* have been available for the purchase of a controlling interest in the mills for which the commission houses sold. This amount compares with the $97,000,000 capitalisation attributed to all woollen and cotton mills in Maine, New Hampshire, and Massachusetts (the mills predominantly selling through Boston) by the U.S. Census of 1870.

Thus, we suggest that the Boston commission houses had the *potential* to acquire a majority equity in somewhat less than 60 per cent of the mills for which they sold. There is no reason, of course, to believe that the commission houses actually locked up all their disposable funds in the mills. We know that the capital of some commission-house partners was invested in a broad variety of property: Amos A. Lawrence, for example, held factory stock at a market value of $166,700 in 1857 as well as $114,500 worth of real estate; the senior partner of George C. Richardson & Co. was said to be a large real estate owner; Joseph Nickerson & Co. made money in railroad stock by 1878.[18]

Some of the commission houses were both marketers and bankers.[19] Many enjoyed considerable liquidity and were able to make loans to the mills. The more important advances from the commission house to the mill came to be, the less likely was it for commission houses to have their funds invested in mill stock.[20] On the whole, then, we argue that the number of mills free from control by commission-house ownership was sufficient for the services of the commission houses to have a competitive market price. This leaves open the possibility of cases, of course, in which, on the basis of control through ownership, selling terms may have deviated from a competitive level.

THE VALUE OF BASIC SERVICES

Table 1 gives a series of prices for the *basic-services* provided by Mason & Lawrence (later Lawrence & Co.) in selling the products of the Cocheco Manufacturing Co., a cotton-print mill, from 1849 to 1883. Column 1 represents the ratio between the mill's payments for the *selling service* (column E) and the wholesale value of the product handled by the commission house (column H). The figures give a monthly average for each commercial year.

Payments by the mill for the *selling service* included two components. First, they include part of the amount which the mill contributed to the general expenses of the commission house — payments on salaries, store rent, taxes, stationery, and so on. The proportion of total general expenses represented by salaries was stable: 53 per cent on the average for the two years 1849-1850; 47 per cent, 1859-1860 and 1869-1870; and 56 per cent, 1879-1880.[21] We have used these proportions in calculating the increment of general expenses represented by salaries of employees (column D). Second, the *selling service* payments contain commissions paid by the mill to a sub-agent or, after May 31, 1859, to an employee of the commission house, who was stationed in New York (column C).

We propose to combine the series of payments to salaried employees (D) and the series of payments to sub-agents (C) into a series representing the cost of the *selling service* as a whole (column

TABLE 1
Average Monthly Payments of the Cocheco Manufacturing Co.
to Lawrence & Co. on Commissions and Salaries
of Employees, 1849-1883

Year	A ($)	B (A% G)	C ($)	D ($)	E (C+D)	F (E% G)	G (A+E)	H ($1,000)	I (E% H)	J (G% H)
1849	1,154	84	132	89	221	16	1,375	76	0.29	1.81
1850	1,026	86	84	81	165	14	1,191	72	0.23	1.67
1851	1,024	81	140	95	235	19	1,259	65	0.36	1.94
1852	1,355	82	210	87	297	18	1,652	85	0.35	1.95
1853	1,358	78	269	108	377	22	1,735	89	0.42	1.95
1854	1,236	77	216	156	372	23	1,608	77	0.48	2.08
1855	1,353	77	231	181	412	23	1,765	85	0.49	2.09
1856	1,239	75	201	207	408	25	1,647	83	0.49	1.99
1857	929	72	162	192	354	28	1,283	61	0.58	2.09
1858	1,335	78	244	133	377	22	1,712	91	0.41	1.88
1859	1,010	76	222	102	324	24	1,334	81	0.40	1.66
1860	967	73	257	94	351	27	1,318	77	0.45	1.71
1861	626	64	242	106	348	36	974	50	0.70	1.95
1862	711	72	196	86	282	28	993	57	0.50	1.75
1863	399	60	184	86	270	40	669	32	0.85	2.10
1864	1,470	83	194	110	304	17	1,774	118	0.26	1.51
1865	1,535	81	222	149	371	19	1,906	123	0.30	1.55
1866	2,360	86	228	161	389	14	2,749	189	0.21	1.45
1867	2,470	86	201	188	389	14	2,859	198	0.20	1.44
1868	2,060	83	182	231	413	17	2,473	165	0.25	1.50
1869	2,180	84	164	235	399	16	2,579	174	0.23	1.48
1870	2,840	87	155	259	414	13	3,254	190	0.22	1.71
1871	3,660	90	134	255	389	10	4,049	209	0.19	1.94
1872	4,230	92	142	231	373	8	4,603	244	0.15	1.88
1873	4,720	92	188	203	391	8	5,111	271	0.14	1.88
1874	4,370	91	225	186	411	9	4,781	250	0.16	1.91
1875	3,940	89	225	282	507	11	4,447	225	0.23	1.98
1876	3,615	88	192	324	516	12	4,131	206	0.25	2.00
1877	3,305	87	167	308	475	13	3,780	189	0.25	2.00
1878	2,620	83	150	388	538	17	3,158	150	0.36	2.10
1879	3,375	86	150	411	561	14	3,936	194	0.29	2.02
1880	4,150	87	167	458	625	13	4,775	237	0.26	2.02
1881	3,480	90	—	392	392	10	3,872	199	(0.20)	1.95
1882	3,480	91	—	355	355	9	3,835	200	(0.18)	1.92
1883	3,425	94	—	235	235	6	3,660	196	(0.12)	1.87

A. Average monthly regular commissions going to partners of Lawrence & Co.
C. Average monthly commissions going to sub-agent in New York (after May 31, 1859, part of salary of employee in New York).
D. Average monthly share of Cocheco Manufacturing Co. in salaries paid to employees by Lawrence & Co. in addition to C.
H. Average monthly gross wholesale value of sales.
For additional notes see Appendix.

E). We assume that this service was performed by these employees and sub-agents with no one else adding much to its performance.

Is this a valid assumption? How was it in reality? We are well informed on the activities of Lawrence & Co.'s sub-agents through their correspondence with the Boston office during the year 1850. Where our information is not sufficient as far as the New York sub-agent, R. H. Snow, is concerned, we can make use of the evidence available for his Philadelphia colleague, W. E. Pratt, who worked in the same capacity.

The sub-agents did provide the selling service in their respective markets. Nobody was there to assist them directly in the promotion of sales. In addition, they helped the home office perform other than *basic services.* They informed Mason & Lawrence on price trends, quoting competing offers, reported on the sales success of competitors, and thus assisted the Boston office in making price decisions for distant markets.[22] They gave their judgment on trends in the development of aggregate demand or on changes in buyers' preferences for particular fabrics[23] and on their taste for particular colours or designs.[24] The Philadelphia sub-agent was personally involved on a few occasions in getting up new styles in prints and he decided on one occasion on the proportion in which different colours were to be printed.[25] Thus, sub-agents helped the commission house to reach decisions on the choice of fabrics. They also investigated the credit standing of buyers, soliciting information on which Mason & Lawrence would be able to base their conclusions.[26] This leaves us with the impression that the sub-agents' earnings (column C) fully covered the value of their salesmanship and may have included an undeterminable value of awareness of a market situation and of future trends and a knowledge of the credit standing of buyers.

What the mill paid on salaried employees (column D) was not related to neatly defined jobs and does not represent a price for a particular service. Instead of asking what activities it could have covered, we ask to what extent it would have covered the costs of selling the goods not sold by sub-agents outside of Boston? The gross wholesale value of sales effected through the Boston office amounted to 71 per cent of the corresponding value of sales effected in New York by the sub-agent during the years 1850-1855.[27] Payments to salaried employees in Boston for these years were 62 per cent of commissions paid to the New York sub-agent. Would an amount equal to 62 per cent of the New York sub-agent's commission have paid for 71 per cent of his New York sales volume if these sales had been made in Boston instead of New York? Average selling costs should fall as sales volume grows, but it was easier to sell the 71 per cent in Boston's narrow market than it was to sell the 100 per cent in New York's wider market. Boston must have been a more comfortable place for making sales at that time than New York. It took quite a salesman to cover the rapidly changing New York market, whereas long established contacts in Boston made selling easier.[28]

It appears safe to say, then, that the amount of payments made to salaried employees approximated the price of the *selling service* as far as provided by the Boston office. Since commissions paid to sub-agents covered a little bit more than just the *selling service* in New York, total payments to sub-agents (column C) and to salaried employees (column D) approximated rather closely the price for the total *selling service* (column E).

Bookkeeping, the second of the *basic services*, was cheap. By the middle of the century a bookkeeper earned a monthly salary of $65.[29] Only one-third of this salary fell to the Cocheco Manufacturing Co., less than 10 per cent of the price of the selling service proper.[30] As to the provision of *transportation service* from the mill to the wholesale markets, it was also cheap as long as it could be left in the hands of a clerk with a salary in the neighbourhood of that of a bookkeeper. Certainly, transportation problems did not rank among the crucial ones a commission house had to face. Amory Lawrence, son of the senior partner of Lawrence & Co., used to write his father lengthy reports on business matters without ever mentioning transportation. But he was personally involved, as a junior partner, even with the 'freight details' until an effort was made to relieve him from his task to which, it was said, 'he was given a good deal of attention of late at a greater expense of time and money than he probably realises'.[31]

We are here quoting a clerk's letter to the senior; a clerk wanted to make sure that at least the boss 'realised' what a burden he was about to take over. We learn from the statement that the clerks could handle freight problems by themselves if the firm so desired. It was the clerks who wrote and signed letters on transportation questions from Faulkner, Page & Co. to N. Stevens & Sons.[32] Another 10 per cent of the price of the *selling service* would thus amply cover the third of the *basic services*. We do not think that elements of exploitation were very significant and that the true value of the *basic services* should thus be looked for in the profits of the partners.

Table 1, column F compares payments to sub-agents and to salaried employees (column E), which we have equated to the total price of the *selling service*, with total payments by the mill for the whole package of services provided by the commission house (column G). Payments to sub-agents and salaried employees were never higher than 28 per cent of total payments up to the Civil War. We shall refer to a possible change over time below. If the combined price of the *bookkeeping* and *transportation* services was, as suggested, not more than one-fifth of the price of the *selling service*, the *basic services* provided by the commission house accounted for only one-third of the amount of total payments from mill to marketing agency. The other two-thirds, probably accruing to the partners, remain to be explained.

THE VALUE OF ADDITIONAL SERVICES

There were three *additional services* provided by the commission house to the mill whose impact on the costs, rents, and profits of the commission house we shall now estimate: (1) giving some security against credit losses of the mill through expert knowledge on the credit standing of buyers (the *credit service*); (2) bringing about financial aid (the *financial service*); and (3) giving advice on the choice of fabrics (the *fabric-advisory service*).

A good record of doing business safely, thanks to sound credit judgment, was certainly important for the success of a commission house. Although good *credit service* was a prerequisite for getting any business at all, it is difficult to believe that, for our particular type of business, it was a very distinguishing factor, one which bound the mills to particular commission houses making for extra profits, since good judgment was common to many houses. A dry goods commission house dealt with a relatively small number of buyers. Francis Skinner & Co. sold the product of the Pepperell Manufacturing Co. to only 240 domestic customers from July 1851 to June 1852.[33] Since the continued patronage of a mill partly depended on it, a marketing agency specialised in dealing with these buyers and was likely to become intimately involved with each of them over time. Ability of buyers to pay in the past was good evidence for their reliability in the near future. This evidence was available to all houses of some experience, and there were many such: thirty-seven out of seventy-four doing business in Boston by 1870 had been in business since at least 1850.[34] Evidence of safe credit standing going beyond a record of past achievements was difficult to come by for anybody.

If *credit service* experience was crucial, newcomers must have found it costly to come up to the common standard. Amos A. Lawrence, upon entering business on his own in 1836, 'travelled into all the U.S. states with 2 business friends to examine credits'.[35] Such newcomers' costs granted established houses a rent. It is at this point where the credit-rating agencies were likely to have their significance; institutions providing some information on credit standings increased following the establishment of Lewis Tappan's Mercantile Agency in 1841.[36] Although the degree of accuracy of the ratings of these agencies is questionable, they were at least able to tell their subscribers how long a potential buyer had been in business without failure and to report changes in the personnel of a firm; that is, they were able to convey a good part of the very substance of an old firm's experience — knowledge of reliability of buyers in the past — to anybody willing to pay their subscription fee. Newcomers' costs of providing *credit service* must have approximated the price of agency information; rents accruing to established houses must have been excluded. And this price was relatively small: originally $50 a year to firms with a trade volume above $50,000 a year and $300 to those with a volume of more than $500,000.

We do not believe, therefore, that credit information weighed heavily in the price of a commission firm's services at the beginning of our period, much less toward the end. The importance of credit information decreased with the length of the credit period and, hence, so did its price.[37] Knowlton gives as the usual credit periods granted by Francis Skinner & Co. in selling cotton fabrics in different years: eight months by 1855; after the panic of 1857 cash, four, six, or eight months; six months by 1859; and thirty days during and after the Civil War throughout our period.[38] Faulkner, Kimball & Co. sold its woollens by 1870 on credit terms of thirty days for the most part also. Out of a sample of 183 sales effected in Boston and New York from January 1 to October 30, 1870, 7 per cent were sold on credit terms of ten days, 56 per cent on thirty days, 26 per cent on sixty days, and 11 per cent on four months.[39] Shorter credit terms reduced the danger of unforseeable developments in the financial standing of a buyer.

A huge share in the price of the package of services provided by a drygoods commission house still remains to be explained. We think that at the beginning of our period the second *additional service*, bringing about financial aid, could account for more than half of the residual in some cases but for much less in the late 1870s. Cost factors — the price of the brokerage service involved in financial aid — were negligible because there was no need for contacting borrowers and the lenders were few and close at hand. But *financial service* was, as long as only a limited number of commission houses was able to provide it, important for two reasons. It attracted business and, therefore, could increase profits on the total package of services performed. It also yielded a substantial rent.

By the middle of the century it was still true that 'the chief credit was with the selling house', not with the mill.[40] The commission house was a better risk for outsiders than was the mill. By interposing its own credit standing, the commission house was able to raise money cheaper than the mill was able to do. Since the commission house was so close to the financial operations of the mill, it did not incur the risks of an outsider. If, therefore, the mill paid the commission house the same rate of interest the former would have had to pay a note broker, then the commission house earned a premium, a 'profit on interest', proportional to the difference between the credit standing of the mill (worse) and the credit standing of commission house (better) in the market. If the mill had only to pay the commission house what the latter paid in the market, it was the mill who at first sight received a benefit. This was the case if the commission house endorsed the mill's notes, thus enabling the mill to discount the notes at a bank at the same rate the commission house would have been granted. For this benefit the mill may have recompensated the commission house in part through higher commissions as long as competition among commission houses did not squeeze out such a recompensation. Here we speak of an 'interest element in commissions'.

'Profit on interest' is empirically feasible. Mason & Lawrence received 6 per cent interest for discounting the Cocheco Manufacturing Co.'s notes, a rate unchanged even in October and November 1857; clearly it was fixed at the level of the legal maximum. The same rate appears later for other types of loans. From June 1, 1844 to November 30, 1852, Mason & Lawrence paid interest on $70,168 employed in its business or invested in the mills on short terms; in the same period they received interest payments on their investments of $90,319. Even without taking into account that some funds were held in non-interest-bearing employments, e.g., as cash, the ratio between the interest rates paid and received was 78:100. If Mason & Lawrence got 6 per cent from the mills, it paid not more than 4.7 per cent to their creditors — a figure which approximates a market rate. A very low proportion of the total interest payments to commission-house creditors went to the partners; most of them, 83 per cent in the period from December 1, 1850 to May 31, 1851, went to banks, insurance companies, or other money lenders.[41]

In contrast, the 'interest element in commissions' can only be inferred from differences in interest rates paid by mills of a given credit standing, either to a commission house or to outsiders, and under the assumption that some proportion of the mill's benefit went to the commission house. Given the fact that commission

TABLE 2
Discounts on Commercial Paper
Paid by Boston Commission Houses and a Textile
Manufacturing Firm, 1875-1879

Firm	1875		1876		1877		1878		1879
	Apr. 26	Nov. 10	Apr. 24	Nov. 20	Apr. 23	—	—	Oct. 1	Feb. 26
Allen, Lane & Co.	6	—	—	—	4½/5	—	—	—	—
Barnes, Ward & Co.	7½	7/7½	—	—	—	—	—	—	—
Dale Bros. & Co.	7	—	—	—	—	—	—	—	—
Danforth, Clark & Co.	6½	—	—	—	—	—	—	—	—
Denny, Poor & Co.	—	—	—	—	3/4	—	—	—	—
Dexter, Abbot & Co.	5½	—	—	4	4	—	—	—	3/3½
Faulkner, Page & Co.	—	—	—	—	—	—	—	—	3/3½
Floyd Bros. & Co.	—	—	—	4½	—	—	—	—	—
Frost & Co.	—	—	—	¹ 4½	5	—	—	—	3/3½
Gowing & Grew	5½	—	4½	4	—	—	—	—	3/3½
Harding Bros. & Co.	—	6/6½	—	5	5	—	—	—	—
Harding, Colby & Co.	5½	—	—	4½	—	—	—	—	—
Holbrook & Co.	5	5½	—	4	—	—	—	4/4½	—
Joy, Langdon & Co.	5½	5/5½	—	4½	4½	—	—	—	—
Kelly, Thomas & Co.	—	—	—	12	—	—	—	10/12	—
Leland, Allen & Bates	6	6	—	—	—	—	—	—	—
Mackintosh, Green & Co.	5½/6	—	—	3½/4	—	—	—	—	—
Minot, Hooper & Co.	—	—	4	—	—	—	—	—	—
Mudge, Sawyer & Co.	—	—	4	—	—	—	—	—	—
Perry, Wendell, Fay & Co.	5	—	—	3½/4	—	—	—	—	3
Richardson & Whitney	12	—	—	—	—	—	—	—	—
Richardson & Co.	5/5½	—	4	—	—	—	—	—	—
Upham, Tucker & Co.	—	—	—	4	—	—	—	—	—
Wentworth & Co.	—	—	—	—	4	—	—	—	3/3½
Whittemore, Cabot & Co.	7½/8	7/7½	—	6½/7	—	—	—	6/6½	—
Wright, Bliss & Fabyan	5/5½	—	—	3½/4	—	—	—	—	—
Lawrence Manufacturing Co.	7	4½/6	3½	3½	4	—	—	4/4½	3½

For notes, see Appendix.

houses apparently charged the maximum legal interest rate, and given the high interest rates in the streets for second-class paper, substantial 'interest elements in commissions' are at least very plausible.[42]

But in the 1870s 'interest elements in commissions' were likely to decrease for three reasons: the mills required less money; they had improved their credit standing; and the commission houses, in an easy money market, were competing for investment opportunities. We referred to the fact that credit periods became shorter over time, hence credit requirements of mills also decreased. Interest rates paid by mills and by commission houses to outsiders approached each other. R. G. Dun & Co. gives at certain dates during the years 1875 to 1879 the discount rates usually paid by a number of Boston commission houses on their paper or on mill paper endorsed by them.[43] Table 2 shows these rates and compares them with rates paid on unendorsed mill paper.[44] We find that the latter ranged among those paid by the very best commission houses.

Much casual evidence for considerable liquidity of commission houses and readiness to assume financial responsibility is available: Mackintosh, Green & Horton were said to have 'what capital they can use to advantage'; Dexter, Abbot & Co. had 'ample means for handling' its accounts; Faulkner, Page & Co. found it difficult to employ all its money. Several firms were reported by R. G. Dun & Co. to buy paper apart from what they took from the mills.[45] Where a large house carried more mills than it easily could supply with funds, it could tap outside resources.[46] What it meant to have outside money available is illustrated by Amory A. Lawrence cautioning his father against accepting a banker's money:[47]

> Don't think we are short of money and must have a large deposit from some one or a line of an outside bank (Beat's for example) for we are not, and if we should borrow, we had better use our own banks, as we shall want but for a few months, and we have not had a loan at any of them for a long time. If you should happen to whisper to Beat that you thought perhaps some time you might want some money he will bother you until you take of him.

Although uncertain as to what portion of the total price of all services the *fabric-advisory service* represented at the beginning of our period, we can now say that it accounted for a large portion in the 1870s, unless either the total price of all services declined over time or the price of the *basic services* increased.

Casual observation of the movement of commission rates does not suggest a decrease.[48] The rates of commission do not, however, say very much about the actual price paid for the services for two reasons. First, the commission payments were obviously less than total selling costs, and part of these costs was charged to the mill in addition to commissions. Just what the commissions were meant to cover was a matter of agreement between the mill and the commission house. Second, even where the type of such an agreement is known, its economic significance still depends upon the internal structure of the commission house. For example, while an agreement may tell us that commissions should exclusively cover the earnings of partner's net of employees' salaries, it does not tell us whether the partners left most of the work to be done to salaried employees or whether new partners were admitted and paid by a share in profits out of commissions.

In order to be on safer ground we turn again to the actual payments of the Cocheco Manufacturing Co. to Lawrence & Co. Adding the figures for commissions to sub-agents (Table 1, column C), the salaries of employees (column D), and the commissions paid to partners (column A), we sum the total monthly payments on commissions and salaries (column G). The last are then related (column J) to the gross wholesale value of sales (column H).

This ratio (column H), between total payments on commissions and salaries and the monthly wholesale value of sales, is considered as the actual price for the package of selling services provided by the selling house. Our series for this price from 1849 to 1883 is not necessarily representative of a general price movement. Shortrun fluctuations and sudden shifts in the price level, like that from 1869 to 1870-1871, can be attributed to particular qualities of the two individual firms. The package of services provided by Lawrence & Co. may have changed over time in an unrepresentative way and hence affected its price. But if we hesitate to take this particular price series as being representative of a general trend, we can at least say that the general trend as reflected in casual quotations of formal commission rates is confirmed in the one case for which we have solid data: the actual price paid by the Cocheco Manufacturing Co. for the services provided by the commission house was as high in the 1870s as it was in the 1850s.

We take for granted that the *transportation service* and the *bookkeeping service* did not assume a greater share in the total price of all services at the end than at the beginning of our period. As to the price of the *selling service*, it might well have increased with the beginnings of more aggressive selling.[49] We were not able to associate the earnings of an individual salesman with as clearly identified a bundle of services in the 1870s, as we were in the 1850s. The only later evidence we have for the earnings of sub-agents, who supposedly were predominantly engaged in bringing about contact with buyers, is taken from rather impressionistic reports of R. G. Dun & Co. Taken as a whole, the reports convey the idea of only a limited financial success among sub-agents: Woodbury & Foss were reported by 1881 to 'make a living' without accun. alating; and by 1885 to 'barely make a living'; C. S. Bartlett & Co. cleared $3,000 in commissions in 1876 and were said to 'make a good living'; Maxwell Lowry was 'doing a good commission business' by 1875, but eight years later R. G. Dun & Co. found that it 'must be close work for him to make a living'; C. J. Davis by 1886 was making 'just about . . . a living'.[50]

Of course, 'to make a living' was a phrase indiscriminately employed by reporters who knew nothing specific. But we learn something about the general image associated in the mind of the reporter with sub-agents as a group; a dramatic rise in sub-agents' earnings would have affected this image somehow. And nothing short of a dramatic rise would have made the *selling service* account for more than one-half of the price of the entire package of services.

THE VALUE OF THE FABRIC-ADVISORY SERVICE

The ability of a commission house to give advice on the choice of fabrics naturally took many forms, and shades in the quality of advice led to a close affilliation of some houses with certain mills. Unlike financial aid or credit information, advice on the choice of fabrics was not easily standardised. It took specialised experience, well-established channels of information, and an individual capable of integrating this information into a vision of coming developments. A house of old standing in a particular field, with the right man at the right place, could offer advantages to a mill not quickly matched by other houses.

If a house thus found itself in a sheltered position, monopolistic profits were likely to persist over time. These profits are hardly measurable except as a residual, that is, with all the difficulties involved before. What may be determinable is the price a commission house had to pay on the special skill of formulating and shaping the advice if the advice was furnished by a particular individual, a 'prophet of fashion'.[51] If such an individual could be identified and his earnings unambiguously associated with this special skill, one would get a lower limit for the value of the *fabric-advisory service,* a figure for the cost element included in the price of the service.

Of course, one would like to avoid the pitfalls involved in looking at the distribution of the net earnings of a commission house among its partners and in taking the share of each partner as a competitive market price for his personal services. A share could include profit and rent elements; it was fixed by agreement hardly responding to changes in a partner's achievements; social considerations and family relationships, may have had a greater influence on it than economic factors. In only one situation of the history of Lawrence & Co. does a share in earnings seem to reflect the economic significance of the specific function fulfilled by a partner. This moment of truth came with the admission of a former employee of a distant firm, a man without means who was not a social peer of the older partners, and with an unusually high reward for his future contributions to the firm's success. Let us see how this situation came about and what it meant.

In 1865, Lawrence & Co. took over a new account and started selling for the recently incorporated Arlington Woollen Mills, later Arlington Mills. The Arlington Woollen Mills started out producing woollen fancy shirtings, flannels, and felted goods. After 1866, it went into worsted and cotton-warp dressgoods. Selling terms in the mid-1870's granted the commission house a commission of 2½ per cent on the sales proceeds and full reimbursements for expenditures on freight, cartage, labels, telegrams and insurance. Yearly commissions of $25,000 on a sales volume of $1,000,000 were thus to cover general commission house expenses like store rent, to the amount of $9,500, and the $8,000 paid out as salaries to two employees dealing with Arlington fabrics. This left a profit of $7,500 to the partners.[52]

We are informed on the functions fulfilled by the salaried employees working on Arlington goods by two statements. The first is a letter of recommendation of 1871 introducing Webster, one of the employees in question, and saying: 'I doubt if anyone in this country knows so much about all descriptions of worsted goods as him . . . I do not know of anyone, so far as I can judge, who would be more capable to superintend the manufacture of worsted goods, order styles, and make sales, than him.' Obviously, Webster was expected, in addition to making sales, to watch the market and guide production. The second statement concerns the other employee, M. H. Dorman, who, by 1873, was complaining about having too little 'Influence on the management of the production'.[53] He, too, apparently formerly had a say in preparing the goods. Thus, the salaried employees attended to problems of styles and production decisions and received part of their salary for doing so.

In sharp contrast to their role in the administration of the Cocheco Manufacturing Co. the partners apparently did not interfere with production problems of the Arlington Woollen Mills.

For one thing, they all were not acquainted with the specific problems of woollen manufacture and had to leave the new problems to new employees. Also, the mill was ably managed by its treasurer, William Whitman, who held office with rare success from 1867 to 1902. There was, thus, no need for the kind of entrepreneurial leadership Amos A. Lawrence was capable of offering. But the mill needed money, and supplying it with financial aid appears to be sufficient explanation, in the first stage of the development of the mill, for the commissionhouse partners' earnings. The financial foundation of the Arlington Woollen Mills was very weak. As late as 1875, the paid-in capital amounted to $200,000 and accumulated profits to $258,000, a guarantee reserve for prospective losses on sales included. These funds hardly covered the fixed assets: the book value of real estate, buildings, machinery, and so on amounting to *$439,000*. The entire working capital of $500,000 had to be provided by outside parties; to a large extent by the commission house.[54]

In the late 1870s the relative importance of the services performed by the selling house to the mill changed, and by 1882 the change became feasible in terms of profit distribution. We have referred to the increasing availability of short-run funds in the 1870s. At the same time, the Arlington Woollen Mills increased its capital stock to $500,000 in 1877 and $750,000 in 1880. A series of spectacular dividend payments, compared with what was usual in the textile industry at the time, of 10 per cent yearly from 1878 to 1881 also improved the mill's credit standing. In fact, by 1879 Arlington's treasurer refused to sell his paper to Lawrence & Co. at a discount rate of 4 per cent 'saying he could do better on the street'.[55]

In April 1881, then, the mill must have felt independent enough to raise some problems with the commission house and to suggest solutions which, at first sight, seemed to aim at breaking up the relations between Arlington and Lawrence & Co.[56] What was at stake was the ability of the commission house to perform the *fabric-advisory service*. This ability was challenged by Whitman in a memorandum of May 9, 1881; at the same time the need for advice was made clear:[57]

> The machinery now at the mill enables me not only to obtain a larger product, but to vary it to meet the constantly changing preferences of customers. The prospective demands of our business indicate the necessity for greater variety of product — smaller quantities of each — higher quality of texture — the exercise of taste and knowledge of the wants of buyers, to a greater degree than heretofore.

I cannot manage this to the best advantage without skilled and intelligent aid. Prominent amongst these requirements is to have persons quick to appreciate any indications of a coming change, either in sorts or colors of the goods, and to suggest the most promising to be made for the immediate future. Such persons can only obtain the requisite skill and knowledge by constant intercourse with buyers and by possessing their confidence. The aid that I require is that of the practical goods merchant. I do not need . . . manufacturing knowledge, but commercial sagacity to guide us to the probable needs of the market, and to sell the goods . . . Now, neither in Boston nor in New York have I the aid that I require, i.e., such a person as I have already described to handle the goods, and be responsible for doing so . . . New York, our largest outlet for goods, needs, I think, immediate care.

Having given this perceptive description of the service he expected his selling house to perform, the mill's treasurer pointed to the man he wanted placed in charge of the selling job in New York: Alfred Ray, hitherto employed in Chicago by Marshall Field & Co.[58]

Ray soon became a partner of Lawrence & Co., responsible for 'the control of the Arlington, absolute control . . . Prices and style' — so agreed the partners — 'We should be second'.[59] If there is any doubt left as to whether Ray was primarily expected, in terms of the treasurer, to 'sell the goods' or 'to guide us to the probable needs of the market', we find evidence for the dominance of the latter function: Ray had not been a salesman or a sales manager with Marshall Field & Co. but purchasing manager of the dress goods department.[60] In that capacity he had become expert in judging demand rather than in making buyers buy.

What did Lawrence & Co. pay for the services of the new man? Ray asked for a yearly salary of $20,000. He was guaranteed this amount and promised, in addition, one-quarter of the increase of profits of 1883 and 1884 over the profits of 1882. His actual share in profits for the first eleven months (January 1-November 30, 1882) amounted to $18,333 and to $24,000 for the first full year. Profits from commissions increased after Ray had joined the firm. But of course the older partners' share in these profits declined. They were credited with $12,000 in 1879; $9,000 in 1880; and $14,000 in 1881. The new arrangement left them with $6,000 in 1882 and with $7,000 in 1883: their earnings from the Arlington Woollen Mills were roughly cut in half.[61] Increase in relative importance of a particular kind of human skill had forced them to transfer profits to the scarce factor, unless they were prepared to quit the Arlington business which they no longer were able to keep through financial ties.

CONCLUSIONS

The general hypothesis and model suggested that much money was paid by the mills for the *fabric-advisory service* of the commission house — perhaps even one-half of the cost of the latter's whole package. The case approach shows that in a particular situation a member of a commission house was paid an extremely high salary (and profit-sharing) for providing that service; indeed, his salary was three times that of the recompensation earned by the mill's top manager, its treasurer.

The strong position of the commission house in the woollen and cotton industries was not just a residual of mercantile capitalism. The characteristics of product innovation in our period and in our industry — continuous adjustment of production to a flow of information on short-run changes of the market — tied up important entrepreneurial activities with an agency close to the market. Not much more was left at the mill in many cases than the trade-school type of technical management in 'command of the intricacies of textile production' as characterised by Navin.[62] And the characteristics of entrepreneurial activity only reflected the basic task with which the industries were confronted: adjustment of a technically mature apparatus to the growing sophistication of a society able to pay for more than the basic needs. Thus, the marketing man appears as the true leader in a process of permanent open-ended change, competitive pressure on his back and profits before him as a reward for a creative idea; profits for the mills, to be sure, but he would get the benefit from them.

APPENDIX TO TABLES

The figures of Table 1 are calculated on the basis of entries in the waste books of Mason & Lawrence (later Lawrence & Co.). Column H gives for each commercial year (December 1-November 30) the average of the monthly gross wholesale values of sales of Cocheco prints effected by the commission house. Column A gives for each year the average of monthly commissions paid by the commission house to the mill; these figures are calculated as percentages of the gross wholesale value of sales in column H on the basis of the formal commission rate. The formal commission rate was 1½ per cent until May 31, 1849, 1¼ per cent from June 30, 1849, to May 31, 1870, 1¾ per cent after June 1, 1870. Until September 30, 1858, the mill paid additional commissions of ½ per cent on sales effected outside of Boston to the commission house. For each year the average of monthly additional commissions has been included in Column A.

Column C shows for each year the average of monthly commissions paid by the mill to the sub-agent in New York from 1849 to May 31, 1859, and after June 1, 1859, the share of the Cocheco Manufacturing Co. as actually fixed by the commission house in the salary of an employee of the commission house in New York. Column D gives the share of the Cocheco Manufacturing Co. in salaries paid to employees of the commission house in Boston. Salaries of employees were charged according to the accounting system of the commission house to a general expense account and the mill accounts were charged for a share in general expenses. On the assumption that each mill's share in general expenses went in equal proportions on the different expense items, we calculated that percentage of general expenses charged to the Cocheco Manufacturing Co. which was paid out as salaries to employees, for four two-year periods: December 1, 1849 to November 30, 1851, 1859/61 1869/71, 1879/81. This percentage figure was quite stable, 53 per cent on the average for the first, and 47 per cent, 47 per cent, and 56 per cent for the other three two-year periods. For each year we took that percentage figure as the basis for the calculation of the payments of the Cocheco Manufacturing Co. on salaries which comes closest chronologically to the particular year. The average monthly value of the share of the Cocheco Manufacturing Co. in total general expenses for each year was calculated as a moving average of the values for May and November of three years.

Table 2 is derived from R. G. Dun & Co's credit rating ledgers for Boston. The reports describe the negotiable instruments in question simply as 'paper' in most cases and occasionally as 'acceptances' or 'endorsements' without specifying their particular character. This paper may have included the following four types: single-name promissory notes issued by the commission house; two-name promissory notes issued by the manufacturing firm and endorsed by the commission house; trade bills used by customers for payment and endorsed by the commission house; drafts drawn by the commission house on buyers. These four types are lumped together under the heading of 'commerical paper.' This term used here does not imply that the paper was only sold in the street; it may have been sold also to banks.

NOTES

1 For the commission payments see, e.g., *Report of Mr William Sturgis' Committee to Twenty-eight Manufacturing Companies* (Boston, 1852), Appendix. For salaries: John S. Ewing and Nancy P. Norton, *Broadlooms and Businessmen: A History of the Bigelow-Sanford Carpet Company* (Cambridge, Mass., 1955), 75, 107; James C. Ayer, *Some of the Usages and Abuses in the Management of Our Manufacturing Corporations* (Lowell, Mass., 1863), 13; Memorandum of Certain Commissions & Salaries Paid by Manuf' Co's August 1, 1848, Amos A. Lawrence Papers (Massachusetts Historical Society, Boston).

2 Arthur H. Cole, *The American Wool Manufacture* (2 vols., Cambridge, Mass., 1926), I, 297-98. The total yardage of cotton cloth produced in the US according to the Census of 1870 was 1,064,000,000, table cloth not included, the yardage of cotton prints and delaines was 482,000,000. We include in the category of cotton fabrics requiring frequent adjustments in style and colour 35,000,000 yds. of lawns and fine muslins and 39,000,000 yds. of ginghams and

checks, so that out discussion applies to roughly one-half of cotton cloth sold to
the trade. US Bureau of the Census, *Ninth Census of the United States*, III,
Statistics of the Wealth and Industry of the United States (Washington, D.C.,
1872), 596, 597, 621.

3 Invoices of prints sent by Cocheco Mfg. Co. to Mason & Lawrence, 1850, Mason
& Lawrence Papers (Mason & Lawrence, 1843-1859; Mason, Lawrence & Co.,
1859-1861; Lawrence & Co., 1861 and thereafter, in Baker Library, Harvard
Graduate School of Business Administration, Boston).

4 Amory A. Lawrence to Amos A. Lawrence, undated   c. 1886 , A. A. Lawrence
Papers.

5 Caroline F. Ware, *The Early New England Cotton Manufacture: A Study in
Industrial Beginnings* (Boston, 1931), 184; Fred M. Jones, 'The Development of
Marketing Channels in the United States to 1920', in Richard M. Clewett (ed.),
Marketing Channels for Manufactured Products (Homewood, Ill., 1954), 26;
Evelyn H. Knowlton, *Pepperell's Progress: History of a Cotton Textile Company,
1844-1945* (Cambridge, Mass., 1948), 81, 82; Joseph Berger (ed.), *Memoirs of a
Corporation: The story of Mary and Mack and Pacific Mills* (Boston, 1950), 16.

6 Henry A. Page to Moses T. Stevens, Nov. 25, 1870, Stevens Papers (business
records of the woollen mills of Nathaniel Stevens, North Andover, 1786-1865,
and his successors, in the Merrimack Valley Textile Museum, North Andover,
Mass.).

7 William R. Bagnall, 'Sketches of Manufacturing Establishments in New York
City and of Textile Establishments in the Eastern States', edited by Victor S.
Clark (Unpublished materials, 4 vols., 1908, in Baker Library, Harvard
Graduate School of Business Administration, Boston), II 1098-1101, 1170-71.

8 *Ninth Census of the United States*, III, *Statistics of the Wealth and Industry of
the United States, passim*.

9 Collective bargaining took place between the commission house A. & A. Lawrence
& Co. and its mills when the latter in 1852 took steps for common action by
twenty-eight manufacturing companies to prevent A. & A. Lawrence from
raising the rate of commissions. The result of this attempt at mobilising some
countervailing power against the leading commission house was a compromise
between A. & A. Lawrence & Co. and the mills for which it sold, but another
commission house, Francis Skinner & Co., felt free to change its terms at the
same time without being bound by the Lawrence compromise. Knowlton,
Pepperell's Progress, 77-79.

10 There were some early cases of direct selling. The partnership B. B. & R. Knight,
Providence, formed in 1852, managed by two brothers, one a merchant, the
other a manufacturer, handled both production at its mills and marketing of the
product to the trade; there are other cases of this brotherly backward or forward
integration. Bagnall, 'Sketches of Manufacturing Establishments', II, 1402-1431.

11 The Number of seventy-four drygoods commission houses in Boston by 1870
includes those firms which, according to *Dockham's US Cotton, Woollen, Silk,
and Linen Manufacturers', Report and Directory, 1870-71* (Boston, 1870), were
actually selling for textile mills, i.e., not only those listed as commission merchants but also those appearing under the title of a manufacturing firm as its
selling agent, provided that they are reported on by R. G. Dun & Co. for doing
primarily a drygoods commission business. R. G. Dun & Co., credit reporting
ledgers for Boston (Baker Library, Harvard Graduate School of Business
Administration, Boston).

12 Robert M. Mason to Amos A. Lawrence, March 9, 1843, A. A. Lawrence Papers;
Henry A. Page to Moses T. Stevens, April 12, 1877, Stevens Papers.

13 Of 74 drygoods commission Merchants doing business in Boston by 1870, 2 had
started out as jobbers, 3 as importers, 4 had combined jobbing and importing

before turning to a domestic commission business, 10 did a mixed business in 1870. R. G. Dun & Co., credit reporting ledgers for Boston.

14 Fred M. Jones, *Middlemen in the Domestic Trade of the United States, 1800-1860* (Urbana, Ill., 1937), 15.

15 The result is a lower limit for the actual figure. The amount of capital invested in the mills for which each commission house sold has been calculated on the basis of capital figures given for incorporated companies in *Dockham's US Textile Directory, 1870-71.* We are assuming that the capital reported by the ninth Census for the cotton and woollen industries of Maine, New Hampshire, and Massachusetts approximates the capital actually invested in all mills selling through Boston houses, in other words, that the capital represented by those mills in those three states not selling through Boston commission houses is about equal to the capital of mills from other states selling through Boston houses.

16 Melvin T. Copeland, *The Cotton Manufacturing Industry of the United States* (Cambridge, Mass., 1912), 215.

17 R G. Dun & Co., credit reporting ledgers for Boston. For a polemic analysis of the creditability of the agency's figures see Thomas F. Meagher, *The Commercial Agency 'System' of the United States and Canada Exposed* (New York, 1876).

18 Property of Amos A. Lawrence, 1857, A. A. Lawrence Papers; R. G. Dun & Co., , credit reporting ledgers for Boston, vol. 4, p. 334 (vol. 73 of Massachusetts series), February 26, 1879 (short Citation used hereafter: Dun & Co., Boston: 4.334(73), 2-26-79; Dun & Co., Boston: 2.886(70), 11·20-78.

19 Dun & Co., Boston: 1.103(67), 4-19-56 (Mudge, Sawyer & Co.); 2.495(69), 11-30-57 (Nevins & Co.).

20 William H. Hilliger, *James Talcott: Merchant and his Time* (New York, 1937), Ewing and Norton, *Broadlooms*, 28, 54, 76, 80, 94. Copeland, Cotton Manufacturing, 210, 212, 215.

21 Calculated on the basis of entries in the ledgers and waste books of Mason & Lawrence and Lawrence & Co. respectively, Mason & Lawrence Papers.

22 R. H. Snow to Mason & Lawrence, July 19, 24 25, 26, August 7, 8, September 10, 13, October 5, 9, 30, 1850, W. E. Pratt to Mason & Lawrence, January 11, February 17, April 4, July 3, October 17, 1850, Mason & Lawrence Papers.

23 Snow to Mason & Lawrence, September 13, 1850, Pratt to Mason & Lawrence, January, 5, 15, 22, 31, February 19, March 16, 18, April 11, October 1, November 4, 1850, Mason & Lawrence Papers.

24 Snow to Mason & Lawrence, October 5, 1850, Pratt to Mason & Lawrence, January 18, 23, February 6, 7, 8, 11, March 20, April 8, July 7, 26, September 2, December 26, 1850, *ibid.*

25 Pratt to Mason & Lawrence, February 18, 25, March 7, 26, April 1, 1850, *ibid.*

26 *Ibid.*, January 12, 21, February 26, 1850.

27 *Ibid.*, waste books, series on monthly wholesale value of total sales and of sales effected in New York; series of commissions paid to the commission house for all sales effected outside of Boston at a given rate of commission of ½ per cent. From this series I have calculated the wholesale value of sales effected outside of Boston, the difference between total sales and sales made outside Boston, and finally the ratio between Boston sales and New York sales.

28 As shown by the experiences of James Talcott. Hilliger, *Talcott, passim.*

29 Joseph B. Wheelock to Amos A. Lawrence, April 7, 1845, A. A. Lawrence Papers; Elva Tooker, *Nathan Trotter: Philadelphia Merchant, 1787-1853* (Cambridge, Mass., 1955), 63.

30 The Cocheco Co. paid 33.8 per cent of the general expenses of the commission house Mason & Lawrence from December 1, 1848 to November 30, 1851, Mason & Lawrence Papers, ledgers B and C.

31 J. F. Dorsey to Amos A. Lawrence, Jan. 28, 1886, A. A. Lawrence Papers.
32 Faulkner, Kimball & Co. (until July 1, 1871, then Faulkner, Page & Co.) to
    N. Stevens & Co., 1867-1880, *passim*, Stevens Papers.
33 Knowlton, *Pepperell's Progress*, 83.
34 R. G. Dun & Co., credit reporting ledgers for Boston. Continuity in the history of
    a commission house has been assumed if the style of its name remained
    unchanged, if the senior partner did not change, if in case of retirement of the
    senior partner the former junior partners continued to do business together.
35 Miscellaneous letters, 1853-1887 and biographical notes on Amos A. Lawrence,
    A. A. Lawrence Papers.
36 For a sketch of the development of credit rating agencies see: Dun & Bradstreet,
    Inc., *The Centennial of the Birth of Impartial Credit Reporting: An American
    Idea* (New York, 1941).
37 Other things being equal. Credit risks may have increased with the territorial
    growth of the market; is it not reasonable to expect that this increase was offset
    by the development of the communication system?
38 Knowlton, *Pepperell's Progress*, 90 f.
39 Faulkner,Kimball & co. to N. Stevens & Co., Stevens Papers. For shortening of
    credit periods in general, See Albert O. Greef, *The Commercial Paper House in
    the United States* (Cambridge, Mass., 1938), 70.
40 Copeland, *Cotton Manufacturing*, 197.
41 Cash books B and C, *passim*, waste book B, May 31, 1870 (interest of 6 per
    cent on unspecified loan), ledger C (interest account), Mason & Lawrence
    Papers. No Individual rates for interest paid to creditors appear on the books.
42 Joseph G. Martin, *Martin's Boston Stock Market: Eighty-Eight Years* (Boston,
    1886), 'Monthly Reports on Money Market', 44 ff.
43 R. G. Dun & Co., credit reporting ledgers for Boston.
44 'Rates paid by Lawrence Manufacturing Company according to entries in Notes
    and Bills payable, 1874-1908'. This single bill book is among the Mason &
    Lawrence Papers, vol. 112.
45 Dun & Co., Boston: 3.477(72), 1-3-76. (Mackintosh, Green & Horton); 1.500
    z/29(68), 9-7-83 (Dexter, Abbot & Co.); 2.599 a/100(69), 9-26-79 (Faulkner,
    Page & Co.); 1,265(68) 11-1-77 (Parker, Wilder & Co.); 15.495(84) 11-1-77
    (Wendell, Hutchinson & Co.); 4.352(73), 11-20-69, 5-1-71, 6-26-73 (White,
    Brown & Co.).
46 Dun & Co., Boston: 16.3(85), 7-2-77 (J. S. & E. Wright & Co.).
47 Amory A. Lawrence to Amos A. Lawrence, 1877, July 3, 1877, A. A. Lawrence
    Papers.
48 Hilliger, *Talcott*, 92; Ewing and Norton, *Broadlooms*, 83, 94, 141.
49 Increasing importance of travelling agents may have affected selling costs. But
    it was the jobbers who mainly employed the commercial travellers in our period.
    Cole, *American Wool Manufacture*, 292; Ewing and Norton, *Broadlooms*, 84,
    94, 136, 152.
50 Dun & Co., Boston: 12-427(71), 7-11-81, 3-26-85 (Woodbury & Foss); 15.176(84),
    11-20-76 (Bartlett & Co.); 2.848(70), 11-10-75, 2.941(70), 2-16-83 (Lowry);
    9.428(78), 3-18-86 (Davis).
51 Berger, *Pacific Mills*, 15.
52 Everton Foster (ed.), *Lamb's Textile Industries of the United States* (2 vols.,
    Boston, 1916), I, 445; 'Memo of an agreement between Messrs. Lawrence &
    Co. & the Arlington Woollen Mills, Sept. 1, 1874', statement on financial
    affairs of Arlington Mills, March 16, 1875, A. A. Lawrence Papers.
53 G. Brewer to Amos A. Lawrence, June 26, 1871, M. H. Dorman to Amos A.
    Lawrence, January 21, 1873, A. A. Lawrence Papers.
54 Statement of the condition of the Arlington Mills, November 30, 1875, *ibid.*

55 Amory A. Lawrence to Amos A. Lawrence, April, 1879, *ibid.*
56 Lawrence & Co. to Whitman, April 30, 1881, *ibid.*
57 Memorandum of Mr Whitman about business, May 9, 1881, *ibid.*
58 Dun & Co., Chicago: 18.255(44), 11-29-78.
59 Amory A. Lawrence to Amos A. Lawrence, December 1, 1881, A. A. Lawrence Papers.
60 Dun & Co., New York City: 3.1283(221), 1-5-82; Chicago: 18.255(44), 11-29-78.
61 Lawrence & Co., to Alfred Ray, July 20, 1881, A. A. Lawrence Papers; waste book, Mason & Lawrence Papers.
62 Thomas R. Navin, Jr., 'Innovation and Management Policies: The Textile Machinery Industry: Influence of the Market on Management', *Bulletin of the Business Historical Society*, XXV (March, 1951), 15-30.

PART THREE

Techniques of
Business Management
and
Organisation

16

Accounting and the Rise of Capitalism: Further Notes on a Theme by Sombart[†]

Basil S. Yamey[*]

Werner Sombart[1] was largely responsible for the broad thesis that systematic or scientific accounting, identified with the double-entry system, played an important part in releasing, activating, stimulating or accentuating the 'rationalistic pursuit of unlimited profits', an essential element in the capitalistic spirit. The main strands in this thesis may be set out as follows: by transforming assets into abstract values and by expressing quantitatively the results of business activities, double-entry bookkeeping clarified the aims of acquisitive business; moreover, it provided the rational basis on which the capitalist could choose the directions in which to employ his capital to best advantage; and finally, it made possible the separation of the business firm from its owners and hence the growth of large joint-stock businesses.[2] Sombart's work gave prominence and prestige to the humble art of accounting by ascribing to it wide economic significance.[3]

In an earlier paper I criticised Sombart's thesis. I tried to show that the claims made for the double-entry system cannot be reconciled with the early practice of the system as illustrated and discussed in texts on accounting published during the first three hundred years after Luca Pacioli's first printed exposition appeared in 1494.[4] I now return to a further examination of the thesis, which,

*From the *Journal of Accounting Research* Vol. 2 (Autumn 1964), pp. 117-36. Reprinted by permission of the editor of the *Journal of Accounting Research* and the author.

†I have benefitted greatly from the comments on an earlier draft of this paper made by Professor W. T. Baxter, Mr Kurt Klappholz and Professor William Letwin.

This paper was first published in *Studi in Onore di Amintore Fanfani,* Dott. A. Giuffre, Milan, 1962, vol. vi, pp. 833-57. It is reprinted here by kind permission of Professor F. Melis of the Comitato Promotore delle Onoranze.

In the present version I have made a few small changes and added some bibliographical references.

since my previous paper, has received some general support from
Professor Federigo Melis, a leading contemporary student of the
history of accounting.[5]

I shall neither analyse Sombart's views concerning the place of
double-entry bookkeeping in the history of ideas[6] — views which to
my mind are too elaborate and fanciful — nor attempt to unravel
the metaphysics attributed to such bookkeeping by Spengler and
others.[7] Discussion of these matters is unlikely to be fruitful; and
these matters, moreover, distract attention from the simple
question provoked by the thesis, namely, the contribution of
double-entry accounting to the solution of problems in business
organisation and administration. I shall try to show that, in the
period covered in this study, this contribution not only was small,
but also that it was not made by those features of the system or in
solving those business problems particularly emphasised by
Sombart. I also suggest, incidentally, that, in the context of the
solution of business problems, double-entry accounting was not
greatly superior to less elaborate methods of accounting. The
argument is illustrated by reference to business accounting records
from the sixteenth to the early nineteenth centuries, and more
particularly to English records.

I.

The calculation of the profits and capital of an enterprise is
given a central place in the development of the Sombart thesis.
Max Weber, in fact, specified that 'a rational capitalistic establishment' was one 'with capital accounting, that is, an establishment
which determines its income yielding power by calculation according
to the methods of modern bookkeeping and the striking of a
balance'.[8] But in fact knowledge of the *total* profit of an enterprise
for a period, either absolutely or in relation to the amount of
capital in the enterprise, is rarely necessary or useful for business
decision-making within that enterprise. In a continuing enterprise,
knowledge of the total or aggregated profitability or rate of return
on capital is not relevant to current decisions which are concerned
with changes in the use of part of the resources at the firm's
disposal; and these, in turn, are related to the expected profitability
of the various separable activities constituting the firm's total
activity and of other activities under consideration. The total profit
position, whether in retrospect or (by extrapolation or otherwise) in
prospect, is undoubtedly more relevant where the termination or
sale of the enterprise as a whole is under contemplation. But this is
not only relatively infrequent, but is also likely to introduce

considerations of an *ad hoc* character which call for special estimates and calculations.

This does not mean, however, that some business men may not from time to time like to review their over-all business results and financial position. But such periodic reviews, whatever satisfaction they may afford the business man, are not likely to bear on the taking of particular decisions affecting the deployment of resources.

But we need not dwell on these general considerations. For whatever value there may be in calculations of total profit or of total capital, it is clear that they can be made independently of a system of double-entry bookkeeping. In this context, double-entry has no inherent superiority over other types of record-keeping. Regardless of the accounting system in use, the total capital of an enterprise can be 'calculated' by making an inventory of its various assets and liabilities at the particular date, attaching appropriate values to each, and reaching a balance by summation. The periodic profit of the enterprise can then be derived by finding the difference between successive inventory totals, after allowing, if thought fit, for intervening contributions and withdrawals of resources by the proprietor.[9] Of course, records of debts owing to or by the business are likely to be necessary to establish the net indebtedness of the business to be included in the inventory, but single-entry bookkeeping supplies this need as effectively as double-entry.

The double-entry system may seem to provide a check on the calculation of total profit from successive inventories by independently throwing up the material for calculating this profit directly; that is to say, details are kept of the various types of incomes and expenditures, and the total profit figure can be ascertained by combining them in the profit-and-loss account. This way of stating the superiority of double-entry would, however, be somewhat misleading. A double-entry ledger contains within itself the material for an independent profit calculation only to the extent that it also contains the material for an inventory of all assets and liabilities. But it cannot contain the materials necessary for a complete inventory: the entries in the asset accounts can provide data of the cost of acquiring the assets but not of their current values at the time of making the capital calculation. If the current values of the assets are specially introduced and incorporated in the calculation, then suitable entries have to be made in the profit-and-loss account to reflect the profits or losses on the revaluation of assets; and thus the profit-and-loss account is no longer an independent check on the calculation of profits (except in an arithmetical sense), but is equally dependent on the results of the external inventory-taking. Conversely, if the asset accounts are not adjusted to reflect current valuations, the capital and balance accounts cannot reflect all the changes in economic values which have occurred.

Sombart was aware of this distinction between the self-contained balance constructed wholly from material in the ledger and the balance based on an external ('ausser buchmässige') inventory-taking.[10] He considered it a serious deficiency that the second type was apparently rare in the first centuries of double-entry bookkeeping.[11] I believe he was mistaken in emphasising the significance of this point. When the accounts are those of a proprietor who supervises the drawing up of the balance account and who is conversant with the details of his enterprise and his resources, then it matters little what value is put against each asset. Even when, as is unlikely, he does not have a fairly good general idea of his *total* resources *before* he starts drawing up his balance, he can gauge his position merely by surveying the enumeration of his assets and liabilities and the descriptions of each — his personal knowledge of the various assets and of the state of markets would dispense with the need for careful current valuations entered into the balance account. This, however, casts serious doubt on the validity of the emphasis in the Sombart thesis of 'quantification' and 'abstraction'.

This doubt is reinforced by more detailed consideration of accounting practices in the sixteenth to eighteenth centuries. Two practices are singled out by way of illustration. First, it seems to have been a fairly common and widespread practice to record claims against debtors at values known to be unrealistically high. This was done so as to have records of the amounts of claims against debtors, even when it was believed that the full amount might never be recovered (or it was known that the full amount was not due currently). This procedure meant that the firm's assets and profits were overstated. But there is no reason to suppose that this incidental result was considered a disadvantage: the business man wanted to have an accounting reminder of the existence of his claims (even if their effective enforcement were doubtful), and was well aware, from the descriptions in the asset-accounts and from his knowledge of his firm's affairs, of the real nature and probable value of these assets. Calculation and quantification were less important that the availability of records for ordinary administration.[12] The second practice concerns the statement in balance accounts of the 'values' of fixed assets like land, buildings, ships and investments in stocks and shares. One treatment of these assets was simply to take the arithmetical difference between the total debits and total credits in the account of an asset as the 'value' of the asset. This meant that the income yielded by the asset was deducted from the cost of the asset, and running expenses added to it — neither income nor expense was treated as an item in the profit calculation. There was no attempt here at valuation or a careful income calculation. The use of this method is not, however, proof of incompetence in accounting; for the same ledger usually shows the use of other and more 'realistic' methods.[13] It does suggest that description of assets (in the titles of accounts) was important, and not their quantification or 'abstraction'; and that the calculation of total assets was low in the hierarchy of purposes served by early double-entry accounting.

Professor Robertson has elaborated the idea of 'abstraction' in accounting. With systematic bookkeeping the various particular and specific assets (different kinds of merchandise or ventures) — 'the true realities of commerce' — 'become mere shadows, they become unreal and the apparent reality seems to lie in book-keeping ciphers. All that the merchant who employs systematic book-keeping sees are money values which increase or grow less . . .'[14] However, if such 'abstraction' had taken place, I suggest it would have made for less rather than more successful decision-making, since the decision-maker would have forfeited the more detailed knowledge of his various affairs and resources, and would have had to view the complexities and detail of reality through the drastically simplifying and possibly distorting screen of his accounts. To-day decision-makers, especially in large firms, have to rely largely on accounting reports and statements for gaining a view of the condition and activities of their enterprise. But how often would they not wish to go behind the 'ciphers' to see the 'true realities' more closely and clearly, since without this knowledge they feel that they are controlling the enterprise with less sensitivity and perceptiveness than they would like.[15] In many cases, of course, remote control may be necessary or desirable when all considerations are taken into account; but it seems to me to be mistaken to regard the process of 'abstraction' as an advantage in itself, as is implied in the elaboration of the Sombart thesis.

Those double-entry ledgers of the seventeenth and eighteenth centuries I have examined do not give the impression that double entry had in fact contributed to the withering away of the commercial 'realities'; and the same seems to be true of earlier ledgers. The detailed entries in the ledgers — the detail is even more emphatic in the journals — and, often, the detailed titles of individual accounts, seem to point the other way. From them the merchant was easily able, if he wished to do so, to reconstruct in some minuteness the course of particular transactions and groups of transactions; in his mind's eye he could relive some past experience, and he could readily visualise the physical attributes and economic circumstances of any particular asset. Abbreviated account-titles and accounting entries appear to be products of later accounting practice (at least in England).

In concluding this section, we revert to its main topic — the calculation of the total profit and the total capital of an enterprise. It might be thought that a system of double-entry records facilitated and so encouraged the regular calculation of these magnitudes. Indeed, there is some suggestion in a few treatises that the possibility of devising a balance account solely on the basis of data in the ledger was sometimes considered an advantage of the system. But, at least among the English records I have examined, there is little to establish that the double-entry system went together with regularity in balancing and in the preparation of summary accounts. The facts about the periodic closing of the profit-and-loss account into the capital account disclosed in the surviving account-books of nine substantial business men are as follows (the dates of the records are in parentheses):

Sir Thomas Gresham (1546-51): not once.
Sir William Calley   (1600-06): once, at end of book.
Sir John Banks   (1657-99): irregularly, 13 times in 43 years (including three times at termination of ledgers).
Sir Robert Clayton   (1669-80): books closed and balanced annually; but there is no separate profit-and-loss account.
Sir Dudley North   (1680-91): not once.
Sir Charles Peers   (1689-94): once, at end of book.
Richard Du Cane   (1736-44): irregularly, six times in nine years.
Peter Du Cane   (1754-58): annually.
William Braund   (1758-74): annually.[16]

The compilation of balance accounts, setting out the assets and liabilities at balancing dates, was generally both less regular and much less frequent. A general impression is that the closing of the accounts and balancing, whether regular or irregular, were concerned at least as much with narrowly bookkeeping purposes (for example, clearing nominal accounts to tidy up the ledger, checking the accuracy of the ledger, or opening a new ledger) as with calculation of the total profit and the establishment of the new capital figure.[17]

II.

Any notion that the double-entry system of accounting is in some sense necessary for the separation of the 'firm' from its proprietors[18] is invalid. Its lack of validity is apparent from the fact that partnership concerns were in operation before the invention of double-entry; and many partnerships have operated without the system since its invention. There is no evidence that the absence of the system involved these 'firms' in any more difficulties (as between the individual proprietors or as between them and their firm) than in other partnerships which used the system. The invalidity is further demonstrated by the fact that some capitalistic joint stock companies have functioned for long periods without double-entry; these include the Dutch East India Company,[19] the Sun Fire Insurance Office of London,[20] the Whitin Machine Company in the United States,[21] and the Capital and Counties Bank in England.[22]

It would also be misleading to suppose that the adoption of the double-entry system by a one-owner firm in some way or other led to the 'depersonalisation' of the firm or gave special emphasis to the separate identity of the firm as distinct from it owner. The double-entry system, though it does call for a capital account in the owner's name, does not enforce the rigorous separation of business assets and activities from the personal assets and activities of the owner outside the business. It was, indeed, the almost invariable practice in the English double-entry account-books of sole proprietorships I have examined to clear personal and household expenditures as well as business expenses through the profit-and-loss account (rather than directly to the capital account); this intermingling of business and other expenses meant that the final net profit figure reflected the net increase in personal wealth rather than the net profit arising from the activities of the 'firm'. A plurality of owners, on the other hand, virtually enforces the separation of business and personal affairs, regardless of the type of bookkeeping employed.

It is unlikely that the 'confusion' of the business firm and its owner had any economic significance,[23] or suggests any attenuation of the capitalistic spirit where it is found. It does, however, illustrate a general point: that the double-entry system does little more than provide a framework into which accounting data can be fitted and within which the data can be arranged, grouped and re-grouped. The system does not by itself determine the range of data to be included in a particular setting, nor impose a particular pattern of internal ordering and re-ordering of the data.[24] Thus little can be inferred simply from the fact that a particular enterprise employed the double-entry system. Sombart seems to have been aware of this (for example in his criticisms of early practice for the lack of thoroughgoing 'inventories'); his broad generalisations, on the other hand, seem to ignore this consideration.

III.

If it could be shown that double-entry accounting did provide material assistance to business men in their choice among the numerous alternative opportunities for the use of the resources, then a major part of the Sombart thesis would be established, and it would be appropriate to credit the invention of double-entry with substantial economic consequences. I shall try to show in this section that the claims made for the system are greatly exaggerated.[25]

In the early practice of double-entry it was usual for separate ledger accounts to be kept for each distinctive type, lot or consignment of goods, for each separate trading venture or temporary partnership, for each ship, and so on. Thus detailed records were available of the results of each of many past business 'activities'. In other words, the detailed compostition of the total profits of an enterprise, as disclosed in the balance of the profit-and-loss account, was to be found in the entries in that account or in the various 'trading' accounts in the ledger. This feature is somewhat comparable to that of modern cost accounting systems designed to disclose the separate profits or losses on each of many different production processes, departments or lines of production. (The early form of double-entry in mercantile accounting proved to be readily adaptable to industrial accounting). The relevant question is whether the information revealed in this arrangement of double-entry ledgers served to improve the ability of the business man to place his resources in those lines of activity where his returns would be maximised.[26]

For discussion of this question it is useful to distinguish three types of situation. The first type is where the business man includes one or more hitherto untried or unexplored lines of activity within the range of alternative opportunities under consideration. It is obvious that he can have no knowledge from his accounts of the likely profitability of the (to him) novel lines of activity. While for other lines of activity he may be able to estimate their future profitability by extrapolation (with such amendment as he thinks fit) of past recorded results, for new lines there can be no accounting guidance. This conclusion also applies, *a fortiori* as it were, where the business man contemplates a novel development or innovation, novel to him as well as to the economy of which he is a part. Steps into the dark or the unknown are perhaps at the heart of capitalistic entrepreneurship — the exploration, induced by the hopes of profits and deterred by the possibilities of losses, of new products, new processes, new methods or new markets. Thus when the business man expresses himself most emphatically as entrepreneur, he is necessarily without benefit of accounting records pertaining to past events and experiences. It is indeed surprising that the role of accounting calculation should have been underlined by Sombart and others as a partial explanation of economic developments in which departures from customary modes of behaviour and the exercise of entrepreneurship were deemed to be crucial. Insofar as the early centuries of capitalism can be characterised as a period of dynamic change from a static base — itself a dangerous simplification — one would have to discount heavily the contribution made by systematic accounting or accounting calculation.[27]

The second type of situation is where the business man is making a choice among alternative lines of activity all of which are familiar to him from past experience. Here his accounting records can provide information of the results of engaging in each of the various lines of activity in the past. But their use as a firm basis for the determination of the relative profitability of different courses of action in the immediate or more distant future depends on the stability of costs and prices over the relevant period. When costs and prices (or the relationship between them) are not expected to remain the same in the relevant future period as in the recorded past, then there is no firm basis for the projection of recorded past results into the future, and the records provide little or no guidance to the business man intent on placing his resources to best advantage. When there is uncertainty about prospective price movements (or changes in cost-price relationships), the business man has to behave 'entrepreneurially'; this type of situation is not unlike the first type discussed above. Success depends not on the availability of accounting records in a particular form, but on the ability to perceive possibilities of favourable price movements, the willingness to risk resources on these possibilities, and flexibility in the deployment of resources. Much turns on rapid assimilation and interpretation of available market information.

The third type of situation is the same as the second, save for the difference that costs and prices (or the relationship between them) are expected to remain stable. Here the records of past results are obviously capable of providing a basis for deciding to discontinue unprofitable lines of activity and to concentrate on the profitable lines. But wherever such stability were to be found, there would be little need for systematic and continuous recording of trading results. Once the relationship between costs and returns in any line had been discovered, there would be no call for the systematic re-calculation of the more-or-less unvarying results of more-or-less routine activities. To summarise, taking the second and third types of situation together; in the former, detailed and systematic accounting analysis of past results would be of little business significance, while in the latter it would be largely unnecessary. One might add that it is the former type of situation which holds out more prospect for attractive profits than the latter (at least in the absence of effective monopoly power).

The foregoing suggests that the systematic accounting of past business results has a decidedly limited part to play in business decision-making. It can be shown, further, that systematic accounting, as in the double-entry system, is not essential for the provision of information about past results or costs in different lines of activity in a business, and about relationships between inputs and outputs. Data on yields of different lines of activity can be collected independently of the business accounts. Thus the Dutch East India Company, which did not keep its accounts by double-entry and whose accounts lacked one of its special components (the profit-and-loss account), after each auction had compilations made of the gross profits secured on each commodity, and also other similar data.[28] Again, where the results or costs of particular activities were thought to be necessary for control or guidance, *ad hoc* arrangements for the necessary records could be made even in a simplified and incomplete set of accounts.[29]

When making a choice between two (or more) courses of action, a business man may for purposes of comparison make *ad hoc* 'calculations' showing their expected results. The calculations, however, are estimates. Their connection with past results recorded in accounts is likely to be tenuous, as we have seen, though *formally* they may take some accounting data as a starting-point for the exercise in forecasting. The entrepreneurial estimates are essentially outside the framework of the business accounts, and independent of any particular system of business accounts.[30]

Evidence of such calculations made in bygone centuries rarely survives for the benefit of historians. Often the calculations would not have been committed to paper, or if they had been committed to paper, they would have had less chance of survival than business accounts; the latter are embodied in volumes, whilst the former would rarely have been kept on an organised, durable basis. But some of these estimates have survived.[31] The most interesting set so far published are those interspersed among the accounting entries in 'A Book for my Remembrance' kept by a farmer, Robert Loder, between 1610 and 1620.[32] These calculations take the form of exercises showing what his profits might have been (on explicit assumptions) if he had followed a different course of action from that actually taken — exercises in jobbing back indulged in to help in deciding future plans.[33] It is interesting that these entrepreneurial calculations should appear in an account-book which, in its purely accounting entries, contains the most elementary form of accounting, the narrative paragraph.[34] It is instructive to find in Loder's remembrance book evidence of a highly-developed spirit of acquisitiveness and of a purposive pursuit of profit together with rudimentary account-keeping. This should indicate — if such indication is necessary — that double-entry, systematic or scientific accounting is not in any way necessary for the flowering of the 'spirit of capitalism'.[35]

The general conclusion to be drawn from the discussion in this section is that accounting records, in the double-entry system or otherwise, could have played no more than a minor part in accentuating the pursuit of profit by enabling the capitalistic business man to select more successfully from among the opportunities open to him. This conclusion is not a criticism of double-entry bookkeeping. It is also not a criticism of its early practitioners, and it certainly cannot be shown that they failed to take advantage of the necessarily limited potentialities of the system in this particular context. The conclusion is inherent in the nature of economic uncertainties and discontinuities, which in turn provide scope and opportunity for the exercise of qualities of entrepreneurship. Indeed, if some of the claims made for double-entry accounting by Sombart were valid, business decision-making would have been rendered more mechanistic and less risky, and to that extent the capitalist entrepreneur would have been less significant.[36]

The general conclusion is not inconsistent with the recognition of the more modest role of business accounts (whether or not cast in double-entry form) both in facilitating enquiries into the working-out of *past* decisions, and also in providing some framework for the budgeting of expenditures involved in impending activities. But this role is quite different from that postulated in the Sombart thesis, if my understanding of the latter is correct.

IV.

Professor Bruchey, in his study of the Oliver double-entry accounting records of early nineteenth century Baltimore, concluded: 'The Oliver accounts aided the partners in their routine problems of business management rather than in the resolution of their entrepreneurial indecisions. These routine problems required the information derivable from each unbalanced account rather than from the total picture of assets and liabilities provided by balance sheets . . . The Oliver structure of accounts provided the means for maintaining an orderly routine in their house of business. When they considered entrepreneurial departures from that routine, factors other than the bookkeeping records which maintained the routine became relevant'.[37] This conclusion would apply fittingly also to those English double-entry ledgers which I have examined. This section considers briefly the *distinctive* contribution of double-entry accounting to the methodising of the management of the more routine problems of business. It is fair to say that this aspect of accounting occupies a subordinate position in the Sombart thesis.

From the point of view of routine administration and the control of assets, the merit of the double-entry system lies in its comprehensiveness and its possibilities for the orderly arrangement of data. In a sense the adoption of the system compels a certain degree of comprehensiveness[38] and orderliness because, as every schoolboy knows, for every debit there must also be a credit.[39] Thus data may be recorded in the system which, but for the compulsion of the system, the business man might at the time prefer to have ignored,[40] and subsequently the availability of the additional data might prove to be useful. And orderliness of arrangement is an obvious help in routine administration.

These qualities cannot be denied. But the superiority of double-entry should not be exaggerated. A system of single entry, with personal accounts for debtors and creditors as well as a cash account, provides a large part of the information necessary in routine administration.[41] Yet such a system would lack the characteristic components of the double-entry system, viz. the profit-and-loss account and the capital account. Again, a set of account-books which may seem untidy, ill-arranged and incomplete to a student today might have been easily manageable by the person who kept them for his own or his master's use. Business men have also been adept at devising *ad hoc* accounting records for controlling particular types of transaction or the use of particular assets, where such control has been necessary for effective administration.[42] Finally, the watchful eye of the proprietor is often a good substitute for detailed accounting records and controls.[43] In brief, the greater comprehensiveness and orderliness of the double-entry system are likely to be relatively unimportant for effective business management when the proprietor is in close touch with much of the detail of his firm.

The double-entry system provides an arithmetical check on the accuracy of account-books. Some of the earlier writers on the system sang the praises of this distinctive feature: 'this way of accounting . . .carries with it its own Proof: And here lies the supreme Excellency and Usefulness of this Mystery'.[44] The self-checking feature is part of the compulsion to 'proper' accounting implicit in the system, and it is clearly of some value, especially in large firms. It is not, however, a major consideration. Moreover, in early practice the discipline of the trial balance was frequently evaded by the correction of any discrepancy in the ledger by the simple expedient of making a balancing single entry or of 'cooking' a figure.[45] This in no way reflects on the business skill of the owner, nor on the probity of the business man who is accountable to himself alone. As Nathan Trotter noted, when making a correcting single entry (in 1845): '. . . and I have *forced* it in this way, much against my wishes, but really I had not time to go thro' a thoro' examination . . . and as the matter lies solely at issue with myself I must reconcile it . . .'.[46]

A final example of the discipline of accounting records is the check on over-spending and the encouragement to economy provided by regular consultation of records of receipts and payments, current and imminent.[47] It should be apparent, however, that the necessary records for this purpose are not peculiar to the double-entry system.[48]

It is scarcely necessary to add that accounting records, whether double-entry or not, are not capable of enforcing economy or good financial management. In the achievement of these results, as in the achievement of other aspects of successful enterprise discussed earlier in this essay, accounting records and accounting systems have only a humble, but nevertheless interesting, contribution to make.

On this note it is fit to end. Sombart was right in drawing attention to accounting methods. He was mistaken in reading too much economic significance into double-entry bookkeeping. This is so even though many, with him, have found the technique to be intellectually attractive, aesthetically satisfying, or provocatively esoteric.

NOTES

1 Werner Sombart, *Der Moderne Kapitalismus*, 6th edition. Munich and Leipzig, 1924, vol. 2.1, pp. 118-19.
2 For more detailed exposition, see Sombart, *ibid.*, pp. 118-25; F. L. Nussbaum,

A History of Economic Institutions, New York, 1933, pp. 159-61; H. M. Robertson, *Aspects of the Rise of Economic Individualism*, Cambridge, 1933, pp. 52-6. See also F. L. Nussbaum, *The Triumph of Science and Reason, 1660-1685*, New York and Evanston, 1962, p. 16: 'A highly motivated form of measurement and one that might be said to have changed the form of economic motivation had been spreading among the Europeans since the fourteenth century: double-entry bookkeeping, which corresponded to the needed kind of measurement in that it was objective and measured something existing independently of the observer'.

3 The influence of Sombart's views may be seen in the following comments of the late Walter Eucken on the economic significance of double entry: 'The knowledge of double-entry book-keeping was a precondition for the south German expansion of the beginning of the sixteenth century. Where this knowledge was lacking or slow to penetrate, as in the Hansa towns, economic development was delayed. It would seem that the conclusion must be that, as the methods of economic calculation improved, a complete transformation occurred in men's attitude to economic life'. *The Foundations of Economics: History and Theory in the Analysis of Economic Reality*, London, 1950, p. 283.

4 Scientific Bookkeeping and the Rise of Capitalism', *Economic History Review*, second series, vol. I (1949), pp. 99-113; reprinted in W. T. Baxter (ed.), *Studies in Accounting*, London, 1950, pp. 13-30.

Professor Raymond de Roover has written: 'Up to now the history of accounting until 1500 has been written on the basis of actual records, and thereafter on the basis of treatises . . . Perhaps a study of . . . later account-books will show that the contemporaneous treatises are no more reliable than the earlier ones in giving a true picture of business organisation in the past'. ('The Development of Accounting Prior to Luca Pacioli according to the Account-Books of Medieval Merchants', in A. C. Littleton and B. S. Yamey (eds.), *Studies in the History of Accounting*, London, 1956, p. 174). Examination of a number of English account-books after 1500 does not suggest that the accounting treatises are likely to mislead, especially if it is borne in mind that a large proportion of the treatises, particularly after 1700, were apparently designed for limited teaching purposes. The only ways in which the treatises might be misleading are, first, that most (but not all) of them confine themselves, for obvious reasons, to exposition of double-entry in terms of a simple arrangement of account-books, whereas in practice more numerous subsidiary books might be kept; and second, that the treatises suggest a high degree of orderliness and system which was not always matched in practice. But these are minor matters so far as concerns analysis of the Sombart thesis. Again, one would not expect the treatises to describe the particular accounting practices of exceptional firms such as the Bank of England and the East India Company. Nevertheless, knowledge of the treatises certainly helps in understanding their extant account-books.

5 F. Melis, *Storia della Ragioneria*, Bologna, 1950, esp., p. 598.

6 See especially Sombart, *ibid.*, p. 119, where it is claimed, for example, that one can detect in double-entry bookkeeping the germ of the ideas of gravitation, the circulation of blood, and the conservation of energy. Oswald Spengler, in *The Decline of the West*, ranked the inventor of the system (thought by him to be Fra Luca Paciolo) 'with his contemporaries Columbus and Copernicus'.

7 For example: 'Double-entry book keeping is a pure Analysis of the space of values, referred to a co-ordinate system, of which the origin is the "Firm".' (Spengler, *ibid.*), and 'The importance of the double-entry system of keeping books lies not in its arithmetic, but in its metaphysics'. C. A. Cooke, *Corporation Trust and Company*, Manchester, 1950, p. 185.

8 M. Weber, *General Economic History*, London, 1927, p. 275.

9 For an early example of this type of profit calculation, see Raymond de Roover, 'The Story of the Alberti Company of Florence, 1302-1348, as Revealed in its Account Books', *The Business History Review*, vol. XXXII (1958), p. 34. A later example is that of the Fugger 'Inventur' of 1527, in which were calculated the firm's capital at the end of 1527 and its profits since the earlier 'Inventur' of 1511; see Jacob Strieder, *Die Inventur der Firma Fugger aus dem Jahre 1527*, Tübingen, 1905, esp., pp. 6-8 and 113-4. For a yet later example, see Arthur Raistrick, *Dynasty of Iron Founders*, London, 1953, pp. 277-8 (referring to the years 1739-45).

The account-book (1616-64) of Thomas Cullum, 'draper, alderman, sheriff, and Restoration baronet', is particularly interesting in that it reveals a regular annual capital and income accounting without double-entry records. At the end of each year Callum calculated the increase in his capital, in effect by deducting his opening net assets from his closing net assets as ascertained by listing and valuation. Part of the change in capital calculated in this way was accounted for specifically by payments such as wages, losses such as bad debts, and particular types of income such as rents; the balancing figure was called, variously, gains from trade, gains from trade and stock, or gains from 'any other stock'. The series of calculations was skilfully done. Callum's other accounting records have not survived; but it is apparent that he did not use the double-entry system. (On Cullum's account-book, see A. Simpson, 'Thomas Cullum, Draper, 1587-1664', *Economic History Review*, second series, vol. XI (1958), pp. 19-34, to which I am much indebted).

An interesting discussion of the minimum records required for successive inventories is in Daniel Defoe, *The Complete English Tradesman*, London, 1745, ch. XXXI.

10 John Mair, an important writer on accounting in the eighteenth century, shows clearly the difference between the two types of balances: 'When a Man begins the World, and first sets up to trade, the Inventory is to be gathered from a Survey of the Particulars that make up his real Estate; but ever after is to be collected from the Balance of his old Books, and carried to the new'. (*Book-keeping Methodiz'd*, 2nd ed., Edinburgh, 1741, p. 5).

11 Sombart, *ibid.*, pp. 115-7. Examination of some seventeenth and eighteenth century double-entry ledgers in England suggests that in practice balance accounts were a mixture of the two types; i.e., balance accounts and profit and loss accounts reflected a mixture of both asset revaluations and unadjusted book values; see my article, 'Some Seventeenth and Eighteenth Century Double-Entry Ledgers', *The Accounting Review*, vol. XXXIV (1959) (now reprinted, with additional material, as a chapter in B. S. Yamey, H. C. Edey and Hugh W. Thomson, *Accounting in England and Scotland: 1543-1800*, London, 1963, pp. 180-201).

Where a firm's activities are extensive and far-flung, it may be difficult and take time for its headquarters to obtain all the data necessary for a complete inventory and profit calculation. This is exemplified in the accounts of the English East India Company. These accounts were kept on a double-entry basis, with the profit-and-loss account closed annually on the 30th June to the general joint stock (i.e., capital) account. The profit-and-loss account for 1751-52 includes the results reported by the Factory in Bombay for the year ended in June 1750. It also includes the profits calculated in the Company's Calico Ledger for the year ended September 1751, and in the Drug Ledger for the year ended August 1750; but nothing from the Tea Ledger. The profit-and-loss account for the next year, 1752-53, includes a further year's Bombay profits, a further year's Calico profits, thirteen months' Drug profits, as well as Tea

Ledger profits for the 22 months ended September 1751. In neither 1751-52 nor 1752-53 (nor in any of the succeeding four years) is there any entry for the results of the Voyage to China and the Voyage to Borneo. (East India Company, General Ledger I (1750-56), Library of the Commonwealth Relations Office, London). It should be apparent that the profit-and-loss totals, and the corresponding capital account totals, could have had no significance for decision-making.

12 A common treatment of doubtful debts is explained, by reference to early accounting treatises, in my 'The Functional Development of Double-Entry Book-keeping', *The Accountant*, vol. CIII (1940), p. 339; see also Yamey *et al., op. cit.*, pp. 105-7. The essence of it was that the balances in the accounts of doubtful or 'desperate' debtors were brought together in a single 'desperate debtors account'. This procedure saved space and trouble when introducing a new ledger, yet reminded the owner of legal claims against debtors.

This treatment of doubtful debts is to be seen in many early ledgers: see Raymond de Roover, *The Rise and Decline of the Medici Bank, 1397-1494*, Cambridge, Mass., 1963, pp. 246, 264, 278 and 292; J. Heers, *Le Livre de Comptes de Giovanni Piccamiglio homme d'affaires Genois, 1456-1459*, Paris, 1959, p. 96; J. Denucé, *Inventaire des Affaitadi, banquiers italiens à Anvers de l'Année, 1568*, Antwerp, 1934, pp. 19, 144 and 149; O. ten Have, *Der Leer van het Boekhouden tijdens de Zeventiende en Achttiende Eeuw*, Delft, 1933, p. 279; Yamey *et at., op. cit.*, pp. 200-201; and Stuart W. Bruchey, *Robert Oliver and Mercantile Book-keeping in the Early Nineteenth Century*, unpublished thesis, Johns Hopkins University, Baltimore, p. 86. The last-mentioned study also provides an interesting example of the extremes to which this type of practice would be taken. The Baltimore merchant, Oliver, bought, for a payment of 20,000 dollars, claims against the British Admiralty for the loss of American ships during the Napoleonic Wars. The face value of these doubtful claims was 80,000 dollars. Oliver immediately raised the asset figure to this full amount, and credited the difference of 60,000 dollars as a profit to the profit-and-loss account (*ibid.*, pp. 102-3).

13 For examples, see Yamey *et al., op. cit.*, pp. 197-9.

14 Robertson, *op. cit.*, pp. 53-4.

15 It may be appropriate to refer here to the following quotation from W. G. Rimmer, *Marshalls of Leeds: Flax-Spinners, 1788-1886*, Cambridge, 1960, p. 278. It touches the present point, as well as others discussed in this paper. The characters are the founder of the business, John Marshall, and his two sons, James and Henry:

'Henry had a passion for statistics, and on becoming a partner in 1831 he had introduced a very elaborate system of accounts and checks which occupied him throughout the year. These recorded in summary form almost every dimension of the firm capable of measurement, and their extent and repetition suggest that compilation became an end in itself and not a tool to facilitate the conduct of business. This misplaced enthusiasm did not matter because the founder continued his own accounts. But after John Marshall's death the partners had no succinct Profit and Loss or annual check account. Instead Henry provided a mine of information, which if it had been digested or communicated to his brothers would have proved useful. But Henry was not communicative, and James found difficulty in following Henry's figures . . . There was fortunately no disagreement over profits. These were still calculated by the balance of assets over liabilities at the annual stock-take. But Henry's devotion to figures reflected his remote, somewhat phlegmatic, attitude towards business. By filtering the performance of the firm in such a way, he readily confused the shadow of his own creation with the substance. He never looked closely at what was going on and when he decided that a particular policy was desirable, . . . he lacked determination and was not prepared to meet the personal cost that would have been called for to push it through'.

Some students of modern accounting practices of large companies have suggested that reliance on accounting statements and data leads to erroneous business decisions which may affect the whole economy. A case in point is the recording of 'paper' profits or losses on stocks of raw materials or goods in times of rising or falling prices. It has been said that business men may not be aware of the realities underlying the situation as disclosed by conventional accounting practices, and that failure to allow for the 'paper' element in profit calculation may give rise to spells of unwarranted optimism or pessimism.

16 Sir Thomas Gresham needs no introduction. Calley was in the cloth trade, a member of the Company of Drapers and of the Merchant Adventurers. He was knighted in 1629. Banks was a wealthy merchant-financier-landowner, and governor of the East India Company. Clayton, described by John Evelyn as 'this prodigious rich scrivener', was member of parliament and also Lord Mayor of London in 1679-80. North was a well-known Turkey merchant and proponent of free-trade doctrine. Peers was a merchant in the Spanish trade, director of the Bank of England, and Lord Mayor of London. Richard Du Cane was a merchant and landowner, member of parliament, and director of the Bank of England. His son, Peter, was director of the Bank and of the East India Company. Braund was merchant, ship-owner, marine insurer, and director of the East India Company and of the Sun Fire Office.

Gresham's account-book is discussed in Peter Ramsey, 'Some Tudor Merchants' Accounts', in A. C. Littleton and B. S. Yamey (eds.), *op. cit.* On the account-books of Banks, Clayton, North, Peers, the Du Canes and Braund, see Yamey *et al., op. cit.,* pp. 180-201. (Calley's surviving ledger is the property of Miss J. M. Calley, J.P., of Burderop Park, Swindon, Wilts. For information on this ledger I am indebted to Mr J. T. Lea, of Salisbury, Wilts. The locations of the other account-books are given in the source articles referred to in this paragraph).

Sir John Banks is the subject of D. C. Coleman, *Sir John Banks: Baronet and Businessman,* Oxford, 1963; his accounts are discussed in an appendix, pp. 201-205.

17 One cannot ascertain whether the merchants or their book-keepers did not sometimes carry out the balancing process (with the compilation of a balance account) outside the ledger, without any formal closing of the ledger or the transfer of the profit balance to the capital account in the ledger. Treatises occasionally refer to such a practice. For example, Richard Hayes has a chapter on 'The Way to balance your Accounts, without shutting up your Ledger'; its concluding sentence runs: ' . . . these Balance Papers are to be carefully laid up in your Escruittore or Desk, to turn to at any Time hereafter, if you should want to know how much your Estate was worth, or in what Posture your Estate lay, in any particular Year'. (*The Gentleman's Complete Book-keeper,* London, 1741, pp. 77-83). I find it hard to believe, however, that 'my' group of merchants would not at least have transferred the profit balance to the capital account in the ledger if and when they made such external calculations.

In my article in the *Economic History Review* (1949) (see note 5 above), I concluded that in early double-entry bookkeeping 'the striking of balance was performed primarily for narrow bookkeeping purposes', (I have been taken to task for this conclusion by Raymond de Roover, 'New Perspectives on the History of Accounting', *The Accounting Review,* vol. XXX, (1955), p. 414, and K. Glamann, *Dutch-Asiatic Trade, 1620-1740,* Copenhagen and The Hague, 1958, p. 252). I now prefer the formulation in the text, largely because it is generally impossible to deduce from the records (or text-book discussions) precisely what was intended and achieved by the procedures in question. In Peers' case, however, the matter is fairly unambiguous. Here the balancing occurred only at the termination of the ledger. On two earlier occasions, however, he carried an amount of profit from the profit-and-loss account to the capital account. On both occasions the detailed journal entries announce that he did not have the time to balance and close his ledger. He only found time when the bookkeeping process required that the ledger be balanced, that is, when it was full.

18 In addition to references in note 2 above, see Cooke, *op. cit.*, p. 46.

19 Glamann, *op. cit.*, p. 244: 'It (the bookkeeping system) was an adapted form of factorage bookkeeping. Externally the Company's general accounts appear as double-entry bookkeeping — there are journals, ledgers and balances in the ledgers — but actually it is not what is understood by double-entry bookkeeping today. There is no capital account, nor any effective profit-and-loss account'. See also W. M. F. Mansvelt, *Rechtsvorm en Geldelijk Beheer bij de Oost-Indische Compagnie*, Amsterdam, 1922, *passim*.

20 P. G. M. Dickson, *The Sun Fire Office, 1701-1960*, London, 1960, p. 120: '. . . A proper double-entry system of bookkeeping, which showed clearly all the assets and liabilities, was adopted for the first time (in 1890) instead of the 'cash' system which had prevailed since the Office's earliest days'.

21 Thomas R. Navin, *The Whitin Machine Works since 1831*, Cambridge, Mass., 1950, p. 150: 'The Whitin company's records were kept on a single entry, cash basis until as late as 1918 . . .'

22 R. S. Sayers, *Lloyds Bank in the History of English Banking*, Oxford, 1957, p. 273: '. . . The Capital and Counties worked on single entry . . .' until its merger with Lloyds Bank in 1918. At this time it had £60 mn. deposits and 473 offices. (*ibid.*, p. 265).

23 Ramsey, in his study of Tudor merchants' accounts writes: 'Much more distinctive is the confusion between the affairs of the business and those of its proprietor, a confusion which comes out strikingly in the treatment of expenses . . . On the other hand, the distinction between business and private affairs would have seemed meaningless to a sixteenth-century merchant, who was not accountable to anyone but himself'. (*op. cit.*, pp. 200-201).

24 With the development of professional accounting and auditing in the nineteenth century, the scope for individual variations within the double-entry framework has been much reduced.

25 For example, Sombart, *op. cit.*, p. 121; and Robertson, *op. cit.*, p. 55: 'Without a proper system of book-keeping profit could only be sporadically pursued, as opportunity offered . . . The use of exact accounts made it possible not only to know at any given time exactly how a business stood, but also to employ rational plans for extensive future operations . . .'.

26 It may be said, in passing, that the detailed records in any case served the purpose of controlling assets. The detailed sub-division of merchandise accounts, for example, provided information of the quantities of goods received and sold or otherwise disposed of, so that the owner could from his records ascertain the quantities which ought to be on hand. Voyage accounts, venture accounts and consignment accounts served the purpose of accounting for money or goods entrusted to or by ship-owners, co-venturers, principals or agents; the accounts were often kept in much detail.

Several voyage accounts in the ledger of Daniel Henchman, an American merchant of the eighteenth century, were left unbalanced (without any calculation of profits); the entries were required, for example, for the control of cargoes and for recording debts to or from the captain, rather than for providing the material for the calculation of profits. (The records are in the Hancock Papers in the Baker Library, Harvard University; cf. W. T. Baxter, *The House of Hancock*, Cambridge, Mass., 1945).

27 One may speculate whether the business man who is pre-occupied with his ledger and its various trading accounts might not be over-cautious as an entrepreneur — he is too busy counting the cost to grasp at new opportunities and to take big plunges. As I have written elsewhere, may we not ask with Sir Roger de Coverly (though not interpreting him literally): 'What can there great and noble be expected from him whose attention is for ever fixed upon balancing his books, and watching over his expenses?' (*The Spectator*, No. 174).

28 Glamann, *op. cit.*, pp. 258 *et seq.* While Glamann seems to emphasise the entrepreneurial importance of these analyses of past results, he does not explain how they could have been used to guide the Company's operations.

29 See, for example, K. H. Burley, 'Some Accounting Records of an Eighteenth-Century Clothier', *Accounting Research*, vol. 9 (1958), pp. 58-9, concerning *ad hoc* cost calculations made during a difficult period; and Richard Pares, *Yankees and Creoles*, London, 1956, pp. 139-40.

30 Entrepreneurial estimates may sometimes call for complicated calculation or arithmetical manipulation. The modern technique of linear programming is an extreme example where estimates of the results of different courses of action are derived only after a complex process of computation. For present purposes it may be noted that the application of the technique is far removed from conventional accounting or the analysis of recorded accounting results.

31 An interesting example in the Tresham papers, ca. 1600, is the comparison of an estimate of the returns on running a flock of sheep with an estimate of the returns on letting the land to a grazier (British Museum, Add. Mss. 39836, ff. 228 and 230; see also Mary E. Finch, *The Wealth of Five Northamptonshire Families, 1540-1640*, Oxford, 1956, p. 75, n. 4). For other examples, see Glamann, *op. cit.*, p. 48, n. 122, and p. 259; Raistrick, *op cit.*, pp. 237-8.

In a recent article Dr E. Stone has discussed profit calculations added to certain manorial accounts in the thirteenth and fourteenth centuries; see, 'Profit-and-Loss Accountancy at Norwich Cathedral Priory', *Transactions of the Royal Historical Society*, 5th series, vol. 12 (1962), pp. 25-48. The usual manorial account contained details of incomings and outgoings of money and, usually separately, of certain categories of goods such as grain and livestock. Its main purposes were to act as a check on the honesty of the official rendering account of his stewardship and as an aid to budgeting. The profit calculations discussed by Stone presumably served different purposes, including that of helping in the making of decisions about the way in which land might be used most profitably. Stone warns that his records may not be typical. Nevertheless, they suggest that there may be some exaggeration in Dr Bridbury's view that 'an accounting system which provided a test of solvency rather than a test of profitability' was among the things that 'conspired to shield the big landlord from having to respond fully to the clamorous opportunities of the age (the later Middle Ages).' One would doubt, in any case, whether a system of accounts could have been as important as the other circumstances referred to by Bridbury, viz., the tenurial system, the system of husbandry, and high prices. (A. R. Bridbury, *Economic Growth: England in the Later Middle Ages*, London, 1962, p. 88).

32 G. E. Fussell (ed.), *Robert Loder's Farm Accounts, 1610-1620*, Camden Third Series, vol. LIII, London, 1936.

33 For example, the following appears after one of these calculations (*ibid.*, pp. 137-8): 'Soe that for aught I canne see or perceave it is certainely my best course, to sowe more wheat & lesse barly . . .'.

34 The form of the accounting is also in marked contrast to the sophistication in

calculation demonstrated in many of the items. For example, since he was often interested in comparisons between alternatives, he included among his costs interest on his capital employed. Again, he omitted charging for the use of certain of his factors of production in particular activities when the alternative to this use would have been idleness (e.g. *ibid.*, pp. 138 and 155). In these (and other) respects his practice is superior to procedures which were to be text-book standards in cost accounting three centuries later.

Loder also charged depreciation in connection with the use of long-lived assets (e.g. *ibid.*, p. 22, '. . . I reckon my horses were the worse in the abovesaid time . . .'), thus answering Professor Mickwitz's question: 'Wie sollte man übrigens ohne doppelte Buchführung eine Amortisation buchen?' (G. Mickwitz, 'Zum Problem der Betriebsführung in der antiken Wirschaft', *Vierteljahrschrift für Sozial- und Wirtschafts-Geschichte*, vol. 32 (1939) p. 15).

35 The 'inborn' spirit in some individuals is also alluded to in the following: 'All Defoe's heroes pursue money . . .; and they pursue it very methodically according to the profit and loss book-keeping which Max Weber considered to be the distinctive technical feature of modern capitalism. Defoe's heroes, we observe, have no need to learn this technique; whatever the circumstances of their birth and education, they have it in their blood . . .' (Ian Watt, *The Rise of the Novel: Studies in Defoe, Richardson and Fielding*, London, 1957, p. 63). It may be noted that Defoe included some discussion of accounts in *The Complete English Tradesman*, but did not refer to double entry.

A. F. Upton, *Sir Arthur Ingram*, Oxford, 1961, is the biography of a highly successful seventeenth century financier. The author writes (p. 172): 'Unlike his friend Cranfield [another leading financier], who was meticulous in keeping his accounts, Ingram seems to have managed without any system of comprehensive accounting . . . The evidence suggests that he kept his accounts in his head, aided by innumerable individual calculations, often on scraps of paper, or the backs of letters . . . The exceptions are found where Ingram had to render formal accounts of public moneys which he handled, and for this purpose he did keep proper ledgers'. (I understand from Professor F. J. Fisher that Cranfield's accounts are not in full double-entry: in particular, his ledger has neither capital account nor profit-and-loss account).

The reader is also referred to Sol Tax, *Penny Capitalism: A Guatemalan Indian Economy*, Washington, 1953, in which an anthropologist describes a largely illiterate community where, to quote Adam Smith as Professor Tax does, 'Every individual is continually exerting himself to find out the most advantageous employment for whatever capital he can command'.

36 It is interesting that in some later writings Sombart emphasised the 'Spannung zwischen Rationalismus und Irrationalismus, zwischen Spekulation und Kalkulation' in the 'capitalistic spirit'. (*Die Zukunft des Kapitalismus*, Berlin, 1934, p. 8). In his earlier discussions of the role of accounting he did not seem to recognise the conflicting elements of speculation and calculation, and this may have contributed to the inflation of his claims for systematic accounting calculation. (I am indebted to Professor B. Hoselitz for this reference).

37 Bruchey, *op. cit.*, p. 120.

38 The qualification is necessary because, as pointed out earlier, the accountant may limit the categories of assets and liabilities and of transactions to be included within a set of accounts. Examples of exclusion of certain business assets are discussed in Yamey *et al., op. cit.*, pp. 181, 182-3 and 185-6; and it is well known that several fixed assets are excluded from the illustrative example of the accounts of a monastery in Angelo Pietra's *Indirizzo degli economi . . .*, Mantua, 1586, so that the recorded capital balance is negative (debit).

39 Sombart quotes, with approval, Schär's statement that double entry converts

bookkeeping into a 'zwangsläufiges System' (*op. cit.*, p. 123).
40 Cf. Alexander Macghie, *The Principles of Book-keeping Explain'd* . . . , Edinburgh, 1718: '*Fictitious or Nominal Accompts* [e.g. expenses, rents received] are such as are contriv'd on Purpose to supply the Defect of a Debitor or Creditor, in all personal or real accompts, seeing that no Accompt can alone consist of a Debitor without a Creditor, or vice versa'.
41 Cf. Raymond de Roover, 'Aux origines d'une Technique Intellectuelle', *Annales d'Histoire economique et sociale*, nos. 44-45 (1937), p. 193:
'Toutes les comptabilités examinées jusqu'ici sont tenues en partie simple. Malgré les défauts inhérents à cette méthode, les marchands du moyen âge surent adapter cet instrument imparfait aux nécessités de leurs affaires et arriver au but, même par des voies détournées. Pour résoudre les difficultés pratiques auxquelles ils se heurtaient, ils trouvèrent des solutions qui nous étonnent par leur souplesse et leur extraordinaire variété. Rien n'est donc plus erroné que la thèse de l'économiste W. Sombart qui prétend que la comptabilité des marchands médiévaux est un tel fouillis (Wirwarr) qu'il est impossible de s'y retrouver. Notre exposé prouve péremptoirement par lui-même l'inanité de cette théorie qui est pourtant à la base de la conception que Sombart se fait du marchand précapitaliste'.
Sombart, incidentally, did not imply that the owner or bookkeeper would have been lost in confusion (*op. cit.*, vol. I, p. 299).
42 See, for example, Burley, *op. cit.*, pp. 55-7.
43 Cf. Alfred Marshall, *Industry and Trade*, 3rd edition, London, 1932 (reprinted), p.366 and footnote:
'For indeed the personal observations, and the instinctive judgments on matters of detail which are within the competency of a small master "whose eye is everywhere", are chief sources of his strength. They enable him with but little effort or outlay to exercise so effective a check on sluggishness and waste, that a large business, conducted on traditional lines, cannot attain to it even by lavish expenditure. This fact was impressed on me in one of the tours which I made formerly in the manufacturing districts of England and some other countries. I may record the extreme instance of the owner of a lock factory, employing some thirty hands. I was directed to him as one whose goods were of high quality, and commanded a price somewhat above the average. His method of working without any clerks, and with but few written accounts, was instructive. His materials were all under lock; and the keys were never out of his control, except when he left them with his sister during his absence from home. He gave out to each man from time to time such material as was appropriate; and he knew without consulting books whether the man made good use of it. He knew this partly by general reasoning, and partly by observation: for in constant presence among the men, he had learnt to measure narrowly the skill, diligence, judgment and carefulness of each. He knew, without any aid from records, almost exactly what each thing produced in his factory had cost him, and therefore what rate of profits he was making on each class of his work: for, his work being all of one kind, he could frame his estimates of indirect outlay on each task by means of his knowledge of the direct outlay on it'.
See also Navin, *op cit.*, p. 158.
44 Stephen Monteage, *Debtor and Creditor made easie* . . ., London, 1682.
45 One or another of these expedients is to be found in four of the eight sets of records discussed in Yamey *et al.*, *op. cit.* referred to in note 16, above. See also evidence of adjusting entries in Denucé, *op. cit.*, pp. 125, 133, 147, 171, 172 and 175. Of the eleven balance accounts shown in de Roover, *Medici Bank*, nine reveal errors in balancing; *op. cit*,. pp. 61, 66, 98, 207, 215, 227, 246, 264, 278, 292 and 336. The corrective entries were relatively small; but this does not

exclude the possibility of larger, partly off-setting, errors in the ledgers.

46 Elva Tooker, *Nathan Trotter: Philadelphia Merchant, 1787-1853*, Cambridge, Mass., 1955, p. 199.

47 Thus William Gordon, *The Universal Accountant and complete Merchant . . .*, 5th ed., Edinburgh, 1787, pp. 15-16:

'When a merchant deals extensively, it is not to be imagined that he can spare time for keeping his own books, but he cannot be supposed to be intimately acquainted with his own affairs if he does not peruse them often. A merchant ought to know, upon all occasions what is in his power to do without embarrassing himself, and have such a general idea of his dealings, and those with whom he deals, that his speculations may be always within his sphere. Were this matter, simple as it may seem to be, sufficiently attended to, we would not see so many failures happen every day. It is want of knowledge in a man's own affairs that makes him rash and adventurous beyond his capital, or even credit, and lands him in a number of difficulties, from which nothing but great abilities, or friends, can extricate him'.

See also the interesting observations in John Locke, *Some Thoughts Concerning Education* 1692, sections 210-11.

48 Loder ended the heading of one of his occasional summaries of 'Money layd out' with the sentence: 'Written for this end that I might see my divers expenses, and soe to prevent them, as much as might be'. (Fussell, *op. cit.*, p. 70; also p. 88).

ADDENDUM

In this addendum I draw attention to various publications bearing on points made in my article, and also discuss briefly some recent contributions to the debate on the Sombart thesis.

(1) Two studies, by Grassby and Pollard, respectively, provide support for several major points in my article.[1] Parts of the discussion in Pollard's informative and profusely illustrated study are marred, however, by a failure to place particular accounting records in the setting of the purposes which they were designed to serve. Moreover, in some places far-reaching but untenable inferences about entrepreneurial motivations and behaviour are drawn from the nature of particular accounting records and practices. For example, the customary calculation of periodic profits and capital by the method of successive inventorisation is said to involve an approach which 'is very far removed from the modern concept of profit maximisation as the driving force of capitalism . . .'[2] Finally, Pollard seems to me to be wrong in implying that with different (i.e. more modern) accounting methods and practices (e.g. in the treatment of fixed assets and their systematic depreciation) his entrepreneurs would have made better management decisions.

(2) The account-book of the English farmer, Robert Loder, referred to above (p. 329) shows how difficult it is to infer a person's motivation and business attitudes from the form or

method of his accounting. In this case the entrepreneurial calculations included in the account-book reveal the profit-mindedness of the farmer. The slightly earlier account-book (1569-73) of a Dutch farmer, Rienck Hemmema, is simpler than Loder's. A detailed study of its contents by the Dutch agricultural historian, Slichter van Bath, shows that Hemmema was as 'capitalistic' as Loder in outlook and drive. In each case simplicity of accounting went with dedicated and successful endeavours to increase the profits of the business.[3]

(3) McKendrick's article on the Wedgwood records, especially of 1782, can serve as an apt illustration of the points made in my article at page 328.[4] Wedgwood's cost estimates and calculations were evidently made outside the ambit of the firm's ordinary accounts and were initiated at a time when business conditions were unfavourable.

(4) Winjum's article moderates considerably the claims made for double entry by Sombart and others, but nevertheless seems to argue that in England the use of the system had important consequences for economic growth.[5] Some aspects of his discussion are commented on here. (a) Many of Winjum's statements refer to various *capabilities* of the double-entry system, without demonstrating at all, or at all convincingly, that the English merchants of his period made use of them.[6] The reader of my article will note that a major part of it serves to show that accounting records not kept by double-entry had the same capabilities. It is of interest that in Winjum's article the only supporting references to the specific contents of surviving account-books are to ledgers which were not kept on the double-entry system.[7] (b) The statement that 'double-entry permits a separation of ownership and management, thereby promoting the growth of large joint stock companies', would have been impressive if it could have been shown that such separation could not and did not occur without double-entry. Winjum's example of the early double-entry records of the Genoese *massari*, which 'reveal just such a separation',[8] is not pertinent: the contemporaneous accounts of many similar bodies (and of other public or quasi-public corporate organisations) in other Italian cities and elsewhere were not kept by double-entry. Moreover, the separation of ownership and management had already occurred in large royal, ecclesiastical and lay estates which did not use the double-entry system or have systematic capital and income accounting. (c) Statements such as that the double-entry system or some of its features 'made the proprietor aware of his contribution to the business and his stake in the outcome of its operations'[9] imply an odd view of the knowledge, mentality and attitude of

merchants who conducted their business without the aid of double-entry accounting. (d) The statement that 'double-entry brought the concept of capital into the accounting records'[10] is incorrect if intended as an historical statement. If it means no more than that the proprietor's capital, and changes in it, are recorded in the double-entry system, it is correct but not illuminating — the proprietor's capital is included in any set of accountng records which include the results of periodic inventorisation. (e) There is no evidence for the statement that 'double entry was generally considered the fairest method in situations where diverse interests were concerned'.[11] The great majority of trading or manufacturing partnerships in Winjum's period almost certainly did not use double-entry accounting. Even in the late eighteenth and early nineteenth centuries, by which time knowledge of the double-entry system would have been widely diffused, many English partnerships did not use the system, and used the reliable method of successive inventorisation to determine the claims of the several partners.[12] In any event, the 'fairness' of accounts depends upon the integrity and reliability of the account-keeper rather than on the system he uses: no system is proof against the wiles of a fraudulent partner. (f) Winjum writes that 'Yamey, Sombart and others who have written on this topic do not specifically identify which concepts of double-entry they accept', and suggests that it is not clear whether they regarded regular calculation of income as a necessary element of the system. He claims that 'if the Sombart thesis is to receive an impartial hearing, it must be evaluated on the basis' of a definition of double-entry in which a regular income calculation is not a necessary constituent.[13] Since I include as examples of double-entry records several extant account-books which do not have regular closures, it is evident that in this respect, at least, I give the Sombart thesis an 'impartial hearing'. (g) Winjum refers to the surviving ledger (1522-1528) of Thomas Howell as if it were a double-entry account-book. However, it is evident from an examination of this ledger that it was not kept on the double-entry system: there is neither capital account nor profit-and-loss account, and there are not two entries for each of the transactions recorded. Winjum's interpretation of the statement made by Howell when he was 'called upon to state his opinion of the ill-kept books of a fellow-merchant in Andalusia'[14] is therefore not valid: since Howell did not keep his own books by double-entry, he could not have been saying something about that system and the comprehensibility to others of records kept on that system.[15] Indeed, Howell's quoted statement relates not to the *keeping* of accounts by some method or other but, rather, to the different matter of the *giving* of an account: '. . . he never sawe any accompt gevyn by any marchaunt . . . but the playnnes therof myght be easelly perceyved by every man that hath any knowledge and not to be gevyn yn suche forme as noo man can understonde yt but hym selfe orelles the marchauntes of Spayn wyll call hym noo playn marchaunt'. The rendering of a statement of his account to a debtor was referred to as the giving of an account — as in part of the title of a chapter in Ympyn's *A notable and very excellente woorke* . . . (1547): '. . . and howe to geve accomte to the debitor . . .'.

(5) A recent text-book on the economic history of Europe illustrates the confusion occasioned by the mistaken belief that the double-entry system was necessary for substantial partnerships and companies. On one page we read of the 'great trading and banking companies of Piacenza, Lucca, Siena, Pisa and above all Florence in the fourteenth and fifteenth centuries'. Of the various firms mentioned, several (e.g. the Bardi and Peruzzi) are known not to have used the double-entry system in their earlier decades (when they were already large). Yet on another page the absence of large and continuing partnerships in other parts of Europe is ascribed, by juxtapositioning, *inter alia* to the fact that double-entry book-keeping was almost unknown.[16]

(6) Kenneth Most's article includes some discussion of my criticisms of Sombart's propositions.[17] (a) It is difficult to determine what Most thinks of my criticisms. On one page we read: 'It will be apparent that we agree generally with Yamey's criticism of the Sombart propositions . . . .' Two pages later we find: 'We have failed to find much substance in Yamey's detailed criticisms of "the Sombart propositions".'[18] (b) It is difficult also to comment on a paper on the Sombart thesis in which it is said that 'it is not essential' in double-entry bookkeeping 'for each individual entry to be made twice, once on each side of an account'.[19] Sombart himself was quite explicit that the double-entry system was 'grounded' in the duality of entries.[20] Most's further elaboraton (in the same paragraph) of his view oɪ ɩhe nature of double entry is confusing and confused. (c) Most draws attention to Sombart's statement that 'double-entry did not grow out of single-entry bookkeeping, the latter being a "crippled" version of the former, and of later date'.[21] I did not refer in my article to this observation (for which there is no solid historical evidence) because it is not relevant to the Sombart thesis, and Sombart did not suggest otherwise. (d) On the question of the separation of a business from its owners, Most refers to the 'spectacle of a succession of British companies acts in the nineteenth century', which, according to him, 'is highly

suggestive, to say the least'.[22] It needs only to be pointed out, however, that these acts did not require that companies should adopt the double-entry system. The requirements on financial reporting in the legislation providing for the registration of companies with limited liability could have been met by 'incomplete' records supplemented by annual inventorisation.[23]

(7) Frederic Lane, in his book, *Venice, A Maritime Republic*, Baltimore and London, 1973, has suggested that double-entry bookkeeping was one of a number of 'improvements in commercial technique' which facilitated the 'use of resident agents instead of travelling merchants'. However, it is difficult to see how *any* system of bookkeeping was capable of allowing a merchant to keep track 'accurately of what his [absent] partners or agents were doing' (p. 140). In any event, the use of distant partners and agents was not confined to merchants who kept their accounts by double-entry (for an interesting example, see H. Thierfelder, *Rostock-Osloer Handelsbeziehungen im 16. Jahrhundert*, Weimar, 1958; and the Fuggers, with 'factories' throughout Europe, did not use double-entry); and merchants who used the double-entry system were not thereby safeguarded against the losses flowing from collaboration with inefficient, extravagant or fraudulent business associates.[24]

NOTES

1 Richard Grassby, 'The Rate of Profit in Seventeenth-Century England', *English Historical Review*, vol. 84 (1969), pp. 721-51; Sidney Pollard, *The Genesis of Modern Management*, London, 1965, chapter 6.
2 Quotation from Pollard, *ibid.*, p. 236. The added statement that 'indeed, the notion of capital as a continuous, let along autonomous, factor is virtually eliminated' invites the question what relevance such a notion has for profit-maximising business decisions. In general, the discussion of the relation between accounting records and decision-making is question-begging because there is no adequate analysis of the *nature* of the information required by the 'rational' decision-maker and the sources of information available to decision-makers in the numerous enterprises referred to in the study. It is pertinent that, according to Pollard (pp. 219-20), surviving *ex ante* estimates of costs and returns, obviously relevant for and connected with decision-making, 'would appear extremely advanced'.
3 On Hemmema, see B. H. Slichter van Bath, 'Robert Loder en Rienck Hemmema', *It Beaken*, vol. 20 (1958), pp. 89-117; and his *Een Fries Landbouw-bedrijf in de Tweede Helfte van de Zestiende Eeuw*, Agronomisch-Historische Bijdragen, vol. 4, Wageningen, 1958.
4 Neil McKendrick, 'Josiah Wedgwood and Cost Accounting in the Industrial Revolution', *Economic History Review*, vol. 23 (1970), pp. 45-67.
5 James O. Winjum, 'Accounting and the Rise of Capitalism: An Accountant's View', *Journal of Accounting Research*, vol. 9 (1971), pp. 333-50.
6 E.g. *ibid*, pp. 344, 348 and 350.

7 *Ibid.*, pp. 343-4.
8 *Ibid.*, p. 348.
9 *Ibid.*, p. 337.
10 *Ibid.*, p. 348.
11 *Ibid.*, p. 349.
12 For two examples, see R. P. Beckinsale (ed.), *The Trowbridge Woollen Industry as Illustrated by the Stock Books of John and Thomas Clark, 1804-1824,* Devizes, 1951, pp. 1 *et seq*; and B. W. Clapp, *John Owens, Manchester Merchant,* Manchester, 1965, p. 3.
13 Winjum, *op. cit.*, p. 335.
14 G. Connell-Smith, 'The Ledger of Thomas Howell', *Economic History Review,* vol. 3 (1951), p. 370.
15 Winjum, *op. cit.*, pp. 334, 348.
16 Jacques Bernard, 'Trade and Finance in the Middle Ages 900-1500', in Carlo M. Cipolla (ed.), *The Fontana Economic History of Europe,* London, 1972, vol. 1, pp. 319, 312.
  Additional examples of substantial long-term partnerships of this early period which did not use double entry are in Tito Antoni, *Il Libro dei Bilanci di una Azienda Mercantile del Trecento,* Pisa, 1967; and Florence Edler de Roover, 'Andrea Banchi, Florentine Silk Manufacturer and Merchant in the Fifteenth Century', *Studies in Medieval and Renaissance History,* vol. 3 (1966), pp. 223-85. Mrs de Roover writes (p. 236): 'To determine profits, Banchi and his partners had to go to the trouble of making a detailed inventory and then preparing a *saldo,* or general financial statement'. She observes that this process was 'more laborious' than that of 'balancing and closing the books' if these had been kept by double entry. This comparison misses the point that keeping the books on the double-entry system might itself have been laborious or difficult for many merchants, and balancing and closing them even more so. (In addition to the examples given in my article, see also J. Gavignac, *Jean Pellet: Commerçant de Gros 1694-1772,* Paris, 1967, p. 36). Moreover, partners would have insisted on a full-scale inventorisation whenever a change in the partnership was to be effected, regardless of whether their books were kept by double-entry or otherwise.
  On the question of the supposedly relative backwardness of the trading methods and arrangements of the Hanseatic (and other non-Italian) merchants in the fifteenth century, because they did not know or use (among other things) double-entry bookkeeping, see the remarks by Blockmans and Lopez in *Finances et Comptabilité du XIIIe au XVIe Siècle,* 1964, pp. 216-9. The former doubts the supremacy of the mercantile and administrative techniques of the Italians. The latter suggests that the Germans did not adopt Italian techniques because their own were good enough: inertia, not ignorance, provides the explanation for the relatively late adoption of Italian practices.
17 Kenneth S. Most, 'Sombart's Propositions Revisited', *Accounting Review,* vol. 47 (1972), pp. 722-34, especially pp. 724-8.
18 Most, *ibid.*, pp. 726, 728.
19 Most, *ibid.*, p. 727.
20 Werner Sombart, *Der Moderne Kapitalismus,* 6th edition, Munich and Leipzig, 1924, vol. 2. 1, p. 113.
21 Most, *op. cit.*, p. 726.
22 Most, *ibid.*, p. 728.
23 For the accounting provisions in the legislation, see H. C. Edey and Prot Panitpakdi, 'British Company Accounting and the Law 1844-1900', in A. C. Littleton and B. S. Yamey (eds.), *Studies in the History of Accounting,* London 1956, pp. 356-79. It is interesting to note that while the non-mandatory model

articles of association of the 1856 act specified that 'accounts shall be kept, upon the principle of double-entry', this provision was dropped in the consolidating act of 1862, and not reinstated in the next revision.
    Ibid., pp. 362, 368.

24 Two of the matters noted briefly in this Addendum — those in paragraphs 4 (g) and 7 — are discussed more fully in my forthcoming 'Notes on Double-Entry Bookkeeping and Economic Progress' in *Journal of European Economic History.*

17

Early Cost Accounting for Internal Management Control: Lyman Mills in the 1850s†

H. Thomas Johnson*

Very little research has been undertaken in the accounting records of industrial firms during the period 1840 to 1890 when manufacturing cost accounting emerged as a specialised tool of management control. Several useful and interesting theses regarding the evolution of cost accounting practice have been suggested by business and accounting historians; generally speaking, such theses are rooted in the study of published sources. Alfred D. Chandler, Jr., for example, has indicated that the small-sized, functionally unspecialised firms typical of American business around 1840 were served adequately by the double-entry mercantile bookkeeping procedures introduced almost 550 years earlier. Such firms did not require the statistical data and the cost accounting methods familiar in the modern enterprise. Chandler has concluded that the need for modern cost accounting arose only after 1850 in railroads and after 1870 in steel, chemical, and metal working industries where oligopolistic markets, complex production processes, and problems of large scale organisation combined to create a high degree of uncertainty and risk. Firms in these industries needed reliable cost data to determine prices, to assess the results of operations and to evaluate capital-intensive technological innovations.[1] Accounting historians who focus on the more specialised, narrow issue of bookkeeping methods similarly argue that modern

*From *Business History Review*, vol. XLVI, No. 4 (Winter 1972), pp. 466-74. Reprinted by permission of the editor of *Business History Review* and the author.

†The Research upon which this paper is based was financed by the Canada Council (research grant S69-1548) — the help thus received is gratefully acknowledged. I wish to thank also Mrs Eleanor Bishop and Mr Robert Lovett for assistance with the textile company records at Harvard's Baker Library; Professors Kevin H. Burley, Alfred D. Chandler, Jr., and Basil Yamey for their advice in the preparation of this article; and Dr Elaine Bowe Johnson for editorial advice.

cost accounting practice did not evolve before the late nineteenth century. They point out that ordinary mercantile double-entry bookkeeping methods were adequate for the external nominal and financial transactions of merchants and traders. These methods did not, however, supply manufacturing firms with data on the results of internal 'transactions' involving the transformation of raw inputs into finished and semi-finished goods. Consequently, many early industrialists estimated manufacturing costs on an *ad hoc* basis, using records and scattered memos that did not form an integral part of the firm's double-entry bookkeeping system. The complete integration of cost and commercial accounts that characterises modern cost accounting could not be achieved until accountants learned how to handle, in the double-entry form, nonpersonal and manipulative transactions (e.g., transferring materials from one process to another and allocating overhead).[2] Progress in the development of the technique was slow. Most accounting historians cite as the earliest example of complete integration of cost and financial accounts in a double-entry system, an accounting text published in 1887.[3]

Clearly the integration of cost and financial records was necessary to the development of modern cost accounting as an important tool of management control. Indeed, one accounting historian has described the transition from mercantile accounting to manufacturing accounting 'as an achievement second only to the original development of bookkeeping according to double-entry principles'. He states further that the adoption of modern cost systems in industrial practices marked 'the expansion of book-keeping (a record) into accounting (a managerial instrument of precision).'[4] It is unfortunate, therefore, that scholars appear not to have given more attention to the needs of industrial cost accounting. In his classic study of accounting history published in 1933, A. C. Littleton noted the paucity of literature published between 1820 and 1885 on cost accounting.[5] S. Paul Garner, commenting over twenty years later on this dearth of studies, also noted that historians interested in the evolution of cost accounting practice have done very little research in nineteenth-century company records. Indeed, it seems that all of the company studies and business histories which have appeared since the early 1930s omit discussion of how industrial firms adapted mercantile bookkeeping to the needs of modern industrial accounting.[6] This gap in the literature of accounting history can be partially bridged, however, by research in the accounting records of nineteenth-century industrial firms. Although such records are scarce, an examination of those available sheds considerable light on manufacturing accounting practice during a period hitherto ignored by accounting historians.

One excellent illustration of an advanced cost accounting system in use before 1860 is provided in the papers of the Lyman Mills Corporation, a cotton textile firm incorporated in Boston in 1854.[7] During the nineteenth century the company maintained its head office in Boston, operated several waterpowered cotton mills along the Connecticut River in Holyoke and sold its finished goods through a commission agent in New York. It is of course conceivable that Lyman Mills was in advance of its competitors in developing a relatively sophisticated cost accounting system at this time. All the available evidence suggests, however, that Lyman Mills was a 'typical' firm in the New England cotton textile industry from the viewpoint of manufacturing, output, marketing, and its switch to 'fine' varieties of fabric after the Civil War.[8] This is to suggest the possibility that Lyman Mills' records examined in the following pages may not be unique and that further research in the records which exist at Harvard's Baker Library and other archives may yield comparable results.

The importance of Lyman Mills' records is twofold. First, they contain the earliest example discovered to date of a completely integrated double-entry cost accounting system and suggest that such a system may have been used widely, long before historians had supposed. Secondly, although Lyman Mills falls outside the oligopolistic type of enterprise which Alfred Chandler links with the emergence of modern cost accounting, we nevertheless find a price-taking enterprise such as Lyman Mills (possibly also its many competitors) adopting what appear to be similar accounting practices. It is platitudinous to reiterate the differences between a textile firm situated in a highly competitive market in an industry with relatively stable technology and organisational patterns and the oligopolists which Chandler says introduced the modern practice of cost accounting. Our primary objective in the following pages is to examine the cost accounting system in use in Lyman Mills after 1856. Secondly, it is our aim to suggest that cost accounting had a function in the middle of the nineteenth century which differs from that linked by Chandler with 'big business'.

The basic accounting records of Lyman Mills date from 1856. These include a double-entry general ledger and sub-ledgers which were kept by the treasurer at the home office in Boston, as well as a double-entry factory ledger with related inventory, payroll, and production sub-ledgers which were kept by the mill agent in Holyoke. Reciprocal entries in the home office and factory ledgers were kept current by means of daily correspondence between the treasurer and the agent. The Holyoke factory ledger includes accounts for current assets, current liabilities, and all operating expenses. The factory ledger also includes two accounts (referred to as 'mill' accounts) which resemble modern work-in-process control accounts. One of the mill accounts was charged with manufacturing costs related to coarse goods production and the other mill account was charged with manufacturing costs related to fine goods production. The Boston general ledger includes not only all the accounts kept in the Holyoke factory ledger, but also additional accounts for plant and equipment, capital stock, long-term liabilities, and profit and loss. Sales and non-manufacturing expense figures were entered only in the general ledger, where they appear in the two mill accounts. Every six months, the books were closed to determine profit and loss.[9]

The two mill accounts were the keystone that supported 'the manufacturing cost system in Lyman's books. Every accounting period, each mill account, one for coarse goods and the other for fine goods, was charged with its respective share of cotton, factory labor, and factory overhead expense. These charges to the mill accounts were transferred from separate control accounts for cotton, payroll, and overhead. For cotton, the largest single item of expense, the mill accounts were charged at the end of a six-month accounting period with the cost of raw material that had been used in production through the weaving stage. 'Cost' was based on the contract price of cotton, including freight and insurance charges, and was calculated semi-annually (after inventory-taking) on a first-in, first-out basis.[10] Payroll charges were distributed to the mill accounts monthly in accordance with a daily record from each mill that shows employee hours for every process (e.g., picking, carding, spinning, warp weaving, weaving, etc.).[11] Factory overhead was distributed to each mill account semi-annually according to several criteria such as floor area, number of looms, and the rated house power of water turbines.[12]

The treatment given to unexpired costs in work in process was more sophisticated in the case of cotton than in the case of factory payroll or overhead. In other words, the cost of cotton that was purchased but was either still in transit, or in bales, or in process up to the weaving stage was charged to inventory and not to current manufacturing expense. The entire amount expended each period on manufacturing payroll and factory overhead, however, was charged to the mill accounts, although a portion of those expenses should have been allocated to work in process. This failure to charge unexpired factory labour and overhead costs to inventory naturally caused profits to be understated in one period and correspondingly overstated in the next. Since the amount of work in process to which these unexpired costs would have been assigned did not change much from one period to another, the net distortion between years because of this practice would have been small. The combined amount of factory labour and overhead was, moreover, a much smaller part of total manufacturing cost than the cost of cotton, which was accounted for properly. The total producion cost charged to the mill accounts each period aproximates quite closely, therefore, the amount designated as 'cost of goods manufactured' in modern manufacturing accounting systems.[13]

Although the amounts charged to the respective mill accounts for cotton, factory labour, and factory overhead are identical in the general ledger and the factory ledger, only the mill accounts in the factory ledger resemble modern work-in-process control accounts. Unlike work-in-process accounts, the Lyman general ledger's mill accounts contain entries for non-manufacturing expenses and sales in addition to entries for manufacturing expenses. Consequently, the mill accounts in the general ledger resemble those early nineteenth-century trading accounts which Littleton and other authorities describe as the 'bridge' between mercantile bookkeeping and modern cost accounting.[14] These accounts provide profit and loss data useful in determining the semi-annual dividend to shareholders, but they do not serve management needs by providing direct information on manufacturing costs. The mill accounts in the factory ledger, however, are charged only with manufacturing expenses and therefore give direct data on production costs as a regular part of the double-entry bookkeeping cycle.

It is notable that regular reports summarising the data from these various cost accounts provided Lyman Mills' management with useful information of production costs. One kind of report, a 'cost of manufacturing statement' which gave a *pro forma* summary of labour, cotton, and overhead charges, was prepared from each mill account every six months.[15] These reports include: labour cost incurred in picking and carding, spinning, warping, and weaving; the cost of cotton used in manufactured goods; and manufacturing overhead charges. The sub-totals for each of these three classes of expense, as well as the total of all expenses combined, agree with the amounts charged to the respective factory ledger mill account. These semi-annual statements on the cost of manufacturing give a detailed breakdown of the items in overhead cost, such as starch, fuel, supplies and teaming. They include, furthermore, data on the cost per pound and per yard of output for each major item of expense. Lyman's accountants also prepared *monthly* cost of manufacturing statements which include all the same data as the semi-annual statements, except that the breakdown of overhead costs is not given.[16] These accountants obtained monthly information on actual labour costs from payroll sub-ledgers. They could not ascertain actual cotton and overhead costs, of course, until physical inventories were taken; normally physical inventory occurred every six months. The total cotton and overhead costs included in the monthly manufacturing statements were therefore calculated by applying estimated costs per pound to the number of pounds of goods manufactured during the month. Figures indicating the pounds of goods manufactured could be obtained from mill production records, and the figures on cotton and overhead cost per pound were taken from the latest semi-annual cost of manufacturing statement. If one makes the reasonable assumption that cotton prices and overhead rates did not change much during most six month periods, then one may conclude that, without having to take physical inventories, Lyman Mills had useful estimates of total manufacturing costs at monthly intervals. Indeed, the monthly cost statements augmented Lyman's regular book-keeping system by providing reliable aggregate data on production cost more promptly that the factory ledger itself.

In addition to producing these aggregate cost data, Lyman Mills also produced periodic information on the unit cost of each cloth style which it manufactured. Although actual unit cost calculations before 1886 are not found in the documents that now remain, the raw data needed to estimate product costs appear in the company's records as early as 1875.[17] Basically, unit cost was based on the average weight of the yarn in each style of cloth that was manufactured. The weight of yarn that was manufactured was readily available in daily production records. The main problem in costing was to determine the cotton, labour, and overhead expense per pound of yarn. It was very easy to determine the cost of cotton, the most important element of cost, since it was accounted for on a cost per pound basis. It was more difficult, however, to allocate labour and overhead expense among the various styles. Basically, the average labour and overhead cost per hank of yarn was calculated every six months; that average cost was multiplied by the number of hanks per pound in each style to get an estimate of the labour and overhead cost per pound.[18] These calculations enabled the company to estimate total cost per pound for each style produced every six months. It was a simple matter to convert the cost per pound figures to cost per yard. The mechanical accuracy of these unit cost calculations was checked by multiplying the estimated unit cost per pound figures by the total pounds of each style produced every six months to arrive at an estimate of the total cost of goods manufactured. The last figure was then compared with the total cost recorded in the plant ledger mill accounts. The difference was never very great, usually less than 3 per cent of total cost in the mill accounts.[19] These product cost statistics, calculated semi-annually at Lyman Mills at least as far back as 1886, are probably less accurate than those one might get from a modern textile mill's process cost accounting system; however, they gave a reasonable idea of relative cost differences between styles and of charges over time in unit costs.

Clearly, the various cost statements described above were superior to the *ad hoc* memos usually pictured as typical of early nineteenth-century 'cost accounting'. The data in Lyman's statements were drawn directly from the company's ordinary double-entry books of account and provided systematic and reliable information on the company's manufacturing operations. Although the statements do not deal with some items of expense, notably depreciation and unexpired conversion costs, in a manner which we would consider appropriate today, certainly these technical shortcomings should not obscure the remarkable efficiency of Lyman's total cost system. Although Lyman's definition of profit and loss does not correspond exactly to the modern concept, the profit and loss figure in Lyman's general ledger was, nevertheless, tied in to the manufacturing cost data in the factory ledger mill accounts. Such a 'tie-in' permitted the management frequent and useful analysis of manufacturing costs and profits.

In conclusion, let us turn to the use made by Lyman Mills of their relatively sophisticated cost accounting system. The evidence provided by the available records gives no indication whatsoever that Lyman Mills used the data thus obtained in the way or for the reasons suggested by Alfred Chandler for the large-scale enterprises which he studied. In other words, Lyman Mills did *not* use cost accounting to evaluate production decisions or to determine the costs and benefits of technological innovation. Indeed, the firm's book values for net investment do not permit meaningful measures of overall rate of return, since capital investments were charged to surplus as rapidly as possible. Nor is there any indication that Lyman's management ever considered calculating return on investment. Similarly, there is no evidence to suggest that they used their unit cost statistics to assess output levels of various styles in the face of changing market prices. As with most textile firms of the period, Lyman's management focused its attention inwards on the shop, and not outwards on the industry. All the evidence examined points to the conclusion that Lyman used its elaborate cost system to facilitate control of internal plant operations: for example, to assess the physical productivity of mill operatives; to assess the impact on operations of changes in plant layout; and to control the receipt and use of raw cotton.[20] Although used primarily to rationalise internal control, Lyman's cost accounting procedure antedates by thirty years a system which until now accounting historians have regarded as the earliest example of a completely integrated double-entry cost accounting format.

NOTES

1 Professor Chandler's comments on the emergence of cost accounting are found in his following works: *Strategy and Structure* (Garden City, N.Y., 1966), 174-185; *The Railroads: The Nation's First Big Business* (New York, 1965), 98-100; *Pierre S. du Pont and the Making of the Modern Corporation*, co-author Stephen Salsbury (New York, 1971), 128-135; 'The United States: Evolution of Enterprise' (unpublished ms., September 30, 1970), secs. II and III.

2 Notable examples of the extensive literature on this issue written by accounting historians are: A. C. Littleton, *Evolution of Accounting to 1900* (New York, 1933), chs. 20 and 21; David Solomons, 'The Historical Development of Costing', in D. Solomons, ed., *Studies in Costing* (London, 1952), 1-36; and S. Paul Garner, *Evolution of Cost Accounting to 1925* (University, Ala. 1954), ch. 2. The orthodox view on cost accounting in the mid-nineteenth century was stated succinctly by Paul Garner in his article, 'Highlights in the Development of Cost Accounting', in Michael Chatfield, ed., *Contemporary Studies in the Evolution of Accounting Thought* (Belmont, Calif., 1968), 216-17: 'During the decades 1820-1880 little can be found which is of interest in the development of cost accounting . . . The absence of striking innovations is rather peculiar, since many lines of industry were rapidly gaining headway . . . It is likely that most manufacturing firms simply modified the then familiar trading account to take care of the factory charges. The ordinary goal was, therefore, the derivation of an interim profit figure rather than the cost of production. Almost no firms had worked out the details of how to show the product flowing from one account to the other on the general ledger'. The cost records of Lyman Mills which are described herein present a considerably different view of mid-nineteenth century cost accounting than the view which Garner outlines.

3 The text is Emil Garcke and J. M. Fells, *Factory Accounts* (London, 1887). Garcke and Fells' cost system is described in Littleton, *Evolution of Accounting*, 348-353. Paul Garner states that the Garcke and Fells book 'probably had more to do with the advancement of cost accounting practices than any other book ever published. One of its most striking features was the procedure for integrating the costing with the financial accounting. This matter had either been ignored, or vaguely mentioned, by previous authorities'. See Garner, 'Highlights', 217-18.

4 Littleton, *Evolution of Accounting*, 359-360.

5 *Ibid.*, 350.

6 Garner, *Evolution of Cost Accounting*, 76-90.

7 These records, housed in Baker Library at the Harvard Graduate School of Business Administration, are described in Robert W. Lovett and Eleanor C. Bishop, *List of Business Manuscripts in Baker Library* (Boston, 1969), 38. In the

following notes, these records are referred to as 'Lyman Collection', with the Baker Library manuscript index reference given.

8 For historical information on the company's operations see Lyman Collection, A-2 (inside front cover) and Constance M. Green, *Holyoke, Massachusetts : A Study of the Industrial Revolution in America* (New Haven, Conn., 1930).

9 Lyman Collection, CA (general ledger) and CB (factory ledger).

10 In some years, particularly after 1887, the balances in the general ledger cotton accounts were written down to market when market values fell below original cost. These write-downs were charged against profits in the general ledger in the year affected, but were not recorded in the factory ledger.

11 Lyman Collection, LC and LT.

12 Lyman Collection, AM (overhead distribution sheets in the semi-annual accounts). Depreciation of manufacturing plant and equipment does not follow modern practice. Expenditures for plant, equipment and major renovations were generally charged to profit and loss in the general ledger in the year they were incurred. Such charges were not entered in the factory ledger and therefore did not affect the data in the company's cost of manufacturing statements (see below). Ordinary repair costs, however, were included in the overhead expense total.

13 Additional information on the transactions in these mill accounts will be supplied to interested readers on request.

14 Littleton, *Evolution of Accounting*, 325.

15 Lyman Collection, MAE (semi-annual).

16 Lyman Collection, MAE (monthly).

17 Lyman Collection, MAF (1886) and MAH-1 (1875). This method of estimating unit costs probably was not described in published sources before the late 1890's. See, for example, William G. Nichols, *Methods of Cost Finding in Cotton Mills* (Waltham, Mass., 1899), 8-18; and James G. Hill, 'Various Systems of Computing the Costs of Manufacture,' *Transactions of the New England Cotton Manufacturers' Association*, 67 (October 5-6, 1899), 132-37.

18 One hank equals 840 yards of yarn.

19 Lyman Collection, MAF.

20 Lyman Collection, PA and PB. For example, see letters from the treasurer to the agent dated December 8, 1884, February 4, 1885, February 19, 1885, May 23, 1885, November 13, 1885, and April 7, 1886 (PB-14 and 15).

18

An Early Victorian
Business Forecaster
in the Woollen Industry [1]

Herbert Heaton*

The two decades following Waterloo witnessed a marked expansion in size and improvement in quality of the provincial newspaper. The economic historian finds little material, except among the advertisements, in the columns of the small four-paged weeklies of the eighteenth century: a strike, a food riot, or an onslaught on machines might merit a place on page three, and a brief list of market prices might be tucked away under the obituary notices: but the greater part of the news was collected, with the aid of a pair of scissors and a pot of paste, from the London journals. After Waterloo economic distress and discontent simply had to be noticed and studied; the number and circulation of papers increased, news-sheets grew larger, and in the growing space devoted to local news, notes about the state of industry, trade, transport, and prices found a place. By the accession of Victoria the leading provincial journals were giving a lot of attention to business annals and analysis, and at least one of them, the *Leeds Mercury*, was employing a textile expert who made his monthly report on the woollen industry a peg on which to hang long, elaborate, carefully reasoned forecasts. For nine years —1835 to 1844 — he described, dissected, and prophesied; and an "evaluation" of his "service" would reveal a score at least as high as that obtained by any branch of Delphic Oracles (Incorporated) during the last decade.

Since at least 1815 the *Mercury*, which was probably the largest provincial paper both in size and circulation, had been printing weekly reports and comments on the state of the cloth market. It had correspondents in all the leading towns and villages, it made special inquiries at times, and the public activities of its proprietor, Edward Baines, brought him in touch with men who could give

*From *Economic History*, Vol. 2 (Jan. 1933), pp. 553-74. Reprinted by permission of the editors of the *Economic Journal* and *The Royal Economic Society*.

inside information. Naturally the news was fullest when trade was bad, and as Baines served on every committee for the relief of the unemployed he searched diligently for signs of recovery. In dark days he sought to cheer his readers with promises of better times just round the corner. When the panic of late 1825 was gathering intensity he reminded them that in the commercial as in the natural world there is a self-adjusting principle. The country has a sound stamina and will be brought back to a rational and desirable state.[2] When the crash had come and most of the local private banks were failing he asked, 'Have we less real wealth than six months ago? Is our land diminished, have we less skill, industry, and talent now than we had then?' Our credit machinery has been damaged, and speculation has claimed its victims, 'but the fundamentals are sound, and 1827 may be as bright as was 1825.'[3] A month later he presented a list of 'symptoms of returning prosperity,'[4] and in September 1826 asserted that trade was gradually reviving, stocks of manufactured goods were low, many more workmen were employed, and 'though we are not yet arrived at prosperity we are advancing towards it with sure and perceptible progress.'[5]

In bright days Baines strove to warn his readers and put out storm signals. In late 1824 he deprecated the 'symptoms of railway madness and speculation' which were filling columns of his paper with notices of company promotions.[6] In early 1825 he reminded those who were tempted to invest in Mexican and South American mines that 'there is a saying in Chile that if a man discover a silver mine he is in great danger of losing his property, and if he find a gold mine he is sure to be ruined.'[7] Beware of prospectuses: 'the arts of stock-jobbing are little understood by the people of London and still less in the country.' 'Impudent frauds, plausible schemes' are afoot: 'innumerable and inconceivable are the tricks:' all is not gold that glitters. He urged the London papers to sift the schemes daily brought before the public,[8] and when they ignored his request scolded them for having 'preserved a remarkable silence' until the mining boom had burst. He blessed the suggestion that a portion of the money collected for each company be put into a separate fund with which to erect a new hospital near Bedlam for the reception of 'those who may sink under the Mining Malady.'[9] When the boom burst he could say 'I told you so,' and regret that 'within the last twelve months one portion of the British public has exhibited a degree of knavery and another a degree of gullibility altogether unparalleled even in the disastrous period of the South Sea mania.'[10]

In Baines' opinion, it was all the more important that the Press should guide and warn its readers, since the State could not and should not attempt to intervene. His *laissez-faire* views were well expressed when in February 1825 the King's Bench ruled that a bank was illegal under the Bubble Act of 1720, and the Lord Chancellor announced that the Government intended to enforce that Act to check the rising tide of company promotion. 'We are extremely jealous of legislative interference to regulate commerical or pecuniary transactions,' said Baines. 'It is certainly desirable to check the rage for speculation, but we much question if any good can be done by acts of parliament. The excesses of speculation soon correct themselves. If men ought to be free in anything, especially in a commercial country, they should be free in the employment of their own money. If there is anything in which they will be cautious, they will be cautious in that. Commercial enterprise is a subject utterly unfit for parliamentary regulations. Proteuslike, it assumes a thousand forms, wields a proboscis of tremendous strength or picks up grain by grain with the most feeble instruments. At one time it flies like an eagle, at another it creeps like a tortoise. In some cases it bears down opposing interests by bulk of capital, in others it insinuates itself with serpentine tortuosity into the chambers of wealth. Yet all these may be honest and legitimate modes of obtaining riches, beneficial both to individuals and to the public. They render it very difficult to impose fetters on this spririt, and show that it ought not to be attempted.'[11]

Trade reports were not always welcomed by the trade. If Baines said business was bad, buyers of wool, cloth, or labour quoted him in support of their demand for lower prices, and thus he offended every seller; if he said trade was improving the sellers demanded more and the buyers were cross; but in either situation the editor was blamed, urged to keep his finger out of the market pie, and even informed that his statements were wrong. In mock despair he finally suggested that he should allot a special part of his columns to each class — buyer, seller, woolstapler, clothier, merchant, wage-earner, and farmer — and warn each class to read only the section printed for its information and guidance.[12] But he could not always turn the tables with a jest, and when in July 1829 he reported that the manufacturers of Leeds were 'tolerably well employed,' some two thousand unemployed men assembled quietly outside the newspaper office and invited Baines to look out of his window.[13] At meetings of the unemployed in that year it was often stated that men who sought work outside Leeds were being advised to go to Leeds, for there work was abundant — Baines says so.[14] And for a brief silly season the endless fight between the Whig *Mercury* and the Tory *Intelligencer* degenerated into a debate on

the topic 'Is trade improving?' — a debate which ended only when
Baines published the results of a questionnaire sent to all the
leading factories.[15]

From the slough of 1826 the textile industry slowly crept. In
some years it advanced three paces and then slipped back two; but
from 1832 recovery was rapid. Between 1832 and 1836 the building
of factories, the construction of machinery, the consumption of
wool, and the influx of population went on at an unprecedented
pace, and Baines therefore decided to supplement his weekly
reports with a monthly survey, the first of which dealt with March
1835, the last with March 1844.[16]

The writer of these reports remains anonymous throughout — so
let us call him Mercurius — but internal evidence reveals his
fitness for the task. He had been actively engaged in the trade for
at least twenty years; his memory went back to the Napoleonic
Decrees, the Orders in Council, the large orders for army cloths in
1813, and the collapse of demand after Waterloo. He knew every
detail of the industry's structure and operation, he was as familiar
with the domestic clothiers as with the factory-owners, and he
frequented cloth halls, woolstaplers' offices, and merchants'
warehouses. He had on his shelves the various blue books dealing
with wool and woollens; he read the *Farmer's Magazine* and
received the monthly letters on business conditions which were now
being sent out by mercantile houses in London, Liverpool, and
Manchester. He was a free trader, a pacifist, and he disliked the
Bank of England, the trade unions, and the agitators for a ten-hour
day.

His final qualification was an ability to translate the language of
the textile area. He knew well the incurable habits of under-
statement in days of prosperity and of over-statement in times of
adversity. He had met men who, after ordering a new phaeton, a
pair of thoroughbred carriage horses, and a gross of port, would go
to market and declare loudly that they were on the brink of
bankruptcy and that the whole industry was on the edge of ruin.
Hence in one of his earliest reports[17] he met the 'usual complaint'
that cloth prices were bad with the comment that the complaint
was 'as old as the trade and as incurable as the unreasonableness
of human expectations': it is 'at all times to be regarded with some
suspicion, and especially when a fair business is doing. It is quite
true that the percentage of profit is small, but it is equally true that
the return on a given capital is much larger than formerly,
payments are much quicker, and the risk is much diminished.' In
1843, when trade was recovering rapidly, he again discounted the
lamentations of the grumblers. 'Of course the lowness of profit is

complained of, which means, rightly interpreted, that the dealer measures the ratio of profit by his own wishes rather than by a law which regards neither wishes nor calculations. We may safely infer that the rate of profit under present circumstances is natural and adequate, though it may be less than tradesmen would like.'[18] Still the old trader found it hard to break the habits of a lifetime, and in July 1843, when dealing with the declining demand for fine and superfine cloths[19] he remarked, 'The fine cloth trade hardly demands notice except to mark the stages of its extinction.'[20] Since such cloths were still being produced and sold, critics accused Mercurius of exaggeration. To this he replied, 'It is true that when we spoke of the stages of extinction we used somewhat hyperbolical language, as do those who declare 'There is no business doing' in dull times. We only claim to be allowed to use our mother tongue as freely as our neighbours, and to have extended to our words and phrases the customary latitude of interpretation.'[21]

Mercurius recognised that in trying to make forecasts he was shouldering a heavy responsibility. 'If our report were confined to a simple statement of the extent and character of the month's transactions, leaving out all inquiry as to the causes of activity on the one hand or of languor on the other, and foregoing all speculation or all calculation as to the future prospects of the trade, our task would be easy and our responsibility light. We have, however, undertaken a more onerous duty than that of mere chroniclers, and we suppose we must pay the penalty of our presumption in occasionally feeling great difficulty in arriving at correct opinions as to the cause or causes of the particular conditions of trade which we have to recall, besides laying ourselves under to light weight of responsibility in hazarding speculations as to the future which may, even in a limited measure, affect mercantile interests. We are not indeed weak enough to think that our monthly lucubrations determine whether sales are to be profitable or not, but we are aware that the public mind is highly sensitive and that even crude and fallacious reasoning or incorrect statements, promulgated with all the weight and dignity of editorial style, under the formality and high pretence of a monthly report, have some influence on the views and conduct of the tradesman, and add somewhat of force to the influences which, whether for good or ill, bear on the body commercial. Our consolation is that we endeavour rather to furnish materials from which to form correct opinions than to force our opinions on the credence of our readers, that we address men more competent than ourselves to deduce just conclusions, and, indeed, that our opinion after all is only taken at its intrinsic value, for what it is worth.'[22]

The years covered by the reports included the boom of 1835-6, the crash of 1836, the partial recovery of 1837-8, and the long, dark days that stretched from 1839 to 1842 or even 1843. In such a period Mercurius is sometimes baffled by the way in which trade disobeys the rules of the game, as, for instance, in July 1835, when the supply of wool and cloth is 'abundant' and buyers are few, yet price does not decline. Sometimes he refuses to predict for lack of material capable of interpretation. 'We frankly confess,' he wrote in May 1837, 'that we do not see our way through the present embarrassments of the woollen trade.' Sometimes the outlook is so black that he has no heart to depict the troubles he sees ahead: 'There is little to record that is good, and little to predict that is encouraging.'[23] But usually he faces his task with courage, analyses the present and the recent past, and projects his graphs into the future.

What were the factors that determined those projections? Mercurius had two large handfuls of them; one lot of forces meant prosperity, the other caused depression, but when both hands were at work simultaneously, a skilful discussion of the conflict of influences was necessary before one could decide whether, for instance, the spring demand would be good or the American fall purchases would be low. At least one forecast was easy: trade in the short run, whether in good times or bad, fluctuated according to the season of the year. The two high spots were the spring and autumn demands. The year began very quietly: bad weather made the movement of raw materials and cloth difficult, and prevented warps and pieces from being dried out of doors. Internal communication in Yorkshire's two great markets — Germany and the United States — was almost at a standstill. Production of cloth was therefore small; the domestic manufacturer went slow, unless he could afford to let his pieces pile up in the cloth hall awaiting a buyer or was convinced that the spring trade would be brisk. In late February the market began to come to life: mechants started filling their orders, the East India Company or its successors placed large contracts for the Oriental market, and German buyers trickled in. Through March, April, and early May demand was brisk, and overtime might be general in domestic workshop, factory, and finishing mill. But when May ended so did the seasonal boom, and June was 'flat.' 'The paucity of buyers of finished goods and the slackness of orders from the country throw a damp on the spirits of the merchants in their dealings with the clothiers. This again cramps the operations of the small clothiers, many of whom are obliged to discontinue manufacturing when their goods accumulate in the halls.'[24] The rural producer therefore turned to his farming work, while many weavers went hay-making and often stopped to harvest, returning to find the autumn demand gathering strength. In July the wholesale buyers began to come into the market; in August the country retailers, having weighed the prospects for the harvest in their districts, came to replenish their stocks; the new season's clip was now in the hands of the woolstaplers, and its price was known. From August to October the market was therefore busy, but with November, 'always the black month in the merchant's calendar,' all was quiet once more, except for visits by London buyers who came to pick up surplus stock in job lots at bargain prices. So the year ended as it had begun.

If production was to be maintained during the summer and winter months of low demand, one must have confidence that the buyers would come in fall or spring, and one must also have capital or credit with which to carry on work and accumulate stock till they came. A forecaster's chief task was therefore that of weighing the evidence on which that confidence should rest or vanish; but he could give little aid to the small producers who sold in the open market and whose reserves would not allow them to work for more than a month without a buyer. Hence he welcomed two tendencies which were rapidly destroying the open market; these were the production of cloths in accordance with orders given by merchants, and the union of manufacturer and merchant in the same person. Both tendencies were at least a century old; there probably never had been a time when all cloths went to the public market, and since at least 1790 merchants had been turning manufacturer, or manufacturers had been stepping into the mercantile class. But both developments had now gained such strength that they were threatening to kill the public market. More important still, they were reducing the extent of the seasonal variations, for 'when the prospect for the autumn trade is good the [merchant-manu-facturers] are generally as fully employed in June and July as any other part of the year, their extensive capital enabling them to accumulate stock in those months for the extra consumption of August, September, and October.'[25]

The second factor controlling trade prospects was the price of wool. Certain simple truths were self-evident. Cheap wool helped trade, dear wool meant costly cloth and therefore injured demand, especially for low-grade woollens and worsteds, for the latter especially competed with linens and cottons and became unsaleable when they were dear unless cotton prices had advanced along with those of wool. But more serious than high price was violent fluctuation in price. A little extra demand over and above the supply 'always makes a great noise in the trade,' and if a sudden rush of orders sent all the manufacturers to the woolstapler clamouring for supplies of raw material, then prices rose far and rapidly. 'Wool is a raw material perhaps more sensitive to variations in the demand than any other. Its quantity can neither be readily diminished nor increased. Great variations in the demand act powerfully in depressing or elevating the price, just as [price] variations act in the way of a large diminution or a large increase of demand for it.'[26] The general outlook for the wool year was determined by the prices paid by English and continental buyers at the wool fairs of Breslau, Stettin, Berlin, Buda Pesth, etc., in late May and early June, at the English fairs which were held during the next two months, and at the auction sales of Australian and other wools in London and Liverpool. But in addition, staplers went round the wool country before the sales and tried to buy supplies, and big manufacturers annoyed the stapler by competing with him both in the farm-yard and the auction room. Even when the textile world knew the price level for the year's sales in bulk, it did not know the probable retail price until the character of the spring and fall demands was apparent. Hence uncertainty as to price movements 'paralyses manufacturing operations betwixt the seasons of principal demand and induces anxious and almost breathless haste during most seasons. Unequal and irregular vibrations in the price of wool and woollens makes the balance of profit and loss almost as little a matter of accurate calculation as the throw of a dicer's box.[27] Violent price movements strained the internal structure of an industry in which wool-stapler, clothier, worsted spinner, worsted manufacturer, and cloth merchant were alternately buyer and seller.

This internal strain was felt in three ways. In the first place, in a period of rising prices the woolstapler demanded more from the clothier; but when the latter tried to recoup himself by passing on the increase to the cloth merchant the merchant resisted stoutly, pointing to the price he had been instructed to pay by his home or foreign clients, and arguing that the ultimate consumer would not pay the price. In the worsted trade the situation was one stage worse, for there the stapler sold wool to the spinner, who sold yarn to the manufacturer, who sold cloth to the merchant, thus giving an additional opportunity for a battle of stubborn men; in fact the most bitter tug-of-war in the whole industry was that between worsted spinners and manufacturers. It was hard work budging staplers and merchants from their posts; experience had taught Mercurius that 'cloth follows the advance on wool slowly and with difficulty; but it falls with wool and often in a greater ratio than the fall in the price of wool warrants.'[28] It had also taught him to sympathise with the merchant's plea, for when coarse woollens reached a comparatively high price their consumption fell heavily and other fabrics took their place.[29] But while the conflict in the market lasted, trading came to a standstill and production dried up. The merchant always assured the manufacturers that wool would soon fall in price, and they could therefore afford to sell at his price; but this information came to be regarded as a new translation of 'Wolf, wolf!' Usually relief came with a fall in the price of wool, a surrender by one of the parties, or a realisation that the consumer needed cloth and was willing to pay more for it.

In the second place, wool from a higher-priced new clip bought in June or July might not reach the cloth hall in the form of a piece until October, *i.e.* just when the autumn demand was petering out. Hence while the clothier must now ask a higher price for his new goods, the merchant was least anxious to buy much or pay more; and in the struggle the clothier could not always hold out till the merchant was willing to accept his terms.

In the third place, the wool supply of some years, *e.g.* 1830, 1834, 1835, and 1836, was inadequate, all the good wools were sold by about Christmas, and only inferior material was available at the stapler's warehouse during the two or three months preceding the arrival of the next clip. The big producers might have laid in a stock large enough to carry them through the wool year, but many of the smaller men, living from hand to mouth, had to scramble for a share of the scanty supply of poor wool, and their competition raised its price accordingly. If the cloths made of this rubbish were ready for market while the spring demand was strong, a fair return might be obtained, but cloth which did not get to the clothier's stand in the hall till May found the demand almost gone and the new wool clip almost ready; hence it had to be sold at a loss or at best at bare production cost; and since merchants were sometimes caught with large stocks of such cloth on hand, both merchant and clothier might have to work for nothing during the last two months of the wool year.[30] Mercurius therefore frequently urged producers to 'let their manufacturing operations be as closely circumscribed as possible from March to July.'[31] Remember, he urged, there is no limit to the possible advance in price, except as the increased price of cloth checks consumption or tends to the substitution of fabrics of silk, cotton, or flax. The tendency of price is to rise highest, and of the quality to sink lowest, in the spring, but there is always greater difficulty at that time in raising the price of cloth to correspond with the advance in the cost of the raw material. If you can market your wares in April or May you will get your money back, but if you are late you will 'infallibly lose.'[32]

The effect of price movements had been clear during the five years before Mercurius took up his duties. Recovery from the slump of 1825 had come slowly, but by 1832 trade had become 'fair to middling' (or in other words very good), especially in the worsted industry, which used English wool only as yet. Throughout the Riding factories and domestic workshops were all fully employed, and new factories were being built on every hand. The demand for wool was enormous, but the supply suddenly ran out. Depressed by the low prices of wool and mutton after 1825, British farmers had neglected their flocks and turned their attention elsewhere. A bad attack of sheep rot in 1831 had depleted flocks still further, and British wool production fell to a low level. But there were on hand stocks which the farmers had refused to sell at 10d per lb, and this reserve, plus the diminished clips of 1831 and 1832, supplied the manufacturers in these years at a moderate price. But the 1833 clip was short, and the old stocks were exhausted. Wool dealers and staplers therefore spent the summer of 1833 scouring the fairs and farms in search of material. The farm price jumped from 36s a tod in June to 44s in August and to 48s in October. This rapid advance scared the merchants; they dare not pay the prices asked for cloth until they knew whether their foreign customers would bear the added burden, and in November they virtually deserted the market. But at Christmas large orders from America and Germany reassured them, and they came back to buy; the staplers therefore went out to find more wool, and in January 1834 were paying 58s or even 60s a tod. This again frightened the cloth merchants and checked trade again to such an extent that mills and shops were closed, thousands of workers walked the streets, and a repetition of the slump of 1825-6 seemed inevitable. 'Wool must come down,' cried merchants and manufacturers; and by 'down' they meant to a shilling a pound as in the years around 1830.[33] 'We can't reduce it,' retorted the staplers; 'We won't let it go down,' said the farmers, and for three months there was complete deadlock. Eventually the staplers gave way a little, foreign orders poured in, compelling merchants to buy cloth and manufacturers to buy wool, and the mills were reopened. Mercurius urged buyers never again to rush into the market in such a pell-mell manner as they had done in 1833; he pleaded for cautious hand-to-mouth buying, and hoped that the manufacturers and staplers would 'try to make money together, and not each try to enrich himself at the other's loss.'[34] And for goodness' sake cease thinking that a shilling a pound is a natural price simply because it ruled from 1828 to 1832. Wool may some day be cheap again, but 'it may perhaps be seriously doubted whether there is yet, either in the increased production of wool or in the diminution of the demand for woollen or worsted fabrics, or in the general condition of trade, or in all these combined, a force sufficiently powerful to bring down the price of wool to the average of 1829-33.'[35] Stability at a moderate level is more important than cheapness, and it 'would be highly conducive to the interest of the trade if wools could be kept steady at the price of January and February last.'

Unfortunately wool did not stand still in price, but continued to advance until the summer of 1836.[36] In April of that year Mercurius reminded his readers of the events of the three preceding years, and warned them there must soon come a pause which would injure those who were buying dear but poor wool. Still prices went up, and cloth-makers raised their prices 5 or 7½ per cent. In August the prophet cried out that wool was at 'an artificial price, *i.e.* a price governed by the intensity of demand and not by the cost of production,' and pleaded with the trade to be satisfied with reasonable profits, 'lest the excessive advances in prices wreck the market.' But the cloth halls and the warehouses were crowded with buyers, orders from America and consignments to that country were unprecedentedly high, so all seemed safe and caution was therefore a hard virtue.

Then, almost in a flash, the car of commerce revealed again its uncanny ability to change from top gear to reverse while moving at full speed. The bank rate was raised to 5 per cent at the beginning of September, and within a month trade and production were headed for that long, dreary depression which lasted, with only brief periods of relief, till 1842-3. During those seven years Mercurius had plenty of time to meditate on the forces which make or unmake prosperity and to scan the horizon for gleams of light. If in boom days he had preached caution, now he tried to record the worst but hope for the best. The slump will not be serious, he predicts in November 1836; there will be no heavy fall in prices. In December he reports that 'we are weathering the storm.' In January 1837 he is 'yet indisposed to admit that any very serious consequences in the way of failures are likely to occur,' but in March he has to admit that trade has been very flat, gloomy and dispiriting, and that any hope of preventing a serious fall in prices is futile. In June he thinks that 'we have reached the bottom of the hill, and consequently our future progress will be one of slow but certain amendment.' In October he is sure that 'the storm has spent itself,' and in November that the home trade will be good in the spring and the foreign trade in the fall. But in March 1838 he has to admit that the home spring demand has been bad; nevertheless, stocks were low in April, so he expected 'a gradual restoration of more prosperous times.' By July he saw 'a sure and rapid return to general activity,' and his eyes did not deceive him. But it was short-lived, and was followed by a much worse relapse, in which the prostration of merchants and manufacturers was 'unparalleled.' In December 1839 he did not 'see any strong grounds for believing we can go much lower, though when we may rise again we can only conjecture.' By August 1840 'alarm is subsiding, men are no longer inquiring with anxious trepidation who is to go next, nor tremblingly alive as to their own danger. We believe that the tide has fully turned.' He was wrong, sadly so, and in February 1842 he estimated that the volume of employment had shrunk to half that of the boom days. But in March he was 'sure this year will witness the first heavings of a tide which will conduct this country to a state of commercial and manufacturing prosperity more palmy and prosperous than it has ever before witnessed.' The Plug Riots of August 1842 seemed to belie this prediction, but it was nearly true; and when in October 1843 he decided that 'the fury of the hurricane of 1837-41 has spent itself' he was right, so right that he soon found it necessary to change his tune to one of caution, and to urge his readers to keep their temperament below fever heat, looking for profit 'rather as the fruit of thriftiness, skill, and prudence than of clever bargaining or bold speculation.'

In these years of tribulation it became evident that no matter how carefully the textile world stepped, its progress was determined in large measure by forces beyond the control of stapler, clothier, and merchant. For there was the business cycle, the wheels of which were turned by speculation and over-trading, while the brake was controlled by the Bank of England. The past teaches us, said Mercurius in February 1837, that 'with the cessation of serious failures (for commercial disease, like bodily, has its regular alternations of excitement and languor) will come gradually but surely a revival of confidence, and then we may calculate on another run of activity and of profit until some new form of speculation or over-trading, or the recurrence of that disposition to meddle with the currency which so often afflicts the Bank Parlour shall once more plunge us into the vortex of commercial embarrassment or perhaps general panic.' Persistent warnings might check speculation and over-trading, and Mercurius took credit to himself for the comparative caution displayed by the local textile trade in 1836 and the consequent absence of serious embarrassment in the early stages of the slump. He had rejoiced at the absence of speculation in land or buildings, the moderate orders for new machinery, and the limited purchases of wool. 'If there has been over-trading we confess we either do not know the

symptoms of that commercial malady, or the disease itself has
assumed a new form.'[37] But no provincial industry could control
completely its own destiny; it was in large crucial part at the mercy
of outside forces, especially Bank policy, the state of the weather,
and the appetite of the United States.

   Mercurius looked on the Bank of England in much the same way
as an American Middle-Westerner looks on the 'moneyed interests'
of lower Broadway and Wall Street — a giant, powerful,
monopolistic, necessary, but pursuing a policy of alternate aid and
hindrance dictated by the desire to swell its profit or save its skin.
The Bank's policy seemed delightfully simple. For a season it
expanded credit, let gold flow out of its vaults into home
circulation or foreign fields; then it became scared at the depletion
of its reserves, and by restricting credit and raising interest rates it
sucked gold back again. Once a safe margin had been established
it repeated the whole process, and trade therefore flourished or
suffered according to whether the Bank was exhaling or inhaling.
Hence it was idle to think of a renewal either in home or foreign
trade so long as the Bank continued its policy of restricting
commercial discounts 'till gold flows in a full tide into its coffers.'
'The revival of home trade depends on the restoration of
commercial confidence, and commercial confidence is impossible
so long as no man dare to calculate on the usual and necessary
banking facilities: and those who expect a revival of foreign trade
without a previous revival of the home trade will do well to study
the advice of the old cookery book — 'How to roast a hare. First
catch it.' We say not that a cautious and guarded renewal of issues
by the Bank of England is not needful now, because we are quite
convinced there has been great mismanagement of the currency,
and not the least faulty that of the Bank of England. But we also
say that there is a point beyond which caution is unwise and
dangerous, that is when the recurrence of a healthy demand for
money is not met by a free and liberal issue.'[38] While admitting
that the joint stock banks had erred grievously by granting
excessive credits and issuing too many notes in 1835-6, Mercurius
was convinced that 'the true cause of the violent derangements in
the currency' was to be found in the Bank's monopoly of the
metropolitan circulation; for while this monopoly did not secure
the Bank against a drain on its reserves in consequence of adverse
exchanges it did allow it 'to continue its issues to the verge of
safety, then enabling it to apply the screw to refill its coffers with
impunity to itself but to the ruin of others.'[39] a System which
'tempts the cupidity of a corporate body in opposition to the
general well-being can only issue in the repeated sacrifice of the

latter. Without a radical change we are fully warranted in expecting after no lengthened series of years a repetition of the horrors of 1826 and 1837.' Obviously, therefore, the question of sound currency legislation cannot long be staved off, 'but will return again and again like a vexed ghost until some sagacious mind extorts the secret of its solution or it be evolved in the natural working of the system.'[40] The sagacious mind of Mercurius had, however, already extorted the secret; it was 'free trade in money,' *i.e.* the issue by joint stock or private banks of notes of £5 or more, payable in gold. Under this new freedom joint stock banks would crop up in London, use their notes to discount commercial paper, and yet be restrained from excess issue by the obligation to pay in gold. Thus the London money market would rest on a broad basis instead of spinning on the tip of a top.

And yet, perhaps with all its faults, the Bank of England might be as much victim as villain, victim of the weather and the harvest. For a defective harvest, such as that of 1838, 1839, or 1840, caused a rapid expansion of food imports; but since there was no corresponding sudden expansion of exports, payment had to be made by shipping bullion abroad. The Bank's reserves were thereby depleted, and it was driven to raise the bank rate and curtail its circulation. Wheat imports alone jumped as follows in the late thirties:—

1836,	242,000	quarters.
1837,	560,000	,,
1838,	1,372,000	,,
1839,	2,875,000	,,

Obviously, 'although ultimately any importation of corn must be paid for by British goods, yet immediately gold will go out in payment, and this will tend to a contraction of the currency and its concomitants — difficulty in procuring discounts and falling prices.'[41] Mercurius therefore urged his readers in late 1838 to shorten sail, and watch the exchange rates and the Bank returns, for the Bank would not again let its stock of specie fall below £3,000,000 or £4,000,000 without taking action; and 'although we think no safe calculation can be made on the prudence of the Bank, we are quite sure its fears will imperatively rule its conduct.'[42] His advice was sound, for by May 1839 the bank rate was up to 5 per cent, by June to 5½ per cent, and by August to 6 per cent. He therefore warned all to expect 'a period of embarrassment of some duration, ruinous to many individuals in the mercantile classes and very trying to the operative population.'[43] He was a true prophet.

If food imports impaired bank funds, dear bread impaired the home population's ability to buy cloth. Mercurius therefore came finally to hang all his forecasts on crop prospects and evolved a harvest theory of the business cycle. In 1839, when food was scarce and costly, and the trade revival of 1838 had vanished, he said, 'It cannot too often or too strongly be impressed on the minds of our merchants and our operative population that the amount of employment for capital and labour is inseparably connected with the amount of food, and in the direct ratio of the amount of the one will be the amount of the other.'[44] Four years later, when good harvests and good trade had returned, he was even more dogmatic. 'The principle has become an everyday truism that the consumption of manufactured fabrics in ordinary circumstances is in the inverse ratio of the price of food. Keep food prices steady and low, and trade will remain steady and good. Preserve the one and you preserve the other.'[45] This theory, he was convinced in 1840, explained 'all the phenomena' of the protracted depression. 'No other theory as to over-speculation or as to the present condition being the final consequences of the excitement of 1835-6 will explain the phenomena.'[46]

In support of his thesis Mercurius studied crop and business conditions since 1790, and found abundant confirmation there. Further, he measured the length of the periods of good harvest and deficient yield; the former had averaged three years each, the latter had run for an average of two years. On these figures prophecy could be based, and in May 1838, after a run of good or even excellent harvests, Mercurius gave warning of lean years ahead. 'In the economy of providence occasional dearth and sterility are part of a plan the wisdom of which we can no more dispute than we can alter the plan itself;' therefore bad seasons are due now.[47] They came. In 1843, when all was smiling once more, the warning note was again sounded. 'We can get a tolerably correct idea how soon another period of deficient harvests will overtake us. We have had two fair crops. Should 1844 be good, the probabilities are that 1845 and 1846 will be bad, one or both. It is against all probability that we shall reach 1847 without a bad, a really bad harvest.' He was not far wrong, for 1845 was bad, and 1846 horrid.[48]

The moral for a country faced with such certainty of recurring disaster was twofold. In the first place, people should take a lesson in humility, 'not soon again to vaunt in the triumph of our manufacturing art or of our mercantile enterprise, seeing how entirely dependent these are on the supply of food which, while it is the product of the simplest application of human industry, is the result of the infinite wisdom of the Deity and one great proof of His

care and beneficence towards His creatures.'[49] In the second place
— much more terrestrial — the Corn Laws should be abolished
and free trade established. Population is rapidly entrenching on the
existing means of subsistence, emigration is an inadequate remedy
for the discrepancy between food and mouths, the necessity of
competing on equal terms with foreign rivals is so urgent, the
prospect of insubordination, outbreak and revolution is so fearful
and imminent, that without throwing down all barriers to
commerce and industry there can be no safety for the nation. We
cannot much longer rely on the native soil to feed us even in good
years. We are rapidly reaching the point where we must become
essentially a commercial people. 'We are in peril if we persist in a
system which was only practicable and bearable whilst our soil
could support its population at a somewhat reasonable rate, and
whilst our manufacturing skill was either unchallenged or only very
distantly approached. We have outlived this condition, and with an
altered national condition we must have an altered national
policy.'[50]

Not even free trade could control the vagaries of the United
States market and tariff. America was Yorkshire's best single
customer; on the eve of the Revolution she bought about one-fifth
of Britain's total exports of woollens and worsteds; at the close of
the century the fraction was two-fifths, from 1822-5 it was
one-third, but in the boom year 1836 it rose to over two-fifths and
exceeded £3,000,000.[51] One-quarter to one-third of the total British
exports to the United States consisted of woollen and worsted
fabrics, which were sent partly in response to orders and partly on
consignment at the sender's risk. Most Yorkshire merchants
preferred to send only goods which were ordered, but some traders
and many manufacturers ventured to try the market by
despatching consignments to be sold by public auction or through
agents on the Atlantic seaboard. In New York, Boston, and
Philadelphia small colonies of Yorkshiremen were to be found,
sons or brothers of West Riding makers or merchants, while
American buyers were frequent visitors to the warehouses of Leeds
and Bradford.

Mercurius therefore watched American developments intently
and with some anxiety. The tariff was a perpetual source of worry,
as was also the national temperament. When in the middle of 1836
American orders were rising to the highest point ever known and
adventurers were pouring consignments across the Atlantic, he
preached caution. 'We are aware that the States are progressing at
an unprecedented rate in wealth and population, but we are quite
convinced that the time is not yet come when as a commercial

country it will cease to exhibit those extreme points of excitement and depression to which it seems more liable than any other nation with which we have dealings.'[52] He was right, for while the woollen exports to the United States in 1836 were over £3,000,000, those of 1837 were barely £1,000,000. When America was down he had great faith in her recuperative powers, and in November 1837 voiced his belief that Americans 'will find a way out of their currency difficulty. They will soon grow tired of doing nothing because conflicting theorists cannot come to an agreement on the proper kind of currency, and will be disposed to put up with one acknowledged to be defective rather than hold the energies of a mighty nation in abeyance till the wranglers agree.' He therefore prophesied that 'our energetic friends across the Atlantic will extricate themselves from their embarrassments ere the autumn is over' and send large orders for the fall of 1838. Again he was right, for the exports rose from £1,000,000 in 1837 to £1,900,000 in 1838 and to £2,200,000 in 1839. But this recovery was too rapid for the prophet's liking, and he felt impelled to warn readers that 'from the varying and unequal character of the demand, its sudden changes and its speculative character, no safe conclusion can be drawn from its present appearance as to its continuance and profitableness, especially as the operation of the Bank of England on the rate of discount has yet to be known and felt in the States.'[53] Again he was right, for on November 9, 1839, the *Leeds Mercury* published an 'Extraordinary' announcing the suspension of specie payments by several leading American banks. This 'measure of fearful import' spread consternation in Liverpool, Manchester, and Leeds, and caused the American woollen purchases to drop from £2,200,000 in 1839 to £1,100,0000 in 1840. They rose to £1,550,000 in 1841, but in 1842 dropped below £900,000. A hard market to serve!

In scanning the European market Mercurius became apprehensive at every threat of higher tariffs or of war. The development of the Zollverein was especially sinister, yet England deserved whatever punishment continental governments inflicted on her. For Mercurius held the free trade view that such countries as America, Germany, and Russia would gladly have remained primary producers, but had been driven into protection by Britain's refusal to buy their food and raw material. 'The tariffs of Europe are our own creation, but although they owe their existence to us, their tenure of existence is not at our disposal. We have sown the dragon's teeth, but the armed men springing from them do not acknowledge subjection to us and will not depart at our bidding.'[54] Foreign industries were advancing relentlessly in efficiency and skill, they had modern equipment, and the advantage England had once enjoyed by being first in the field with the new textile machines was rapidly disappearing. Hence the export of certain kinds of woollens, especially to Europe, seemed in the early forties to be 'in a process of extinction';[55] only for worsteds, made of English wool, was there any hope, and foreigners could now buy that wool and learn to make their own worsteds. Every tariff discussion abroad, therefore, made Mercurius nervous; let the British Government checkmate higher tariffs by lowering its own, and let the woollen trade awake, improve and cheapen its wares, before all its foreign market was gone.

Revolutions and threat of war always led Mercurius to recall the days before 1815. In 1840 the problem of what to do with Mehemet Ali threatened to plunge Europe into conflict, for France was with Mehemet but the other big Powers were against him. Mercurius therefore held his breath till October, when the fear of war diminished, and expressed his surprise that his fears had not been shared by his fellow-countrymen. Those who remember the wars with the United States and France know what war means. But most businessmen of today are too young to have that knowledge. If they had realised the danger they would have protested forcefully. "We are not sanguine enough to hope that the perception of the evils of war to a manufacturing and commercial country is so general or so strong as to render the recurrence of that worst of social evils unlikely or impossible. But of this we are convinced, that few would remain at its close unconvinced at least of the utter folly of war, if not of its deep criminality."[56]

One final influence with which a textile forecaster had to reckon was fashion. For centuries Yorkshire had been manufacturer for the masses; its staple product was low and medium-grade cloths. But during the first three decades of the nineteenth century — and especially during the third — great and successful efforts had been made to produce high-grade fabrics. Spanish or Saxon wool was used, finishing machinery was designed, and cloth was submitted to a long series of finishing processes from which it emerged firm as billiard cloth, opaque as blotting-paper, long of life, costly, and worthy the best attention of a good tailor. Yorkshiremen at times even equalled the West of England in this field of production, and some manufacturers built large mills especially for the production of these cloths. But in the 'thirties 'the gentlemen who lead the *ton* in Bond Street and other fashionable parts of the metropolis' turned away from these costly fabrics to new types of cloth. For outdoor wear in bad weather the macintosh, whether cape or coat, displaced the heavy impervious double-milled cloth overcoat.

Critics might say the macintosh was injurious to health and
Mercurius was sure 'it would have puzzled the ingenuity of
Hogarth to find the line of beauty in any man, tall or short, fat or
lean,' who wore a macintosh.[57] Underneath this new protector men
and women began to wear clothes made of tweeds, pilots, beavers,
or worsteds. These cloths were made of cheaper wool, they were less
firmly woven, and little time or labour was spent in milling and
finishing them; they were lighter in weight, and in comparison with
the old fabrics were almost as a piece of cheese cloth is to a piece of
felt. Many of them had woven or printed patterns and were
described as 'fancies'; the worsteds had a cotton warp, and, thanks
to improvements in pattern designing and in machinery for
spinning and weaving worsteds, were of 'unparalleled cheapness
and beauty.' Garments of these cloths were made more loosely
fitting, and to the lover of good tailoring were so unsightly and
coarse that there was 'little difference between the beau and the
drayman.'[58] But the new fabrics and fashions gave ease and
comfort, added variety to the colour of garments, and were so
cheap that a new suit or dress could be bought more frequently.

This change in dress habits was apparent during the boom of
1833-6, but as the Yorkshire and West of England makers of
high-class cloths were selling their wares no alarm was felt. When
depression came these makers attributed the prolonged lack of
orders to the general state of trade. But Mercurius was of a
different opinion. Double-milled fine and superfine cloths would
never regain their old popularity; broadcloth had had its day, the
taste for the new kinds was 'now established, and a recurrence to
the old fashion of wearing heavy milled cloths can hardly be
expected.'[59] We may regret this, for the amount of labour required
to make and finish a fine cloth is four or five times greater than
that bestowed on pilots, beavers, and tweeds; and the closing of
mills and finishing shops in Leeds is therefore a tragedy.[60] But
waiting and whistling will not reopen them. It is 'time for all to
look the danger in the face and probe the evil to the bottom';[61] it is
obvious that a change in the direction of Leeds capital and labour
is necessary; the fine cloth maker must change his course or find
his occupation gone.[62] 'But this calls for such a display of energy
and enterprise as has been woefully lacking . . . If ingenuity were as
rife in the woollen trade as in the cotton and worsted, the former
trade might experience a great accession of prosperity . . . There is
room and verge enough for taking the lead if energy be used.'[63] The
cotton and worsted men have gone forward in search of taste,
beauty, and colour 'more rapidly than the woollen; the stationary
unimproved character of the latter trade is its opprobrium.' Can it

be removed? Yes, by producing fine fancy woollens instead of good but homely plain blacks, blues, olives, bottle-greens, and the like. Study the designs of the cotton and worsted men; create a class of artists of design; improve the standards of workmanship, and concentrate efforts on the production of an efficient power-loom. 'The power-loom has not yet had its fair trial in woollen fabrics: we are persuaded it will one day supersede the hand-loom, and the fine descriptions of fancy woollens present the opportunity for further experiment.'[64]

This advice was followed by some producers, but the old hands in the fine cloth trade had become too cramped to be capable of such flexibility. There was nothing like broadcloth. Hence while Huddersfield, Halifax, Bradford, and many of the clothing villages continued to cater for diversity of taste and changes in fashion, Leeds clung to its fines and superfines. More was needed than the pleadings of a forecaster to move second and third generation mill-masters. That 'more' was the sewing-machine and the ready-made clothing industry, which enlarged enormously the demand for cheaper fabrics and cut still lower the sale of high-grade cloths. It is one of the ironies of textile history that this industry should be born in Leeds.

NOTES

1 Most of the material used in this article was collected during 1931-2 while the writer was in England holding a Fellowship from the Guggenheim Memorial Foundation. His thanks are due to the Foundation and to the Chief Librarian and staff of the Leeds Reference Library.
2 Oct. 29, 1825 3 Feb. 4, 1826 4 Mar. 11, 1826
5 Sept. 23, 1826 6 Dec. 24, 1824 7 Jan. 15, 1825
8 Jan. 22, 1825 9 Feb. 5, 1825 10 Nov. 19, 1825
11 Feb. 12, 1825 12 Sept. 23, 1826
13 July 25, 1829.
14 Nov. 28, 1829
15 Oct. 31 and Nov. 28, 1829.
16 The reports sometimes occupied only a quarter of a column, but occasionally they filled a whole column or even more.
17 Report for May, 1835.
18 Report for October 1843.
19 See the concluding paragraphs of this article.
20 Report for July 1843.
21 Report for September 1843.
22 March 4, 1837.
23 Report for June, 1842.
24 Report for June, 1835.
25 July 4, 1835.
26 Report for January 1844.
27 Report for July 1835. On wools selling at less than 2s 6d per lb. an increase of 3d in

the price might raise the price of low and middle-priced cloths by at least 5 per cent. (Report for June 1836.)

28 Report for July 1838.
29 Report for April 1839.
30 May 7, 1836.   31 Feb. 6, 1836.   32 Feb. 6, 1836.
33 May 3, 1834. Wool bought at 36s a tod was sold by the stapler at 13d to 20d per lb. according to quality. Wool bought at 60s sold at 22d to 29d.
34 Sept. 5, 1835.
35 July 4, 1835.
36 The price in 1834 was 45 to 50 per cent. above the 1828-30 level: in early 1835 it dipped to 30 per cent., but rose above the 1834 level in 1836. Dyestuffs also became much more costly. As cotton prices also rose, worsted fabrics could be sold higher without fear that cottons would deprive them of the market.
37 May 7, 1836.
38 February report, 1837.
39 December report, 1837.
40 September report, 1837.
41 March report, 1838.
42 December report, 1838.
43 June report, 1839.
44 December report, 1839.
45 August report, 1843.
46 November report, 1840.
47 May report, 1838.
48 November report, 1843. The annual average price of wheat was 1845 = 50s 10d per qr., 1846 = 54s 8d per qr., and 1847 = 69s 9d per qr.
49 August report, 1837.
50 February report, 1840.
51 Total exports of woollens and worsteds = £7,639,000 (declared value). Exports to U.S.A. = £3,175,000.
52 June report, 1836.
53 June report, 1839. The bank rate had been raised to 5½ per cent. in June.
54 Jan. 6, 1844.
55 *Ibid.*
56 October report, 1840.
57 September report, 1837.
58 July 30, 1842, and Aug. 6, 1842.
59 October report, 1841.
60 Aug. 6, 1842.
61 February report, 1843.
62 November report, 1842.
63 October report, 1843.
64 November report, 1842.

19

A Manchester Merchant and his Schedules of Supply and Demand

B. W. Clapp*

Demand and supply schedules are common enough in economics textbooks, and the facts of economic life show that such schedules do represent the economic behaviour of man in the mass. It is not often, however, that we can watch a firm laying down explicit demand and supply schedules in the manner of a treatise on economics.

Table I shows the highly elastic demand schedule for American cotton on which Owen Owens and Son of Manchester in 1821 instructed their partner in Philadelphia to base his purchases.[2] The Manchester firm had not in 1821 had a great deal of experience of foreign trade, and its appetite increased by measured steps of 200

Table I

Price (cents. per lb.)	Demand (bales)
11	1,200
11¼	1,000
12	800
12½	600
13	400
13½	200

Table II

To cost in Liverpool (pence per lb.)	Demand (bales)
5¼	2,000
5½	1,000
5¾	200

bales for every fall of ½ cent per lb in the price of cotton. Over the next quarter of a century the firm devised, as its stock of

*From *Economica*, N.S. Vol. 29, No. 114 (May 1962), pp. 185-7. Reprinted by permission of the editors of *Economica* and the author.

experience accumulated, demand schedules to a variety of patterns.
For example, it could exaggerate still further the elasticity of its
demand, as in the following order sent to its New York agents in
April, 1840[3] (Table II).

The success of operations in the cotton market depended to a
large extent on the operator's ability to allow correctly for the size
of the prospective American cotton crop. The prudent importer
would vary his offer price inversely with the probable result of the
American crop. By 1840, John Owens was the only active partner in
the firm of Owen Owens and Son, and from the autumn of that
year regularly made allowances for the size of the American crop in
the orders he gave. He took account of three possibilities — a large
crop, an average crop, and a deficient crop. Basing his calculations
on an average crop he laid down the familiar schedule, in this case
100 bales at 6d to 6⅛d, rising sharply to 2,000 bales at 5½d to
5⅝d. If the crop was likely to exceed two million bales these prices
were to be reduced by one farthing; if the crop fell below one-and-
three-quarter million bales, a farthing was to be added to the offer
price.[4] In course of time, Owens came to believe that he could
profitably narrow the margins within which he operated. In
January, 1844, he was willing to buy from 500 to 2,000 bales of
cotton at prices ranging from 5d down to 4½d — given an average
crop; if the crop fell below 1,850,000 bales, his agent could add a
farthing to these prices, but if the crop exceeded 2,100,000 bales,
the order was to be cancelled outright.[5]

John Owens used the same technique for the purchase of flour
and of wheat, and his demand schedules were always highly elastic.
In 1839, for example, he was willing to buy 3,000 barrels of
American flour at $5, but only 500 barrels at $5.75.[6] In 1845, he
gave instructions for the purchase of Egyptian wheat: the amount
he was prepared to buy ranged (by steps of 1,000 quarters and a
shilling) from 10,0000 quarters at 18s 0d to 4,000 quarters at 24s
0d.[7] It is possible that he followed similar principles in the purchase
of manufactures, but the evidence is very scanty because he met his
suppliers face to face and did business by word of mouth rather
than by letter. Moreover, he was in constant touch with the
Manchester market for cotton yarn and goods, and could keep a
closer watch on the markets of Rochdale, Leeds, and London than
on those of New York, Charleston, and Alexandria. He could pick
up bargains day by day or week by week, and did not have to draw
up a once-for-all statement of his demands.

As a seller — of cotton, tea, wheat, or railway shares — Owens
had to act, as he did when buying these commodities, through
agents. He was not a bad judge of cotton, but cotton-importing was

a Liverpool business and only from time to time did he personally negotiate sales in Manchester. He had no means at all of judging the quality of the wheat he had bought, or of the tea remitted to him in return for textiles that he had consigned to China. He was a highly successful speculator in railway shares, but had to leave the actual purchase and sale of stock to professional agents. In all these dealings, then, a supply schedule would be a useful guide to his agents, and sometimes he provided a simple scheme, though his usual practice was to watch the market and release supplies in driblets as and when prices rose. Dealings in tea he conducted through an agent in Mincing Lane. His stock of tea was never large and it would have been a futile exercise to draw up elaborate schedules for a mere hundred chests. In October, 1839, he was willing to sell 50 chests at 2s 10d a lb or 100 chests at 3s; by the following January, when relations with China, already bad, had deteriorated further, Owens was 'greatly apprehensive the suspension of trade with China will be long protracted and that the Chinese will be found very obstinate and unmanageable.' He would not now part with more than 50 chests of tea at 3s or with 100 at 3s 3d.[8] On at least one occasion he instructed his stockbroker to sell shares on a similar basis. In August, 1845, speculation in railway shares was at its height,[9] and John Owens was busily engaged in the pastime. One of his most substantial holdings was in the London and Birmingham Railway, the shares of which had appreciated sharply since he first began buying in 1840. Owens was ready to sell 100 quarter-shares at 37, 50 at 36½, or 20 at 36.[10] As with demand, so with supply, he was prepared to react sharply to small changes in price.

There is no reason to suppose that Owens was behaving oddly in trying to buy and sell to a plan that emphasised the price elasticity of his wants or willingness to sell. There was nothing self-conscious about the letters in which he gave orders to agents at home and overseas, and it is probable that other Manchester merchants followed a similar policy. It is interesting, and perhaps a little surprising, that the idea of price-quantity schedules of supply and demand, so familiar to them, should have found its way into works on economics only towards the end of the nineteenth century.

NOTES

1 This Note is based on the Owens MSS, the property of the University of Manchester.

2 Owens to Thomas Owen, 30th September, 1821. This and the following tables are adapted with only minor changes from material in the firm's letterbooks.

3 Owens to Oakeys and Robinson, 14th April, 1840.

4 Owens to Leech, New Orleans, 30th September, 1840.
5 Owens to Gourdin, Matthiessen & Co., Charleston, 3rd January, 1844.
   In the autumn of 1845, when the business outlook was uncertain, Owens changed
   his policy and procedure. He proposed to limit his risks by buying a fixed quantity
   of cotton, varying his offer price inversely with the size of the American crop. As
   a further precaution against loss he instructed his agents to make no purchases at
   all if the crop should exceed 2½ million bales. (Owens to Gourdin, Matthiessen &
   Co., 18th October, 1845.)
6 Owens to Oakeys and Robinson, 15th November, 1839.
7 Owens to A. Tod, Alexandria, 6th August, 1845.
8 Owens to Corrie and Co., 2nd October, 1839, and 11th January, 1840.
9 D. Morier Evans, *The Commercial Crisis, 1847-1848*, second edition, 1849, pp. 12
   and 20.
10 Owens to Johnston Bradley and Walker, 5th August, 1845.

20
The Social Organisation of Credit in a West African Cattle Market[1]
Abner Cohen*

Credit is a vital economic institution without which trade becomes very limited. In the industrial Western societies, where it is highly developed, it operates through formal, standardised arrangements and procedures by which the solvency of the debtor is closely assessed, securities against possible default are provided, and the conditions of the agreement are documented and endorsed by the parties concerned. Ultimately, these arrangements and procedures are upheld by legislated rules and sanctions administered by central, bureaucratised, fairly impartial, efficient, and effective courts and police. In West Africa, on the other hand, where long-distance trade has been fostered by varying ecological circumstances, such organisation has not yet evolved, particularly for long-distance trade. Nevertheless extensive systems of credit have been developed.

I discuss in this paper the organisation and operation of credit in one Nigerian market which I studied intensively. After a preliminary description of the formal organisation of the market and of the credit by which it functions, I discuss some non-economic social relations which, while formally exterior to the market situation, are in practice built into the structure of the credit system in such a way that they make its functioning as a going concern possible.

Nearly 75,000[2] head of cattle are sold every year in the cattle market of Ibadan, capital of the Western Region of the Federation of Nigeria. The forest belt of West Africa, of which Ibadan is part, is infested with the disease-carrying tse-tse fly which is fatal to cattle. The inhabitants depend for their beef supplies on herds of cattle brought from the savannah country, hundreds of miles to the

*From *Africa*, Vol. XXXV, No. 1 (Jan. 1965), pp. 8-19. Reprinted by permission of the editor of *Africa* and the author.

north. These herds are collected mainly from the semi-nomadic Fulani by Hausa dealers from Northern Nigeria and are then brought south to be sold with the help of local Hausa middlemen. In the Ibadan market, which is locally known as 'Zango',[3] the buyers are Yoruba butchers and are total strangers to the Hausa dealers. Nevertheless, all sales are on credit and there is always an outstanding total amount of about a hundred thousand pounds current debt.[4] No documents are signed and no resort is made to the services of banks or to the official civil courts, and the whole organisation, which has developed over the past sixty years, is entirely indigenous.

The cattle are brought to Ibadan either on foot or by train. In the market there is a sharp distinction between the two categories of cattle, not only in price but also in the organisation and the scale of the business. After about five weeks of continuous travel, the foot cattle[5] arrive at the market thin, weak, and already having been exposed, for many days, to the disease[6] as they penetrated the forest area. The manoeuvrability in selling them is therefore limited in both time and place and dealers are always eager to sell. This eagerness is further enhanced by the need of the dealers to release, as soon as possible, the capital invested in the herd in order to have a quicker business turn-over. In recent years, cattle have increasingly been brought south by train, but between 30 and 40 per cent still come on foot, either because they are brought from districts which are remote from a railway line, or because no train wagons happen to be available at the time. The principal advantage of bringing cattle on foot is that part of the herd can be sold on the way to small towns and villages which are not served by the railways or which are not large enough to have cattle markets.[7]

Foot cattle are brought by smaller-scale Hausa dealers, each dealer making an average of four journeys to Ibadan in a year, bringing to the market each journey an average of seventy head of cattle.[8] The herd is driven by hired Fulani drovers, an average of one drover[9] for every twenty-five head. The head owner walks with his cattle as far as Ilorin, where he usually parts with the caravan and starts a reconnaissance trip, by lorries and mammy wagons, along the ninety-five-mile route to Ibadan., stopping at the cattle markets in Ogbomosho and Oyo, and also at other, smaller towns, choosing the most advantageous place to sell. The more southerly the place, the higher the price, but the greater the hazards to the health of the cattle and the longer the period in which the capital is engaged.

The train cattle[10] are either brought by smaller-scale dealers, who travel with the herd, or are sent by relatively larger-scale dealers to their permanent agents in Ibadan. The cattle are transported in special wagons, each wagon accommodating between twenty and thirty head.[11] The herd in each wagon is looked after by an attendant[12] whose main task is to guard the beasts against theft. The journey to Ibadan takes two to three days and the few cattle who show signs of sickness in the meantime are slaughtered and sold in the several intervening stations, where local butchers are always waiting for such opportunities.

According to men in the business, the life expectancy of cattle after arriving in Ibadan is about two weeks for those brought on foot and about two and a half months for those brought by train. Train cattle therefore fetch a higher price than foot cattle of the same size and quality, particularly because they are demanded by butchers, not only from Ibadan, but also from neighbouring towns and villages. Also, when prices in Ibadan are unfavourable train cattle can be taken south as far as Lagos.

Despite the sharp distinction in the market between the two categories of cattle, the organisation of credit is essentially similar in both cases.

When the cattle dealer,[13] whether he is the owner of the herd or only an agent of the owner, is in Ibadan he lodges with his usual 'landlord' in the Hausa Quarter. The word 'landlord' is a literal translation of the Hausa term *mai gida*, but the *mai gida* plays several kinds of roles in the cattle business which are not denoted by the English translation and need to be analytically separated. In the first place, the *mai gida* is a house-owner, having, besides that in which he and his family live, at least one more house for the accommodation of his dealers from the north. Of the twelve cattle landlords who operated in Zango in 1963, one had six such houses, a second had four, two others had two houses each, and the rest had one each. The landlords usually own additional houses in which their assistants, clerks, servants, malams, and other men of their entourage are accommodated, free of charge. The landlord also provides three meals a day for his dealers and entertains them in the evenings, but this function as inn-keeper is by no means the most fundamental of his roles.

The landlord is also a middleman[14] who mediates between his dealers and the local butchers in the market. Each landlord has for this purpose a number of middlemen[15] working under him, but responsibility for their business conduct remains always with him. Thus, when the herd of the dealer arrives at the market, the landlord entrusts its sale to one of his middlemen. The dealer then accompanies the middleman in the market and remains with him until the whole herd is sold. But no transaction can be finally concluded without the approval of the landlord.

Here we come to the role of the landlord as insurer or risk-taker, which is the most crucial factor in the operation of the whole market. As sale is on credit, the landlord is the guarantor that the money will eventually be paid, and that if the buyer should default, he would pay the full amount to the dealer himself. This obligation means that he must be very well acquainted with the buyers, and it is only through long experience in the business that he comes to acquire the necessary knowledge. He has to know not only where a buyer slaughters the cattle, or where he has his shop or market stall, but also where he lives, who are his relatives and associates, what is the size of his business, and how honest and trustworthy he has proved himself to be in his dealings so far. In this way, every butcher in the market is informally graded by the landlords and their middlemen on a scale of credit-worthiness from nil up to about £1,000 of credit, for a period of up to four weeks. No sane landlord would give a butcher credit in excess of the latter's 'quota'. Misjudgment in this respect can ruin the business house of the landlord. This actually happened early in 1963 to one of the landlords, when a number of butchers who had bought cattle through him defaulted, and he eventually failed to pay the money himself to the dealers. These stopped lodging with him and complained to the Chief of the Cattle Market. He finally sold his only house of strangers to meet his obligations and became an ordinary middleman.

Thus landlords need to have not only a precise assessment of the buyer's social background and of his business conduct in the past, but must also be continuously vigilant as to his day-to-day purchases in the market. For while a dealer is attached to one landlord at a time, the butcher is free to buy through any landlord, and he usually makes his purchases through many landlords. It is conceivable, therefore, that he may succeed in buying, within a short period of time, from several unsuspecting landlords in excess of the limits of his credit-worthiness. The only way in which the landlords can meet this potential danger is by the continuous exchange of business information. No formally institutionalised channels for such an exchange exist in the market, but the objective is nevertheless achieved through informal relations.

Landlords interact very intensively among themselves, since it is in the nature of their business both to compete and to co-operate. They compete fiercely over business, and countless disputes arise among them over what they describe as 'stealing of dealers.' Generally speaking, a dealer has one landlord to whom he is accustomed to entrust the sale of his cattle whenever he comes to

Ibadan. This attachment of a dealer to one landlord usually holds for years and sometimes continues to hold between their sons when they die. Landlords do much to keep their dealers attached to them, offering them various services, some of which have little to do with the cattle business. When a dealer finally goes back to the North, after selling his cattle, his landlord gives him a present, the minimum standard being a bottle of French perfume costing (as in 1963) 18 shillings.[16] But some dealers, particularly those of foot cattle who come to Ibadan only occasionally, *do* change their landlords, for one reason or another, and sometimes landlords send emissaries as far as Ilorin to meet such dealers, offer them presents, and direct them to lodge with their masters.

Disputes between landlords over dealers have often led to political crises within the Hausa Quarter. The basic principle of political grouping among the 5,000 Hausa of the Quarter is that of the client-patron relationship, which is essentially diadic, holding between the patron and each client separately, without leading to the formation of corporate groups. A man's clients are his employees, attendants, and tenants. The patrons of the Quarter are the thirty landlords, in the various economic fields, who control much of the employment and of the housing of the rest of the population. Each one of them is the head of what may be described as a 'house of power'. Clients often 'change house', i.e. change their allegiance from one landlord to another, which often means literally moving from one house to another. Generally speaking, landlords are old residents in Ibadan while most of their clients are new migrants.[17]

The landlords and their clients pay allegience to the House Chief of the Quarter,[18] who mediates between them and the authorities, adjudicates — with the help of his advisers — in cases of disputes within the Quarter, and appoints men to titled positions who regulate communal affairs. One of these positions is that of the 'Chief of the Cattle Market',[19] who is responsible for keeping order in the market and who arbitrates in cases of disputes within it.

Of all the patrons, the cattle landlords are the most powerful as they have dominated the Quarter politically ever since its foundation in 1916. The Chief of the Quarter has always been a cattle landlord and, since 1930, he has also been the Chief of the Cattle Market.[20]

The cattle business is thus directly involved in the politics of the Quarter. The same men who meet in the cattle market as landlords confront each other in the Quarter as political leaders, and their behaviour in the one role affects their behaviour in the other. For example, one of the duties of the Chief of the Quarter is to give accommodation to any Hausa stranger who comes to him, and the

Chief runs many houses for this specific purpose. When a new cattle dealer comes for the first time to Ibadan and lodges in one of these houses, as a stranger, it is only natural that he should eventually sell his cattle through the Chief, in the latter's role as cattle landlord.

Within the context of the Quarter, one major source of dispute between the landlords has been the struggle for the control over houses, since from the early 1930's these have become relatively scarce because of overcrowding. A man needs housing in the Quarter to secure membership of the community, to establish himself in business, to gather clients around him, to enlarge his family by marrying more wives, to foster the sons and daughters of his kin, and to accommodate malams whose services in the mystical world are indispensable to his success and well-being. Thus, command over housing is in no small measure command over economic and political power. When the Quarter was first established, the land, which had been allotted for the purpose by the city's native authority, was distributed in equal plots among the first settlers. But since then many changes have taken place in the ownership and distribution of houses and land. In 1963 only five of the many hundreds of houses of the Quarter were registered as deeds. There were no documents of any kind to establish ownership over the rest of the houses. Most of the orginal houses and plots have changed hands many times through sale or death of their owners. The houses of persons who died without leaving heirs have been 'inherited' by the Chief of the Quarter, who is presumed to use them for the general welfare of the community. In this way the Chief has come to control scores of houses in which he accommodates, rent free, several hundreds of people who have in this way automatically become his clients. Landlords thus struggle over the ownership of houses in the Quarter because these are the means to political and economic power.

In the cattle market the landlords also compete over the buyers and each landlord has a number of young men who act as 'advertisers', trying to draw the attention of the butchers to the herds marketed through their employers. But landlords are at the same time forced to co-operate in the market in several respects, the most important being to present a united front vis-a-vis the butchers. These are very powerfully organised through an association which has played an important role within the Ibadan polity and only a strong landlords' front can keep the necessary balance in the market.

The market is held twice a day, once in the morning, between 9 and 10, and again in the afternoon, between 5 and 7. These official hours are enforced by the Chief of the Market.[21] But landlords come to the market about an hour before each session to sit informally together and 'joke', often very clumsily, and it is in the course of this joking that much of the vital information on the buyers is exchanged.

Another informal channel through which business information is exchanged is the interaction between the clerks. Every landlord had a clerk[22] whose main duty is the registration of sales and the collection of money from the debtors. As soon as a transaction is concluded, the middleman involved calls the clerk of his landlord to note down the details. These include the date of the transaction, name of dealer, name of middleman, name and address of buyer, the number of cattle sold, the price and total amount as well as the exact time and place of payment.[23] The clerk occupies a central position within the structure of the 'business house' because, while the middlemen and the other assistants are individually related to the landlord and are not formally related to each other, the clerk is formally related to everyone within the house, and thus knows about all the transactions concluded through the house. Being also the collector of substantial amounts of money, he is always a man who is fully trusted by the landlord. Of the twelve landlords in the Ibadan market, three have their own sons as clerks, two their 'fostered'[24] sons, and three perform the task themselves. The clerks are young, educated 'in Arabic'[25] and are Ibadan-born. They speak Yoruba as well as Hausa and belong to the same age-group. Sharing the same background, they belong to the same group whose members pray, eat, learn, and seek entertainment together.[26] They thus meet in various social situations every day and in the course of their interaction they exchange information about the solvency of the butchers, which they eventually pass on to their respective masters.

These exchanges of information, however, relate only to the behaviour of the butchers in the past and it is conceivable that a butcher may in one hour buy from several landlords who, in the pressure of business, may not realise that he is exceeding his limits. A protection against such a possibility is obtained through the informal activities of, and interaction among, the 'boys',[27] who perform various jobs in helping their landlord and his middlemen in the market. These 'boys' can be seen everywhere in the market, and indeed the literal meaning of the Hausa word *kankamba* is 'going hither and thither'. Their tasks take them to many parts of the market and they mingle with the 'boys' of other landlords. When, in the course of their activities, they notice a butcher who, having already bought cattle in other corners of the market, comes to buy also from their landlord, then they alert the middlemen to the impending danger.[28]

Thus, joking and gossiping between the landlords, informal meetings among the clerks, and the activities of the 'boys' serve as means of disseminating business information and help to guard against the hazards of credit.

But the conflicting interests of the landlords are implicit even in this very fundamental issue of exchanging information about the butchers' purchases, and it sometimes happens, though not often, that a landlord tries to suppress information. I witnessed in 1963 a case of a butcher who failed to pay, on time, a debt of a few hundred pounds to a landlord, but promised to do so as soon as his business improved. The landlord withheld this news from the other landlords, since otherwise these would have refrained from selling cattle to the butcher, who would thus have been without business and would have failed to settle his original debt. An unsuspecting landlord eventually sold cattle to the butcher in question, who duly settled his debt to the first landlord but defaulted in payment to the second. When the first landlord was later blamed for his unethical conduct he replied that no one had asked him to give the information which he had withheld. The landlord who suffered in this case had himself acted as his own clerk and had therefore no means of knowing of the default of the butcher except from the first landlord. Landlords are thus sometimes in an invidious position about revealing information concerning their sales.

The credit is given for a period of two to four weeks.[29] Dealers in foot cattle usually remain during this period accommodated and fed by the landlord, and when the money is finally collected it is kept by the landlord until the dealer arranges transport for himself to go back to the North.[30] Dealers in train cattle often go back to the North as soon as their cattle are sold and collect the proceeds when they come back with the next herd.

The landlord receives no direct reward whatsoever from the dealer for accommodation, food, mediation, banking, or risk-taking. On the contrary he gives the dealer not only presents but also part of his own earning from the sale of the cattle. The landlord's remuneration is a fixed commission, known by the Hausa term *kudin lada* or simply *lada*, which he collects from the buyer, in cash, on the conclusion of the sale. During 1963 the commission in Ibadan was 13 shillings on each head of cattle, irrespective of the price. From this amount the landlord pays 3 shillings to the middleman who arranged the transaction, about a shilling to the clerk and the 'boys', 2 shillings to the dealer himself, and retains the rest to cover his expenses and to remunerate himself for the financial risks he has taken in assuring the credit.[31]

This credit arrangement is not fool-proof and cases of default occur, but, barring political or economic upheavals, the risks are greatly reduced by a variety of factors.

In the first place a loss is always distributed among several individuals because a butcher is usually indebted not to one landlord but to many, and a dealer's herd is sold not to one butcher but to many butchers. Thus, if a butcher defaulted the loss would be shared by the several landlords who gave him credit. The incidence of the loss is spread still wider when the case is eventually arbitrated, and in nearly all the cases I have recorded the dealer was made to share in the loss even though the formal principle is that the whole loss should be borne by the landlord.[32] I am talking here of loss, but it nearly always happens that an arrangement is reached, as a result of arbitration, by which the butcher undertakes to pay his debt by instalments over several months. During these months he is allowed to buy from the market but must pay in cash.

Unless a butcher is prepared to go out of the business altogether he is forced to abide by such an arrangement, since according to municipal rules he would forfeit his licence as a butcher if he did not slaughter at least one beast every week. This is a very important source of pressure on him because a licence is very difficult to obtain and is also very expensive. He cannot evade payment by buying cattle elsewhere. The Hausa throughout the region, indeed throughout southern Nigeria, monopolise the sale of cattle and control all cattle markets. These markets, together with the Hausa Quarters to which they are attached, constitute a widespread network of highly interrelated communities. In each of the three large cattle markets which are within a radius of sixty miles of Ibadan (Ogbomosho, Oyo, and Abeokuta) the Chief of the Cattle Market is himself the Chief of the Hausa Quarter, as well as being a cattle landlord. Thus, when the landlords in the Ibadan market decide not to sell to a defaulting butcher, they usually send a word to the neighbouring cattle markets about him and if he ever appeared there no one would sell to him even if he paid cash.

An equally important form of pressure on individual defaulters comes from the butchers themselves, who are organised in eight slaughter-houses, as well as within the overall occupational association. When one butcher defaults, the landlords are often forced to retaliate by declaring a temporary boycott of all the butchers within his slaughter-house. I witnessed one such case in 1963 when a butcher failed to pay a debt of about £700 which he owed to many landlords. In their gossiping time one day the landlords decided to refuse selling any cattle to the whole slaughter-house of the defaulting butcher in order to mobilise the pressure of his colleagues on him. This action was so effective that the butchers involved, together with the chief of the whole Association,[33] as well as the defaulting butcher, came to the Chief of the Hausa Quarter, in his capacity as Chief of the Cattle Market, on the same evening and an arrangement was made there and then to settle the matter. Indeed it happens sometimes that when a butcher shows signs of financial difficulties, some of his colleagues within the same slaughter-house will caution some of their trust-worthy middlemen not to sell to him. Thus, the butchers on their part watch each other's conduct in business and can exert a great deal of pressure on potential defaulters.

The market is therefore not seriously disturbed by the occasional default of individual butchers. Indeed, from the study of cases seen against the background of the history of the market organisation, it appears that occasional default (as crime in Durkheim's analysis)[34] has led to continual re-examination and retightening of the control mechanisms in the market and thus made the continuity of the credit system possible. The cattle landlords' main worry is not the individual defaulter but the sudden collapse of the market as a result of a concentrated hostile action on the part of the butchers.[35] The position of the landlords is particularly vulnerable, since the pressure which they can exert on the butchers is limited in degree and is not without its dangers. This is because the cleavage in the market between buyer and seller, debtor and creditor, is also a cleavage between Yoruba and Hausa and, indeed, both sides describe their mutual relationships in tribalistic terms. The land-lords often talk of the 'machinations' and the 'treachery' of the Yoruba and the butchers of the 'exploitation' and 'greed' of the Hausa. When the Ibadan cattle landlords appeal for support and solidarity from the cattle landlords in other markets in the region they actually do so not in the name of the profession but in the name of Hausa-ism, and the communication between the markets is affected through the respective Hausa chiefs, acting *as* Hausa chiefs, and not as chiefs of the cattle markets.

In the same way, the butchers confront the landlords as a tribal group and rely on the support of various other Yoruba groupings in this confrontation. The butchers resent the fact that it is they, and not the Hausa sellers, who are made to pay the commission to the landlords, and for years they have been agitating against it. In this agitation they have often succeeded in mobilising support from the press and from the city's traditional chiefs, who on several occasions in the past reminded the Hausa that they were strangers, that the Quarter stood on the Olubadan's land, that if they did not behave they would be made to leave, and so on. The landlords are always afraid that the city council or the regional government may impose on them new taxes or new restrictions on the movement and sale of cattle, or that they will decide to remove the Hausa Quarter or to 'scrap' it altogether.

The cattle landlords have not been passive in the face of such threats. When during the 1950's the butchers affiliated themselves within the predominantly Yoruba Action Group Party, which was until 1962 in power in the Western Region, the Hausa landlords reacted not only by joining the same party themselves, but also by dragging almost the whole Hausa Quarter with them in joining it, and in successive elections the Ibadan Hausa gave their votes to it.[36] In the 1961 election for the Ibadan local council, 93 per cent. of the votes in the Quarter went to the Action Group candidate. Within the party, the Hausa eventually formed a strong pressure group. According to the 1952 Census of Nigeria there were in the Western Region nearly 41,000 Hausa residents and even then it was realised that there were many more Hausa who for a variety of reasons had not registered themselves. In 1953 the chiefs of all Hausa communities in the Region formed a joint Hausa association[37] and unanimously elected the Ibadan Hausa Chief as their chairman. This occurred on the eve of the 1954 Federal Election and there is little doubt that the association played an important role in mobilising Hausa support for the party chosen by their chiefs. At that time the Action Group was struggling to establish itself, not as a regional, but as a national, party which was to gain the support of the masses from the other tribes of the Federation of Nigeria. For that purpose the party fought particularly hard to gain a foothold in Hausaland in the North, as that region contained more than half the population of the Federation. A party with such objectives could not allow the persecution of a Hausa minority in its own capital. Thus, the party not only prevented hostile action being taken against the cattle landlords, but even tried to prevent individual butchers from defaulting, by exerting pressure on these to honour their obligations, and sometimes by granting loans to those among them who did not have the cash to pay.

The risks of the credit system have thus made it necessary for the cattle landlords to act politically within the Hausa network of communities, as well as within the Ibadan, the regional, and the national polities. To do so, they have had to act not on occupational but on tribal lines, and it has therefore been essential for them to control the Chieftaincy of the Hausa Quarter. Under the prevailing conditions it is only through the Chieftaincy that political interaction with other Hausa communities, on the one hand, and with the Yoruba, on the other, can be effected.

The cattle landlords are few in number and, together with all their middlemen, clerks, and assistants, constitute only 6 per cent. of the working Hausa male population of the Quarter.[38] And yet they have always been so dominant that the history of the Quarter is to a great extent the history of the cattle trade in Ibadan. From the very beginning of Hausa settlement in Ibadan, at the beginning of the present century, until today, the Chief of the Quarter has always been a cattle landlord. And this is the case not only in Ibadan but also in the other Hausa communities in those Yoruba towns where a cattle market exists. Indeed it was initially this sociological problem, i.e. 'How is it that a handful of cattle landlords have come to dominate the whole Quarter politically?', which led me to study the organisation of the cattle market.

There are various factors involved in this phenomenon, but it is beyond the limits of this paper to discuss them in detail. It is sufficient to point out that the landlords not only 'need' the Chieftaincy because of its role in the organisation of credit, but also have the power and the organisation to dominate the Quarter. They interact among themselves most intensively, as they meet in a relatively small place (the market) twice a day, seven days a week. In contrast, the kola landlords, for example, who run business on similar lines and who, as an occupational group, constitute nearly 18 per cent.[39] of the working Hausa males in the Quarter, and certainly command greater wealth, do not have opportunities to interact so frequently and so intensively, since they have to leave the Quarter every morning and disperse in all directions within a radius of about forty miles in quest of supplies. They also operate mainly with cash and, since they are dealing in a local product for export from the area, whenever credit is involved, they are the debtors, not the creditors, and hence are not impelled to political action to the same degree as are the cattle landlords, who seem to be always beset by great anxieties over the thousands of pounds of credit which continuously weigh on their conscience. Another factor which should be taken into account is that of continuities from the past. The cattle landlords and middlemen were among the very first of the Hausa migrants to Ibadan. In a census taken in the Quarter in 1916, a few months after its establishment, 56 out of 261 (20 per cent.) Hausa males were described as cattle traders, which means that men working in the cattle trade constituted a much higher proportion of the working population in the past than today. On the other hand, the kola men came to the Quarter mainly during the past generation, since kola has been grown in the Western Region of Nigeria only in recent decades. For the cattle landlords, seniority in the Quarter has meant greater opportunities for acquiring houses, for rallying clients, and for establishing connections with local sources of power and authority. These are advantages which help the cattle landlords, within the contemporary situation, to control the Quarter.

I am not arguing here that the majority of the Quarter blindly align themselves for political action behind the cattle landlords, to the latter's private interests. I am only suggesting that, because of their role in the cattle market, the cattle landlords are more politically active and better organised for political action than any other group within the Quarter. They are also the group most sensitive to any changes in Hausa-Yoruba relations. When the 1962 emergency situation in the Western Region of Nigeria came to an end, in January 1963, and the former Prime Minister, Chief Akintola, returned to his previous position in Ibadan, the cattle landlords and middlemen, who had been ardent Action Groupers until the emergency, went *en masse*, taking with them any Hausa they could mobilise, to greet the returning Premier and to express allegiance to him and to his party (at the time the UPP), which had emerged in opposition to the Action Group. They did this not as cattle men but as Hausa, representing the whole Hausa Quarter. It is significant, incidentally, that at the doors of the Premier they came face to face with another delegation who had also come to express their allegiance — it was the delegation of the Yoruba butchers.

The cattle landlords have very serious reservations about submitting their disputes with the butchers to the civil courts. There are many reasons for this attitude. When a butcher defaults he is usually indebted to many dealers from whom he has bought cattle. As these dealers are the legal creditors, it is they, not the landlords, who should apply to the courts for adjudication, which means that a number of dealers should act jointly in order to pursue their case against the defaulting butcher. But this is highly impracticable. The amount due to each dealer from the defaulting butcher is relatively small, while the expenses of adjudication are high. Furthermore, court procedure is long and the dealers, whose residence is usually far in the North, cannot wait in Ibadan indefinitely. There is also the problem of language and cultural differences. Furthermore, the landlords believe that court rulings in cases of this nature are not effective, since a butcher who pleads that he has no money can be asked to pay only a few pounds a month to his creditors until an amount of hundreds of pounds could be finally settled.[40]

Arbitration by the Chief of the Market, on the other hand, is prompt, convenient, and effective. It is performed by a Hausa, but in nearly all cases of dispute, the Chief of the Butchers, a Yoruba, participates in the arbitratory process. The ruling of the Chief of the Market is final and is nearly always honoured.[41]

Thus the organisation of credit in the market is ultimately upheld, not by the civil courts, but by what may be labelled as 'tribal politics'. In the market, debtors and creditors face each other as tribesmen as well as business men. This double cleavage is basic to the operation of the credit system. It is the product of a number of processes which have driven the Hausa out of the butchering business, on the one hand, and prevented the Yoruba from performing the functions of the cattle landlords, on the other. Until the early 1930's many of the butchers of Ibadan were Hausa, and the Quarter's Hausa 'Chief of the Butchers' was a very powerful man. But today there is only one Hausa butcher[42] in the city, and the title 'Chief of the Butchers' within the Quarter has sunk into insignificance.[43] On the other hand, all the attempts that have been made every now and then by some ambitious Yoruba to act as cattle landlords or even as cattle dealers have completely failed.

I have attempted to show that in order to understand the operation of credit in the cattle market in Ibadan we need to consider such phenomena as informal gossiping and joking, age-grouping, and inter-tribal politics. These are essentially non-economic factors which seem to be exterior to the market situation. In considering credit in Western society, it is equally essential to take into account some non-economic factors, but because of the highly developed centralisation, communication, and bureau-cratisation, these factors are fundamentally the same throughout the society and there is therefore one unitary system of credit. In his analysis, the economist can thus regard these factors as constant, take them for granted, and never mention them. In a pre-industrial society, on the other hand, there are many systems of credit, each having its own structure which consists of both formal and informal relations. This is why, in order to explain such a system, the economist has to rely much on anthropologists or become one himself.

1 The material on which this paper is based was collected in the course of field study among Hausa migrants in the Western Region of Nigeria between September 1962 and November 1963. I am grateful to the School of Oriental and African Studies, University of London, for financing the project and to the Nigerian Institute of

Social and Economic Research and the University of Ibadan for their invaluable help in carrying it out.

2 This is an approximate figure which is higher by about 12 per cent. than that obtained from the records of the veterinary service offices.

3 Throughout the Western Region of Nigeria the cattle markets are locally known by the Hausa word *Zango* (literally meaning a camping place of caravan or lodging place of travellers), while the local Hausa quarter is known as *Säbo*, short for *Säbon Gari*. In Ghana, on the other hand, the word *Zango*, which is usually pronounced as *Zongo*, is used for the native strangers' quarter which is often predominantly Hausa.

4 This, again, is an approximate figure derived from the number of cattle sold in the market, the average price per head, and the average length of the period of credit.

5 *Shänun Rosa*.

6 Trypanosomiasis.

7 According to figures from the veterinary service offices, for the years 1959 to 1962, 20 per cent. of all the cattle which started the journey from the North towards Ibadan as the final destination did not actually reach Ibadan, which means that they were sold on the way. As nearly all the cattle brought by train eventually arrive at Ibadan, this percentage represents the foot cattle which are sold on the way. This means that about 50 per cent. of the foot cattle originally destined for Ibadan are sold on the way.

8 These figures are from a survey covering 118 dealers in foot cattle.

9 *'Dan köre*.

10 *Shänun Jirgi*.

11 Depending on the size of the animals. Usually the horns of the cattle are cut short before the journey so that more cattle can be accommodated in a wagon, and in the market, train cattle can usually be easily identified by their shorter horns.

12 *'Dan taragu*, literally 'son of the wagon'.

13 *Mai shänu*.

14 *Dilläli*.

15 Between them, the twelve cattle landlords operating in Ibadan in 1963, had fifty-two middle-men working for them. The senior among these middlemen had assistants under them, as they were usually given more cattle to sell than were the junior middlemen. Some of these senior middlemen provided food, cooked by their own wives, to the dealers who were 'allotted' to them, and they therefore received a greater proportion of the commission. There were a few middlemen in the market who were not attached to any particular landlord but who worked on a temporary basis for landlords who had more business on their hands than could be dealt with by their permanent middlemen.

16 It is customary for Hausa *men* to wear perfume.

17 According to census material which I collected in 1963, only 12 per cent. of the Hausa migrants in the Quarter had been in Ibadan for twenty years or more.

18 Known as *Sarkin Hausäwa* and sometimes as *Sarkin Säbo*.

19 *Sarkin Zango*.

20 These two positions, the *Sarkin Säbo* and the *Sarkin Zango*, have become so involved in each other that in some situations it is difficult to separate them, even analytically.

21 The beginning and the ending of a session are announced by a whistle blown by one of the 'boys' of the Chief of the Market.

22 Known as *mälam*, in the sense of 'literate', not of 'religious functionary'.

23 The register in which these details are written down serves as a reminder, not a document. The details are neither checked nor ratified by the buyers.

24 Child fostering is very widespread among the Hausa.

25 All education in the Hausa Quarter is 'Arabic' education which consists mainly in

learning to read the Kor'an and to write in Arabic.

26 The overwhelming majority of the Hausa in Sabo adhere to the Tijaniyya order which enjoins intensive collective ritualism and ties initiates to a ritual leader known as *mukaddam*. Groupings emerging in the course of ritual performance tend to become fraternities whose members co-operate in many social fields.

27 *Kankamba.*

28 The butchers are always under constant observation by the landlords and their subordinates. The absence of a butcher for three or four days in succession is always marked with suspicion in the market.

29 As the Hausa are Muslims, the dealers do not in principle charge interest for the credit they give to the butchers. But cash price is always lower than credit price by £1 to £3 for a head of cattle which is usually sold at £20 to £40.

30 Landlords often keep in their houses several thousands of pounds, in cash, for their dealers. The money is kept in simple wooden chests which are protected from thieves by amulets prepared by the malams and are also watched night and day by trusted attendants.

31 There are slight variations in the distribution of the commission between foot cattle and train cattle.

32 A landlord would run the risk of losing all his dealers if he did not meet his obligations. The payment of compensation to the dealers is always by monthly instalments, in accordance with the ruling of the Chief of the Market in the case.

33 The *Sarkin Päwa*. The incumbent of the office is of course a Yoruba man.

34 See E. Durkheim, *The Rules of Sociological Method*, pp. 64-75, translated by S. A. Solovay and J. H. Mueller, and edited by G. E. G. Catlin, The Free Press, Glencoe, Illinois (1950).

35 Such an action is not unlikely to happen. It happened in 1963 in the Abeokuta cattle market, when the butchers stopped paying their debts to the dealers and completely paralysed the market for about five weeks, until the two sides accepted arbitration by the Ibadan Hausa Chief. The dispute arose when some of the Hausa cattle landlords attempted to enter the butchering business by slaughtering a number of cattle and selling the meat to local retailers. The arbitrator eventually ruled that no slaughtering should be done by the landlords.

36 Men in the Quarter do not conceal the fact that in their political behaviour they follow the instructions of their patrons unquestionably.

37 The association was formally called 'The Federal Union of the Western Sarkis Hausawa'.

38 Ninety-seven out of a total of 1,570. The figures are from a general census which I took in Sabo with the help of local assistants.

39 285 out of a total of 1,570.

40 The landlords often skip over most of these factors and dismiss the case for submitting disputes to the courts by saying: 'After all these are *Yoruba* courts.'

41 One of the most striking phenomena I witnessed in this respect was the obedience which the Yoruba butchers showed towards the Hausa Chief, whose authority was so strong that he could send his messenger and summon any butcher to his office.

42 Besides this licensed butcher there are a few Hausa men who work as 'meat cutters', buying wholesale from Yoruba butchers and selling within the Quarter or in the neighbouring Mokola Quarter.

43 The case of dispute between the local Yoruba butchers and the Hausa cattle landlords mentioned in footnote 2, p. 16, points in the same direction.

PART FOUR

Special Appendices

APPENDIX ONE
Interpreting Accounting Data and Business Records

Those involved in business history research quickly recognise the need for theory and measurement as aids to control or to direct the interpretation of accounting data and business records.

This appendix is intended as a guide to the interpretation of business accounts and the secondary records which may be derived from book keeping entries or other primary sources. With increasing attention (by business analysts, accountants, government agencies and those with financial interests in firms) being devoted to the disclosure, consistency and comparability of accounting reports, the practices of measurement, allocation and assessment of performance must be of crucial importance to a business historian. Similarly, more recent developments in the theory of the firm, industrial structure, decision-making and the relationships between firms and other areas of their trading environment are of relevance to the methods of business history research and the questions it poses. Just how relevant this interdisciplinary literature is depends in part on the awareness of the researcher of its existence and the demonstration of its usefulness. Many of the readings in this selection show that both of these conditions have already been met. The list of references given below is designed to further this possibility of challenging the data, the theory and the established evidence with the best techniques of analysis available.

For an introduction to interpreting account-books and accounting practices, B.S. Yamey's useful commentary in *Business History* (The Historical Association, Revised Edition, 1971), pp.33-9, should be consulted. By contrast, and with a view to using models to describe or explain systems depicted by accounting data, a book by John Flower entitled *Computer Models for Accountants*. (Accountancy Age Books, Haymarket Publishing Ltd., 1973), shows how simple representations of reality can provide insight for explanation and control. Many of the techniques of analysing business data, including simulation models, cost-benefit analysis, capital budgeting procedures, mathematical programming, and statistical cost analysis, have their uses in manipulating historical business data. And the development of theory and the extension of empirical knowledge in the fields of operations, research, finance, managerial economics, accountancy, micro-economic theory and industrial structure and organisation and applicable, as evidence and a framework, for research in business history.

The books listed in the first part of the reading guide are intended to draw attention to some of the literature on the above-mentioned techniques and from proximate fields of research. The sections dealing with journal articles are more specialised. The articles included fall into three groups. The first deals with interpreting accounts, records and measures of performance which are used for the purposes of internal management and control. Some of the problems discussed include methods of attributing costs and revenues to divisions or products, methods of tracing the sources of variations in cost, methods of accounting for cost allocation over time and the effects that some of these methods may have in possibly biasing any judgment on performance at a more aggregate level.

Many of the financial ratios which are calculated to describe financial structure and performance are the joint product of methods of allocation and cost control used internally and methods of valuation, recording and disclosure used in the preparation of published accounts. Because much periodic recording is based upon historical prices rather than the market prices of equivalent stocks or assets, both inflation and changes in methods of valuation and presentation may lead to a lack of comparability between firms or over periods of time. The difficulties of interpretation occasioned by changes in the unit of account are discussed in Appendix Two.

The uses and limitations of financial ratios are important to a business historian. Once prepared, they are often the only benchmark by which he can chart the changes in profitability or financial structure of the organisation and relate them to other types of evidence (e.g. minute books or the economic context) which may have determined this financial outcome. The relationships among the variables used in such ratios are also important for the business historian wishing to trace the origins and causative directions of change. Also, methods of organising this data, whether for example in a funds statement showing changes in assets and liabilities or by use of a mathematical programming model to show constraints on raising capital or increasing production and sales, are useful techniques for distilling the particular or general features of the organisation over time or groups of firms at a point in time. The potential of these techniques is limited only by the quality of the data and the inventive application of the researcher.

(a) Books

Archibald, G. C. (ed.), *Theory of the Firm* (Penguin Education, Harmondsworth), 1971.

Baumol, W. J., *Economic Theory and Operations Analysis*, 2nd Edition (Prentice-Hall, Englewood Cliffs, N. J.), 1961.

Baumol, W. J., *Business Behaviour, Value and Growth* (Harcourt, Brace and World), 1976.

Bierman, H. and Smidt, S., *The Capital Budgeting Decision: economic analysis and financing of Investment Projects* (Macmillan, New York), 3rd Ed. 1971.

Brown, Murray, *On the Theory and Measurement of Technological Change* (Cambridge University Press), 1966.

Burn, Duncan (ed.), *The Structure of British Industry. A Symposium*, volumes 1 and 2 (Cambridge University Press), 1958.

Chandler, A. D. Jr, *Strategy and Structure* (M.I.T. Press, Boston), 1965.

Chandler, A. D. Jr; Bruchey, S. and Galambos, L. (eds.), *The Changing Economic Order: Readings in American Business and Economic History* (Harcourt, Brace and World), 1968.

Clarkson, G. P. E. (ed.), *Managerial Economics* (Penguin Education, Harmondsworth), 1968.

Cowling, Keith (ed.), *Market Structure and Corporate Behaviour: Theory and Empirical Analysis of the Firm* (Gray-Mills Publishing Ltd., London), 1972.

Cyert, R. M. and March, J. G., *A Behavioural Theory of the Firm* (Prentice-Hall, Englewood Cliffs, N.J.), 1963.

Deakin, B. M. and Seward, T., *Productivity in Transport*, University of Cambridge Department of Applied Economics, Occasional Paper no. 17 (Cambridge University Press), 1969.

Edwards, E. O. and Bell, P. W., *The Theory and Measurement of Business Income* (University of California Press), 1961.

Eichner, Alfred S., *The Emergence of Oligopoly. Sugar Refining as a Case Study* (The Johns Hopkins Press, Baltimore), 1969.

Evely, R. and Little, I. M. D., *Concentration in British Industry: An Empirical Study of the Structure of Industrial Production, 1935-51* (Cambridge University Press), 1960.

Flower, John, *Computer Models for Accountants* (Haymarket Publishing Ltd., London), 1973.

Fuchs, Victor, R. (ed.), *Production and Productivity in the Service Industries*, Studies in Income and Wealth, volume 34 (Columbia University Press, New York), 1969.

George, K. D., *Productivity in Distribution*, University of Cambridge Department of Applied Economics, Occasional Paper no. 8 (Cambridge University Press), 1966.

George, Kenneth D., *Industrial Organisation: Competition, Growth and Structural Change in Britain* (George Allen and Unwin Ltd., London), 1971.

George, K. D. and Hills, P. V., *Productivity and Capital Expenditure in Retailing*, University of Cambridge Department of Applied Economics, Occasional Paper no. 16 (Cambridge University Press), 1968.

Griliches, Z. and Ringstad, V., *Economies of Scale and the Form of the Production Function: an econometric study of Norwegian Manufacturing Establishment Data* (North-Holland, Amsterdam), 1971.

Hadley, G., *Linear Programming* (Addison-Wesley, Reading, Mass.), 1962.

Hadley, G., *Nonlinear and Dynamic Programming* (Addison-Wesley, Reading, Mass.), 1964.

Hadley, G. and Kemp, M. C., *Finite Mathematics in Business and Economics* (North-Holland, Amsterdam), 1972.

Hart, P. E. (ed.), *Studies in Profit, Business Saving and Investment in the*

United Kingdom, 1920-1962, volumes 1 and 2 (George Allen and Unwin Ltd., London), 1965 and 1968.

Hart, P. E.; Utton, M. A. and Walshe, G., *Mergers and Concentration in British Industry*, The National Institute of Economic and Social Research, Occasional Paper no. XXVI (Cambridge University Press), 1973.

Heward, J. H. and Steele, P. M., *Business Control Through Multiple Regression Analysis* (Gower Press, London), 1972.

Johnston, J., *Statistical Cost Analysis* (McGraw-Hill, New York), 1960.

Lancaster, K., *Consumer Demand: a New Approach* (Columbia University Press, New York), 1971.

Littleton, A. C. and Yamey, B. S. (eds.), *Studies in the History of Accounting* (Sweet and Maxwell Ltd., London), 1956.

March, J. G. and Simon, H. A., *Organisations* (John Wiley, New York), 1958.

Marris, R., *The Economic Theory of 'Managerial Capitalism'* (Macmillan, London), 1964.

Marris, R. (ed.), *The Corporate Economy; growth, competition and innovative potential* (Macmillan, London), 1971.

Merrett, A. J. and Sykes, A., *The Finance and Analysis of Capital Projects* (Longmans, London), 1963.

Merrett, A. J. and Sykes, A., *Capital Budgeting and Company Finance* (Longmans, London), 1966.

Mishan, E. J., *Cost-Benefit Analysis: an Informal Introduction* (George Allen and Unwin Ltd., London), 1971.

Needham, Douglas (ed.), *Economic Analysis and Industrial Structure* (Holt, Rinehart and Winston, Inc., New York), 1969.

Nelson, Ralph L., *Concentration in the Manufacturing Industries of the United States* (Yale University Press, New Haven), 1963.

Penrose, Edith, T., *The Theory of the Growth of the Firm* (Basil Blackwell, Oxford), 1959.

Penrose, Edith T., *The Growth of Firms, Middle East Oil and Other Essays* (Frank Cass, London), 1971.

Pratten, C. F., *Economies of Scale in Manufacturing Industry*, University of Cambridge Department of Applied Economics, Occasional Paper no. 28 (Cambridge University Press), 1971.

Rosenbluth, Gideon, *Concentration in Canadian Manufacturing Industries*, National Bureau of Economic Research, Number 61, General Series (Princeton University Press, Princeton), 1957.

Rowley, Charles K., *Readings in Industrial Economics*, volumes 1 and 2 (Macmillan, London), 1972.

Rowthorn, Robert (and Hymer, Stephen), *International Big Business 1957-1967: a Study of Comparative Growth*, University of Cambridge Department of Applied Economics, Occasional Paper no. 24 (Cambridge University Press), 1971.

Rybczynski, T. M. (ed.), *A New Era in Competition* (Basil Blackwell, Oxford), 1973.

Solomons, D., *Divisional Performance: measurement and control* (Financial Executives Research Foundation, New York), 1965.

Salter, W. E. G., *Productivity and Technical Change* (Cambridge University Press), 1960.

Sutherland, Alister, *The Monopolies Commission in Action*, University of Cambridge Department of Applied Economics, Occasional Paper no. 21 (Cambridge University Press), 1969.

Tisdell, Clement Allan, *The Theory of Price Uncertainty, Production and Profit* (Princeton University Press, Princeton, N.J.), 1968.

Townsend, H. (ed.), *Price Theory* (Penguin Education, Harmondsworth), 1971.

Tucker, K. A. and Yamey, B. S. (eds.), *Economics of Retailing* (Penguin Education, Harmondsworth), 1973.

Utton, M. A., *Industrial Concentration* (Penguin Books, Harmondsworth), 1970.

Wagner, Leslie and Baltazzis, Nikos, *Readings in Applied Micro-economics* (The Clarendon Press, Oxford), 1973.

Yamey, Basil S. (ed.), *Economics of Industrial Structure* (Penguin Education, Harmondsworth), 1973.

(b) Journal Articles

Ball, Ray, 'Index of Empirical Research in Accounting', *Journal of Accounting Research*, vol. 9, no. 1 (1971), pp. 1-31.
(i) Cost Allocation, Control and Measures of Internal Performance.

Benston, George J., 'Multiple Regression Analysis of Cost Behaviour', *Accounting Review*, vol. 41 (1966), pp. 657-72.

Brief, Richard P. and Owen, Joel, 'A Least Squares Allocation Model', *Journal of Accounting Research*, vol. 6, no. 1 (1968), pp. 193-99.

Brief, Richard P. and Owen, Joel, 'On Bias in Accounting Allocations under Uncertainty', *Journal of Accounting Research*, vol. 7, no. 1 (1969), pp. 12-16.

Bromwich, M., 'Measurement of Divisional Performance: A Comment and an Extension', *Accounting and Business Research*, vol. 3, no. 10 (Spring, 1973), pp. 123-32.

Chin, John S. and De Coster, Donald T., 'Multiple Product Costing by Multiple Correlation Analysis', *Accounting Review*, vol. 41 (1966), pp. 673-80.

Comiskey, Eugene E., 'Cost Control by Regression Analysis', *Accounting Review*, vol. 41 (1966), pp. 235-38.

Demski, Joel S., 'Decision-Performance Control', *Accounting Review*, vol. 44 (1969), pp. 669-79.

Dyckman, T. R., 'The Investigation of Cost Variances', *Journal of Accounting Research*, vol. 7, no. 1 (1969), pp. 215-44.

Flower, J. F., 'Measurement of Divisional Performance', *Accounting and Business Research*, vol. 1, no. 3 (Summer, 1971), pp. 205-14.

Hart, H., 'Capacity Concepts and Overhead Costs', *Business Ratios*, vol. 3, no. 1 (Autumn, 1969), pp. 13-23.

Jensen, Robert E., 'A Multiple Regression Model for Cost Control-

Assumptions and Limitations', *Accounting Review*, vol. 42 (1966), pp. 265-73.

Jensen, Robert E. and Thomen, C. Torben, 'Statistical Analysis in Cost Measurement and Control', *Accounting Review*, vol. 43 (1968), pp. 83-93.

Johnson, Orace, 'A Consequential Approach to Accounting for R & D', *Journal of Accounting Research*, vol. 5, no. 2 (1967), pp. 164-72.

Koplan, Robert S. and Thompson, Gerald L., 'Overhead Allocaticn via Mathematical Programming Models', *Accounting Review*, vol. 46 (1971), pp. 352-64.

Langhold, Odd., 'Cost Structure and Costing Method: An Empirical Study', *Journal of Accounting Research*, vol. 3, no. 2 (1965), pp. 218-27.

Livingstone, John Leslie, 'Matrix Algebra and Cost Allocation', *Accounting Review*, vol. 43 (1968), pp. 503-08.

Ozan, T. and Dyckman, T., 'A Normative Model for Investigating Decisions Involving Multiorigin Cost Variances', *Journal of Accounting Research*, vol. 9, no. 1 (1971), pp. 88-115.

Ronen, Joshua and McKinney, George, 'Transfer Pricing for Divisional Autonomy', *Journal of Accounting Research*, vol. 8, no. 1 (1970), pp. 99-112.

Ronen, Joshua, 'Capacity and Operating Variances: An Ex Post Approach', *Journal of Accounting Research*, vol. 8, no. 2 (1970), pp. 232-52.

Samuels, J. M., 'Opportunity Costing: An Application of Mathematical Programming', *Journal of Accounting Research*, vol. 3, no. 2 (1965), pp. 182-91.

Shillinglaw, Gordon, 'The Concept of Attributable Cost', *Journal of Accounting Research*, vol. 1, no. 1 (1963), pp. 73-85.

(ii) Financial Ratios: Their Use and Limitations

Beaver, William H., 'Market Prices, Financial Ratios and the Prediction of Failure', *Journal of Accounting Research*, vol. 6, no. 1 (1968), pp. 179-92.

Beaver, William H., 'Financial Ratios as Predictors of Failure', *Empirical Research in Accounting: Selected Studies* (1966), pp. 71-112.

Benishay, Haskel, 'Economic Information in Financial Ratio Analysis: a note', *Accounting and Business Research*, vol. 1, no. 2 (Spring, 1971), pp. 174-79.

Bird, Peter, 'What is Capital Gearing?', *Accounting and Business Research*, vol. 3, no. 10 (Spring, 1973), pp. 92-97.

Chambers, D. J., 'The Joint Problem of Investment and Financing', *Operational Research Quarterly*, vol. 22, no. 3 (1971), pp. 267-295.

Horrigan, James O., 'Some Empirical Bases for Financial Ratio Analysis', *Accounting Review*, vol. 40 (1965), pp. 558-68.

Horrigan, James O., 'A Short History of Financial Ratio Analysis', *Accounting Review*, vol. 43 (1968), pp. 284-94.

Kendall, Henry, 'The Use of Ratios in the Printing Industry', *Business Ratios*, vol. 1, no. 2 (Summer, 1967), pp. 15-20.

Lev, Baruch, 'Industry Averages as Targets for Financial Ratios', *Journal of Accounting Research*, vol. 7, no. 2 (1969), pp. 290-99.

(iii) Financial Control, Disclosure and
External Performance

Amey, L. R., 'Interdependencies in Capital Budgeting', *Journal of Business Finance*, vol. 4, no. 3 (1972), pp. 70-86.

Barron, M. J., 'Profitability, The Profit Margin and Turnover Ratio — An Empirical Investigation', *Business History*, vol. 2, no. 2 (Summer, 1968), pp. 16-24.

Bar-Yosef, S., 'Value Added and Return on Capital as Measures of Managerial Efficiency: Comment', *Journal of Business Finance*, vol. 4, no. 2 (1972), pp. 71-74.

Bayliss, R. W., 'Input-Output Analysis as an Aid to Financial Control', *Accounting and Business Research*, vol. 2, no. 5 (Winter, 1972), pp. 53-9.

Beattie, D. M., 'Value added and Return on Capital as Measures of Efficiency', *Journal of Business Finance*, vol. 2, no. 2 (1970), pp. 22-28.

Bromwich, M., 'Capital Budgeting — a Survey', *Journal of Business Finance*, vol. 2, no. 3 (1970), pp. 3-26.

Dunning, J. H. and Barron, M. J., 'A Productivity Measure of Business Performance', *Business Ratios*, vol. 1, no. 3 (Autumn, 1967), pp. 11-15.

Falk, Haim, 'Financial Statements and Personal Characteristics in Investment Decision Making', *Accounting and Business Research*, vol. 2, no. 6 (Spring, 1972), pp. 209-22.

Felix, William L. Jr, 'Estimating the Relationship between Technical Change and Reported Performance', *Accounting Review*, vol. 47 (1972), pp. 52-63.

Feltham, Gerald, A. and Demski, Joel S., 'The Use of Models in Information Evaluation', *Accounting Review*, vol. 45 (1970), pp. 623-40.

Grinyer, J. R., 'The Cost of Equity Capital', *Journal of Business Finance*, vol. 4, no. 4 (1972), pp. 44-52.

Hart, P. E., 'Competition and Rate of Return on Capital in U.K. Industry', *Business Ratios*, vol. 2, no. 1 (Spring, 1968), pp. 3-11.

Holmes, Geoffrey, 'Earnings per share: A Measure of Sustainable Growth', *Accounting and Business Research*, vol. 1, no. 2 (Spring, 1971), pp. 118-44.

Ijiri, Y.; Levy, F. K. and Lyon, R. C., 'A Linear Programming Model for Budgeting and Financial Planning', *Journal of Accounting Research*, vol. 1, no. 2 (1963), pp. 198-212.

Jensen, Robert E., 'A Cluster Analysis Study of Financial Performance of Selected Business Firms', *Accounting Review*, vol. 46 (1971), pp. 36-56.

Kinney, William R. Jr, 'An Environmental Model for Performance Measurement in Multi-Outlet Businesses', *Journal of Accounting Research*, vol. 7, no. 1 (1969), pp. 44-52.

Lawson, C. H., 'Published Accounting Data and the Measurement of Performance', *Business Ratios*, vol. 3, no. 2 (Summer, 1969), pp. 5-7.

Peles, Yoram, 'Amortisation of Advertising Expenditures in the Financial Statements', *Journal of Accounting Research*, vol. 8, no. 1 (1970), pp. 128-37.

Rosen, L. S. and De Coster, Don, T., ' "Funds", Statements: A Historical Perspective', *Accounting Review*, vol. 44 (1969), pp. 124-36.

Samuels, J. M., 'An Empirical Study of the Cost of Equity Capital', *Business Ratios*, vol. 2, no. 1 (Spring, 1968), pp. 12-15.

Summers, Edward L. and Deskins, James Wesley, 'A Classification Scheme of Methods for Reporting Effects of Resource Price Changes', *Journal of Accounting Research*, vol. 8, no. 1 (1970), pp. 113-17.

Williams, Edward E., 'Cost Capital Functions and the Firm's Optimal Level of Gearing', *Journal of Business Finance*, vol. 4, no. 2 (1972), pp. 78-83.

Wright, F. K., 'Measuring Asset Services: A Linear Programming Approach', *Journal of Accounting Research*, vol. 6, no. 2 (1968), pp. 222-36.

Yu, S. C., 'A Flow-of-Resources Statement for Business Enterprise', *Accounting Review*, vol. 44 (1969), pp. 571-82.

APPENDIX TWO
Allowing for Changes in the Unit of Account and Measuring Income, Assets and Liabilities

The measurement of accounting data in common units of value is designed to facilitate comparisons across activities of a similar nature and for the same organisation over time. If the supply and demand conditions in money, labour, land, capital and goods markets were constant over time and if information pertaining to these conditions was consistently and comprehensively recorded and disclosed on the same basis, there would be little need to adjust accounting and business records to remove bias or fictitious changes in value. Unfortunately, for the business historian, neither are the real market effects nor are changes in the basis of reporting so unambiguously revealed.

Ideally, the business historian would like to standardise his data to remove changes in money values (as distinct from the relationships expressing changes in real quantities) and to ensure that methods of valuing inventories, debtors, fixed assets and goodwill are consistent among firms (for cross-sectional analysis) or over different periods of his analysis (for time series data). This rectified data then represents the remaining effects of supply and demand and decision-making in changing the real price and quantity intercepts of these relationships. Theories of response to various economic contexts, legal conditions of offer and acceptance and financial claims to and the utilisation of real resources can then be evaluated with greater interpretative clarity.

Much of the data of business decision-making is not amenable to such treatment. This is so for a number of reasons. First, it is not always possible to obtain a suitable index by which to re-weight or revise the given series. Secondly, it may be that several possible indices may be used or constructed to standardise the data, each of which has various limitations and merits. Thirdly, it may be that the application of the standardising procedure would not materially alter the interpretation given to the series or the relationships. In the last instance, it is therefore a superfluous exercise, apart from the confirmation that the unit of account is significantly invariant with respect to the chosen index. Thus the justification for not allowing for changes in measurement constructs, accounting procedures, or the real value of the units, may be one or many of the above three reasons.

Another set of reasons may also apply, especially when historical records and management practices suggest that changes in prices, expressed in terms of money values alone, result in a lack of response, a proportionate response or the development of a form of expectation about further changes in the price level. For example, if management interprets its performance in average money terms or the result of each year expressed as a percentage change on the previous year in money values, the decisions taken must be reconstructed and interpreted in a different way from decisions taken assuming that they watched for underlying real trends or re-based each year's performance by allowing for money price changes. However, if the former is the case, it may be a revealing exercise to question how far management decisions might have been altered if allowance had been made for the biased measures of performance, structure or the net value of assets. Similarly, capital budgeting decisions may be affected by the extent to which inflationary tendencies are allowed for and by which methods.

There is no easy answer to the problem of discovering how well financial measures report real relationships and the degree of managerial control or financial disclosure exercised in generating the data. The problems of measuring income in current terms, allowing for elements of wear and tear, obsolescence, or capital gains, revaluing assets or goodwill and comparing leases with asset services which are owned must be studied in the particular context of the ways the business records have been prepared, what they were used for and how they have survived.

The references given in this appendix relate largely to problems of interpreting measurement and reporting in current accounting practice. They are intended only as a starting point for those wishing to scrutinise critically any data they are using in research programmes or projects. In many cases, they show that it is possible and useful to standardise data for changes in the unit of account or to splice series prepared on different bases. But when it comes to finding out how far decisions have been affected by changes in the unit of account, business historians may well be able to contribute as much as accountants, economists or management.

Anton, Hector, R., 'Some Aspects of Measurement and Accounting', *Journal of Accounting Research*, vol. 2, no. 1 (1964), pp. 1-9.

Benjamin, James, 'The Effects of Using Current Costs in the Measurement of Business Income', *Accounting and Business Research*, vol. 3, no. 11 (Summer, 1973), pp. 213-17.

Bierman, Harold, Jr, 'Recording Obsolescence', *Journal of Accounting Research*, vol. 2, no. 2 (1964), pp. 229-35.

Bromwich, M., 'Inflation and the Capital Budgeting Process', *Journal of Business Finance*, vol. 1, no. 2 (1969), pp. 39-46.

Chambers, R. J., 'Measurement in Accounting', *Journal of Accounting Research*, vol. 3, no. 1 (1965), pp. 32-62.

Duvall, Richard M. and Bulloch, James, 'Adjusting Date of Return and Present Value for Price-Level Changes', *Accounting Review*, vol. 40 (1965), pp. 568-73.

Lee, T. A., 'Accounting for Goodwill: An Empirical Study of Company

Practices in the United Kingdom — 1962 to 1971', *Accounting and Business Research*, vol. 3, no. 11 (Summer, 1973), pp. 175-96.

McDonald, Daniel L., 'A Test Application of the Feasibility of Market Based Measures in Accounting', *Journal of Accounting Research*, vol. 6, no. 1 (1968), pp. 38-49.

Moonitz, Maurice, 'Price-Level Accounting and Scales of Measurement', *Accounting Review*, vol. 45 (1970), pp. 465-75.

Most, Kenneth S., 'The Valuation of Inventories', *Journal of Accounting Research*, vol. 5, no. 1 (1967), pp. 39-50.

Myddelton, D. R., 'Short Cuts in Adjusting Accounts for Currency Debasement', *The Investment Analyst*, no. 29 (May, 1971), pp. 8-15.

Myddelton, D. R., 'Consolidated Nationalised Industries Accounts 1948-1970. Published Figures Adjusted for Currency Debasement', *Accounting and Business Research*, vol. 2, no. 6 (Spring, 1972), pp. 83-109.

Staubus, George J., 'The Measurement of Assets and Liabilities', *Accounting and Business Research*, vol. 3, no. 12 (Autumn, 1973), pp. 243-62.

Vatter, W. J., 'Accounting for Leases', *Journal of Accounting Research*, vol. 4, no. 2 (1966), pp. 133-48.

Wilkes, F. M., 'Inflation and Capital Budgeting Decisions', *Journal of Business Finance*, vol. 4, no. 3 (1972), pp. 46-53.

APPENDIX THREE
Select Bibliography for Further Reading

It is not intended that this bibliography should be a comprehensive guide to sources or archive material or even to published studies that relate to some areas of business history. Rather, it is a complement to those readings selected for inclusion in this volume. Along with the material cited by the contributors, it provides a demonstration of methods and approaches that have been employed in business history research.

Neither is there any reference to particular studies in business history of book length. For readers interested in consulting these examples, reference may be made to the useful booklet by T. C. Barker, R. H. Campbell, P. Mathias and B. S. Yamey, entitled *Business History* (The Historical Association, Revised Edition, 1971) and the Social Science Research Review entitled *Research in Economic and Social History* (Heinemann, 1971).

However, the first part of the bibliography does refer to book-length studies or collections which may be consulted as general guides to objectives, methods and the practice of business history research. This section is followed by a list of articles from journals on the same themes.

The remainder of the selection is concerned with some of the topics and subjects of primary interest which have been investigated in the writing of business history. The examples are all taken from journals. The arrangement of the groups is intended to roughly correspond with the sequence and major focus of the contributions selected for this set of readings. There is, necessarily, some overlap and often a referenced article may almost equally well cover two or more of the sub-headings of the reading guide. The title of the article, in some cases, may indicate this relatedness but the only certain check on relevance is, of course, to read the material in question.

Early examples of business history research are included on the assumption that recent studies have no exclusive claim on the more appropriate and improved deployment of methods of analysis, data manipulation or ways of verifying events. They also often highlight the constraints of data availability and the particular purposes of the writer in delimiting the means of treatment and avenues of interpretation.

For those who are interested in applying methods of analysis to various types of data, Appendix One: Interpreting Accounting Data and Business Records, and Appendix Two: Allowing for Changes in the Unit of Account, may be referred to. From these references the potential usefulness of quantitative approaches of various types may be assessed. The emphasis is on what research in business history may yield in the form of empirical results from an infusion of additional perspectives, exploratory directions of analysis and presentation, and the extended use of statistical testing and theoretical framework.

The bibliography is arranged as follows.

Appendix Three: Select Bibliography for Further Reading

A. Studies in Business History: Books
B. Studies in Business History: Articles
   Part One: Business History as a Subject
      (i) The Development and Uses of Business History
      (ii) Objectives and Methods of Business History
      (iii) The Practice of Business History
   Part Two: Business Organisation, Growth and Structure
      (i) Energy, Raw Materials and Primary Production
      (ii) Secondary Activities
         (a) Fibre Industries
         (b) Metal Industries
         (c) Producer Goods
         (d) Consumer Goods
      (iii) Tertiary Activities
         (a) Transport, Construction and Communications
         (b) Banking, Finance and Insurance
         (c) Trading, Marketing and Retailing
      (iv) Business Organisation and Growth
         (a) Technical Progress and Scale
         (b) Investment, Productivity and Structural Features
         (c) Competition and Regulation: Science and Government
         (d) Entrepreneurship
   Part Three: Management Practices and Techniques

A.   Studies in Business History: Books

Andreano, R. L. (ed.), *The New Economic History: Recent Papers on Methodology* (John Wiley, New York) 1970.
Aydelotte, W. O., *Quantification in History* (Addison-Wesley, Reading, Mass.) 1971.
Aydelotte, William O.; Bogue, Allen C. and Fogel, Robert W. (eds.), *The Dimensions of Quantitative Research in History* (Princeton University Press, Princeton) 1972.
Barker, T. C.; Campbell, R. H.; Mathias, P. and Yamey, B. S., *Business History*, Revised Edition (The Historical Association, 1971).
Business History Review: Special Issues — Vol. 36, Nos. 1 and 2 (1963) 'Fashion'; Vol. 37, Nos. 1 and 2 (1964) 'Government-Business'; Vol. 39, No. 1 (1965) 'Transportation'; Vol. 47, No. 2 (1973) 'Canada'.

Cain, Louis P. and Uselding, Paul J., *Business Enterprise and Economic Change. Essays in Honour of Harold F. Williamson* (The Kent State University Press, Ohio) 1973.

Coleman, D. C., *What has happened to Economic History?* (Cambridge University Press, Cambridge) 1972.

Dollar, C. M. and Jewsen, R. J. N., *Historian's Guide to Statistics: Quantitative Analysis and Historical Research* (Holt, Rinehart and Winston, New York) 1971.

Dyos, H. J. and Wolff, Michael (eds.), *The Victorian City*, Vols. 1 and 2 (Routledge and Kegan Paul, London) 1973.

Floud, Roderick, *An Introduction to Quantitative Methods for Historians* (Methuen and Co. Ltd., London) 1973.

Fogel, R. W. and Engerman, S. L. (eds.), *The Reinterpretation of American Economic History* (Harper and Row, New York) 1971.

Gould, J. D., *Economic Growth in History: Survey and Analysis* (Methune and Co. Ltd., London) 1973.

Landes, D. S. and Tilly, C., *History as Social Science* (Prentice-Hall, Englewood Cliffs, N.J.) 1971.

Lovett, R. W., *American Economic and Business History. A Guide to Information Sources* (Gale Research Company, Detroit) 1971.

Macmillan, D. S. (ed.), *Canadian Business History. Selected Studies, 1947-1971* (McClelland and Stewart Ltd., Toronto) 1972.

McCloskey, D. N. (ed.), *Essays on a Mature Economy: Britain after 1840* (Methuen, London) 1971.

Payne, Peter L. (ed.), *Studies in Scottish Business History* (Frank Cass, London) 1967.

Payne, P. L., *British Entrepreneurship in the Nineteenth Century* (Macmillan, London) 1974.

Research in Economic and Social History, Reviews of Current Research. Social Science Research Council (Heinemann, 1971), especially pp. 19-32 and 69-75.

Rowney, D. K. and Graham, J. Q. Jr (eds.), *Quantitative History: Selected Readings in the Quantitative Analysis of Historical Data* (Dorsey Press, Homewood, I11.) 1969.

Taylor, George Rogers and Ellesworth, Lucius F. (eds.), *Approaches to American Economic History* (The University of Virginia Press, Charlottesville) 1971.

Temin P. (ed.), *New Economic History* (Penguin Education, Harmondsworth) 1973.

B. Studies in Business History: Articles

Part One: Business History as a Subject
(i) The Development and Uses of Business History

Ashton, T. S., 'Business History', *Business History*, vol. 1, no. 1 (1958), pp. 1-2.

Barker, T. C., 'Business History and the Businessman', *Business History*, Vol. 1, no. 1 (1958), pp. 16-20.

Birch, Alan, 'Writing a Company History', *Business Archives and History*, vol. 1, no. 2 (1956), pp. 16-21.

Briggs, A., 'Business History', *Economic History Review*, Second Series, vol. 9, no. 3 (1957), pp. 486-98.

Butlin, N. G., 'Borderlands or Badlands? Rejoinder to Professor Cochran', *EEH*, 1st Series, vol. 3, no. 1 (1950), pp. 44-50.

Cochran, Thomas C., 'The Economics in a Business History', *Journal of Economic History*, vol. 5 (1945), Supplement, pp. 54-65.

Gras, N. S. B., 'The Businessman and Economic Systems', *Journal of Economic and Business History*, vol. 3 (1930-31), pp. 165-84.

Gras, N. S. B., 'Business History', *Economic History Review*, First Series, vol. 4, no. 4 (1934), pp. 385-98.

Hartwell, R. M., 'The Use of Business History', *Business Archives and History*, vol. 1, no. 4 (1958), pp. 20-26.

Hoselitz, Bert F., 'The Early History of Entrepreneurial Theory', *EEH*, 1st Series, vol. 3, no. 3 (1951), pp. 193-220.

Hower, Ralph M., 'The Boston Conference on Business History', *Journal of Economic and Business History*, vol. 3 (1930-31), pp. 463-80.

'N. S. B. Gras, 1884-1956', *Business History Review*, vol. 30, no. 4 (1956), pp. 357-60.

Payne, P. L., 'The Uses of Business History: A Contribution to the Discussion', *Business History*, vol. 5, no. 1 (1962), pp. 11-21.

Redlich, Fritz, '"Quantitative" and "Qualitative" Research in Economics: Meaning and History of the Terms', *EEH*, 1st Series, vol. 9, no. 4 (1957), pp. 229-40.

Soltow, James H., 'The Business Use of Business History', *Business History Review*, vol. 29, no. 3 (1955), pp. 227-37.

Supple, B. E., 'The Uses of Business History', *Business History*, vol. 4, no. 2 (1961), pp. 81-90.

Williamson, Harold F., 'The Uses of Business History', *Business History*, vol. 7, no. 1 (1964), pp. 57-8.

(ii) Objectives and Methods of Business History

Basmann, R. L., 'The Role of the Economic Historian in Predictive Testing of Proffered "Economic Laws"', *EEH*, 2nd Series, vol. 2, no. 3 (1965), pp. 159-86.

Bell, Peter F., 'The Direction of Entrepreneurial Explorations. A Review Article', *EEH*, 2nd Series, vol. 5, no. 1 (1967), pp. 3-11.

Chandler, Alfred D. Jr and Redlich, Fritz, 'Recent Developments in American Business Administration and Their Conceptualisation', *Business History Review*, vol. 35, no. 1 (1961), pp. 1-27.

Church R. A., 'Themes and Perspectives', Chapter Six of *Kendricks in Hardware. A Family Business: 1791-1966* (David and Charles, 1969), pp. 304-29.

Cochran, Thomas C., 'The Entrepreneur in Economic Change', *EEH*, 2nd Series, vol. 3, no. 2 (1966), pp. 25-38.

Coleman, D. C., 'Comparisons and Conclusions', Chapter 12 of *Courtaulds*, vol. 1 (Oxford University Press, 1969), pp. 261-74.

Cole, Arthur H., 'Conspectus for a History of Economic and Business Literature', *Journal of Economic History*, vol. 17 (1957), pp. 333-88.

Cole, Arthur H., 'Business History and Economic History', *Journal of Economic History*, vol. 5 (1945), Supplement, pp. 45-53.

Cole, Arthur H., 'Meso-economics: A Contribution From Entrepreneurial History', *EEH*, 2nd Series, vol. 6, no. 1 (1968), pp. 3-33.

Cole, Arthur H., 'Aggregative Business History', *Business History Review*, vol. 39, no. 3 (1965), pp. 287-300.

Conrad, Alfred H. and Meyer, John R., 'Economic Theory, Statistical Inference and Economic History', *Journal of Economic History*, vol. 17 (1957), pp. 524-53.

David, Paul, 'The Use and Abuse of Prior Information in Econometric History', *Journal of Economic History*, vol. 32, no. 3 (1972), pp. 706-27.

Davis, Lance E.; Hughes, J. R. T. and Reiter, S., 'Aspects of Quantitative Research in Economic History', *Journal of Economic History*, vol. 10 (1960), pp. 539-47.

Desai, M., 'Some Issues in Econometric History', *Economic History Review*, Second Series, vol. 21, no. 1 (1968-69), pp. 1-16.

Evans, G. Heberton Jr, 'Business Entrepreneurs, Their Major Functions and Related Tenets', *Journal of Economic History*, vol. 19, no. 1 (1959), pp. 250-70.

Glade, William P., 'Approaches to a Theory of Entrepreneurial Formation', *EEH*, 2nd Series, vol. 4, no. 3 (1967), pp. 245-59.

Gould, J. D., 'Hypothetical History', *Economic History Review*, Second Series, vol. 22, no. 2 (1969-70), pp. 195-207.

Hidy, Ralph W., 'The Road We are Travelling', *Journal of Economic History*, vol. 32, no. 1 (1972), pp. 3-14.

Hughes, Helen, 'Business History or the History of Business', *Business Archives and History*, vol. 3 (1963), pp. 1-19.

Hutchins, John G. B. 'Business History, Entrepreneurial History and Business Administration', *Journal of Economic History*, vol. 18 (1958), pp. 453-66.

Johnson, Arthur M., 'Agenda for the 1970s: The Firm and the Industry', *Journal of Economic History*, vol. 31, no. 1 (1971), pp. 106-17.

Johnson, Arthur M., 'Where Does Business History Go from Here?', *Business History Review*, vol. 36, no. 1 (1962), pp. 11-20.

Krooss, Herman E., 'Economic History and the New Business History', *Journal of Economic History*, vol. 18 (1958), pp. 467-85.

Mills, C. Wright, 'The American Business Elite: A Collective Portrait', *Journal of Economic History*, vol. 5 (1945), Supplement, pp. 20-44.

Redlich, Fritz, 'The Role of Theory in the Study of Business History', *EEH*, 1st Series, vol. 4, no. 3 (1952), pp. 135-44.

Redlich, Fritz, 'Approaches to Business History', *Business History Review*, vol. 36, no. 1 (1962), pp. 61-70.

Smith, Howard R., 'A Model of Entrepreneurial Evolution', *EEH*, 2nd Series, vol. 5, no. 2 (1967), pp. 145-57.

Stout, Donald E., 'Are Business History and Economic Theory Compatible?', *Business History Review*, vol. 29, no. 4 (1955), pp. 285-97.

Walton, Clarence C., 'Business History: Some Major Challenges', *Business History Review*, vol. 36, no. 1 (1962), pp. 21-34.

von Tunzelmann, G. N., 'The New Economic History: An Econometric Appraisal', *EEH*, 2nd Series, vol. 5, no. 2 (1967), pp. 175-200.

Wohl, Richard R., 'The Significance of Business History', *Business History Review*, vol. 28, no. 2 (1954), pp. 128-40.

(iii) The Practice of Business History

Atherton, Lewis E., 'The Research Center in Entrepreneurial History: A Personal Appraisal', *EEH*, 1st Series, vol. 7, no. 2 (1954), pp. 105-10.

Baughman, James P., 'Recent Trends in the Business History of Latin America', *Business History Review*, vol. 39, no. 4 (1965), pp. 425-38.

Birch, Alan, 'The Study of Business History in Australia', *Business Archives and History*, vol. 2 (1962), pp. 65-76.

Blainey, Geoffrey, 'The Future of Australian Business History: a writer's view', *Business Archives and History*, vol.1, no. 5 (1959), pp. 12-15.

Cochran, Thomas C.; Aitken, Hugh G. J. and Redlich, Fritz, L., 'The Research Centre in Retrospect', *EEH*, 1st Series, vol. 10, nos. 3-4 (1958), pp. 105-06.

Fischer, Wolfram, 'Some Recent Developments of Business History in Germany, Austria, and Switzerland', *Business History Review*, vol. 36, no. 4 (1963), pp. 416-36.

Fishlow, Albert and Fogel, Robert W., 'Quantitative Economic History. An Interim Evaluation. Past Trends and Present Tendencies', *Journal of History Review*, vol. 41, no. 1 (1967), pp. 94-103.

Fohlen, Claude, 'The Present State of Business History in France', *Business History Revies*, vol. 41, no. 1 (1967), pp. 94-103.

Htuchins, John G. B., 'Recent Contributions to Business History in the United States', *Journal of Economic History*, vol. 19, no. 1 (1959), pp. 103-21.

Hyde, Francis E., 'British Business History: A Review of Recent Books', *Business History Review*, vol. 36, no. 3 (1963), pp. 240-50.

Klompmaker, H., 'Business History in Holland', *Business History Review*, vol. 37, no. 4 (1964), pp. 501-10.

Landes, David S., 'Entrepreneurial Research in France', *EEH*, 1st Series, vol. 3, no. 1 (1950), pp. 24-34.

Porter, Glenn, 'Recent Trends in Canadian Business and Economic History', *Business History Review*, vol. XLVII, no. 2 (1973), pp. 141-57.

Porter, Kenneth Wiggins, 'Trends in American Business Biography', *Journal of Economic and Business History*, vol. 4 (1931-32), pp. 583-610.

'Survey of the Teaching of Business History in Colleges and Universities in the U.S., Canada, Australia and Japan', *Business History Review*, vol. 36, no. 2 (1962), pp. 359-71.

Tauman, Merab, 'A Critical Comment on Australian Business Histories', *Business Archives and History*, vol. 1, no. 9 (1961), pp. 57-65.

White, H. L., 'A Summing Up of the First Australian Conference on Business History', *Business Archives and History*, vol. 1, no. 5 (1959), pp. 21-23.

Woodruff, W., 'History and the Businessman', *Business History Review*, vol. 30, no. 3 (1956), pp. 241-59.

Woodruff, W., 'Capitalism and the Historians', *Journal of Economic History*, vol. 16 (1956), pp. 1-17.

Part Two: Business Organisation, Growth and Structure

(i) Energy, Raw Materials and Primary Production

Bateman, F., 'Improvement in American Dairy Farming, 1850-1910: a quantitative analysis', *Journal of Economic History*, vol. 28 (1968), pp. 255-73.

Bateman, F., 'Labour Inputs and Productivity in American Dairy Agriculture, 1850-1910', *Journal of Economic History*, vol. 29 (1969), pp. 206-29.

Butt, J., 'Technical Change and the Growth of the British Shale-Oil Industry (1680-1870)', *Economic History Review*, Second Series, vol. 17, no. 3 (1964-65), pp. 511-

Buxton, N. K., 'Entrepreneurial Efficiency in the British Coal Industry between the Wars', *Economic History Review*, Second Series, vol. 23, no. 3 (1970), pp. 476-97.

Chapman, Dennis, 'William Brown of Dundee, 1791-1864: Management of a Scottish Flax Mill', *EEH*, 1st Series, vol. 4, no. 3 (1952), pp. 119-34.

Chapman, S. D., 'The Pioneers of Worsted Spinning by Power', *Business History*, vol. 7, no. 2 (1964), pp. 97-116.

Court, W. H. B., 'A Warwickshire Colliery in the Eighteenth Century', *Economic History Review*, First Series, vol. 7, no. 2 (1936-37), pp. 221-28.

Daniels, G. W. and Ashton, T. S., 'The Records of a Derbyshire Colliery, 1763-1779', *Economic History Review*, First Series, vol. 2, no. 1 (1929-30), pp. 124-29.

Du Boff, R. B., 'The Introduction of Electric Power in American Manufacturing', *Economic History Review*, Second Series, vol. 20, no. 3 (1967), pp. 509-18.

Eddie, S., '"Farmers" response to price in large-estate agriculture: Hungary, 1870-1913', *Economic History Review*, Second Series, vol. 24 (1971), pp. 571-88.

Hyde, Charles K., 'The Adoption of Coke-Smelting by the British Iron Industry, 1709-1790', *EEH*, 2nd Series, vol. 10, no. 4 (1973), pp. 397-418.

Hyde, Charles K., 'The Adoption of the Hot Blast by the British Iron Industry: A Reinterpretation', *EEH*, 2nd Series, vol. 10, no. 3 (1973), pp. 281-94.

John, A. H., 'Iron and Coal on a Glamorgan Estate, 1700-1740', *Economic History Review*, First Series, vol. 13, no. 1 (1943), pp. 93-103.

Mathias, P., 'Agriculture and the Brewing and Distilling Industries in the Eighteenth Century', *Economic History Review*, Second Series, vol. 5, no. 2 (1952-53), pp. 249-57.

Mingay, G. E., 'The Size of Farms in the Eighteenth Century', *Economic History Review*, Second Series, vol. 14, no. 3 (1961-62), pp. 469-

Musson, A. E. and Robinson, E., 'The Early Growth of Steampower',

Economic History Review, Second Series, vol. 11, no. 3 (1958-59), pp. 418-39.

Parker, W. N. and Klein, J. L., 'Productivity Growth in Grain Production in the United States, 1840-60 and 1900-10', *Output, Employment and Productivity in the United States after 1800*. Studies in Income and Wealth, vol. 30, National Bureau of Economic Research 1966, pp. 523-46.

Primack, M., 'Farm Capital Formation as a Use of Farm Labour in the United States, 1850-1910', *Journal of Economic History*, vol. 26 (1966), pp. 348-62.

Raybould, J. J., 'The Development and Organisation of Lord Dudley's Mineral Estates, 1774-1845', *Economic History Review*, Second Series, vol. 21, no. 3 (1968), pp. 529-44.

Reed, Peter Mellish, 'Standard Oil in Indonesia, 1898-1928', *Business History Review*, vol. 32, no. 3 (1958), pp. 311-37.

Sutherland, L. Stuart, 'Sir G. Colebrooke's World Corner in Alum, 1771-73', *Economic History*, vol. 3 (1934-37), pp. 237-58.

Taylor, A. J., 'Labour Productivity and Technical Innovation in the British Coal Industry, 1850-1914', *Economic History Review*, Second Series, vol. 14, no. 1 (1961-62), pp. 48-70.

Temin, P., 'Steam and Water power in the Early Nineteenth Century', *Journal of Economic History*, vol. 26 (1966), pp. 187-205.

(ii) Secondary Activities
(a) Fibre Industries

Burley, K. H., 'An Essex Clothier of the Eighteenth Century', *Economic History Review*, Second Series, vol. 11, no. 2 (1958-59). pp. 289-301.

Chapman, S. D., 'Fixed Capital Formation in the British Cotton Industry, 1770-1815', *Economic History Review*, Second Series, vol. 23, no. 2 (1970), pp. 235-66.

Coleman, D. C., 'An Innovation and its Diffusion: The "New Draperies"', *Economic History Review*, Second Series, vol. 22, no. 3 (1969), pp. 417-29.

Daniels, G. W., 'Valuation of Manchester Cotton Factories in the Early Years of the Nineteenth Century', *Economic Journal*, vol. 25 (1915), pp. 626-26.

Daniels, G. W., 'The Early Records of a Great Manchester Cotton-Spinning Firm', *Economic Journal*, vol. 25 (1915), pp. 175-88.

David, Paul, 'The "Horndal Effect" in Lowell, 1834-1856: A Short-run Learning Curve for Integrated Cotton Textile Mills', *EEH*, 2nd Series, vol. 10, no. 2 (1973), pp. 131-50.

Doane, David P., 'Regional Cost Differentials and Textile Location: A Statistical Analysis' *EEH*, 2nd Series, vol. 9, no. 1 (1971), pp. 3-34.

Feller, I., 'The Draper Loom in New England Textiles, 1894-1914: a study of diffusion of an innovation', *Journal of Economic History*, vol. 26 (1966), pp. 320-47.

Heaton, H., 'Benjamin Gott and the Industrial Revolution in Yorkshire', *Economic History Review*, First Series, vol. 3, no. 1 (1931), pp. 45-66.

Heaton, H., 'Benjamin Gott and the Anglo American Cloth Trade', *Journal of Economic and Business History*, vol. 2 (1929-30), pp. 146-62.

Lane, F. C., 'The Rope Factory and Hemp Trade of Venice in the Fifteenth and Sixteenth Centuries', *Journal of Economic and Business History*, vol. 4 (1931-32), pp. 830-47.

Mann, J. de L., 'A Wiltshire Family of Clothiers: George and Hester Wansey', *Economic History Review*, Second Series, vol. 9, no. 2 (1956-57), pp. 241-53.

Sutherland, Alister, 'The Diffusion of an Innovation in Cotton Spinning', *Journal of Industrial Economics*, vol. 7, no. 2 (1959), pp. 118-35.

Taylor, A. J., 'Concentration and Specialisation in the Lancashire Cotton Industry, 1825-1850', *Economic History Review*, Second Series, vol. 1, nos. 2 and 3 (1948-49), pp. 114-22.

Vitkovitch, B., 'The U.K. Cotton Industry, 1937-1954', *Journal of Industrial Economics*, vol. 3, no. 1 (1954), pp. 241-65.

Williamson, Jeffrey G., 'Embodiment, Disembodiment, Learning by Doing and Returns to Scale in Nineteenth-Century Cotton Textiles', *Journal of Economic History*, vol. 32, no. 3 (1972), pp. 691-705.

Wilson, C., 'Cloth Production and International Competition in the Seventeenth Century', *Economic History Review*, Second Series, vol. 13, no. 2 (1960-61), pp. 209-21.

Wright, G., "An Econometric Study of Cotton Production and Trade, 1830-60', *Review of Economics and Statistics*, vol. 53 (1971), pp. 111-20.

(b) Metal Industries

Barloom, Marvin J., 'The Expansion of Blast Furnace Capacity, 1938-52: A Study in Geographical Cost Differentials', *Business History Review*, vol. 28, no. 1 (1954), pp. 1-23.

Barloom, Marvin J., 'Institutional Foundations of Pricing Policy in the Steel Industry', *Business History Review*, vol. 28, no. 3 (1954), pp. 214-35.

Crossley, D. W., 'The Performance of the Glass Industry in Sixteenth-Century England', *Economic History Review*, Second Series, vol. 25, no. 3 (1972), pp. 421-33.

Donnachie, I. L. and Butt, J., 'The Wilsons of Wilsontown Ironworks (1779-1813): A Study in Entrepreneurial Failure', *EEH*, 2nd Series, vol. 4, no. 2 (1967), pp. 150-68.

Fogel, R. and Engerman, S., 'A Model for the Explanation of Industrial Expansion During the Nineteenth Century, with an Application to the American Iron Industry', *Journal of Political Economy*, vol. 77 (1969), pp. 306-28.

Hammersley, G., 'Technique or Economy? The Rise and Decline of the Early English Copper Industry, ca. 1500-1660', *Business History*, vol. 15, no. 1 (1973), pp. 1-31.

Harris, J. R., 'Copper and Shipping in the Eighteenth Century', *Economic History Review*, Second Series, vol. 19, no. 3 (1966), pp. 550-68.

Hunter, L. C., 'Financial Problems of the Early Pittsburg Iron Manufacturers', *Journal of Economic and Business History*, vol. 2 (1929-30), pp. 520-44.

Johnson, B. L. C., 'The Foley Partnerships: The Iron Industry at the End of the Charcoal Era', *Economic History Review*, Second Series, vol. 4, no. 3 (1951-52), pp. 322-40.

Livesay, Harold C., 'Marketing Patterns in the Antebellum American Iron Industry', *Business History Review*, vol. XLV, no. 3 (1971), pp. 269-95.

Mancke, Richard, 'The Determinants of Steel Prices in the U.S.: 1947-65', *Journal of Industrial Economics*, vol. 16, no. 1 (1967), pp. 147-64.

Raistrick, A. and Allen, E., 'The South Yorkshire Ironmasters (1690-1750)', *Economic History Review*, First Series, vol. 9, no. 2 (1935), pp. 168-185.

Redlich, Fritz, "A German Eighteenth-Century Iron Works During its First Hundred Years', *Business History Review*, vol. 27, nos. 1 and 2 (1953), Part I, pp. 69-96, Part II, pp. 141-57.

Yamamura, Kozo, 'The Founding of Mitsubishi: A Case Study in Japanese Business History', *Business History Review*, vol. XLI, no. 2 (1967), pp. 141-60.

(c) Producer Goods

Aldcroft, Derek H., 'The Performance of the British Machine-Tool Industry in the Interwar Years', *Business History Review*, vol. 40, no. 3 (1966), pp. 281-96.

Logan, J. C., 'The Dumbarton Glass Works Company: A Study in Entrepreneurship', *Business History*, vol. 14, no. 1 (1972), pp. 61-81.

Musson, A. E., 'An Early Engineering Firm', *Business History*, vol. 3, no. 1 (1960), pp. 8-18.

Payne, Peter L., 'George Spencer, Merchant and Rubber Spring Manufacturer, 1852-1891', *EEH*, 1st Series, vol. 10, no. 2 (1959), pp. 81-89.

Penrose, Edith T., 'The Growth of the Firm — A Case Study: The Hercules Powder Company', *Business History Review*, vol. 34, no. 1 (1960), pp. 1-23.

Saul, S. B., 'The Market and the Development of the Mechanical Engineering Industries in Britain, 1860-1914', *Economic History Review*, Second Series, vol. 20, no. 1 (1967), pp. 111-30.

Trebilcock, R. C., '"Spin-off" in British Economic History: Armaments and Industry, 1760-1914', *Economic History Review*, Second Series, vol. 22, no. 3 (1969), pp. 474-90.

(d) Consumer Goods

Arnould, Richard J., 'Changing Patterns of Concentration in American Meat Packing, 1880-1963', *Business History Review*, vol. XLV, no. 1 (1971), pp. 18-34.

Church, R. A., 'Messrs Gotch and Sons and the Rise of the Kettering Footwear Industry', *Business History*, vol. 8, no. 2 (1965), pp. 140-49.

Church, R. A. 'Labour Supply and Innovation 1800-1860: The Boot and Shoe Industry', *Business History*, vol. 12, no. 1 (1970), pp. 25-45.

Church, R. A. and Smith, B. M. D., 'Competition and Monopoly in the Coffin Furniture Industry, 1870-1915', *Economic History Review*,

Second Series, vol. 19, no. 3 (1966), pp. 621-41.

Harrison, A. E., 'The Competitiveness of the British Cycle Industry, 1880-1914', *Economic History Review*, Second Series, vol. 22, no. 2 (1969), pp. 287-303.

Porter, Patrick G., 'Origins of the American Tobacco Company', *Business History Review*, vol. XLIII, no. 1 (1969), pp. 59-76.

See, Henri, 'Hat Manufacturing in Rennes, 1776-1789: Its Financial and Commercial Organisation', *Journal of Economic and Business History*, vol. 1 (1928-29), pp. 208-40.

Spencer, U. M., 'A La Mode — A Study of the Ladies' Hat Industry', *Accounting Research*, vol. 9 (1958), pp. 45-9.

(iii) Tertiary Activities

(a) Transport, Construction and Communications

Aldcroft, Derek H., 'Efficiency and Enterprise in British Railways, 1870-1914', *EEH*, 2nd Series, vol. 5, no. 2 (1967), pp. 158-74.

Alford, B. W. E., 'Business Enterprise and the Growth of the Commercial Letterpress Printing Industry, 1850-1914', *Business History*, vol. 7, no. 1 (1964), pp. 1-14.

Fearon, Peter, 'The Formative Years of the British Aircraft Industry', *Business History Review*, vol. XLIII, no. 4 (1969), pp. 476-95.

Fogel, R. W., 'A Quantitative Approach to the Study of Railroads in American Economc Growth: a report of some preliminary findings', *Journal of Economic History*, vol. 22 (1962), pp. 163-97.

Higham, Robin, 'Quantity vs Quality: The Impact of Changing Demand on the British Aircraft Industry, 1900-1960', *Business History Review*, vol. XLII, no. 4 (1968), pp. 443-66.

Holmes, Oliver W., 'Levi Pease, The Father of New England Stage-Coaching', *Journal of Economic and Business History*, vol. 3 (1930-31), pp. 241-63.

Hutchins, John G. B., 'The American Shipping Industry Since 1914', *Business History Review*, vol. 28, no. 2 (1954), pp. 105-27.

Irving, R. J., 'British Railway Investment and Innovation 1900-1914', *Business History*, vol. 13, no. 1 (1971), pp. 39-63.

Klein, Maury, 'Southern Railroad Leaders, 1865-1893: Identities and Idealogies', *Business History Review*, vol. XLII, no. 3 (1968), pp. 288-310.

Lee, A. J., 'The Management of a Victorian Local Newspaper: the Manchester City News, 1864-1900', *Business History*, vol. 15, no. 2 (1973), pp. 131-48.

Livesay, Harold C., 'The Lobdell Car Wheel Co., 1830-1867', *Business History Review*, vol. XLII, no. 2 (1968), pp. 171-94.

Mercer, L., 'Rates of Return for Land-Grant Railroads: the Central Pacific System', *Journal of Economic History*, vol. 30 (1970), pp. 602-26.

Musson, A. E., 'Newspaper Printing in the Industrial Revolution', *Economic History Review*, Second Series, vol. 10, no. 2 (1957-58), pp. 411-26.

Neal, L., 'Investment Behaviour by American Railroads, 1897-1914', *Review of Economics and Statistics*, vol. 51 (1969), pp. 126-35.

Niemi, A., 'A further look at Interregional Canals and Economic Specialisation: 1820-1840', *EEH*, 2nd Series, vol. 7 (1970), pp. 499-520.

North, D., 'Sources of Productivity Change in Ocean Shipping, 1600-1850', *Journal of Political Economy*, vol. 76 (1968), pp. 953-70.

Schaefer, Donald and Weiss, Thomas, 'The Use of Simulation Techniques in Historical Analysis: Railroads versus Canals', *Journal of Economic History*, vol. 31, no. 4 (1971), pp. 854-84.

Walton, G., 'A Measure of Productivity Change in American Colonial Shipping', *Economic History Review*, Second Series, vol. 21 (1968), pp. 268-82.

Walton, Gary M. and Mak, James, 'Steamboats and the Great Productivity Surge in River Transportation', *Journal of Economic History*, vol. 32, no. 3 (1972), pp. 619-40.

(b) Banking, Finance and Insurance

Adams, Donald R. Jr, 'The Bank of Stephen Girand, 1812-1831', *Journal of Economic History*, vol. 32, no. 4 (1972), pp. 841-69.

Barbour, Violet, 'Marine Risks and Insurance in the Seventeenth Century', *Journal of Economic and Business History*, vol. 1 (1928-29), pp. 561-96.

Boyd, J. P., 'Connecticut's Experiment in Expansion: The Susquehannah Company, 1753-1803', *Journal of Economic and Business History*, vol. 4 (1931-32), pp. 38-69.

Davis, Lance E., 'Sources of Industrial Finance: The American Textile Industry, A Case Study', *EEH*, 1st Series, vol. 9, no. 4 (1959), pp. 189-203.

Davis, Lance E., and Payne, Peter L., 'From Benevolence to Business: the Story of Two Savings Banks', *Business History Review*, vol. 32, no. 4 (1958), pp. 434-43.

Fisk, H. E., 'Fisk and Hatch, Bankers and Dealers in Government Securities, 1862-1885', *Journal of Economic and Business History*, vol. 2 (1929-30), pp. 706-22.

Gill, C., 'Blackwell Hall Factors', *Economic History Review*, Second Series, vol. 6, no. 3 (1953-54), pp. 268-81.

Jones, W. J., 'Elizabethan Marine Insurance', *Business History*, vol. 2 (1959), pp. 53-66.

Joslin, D. M., 'London Private Bankers, 1720-1785', *Economic History Review*, Second Series, vol. 7, no. 2 (1954-55), pp. 167-86.

Lovell, Michael C., 'The Role of the Bank of England as Lender of Last Resort in the Crises of the Eighteenth Century', *EEH*, 1st Series, vol. 10, no. 1 (1957), pp. 8-21.

Maywald, K., 'Fire Insurance and the Capital Coefficient in Great Britain, 1866-1952', *Economic History Review*, Second Series, vol. 9, no 1 (1956-57), pp. 89-105.

McCasker, John J., 'Sources of Investment Capital in the Colonial Philadelphia Shipping Industry', *Journal of Economic History*, vol. 32., no. 1 (1972), pp. 146-57.

Robertson, H. M., 'Sir Bevis Bulmer: A Large-Scale Speculator of Elizabethan and Jacobean Times', *Journal of Economic and Business History*, vol. 4 (1931-32), pp. 99-120.

(c) Trading, Marketing and Retailing

Blackman, Janet, 'The Development of the Retail Grocery Trade in the Nineteenth Century', *Business History*, vol. 9, no. 2 (1966), pp. 110-17.
Blomquist, Thomas W., 'The Drapers of Lucca and the Marketing of Cloth in the Mid-Thirteenth Century', *EEH*, 2nd Series, vol. 7, nos. 1 and 2 (1969-70), pp. 65-73.
Cohen, Ira, 'The Auction System in the Port of New York, 1817-1837', *Business History Review*, vol. XLV, no. 4 (1971), pp. 488-510.
Daniels, G. W., 'The Trading Accounts of a London Merchant in 1794', *Economic Journal*, vol. 33 (1923), pp. 516-22.
Dixon, D. F., 'Petrol Distribution in the U.K., 1900-1950', *Business History*, vol. 6, no. 1 (1963), pp. 1-19.
Dixon, D. F., 'Gasoline Marketing in the United States — The First Fifty Years', *Journal of Industrial Economics*, vol. 13, no. 1 (1964), pp. 23-42.
Fussell, G. E., 'The London Cheesemongers of the Eighteenth Century', *Economic History*, vol. 1 (1926-29), pp. 394-98.
Jack, Andrew B., 'The Channels of Distribution for and Innovation: The Sewing Machine Industry in America, 1860-1865', *EEH*, 1st Series, vol. 9, no. 3 (1957), pp. 113-41.
Lovett, Robert W., 'Storekeeping in a Marine Seacoast Town: Records of the W. G. Sargent Company', *Business History Review*, vol. 17, no. 2 (1953), pp. 121-23.
McKendrick, N., 'Josiah Wedgwood: An Eighteenth Century Entrepreneur in Salesmanship and Marketing Techniques', *Economic History Review*, Second Series, vol. 12, no. 3 (1959-60), pp. 408-33.
Nef, J. U., 'Dominance of the Trader in the English Coal Industry in the Seventeenth Century', *Journal of Economic and Business History*, vol. 1 (1928-29), pp. 422-33.
Norris, James D., 'One-Price Policy among Antebellum Country Stores', *Business History Review*, vol. 36, no. 4 (1962), pp. 455-58.
Payne, Peter L., 'The Role of the Salesmen and the Commission Agent in the Early Years of the British Rubber Mechanicals Industry', *EEH*, 1st Series, vol. 7, no. 4 (1955), pp. 205-14.
Pollins, H., 'The Marketing of Railway Shares in the First Half of the Nineteenth Century', *Economic History Review*, vol. 7, no. 2 (1954-55), pp. 230-39.
Porter, J. H., 'The Development of a Provincial Department Store, 1870-1939', *Business History*, vol. 13, no. 1 (1971), pp. 64-71.
Resseguie, Harry E., 'Alexander Turney Stewart and the Development of the Department Store, 1823-1876', *Business History Review*, vol. 39, no. 3 (1965), pp. 301-22.
Robinson, E., 'Eighteenth-Century Commerce and Fashion: Matthew Boulton's Marketing Techniques', *Economic History Review*, Second

Series, vol. 16, no. 1 (1963-64), pp. 39-60.

Simpson, A., 'Thomas Callum, Draper, 1587-1664', *Economic History Review*, Second Series, vol. 11, no. 1 (1958-59), pp. 19-34.

Smalley, Orange A., 'Market Entry and Economic Adaptation: Spiegel's First Decade in Mail Order', *Business History Review*, vol. 35, no. 3 (1961), pp. 372-401.

Sutton, G. B., 'The Marketing of Ready Made Footwear in the Nineteenth Century', *Business History*, vol. 6, no. 2 (1963), pp. 93-112.

Twyman, Robert W., 'Potter Palmer: Merchandising Innovator of the West', *EEH*, 1st Series, vol. 4, no. 2 (1952), pp. 58-72.

(iv) Business Organisation and Growth
(a) Technical Progress and Scale

Aldcroft, Derek H., 'Technical Progress and British Enterprise, 1875-1914', *Business History*, vol. 8, no. 2 (1965), pp. 122-39.

Aldcroft, D. H., 'Factor Prices and the Rate of Innovation in Britain, 1875-1914', *Business History*, vol. 9, no. 2 (1966), pp. 126-31.

Baldwin, George B., 'The Invention of the Modern Safety Razor: A Case Study of Industrial Innovation', *EEH*, 1st Series, vol. 4, no. 2 (1952), pp. 73-102.

Bateman, F.; Foust, J. D. and Weiss, T. J., 'Large-Scale Manufacturing in the South and West, 1850-1860', *Business History Review*, vol. XLV, no. 1 (1971), pp. 1-17.

Carter, C. F. and Williams, B. R., 'The Characteristics of Technically Progressive Firms', *Journal of Industrial Economics*, vol. 7, no. 2 (1959), pp. 87-104.

Chandler, Alfred D. Jr, 'The Beginnings of "Big Business" in American Industry', *Business History Review*, vol. 33, no. 1 (1959), pp. 1-31.

Chandler, Alfred D. Jr and Galambos, Louis, 'The Development of Large-Scale Economic Organisations in America', *Journal of Economic History*, vol. 30, no. 1 (1970), pp. 201-17.

David, P. and Van de Klundert, T. H., 'Biased Efficiency Growth and capital-labour substitution in the U.S., 1899-1960', *American Economic Review*, vol. 55 (1965), pp. 357-94.

Ferguson, C. E., 'The Relationshop of Business Size to Stability: an Empirical Approach', *Journal of Industrial Economics*, vol. 9, no. 1 (1960), pp. 43-62.

Gras, N. S. B., 'The Rise of Big Business', *Journal of Economic and Business History*, vol. 4 (1931-32), pp. 381-408.

Greenwald, William I., 'The Impact of Sound upon the Film Industry: A Case Study in Innovation', *EEH*, 1st Series, vol. 4, no. 3 (1952), pp. 178-92.

Nef, J. U., 'The Progress of Technology and the Growth of Large Scale Industry in Great Britain, 1540-1640', *Economic History Review*, First Series, vol. 5, no. 1 (1934), pp. 3-24.

Payne, P. L., 'The Emergence of the Large-Scale Company in Great Britain, 1870-1914', *Economic History Review*, Second Series, vol. 20, no. 3 (1967), pp. 519-42.

Phillips, Almarin, 'Concentration Scale and Technological Change in Selected Manufacturing Industries, 1899-1939', *Journal of Industrial Economics*, vol. 4, no. 3 (1956), pp. 179-93.

Rosenberg, Nathan, 'Factors Affecting the Diffusion of Technology', *EEH*, 2nd Series, vol. 10, no. 1 (1972), pp. 3-34.

Schmookler, J., 'Economic Sources of Inventive Activity', *Journal of Economic History*, vol. 22 (1962), pp. 1-20.

Uselding, Paul and Juba, Bruce, 'Biased Technical Progress in American Manufacturing', *EEH*, 2nd Series, vol. 11, no. 1 (1973), pp. 55-72.

Walton, Gary M., 'Obstacles to Technical Diffusion in Ocean Shipping, 1675-1775', *EEH*, 2nd Series, vol. 8, no. 2 (1970), pp. 123-40.

(b) Investment, Productivity and Structural Features

Allen, G. C., 'Methods of Industrial Organisation in the West Midlands', *Economic History*, vol. 1 (1926-29), pp. 535-53.

Ashton, T. S., 'The Domestic System in the Early Lancashire Tool Trade', *Economic History*, vol. 1 (1926-29), pp. 131-40.

Birch, Alan, 'Carron Company 1784-1822: The Profits of Industry During the Industrial Revolution', *EEH*, 1st Series, vol. 8, no. 2 (1955), pp. 66-79.

Birch, Alan, 'Carron Company 1784-1822: A Reply', *EEH*, 1st Series, vol. 9, no. 1 (1956), pp. 46-49.

Campbell, R. H., 'Financing the Carron Company', *Business History*, vol. 1, no. 1 (1958), pp. 21-34.

Chandler, Alfred D. Jr., 'Patterns of American Railroad Finance', *Business History Review*, vol. 28, no. 3 (1954), pp. 248-63.

Chandler, Alfred D. Jr, 'The Structure of American Industry in the Twentieth Century: A Historical Overview', *Business History Review*, vol. XLIII, no. 3 (1969), pp. 255-98.

Channon, Geoffrey, 'A Nineteenth-Century Investment Decision: the Midland Railways London Extension', *Economic History Review*, Second Series, vol. 25, no. 3 (1972), pp. 448-70.

Chapman, S. D., 'The Transition to the Factory System in the Midlands Cotton-Spinning Industry', *Economic History Review*, Second Series, vol. 18, no. 3 (1965-66), pp. 526-43.

Daly, M. T. and Webber, M. J., 'The Growth of the Firm Within the City', *Urban Studies*, vol. 10, no. 3 (1973), pp. 303-17.

Davis, L., 'The Capital Markets and Industrial Concentration: The U.S. and U.K., a Comparative Study', *Economic History Review*, Second Series, vol. 19, no. 2 (1966), pp. 255-88.

Davis, Lance Edwin, 'Stock Ownership in the Early New England Textile Industry', *Business History Review*, vol. 32, no. 2 (1958), pp. 204-22.

Dunning, J. H. and Utton, M. A., 'Measuring Changes in Productivity and Efficiency in U.K. Industry, 1954-63', *Business Ratios*, vol. 1, no. 2 (Summer, 1967), pp. 21-9.

Feller, Irwin, 'Urban Location of United States Invention, 1860-1919',

EEH, 2nd Series, vol. 8, no. 3 (1971), pp. 285-303.

Hall, A. R., 'Note on "Carron Company 1784-1822: The Profits of Industry During the Industrial Revolution" by A. Birch', *EEH*, 1st Series, vol. 9, no. 1 (1956), pp. 44-45.

Higgs, Robert, 'Williamson and Swanson on City Growth: A Critique', *EEH*, 2nd Series, vol. 8, no. 2 (1971), pp. 203-11.

Hinderliter, Roger H. and Rockoff, Hugh, 'The Management of Reserves by Banks in Ante-bellum Eastern Financial Centers', *EEH*, 2nd Series, vol. 11, no. 1 (1973), pp. 37-54.

Holderness, B. A., 'Landlord's Capital Formation in East Anglia, 1750-1870', *Economic History Review*, Second Series, vol. 25, no. 3 (1972), pp. 434-47.

Jefferys, J. B., 'The Denomination and Character of Shares, 1855-1885', *Economic History Review*, First Series, vol. 16, no. 1 (1946), pp. 45-55.

Laffer, Arthur B., 'Vertical Integration by Corporations, 1929-1965', *Review of Economics and Statistics*, vol. 51 (1969), pp. 91-3.

Larson, Henrietta M., 'S & M Allen — Lottery, Exchange, and Stock Brokerage', *Journal of Economic and Business History*, vol. 3 (1930-31), pp. 424-45.

Livesay, Harold C. and Porter, Glenn, 'The Financial Role of Merchants in the Development of U.S. Manufacturing, 1815-1860', *EEH*, 2nd Series, vol. 9, no. 1 (1971), pp. 63-87.

McLlelland, Peter D., 'Social Rates of Return on American Railroads in the Nineteenth Century' *Economic History Review*, Second Series, vol. 25, no. 3 (1972), pp. 471-88.

Mercer, Lloyd J. and Morgan, W. Douglas, 'Internal Funds and Automobile Industry Investment: An Evaluation of the Seltzer Hypothesis', *Journal of Economic History*, vol. 32, no. 3 (1972), pp. 682-89.

Neal, Larry, 'Trust Companies and Financial Innovation, 1897-1914', *Business History Review*, vol. XLV, no. 1 (1971), pp. 35-51.

Niemi, A., 'The Development of Industrial Structure in Southern New England', *Journal of Economic History*, vol. 30 (1970), pp. 657-62.

Niemi, Albert W. Jr, 'Structural Shifts in Southern Manufacturing', *Business History Review*, vol. XLV, no. 1 (1971), pp. 79-84.

Niemi, Albert W. Jr, 'Structural and Labour Productivity Patterns in United States Manufacturing, 1849-1899', *Business History Review*, vol. XLVI, no. 1 (1972), pp. 67-84.

Olmstead, Alan L., 'Investment Constraints and New York City Mutual Savings Bank Financing of Antebellum Development', *Journal of Economic History*, vol. 32, no. 4 (1972), pp. 811-40.

Pollard, S., 'Fixed Capital in the Industrial Revolution in Britain', *Journal of Economic History*, vol. 24 (1964), pp. 299-314.

Pollins, H., 'The Finances of the Liverpool and Manchester Railway', *Economic History Review*, Second Series, vol. 5, no. 1 (1952-53), pp. 90-97.

Porter, Patrick G. and Livesay, Harold C., 'Oligopoly in Small Manufacturing Firms', *EEH*, 2nd Series, vol. 7, no. 3 (1970), pp. 371-79.

Richards, E. S., 'The Finances of the Liverpool and Manchester Railway Again', *Economic History Review*, Second Series, vol. 25, no. 2 (1972), pp. 284-92.

Siegenthaler, Jurg K., 'A Scale Analysis of Nineteenth-Century Industrialisation', *EEH*, 2nd Series, vol. 10, no. 1 (1972), pp. 75-108.

Shannon, H. A., 'The Limited Companies of 1866-1883', *Economic History Review*, First Series, vol. 4, no. 3 (1934), pp. 290-316.

Shannon, H. A., 'The Coming of General Limited Liability', *Economic History*, vol. 2 (1930-33), pp. 267-91.

Shannon, H. A., 'The First Five Thousand Limited Liability Companies and Their Duration', *Economic History*, vol. 2 (1930-33), pp. 396-424.

Stilwell, F. J. B., 'The Location of Industry and Business Efficiency', *Business Ratios*, vol. 2, no. 3 (Winter, 1968), pp. 5-17.

Supple, Barry E., 'A Business Elite: German-Jewish Financiers in Nineteenth-Century New York', *Business History Review*, vol. 31, no. 2 (1957), pp. 143-78.

Swanson, Joseph A. and Williamson, Jeffrey G., 'A Model of Urban Capital Formation and the Growth of Cities in History', *EEH*, 2nd Series, vol. 8, no. 2 (1970), pp. 213-22.

Swierenga, Robert P., 'The "Western Land Business": The Story of Easley and Willingham, Speculators', *Business History Review*, vol. XLI, no. 1 (1967), pp. 1-20.

Temin, P., 'Labour Scarcity and the Problem of American Industrial Efficiency in the 1850s', *Journal of Economic History*, vol. 26 (1966), pp. 361-79.

Todd, G., 'Some Aspects of Joint Stock Companies, 1844-1900', *Economic History Review*, First Series, vol. 4, no. 1 (1932), pp. 46-71.

Uselding, Paul, 'Factor Substitution and Labour Productivity Growth in American Manufacturing, 1839-1899', *Journal of Economic History*, vol. 32, no. 3 (1972), pp. 670-81.

Weiss, Thomas, 'Urbanisation and the Growth of the Service Workforce', *EEH*, 2nd Series, vol. 8, no. 3 (1971), pp. 241-58.

Williamson, Jeffrey G., 'Consumer Behaviour in the Nineteenth Century: Carrol D. Wright's Massachusetts Workers in 1873', *EEH*, 2nd Series, vol. 4, no. 2 (1967), pp. 98-135.

Williamson, Jeffrey G. and Swanson, Joseph A., 'The Growth of Cities in the American Northeast, 1820-1870', *EEH*, 2nd Series, vol. 4, no. 1 (1966), Supplement.

(c) Competition and Regulation:
Science and Government

Alford, B. W. E., 'Government Expenditure and the Growth of the Printing Industry', *Economic History Review*, Second Series, vol. 17, no. 1 (1964-65), pp. 97-112.

Allen, G. C., 'An Eighteenth-Century Combination in Copper-Mining', *Economic Journal*, vol. 33 (1923), pp. 74-85.

Burn, D. L., 'The Genesis of American Engineering Competition, 1850-70', *Economic History*, vol. 2 (1930-33), pp. 292-311.

Cain, P. J., 'Railway Combination and Government, 1900-1914', *Economic History Review*, Second Series, vol. 25, no. 4 (1972), pp. 623-41.

Calhoun, G. M., 'Risk in Sea Loans in Ancient Athens', *Journal of Economic and Business History*, vol. 2 (1929-30), pp. 561-84.

Dunning, John H., 'U.S. Subsidiaries in Britain and Their U.K. Competitors', *Business Ratios*, vol. 1, no. 1 (Autumn, 1966), pp. 5-18.

George, K. D., 'Changes in Industrial Concentration, 1951-1958', *Journal of Industrial Economics*, vol. 15, no. 3 (1967), pp. 200-11.

George, P. J. and Oksanen, E. H., 'Saturation in the Automobile Market in the Late Twenties: Some Further Results', *EEH*, 2nd Series, vol. 11, no. 1 (1973), pp. 73-86.

Hannah, Les, 'Takeover Bids in Britain Before 1950: An Exercise in Business "Prehistory"', *Business History*, vol. 16, no. 1 (1974), pp. 65-77.

Jacoby, Neil H., 'The Relative Stability of Market Shares: A Theory and Evidence from Several Industries', *Journal of Industrial Economics*, vol. 12, no. 2 (1964), pp. 83-107.

Johnson, Arthur M., 'Government-Business Relations: An International Approach', *Business History Review*, vol. 36, no. 1 (1964), pp. 1-4.

Jones, S. R. H., 'Price Associations and Competition in the British Pin Industry, 1814-40', *Economic History Review*, Second Series, vol. 26, no. 2 (1973), pp. 237-53.

Kirby, M. W., 'The Control of Competition in the British Coal Mining Industry in the Thirties', *Economic History Review*, Second Series, vol. 26, no. 2 (1973), pp. 273-84.

Kirby, M. W., 'Government Intervention in Industrial Organisation: Coal Mining in the Nineteen Thirties', *Business History*, vol. 15, no. 2 (1973), pp. 160-73.

Mercer, Lloyd J. and Morgan, W. Douglas, 'Alternative Interpretations of Market Saturation: Evaluation for the Automobile Market in the Late Twenties', *EEH*, 2nd Series, vol. 9, no. 3 (1972), pp. 269-90.

Musson, A. E. and Robinson, E. 'Science and Industry in the Late Eighteenth Century', *Economic History Review*, Second Series, vol. 13, no. 2 (1960-61), pp. 222-44.

Navin, Thomas R. and Sears, Marian V., 'A Study in Merger: Formation of the International Mercantile Marine Company', *Business History Review*, vol. 28, no. 4 (1954), pp. 291-328.

Passell, P. and Schmundt, M., 'Pre-Civil War Land Policy and the Growth of Manufacturing', *EEH*, 2nd Series, vol. 9 (1971), pp. 35-48.

Sigsworth, E. M., 'Science and the Brewing Industry', *Economic History Review*, Second Series, vol. 17, no. 3 (1964-65), pp. 536-50.

Tzoannos, J. and Samuels, J. M., 'Mergers and Takeovers: The Financial Characteristics of Companies Involved', *Journal of Business Finance*, vol. 4, no. 3 (1972), pp. 5-16.

Utton, M. A., 'Diversification, Mergers and Profit Stability', *Business Ratios*, vol. 3, no. 1 (Autumn, 1969), pp. 24-8.

Utton, M. A., 'Some Features of the Early Merger Movements in British Manufacturing', *Business History*, vol. 14, no. 1 (1972), pp. 51-60.

Wesley, Edgar B., 'Government Factory System among the Indians', *Journal of Economic and Business History*, vol. 4 (1931-32), pp. 487-511.

Wray, Margaret, 'Uncertainty, Prices and Entrepreneurial Expectations — An Applied Study', *Journal of Industrial Economics*, vol. 4, no. 2 (1955), pp. 107-28.

(d) Entrepreneurship

Alexander, Alec P., 'The Supply of Industrial Entrepreneurship', *EEH*, 2nd Series, vol. 4, no. 2 (1967), pp. 136-49.

Aldcroft, D. H., 'The Entrepreneur and the British Economy, 1870-1914', *Economic History Review*, Second Series, vol. 17, no. 1 (1964-65), pp. 113-34.

Belshaw, Cyril S., 'The Cultural Milieu of the Entrepreneur: A Critical Essay', *EEH*, 1st Series, vol. 7, no. 3 (1955), pp. 146-63.

Buxton, Neil K., 'Avoiding the Pitfalls: Entrepreneurial Efficiency in the Coal Industry Again', *Economic History Review*, Second Series, vol. 25, no. 4 (1972), pp. 669-73.

Buxton, Neil K., 'Entrepreneurial Efficiency in the British Coal Industry between the Wars: Reconfirmed', *Economic History Review*, Second Series, vol. 25, no. 4 (1972), pp. 658-64.

Cochran, Thomas C., 'Nineteenth Century Railroad Entrepreneurs', *EEH*, 1st Series, vol. 3, no. 1 (1950), pp. 1-23.

Coleman, D. C., 'Gentlemen and Players', *Economic History Review*, Second Series, vol. 26, no. 1 (1973), pp. 92-116.

Evans, G. Heberton, Jr, 'A Century of Entrepreneurship in the United States, c. 1850-1957', *EEH*, 1st Series, vol. 10, no. 2 (1957), pp. 90-103.

Jaher, Frederic C., 'Businessman and Gentleman: Nathan and Thomas Gold Appleton — An Exploration in Intergenerational History', *EEH*, 2nd Series, vol. 4, no. 1 (1966), pp. 17-39.

Johnson, W., 'Entrepreneurial Efficiency in the British Coal Industry between the Wars: a Second Comment', *Economic History Review*, Second Series, vol. 25, no. 4 (1972), pp. 665-68.

Kirby, M. W., 'Entrepreneurial Efficiency in the British Coal Industry Between the Wars: A Comment', *Economic History Review*, Second Series, vol. 25, no. 4 (1972), pp. 655-57.

Mathias, Peter, 'The Entrepreneur in Brewing', *EEH*, 1st Series, vol. 10, no. 2 (1957), pp. 72-80.

Marburg, Theodore F., 'A Study of Small Business Failure: Smith and Griggs of Waterburg', *Business History Review*, vol. 28, no. 4 (1954), pp. 366-84.

McKay, John P., 'John Cockerill in S. Russia, 1885-1905: A Study of Aggressive Foreign Entrepreneurship', *Business History Review*, vol. XLI, no. 3 (1967), pp. 243-56.

McCloskey, Donald N. and Sandberg, Lars G., 'From Damnation to Redemption: Judgments on the Late Victorian Entrepreneur', *EEH*, 2nd Series, vol. 9, no. 1 (1971), pp. 89-108.

Rae, John B., 'The Engineer-Entrepreneur in the American Automobile

Industry', *EEH*, 1st Series, vol. 8, no. 1 (1955), pp. 1-11.

Sears, Marian V., 'The American Businessman at the Turn of the Century', *Business History Review*, vol. 30, no. 4 (1956), pp. 382-443.

Silk, Alvin J. and Stern, Louis William, 'The Changing Nature of Innovation in Marketing: A Study of Selected Business Leaders, 1852-1958', *Business History Review*, vol. 36, no. 3 (1963), pp. 182-200.

Wilson, Charles, 'The Entrepreneur in the Industrial Revolution in Britain', *EEH*, 1st Series, vol. 7, no. 3 (1955), pp. 129-45.

Part Three: Management Practices and Techniques

Baughman, James P., 'Early American Checks: Forms and Functions', *Business History Review*, vol. XLI, no. 4 (1967), pp. 421-35.

Brief, Richard P., 'The Origin and Evolution of Nineteenth-Century Asset Accounting', *Business History Review*, vol. 40, no. 1 (1966), pp. 1-23.

Burley, K. H., 'Some Accounting Records of an Eighteenth-Century Clothier', *Accounting Research*, vol. 9 (1958), pp. 50-60.

Cauley, T. J., 'Early Business Methods in the Texas Cattle Industry', *Journal of Economic and Business History*, vol. 4 (1931-32), pp. 461-86.

Chandler, Alfred D. Jr, 'Management Decentralisation: An Historical Analysis', *Business History Review*, vol. 30, no. 2 (1956), pp. 111-74.

Chandler, Alfred D. Jr, 'The Railroads: Pioneers in Modern Corporate Management', *Business History Review*, vol. XXXIX, no. 1 (1965), pp. 16-40.

Comiskey, E. E. and Groves, R. E., 'The Adoption and Diffusion of an Accounting Innovation', *Accounting and Business Research*, vol. 2, no. 5 (Winter, 1972), pp. 67-77.

Crossley, D. W., 'The Management of a Sixteenth-Century Iron Works', *Economic History Review*, Second Series, vol. 19, no. 2 (1966), pp. 273-88.

Edwards, James Don, 'Public Accounting in the U.S. from 1913 to 1928', *Business History Review*, vol. 32, no. 1 (1958), pp. 74-101.

Eilbirt, Henry, 'The Development of Personnel Management in the United States', *Business History Review*, vol. 33, no. 3 (1959), pp. 345-64.

Ekelund, Robert B. Jr, 'Economic Empiricism in the Writing of Early Railway Engineers', *EEH*, 2nd Series, vol. 9, no. 2 (1972), pp. 179-96.

Fisher, F. J., 'Some Experiments in Company Organisation in the Early Seventeenth Century', *Economic History Review*, First Series, vol. 4 no. 2 (1933), pp. 177-94.

Hagedorn, Homer J., 'The Management Consultant as Transmitter of Business Techniques', *EEH*, 1st Series, vol. 7, no. 3 (1955), pp. 164-73.

Hawkins, David F., 'The Development of Modern Financial Reporting Practices among American Manufacturing Corporations', *Business History Review*, vol. 36, no. 3 (1963), pp. 135-68.

Lee, T. A., 'The Historical Development of Internal Cost Control from the Earliest Times to the End of the Seventeenth Century', *Journal of Accounting Research*, vol. 9, no. 1 (1971), pp. 150-57.

Lynn, Robert A., 'Installment Credit Before 1870', *Business History*

Review, vol. 31, no. 4 (1957), pp. 414-24.

McKendrick, N., 'Josiah Wedgwood and Cost Accounting in the Industrial Revolution', *Economic History Review*, Second Series, vol. 23, no. 1 (1970), pp. 45-67.

Pelzer, L., 'Financial Management of the Cattle Ranges', *Journal of Economic and Business History*, vol. 2 (1929-30), pp. 723-41.

Porter, J. H., 'Management, Competition and Industrial Relations: The Midland Manufactured Iron Trade 1873-1914', *Business History*, vol. 11, no. 1 (1969), pp. 37-47.

Redlich, Fritz and Webster M. Christman, 'Early American Checks and an Example of Their Use', *Business History Review*, vol. XLI, no. 3 (1967), pp. 285-302.

Shelton, John P., 'The First Printed Share Certificate: An Important Link in Financial History', *Business History Review*, vol. 39, no. 3 (1965), pp. 391-402.

Stone, Willard E., 'An Early English Cotton Mill Cost Accounting System: Charton Mills, 1810-1889', *Accounting and Business Research*, vol. 4, no. 13 (Winter, 1973).

Sutherland, L. S., 'The Accounts of an Eighteenth-Century Merchant', *Economic History Review*, First Series, vol. 3, no. 3 (1932), pp. 367-87.

Wedgwood, H. C., 'Josiah Wedgwood, Eighteenth-Century Manager', *EEH*, 2nd Series, vol. 2, no. 3 (1965), pp. 205-26.

Yamey, B. S., 'Scientific Bookkeeping and the Rise of Capitalism', *Economic History Review*, Second Series, vol. 1, no. 2 and 3 (1948-49), pp. 99-113.

EEH   =   Explorations in Entrepreneurial History
           (now Explorations in Economic History)

Author Index

General Index

Accounting, accounts, 46; the rise of capitalism and, 319-45; 'abstraction' in, 323; cost, for internal management control, 347-55; 'work-in-process', 351

Accounting data and business records, interpreting, xv-xvi, 401-2; measurement of, 403-4

Agricultural credit, 279

Ainsworth, George, 154, 156, 157, 159

Alabama Great Southern railroad, 253, 257, 258, 263

Amalgamated Ironworkers Union, 168

American Ice, 190

American manufacturing, vertical integration in, 184-91

American Sugar Refining, 186

American Tobacco, 190

Anderson, Joseph, 285

Applied micro-economics, ix

Apprentices, 132

Arbitration and conciliation, 168

Arkwright, Richard, 136, 137

Arlington Woollen Mills, 307-9

Arro Oil and Refining Company, 208

Arts, connections between business and, 6

Ashton, Thomas, 108, 109

Assembly-line manufacture, 174, 180-1, 199

Assets, of Southern Railroads, 250, 252, 253, 258-60, 265; statement in balance accounts of 'values' of, 322-3

'Association for the Promotion of Order', 139

Atlantic Refining Company, 193, 195, 196-7, 197, 199, 200, 203-4, 206, 209, 210, 212, 216, 217, 220

Australian business history, 45

'Automatic temple', 101

Automobile industry, American, 189, 199

B. and L. Oil Company, 203

Backward integration, 218, 281; of Consett Iron Co., 159-63; in American manufacturing, 186, 188; in American oil companies, 202

Bad language, prohibition of, 140

Ballard and Hall, commission merchants, 283

Bank of England, Mercurius's views on, 368-9

Bank of New York, 272, 280

Banks, commercial, 5; loans to manufacturers by, 272-3, 278, 279, 280

Banks, Sir John, 324

Barber Asphalt Corporation, 210

Bartlett, C. S. and Company, 306

Booth, Alfred, and Company, 16, 21, 24

Boron Oil Company, 216

Beacon Oil Company

Bessemer steel-making, 153, 154

Bethlehem rail mill, 274

Big Enterprise in a Competitive System (Kaplan), 184

Bills of exchange, 9, 279

Bills of lading, 7, 9

Binding money (in coalmining), 72

Blacklists, 134

Blanket-making see Woollen industry

Bleaching, 92, 107-8

Blincoe, Robert, 132, 136

Board of Ordinance, purchase of blankets and woollen cloths by, 225, 228-30

Bolling, John, 132